A LIFE IN TWO CENTURIES

Books by Bertram D. Wolfe

THE BRIDGE AND THE ABYSS: *The Troubled Friendship of Maxim Gorky and V. I. Lenin,* 1967

CIVIL WAR IN SPAIN, 1937

COMMUNIST TOTALITARIANISM, 1961

DIEGO RIVERA, 1947

DIEGO RIVERA: HIS LIFE AND TIMES, 1939

THE FABULOUS LIFE OF DIEGO RIVERA, 1963

AN IDEOLOGY IN POWER: *Reflections on the Russian Revolution,* 1969

KEEP AMERICA OUT OF WAR, 1939 *(with Norman M. Thomas)*

KHRUSHCHEV AND STALIN'S GHOST, 1956

LENIN AND THE ORIGINS OF TOTALITARIANISM, 1966

MARXISM: *One Hundred Years in the Life of a Doctrine,* 1964

Mundo sin Muerte, 1942

PORTRAIT OF AMERICA, 1934 *(with Diego Rivera)*

PORTRAIT OF MEXICO, 1937 *(with Diego Rivera)*

El Romance Tradicional en Mexico, 1925

SIX KEYS TO THE SOVIET SYSTEM, 1956

STRANGE COMMUNISTS I HAVE KNOWN, 1965

THREE WHO MADE A REVOLUTION: *Lenin, Trotsky, Stalin,* 1948, revised edition, 1964

A LIFE IN TWO CENTURIES

BERTRAM D. WOLFE

An Autobiography

Introduction by

Leonard Shapiro

SD

STEIN AND DAY/*Publishers*/New York

First published in 1981

Designed by David Miller
Printed in the United States of America
Stein and Day/*Publishers*/Scarborough House
Briarcliff Manor, N.Y. 10510

Library of Congress Cataloging in Publication Data

Wolfe, Bertram David, 1896–1977.
A life in two centuries.

Autobiographical.
1. Wolfe, Bertram David, 1896–1977. 2. Socialists
–United States–Biography. I. Title.
HX84.W64A35 335'.0092'4 [B] 78-7420
ISBN 0-8128-2520-9

CONTENTS

Contents

LIST OF ILLUSTRATIONS

INTRODUCTION

BY LEONARD SCHAPIRO

Of the many facets of the long and adventurous life of Bert Wolfe the one which reveals itself again and again is his love of Spain, its literature and its culture. I do not mean only, or so much, in his work—though he wrote and lectured perceptively on Spanish literary topics. I mean because he inevitably calls to mind, for those who knew him, the noble figure of Don Quixote. The image of Don Quixote has for centuries dominated Spanish thought. Cervantes embodied in this figure, in whom sadness mingles with laughter, a deep-seated ideal of a nation, of humanity perhaps—sadness because the noble endeavors so often end in disaster, and laughter because it is the only way for man to discharge the tension of frustration, and the tragedy of the unattainable good. Don Quixote lives for truth, for struggle against injustice. He sometimes tilts at windmills, believing them to be giants. Very well, his author seems to be saying, but which of us, looking back on his life, can be certain that he was always able to distinguish the windmills from the giants? The essence of life lies in the sincerity, in the strength of the conviction. The results of our actions lie with the fates: our only duty is to arm and to go into battle.

As I remember Bert Wolfe and as these memoirs have now reminded me, I think he would have agreed with this view, which is the view of Turgenev in his remarkable essay on Don Quixote and Hamlet. I suppose to this generation Wolfe is known primarily for his critical and historical writings on Marxism and communism, principally the Soviet variety. I will return to this aspect of his work in a moment. These memoirs are not, however, concerned with this phase of his life, which started in 1948 with the publication of *Three Who Made a Revolution*. By that date Wolfe was already 54, with much active and exacting experience behind him: it is this part of his career that is dealt with in this story of his life which he unhappily did not live to complete. It is an account of an American Don Quixote, who fought sincerely for truth and justice as he saw it and who enriched the fabric of American life by his indomitable spirit and his unquenchable love of liberty.

If an outsider who has learned to love America may be allowed to pontificate, Americans are at once the most conformist and the most individualistic of people. They conform over large areas of life because this is the only way to weld together a nation out of the disparate elements that flow from all corners of the earth to the shores of their continent. Yet, at the same time, there arise from the midst of these people individuals who reject conformity, repudiate accepted standards, and fight relentlessly for the liberty to assert the truth as they see it. These are the people, often wrong, often misguided, who, like Don Quixote, captivate by their sincerity and by their selfless devotion to the pursuit of the truth as they see it, regardless of the consequences to themselves. It was men and women like these who were to be found among the pioneers of American communism because they believed that in answering the call that went out from Russia in 1917 they could help to lay the foundations for a better, more just, more humane America. They discovered in time that the Russia molded by Stalin did not want idealists who thought for themselves, but obedient and cynical operators who did what they were told. They learned that Stalin was little interested in American well-being, let alone in justice of any kind, and pursued solely the interests of Communist, and especially his own, malignant power over Russia. And so they broke with the illusion—with the illusion, but now with the ideal, as far as Bert Wolfe was concerned. Enriched by his experience, he eventually threw himself with the zest that characterized everything he did into instructing and warning his fellow Americans against the blandishments of the Soviet Communist lie to which he had himself for a time fallen a victim.

A part, but only a part, of these fascinating memoirs is concerned with this story—an important story, because it depicts the path that was traversed by so many American and European intellectuals between the wars. But I find particularly absorbing the account of the boyhood and student days in Brooklyn and in City College, of this brilliantly gifted, restless child of immigrant German-Jewish parents, growing to manhood in the world that was never to be the same again after World War I—the Great War, as it was called. Then there were the years in Mexico so vividly reflected in Wolfe's other writings and especially in his books on the painter Diego Rivera, with whom he later collaborated to write a book on Mexico. Two chapters of these memoirs, the last that he lived to complete, deal with the Spanish Civil War. Yet the most significant testimony of this life is after all about the involvement with communism: the years in Russia among the Bolshevik leaders and the break with Stalin and his apparatus. Many former Communists have written their memoirs. None that I know approximate to these for vividness of style and perception. None illuminates so brilliantly the gulf that yawns between Leninism in its developed form—Stalinism—and the idealism that drew many sensitive, sincere, and honest young men and women for a time to enlist on the side of Soviet Russia. In dealing with this phase of his life Bert Wolfe uses the same rigid standards of truthfulness and sincerity that he applied to all his work. There is not a trace of self-justification, and rightly so. For it was out of the experience of communism in action that there emerged the scholar who will be remembered and honored as long as respect for truth prevails among those engaged in the study of the contemporary world.

The impact of *Three Who Made a Revolution,* the first of the many important works on Soviet communism that Bert Wolfe wrote, was enormous. It told, literally for the first time, the authentic story of bolshevism and its leaders in the years before the capture of power in 1917. Strange to relate, no one had done this before, though the facts were discernible by those with the industry and honesty to search for them. But they had hitherto been ignored, submerged in the mythology in which so much history of political movements is usually enveloped. Wolfe's book was published at the very dawn of the revival of the study of the Soviet Union, which followed the flood of nonsense generated by well-meaning enthusiasts for wartime comradeship who assumed that military valor and integrity in politics necessarily went together. *Three Who Made a Revolution* showed that the defects of Soviet communism were not temporary aberrations in a potentially perfect system, but vices inherent in the very mechanism of power that Lenin and his followers had created. It set a fashion in meticulous and objective research into the past of modern Russia that numerous scholars have since followed. Above all, it reminded a generation which, in the aftermath of World War II, was inclined to cynicism and disillusionment that in the study of history, at least, such old-fashioned virtues as truth, sincerity, justice, and respect for the dignity and worth of man still had to prevail if a true picture was to emerge from the pen of the historian.

These were the qualities first revealed in *Three Who Made a Revolution.* They continued to shine out of the many works devoted to the history of Marxism and Soviet communism, both books and articles, with which Wolfe embellished American scholarship in the thirty years of life that remained to him after the end of the war. With the support of his wife Ella, whose devotion and help for nearly 60 years enabled him to overcome more than man's normal share of ill health, he labored honestly and brilliantly in the historian's vineyard. But these memoirs serve to remind us, by the variety of their interest, by their integrity, by their richness of episode and acuteness of observation, that a life of intense action had gone to make the scholar. Truly can it be said of Bertram Wolfe, in the words of Don Quixote, ". . . *muchos son los caminos por donde lleva Dios a los suyos al cielo*"—"Many are the paths along which God raises his own up to heaven."

IN PLACE OF AN AUTHOR'S INTRODUCTION

I see no reason why the reader should be interested in my private life. The unexpected vicissitudes of that life have led me to take up more trades and professions than the average American, but in our mobile society this is not particularly notable. I was born, succeeded in growing up without undue strain, have known happiness and sorrow, have lived long, and soon shall die. But there is nothing unusual about that. In whatever occupation fate threw me, I have pursued excellence, feeling at moments that I was touching the hem of her garment yet never catching up with her. That pursuit, too, can be of little interest to others. Moreover, I do not belong to that class of autobiographers who feel that every time they sneeze the earth shakes. Hence I shall confine my account to those adventures which are of public interest whether because they involve contact or conflict with great men, or because they brought me close to the epicenter of great events that have absorbed the interest and determined the fate of millions in our time. Being somewhere near the epicenter does not imply that I had any significant role in bringing about the earthquakes, merely that I was in the midst of them, a close and intensely interested observer who had unusual freedom of movement through the turmoil, reported on it in writing, and spent much of the rest of my life reflecting on and deepening my understanding of what I had witnessed.

As a historian I early learned how unreliable autobiographies are, how often the unconscious and the conscious collaborate in rewriting deeds and events closer to the heart's desire. Yet I hope to keep this awareness ever in mind as I write, to be as self-critical of my memory as I have always been of my style, and to use the same historian's method (old documents, clippings, minutes, accounts of others, and similar evidence) to check the wayward impulses and the apologetic inclinations of memory. Where others see an event differently I shall let them speak; where I am in doubt, I shall let the reader know of my uncertainty; in any case I do not see why it should be impossible for an honest man with a historian's training to tell the truth about events in which he has participated and about his part in them. At least this is what I shall try to do.

Since this is not primarily my private life but a series of personal experiences and adventures in the life of our time, I shall have no need to follow chronology but will pursue separate adventures, thoughts, and themes whither they lead, bearing in mind that some of these experiences are remote from the experiences and life span of many of my readers. In making these sometimes ancient, sometimes bizarre and exotic happenings live for them, I shall in some measure reappraise them and relive them myself. That I suppose is one of the pleasures of writing an autobiography.

As with all my books, I have written much of this in reveries late at night when the controls of rigorous logic and daily cares are relaxed and the mind unfettered floats where it will, finding forgotten things to remember and its own way of saying them. Often I have tried this method in writing poetry, too, but what seemed iridescent in the small hours of the night lost its sheen in the cold light of the next day, so that I have never published a poem. But in prose, and especially in the writing of history, I feel that my relaxed subconscious has contributed much to my writing, giving me some of my clearest thoughts and most felicitous expressions. Sometimes, I have found to my astonishment that questions I left unsolved as I fell asleep have solved themselves while I slept. At other times the cool self-critical light of morning has made me scrap much of what pleased me inordinately the night before. This combination of memory and reverie and strict checking of both has been pursued throughout this autobiography. What is left of this interplay I offer the reader with the assurance that I have done the best that memory, reverie, critical consciousness, and historical checking can produce in such a writer as the undersigned.

Bertram D. Wolfe
Hoover Institution on War,
Revolution and Peace

A LIFE IN TWO CENTURIES

1

"WH-WHAT CENTURY?"

When Hitler double-crossed Stalin and invaded Russia on the night of June 21–22, 1941, Joseph Stalin was pushed into our camp. We Americans, in our infancy as a world power, tend to think in terms of unlimited aims and absolute moral rightness and wrongness in every conflict. All our allies must perforce be "good guys" and all our opponents "bad guys," without shadings or qualifications. Yet for me, who knew Stalin personally and had fought with him in Moscow for five long months (that was in 1929, before he had perfected his technique for cutting short discussion!), his entry into "our camp" created a problem. How was I to convince my countrymen that he had not become a democrat merely because he desperately needed our help against his perfidious partner of yesterday? How was I to make clear that he had not suddenly become a "good guy"? Or that the great Russian land, with its millionheaded armies, its soldiers always so stubborn for defense, and its immortal general staff, General Mud, General Distance, and General Winter, was likely to prove unconquerable under Stalin's leadership and dominion as under the tsars, a marvelous ally for war but, even more than under the tsars, a dangerous partner for making a decent peace?

The attack on Pearl Harbor that was to put us Americans into the war was still five months away when Harry Hopkins made his first quick trip to Moscow from London as the President's personal representative, in order to ask Stalin: "How can we most expeditiously and effectively make available the assistance which the United States can render to your country . . . all possible aid in munitions, armaments, and other supplies . . ." so that Stalin would know that we mean business in a long-term supply job? There were to be "no conditions," Harry Hopkins wrote to the President, no discussion of "future frontiers or spheres of influence."

With Stalin's armies at that moment retreating on all fronts; with his front-line planes and tanks smashed and his front-line shock troops surrendering by the millions; with America still at peace with Germany, Japan, Italy, and Russia—this would have been the time for stipulating terms for a decent peace, and guaranteeing that all the imposing panoply of war we were about to provide not be used to conquer any of Russia's neighbors. This would have been the time for stipulating that Latvia, Estonia, and Lithuania be restored to sovereignty, and that Poland be restored with her original frontiers and with a government freely chosen by her own people. As a political realist Stalin felt that such an agreement might be demanded. Having heard the generous offer, he asked Hopkins point blank: "And what do you want in return for all this?" Hopkins answered: "I have come not to discuss conditions but to get as complete a list as possible of all Russia's needs in tanks, planes, trucks, antiaircraft guns, machine guns, and all sorts of equipment, materials, and supplies." With generous trust and all unconsciously, at that moment we laid the foundations for the major evils that have frustrated all attempts to make a decent peace since the end of World War II.*

The problem became still more pressing for me when, on December 7, 1941, the Japanese made their surprise attack on Pearl Harbor, leaving our mighty Pacific fleet and air force a heap of ruins. The date did not "live in infamy" as Roosevelt had said it would in his war message to Congress delivered on December 8, for until our century, surprise attacks to open a war had been the rule rather than the exception. Moreover, in our own century, in the year 1904, Japan had already made just such a surprise attack on Russia's Pacific fleet. In any case, famous leaders and policies go, but nations remain, and our truly enlightened occupation of Japan was to end with that country's becoming a friendly and to a large extent an allied nation.

Until Pearl Harbor, Norman Thomas and I had been playing active roles on the governing board of the Keep America Out of War Congress and had just written and published together a book entitled *Keep America Out of War* (New York, 1939). On the morning of December 8, even before the President delivered his war message to Congress, Thomas and I talked it over on the phone. We agreed that America was in fact at war and that an emergency meeting of our governing board should be called to dissolve that body. As for our coauthored book, despite Daniel Bell's quip in the *New Leader* ("Have you seen the new Thomas Wolfe book? With such a name it is bound to succeed"), almost none of the review copies were ever reviewed, while along with them the whole first and final printing dropped noiselessly into the sea.

Norman Thomas formed a new group called the Post-War World Council which, or so it seems to me, made little contribution except to strengthen illusions about the forthcoming United Nations and "One

* A report on Harry Hopkins's visit to Stalin in July 1941 is to be found in Robert E. Sherwood, *Roosevelt and Hopkins* (New York, 1948, Chapter XIV, pp. 301–65). Hopkins was already dead when Sherwood wrote this, but he had listened to Hopkins's account of the meeting with Stalin and was given access to Hopkins's partially completed autobiography and all his notes and papers.

World." Some 21 years later, on November 2, 1962, Norman would write to me ruefully: "I read your article in *Foreign Affairs* on 'Communist Ideology and Soviet Foreign Policy' . . . with that assent . . . that I usually feel compelled to give when you speak on Russian affairs. I myself only wish that I had pushed harder my criticisms of the Allied approach to peace with its unnecessary concessions to Stalin's empire building."

As for me, I turned my full attention to the problem of trying to alert my countrymen to the fact that though Stalin made a wonderful ally for winning the war, we must not let our moral debt to the Russian people obscure the moral issues of a decent peace, or grief for countless millions would come of it.

How could a lone wolf make himself heard amid the din of war, the fear of invasion of our "defenseless" West Coast, and all the sounds of a great nation girding itself for battle? I wrote asking for lecture dates to the universities, the women's clubs, the foreign-affairs councils that had hitherto welcomed my talks. Not one of them would permit me to speak on Russia and the Peace. I wrote an article, "Stalin at the Peace Table," completing it at the end of the same month of December in which Pearl Harbor was bombed. Violating the one-sided rule that tries to oblige freelance writers to submit their work to only one magazine at a time, I sent a copy to every editor who had ever asked me for an article or published any of my work.

I had no need to worry that several might accept it at the same moment, thus causing me embarrassment. Indeed, all copies of the article bounced back at once, with or without a coldly worded rejection slip. I visited each editor whom I knew personally. They told me with varying degrees of gruffness, "We're not talking about the making of the peace. We're talking about winning the war." "In that case," I retorted, "we will *win* the war, as we did the last one, but we will *lose* the peace."

My warning fell on deaf ears. A frustrating year went by, and another got under way, yet I made no headway in getting a speaking date or getting my article into print. Then two miracles occurred of the kind that made me remember one of my mother's favorite ego-building remarks to me: "Only God takes care of fools like you!"

The San Francisco poet Kenneth Rexroth, who had been writing endless unsolicited letters to both Richard Rovere and me, discovering one day as he addressed them that we lived on the same street, commanded us to get together. When we met, Rovere had just been made editor of the obscure magazine *Common Sense* (circulation between ten and fifteen thousand). He was editor only for part of 1943 and 1944, but that was a crucial time for me as a frustrated author. On one of our walks along the waterfront below Brooklyn Heights, I told him of my difficulty. "Dick," I said, "if only because you are my friend, or because you believe in freedom of communication, you must publish my article." He read it and returned it with the words, "I don't like it."

"Just the same," I urged, "if not out of friendship, then out of conscience, you must help me break through the voluntary censorship which the entire press has imposed upon itself—and me."

"Well, if you'll let me take out some of the worst expressions . . ." and pulling from his coat pocket the thick black soft drawing pencil that was the tool of his trade, he began to translate me into language more acceptable to him.

My first sentence had read: "To begin with there will be no peace table." He changed it to read: "To begin with there *may* be no peace table." I winced. Yet I recognized the difference in our temperaments, and his greater uncertainty and tentativeness, and I had perforce to allow for the fact that he had not seen the dictator close up, angry and threatening, as I had, nor studied his ways.

"Dick, I get the idea. Let me rewrite it myself and see if I can't make it into a piece acceptable to you without its becoming unacceptable to me." I transformed it quickly into the article that was featured without further change in the issue of *Common Sense* of May 1943. Thus, a year and five months after I had written it, I managed to get the essence of my thought into print, creating such a stir as an obscure writer may create when, out of 133.4 million Americans, he manages to reach—perhaps—some ten or fifteen thousand.

I grieved deeply over the loss of the first sentence, "To begin with there will be no peace table," for it was arresting and, I felt sure, correct. Indeed, there has been no peace table. And to this day, still no peace. Over 30 years later, as I read the article once more for the present book, I remembered how I had relived the anguish of Cassandra, who knew the double misfortune of foreseeing the future and not being believed. It was a pang I was to feel many times thereafter. And small comfort to know that those who ignored such warnings were playing out another archetypal role of Greek legend, the role of Tantalus, for when they bent to drink of the waters of peace, the waters receded, and Cassandra could resume her croaking.

Despite the loss of the first sentence and the change of tone throughout, the article did convey my warning, and was featured on the cover. Dick Rovere and I remained friends as before.

Suddenly and unexpectedly, out of this obscure article in an obscure magazine of derisory circulation came another lucky break. My mother's God must have been taking care of His fool again, for Edward Duckles, a quiet, earnest, busy Quaker activist, Southern field worker for the American Friends Service Committee, director of an international seminar on foreign affairs in North Carolina, broke his leg. Confined to his bed for the nonce, he had time to read. His wife, Jean, like him an earnest, quiet Quaker activist, playing nurse to him, brought him the May *Common Sense* with the comment, "Ed, here's a man writing about peace in the midst of war. I think we should invite him to our institute."

Out of the blue came Duckles's invitation to spend a week at Guilford College, Guilford, North Carolina, to act as "resource man on Russia" and give, besides, an evening talk, open to the nearby community, on "Russia at the Peace Table." Thus in June or July 1943, out of the inscrutable ways of fate, I received a modest platform, and became unwittingly a fellow traveler of the Quakers for the duration of the war.

I MEET SOME MOVIE ACTRESSES

Another ten months of baffling speechlessness and inability to get a word into print. Then, in May 1944, Ed Duckles sent me a second invitation to Guilford. "Don't you ever send people to California?" was my impertinent answer. A week or so of silence, then a third surprise: from Ray Newton of the American Friends Service Committee Headquarters in Philadelphia. "We have arranged dates for you in Seattle, Portland, Eugene, Oakland, San Francisco, and Whittier, and at an International Students Institute in a ranch house north of Taos in New Mexico. The San Francisco date is a Jewish Forum for which separate financial arrangements will be made by the forum. The others are Institutes of International Relations, at which you will stay for three to five days each. The honorarium is $100 for each stop, plus all expenses. There will be another Russian expert at each Institute with a viewpoint different from yours." I knew that the "other expert" would be able to wave two banners, the Red Flag and the Red, White, and Blue, and I could wave no flags but would be giving an unwelcome message of gloom. But I was happy to have at last a wider platform and some West Coast audiences.

As soon as the announcements were printed by the different institutes, the Communist party, which must have taken note of my article in *Common Sense,* sent a message to Harry Bridges, then a member of the Communist party and head of the West Coast longshoremen's union, instructing him that he must stop me from delivering any West Coast talks on "Russia at the Peace Table." In Seattle there was a two-day battle, won by me with the loyal support, strictly limited to passive resistance, of the Seattle Friends' Meeting and ultimately of the aroused citizens of Seattle. The damage to the Communist party, which in the state of Washington had infiltrated the Democratic party and elected both a congressman, Hugh Delacy, and a state senator, Thomas C. Rabbit, was so serious that they called off the other confrontations, permitting me to continue almost undisturbed down the rest of the West Coast.

Audience and controversy differed from meeting to meeting, but when I finally got to Whittier College in the Greater Los Angeles area, my auditors were quiet to the verge of somnolence. The hall was filled with what seemed to be comfortably religious people, middle-aged and elderly men and women, the latter plainly, even dowdily dressed. Still, on one side of the hall there was a group of a half dozen uncommonly pretty young women, fashionably and elegantly clad. The contrast intrigued me. Who were they? What were they doing in Whittier, spending five days at an

Institute of International Relations run by the American Friends Service Committee? The rest of the audience dragged heavily behind me as I pursued my thought. But the pretty girls raced ahead of me, often starting to laugh at my witticisms before I had completed a humorous side remark. Except for being more uniformly pretty and more elegantly dressed, they were like any group of girl graduate students in an honors course.

On the last day of the institute, the group crowded around the lectern. One spoke for all. "We girls want to thank you for what you have done for us."

"Who are you girls? And what have I done for you?"

"We're movie actresses. You wouldn't know our names; we're only beginners; we play bit parts. But we are trying to learn acting. The only place that teaches acting seriously is Actors' Lab. It's controlled by Communists, and they're always trying to feed us Communist propaganda on the side. Our five days with you have given us an antidote that will last us for a lifetime. Now we can study acting and not worry about the propaganda."

I had no time to savor the compliment, for the same spokeswoman continued, "Now can I ask you a question? You speak like a native American. How is it that you know so much about Marx and Engels and Lenin and Trotsky and Stalin, so much about their writings and doings?"

"You're asking me for an autobiography, miss. I can't recite it standing on one foot, so suppose you have a drink with me and I'll try to give you a thumbnail sketch." A drink at Whittier was either orange juice or soda pop. As I soothed my weary throat with orange, I searched for a short answer.

"To begin with, I must tell you that I was born in another century." The girls were astounded. "Wh-what century?" their spokeswoman faltered.

"Would you mind telling me when you were born, young lady?"

"I was born in 1925."

"Of course, then you wouldn't know any other century. Still, you're right to ask, for I was born in 1896, and the century I'm thinking of is not the round-numbered century of the calendar. As a historian, I think of 'the grand century of peace and progress' in which I was born, as beginning in 1815, when Napoleon fell, and ending for Europe in 1914, for America in 1917, when I reached 21.

"I was born when the century of the calendar was nearly at an end, but *la Belle Epoque*, as the French called it, was to last another 19 years in Europe, and almost a quarter of a century for me, in America. Spiritually I was brought up and educated in that 'grand century of peace and progress.' In school, high school, and college, I was taught that since there had been no general war in Europe for 100 years after the fall of Napoleon, the twentieth century would surely be too civilized for war."

The girls laughed. Had I not just been explaining to them in the lecture hall that the twentieth century was a time of troubles? That the long peace had been interrupted not merely by a general European war, but by the first total war in history? That the war had ended in a false peace, breaking down into lesser yet violent and bitter wars, and revolutions? Far from making the world safe for democracy, total war had begotten the first totalitarian regimes. Then the leaders of the two totalitarian regimes, Stalin and Hitler, by partitioning Poland and making secret agreements to partition between themselves as much of Europe and the world as possible, had initiated the Second World War, in which we were still engaged. My central theme had been the danger that the second total war, still in progress, might easily issue into yet another false peace, with the possibility of yet a third total war before our century was over.

"Don't laugh, girls. The expectation that at long last the scourge of war was about to be banished from the earth was general as the nineteenth century drew to a close and the twentieth began. If the belief has proved fatuous, it was a belief shared by philosophers and politicians, by my teachers and my classmates, and by such thinkers and practical men of affairs as Andrew Carnegie, Herbert Hoover, David Starr Jordan, and Woodrow Wilson. In 1910, when Andrew Carnegie was desperately trying to give away all his money in order to die a piously poor man, he added to his other foundations an Endowment for International Peace. All he gave it was ten million dollars, but, canny Scotsman that he was, he worried about the residue after war had been abolished! 'When the establishment of universal peace is attained,' he wrote in the deed of trust, 'the revenue shall be devoted to the banishment of the next most degrading evil. . . .' And as late as February 1914, when he set up a Church Peace Union with a mere two million, he instructed its trustees to 'divert [what would be left over] to relieving the deserving poor.' " Again I was interrupted with laughter, which called for another round of drinks.

"And Herbert Hoover," I resumed, "when war actually broke out, was convinced that the world had blundered into it out of ignorance. If enough scholars would make a thorough study of how that happened, he thought, it would never happen again. As a Quaker, he accepted no direct war work, but he became the greatest organizer of philanthropies in all history by undertaking war relief in 45 countries. Wherever he and his assistants went, he gathered pamphlets, manifestos, journals, government documents, books, and every kind of fugitive material on the war and its attendant lesser wars and revolutions. That is the origin of the Hoover War Library at Stanford, which I have come to California to examine, to see if I will find it useful to work there. But despite all the documents and all the famous scholars who have used them, here we are in our second total war, and our century not yet half over."

I had talked enough, I thought, but the one who had acted as spokeswoman chided, "You haven't answered our question." She was right, of course, so I launched into a second Brobdingnagian "thumbnail sketch."

"Our President," I continued, "when I reached 21 in 1917 was Woodrow Wilson. Originally elected in 1912 on purely domestic issues and engrossed in reforms which he called the New Freedom, he looked with annoyance as well as moral shock at the war that had broken out in Europe. Like Carnegie and Hoover he was convinced that he could find measures to put a stop to it and ensure that so barbarous a thing could be prevented from ever happening again. Just before Christmas 1916, he addressed a note to all the belligerents telling them with asperity that the carnage had gone on long enough, and that it was high time to make a decent compromise peace, without rancor and without victory for either side, and to set up an organization, which we too would join, that would be 'a guarantee against the kindling of any similar conflict in the future.' 'The peace,' he told the Senate late in January 1917, 'must be permanent and universal and preserved by a definite concert of powers which will make it virtually impossible that any such catastrophe should ever overwhelm us again.'

"In 1914, I was a sophomore at college. On a Saturday afternoon, the first day of August, I was hanging out of a summer trolley car bound for the grass tennis courts in Prospect Park, one hand holding a racket, the other an outside pole of the car, when a newsboy rushed past with an *Extra* bearing the huge word WAR on the first page. Switching my racket to the arm holding the pole, I fished for a penny, then read the brief story with incredulity and anger.

" 'Thank God this is a republic,' I said. 'We will never get into it!'

"For the next two years I watched as we sold munitions and supplies to one side and not the other, and as a consortium headed by the House of Morgan floated war-loan bonds for the same Allied side, thus creating a strong material interest in its victory. In the presidential election of 1916 once more our people voted clearly against America's entrance into the monstrous holocaust. Woodrow Wilson conducted his campaign for re-election on the single slogan 'He kept us out of war.' Yet he was no sooner inaugurated for his second term than he sent a war message to Congress. At that time it seemed sheer deception, but in retrospect I see it also as a change of heart on Wilson's part. Only at that moment did my nineteenth-century illusions come to an end.

"In January 1917, I turned twenty-one. Nineteen seventeen was a turning point in America's history and the history of the world, a turning point, too, in my personal history. Though my interests had been literary, not political, though I had not been in the habit of reading foreign news, nor of reading the daily papers at all, I now founded with some of my contemporaries a journal concerned with foreign news, war aims, conscription, wartime legislation, the causes of the war, how we got into it, and how it was changing our national life. The journal was called *Facts: The People's Peace Paper.* It was a strange combination of ignorance, earnest thought and study, and historical insights that until then I did not know I possessed. It constituted my first reluctant entrance into the field of history.

"That same year, Russia left the war. I knew nothing about Russia except for her novelists, but the fact that Lenin took Russia out of the war and announced that he was declaring war on war itself and on 'the war-making system,' caused me to open a large credit to the new rulers of Russia, as yet unknown to me.

"Those two large events, America's entrance into and Russia's exit from the war, gave the initial spin to the trajectory of my life. Since then more than a half century has elapsed, much of which I have spent trying to find the truth about the events in which I was then caught up, to find what it was I knew and didn't know about our time of troubles, and, hardest of all, to find what it was I knew that wasn't so. My talks to you here at Whittier are part of the harvest I have gleaned. That must answer your question, miss, and the questions I see in the faces of the rest of you, for that's all the autobiography I can give you now." And that was the first thumbnail sketch of the autobiography I am writing at this moment.

"*Wh-what century?*" I repeated to myself in amusement as I bade good-bye to the young movie actresses, the first I had ever met. They were going swimming and had invited me to go with them in a nearby pool on a Hollywood estate. I thought briefly of the wispy two-piece bathing suits they would be wearing, then just becoming popular in Hollywood, a style that would not even get its name until a half dozen years later when we dropped a test atom bomb on the atoll of Bikini. And then it was well named; for me who had been born in the nineteenth century the bikini was an atom bomb of a bathing suit.

As I thought of their bikinis, my mind went back to an episode of my childhood. The year was 1899 or 1900, I was going swimming at Brighton Beach with my sister, Lillian, eight years my senior. When she stepped out of the bathhouse, she was wearing a wide, round, shirred bathing cap shaped like a sailor's hat, a blouse with leg-of-mutton sleeves, a knee-length skirt under which were dark-blue woolen bloomers, and a pair of cloth bathing shoes. A policeman stopped us before we could reach the waterline and ordered her off the beach for *indecent exposure,* because she was not wearing stockings! From that raiment of my modest sister so overdressed by present standards yet expelled from ocean and shore for lack of stockings, to the age of the bikini—the two modes bespeak the two different ages in which I have lived my life.

I LEARN ABOUT MARGARET SANGER

My mother earnestly taught us that lying was sinful and we must always tell the truth—except to large corporations, or in order to get a job. It was all right, it seemed, to pretend to be under six as long as you could go free on the trolley or the elevated, or under 12 to get half fare on railroads. It was all right to pretend to be older than you were if that helped you to get a job. To a family that had lived through two depressions—that from 1893 to 1898 and the crisis of 1907 and 1908—getting a job was a serious matter and any stratagem that might help was deemed permissible.

We were a poor family; every cent any of us could earn was contributed to the family purse, managed with unrelaxing care by my mother. With a family of six, including three growing boys and a girl, and my father able to turn over to my mother in good times only eight dollars a week to feed and clothe us and pay the rent, what we children earned was never pocket money. From the age of nine I worked before and after school delivering papers. During the summers I sold newspapers and, as soon as I looked old enough, I got a job as a newsboy and candy butcher on the Long Island Rail Road, and then as a messenger boy for Western Union. When my older sister and brother reached the crucial age of fourteen, which enabled them to get working papers, their schooling ended. I was the first in my family who ever got to high school and college. At the age of 16, being just barely tall enough and weighing within ounces enough to pass the physical, I pretended to be 18 and took the examination for postal clerk, which, like all exams, I passed easily. Thus at 18 I was already appointed and working after school and during summer vacations as a full-time substitute postal clerk to help meet the family needs while going to college.

One day in April 1914, as I was working in the General Post Office with "all hands" during the late-afternoon rush hour on the all-important first-class mail, an unprecedented order was given us by the superintendent to drop the privileged financial-district rush mail and go down to "The Hole" for a special emergency assignment. I was working in the old General Post Office building in City Hall Park, and my normal assignment for six hours of the eight-hour day was "killing slugs," i.e., hand-canceling stamps on parcels in The Hole, a huge cellar or basement with only tiny grated windows, innocent of all cross ventilation, and of course without air conditioners, a device that had not yet been invented. Because clerks had fainted there on hot days, a rule was adopted while I was working in the hole that we were to go up and outdoors for air for ten minutes in every hour, except at the end of the first hour and the beginning of the last of our eight-hour day. That was the rush hour, when all hands, except the clerks tending windows, were ordered to handle the sacrosanct first-class mail dumped in mountains between four-thirty and six-thirty from the downtown business offices. This rush hour provided a great relief for me. I would go from the cellar to the well-lighted, better-ventilated main floor, to face up the incoming first-class mail so that all the stamps faced the same way, to be swallowed by a lickety-split machine that canceled them.

But now, unprecedented in the history of the General Post Office, all of us who were not tending windows were ordered to abandon the top-priority financial-district mail still pouring in in boxes, bags, and banded bundles. In the cellar the super mounted a table to instruct us on the sudden emergency assignment:

"I want you fellows to take every piece of second- or third-class mail, every newspaper or magazine that is wrapped in a circular wrapper open at both ends, hold it up to the light, and see if another piece of mail is wrapped up inside it. We're looking for copies of an eight-page sheet called *The Woman Rebel.* This is their first issue and it carries the dateline March 1914. The solicitor has declared it obscene and unmailable under Section 89 of the P.L. and R. (Postal Laws and Regulations), but the bitch who edits it, name of Margaret Sanger, after getting the official notice, has been trying to fool us by mailing it wrapped up in respectable newspapers and magazines. Whenever you see a piece of mail inside another, don't pull it out but take the whole piece over to this table. If there's a lot of them we'll put up extra bags and boxes. *Don't let any get through!*"

This was exciting! I no longer minded being dragged down into The Hole again without my accustomed respite. I did as I was told, but after I had found a few pieces containing the contraband journal, I extracted one and took it to the men's room to see what monstrous obscenity had caused the excitement.

I looked in vain for obscenity. The magazine was poorly edited and diffuse, as if its editor were only beginning to zero in on what was to be her special target for the rest of her life. The masthead contained the slogan "NO GODS NO MASTERS." The journal would aim to "stimulate working women to think for themselves and build up a conscious fighting character . . . teach young girls from fourteen to eighteen what constitutes clean living without prudishness . . . show what social force is at play to cause large scale prostitution . . . advocate the prevention of conception and impart such knowledge in the columns of this paper. . . ." That must be it, of course; that promise was the aim that earned the verdict "unmailable," though there was no contraceptive information whatsoever in this first issue. All discussions of sex were decent and delicate to the verge of prudery. On one page there was yet another, more diffuse statement of aims reading:

"The Rebel Women claim: the Right to be lazy; the Right to be an unmarried mother; the Right to destroy; the Right to create; the Right to love; the Right to live." There were a number of contributions and fillers manifestly selected by the editor. "The IWW Preamble" vying with the vague "pagan-liberal" slogans of Greenwich Village. But the first page and the last, made up of unsigned editorials written by one Margaret Sanger, made clear what the destiny of the journal and its editor was to be.

I was only 18 when I engaged in this intensive search for concealed copies of *The Woman Rebel,* and I had never heard the name of Margaret Sanger. Now her crusading zeal and the no less dedicated zeal of Post Office solicitors, superintendents, police, and magistrates would guarantee that her name was never to fade from my memory. There were many others who worked with her or acted separately in the same cause, but thenceforward she would devote herself to nothing else and was tireless in keeping her name and her cause in public view, until to say "Margaret Sanger" was to think *Birth Control,* spelled in one's mind as she always spelled it, with two capital letters. At first smart-aleck newspapermen mocked at her ("Not only should she be barred from the mails but males should be barred from her," wrote one of them); later they reported her doings matter-of-factly, and much later with reluctant or ungrudging admiration. But they never seemed to realize that the suppression of this poorly edited, single-minded, crusading journal might well be regarded as the Zenger case of the twentieth century.

Arrayed against her was a multitude of statutes; the tenets of the Catholic Church, so well entrenched in the political machines and among the police and magistrates of many of our big cities; the fanatical zeal of Anthony Comstock, secretary of the Society for the Suppression of Vice and author of the Comstock Law of 1873; and the then prevailing notion that population growth was the measure of a nation's greatness and a city's progress. Not until a quarter century had elapsed from the publication and suppression of that first issue of *The Woman Rebel* did Margaret Sanger's cause make its first important step on the road to legality and respectability. In 1936 the United States Court of Appeals, in a case known as *The United States* v. *One Package,* reversed the conviction of Dr. Hannah Stone, who had committed "the criminal act of importing a package of contraceptive diaphragms from England." The charge had been made under the Comstock Act of 1873, which made the importation, or offering for sale, or even any description of such simple devices, an act of obscenity. The court's ruling in the case was narrow, for it decided that in this particular instance the action was not obscene because Dr. Stone was a duly licensed physician and had imported the diaphragms lawfully for use in the treatment of one or more patients. Circumspect, yet a breakthrough. All the same, Margaret Sanger, her publications, and her clinics continued to have troubles with police and courts, and with such crusaders for "public decency" as Comstock and John Singer Sumner.

During an entire half century, people of my own and succeeding generations still had to choose whether they wished to devote their time and energy to test cases, or engage in under-the-counter purchase from druggists they knew, or find out from such writers as the English birth-control crusader Marie Stopes where such devices as diaphragms and suppositories could be legally bought in England. The English firms connived at our lawbreaking by wrapping their products in misshapen packets of the *London Times* or *Manchester Guardian,* many copies of which traveling in hot weather and in the holds of coal-burning ships were likely to arrive with melted cocoa butter making the outer pages of the packet suspiciously translucent.

All through the sixties the battle against freedom to publish information, freedom to sell contraceptive devices, freedom for doctors and nurses to make such information and such materials available, and the right of women to control their own bodies, continued to be waged in many cities and such states as Massachusetts and Connecticut. By 1966, when Margaret Sanger, worn out by the weight of her years and battles, died quietly in Arizona, her victory seemed well nigh universal.

In 1969, when I made a trip to New York to prepare the shipment of my books and papers to the Hoover Library, I got visual evidence that I was now living in another century from the one in which I was born. As I sat in the subway, my eye lighted on a placard put up by the city authorities:

YOU CAN DECIDE
HOW MANY CHILDREN YOU WANT.
INFORMATION ABOUT BIRTH CONTROL
IN YOUR NEIGHBORHOOD.
CALL 777-2015

FAMILY PLANNING INFORMATION SERVICE

I made a note of the date—September 18, 1969, some 55 years after that day in April 1914 when the superintendent of the General Post Office had set me, an 18-year-old youth, to hunting down concealed copies of the first issue of *The Woman Rebel* in which Margaret Sanger opened her "obscene" and "criminal" campaign. And on August 6, 1970, the United States Court of Appeals for the First Circuit ruled unconstitutional the broad language of the 125-year-old Massachusetts law to punish "crimes against decency, chastity, morality, and good order" and set aside the 1967 conviction of birth-control crusader William A. Baird. He had given without prescription a tube of contraceptive foam to an unmarried Boston woman student and publicized his action to test the constitutionality of the law. Strange to relate, the Civil Liberties Union refused to take his case, but many lawyers offered to serve him without compensation. How new the "new century" was is testified to with unconscious irony by the fact that only one week before this decision, the Supreme Judicial Court of Massachusetts had once more upheld the constitutionality of the selfsame 125-year-old statute. The new decision held that the statute, since it had been construed to dictate whether individuals might learn about, purchase, and use contraceptives, "conflicts with fundamental human rights; in the absence of demonstrated harm, we hold it beyond the competency of the state." The opinion of the court written by Chief Judge Bailey Aldrich, was unanimous. And the idea that there were some things that should be held to be "beyond the competency of the state" was never to leave my mind again.

2

FUTUROLOGY: THE NINETEENTH CENTURY LOOKS FORWARD TO THE TWENTIETH

> Most of the turning points of history, great and small, were surprises to both their participants and the analysts of the day, whatever their doctrine.
>
> —Kenneth Arrow

There is a fascination to a little row of zeros that makes scholars commit themselves to enterprises of which they might otherwise be wary. It is understandable that we should think highly of a zero, and of the number ten, for during countless centuries they have enabled men to count, to sum, and to record the passage of time. The Aztecs and the Mayans, perhaps because their climate encouraged them to go barefoot, raised the number of digits to twenty and reckoned time and tribute in twenties. Hence, we should not wonder at the double fascination of the coming millennium that begins with the year 2000. By 1960, with that millennium still four decades away, many of our political scientists and sociologists could contain themselves no longer, and a new-*ology* was born and baptized: futurology. My friend Daniel Bell deserted his fruitful contemplation of *Work and Its Discontents* and his less rewarding efforts to demonstrate *The End of Ideology*, in order to make himself captain of an impressive crew of explorers of a century and millennium yet unborn. In France another friend, Bertrand de Jouvenel, abandoned his fascinating study *Power* to publish *Futuribles* and a monthly journal, *Analyse et Prévision*. The Social Science Research Council set up its Committee on the Next Thirty Years; the Ford Foundation made a large investment in futurology; the Prophecy Institute at Cornwall on the Hudson published "A Framework for Speculation" under the title *The Year 2000;* and a reference-work publisher in Germany sent out a prospectus on a coming *Who's Who in Futurology*. How one can get into this venturesome company is not made clear by the publisher, but I imagine anyone may qualify who makes bold to publish a book on the next century or millennium. "Nice work if you can get it," I might be moved to say were it not for the memory of how badly our nineteenth century fared when we projected its expectations concerning the twentieth.

It seems strange now to contemplate how confident we were, we who inherited the presuppositions of the eighteenth century and were born into the certitudes of the nineteenth, when we thought of the coming wonders of the hundred years that were to begin with the year 1900. In 1781 Edward Gibbon could write while England was engaged in yet another war with France and was losing her 13 colonies on the Atlantic seaboard:

> In war the European forces are exercised by temperate and indecisive contests. The balance of power will continue to fluctuate, and the prosperity of our own or the neighboring kingdoms may be alternately exalted or depressed; but these partial events cannot essentially injure our general state of happiness, the system of the arts and laws and manners, which so advantageously distinguish above the rest of mankind the Europeans and their colonists.

It is not because Gibbon did not know of war, for he had just earned a captaincy in the Seven Years War. Nor was he unaware of the decline and fall of empires, since his great life work was the study of the decline and fall of Rome. Yet in the optimistic milieu in which he was brought up, there was no possibility of his imagining that the British Empire might also decline and fall.

Compare his words with those of Paul Valéry, writing in 1922 in France, a France at that moment victorious after the first total war of our century:

> The storm has ended, yet we are still restless and full of care. . . . We have only vague hopes but clear fears. No thinking man can avoid the darkness. . . . We know not what will come, and not without reason, we are afraid of the future. . . . It can be said that all the foundations of our world have been shaken. Something more essential than the replaceable parts of a machine has worn out. . . .

THE LIGHTS GO OUT

On August 3, 1914, Sir Edward Grey stood looking out of his chancellery window at the lowering night and, though bombing planes were but boxkites then, the first blackout was beginning. "The lights are going out all over Europe," he said, "never to be rekindled in our generation." Now we know that the darkness was to last for many generations, for its pall hangs over us still.

It was *la Belle Epoque* that was blacking out, along with the self-styled "grand century of peace and progress" and two centuries of confident optimism. Ending that night was our futurological prophecy that the twentieth century would be "too civilized for war." Ending too was one of the strongest and most deeply rooted and widespread of all the futurological certitudes, the dreams of international scientific socialism. And many other dreams to which the eighteenth century had given rational form and the nineteenth made such seeming progress in realizing: dreams of cosmopolitanism and internationalism; of the free movement of men, ideas, and goods in an ever widening and ever more open society. Gone the dream of a limited state circumscribing its powers and regulations, submitting to steadily increasing control from below and the strengthening of curbs on dictatorial, arbitrary, bureaucratic, and autocratic power. But today forced-labor and concentration camps at the heart of Europe have replaced the hope of the abolition of all forms of involuntary servitude. Two total wars have so brutalized our age that there actually exists a kind of terror international in which Japanese terrorists can replace Arab terrorists to machine-gun an Israeli airport, the largest number of their victims being Roman Catholics from Puerto Rico making a pilgrimage to Jerusalem. The map of the world that was incomplete without the blessed isles of Utopia has been replaced by a map with the bleak islands of Dystopia, and to build such islands at the very heart of the great civilizations have arisen arrogant and dehumanized "sciences" that assure us of the total manipulability of man, with "concerned scientists" as self-appointed manipulators—scientists with the ability to transform genes and viruses with DNA without knowing what new and monstrous things may come of it.

Those who came to maturity in the epoch between the two total wars, or in the succeeding time of troubles in which we now live, find it hard to imagine a century in which peace, solid and relaxed, seemed the normal state of affairs, and war but a temporary interruption. To be sure, in the long peace between 1815 and 1914 there were several wars at the heart of Europe, but they had limited aims and intentions, were looked on as disturbances of the normal state, set their goals as the signing of a peace treaty and a fresh agreement, and ended quickly with comparatively generous peace terms that left the political and social structure, and the map of Europe itself, basically unaltered, the vanquished recovering as quickly as the victorious. It was with this in mind that Clausewitz wrote that each war should end with a fresh equilibrium or balance of power of the age-old "Republic of the States of Europe."

Back in 1912, when I began my study of French at City College, I read a story of the Franco-Prussian War of 1870–71 that contained the following episode: On March 1, 1871, a French writer is sitting in a garret facing on one of the main arteries of Paris; he hears the sound of tramping boots and martial music; he goes to the window and sees the gray uniforms of Prussian soldiers occupying the City of Light. In disgust, he watches the parade for a moment, then closes the window, goes back to his table, and resumes his writing. I don't remember the writer's name, the story may be apocryphal, but it was written to suggest a time when fighting was the business of specialists called soldiers, and writing the business of poets and novelists.

When Clausewitz wrote the words repeatedly cited by Lenin, "War is the continuation of policy by other means," he was saying that the policy of peacetime should govern the rational aims and set the limits on a war which had interrupted the policy or politics of peace. In the first article he published, anonymously, he wrote:

> What seems to be the purpose of all the development of the art of war consists exclusively in the following: to subject the events (in general, the interplay of forces) to the control of a reasonable will, to make them more and more independent of the play of chance.

But during the first total war of our century, a new breed of "military theorist" would appear in the shape of V. I. Lenin to rip out of its context and stand on its head his oft-repeated, solitary quotation from Clausewitz. For Lenin the policies of peace were the policies forced upon him by his inability to find as yet the occasion for engaging in all-out or total war. The policies and politics of peace (in German as in Russian one and the same word covers both *politics* and *policy*) are to him but the policies aiming to bring about "the final conflict," the policy of a longed for war to that end that has not yet burst into full flower. A time of peace was a time to form his detachments, to stir their passions and hatreds, to train his cadres, to exercise and drill them, to steel their fighting spirit, to initiate them in preliminary skirmishes, deeds of arms, dress rehearsals, practice actions, preparing for open war. Thus did Lenin turn Clausewitz upside down.

Since Andrew Carnegie had been so generous in setting up public libraries near whatever run-down neighborhood I happened to live in (for which, even after I had learned of his ignominious role in the Homestead Steel strike, I continued to bless his memory), I read everything in that amazing array of books that a generous citizenry was taxing itself to buy for me, everything I could lay hands on, with no discernible limitation except that I as a little boy could take out no more than one work of nonfiction and one of fiction per day. Many an afternoon I spent long happy hours in Tompkins Square Park finishing both of the precious treasures, then argued, sometimes in vain, with "teacher" (the librarian) that I really had finished them and wanted to return them and get two others to read that night.

I read history, too, but it was never current history, for the libraries I frequented bought only the work of historians whose worth had been "proved by time." Nor did I read newspapers or magazines since they seemed much inferior to the marvelous books pressing to be read. Moreover the newspapers had almost no foreign news in those days of innocence, only love nests, divorces, murder trials, municipal and national corruption, and other such trivia, and I early outgrew the funnies. Hence I fondly believed that wars were the sport of kings for which democratic republics would have no use. I knew we had been in a war with Spain when I was too young to understand it, but that had been more like a parade of victories in which our boys died only of rotten beef or yellow fever or malaria, and Spanish cannonballs always fell into the sea far short of our great ships.

WAR BECOMES TOTAL

Yet the "sport of kings" had been but a moderate sport compared with the wars of entire peoples, after the French Revolution brought the people to the center of the stage. Whereas dynastic wars could be settled swiftly by the son of one house marrying the daughter of another, and conflicts over a strip of land could be ended by the victorious occupation of the strip by the better army or by its partition, or an exchange of one piece of territory for another, the wars of the French Revolution and Napoleon ultimately put 3 million people into battle, while the war that began in Europe in 1914 engaged from the outset entire populations and was fought under vast ideological banners for no lesser stakes than predominance in Europe and in the world.

Most Americans did not seem to take the failure of European civilization as seriously as I; most of us went on doing what we had been doing before. We thanked God for having created Columbus and the Atlantic Ocean to keep us out of the mess. Or thanked our forefathers for the foresight they had shown in emigrating from Europe. To a tune lifted from Bizet's *Carmen* America sang lightheartedly:

> I'm sorry that there must be war,
> I don't know what they're fighting for,
> But I'm glad my wife's in Europe,
> Where she can't get back,
> Where she can't get back . . .
> Where she can't get back no more.

But she got back, as I discovered when I was compelled to work all day and all night "dragging ship," that is, dragging mailbags from the delivery platform to the mail chute the day the first ships finally got through the double blockade.

After we got used to scenes of battle carnage, denuded forests, and war news flashes, the song that really swept the country ran:

> I didn't raise my boy to be a soldier,
> I brought him up to be my pride and joy,
> Not to raise his musket to his shoulder,
> To shoot some other mother's darling boy.

Yet America was not as carefree as her songs. The more sensitive among us grieved at the breakdown of European civilization. Gradually too, I became aware of the fact that this war was different from all earlier wars, that it was not a "more-or-less war" but an "absolute war." Not thrones nor strips of land, nor the reestablishment of a balance of power in the "Republic of the States of Europe," nor the return to a *status quo ante*, but Right and Wrong, Truth and Error, Good and Evil, Orthodoxy and Heresy, Aggression and Innocence, Past and Future, Faith and System and Way of Life were held to be in contest with each other. When antagonists raise such banners, does not compromise become shameful or impossible? When service in the army becomes no longer a task of specialists but a democratic and universal obligation, when the memories and solidarities, affections and antagonisms of entire peoples are engaged, when universal suffrage makes foreign affairs no longer the trade of trained diplomats and practical negotiators but matters to be submitted to the emotions and passions, the swift judgments and catchy slogans of inexperienced multitudes, no minor adjustments of territory, no tolerance, no give and take, no specific and limited aims seemed any longer possible; nothing but all-out victory, complete surrender, total occupation and subjection to not yet formulated war aims. In short, as I realized each day more keenly, Europe was entering into an age of total war.

What brought this home most intensely to me was a series of flattering yet disturbing experiences at our college. To the Great Hall of the College of the City of New York came a succession of distinguished scholars to convince us that the cause of Germany and Austria-Hungary, or the cause of Belgium, France, England, and Russia, was just, and should become our cause as well. Of the Americans who spoke to us the most distinguished and impressive was the historian Charles A. Beard. In a single, spellbinding hour he summed up forty or fifty years of history to persuade us that the unification of Germany under the aegis of Prussia and the Hohenzollern dynasty had consolidated autocracy and militarism and transformed the land of Goethe, Schiller, and Heine, of Bach, Beethoven, and Mozart, into the land of the Prussian drillmaster and the *Junker*. He charged the Central Powers with responsibility for bringing on the war. He made vivid the plight of neutral and harmless Belgium, and demonstrated that Austria's ultimatum to Serbia was deliberately formulated in terms that no self-respecting sovereign country could accept. Our acting president, Adolph Werner, head of the German department and great humanist for whom I felt a deep affection (he was one of my favorite teachers and I one of his favorite students), was so angry at the "abuse" of the Great Hall lecture platform for "propaganda purposes" that he issued a prescript that Professor Beard should not be invited again, and that the bellicose debate in a land whose President had asked us to be "neutral in thought and deed" should cease at once.

But the debate would not be stilled. In 1915, to the Great Hall of our college came two philosophers of great distinction to win our spirits to their respective sides. One was Henri Bergson, sent to us by the government of France. Bergson was already known to me by reputation as an analyst of laughter, as a philosopher of dynamic activism, as the author of works on durational time, on motion and change, on free will, on creative evolution, as a thinker who had given us a whole new vocabulary and set of concepts, a philosopher destined, a little too belatedly, to get a Nobel Prize for Literature. Germany sent us a less colorful philosopher, already a Nobel Prize winner, Rudolf Eucken, who had achieved some distinction for his discussion of Aristotelian method, and greater reputation for his idealism and moral philosophy, and his fashionable buttressing of religion in an increasingly skeptical age.

Of course, we were flattered to be addressed by these eminent men. Though I had already won the Ward medals in German literature and moral philosophy, and was president of the Deutscher Verein, Eucken made little impression on me. Though I was a mere beginner in French, in which I could win no college medal if I should live to be a hundred, it was Bergson who captured my imagination. But neither the historian Beard nor the philosophers Eucken and Bergson won our support for their respective sides. In my spirit there was growing despair for Europe's culture, and growing awareness that this was a new kind of war, as I contemplated the fact that philosophers were enlisting their wisdom as war propagandists; historians rewriting their country's and their enemy's past; scientists signing manifestos on wartime atrocities real and imaginary; novelists and poets donning uniforms and dipping their pens in blood-red ink.

Only over the course of years did I come to realize that it was not just one single all-embracing war, but an age of total wars into which we were entering, and that much of my young manhood and maturity would be devoted not to the "pure" literary pursuits of which I had dreamed, but to vain and futile efforts to keep America out of "Europe's bloody wars," and to try to prevent such wars from recurring.

Having had my expectations and beliefs formed in the nineteenth century, that "grand century of peace and progress," and in the splendid afterglow of *la Belle Epoque*, and coming to maturity in the Age of Total Wars, I was driven by indignation and by hope to make the effort, to forgo my dreams of contributing to literature in its "purer" sense, and turn my literary efforts into history, political analysis, sociology, and kindred fields, hoping at the same time to make of my histories and other writings works of genuine literature, and to leave the English language if not better, at least not worse, than I found it when I was born to its great heritage. Nor do I give up altogether the hope that the body of work I leave behind may yet serve in some small measure to aid my country and mankind to climb out of the shadow of the *smutnoye vremya*, the Time of Troubles, in which most of my own years have been spent.

As in the bloody centuries of the "holy" wars between Cross and Crescent and the century and a half that succeeded the split in European culture and faith in which Protestant and Catholic princes of church and state had to learn that the "true faith" could not conquer by the sword, now once more a long period of localized and limited wars in a stable "Republic of the States of Europe" was giving way to an age in which ancient thrones and empires disappear as if they had never been, an age beset by clashing arms and doctrines. Once more confidence yields to uncertainty, and relative indifference, tolerance, transaction, and compromise to a new age of force. And history, as Stephen Dedalus says, becomes "a nightmare from which I am trying to awake."

PROPHETS OF VIOLENCE

Before long there were prophets on hand to tell us of it. "The age of discussion ends," wrote Spengler with *Schadenfreude* (joy in evil), "and the age of 'election as revolution in legitimate forms' now leads to one in which mankind 'elects' its destiny once more by the primitive methods of violence." Lenin, also writing with *zloradstvo,* the same joy in evil, bade his most faithful wartime lieutenant Shlyapnikov bear in mind that "the epoch of the *bayonet* has come, which means that it is *with this weapon* that we must fight." Then, in a world begotten by total war, would come other men, like Mussolini, to proclaim that "a revolution is an *idea* with bayonets"; Mao Tse-tung, to omit Mussolini's *idea* and proclaim nakedly that "power comes out of the barrel of a gun"; Hitler, to pronounce our epoch "a time when not the mind but the fist decides." The few thinkers in the nineteenth century who dimly foresaw this age did not gloat like these (gloat is the nearest English equivalent to proclaiming with *Schadenfreude* or *zloradstvo),* for men like Herzen wrote their flashes of prophecy in fear or, like Henry Adams, in resignation.

The first total war, which was to "make the world safe for democracy," actually aborted the nascent democracy of countries like Germany and Russia, begetting in them the first totalitarian regimes in history. These in turn, reaching out their hands to each other in the Stalin-Hitler Pact, brought on the second total war. Yet I feel that the initial responsibility must not be laid on the two totalitarian powers who were by-products of the first total war, but on the failure of our civilization itself, a failure that brought on the first total war, which begot the two totalitarianisms. Before there could be what Churchill called "the bloody-minded professors of the Kremlin," there had first to be the bloody mess in Flanders, where, as Britain's wartime leader, Lloyd George, would write: "Nothing could stop Haig's compulsion to send thousands and thousands to their death against the enemy's guns in the bovine and brutal game of attrition."

The children of our new age are growing up in an altogether different world from that of my childhood, a world in which "war is the health of the state," in which soldiering has ceased to be a specialized and somewhat misprized profession, but has become a normal part of every able-bodied man's experience, in which life is chained to the expectation, or apprehension, that peace may be but a troubled breathing spell between wars.

Thus in August 1914 began the age of the bayonet, the rocket, and the bomb. It began with a brief dream of a *Blitzkrieg* to be "over by Christmas," followed by four long terrible years of a frozen war of position, bloody brutalizing years that were to accustom us to brutality in our daily lives, in our streets, our neighborhoods, our discussions, our classrooms, our campuses, terrible years in which statesmen and generals treated all male citizens as so much human matériel to be expended without stint or calculation in the pursuit of undefinable and unattainable objectives, savage hopeless years with absolutely no end in sight—until America suddenly tipped the scales with the entry of fresh troops into the worn, decimated battle lines.

In the trenches men learned the art of sniping, the art of mugging, the art of making and throwing bombs, of making delayed-action booby traps and incendiaries, of sticking in of knife and bayonet. Later, as the training became more universal and the weaponry more sophisticated, any crackpot with a rifle equipped with a telescopic sight might shoot a president from a distance and, except by accident or blunder, escape detection. Men learned to accept as commonplace the ruthless logic of mutual extermination, to master their fear of sudden death and their revulsion at inflicting it, to develop a monstrous indifference to suffering, their own as well as that of others.

Without this spread of the psychology of the trenches and the strain of endless, all-consuming, all-demanding, stalemated total war, a Lenin and a Hitler might have gone down in history as one more page each in a book of terrors and hatreds, a page for Lenin alongside of Bakunin and Nechayev, lesser perhaps than Bakunin but greater and more scrupulous than Nechayev.

But war was Lenin's opportunity. Universal military discipline made his vision of military discipline in the party, in the state, and in all of public life, made, too, his requisitioning during the first period of "war communism" of every sheaf of wheat and every inkpot, seem less alien and less unworkable. Total war's brutal conception that entire peoples, men, and women, and children, are "the enemy," made his idea of the extermination of entire classes seem less shocking.

Universal war so brutalized modern man that it became possible to beguile men into fresh brutalities by their resentment against brutality. Now that all things seemed subject to the arbitrament of bullet and bayonet and bomb, why not war and peace and "the system" that had made the sterile carnage possible, or, according to Lenin, inevitable?

As a historian I may try to console myself by remembering the long and bloody history of man's wars on his fellow man, but there is no comfort in it, for the scale is different and the spirit, too. At the end of the Napoleonic Wars, all the nations of Europe together had a total of 3 million men under arms. But in our first total war, more than five times that many made up the numbers of the killed and wounded alone. World War II involved the total conscription of labor and manpower. Its aim, if that's the word for it, involved the total annihilation of all the centers of industry and population of the enemy that could be effectively reached by shells, or missiles, or bombs. As for a possible Third World War with weaponry that makes science fiction seem the work of impoverished imaginations, my own imagination falters.

A VANISHED WORLD

How remote now seems that world into which I was born, in which one could buy a ticket to anywhere on the face of the earth—except Turkey or Russia—without presenting an identity card, a passport, or a visa. If one did not have the price, one could present oneself to a ship's purser and ask for a job as a workaway, as, by stowing away until the pilot was dropped, I was able to do as late as 1924, when traveling from Mexico to Moscow. But in general the free and open world remained thus open only until 1914 in Europe and 1917 in the United States. Then total war with its psychological warfare, its espionage, its sabotage by "tourists" and terrorists of industrial and military objectives, made even the freest and most relaxed of governments dictatorial in matters of the free exit and entrance of its citizens as well as foreigners. Up to 1914 a passport was a luxury, a privilege of the envoy or of the wealthy traveler, in which his government introduced him and commended him to the hospitality of foreign officials, never a necessity for the humbler citizen or the refugee seeking some spot on the planet where he might come to rest and resume his full status as a human being.

My existence in my young manhood was attested to by my mere physical presence, without documents, forms, permits, licenses, orders, lists of currency carried in and out, identity cards, draft cards, ration cards, exit stamps, customs declarations, questionnaires, tax forms, reports in multiplicate, or other authentications of my birth, being, nationality, status, beliefs, color, creed, right to be, enter, leave, move about, work, trade, purchase, dwell. The middle ages, to be sure, had known fixity of many kinds. But our nineteenth century had been the great century of the loosening of the bonds, of *laissez-faire*, of individual autonomy, of freedom of movement of men, money, and ideas—and our confident nineteenth-century futurology bade us believe that the twentieth century would be freer still.

There is incredulous wonder in the eyes of young men and women when I tell them that in my youth I could go around the world, except for only two countries, without a document. A lost world? I for one have never accepted the passport system and all the barbed wire of documents. They are by-products of the universal bureaucratization of life, of total war and totalitarianism, and we cannot take one step toward a return to a more truly open society without abolishing the compulsory passport and visa and reducing the maze of documents that threaten to drown us. Moreover, the whole wasteful process that consumes the time of millions of bureaucrats in many lands, has never yet stopped a Communist, a dope smuggler, a bail jumper, a spy, from making his trip. Criminals, and spy rings, and agents of foreign powers know how to forge or purchase passports. With our impressive open frontiers with Canada and Mexico, who but scholars, innocents, tongue-tied or vociferous travelers, or Simple Simons, can be stopped by paper walls? Unregenerate therefore after more than half a century of travel and observation, and after getting to Russia without a passport from my government, and into Spain during the Spanish Civil War with a passport stamped "Not valid for Spain," only to be asked on my return by a high official of our State Department to report on what I had just seen where I was not supposed to be, I oppose the passport system still. Nor do I altogether despair of seeing in the remainder of my lifetime some hesitant steps made by my country and by England, perhaps by all the NATO countries, toward the loosening of the bonds. In fact, in the last few years some such steps, hesitant, feeble, and scarcely noted, have been taken.

3

THE EDUCATION OF A BROOKLYN BOY AT THE TURN OF THE CENTURY: I. Cemeteries and Swamps

Until I turned sixteen and began going to the College of the City of New York, Brooklyn was my city, and the limits of my physical world. Much of my education I got from its streets, its cemeteries, its wooded hills, its marshes, much of it from its schools, its libraries, its museums, the ten-cent galleries of its stock-company playhouses, and my fellow Brooklynites.

Contrary to the opinion disseminated by vaudeville comics, Brooklyn was no mean city. Before it joined Greater New York on January 1, 1898, to its undoing, it was the third or fourth largest city in the United States, with a sizable cultural life of its own. At the moment of its self-immolation it possessed some 1.2 million inhabitants to the greater city's 3.4 million, the latter figure being reached only by adding the newly annexed Brooklynites. It had, and still has, its own excellent library system, schools and high schools and colleges; a museum that has exhibits in both the arts and the sciences; a children's museum which as far as I know is unmatched in the other four boroughs, and is still functioning; the Brooklyn Academy of Music, now in slow decline; its own theater district, now deserted but once possessing theaters both for traveling companies and stock companies; annual big outdoor tent circus visits, and exciting circus parades, of both Barnum and Bailey and Ringling Bros., that eclipsed the indoor circuses in Madison Square Garden; and it still boasts the possession of the benevolent Pratt Institute of Arts and Sciences and Pratt Library, which are in some ways comparable yet superior to the Cooper Institute at Cooper Union in Manhattan.

Besides, it had such attractions as a unique accent, now slowly losing ground to the blows of radio and television and the influx of Negroes and Puerto Ricans and other peoples with accents of their own; a unique and comical baseball team, which has since deserted Ebbets Field and the city of its birth and true fame; and a long and hospitable string of cemeteries that run through its wooded northern hills, all of which have been the source of most of the music hall and journalistic jokes concerning Brooklyn. It, and not Manhattan, was, and still is, the great world seaport with a long and varied coastline of hills and beaches, and docks where ships are loaded and unloaded for traffic with distant ports and seas, ships bearing such imagination-kindling names for a little boy as *Gran Colombiana* and *Yamato Maru.* If New York is known to the world as a great seaport, it is Brooklyn that makes it so.

When I delivered newspapers in the early 1900s, with Brooklyn for almost a decade no more than a borough, there were still four Brooklyn dailies bought by many of my customers: the *Brooklyn Eagle,* the *Brooklyn Times,* the *Brooklyn Citizen,* and the *Brooklyn Standard Union.* The *Brooklyn Eagle,* from 1841, when it was founded, until the 1920s, was one of America's truly great newspapers. In its days of greatness it offered a full coverage of national and foreign news as well as an amazingly detailed amount of Brooklyn and Long Island local news, issued an annual almanac in no way inferior to the still surviving *World Almanac,* crusaded against political bosses and political corruption, fought for the Brooklyn Bridge, which was to be a contributor to its ultimate death, and gave Brooklyn a strong sense of community, a knowledge of its own life as a great city, and a feeling for its history and traditions. It served Brooklyn well, and among its editors included Walt Whitman, who served America well. It took in its stride the loss of advertising as the result of some of its crusades against greed and corruption, and in 1955 finally died a hard and lingering death (as so many of the Manhattan newspapers did), as a result of the ever greater centralization in Manhattan of the city's cultural life, the competition of new media such as radio, and the unforesightful demands of the typographical unions and the newspapermen's guild. If ever the greater city should really develop a more localized community life again, something like a resuscitated *Brooklyn Eagle* will be needed once more.

In my boyhood there remained an empty lot on Berriman Street in East New York (on which street I lived from my ninth year to my twenty-first), where a tethered billy goat waited for me to pass with my four Brooklyn dailies and my Greater New York journals to feed him such delicacies as the slender strips of paper that I tore from their margins before I delivered the printed matter to my customers.* But I must admit that the goat, though born in Brooklyn even as I was, really showed no special dedication to the Brooklyn dailies, eating with equal relish the Manhattan English-language journals and strips from the *Jewish Daily Forward,* the German *Staatzeitung,* and *Il Progresso Italiano.* My mother, when I commented on this, assured me that "goats will eat anything, even tin cans," an assertion which I never swallowed any more than the goat did.

* An article in the Soviet journal *Sel'skaya Zhizn'* of June 1, 1936, presents American and English boys who deliver newspapers as "children who have forgotten how to laugh." That is enough to make a goat laugh, and the young boy I am describing laugh with him.

Brooklyn possessed too, when I was born, the beautiful Brooklyn Bridge, opened in 1883, still one of the architectural and functional wonders of the world, a bridge that Brooklyn alone dreamed up and paid for, paying also with the lives of its two dreamers, the Roeblings father and son, the father dying of tetanus poisoning after his leg was crushed by a ferry boat against the dock of the old Brooklyn ferry, and the son suffering lifelong crippling from "caisson sickness" (the bends) contracted when he descended into a caisson to see if the excavation was really bone-dry from compressed air before a giant pillar was lowered into it, thereafter spending the rest of his life directing the construction with a spyglass from a Brooklyn Heights window and watching the inauguration ceremonies by telescope from his bed. At the bridge's opening Seth Low, mayor of Brooklyn, said, "No one shall see it and not feel prouder to be a man." The restful beauty of its web of steel and towering arches of stone was the beginning of Brooklyn's downfall, and is its monument. That, along with two unbeautiful bridges not built nor dreamed up by Brooklyn, plus five or six subway tunnels, has drained so much of the cultural life from Brooklyn to Manhattan, consolidating the theater districts there, destroying all the daily newspapers that Brooklyn harbored, leaving Brooklyn merely the greatest borough of the greatest city in the United States, a borough which, taken by itself, still would be the fourth largest city in the entire country.

I must say a word about Brooklyn's famous accent. Although it is known as Brooklynese, the famous *ŏi* sound for *er* and *ir* derives from Anglo-Saxon and was brought to America, like so many of our regional accents, from parts of old England. It is spoken in Virginia by some sector of the old Virginian aristocracy, and along a section of the coast of New Orleans by mysterious "Brooklynites" who will tell you, "Why, I never was in Brooklyn in my life!"

Personally, I do not possess the characteristic Brooklyn accent because in my childhood, unconsciously, I set out to speak what I took to be the cultured speech of my teachers and educated Americans generally. Yet I can speak Brooklynese if I wish to, and my older brother still had no way of pronouncing my first name except to call me "Boit." The long *oi* spelling of the Brooklyn "Boids" and "Boits" does not give a correct notion of the sound, but I suppose it is the nearest that newspapers and vaudeville comedians have been able to get. If the reader would like to pronounce the sound as a true Brooklynite does, let him take a word with an *r* in it such as *third* or *bird,* suppress the *r* completely, but not the influence of the *r* on the vowel that precedes it, and he will exactly reproduce the sound which characterizes Brooklynese, something like the *eu* in the French word *feu.*

Of course, there are other niceties about Brooklynese that might be mentioned, such as saying *Greenpernt* for *Greenpoint, hearsting* flags on

Decoration Day, calling the hereditary rival baseball team the *Jints,* or voicing the *g* in sin*ging,* or speaking of *gole joolry,* but the real shibboleth has always been the *er* which occurs in my first name.

Nowadays Brooklyn is so hard up for teachers that the examination for a license is virtually limited to using a stethoscope to see if a candidate is still breathing. But in order to keep speakers of Brooklynese out of teaching when I took the examination to teach English in high school back in 1916, I was given such tricky tongue twisters as: "The dirty boy from New Jersey sold soiled *Worlds* and *Journals.*" I was made to recite a verse which told of the "Swinging and the ringing of the bells, the clanging and the banging of the bells." And what the bells were ringing—to the confusion of those who were tensely suppressing their habit of sounding a palatal *g* in *ing*—was "Linger longer, Lou"—a mean trap, since only here did the *g* have to be sounded. I passed the exam all right, for I was free from Brooklynese, yet I suppose I ought to confess that all my life there has remained one pair of words, and only one, namely, *adjoin* and *adjourn,* that compels me to hesitate an imperceptible second before deciding whether we are to *adjoin* to the *adjourning* room or *adjourn* to the *adjoining* one, and while I hesitate, etymology helps me to decide whether the root I want is the French *jour* or the English *join.* This Brooklynese confusion with a solitary pair of words in our language seems likely to haunt me to the end of my days.

MY DEBT TO BROOKLYN'S CEMETERIES

Let not professional jokesters laugh at Brooklyn's chain of cemeteries, either, nor at her bedrooms, in one or the other or both of which so many of those who work in Manhattan come to rest. It was in that necklace of final resting places that one Brooklyn boy from a world made all of paving stones and cobblestones found his first green woods, his first excitement at the wonder of spring buds on the trees, frogs' eggs in the ponds, the first splendors of Easter sunshine that not only warmed, but seemed, as the first spring sunshine sometimes does, to melt the heart to overflowing. It is in these cemeteries, and later in New England churchyards, that I built fantasies around skimpy epitaphs, and especially pondered the feelings of one of the departed who had engraved on her headstone:

> Stranger, as you pass me by,
> As you are now, so once was I,
> As I am now, so you will be,
> So think on death, and follow me. . . .

Nor could I tell what the mood of the not particularly devout author was, nor where following her would get me.

Wandering amid these sun-drenched hills, with their modest rows of white headstones alternating with a pride of pompous and ornate tombs, I puzzled over the fact that some folk felt that they still had "class" after they lay moldering in the ground. I tried to figure out why people lying in all-leveling death primly tuck themselves in their shrouds to hold themselves apart from those of other creeds and colors. I marveled to find that here the Chinese, living and dying on American soil and being buried in American ground, yet had a cemetery of their own. There, one of those "Easter-spring" days, I came upon a number of Chinese of both sexes and all ages picnicking on the graves of their beloved dead, roasting suckling pigs, sharing the good-smelling brown flesh with those they were honoring, decorating the graves with bowls of rice and cakes and fruit, long fragrant sticks of burning incense, and gay red-and-gold-colored paper squares. (As I was setting down my memories of this exotic scene, I took this passage to the girl at the information desk of the Chinese library in the Lou Henry Hoover Building to check the accuracy of my childhood memories of more than two-thirds of a century ago, to see if I had not dreamed them up or embellished them. She assured me that my boyhood memories were accurate. The red squares of paper, she said, honored dead fathers whose names were brushed on them in Chinese characters, while the little squares of gold represented money to be used by the dead in the other world. The ceremony was both solemn and festive, taking place every spring on a different date according to the Chinese moon calendar, and known as Ching Ming.)

That adventure took place some 60-odd years ago, but the thrill is still vivid of the unexpected sight, and of my boyish delight in discovering signs of a festive mood rather than one of sorrow, as those Chinese families remembered and feasted with their honored dead. It was my first perception, later to be deepened in Mexico, that attitudes toward death and the dead might differ greatly from land to land and culture to culture. With that awareness came a sudden, if still only partial, release from the morbid fear of death which my mother had instilled in me from her own oft-repeated macabre fantasy that she might be buried alive while in a coma and come to consciousness in her coffin deep in the earth, only to cry out and beat her fists on her coffin lid in vain.

The joys of bud-hunting, the discoveries of crocuses, jack-in-the-pulpits, the strange red-and-orange skunk cabbage blossoms, the young fiddleheads of the cinnamon fern, choke cherries, in my ramblings through and around the cemeteries of Cypress Hills, all these made a cemetery seem a pleasant tramping ground. If it got dark while I was still traversing some graveyard, I knew no fear of ghosts nor need to whistle to keep my courage up as I sought my way back to "civilization." In 1939, when I wrote my only novel, *World Without End,* it began with a prologue called "Death and the Author" that showed the familiar terms on which I was with Death, as Death had revealed itself to me in those first cemetery walks; and then as Death revealed itself in the great Mexican festival called the Day of the Dead (actually a week-long fiesta), and in the Dance of Death, when I got to know the dance through my later studies in medieval literature, painting, and intellectual history. I did not find the same death-friendliness or familiarity, or the same sense of quiet ease in a cemetery in any other American writer, until I met young Peter Beagle, son of two old friends, successful novelist at 19, who had looked out of his window daily at Woodlawn Cemetery throughout his boyhood and gone so often with his mother on walks in Woodlawn as the nearest green strip of land, and there formed his fantasies concerning the cemetery and its inhabitants. Those walks and fantasies were the stuff from which came his gem of a first novel, *A Fine and Private Place,* the principal characters of which are two shades who are in love with each other and an old man, still alive, who has entombed himself in a cemetery mausoleum to escape from the inhospitable world, and has learned there to communicate with the shades of the young lovers.

THE JOYS OF BROOKLYN'S MARSHES

No laughing matter to me either are Brooklyn's swamps, marshes, creeks, rivulets, and wetlands that ran in my boyhood from the foot of Crescent Street, less than a mile from my home, down to Jamaica Bay. I reached that paradise for boyhood adventure at the age of nine, when the family, its income augmented by the wages of my older brother and sister, was able to buy—with heavy first and second mortgages—an old two-story frame building at 148 Berriman Street in East New York.

The new home introduced many changes into our lives, above all into mine. My father could take his horse and wagon through a regular alleyway to the rear of our home, where there were both a shed and a stable, instead of driving, as he had been doing, with horse and wagon through the large hallway of our old tenement house to a skimpy back yard of stone and dirt, with old-fashioned outhouses in lieu of indoor toilets, and a single stall with a hayloft for the horse. There was a peach tree in the new yard with real peach blossoms and peaches, and an overhanging pear tree next door from which we picked the overhanging pears. (Years later I was to learn that this was not theft but a perfectly legal response to the "trespass" of the intruding branches.) There were a giant peony bush (pronounced *piney* in Brooklyn), fences to mend and paint, and other attractions to keep a boy of nine busy and absorbed. We had a real bathtub on the second floor and I no longer had to bathe in the presence of the whole family in the kitchen washtub, from which a central partition was removed for the purpose of making it big enough for me, and my parents could stop using the public baths. It was my sister, I suppose, who decided that at the age of nine it was time, as there was now space, for me to sleep not with her but with my younger brother, with my father and older brother in the other bed, in a "men's" bedroom. All this spelled real luxury until two orphan cousins came to live with us, and then there were beds in the living room (folding beds, of course), and mattresses on the floor of our bedroom. Still, it was affluence.

Suddenly, I found myself the "oldest" in the family, with my older brother too big for the chores or away at gainful work. It was I who now cleaned the stable, earned the bit of pocket money, saw that the horse had rock salt and bran and clean straw to lie on, learned to chop open the tight wire on a bail of hay and leap out of its path when it "went haywire"—an expression many urbanites use today without knowing its meaning. I learned to use a chisel, hammer a nail in straight, mend the rickety fence, fix almost any broken gadget with "make-do" materials. It was a great surprise to me, when I grew up, to find that my intellectual friends who had grown up as city boys were unable to put in a washer, fix a piece of equipment, or hammer any nail but their thumbnail. I have always been thankful for having learned to use my hands along with my head, and even for the gift, which I have never lost, of fashioning out of improbable odds and ends a substitute or "make-do" replacement for a missing object, when the hardware store was closed, or too expensive, or too far away.

I suppose I should report that although my father always had to have a horse to deliver his drygoods and notions to the little stores that were his customers, my attempt to learn to ride horseback ended in an immediate and decisive fiasco. Without stirrup or saddle, I managed to pull myself up somehow on our horse's bare back, but instead of following my instructions (I had no bit or bridle on him either), he looked at his little friend in astonishment, then headed for his stall. Since the stable door was low and narrow I was ignominiously brushed off: thus ended once and for all my training as a cavalryman.

Another momentous novelty in my new life was the fact that East New York, today a teeming ghetto interspersed with ruined former dwellings, was then largely empty, or filled with small, two-story frame houses, empty lots, no tenement buildings. And just beyond was the old city line dividing Brooklyn from Queens, an ancient aqueduct and an aqueduct trail, with no buildings lining it, and real growing corn and milk cows and truck farming. To the north were the hills of Highland Park, the Cypress Hills cemeteries, and a reservoir, beyond that the deeply quiet foot trails and woodlands of Forest Park, and the storybook buildings just being put up by the Russell Sage Foundation in what is now the forgotten nucleus of teeming Forest Hills. Artesian-well water came to us from the aqueduct (has any water ever tasted so sweet and pure and cold?), and there were wildflower fields of goldenrod, wild grapes, dandelions, sweet clover, Queen Anne's lace (how dressed up she must have been!), and all the variegated splendors of the Long Island spring, summer, and autumn foliage.

Not having pocket money but possessing the hunger of an active boy in the woods on my journeys of exploration, I was fortunate enough to have a mother who taught me to recognize many edible plants and berries and fruits and nuts which one could find growing wild. She cautioned me against tasting brightly colored berries that were unfamiliar (a caution no longer handed down from generation to generation) but taught me to recognize the chokecherry, the pucker-sour wild crabapple, the edible blossomhead of the sweet clover, the halberd-shaped sorrel leaf (sour grass) from which Russian and Eastern Jewish cooks made *shchav* (generally spelled *tschav* on restaurant menus), pepper grass, the nasturtium leaf, raw carrots (properly scraped with your jackknife), ears of uncooked corn when the color of the beard showed that they were ripe, mickeys (potatoes with skins charred black in a bonfire with inside whiteness all fluffed from the heat), and a dozen other woodland or farmland goodies. (The farmers on Long Island then, like the fruit farmers in the Santa Clara valley in the twenties, did not object to your taking an ear or a root or a tomato or a piece of fruit or two, so long as you didn't carry a sack or basket with the intention of filling it.) My mother knew so much lore of wild growing things because she was born in Kingston, New York, in 1861, when Kingston was little more than an overgrown village, and it was just a short walk over the frozen Hudson to Roundout, and on the Western Shore there were in her day not realty developments and hard paved roads, but hills and lakes and partial clearings for farms, in any direction she might walk. Thus armed with a tradition of the lore of edible herbs and roots and berries, a small boy never went altogether hungry even if he didn't have the pocket money to stuff himself with pretzels and bolivars and candy, or prefabricated slabs of hamburger or the present-day abomination still masquerading as a frankfurter.

Much as I loved the hills and forest quiet of the northern ridge of Long Island, it was the marshes to the south that taught me most and gave me my happiest afternoons from my ninth year until my sixteenth, when the courtship of the girl who was to become my wife took me back down to the teeming ghetto of Williamsburg again, while the long trek or trot on foot to the Warwick Street station of the Long Island Rail Road, then by subway from that end of the line to 137th Street, brought me each day to the College of the City of New York. New interests, new sources of knowledge, new love, but my old love affair with the woods and hills of northern Long Island and the swamps and inlets of its South Shore never ceased.

At the foot of Crescent Street stood the ruins of a huge old mill, its waterwheel gone and its walls crumbling to decay, but with raceway still running, and vast and dusty windowless storage rooms echoing with muffled mystery to one's shouts, while the sunlight slanted into the obscurity with motes flying in it, giving the dim light a tenuous volume. To my book and dream-fed imagination this was my Melrose and Tintern Abbey and my tall tower (two stories high was enough!) of Philippe le Bel. From there to the distant and wide horizon ran wetlands, marshes, swamps, and—or so I was warned by my mother—possibly quicksands, which, once you stepped in them, the more you struggled to get out, the faster you sank, to be swallowed up without a trace.

The whole area was crisscrossed by creeks and rivulets and cut by drainage ditches not too wide for an active and agile boy to jump over, with the added thrilling hazard that the other side might be too slippery and muddy for one to get a secure foothold when he leaped. There was a wider tidal inlet, or creek, lined on the higher side by wood huts mounted on piles, old, unpainted, cracked, and peeling from the sun, but still habitable and inhabited by people with a rowboat or an outboard motor boat hitched to their meager land and meagerly furnished hideaways, which boat at low tide would rest on the gray sandy mud. The little boats were named after girls, the crumbling wooden huts bore such shingles as *Bide-a-wee, At Rest at Last, Snug Harbor,* and *Dew Drop Inn.* Ramshackle as they were, and unimaginative as their shingle names might be, they were adventure and romance to a small boy, too.

Undaunted or unbelieving in my mother's quicksands, from the Old Mill I would begin my journey through the marshes toward Jamaica Bay; jumping over inlets and irrigation drains; pausing at streams to catch killies (minnows), or to wait for unquenchable curiosity to bring a fiddler crab out of his hole, fiddler foremost, after which it was easy to close the hole with a jackknife and catch the fiddler crab; collecting starfish and other exciting shells; gathering bulrushes or cattails to save for torches when they had been dried and dipped in oil; pausing to listen to the rustle of the reeds and tidal streams and to rest my eyes on the long, low horizon so characteristic of tidal lands; penetrating ever deeper and deeper into the marshland. The brackish inlets had baby fish of many species to angle for with homemade fishline and fishhook. As the journey continued there would be coots and gulls, and geese, and terns, and other shore birds to watch. Only the terns were a bit frightening, for if one approached unwittingly one of the grassy sunlit flats on which they had made their nests and had their eggs or young, a sentinel tern would rise screeching high into the sky, then hundreds of terns would dive-bomb at my head while I waved my arms to exhaustion to shoo them off, until I had gotten safely clear of their nests and their shrieking.

In the restful seeming monotony of the wetlands there were endless varieties of flying, hopping, flitting, and crawling creatures; there were reeds, sedges, lupine, and all manner of growing things found only in swamps, along with one or two unexpected clusters of standing trees that had been missed by the lumberman's saw and ax, stands of scrub oak and pine, blackjack oak and white birch, whose bark, peeled with a jackknife, made wonderful torches for illuminating the night, without dissipating the encompassing darkness; elderberries, waxberries, sassafras, bay leaves and bayberries, sumach, goldenrod, and all sorts of strange plants that had learned to live with and resist flood tides, desert dryness of sand dunes, high winds racing through the open spaces.

In the stands of trees were sometimes birds of passage resting for a day from their annual round trip to the North in the spring, to the South in the fall. When they came to rest on this Long Island halfway station, they gave the trees an unexpected brilliance of plumage, movement, and music, especially at twilight. With Cabell's Jurgen, I can say that "I have it on the best of authorities that the dawns were also beautiful," but I never saw the sun rise over Jamaica Bay and its moorlands. Most unforgettable of all these experiences was the day I chanced upon my favorite patch of woodland near sunset and found every branch of every tree aflame with scarlet tanagers resting on their way to New England, bound perhaps for Gloucester moors, of which William Vaughn Moody wrote in his memorable poem of the same name, "Yon green-gold flash was a vireo, and yonder flame where the marsh flags grow, a scarlet tanager."

Finally, all this leaping, and slipping, and wading with shoes laced over my shoulder would bring me to paradise itself, a beautiful strip of yellow-white sandy shore called Nassau Beach, where I and such friends as I could induce to accompany me could go swimming without bathing suits, since no girls and no adults were ever known to undertake the arduous pathless trip through the swamps. Then we would build a big crackling fire of driftwood and dried seaweed (how quickly one dried in the sun and warmth without a wet bathing suit!) and roast green apples, mickeys, and ears of corn gathered from the few farms we passed, or whatever our collective larder could scrape together. Only the road back had its difficulties, for there was often the question of whether a tidal inlet might fill too full to wade through, and there were the mosquitoes that, as soon as the sun grew dim, rose in clouds to gather about my head, for I had a thinner skin and exuded more body heat than my friends, which apparently made me seem the desirable target. Without them, I should have needed no paradise after death. Indeed, even with them, these marshes were paradise enough.

From some of the glimpses I have gotten while flying into Kennedy Airport on the edge of Jamaica Bay, and from an uneasy inspection of the borderlands of my boyhood paradise as it is today, it seems to me that the venerable ruins of the Old Mill no longer exist, that Crescent Street has been extended into the wetlands, and that there is a labyrinth of two-story dwellings and high-rise apartments beyond New Lots Road which was in my boyhood the boundary of the old borough's built-up area. The old aqueduct and farms have disappeared under unfeeling pyramids of streets and sewers and pavements and asphalt roads and incipient beehive slums. Where once the gulls and terns and geese and coots, and the rarer herons and kingfishers, flew and floated, dived and sought their food, and marshaled their comical flotillas and graceful flocks, where muskrats, raccoons, even possums, and fish and waterfowl, found their food and resting places, breeding grounds, and meeting places (what solemn confabulations and caucuses the more gregarious birds would convoke on a bit of sandy flat!), there is now asphalt and tar and concrete and cobblestones and brick and rubble. Creeks that once sheltered and fed fiddler crabs, mussels, killies, and the myriad newly hatched small fry of all the world of fish, have been largely dredged, widened, straightened of their lovely curves, lined with elegant marinas with spick-and-span boathouses sheltering noisy power yachts.

One of the less felicitous measures of our greatness is the fact that our country produces a larger total and per capita refuse than any other country in the world, perhaps more than all of them put together. Much of the water in what is left of the creeks is foul with human excrement and garbage and spilled fuel in which no young fish can surface or breathe. Inlets over which I leaped are filled in or cut sharply into geometric channels. The banks and hummocks, with all their sedges and reeds and other growing things, are strewn with rotting dories, old rubber tires, and rubble of every conceivable description, with beer cans and ugly brown masses of human waste vying for first place. Where once there were the romantic tiny shacks with the friendly names there are realty developments, brick apartment buildings, and fuel tanks. There are dredges and derricks, pile drivers and bulkheads, filthy sanitary landfill, sucked-up sand and raw sewage, jet fuel and oil from the Kennedy airfield. Some sixteen hundred pipes and four or more partial-treatment sewage plants pour into beautiful Jamaica Bay and its wetlands the detritus of Nassau County, the sludge and muck, the "black mayonnaise," more terrible than my mother's quicksands, that covers much of the bottom of the inner bay. The once virginal marshes bloom with newspapers, cardboard, and tin cans, plastic bottles (with no romantic messages in them such as we hopefully used to set afloat), broken glass, rotting lumber, rusty spikes—all the signs and shards for future archaeologists to decipher our mass-production-of-refuse civilization.

The margins of Jamaica Bay are by nature marshlands. Marshes are born only once. It takes decades of ages to produce one, but a marshland can die of neglect or greed or "progress" in less than a generation. Already there is the Cross Bay Boulevard bisecting the bay, and a railway trestle to the Rockaways. Greedy realtors, hungry for new lands with a "sea breeze," to fill in with refuse and build on them high-rise apartments, contend with or tacitly combine with the ruthless rulers of the Kennedy Airport, already a nightmare of overgrowth, reaching out its tentacles to plot three new runways stretching out into the bay and enveloping it.

Yet the great bay with its surrounding marshes, its connection with the great Atlantic, its mighty tides that rip out rubbish and pour in fresh water, does not die so easily. Salt marshes, swift channels, strong tides, and broad expanse of bay are remarkable for their capacity to withstand continued and successive assaults of sewage and oil spill, to absorb pollutants as plant food that converts into food for marine animals and then for aquatic birds. The marshes with their spartina grass and their other hardy aquatic growths actually serve as a secondary sewage-treatment system, and there are a few holes so deep that much of the heavier sludge settles into them, leaving the upper waters pure enough for marine life. Each day the mighty tides sweep in from the Atlantic and the deep channels, carry fresh nutrients and oxygen, and scrub the bay of much of its filth. Since Parks Commissioner Robert Moses won his battle to reserve nine thousand acres as a watery parkland and President Nixon came to declare the whole surrounding area a national park, the tide—no pun intended—has visibly turned. Dr. René Dubos, Rockefeller University biologist, Elinor Guggenheimer, former city planning commissioner, Assemblyman Posner, representing the Rockaways that want clean swimming and unpolluted water at their doors, and, perhaps most important, Herbert Johnson, a Parks Department employee who has charge of the nine thousand acres, have added a crusading spirit to the cleansing sweep of the tides. They, and a group calling itself the Green Ribbon Panel, are giving battle to realtors, to Kennedy Airport officials, and to army engineers. Edible herring is still being caught off Broad Channel, birds have returned that had disappeared. Herbert Johnson has planted trees and marine grasses on the man-made garbage-dump islands that the city laid down in the bay, and he has counted hundreds of marine and land birds on the new woodlands of his own personal unordered and unauthorized planting. By 1960 some sixty species of such birds were reported in this reviving wildlife sanctuary, and by the middle of the 1970s the number of species counted in the marshes and newly planted shrubbery was over three hundred. That amateur ornithologist Herbert Johnson, newly retired, was made the guest of honor of the Linnaean Society in March 1973, at their annual meeting at the American Museum of Natural History. Despite airport officials, realtors, and army engineers, the beautiful islands, waters, and marshlands of Jamaica Bay seem sure to survive. There is a better than even chance that youngsters yet unborn may find again some of the marshland paradise I found in my own youth. René Dubos calls it a major success story in the generally bleak picture of ecological despair and deterioration.

BROOKLYN'S ARTISTIC POVERTY

There were no pictures on the walls of the flat at 260 Ellery Street in Williamsburg, Brooklyn, in which I was born. Of course, there was a calendar with a picture of dubious esthetic quality, an embroidered sampler duly framed, which read *Vom Aufgang bis zum Niedergang der Sonne soll der Name des Herrn gepriesen sein;* a "family tree" in a frame—a tiny tree six or eight inches high made of loops of hair of different female ancestors, now red, now brown, now white, with the names of the respective ancestors lettered in gold next to each branch of the little tree; an enlarged photo of my father, rather handsome, with curly hair which had largely disappeared before I was born, and an oversized mustache requiring a mustache cup to keep it clean when he drank his coffee. The flats of our neighbors were still poorer than ours. When one of my better-off relatives bought a picture to hang on her wall, I acquired my first bit of esthetic critical vocabulary from her, "It's a genuine oil painting."

The first works of art I remember seeing I found in the Brooklyn Institute of Arts and Sciences (now simply the Brooklyn Museum) on the main boulevard running to Prospect Park, within walking distance—some four or five miles each way—for a carfareless and tireless walker in the streets of Brooklyn. All I remember of my hushed boyhood visits there are some nude Grecian statues, most of them dressed up for the prudish with a solitary fig leaf, and one huge canvas that seemed to occupy an entire wall of one of the galleries. It was a battle scene, not the glory of battle but its misery, not the adrenaline-bolstered bloody clash but the desolate aftermath. The painting was entitled *The Road of the War Prisoners* and the painter was the Russian Vasily V. Vereshchagin. The painting was as huge as I remembered it to be, for a devoted curator has responded to my queries by sending me a photograph together with the information that it is 72 inches high and 132 inches wide (6 feet by 11). It consisted of low hills covered with half-melted and refrozen snow, and was better than most of Vereshchagin's poorly structured pictures, thanks to the close-knit composition bound together by a curved road filling the entire bottom of the painting, narrowing as it curved upward past the center and disappeared, still curving, at the upper left of the canvas. Along the road, further strengthening the composition, was a line of telegraph poles and a scatter of frozen corpses of men who had dropped by the wayside, while on the telegraph lines and in clusters near the corpses were what looked to me like vultures, but may well have been ravens or crows.

The painter, born in 1842 and still living in the early twentieth century when I repeatedly contemplated his painting, was a member of the Society of Wanderers, or, more formally, Society of Circulating Exhibits. They had broken with and defied the academy where officially recognized painters were hung, painted subjects of their own choosing, and set up their own society to exhibit their own less academic paintings, most of them characterized by an anecdotal character and a social message. Vereshchagin was not the best of the lot but he was probably the best known at the time for his pacifism, his "progressive realism," and his endless output of huge battle canvases of which this was one. What the war correspondent with his camera and television eye does today was his self-appointed task executed with paint and brush on vast expanses of canvas—always big enough to steal the show at any traveling exhibition. His first subjects were taken from the Russo-Turkish War of 1877 and '78; he covered our war with Spain and Theodore Roosevelt's overpublicized charge up San Juan Hill, and later our war against the Filipino guerilla leader Aguinaldo. The only reason he did not cover the Boer War was that the British would not let him get near the front. He met his death, still on the firing line, painting naval battle scenes in the Russo-Japanese War, when the flagship of the Russian fleet on which he had set up his easel was sunk by a Japanese surprise attack off Port Arthur in 1904.

At any rate, the statues and paintings in the Brooklyn Museum, more anecdotes to me than paintings, were all the education in appreciation of art that I got until the vicissitudes of life flung me into that plastic land Mexico, into close contact with the powerful, awe-inspiring sacred art of pre-Conquest peoples and into the company of Diego Rivera, José Clemente Orozco, Alfaro Siqueiros, Rufino Tamayo and the galaxy of artists of the Mexican Renaissance, in the year 1922. Immersion in the Mexican milieu gave me an understanding and feeling for the art of many lands and times and changed my vision of the external world. The Brooklyn boy's education in the arts may be equated to zero until, in his middle twenties, he suddenly found himself teaching and studying and exploring in Mexico.

4

THE EDUCATION OF A BROOKLYN BOY AT THE TURN OF THE CENTURY: II. Schools and Gangs

I learned to recite the alphabet at three, eliciting gaiety in the family when I followed *"h, i, j, k"* with *"lemon 'n' tea,"* which I thought I had heard as the next burst of letters. At four I learned to read, thanks to pestering my sister. She was 12 then, and she told me tales that filled me with wonder. "Lillie, tell me a story," I would cry whenever I laid eyes on her.

"I don't know any more, I've told them all."

"Tell me one again. Or read me a story."

"If you want so many stories, why don't you read them yourself?"

"Why don't you teach me how?"

"I will!" And picking up a child's reader, she took me to the steps of the schoolhouse to teach me words, sounds, the mystery of silent letters. I needed no urging. Soon I could read my own stories and enter into the enchanted world of books.

Though I was constantly daydreaming, I was not given to the usual visual dreaming when asleep. My dreams were made up of conversations with people whom I did not see but somehow knew to be who or what they were, for from early childhood I had almost no visual imagery nor visual memory, making do with words, supplemented by rudimentary kinesthetic imagery. The last vivid visual dream I remember having occurred when I was four. My father got two tickets for a *Schwabenfest*, a Swabian folk festival, in which the devil appeared on the stage, frightening me out of my wits as he pointed a finger at me, or, as it seemed to me, at a finger on my left hand. I screamed so loud that I had to be taken home. That night I saw the devil in a nightmare, not red as on the stage but a pallid, gray shadow of a devil. He pointed at my hand, and I awoke with a cut or sore on the finger he had pointed at. This gave me cause to wonder, yet the cut healed as swiftly and as naturally as any other. But I could not be persuaded to go to next year's *Schwabenfest* lest I meet the devil again, for my mother had made me believe in the devil more intensely than in God, and I was taking no chances. Thereafter I never had another vivid visual dream, scarcely even a faint one, until old age when my childhood capacity for verbal and kinesthetic and faintly visual dreams returned to me. My dreams today are largely verbal, I address audiences I do not see, talk with people who are not there, traverse regions that are but shadows of shadows, and have no nightmares.

My lack of visual imagery has been a grave handicap in chess, in solid and spatial geometry, in countless other activities. I have never been able to conjure up faces and scenes while I am away from them, though I invariably recognize people and places when I see them again. It takes a special effort on my part to make a purely verbal or mental note of the characteristics that distinguish a face or a scene, or the landmarks on a road or in a forest, if I want to remember them; thus I have strengthened my verbal imagery to make up for the lack of a visual imagination. My topographical sense is close to zero: I can take the right road in the wrong direction more often than any other driver I know. Yet I know what words can do to evoke visions in others, as I proved to myself in my writing of *The Fabulous Life of Diego Rivera.* For instance, my picture of his native Guanajuato with which the book opens: its granite hills, their sharp outline against the sky, the little city with streets beginning immediately to climb into the hills—all this was written from notes made by me while studying a panoramic photograph of the city which I found in Diego's files, supplemented by verbal notes made while contemplating similar mountain ranges with a clear-cut line between them and the luminous sky, in other mountain vistas of Mexico:

> Guanajuato is flooded with light. The sun beats down with brilliant intensity upon its flat-roofed houses, fills with purple darkness their windows and doorways, gives bulk to solid forms, draws clean lines that separate surrounding hills from light-drenched sky. The valley in which the city dozes is seven thousand feet above the sea. Narrow cobblestone streets circle through the old center, then begin to climb into the hills. At the outskirts, trees become discouraged; ridges rise bare and brown into a sky deep, remote, free from haze, standing out sharp against the light-filled emptiness of space. He whose eyes have been nourished on these clear forms and solid volumes and light-filled space will never be altogether at home in the pale yellow sunlight and soft outlines of Paris treetops and towers where the light has been diffused by haze that forever hints of rain. . . . A boy born here can never really find himself as a painter until he has rediscovered the strongly defined forms, pure colors, clear atmosphere, and omnipresent flood of light that gives solidity to all the objects it illumines without seeming to appear upon the scene at all.

That brief description has made Guanajuato live again for many who have seen it, but I had never been to Guanajuato when I wrote it, nor have I been there to this day.

There were no books to speak of in my home. There was a small prayerbook in English and Hebrew, of which I could read only the English, dull because it was an execrable translation and because each Saturday morning, facing toward the east, I read the same brief ceremonial prayer of several pages and the same two psalms over and over because my mother felt that they were ritually prescribed. No one ever explained to me the tribal nature of the Hebrew God nor the covenant between Him and Abraham, so I could not understand addressing the Deity in the terms of the prayer as "O Lord, our God, the God of our fathers, the God of Abraham, the God of Isaac, the God of Jacob. . . ." Besides the prayerbook there was a pictorial history of the American navy in two volumes, always heroic, always virtuous in the sentiments of its heroes and unsailorlike in the language they used; and there were *The Woman in White* and *The Moonstone* by Wilkie Collins; a novel in tedious verse by Edward Robert Bulwer-Lytton called *Lucile: The Prisoner of Devil's Island,* dealing with the case of Captain Dreyfus, to me who knew little of the long, tormented history of the Jewish people, the most terrible story of anti-Semitic persecution, until the Beilis case of the next century in tsarist Russia, and until both of these were submerged into nothingness by the Hitler holocaust. There was not even a dictionary in the house until one of my sister's suitors gave me a Webster's *Academic* as a present on my thirteenth birthday. How this nondescript library got into my home I cannot imagine, unless my father accepted the volumes in satisfaction of some debt of a bankrupt customer, for no one in my home ever thought of buying a book.

On such meager fare my newborn love of letters would scarcely have flourished, were it not for schoolbooks (I was fascinated by all of them—geographies, histories, readers, literary texts, everything!)—and were it not for the free public libraries, for which I am eternally grateful to Andrew Carnegie who built and endowed them, and to the people of Brooklyn and the Greater City who taxed themselves to keep the shelves full to overflowing and to hire deeply dedicated people as librarians, a race apart of devoted men and women, full of knowledge and sometimes of wisdom, knowing what was in their books, ever ready to help and encourage shy little boys. All my life I have been helped by them in every library I have worked in, and I have nothing but admiration for their tribe, self-chosen servitors who are delighted if you ask for their help. When I consider how much I owe to libraries and librarians, I am deeply ashamed at present of my giant, wealthy native city for skimping on the funds that would be necessary to keep its libraries open evenings and Saturdays and Sundays, since free libraries functioning at the full are an important part of the soil a free society needs to flourish.

Reading opened up the world to me, transporting me from a few mean streets in a Williamsburg ghetto to the wide expanse of the world with its "seven wonders" and its march of civilizations, and from my brief moment of time on the face of the earth to the whole expanse of time in which man has lived and set down his record or left behind some durable remains of his living. The row on row of novels and plays and poems and other works of "fiction and nonfiction" opened to me the hearts of men, their schemes and dreams, their tragedies and failures, their moments of meanness and greatness.

What to read first? There was no one in my family to tell me. Teachers and librarians answered my questions but I didn't know what questions to ask. So I read and read and read, at random, unceasingly: by authors when one of an author's books pleased until I wearied of him, or ran out of his works; by genres until I discovered the monotonous sameness in some of them, or their triviality—how I could almost unfailingly solve a murder mystery, for example, within a few pages of clues, by picking on the least suspect to be the villain. I read trash, vulgarity, coarse comedy, dime novels, masterpieces, sickly sentimental and unreal love stories, and deathless tales of love that made it impossible for me thereafter to separate sex from love.

There was no toilet paper in our poor household so I read every scrap of newspaper that served as substitute in the outhouses in the back yard of our tenement house. My older brother liked me to read aloud to him from "dime novels" (actually a nickel apiece when new, with their covers still on, and two for five when they had lost their covers), which he bought with the bit of pocket money he earned—ten cents a month for cleaning out the stable where my father kept the one horse he used to deliver drygoods and notions to storekeepers.

My brother bought *Jesse James* and *Nick Carter* and *Old King Brady* and *Young Glory* and *The Liberty Boys, Pluck and Luck, Work and Win,* and *Snap,* which last was meant to be humorous, and all the other series for boys of all ages that were being turned out as if from a word machine by men who earned a miserable living as men of letters. My brother was four years my senior but a poor reader because his eyesight was bad as the result of my sister's having injured one of his eyes in babyhood with a red-hot poker, which somewhat affected the vision of the other eye also. But he liked stories, so I would sit on a Tompkins Park bench with him and read aloud as much as my newfound knowledge of the art of reading would permit. I recognized more words than I could pronounce and pronounced or sought to pronounce words I could not recognize, but I read aloud whatever he purchased. I remember a Jesse James story in which there was a character obnoxious to the protagonist, whose name was Green. "Jesse James hated a spy," I read, "especially when he was a deteceive." "A what?" asked Paul. "A deteceive," I repeated. "What's a deteceive?" he demanded. "A deteceive? I don't know either, but that's what it says, and whatever they are, Jesse James hated them." It took some time until I learned that what Jesse James hated was more generally known as a *detective.* Given his occupation, I could not blame Jesse, nor make up my mind whether I should hate or like a detective if I ever met one.

That was the trouble with all that reading without a mentor. Even when I got to high school I remember proudly volunteering an answer in an English history course, "The members of the clergy," I said, "were tried in special eccliastical courts." "Why, Bertram!" said my teacher. "I am ashamed of you!" It was not until I got home and opened my Cheney's *History of England* to find out why the generally friendly Mr. Rogers was ashamed of me that I learned that I should have said *ecclesiastical.* Such are the hazards of self-education, which I still hold, despite all its perils, to be the best and in the long run the only true education. As for reading so much trash in my omnivorous journey through the world of books, I am sure that it helped me to develop my taste for good literature. The books of mechanical formula, identical plot, lifeless character, soon lost interest and I gradually learned what made a given book live and another not worth reading. I am convinced that if a child with a love of reading is turned loose amid books, he will find his way and be none the worse for the hazards of the journey. Unfortunately, television does not give the child the same chance that the endless rows and rows and tiers and tiers of books in a library do.

My wide-ranging reading eased my way through school so that it seemed natural to be at the head of the class, to have friendly teachers, to skip a class or two. The eight-year elementary-school course I finished in seven years, the four-year high-school course in three and a half, and the four-year arts baccalaureate at the College of the City of New York in three and a half years, and I began to teach English in high school two weeks after I turned twenty. I had to grow a mustache to distinguish myself from similar tall, lanky youths in the senior class there. Extra hair wouldn't help a young high-school teacher much today.

There were no hard subjects or unpleasant ones in elementary school. When the mind is young it finds it easy to memorize almost anything, provided the memorizing is motivated by a few words of explanation. It would be intolerably dull to memorize the multiplication table in adulthood, but when one is young it is easy. Long division, square root, proper and improper fractions, doing arithmetic in your head, spelling in our preposterous orthography, all proved simple. If any reader should wonder why I call our orthography and pronunciation preposterous, let him consider the story told me by a Russian émigré concerning another Russian escapee who began to doubt the wisdom of his flight as soon as some kind soul started to teach him on the boat: "Thought, *thawt;* through, *thru;* though, *tho;* tough, *tuff;* slough, *slou* and also sluff. . . ." After he got through the thicket of immigration, he walked up Broadway until he reached a movie house on the marquee of which he painfully spelled out "Greta Garbo in N-I-N-O-C-H-K-A Pronounced Success!" He turned on his heels, marched back down Broadway to the ship, and asked to be taken back to Russia.

I won spelling matches though I did not have the gift of visualizing the words as they were called out, but I had learned to make up for that by mentally pronouncing silent letters when I was writing a word, for example saying *fry-end* for *friend* as I wrote. In those days a prize might be no more than a wooden penholder with a steel penpoint, but the real prize consisted in the confirmation of excellence. I enjoyed exercises such as diagramming sentences for syntax and meaning and in 1972 was startled to read that two of Noam Chomsky's disciples made a verbal fuss about the niceties of diagramming such sentences with slightly different structural lines than those of their master. In differing with him in these momentous niceties, both disciples, already professors in their own right, called their master a "genius." Certainly the tribute was out of place in such a discussion of things that I had already learned in my boyhood more than two thirds of a century earlier. I was reminded of the famous dialogue between the two Russian clowns Bim and Bom when Stalin and Zhdanov were beginning to claim that the Russians had invented everything. Bim appeared on the stage wearing a big cardboard replica of the Order of Lenin. "Bim, you got the Order of Lenin! What for?" "*I* invented the umbrella." "Aw, that was invented ages ago." "I'm the first man to invent the umbrella the second time." The audience roared and applauded. But a few months later, Bim and Bom were more careful about the targets they chose for their unfailing barbs of wit. Eventually they seemed to disappear from the world of mummery.

In arithmetic I invariably "proved" my answers by reversing the arithmetical operations as I did them. Later, when I got to high school and began to study my first foreign language, German, I engaged in similar self-teaching by translating passages from the German in writing, laying the English aside until it got cold, then translating back to German and comparing my grammar and even my style with the original. This extra effort at self-education paid off in more ways than one. When I got to City College I early won the Ward Medal as "the student of greatest proficiency in German language and literature" and, more important, the friendship of Adolph Werner, the great humanist and inspiring teacher who headed the German department. And in 1929, when I found myself in Moscow engaging in a fight with Joseph Stalin and discovered that the German translators were making a mockery of my words, though I had no practice in speaking German, I ventured to switch to that *lingua franca* of most of my auditors. My long reading of works of German literature, and texts of Marx and Freud that had not yet been translated into English, had taught me to think in German and saved me from disgrace with this my first address—of an hour's duration—in the German tongue.

IT'S HARD TO BE A JEW

When we moved to Berriman Street in East New York in the ninth year of my life (or rather the tenth, for I turned nine in January) and entered our new home, we instantly became notorious as the first Jews on the block. The area was inhabited by Irish and Italians and Negroes, with a sprinkling of early Americans, and the street next to ours, Atkins Avenue, was the hangout of the Irish-American Atkins Avenue Gang, looking for suitable ways to liven their life on the streets. I had never had any special awareness of Jewishness in Williamsburg, except for the puzzling fact that I was not allowed to write on the Sabbath (Saturday), not take butter with meat, and not do other things that seemed simple and innocent to me, for which prohibitions it never occurred to my mother to offer such explanations as were inherent in the six days of creation and the seventh day of sacred rest and refreshment, and other biblical and talmudic tales and precepts. In our new neighborhood my older brother, Paul, became "Sheeny Wolfe." When I saw him attacked by the gang on the empty lot on our block, I came with my feeble reinforcement to help him, arming myself with an old stovepipe I found lying there, with which I belabored his attackers. Their wrath turned toward me and I inherited my older brother's title, especially when he began to go to work and ceased to be a visible target. The animus against me was much worse than against him, for I possessed certain especially annoying characteristics that aroused the gang's animosity. I always seemed to know the answers in the classroom but zealously prevented neighboring boys from peering over my shoulder and copying my answers, then made matters worse, according to the gang code of honor, by threatening, on my mother's urging, to tell the teacher if they persisted in copying from me. I do not wonder in retrospect that they chose me as the predilect gang target.

As the gang hostility increased along with the pleasure of "Wolfe-hunting," I had to fight my way to and from school, aided by a growing fleetness of foot and a catstick (a sawed-off broom handle), which I kept concealed in the right leg of my bloomers. These things were part of my education: swiftness of foot, skill in running a gauntlet (while with a catstick I delivered hard blows), and courage in the face of overwhelming odds to which I could not capitulate. Yet sometimes I came to class late with a bloody nose or a discolored eye, vainly trying to wipe tears away and conceal the physical battering. The teacher said nothing about my lateness, for girls who had witnessed the fray (ours was a mixed class of girls and boys) would already have told the teacher of my plight.

What with growing skill with the catstick, increasing fleetness of foot, the sympathy of the girls in the class who tried to shame their classmates because of the unfair odds of the gang hunt, and a visit by my mother to the local Democratic precinct leader, an Irishman who was the father of the leader of the Atkins Avenue Gang, I found life not unbearable. Another weapon stood me in good stead: I was better than any of the gang in repartee and in swift retort to insults intended to humiliate me. This, too, was later to serve me well on the platform when my audience contained some little band determined to heckle me or prevent me from speaking. My mother attempted to console me with one of the innumerable proverbs that she trotted out for every one of life's occasions—in this case, "Sticks and stones will break your bones, but names will never hurt you." If the hurt was intended to be physical, she was right, but if it was meant as a hurt to the spirit, then my skill in repartee fended for me.

Part of my mother's efforts to prepare us children for the problems and vicissitudes of life was to arm us with such proverbs, and despite the frequent contradictions in this accumulated folk wisdom, e.g., *"Look before you leap"* and "*He who hesitates is lost,*" they often served me after their fashion. Thus when I was setting up the Ideological Advisory Staff of the Department of State and had to tell promising applicants that it would take about six months in those parlous McCarthy days to clear them for security, and they asked, "How do I live meanwhile?" my mother seemed to stand at my elbow and bid me say compassionately, "Live, horse, till the grass grows."

As for her "names will never hurt you," I really believed that one until I examined the choice vocabulary of prosecutor Andrei Vyshinsky in the great purge trials in which Stalin exterminated all of Lenin's closest collaborators. When I read Vyshinsky's summation calling the Old Bolsheviks, every one of them his better, "a foul-smelling pile of human garbage . . . the last scum and filth of the past . . . covered with the blow-flies of German, Japanese, and Polish espionage . . . accursed offspring of the fox and the pig . . . must be shot like dirty dogs! Our people demand only one thing, crush the accursed reptiles!"—then I realized that names too may be used to deprive human beings of their humanity and make it easier to kill them.

My readers must not imagine that the Atkins Avenue Gang was anything like the gangs that invade the New York schools today. There were no handguns, no muggings, no demanding of a nickel or a quarter under penalty of slashing your face with a switchblade knife if you didn't have it (I wouldn't have had it), no sexual attacks on teachers or girls in the school, no carrying of gang wars into corridors or classrooms, no fatalities. Fists and epithets and dirty words or offensive ones were the weapons. The members of the gang, once they entered the school, in the main obeyed their teachers, feared a pink card that would send them to the principal's office, mocked at but feared the truant office and the reform school. Cheating was the high crime in the classroom, and after that, inattention, talking to your neighbor, passing of notes, hurling chalk or erasers when the teacher's back was turned. Although I heard of teachers slapping an extended palm with a ruler as a means of discipline, I never witnessed such an act of corporal punishment. Nor did the principal possess a paddle to spank a recalcitrant with as he still does in California. My situation was never really dangerous despite the gang ambushes.

Public School 64, a few blocks from my home, was a primary school in the process of growing into a full-fledged eight-year grammar school. Each year, when I was about to be transferred to some other school, they added another grade, and our same mixed class, and sometimes our teacher, were promoted together. The gang and its favorite quarry got more used to each other, while the restraining influences I have alluded to grew in effectiveness. When we reached the graduating class, two events strengthened and made manifest the growing tolerance.

We were reading *The Merchant of Venice,* a work that Jewish organizations have sometimes asked to be barred from school study as promoting race prejudice. Our teacher decided to have us act the courtroom scene and invite our parents, relatives, and friends to attend. The teacher asked me, perhaps after internal debate, whether I would play the part of Shylock. I was glad to accept. Overcoming my bashful stage fright, I acted the part with feeling. Perhaps Shakespeare intended to write just another anti-Jew play as successful as Marlowe's *The Jew of Malta,* but, as always with Shakespeare, his characters assumed a full-bodied life of their own. I took advantage of this fact, and delivered the speech beginning, "Hath not a Jew eyes? Hath not a Jew hands, organs, dimensions, senses, affections, passions?" with such feeling that the entire class, and the visiting parents, were moved by it. The cultured parent of one of my classmates, a Mrs. Shelter, quite turned my head by saying, "You were as good as Robert Mantel" (the then popular Shakespearean actor). Of course, I knew it could not be so, but I was flattered just the same. I remember the Shelter name because of her generous praise and because her son, Raymond Shelter, had so large a weekly allowance that he sometimes paid my admission, a whole nickel in those days, in order to have my company at the movies. They were the first movies I ever saw.

A little later a more crucial test came, when one of the girls nominated me for president of the graduating class. Our teacher, Mrs. Schrader, who I imagine must have secretly intervened with some of the tougher of my gang classmates on my behalf, now asked me to see her after school. "Bertram," she said, "in view of the antagonism and prejudice against you and the hard time they have been giving you, I think it best for you to decline the nomination next week at the next session of the class club."

Her suggestion filled me with indignation. "Let them vote me down," I said, "but I have as much right to run as any of the others. I will not withdraw." At the next meeting a miracle happened. One by one the other nominees withdrew in my favor. I was elected class president by a unanimous vote: even Johnnie McGrane, Chick Ennis, and Pat O'Brien, leaders of the Atkins Avenue Gang, raised their hands with the others.

Then a second wonder occurred. A Negro girl, Irene McCoy, more mature by four or five years than any of the rest of us, whose family had moved up from the South largely to give her a chance for an education denied to her in her native home, was nominated for vice-president. She had always vied with me for first place in spelling matches, in geography, history, arithmetic, and even composition. She was elected unanimously, too, amid general applause, for our classmates seemed conscious of the fact that in electing us they had done something unusual. What electioneering had gone on among them during the week between nominations and elections I do not know, but clearly the boys and girls, in their school setting, were judging by different standards from those prevailing in the street.

After my personal plea as Shylock and my elevation to the class presidency, I was met with a new tolerance by the Atkins Avenue Gang, who began to seek their quarry elsewhere, though they would not have accepted me as a member had I wanted to join. By the standards of the street I could not have made it.

I excelled in all my subjects except music. Though I had songs in my heart, they came out flat and off-key when I tried to sing them when alone. In school I let the others do the singing. I could not carry a tune nor hit the note I heard within me. I loved school where I was learning so many wonderful things, but when I heard that a music teacher was to come and listen to each individual voice to place us as soprano, alto, tenor, or bass for group singing, I played sick after a normal breakfast, and said I could not go to school. Seeing through my transparent lie, my mother threatened to "chase me to school with a strap." With reluctant feet I went off to the ordeal. The music teacher had us all sing at once, putting her ear close to each boy's or girl's mouth, then pronouncing her verdict. I opened my mouth with the rest of them, moved my lips to form the words of the song, but permitted no sound to escape my gullet. The teacher listened and listened at my mouth while the whole class sang. She looked at me, and there I was with my mouth open, my lips articulating the words, my face set in song. She listened again, longer this time, then at last oracularly pronounced the word to the classroom teacher: "Alto." Thereafter, false or flat or off-key or falsetto, I was *alto*.

Though I could not carry a tune and could venture to let song ring out only when I was surrounded by the chorus of my classmates, the lessons of the music teacher and our classroom singing were not altogether lost. As I walk in the woods I often find myself singing without sound some of the more beautiful songs I learned in my childhood. Our songbook contained songs by Goethe, and he was set to music by German composers and well translated by English poets. When I read German poetry I found Goethe's *Ein Veilchen auf der Wiese stand* to be "A violet on the mead just blown" that I had learned in my boyhood. The songs of Robert Burns made their mark on my memory, both words and music, long before I knew the name of Robert Burns, and songs like "Flow Gently, Sweet Afton" still resound in my ears. When I first went to see Mozart's *Don Giovanni* there was a moment of exquisite delight when the musicians played the minuet in Giovanni's ballroom as music without words, and I heard the words I had sung in my childhood:

Folks great once danced the Minuet,
Proud of their gorgeous etiquette,
Nor deemed that Time would ere forget
That they were fair and brave.
Time heard and whispered as he passed,
Great deeds alone are doomed to last,
Useless things and small all hurry fast,
To their forgotten grave.

No, the time was not wasted even on a tone-deaf youngster, but it is a pity that our teachers never thought of telling us a little about Goethe and Heine and Mozart and all the great composers and poets who had found their way into our songbooks.

TO BE A WRITER OR TO BE FAMOUS?

As I moved from class to class and saw the end of my elementary schooling approaching, the problem arose whether my formal education should stop with graduation. I had turned thirteen a week or two before I graduated, and I could not get working papers for another year. No one in my family had ever gone beyond elementary school. Despite my newspaper routes morning and evening, I did not contribute much to the family treasury. It was expected that I too would seek full time employment as soon as I got my working papers.

But what to do between my thirteenth and fourteenth years? How continue my education? Secretly I nourished two ambitions that contended with each other for the possession of my spirit: to be a writer or to be "famous."

A number of my teachers had encouraged me to be a writer, perhaps unwittingly. One of them was a Miss Rentum. She had me read every composition aloud to the class but made me rewrite every composition at least twice because of my always legible but never neat or very regular handwriting. At home my mother and sister had taught me to write a deep cursive forward slant. Then three successive schools had taught me to write vertically with perpendicular strokes, next a Spencerian hand with shaded strokes from the wrist, and finally after drawing many rapid ovals, to write by the Palmer method—a series of warring methods that left my handwriting a shambles, except for my conviction that since I wrote for others to read, however it looked, my writing must be legible. So it is today, always frightening the reader at first glance, until he discovers that every letter and every word is legible. One day an inspector visited our class as we were writing. In a whisper I was not supposed to hear I heard Miss Rentum say, "You want to see something interesting? Look over the shoulder of the little boy in the first row, first seat. It looks as if a hen had walked in a mud puddle, then all over his paper. But what he writes, he writes like an angel." She never knew how much that whisper encouraged me to believe that I might become a writer.

But a famous man? To be famous at that moment was to be like Thomas Edison, to make inventions that would light men's homes (we were still using gaslight), lighten men's burdens, preserve beautiful voices that might outlast the too-brief lives of great singers. . . . I would study electrical engineering and become a famous inventor. I made magnets, homemade compasses, crude electric motors out of wires and metals and other materials found in a nearby freight yard, and imagined I was preparing myself to become a famous inventor. When I reached the seventh grade I told my mother and my teacher that I wanted to enter Cooper Union upon graduation. "Tuition is free. All you need is an elementary-school diploma and an examination in algebra and geometry." My mother wavered. "You have always done well in school. Maybe electrical engineer is a good-paying profession. But if you ever flunk . . ." From my teacher I borrowed an algebra book with answers in the back and went all through algebra. Then I borrowed a geometry text, and went through that. Upon graduation I took my diploma and presented myself at Cooper Union for the exams in algebra and geometry. They looked at this little boy who had ceased to be twelve only two weeks earlier and said with obvious amusement, "We don't admit anybody so young. Come back when you are sixteen and we'll give you the examination."

I was in despair! Good-bye electrical engineering. Good-bye fame. Good-bye education. Who could afford to wait three years? But then who could afford to wait another year for working papers?

I talked it over with my mother. "Let me go to high school until I am sixteen." My mother hesitated, then said, "All right. You'll work after school and during the summer. You'll go to high school. But if you ever flunk a single subject, out you go." Agreed. On the principal's recommendation, I went to Boys' High School, then the best for bright boys eager to learn. Latin, German, ancient history, medieval and modern history, English history, American history, physics (so easy for the embryonic electrical engineer who found that he had been reading a lot of physics), biology, algebra, geometry (what could they teach me that I had not learned already?), high-school English, classics of English literature—high school opened an entire new world to me. Goodbye inventions, goodbye fame, I would become a writer. Since a poor boy couldn't make a living by writing, at least not for years, I decided to become an English teacher with a minor in German language and literature, and I thanked my mother's God who takes care of fools like me for keeping me out of Cooper Union.

5

I LEARN THAT NOBODY IS WATCHING ME

As I moved into adolescence, I developed a growing concern with sin, and a longing for a deeper religious feeling. But what did it mean for me to be religious or cultivate religious feelings?

My father seemed quietly indifferent, content with being a "twicer," a Jew who went twice a year to one of the makeshift temporary synagogues that sprang up during the High Holidays, Rosh Hashana, the Jewish New Year, and Yom Kippur, the Day of Atonement, fasting on the latter holiday, satisfied that the Jewish dietary laws were followed in his household, though he did not observe them outside of it. I never heard a religious thought from his lips. My mother was more zealous, but less informed. Father knew enough Hebrew to read the solemn festival prayers, but she did not. He had run away from his home and family in the then German town of Kempen in Posen (now the Polish Poznan), where he was born on May 30, 1861. It was on his thirteenth birthday that he ran away because his stepmother would not give him a new suit for his formal entrance into religious adulthood, though his two older brothers had gotten new woolen suits for their bar mitzvah solemnities while his real mother was still alive. He ran off to America, working his way on a German ship, then apprenticing himself to an immigrant German peddler who took him off in a wagon laden with goods to be sold at farmhouse doors (there were no autos then and the goods had to go to the farmers, not they to town). Each day my father took a basket of shoestrings, collar buttons, safety pins, spools of cotton, papers of needles and pins, and other notions, and went to visit farms off the wagon road. Each night he met the peddler at an appointed place. They slept in or under the wagon as weather dictated, and resumed their journey next morning. But one night deep in the southern Appalachians the peddler did not meet his boy at sunset, whether by accident or design, and my father was on his own with nothing but a basket full of notions, and a vocabulary barely adequate for peddling them. From the southern Appalachians he worked his way back to New York, picking up odd jobs on farms and sleeping in barns. By the time he got to New York, he had lost the top of his left thumb to an ax; his English was better than his rapidly fading German; and he was an American. He was not highly literate either in his native German or in Hebrew, and, although the province of Posen was overwhelmingly Polish, he knew no Polish except for one or two curse words. At thirteen, his education in his native German tongue, in the Jewish religion and Hebrew, and in the traditions of his people, ceased altogether.

Although my mother was our teacher in what she took to be the Jewish religion, she knew even less than my father concerning their creed. She did not have to learn to be an American in the Appalachian Mountains, for she was born in Kingston, New York, in 1861, of parents who had left Germany for America in 1848. Kingston was then a small closely knit community; her parents and their sons and daughters were a part of that community. Her father, Ber Samter, ran the general store in the center of the little town, and was known to all the inhabitants thereof as Uncle Bear. He was dead when I was born and so much the revered patriarch of our family that a number of my cousins as well as I, were named after him. My mother shrank from the thought of turning me into a miniature zoo by calling me Bear Wolfe, so from one of the novels she had read she picked the name Bertram. All my cousins named after "Uncle Bear" were called Bernard.

My mother was taught by my grandmother a mixture of stern German family discipline ("Children should be seen and not heard"; "Don't question, don't argue, don't talk back"; "Honor thy father and mother") and some rigid rules concerning the Jewish dietary laws and the proper observance of the Sabbath and other religious holidays. Outside of that, she was an American girl, a native of Kingston, a product of its schools, its social groups, its opinions, its Americanism. She sometimes spoke of God to us, but He seemed to be a God who was mainly occupied with watching us to see that we did not disobey His Commandments. He was all-seeing, we could not hide any secret actions from Him even if we hid in the coal bin in our cellar. Apparently, he kept for each of us a ledger page on which all our trespasses were noted. That we might acquire entries on the asset side of the ledger never seemed to occur to my mother. Her God was a stern one, His watch unceasing, His injunctions precise and rigorous. He was not a God of love and mercy, but of justice and punishment, hence I could not deepen my religious feelings by love of God, only perhaps by fearing and more scrupulously obeying Him.

Except for honoring my father and mother, all the precepts and commandments were negative thou-shalt-nots. They included not so much the Ten Commandments, whose violation was unthinkable in our puritanic household, but such prohibitions as "You must not eat butter or milk with meat, nor for three hours thereafter"; "You must not ride on a train or trolley car on a Jewish holiday"; and "You must not eat a variety of foods that all our friends and neighbors seem accustomed to eat." And, most vexatious to me, "You must not write down a word or take pen or pencil or crayon or paintbrush in hand from Friday night at sundown to Saturday night at sunset." Why these restrictions were laid upon us my mother never explained, perhaps had never been taught. How could she know of the dense and elaborate literature of interpretation that rabbis had deduced from the single injunction, thrice repeated in the Old Testament, "Thou shalt not seethe a kid in its mother's milk"? Or know that out of that single command had grown up the whole lore and practice and exacting code concerning the separation of a meat meal by three hours, and among the more zealous practitioners by six hours, from the consuming of milk or any of its products? How could she explain to us children why she had four sets of dishes with their respective utensils and dish towels, two for every-day milk meals and meat meals, and yet two others for the Passover meals of milk and meat?

Had she explained to me that the word Sabbath was derived from the Hebrew word *Shabbat* (in Sephardic Hebrew) or *Shabbos* (as my mother pronounced it in Ashkenazic Hebrew) meant simply *rest;* had I known that the Sabbath was so called because God had created the world in six days and on the seventh had felt the need of resting and being refreshed, and that therefore, He, or His rabbinical spokesmen in His name, had enjoined on us a complete and blessed rest on the seventh day, I might still have questioned why I was not permitted to write on Saturday, but I would have found the idea of a day of rest for God and a day of rest for man an engaging one. Perhaps at this point I should admit that in writing the present book I have been doing my best and most peaceful writing on the two Sabbaths, Saturday and Sunday, when nobody phones me in my office, nor comes to chat, nor to seek my counsel. The Sabbaths for me are days of rest in peaceful and joyous work. Perhaps that is one of the privileges of the intellectual life: we intellectuals are, it seems, so well organized that we have conquered the seven-day work week, and rejoice in it. What other union or trade can boast as much?

If this was all the religion my mother and father had acquired and all my mother was able to transmit to me, how was my yearning for a deeper religious faith to be satisfied? I longed for a prouder tradition, for more faith and understanding, for more poetry than was in her creed. I sensed that the Jews had not been held together through all the fearful vicissitudes of their history by this meager code. I felt that there must have been something bordering on the miraculous in the fact that the Jews had lived under so many great empires and civilizations, all of which had perished, while this weak, defenseless, and peaceable people continued to survive. Surely there must be more to my heritage than my mother had been able to transmit to me. But all I could find in the inheritance was a possibility of deeper zeal in obeying unexplained commandments and prohibitions and ill-comprehended rituals. Debating this question with myself when I was ten years old, all I could come up with was a proposal to my mother that she should permit me to fast like the grown-ups for a full 24 hours from sundown to sundown on Yom Kippur. "No, you are not old enough," she replied. "You do not fast from sundown to sundown until you are thirteen." Seeing my disappointment and no doubt welcoming my unexpected zeal, my mother added, "After you turn eleven next January, you may fast a half day. From sundown on Yom Kippur eve you will not touch food or water until noon on Yom Kippur day. Then I will give you your lunch." I accepted the concession as a step in the deepening of my religion. But, by the time I turned 11 on my next birthday, I did not reach the great Day of Atonement of the following autumn with my zealous desire to fast intact. A crisis supervened on the Rosh Hashanah of that year which comes a week before Yom Kippur, a crisis that left a deep and indelible mark on my spirit.

Taking further advantage of my newfound zeal, my mother said to me on the holy eve of the Jewish New Year, "You are old enough now to go with your father to the synagogue on Rosh Hashanah. Take the prayer-book with you and say the same prayers as you say for Shabbos, and read some more of the psalms."

"But that will take only a quarter of an hour, and Dad stays in the synagogue all day until sundown."

"No matter, you will hear the cantor chant, the rabbi and the congregation pray aloud, and at sunset you will hear the blowing of the ram's horn. It is written that every Hebrew male must hear the shofar blown on *Rosh Hashanah.*"

I went with my father, read my sparse prayers and psalms, browsed through the rest of my little Book of Common Prayer which seemed dull and prosy after the snatches of Bible reading I had begun in the public library, contemplated the prayer shawls and the elaborate silk caftans of the more prosperous or more zealous, contemplated their skullcaps, the unwonted spectacle of the entire congregation bowing incessantly out of time with each other as they chanted aloud their seemingly endless prayers and incantations. Of these I understood not one word. I was bored to death. My religious zeal was in peril if this was all I could get out of the sacred service.

Only once was there a single unmistakable word, one word only, which I understood, and with it came a moment of unexpected drama. As they chanted their incomprehensible and interminable prayers, suddenly, loud and clear, I heard from my father's lips the solitary intelligible word "*Brooklyn!*" The din of incantation and prayer grew deathly still; all eyes turned from the Ark of the Covenant and the prayerbooks to stare at my father, most with angry looks, a few with amusement in their eyes. There was a tense moment of hushed shock, then they returned to their prayers. Only years later did I understand that my father had altered what were perhaps the most sacred words in the entire Rosh Hashanah ceremony, the cry of all the dispersed Jews of the Diaspora, "*Next year in Jerusalem!*" Whether out of a sense of humor (one of his traits to which I owe much) or out of frankness, he had expressed his true wish and expectation, "*Next year in Brooklyn.*"

Boredom settled down on me again amid the alien chanting until at last a brilliant and pious thought struck me. What was I doing here listening to chants and shouts I did not understand? What could be religious in hearing a din of sounds without meaning? I would walk out, go to the Arlington Library, the shelves of which I had scrutinized so often that I knew by heart what books were in what places. I would go to the two-foot-high tomes of the English translation of the Babylonian Talmud, one volume of which I remembered bore the title *Tract Rosh Hashanah.* There I thought I would penetrate the mysteries and discover the sacred meaning of this most holy day; there and then I would truly become a part of the congregation to which my mother had sent me. At last I was to set out on the high road to faith and meaning, to beauty and fervor, to the poetry and song that sustained my fellow Jews and kept them together despite suffering and persecution.

I slipped out of the synagogue, ran through the streets, bounded up the steps of the library, went straight to the shelf harboring the Babylonian Talmud, and selected that one of its tall volumes that bore the legend *Tract Rosh Hashanah.* It was too forbiddingly big to be read through in an afternoon, so I opened it at random—after all, Rosh Hashanah was a two-day holiday and I could start earlier tomorrow. My eyes fell, by luck—or was it God's grace?—upon the section that my mother had assured me dealt with the most sacred of Rosh Hashanah ceremonies, the sounding of the ram's horn, the closing climax of the celebration of the New Year. With joy I began to read the holy work, confident that it would light up my spirit.

CONCERNING THE HORN AND THE TRUMPET

My expectation soon gave way to bewilderment and dismay. Yet I read on and on as one continues to press on when lost in a labyrinth.

Learned rabbis were arguing with each other, commenting on each other's comments on yet other rabbis' comments, on single sentences or phrases in a sacred text. One said that any kind of horn might be used on New Year's Day except a cow horn; another that the horn must be that of a ram; another that it must be the straight horn of a wild goat; yet another insisted that the horn must be crooked and only from a ram. The mouthpiece might be inlaid with gold, but the gold must not touch the mouth, or the horn could not be used. Followed a discussion on mouthpieces, covered with silver to blow on a wild goat's straight horn for Jubilees, but of gold to sound a crooked ram's horn for New Years. My head spun.

What, I wondered, was a Jubilee and how did it get into the sounding of the horn, or horn and trumpet, on New Year's Day? In time I learned that the Jubilee came every seventh New Year, a particularly solemn and beautiful New Year's Day, in which every Jew must free his slaves and pardon all debtors their debts to him. I read on and on but could not find out which rabbi had triumphed between ram and goat, nor the metaphorical meaning of the crooked and the straight. One thing at least pleased me: in the Talmud there was not the rigid, dogmatic, intolerant orthodoxy of my day. It was apparent that equally learned and equally pious men could discuss amiably and amiably disagree with each other on the meaning of a phrase while they retained respect for one another. That at least would lighten for me the burden of being a Jew.

For a brief moment my heart was lifted up by a sudden switch from disputations concerning punctilious prescriptions to a line of poetry from one of the Psalms of David, "With trumpets and sound of horn make a joyful noise before the Lord. . . ." But my spirits drooped again when I learned that the Lord could be found only in His Temple, and that the Temple had been destroyed, so that one could no longer stand before Him and make a joyful noise with both trumpet and ram's horn! The trumpet, the more musical and joyous of the two instruments, was out.

Next came the problem of what a Jew might do if he found himself at the bottom of a pit on New Year's Day and wished to celebrate the ceremony of the ram's horn. If the horn was sounded inside the pit, both he who sounded it and those who, leaning over the pit's mouth, heard the sound, or even part of it, might be held to have done their duty. On the other hand, if one heard part of the brief flourish of two sounds before daybreak and the other part after daybreak, he might not feel that he had done his duty, for the night was not a proper time for the sounding of the horn. I paused to wonder what a good Jew could be doing at the bottom of a pit on so holy a day, but did not learn until later that the Babylonian masters were accustomed to throw their captive Jewish slaves into a pit or cistern as a punishment and mark of contempt, and that they also threw lepers into their pits and cisterns. Under such circumstances, it was deeply moving to think of a Jew trying to sound, or to hearken to the sound of a sacred horn on his Holy Day.

I drowsed next over smallish-seeming subtleties about patched and mended horns, but my drowsy senses awakened with astonishment when I came to a passage reading:

> All are obliged to hear the sounding of the trumpet, priests, Levites, and Israelites, converts, freed slaves, a hermaphrodite, and one who is half slave and half free. A sexless person cannot sound the horn in behalf of those like or unlike himself, but a hermaphrodite can act on behalf of those of the same class, but not of any other.

I copied the puzzling passage to study it. What were hermaphrodites? Why could a hermaphrodite sound the ram's horn only for other hermaphrodites, and not for other people? What was a sexless person? Why was a sexless person called "it"? Why could a sexless person not sound the horn for others, not even for other sexless persons? With those bewildering words on my mind I closed the big Tract, no wiser than before. Unlike the chant in the synagogue, I understood the words, or most of them, but I understood no more of the holiness of the Holy Day than I had before. Moreover, it was getting late and dinner would be served as soon as the ram's horn signaled the end of the services and my father returned from the synagogue.

When I got home, breathless and full of questions, Father was not yet there. "Ma," I asked without pausing to catch my breath, "what's a hermaphrodite?"

"A *what?*"

"A hermaphrodite."

There was a long silence. "Maybe you mean *morphodite?*" (Like me, my mother encountered many words in her reading that she had never heard pronounced.) "Maybe I do mean *morphodite,* but it looked to me like *hermaphrodite.*"

"*Where* did you find that word?" she demanded severely.

"In the Talmud—the Babylonian Talmud."

"And *where,*" she demanded more sternly, "did you see the *Talmud?*"

"In the library."

"*When* did you go to the library?"

"Today. I didn't understand a single word that was being shouted in the synagogue, so I went to the library and got out *Tract Rosh Hashana* of the Talmud. It's in English. I thought it would help me understand what Rosh Hashana is about, really feel the holiness of the Holy Day, understand the prayers and the chants and the meaning of the blowing of the shofar."

My mother's face contorted with anger. "Don't you know," she cried, "that you're not supposed to go to a library on a Jewish holiday? Don't you know you're not supposed to *enjoy yourself* on a Jewish holiday?"

No, I did not know it, nor did I quite believe it, but I was speechless. I couldn't explain to my mother how I felt. I could not explain it even to myself. I left her presence without a word, left the house to walk in the streets, for the first time in my life without partaking of the family dinner.

THE BEGINNING OF DOUBT

I walked the streets for hours, then for many days and nights, thinking, thinking, asking questions for which I found no answers, thinking thoughts I scarcely dared think through, questioning the very sources of my mother's injunctions, her authority, her understanding of what she had taught me. For the next two or three years the interior dialogue continued, and I was powerless to end it. I was afraid to think my thoughts through to the end, yet I could not stop. For a while the nights were like the days as I lay wide-eyed in the darkness, trying to think through thoughts which perhaps had no answers, thoughts that opened forbidden and terrifying vistas. When I went on my newspaper route mornings and afternoons, I hurled my rolled-up newspapers mechanically, leaving them, I suppose, at the right doorsteps, since there were no complaints, but guided only by habit, while my thoughts and attention were far away from the *Journal,* the *World*, the *Eagle*, the *Staatszeitung*. Every moment I could spare from my newsboy work, every moment I robbed from neglected homework, was spent walking through the streets of the city, around the reservoirs, through Highland and Forest parks, trying to think my way through the maze of questions which the questioning of my mother's religion had opened up. Instinctively I avoided my beloved salt marshes that might have given me solace, for it was dangerous to travel through swampland, and leap over mud slicks and streamlets, unless you gave full attention to what you were doing. For the rest, I did not even notice where I walked, too absorbed with unaccustomed thoughts. The turmoil was like a religious conversion in reverse.

My mother's fateful words kept ringing in my ears. *Don't you know that you dassent* (my mother's word for *dare not* or *must not*) *go to the library on a Jewish holiday?* Why not? What was wrong with reading on a holiday, if what one read was a good book? Are we Jews not known as "the People of the Book"? What's wrong with reading the holy Talmud in a language I can understand, if the Talmud is exactly what they are reading in the synagogue in a language they understand? What could be wrong in going to the library to read the *Tract Rosh Hashanah* on Rosh Hashanah itself? What could be wrong with my purpose, reading to master the mysteries of my faith, to understand the rites, the prayers, the songs, the ceremonies being conducted in the synagogue, to learn the very meaning of the holiday itself, to share its solemnity and its joy and communion with my fellow Jews, the members of my father's congregation?

To share its solemnity and joy by comprehending its meaning. . . . I heard my mother's voice, stern and angry: "*Don't you know you're not supposed to enjoy yourself on a Jewish holiday?* For answer I heard the words of *Tract Rosh Hashanah* bidding my people, and me myself, "*with trumpets and horn to make a joyful noise before the Lord. . . .*" What was Rosh Hashanah if not a day for rejoicing at the coming of the New Year, for joy at the opportunity to repair the mistakes and injustices of the year that had passed and make the coming year better than the one that was ending? And what were those especially holy seventh sabbatical New Year's Days, the solemn Jubilee Year, and the yet more solemn seven times seventh Jubilee Year, but a time of righteousness, forgiveness, and joy, when "every man shall be returned to his possessions," and all debts shall be wiped out and all slaves freed?

No matter how I turned those two utterances of my mother, against reading and against joy, over in my mind, no matter how I sought to understand her anger at my attempt to deepen my religious understanding and my faith, always I came to one and the same conclusion.

"Why," I said to myself at last, "that woman"—using the third person for the first and only time in my life concerning my mother, as if a great gulf had sprung up between me and the author of my being and source of my faith—"that woman is simply not religious at all. She doesn't know what religion is, nor what religious feeling is. She doesn't understand that she is rebuking me for trying to become more deeply religious."

But where was that thought leading me? If my mother was not religious at all, what reason had I to be religious? If my mother was the source of my belief that I was a Jew, and the source revealed itself as dried up, what reason had I to accept all the dry rules devoid of spirit which she had indoctrinated into me? If no waters of religious feeling gushed forth from the source, how could my faith itself be anything but dry and barren?

What remedy? *To think everything out for myself?* To read the Old Testament from end to end, to examine it in the light of my unripe and green reason? To see how its passages had been interpreted by all those rabbis who seemed so barrenly legalistic themselves in my first encounter with them? To ask myself whether the ram's horn and the goat's horn were sacred instruments for the New Year and the Jubilee Year because they were the most musical? Or whether they were the only ones available to the ancient pastoral and captive people of the Babylonian captivity? And whether they could not be replaced in our day by more splendid and joyous musical instruments, more suitable for rejoicing and lamentation? Was it merely because once set down in Hebrew script and commented on by so many learned rabbis, it now became impossible to examine their music and appropriateness? Or was there some deeper and better reason why it should be only the ram's horn and the goat's horn and two trumpets if the Temple were rebuilt? If I now questioned my mother's creed, how many other frightening questions did that open up?

What creed could I now accept? Should I examine all creeds for an answer? Had any other creed a greater warrant than mine? Were all of them thus believed because one was born into a family that professed it? After a number of days of such turmoil and fear, I became less afraid of the forbidden and unbidden, and decided that I could not know peace again unless I followed wherever they led.

As soon as I had made up my mind to follow my thoughts wherever they might lead me, conclusions began to come fast, and they were unexpectedly sweeping in scope. Now, near the tailend of my life, one of them may be an open question for me still, but in my eleventh, twelfth, and thirteenth years I did not shrink from trying to answer them.

"Why am I a Jew?" I asked myself, and answered, "Because I was born to Jewish parents who told me so. If I had been born in a Catholic family, I would have been a Catholic; in a Protestant family, a Protestant; in a Mormon family, a Mormon. How do I know that the Old Testament is God's word, and the New not? Perhaps they are both legends like the Greek legends I have been reading." I turned these puzzles over and over in my mind, and could find no answer except to conclude that I must read the Holy Bible from end to end, both the Old Testament and the New, then examine and reexamine the creed I had been taught in such pitiful fragments, to see if I really believed it.

And if not? If not I would have to examine all the other religions to which I might have access, to see if any of them would convince and satisfy. And if none and no mixture of them satisfied, then I might have to decide whether it would be possible to live without any religion at all.

For a year or more I struggled against considering yet another question that kept obtruding and would not go away: *How did I know there was a God?*

Of course, I had been told so, but now that I was questioning all that I had been told, why exclude that question? I needed a better reason than the say-so of my mother and my elders, many of whom acted as if they did not believe in God themselves.

A better reason? Yes, there was one: the existence of the universe, its splendors, its mysteries, its terrors. How could I imagine anything or anybody without a beginning and without a Creator? Yet how did I know that the universe that was here when I was born, for me to be born into, had not existed always? What did I know beyond the fact that it existed when I was born and would exist after I died? Why did it have to have a Creator?

Did it help any to say that it must have had a Creator? Would I not then run up against the question of who created Him, or whether He did not have to be created? Was He, whom I had never seen and found impossible to contemplate with my senses, any easier to imagine than the universe that I saw and in part knew? How far must I push back before I came to something, or Someone, that must have existed from the beginning of time and would exist forever? How could I decide whether the God of whom suddenly I seemed to know nothing had existed from everlasting to everlasting, or whether the universe, visible and tangible, of which I knew quite a lot, had existed from everlasting and would exist to everlasting? My voracious and random reading in libraries added food for thought and matter for bewilderment. I came upon the marvelously simple exposition of the Darwinian theory in Clodd's *Primer of Evolution*; I knew something about atoms and molecules and their multiple and their random combinations. I knew something of nebulae. I was puzzled at the thought of a God who was omnipotent, yet had to take six days to create the universe instead of a single instant of His will, and then was so tired out that He had to rest on the seventh day to be refreshed. In the poverty and misery of the Williamsburg tenement in which I had lived until the preceding year I saw much that I thought a just God would not have created or permitted. Was God running the universe, I wondered, or letting it run itself? Did the Creator of the universe really have time or desire to watch little me and keep a black book of my faults, where he noted that I wrote on Shabbos, the day He had dedicated to rest, or that I ate pork, or shellfish, or drank milk right after I finished my meat? Now that I thought about it, could I really believe that the Creator of all things that lived and all the planets and galaxies and stars could also concern Himself with watching and noting down every misstep or peccadillo of little me and millions, nay billions, of other people like me? Were we not giving ourselves too much importance when we thought, as my mother did, that the Creator of the sun and the moon and the stars and the vast, mysterious universe with all its wonders, had nothing more important to do than to watch whether I wrote a story or kindled a flame on one of the seventh-day anniversaries of the day on which He had rested? or time me to see whether I waited five or three hours after eating meat before I touched milk, or whether I waited only five or three minutes to put milk in my coffee after I had finished my meat? Was that a godlike task? As these questions forced themselves into my consciousness, I felt an upsurge of relief. "Why, nobody is watching me!" I cried aloud in the street where I was walking. And though a number of passersby stopped to stare at the little boy who had cried out to an unlistening sky that nobody was watching him, I was not abashed, nor did the joy at sudden freedom from a great weight diminish.

But in the next instant, a half-formulated new care took the place of the care that had vanished: Who then was going to watch me and guide me and provide rules for my actions and impulses? But I succeeded in pushing the new puzzle from my mind, taking joy in my new freedom, and pride that the task was now my own to work out rules and guidelines and a code to guide my own conduct.

With that, a number of thoughts began suddenly to jell, thoughts, half thoughts, and fragments, cohering for a brief space and seeming to support and reinforce each other as if their mere coherence were a warrant for the soundness of all of them.

Nobody was watching me, I told myself again and again. There is no stern and grim celestial bookkeeper, quill pen always hovering over a black book with my name on it and with no space for assets and merits but only for liabilities, sins, and transgression. But in that case there is no devil either! And no hell with fiery caldrons, fiends and demons, boiling oil, searing flames that torture but never consume, no pitchforks nor hot tongs nor any of the rest of the apparatus of torment through all eternity that my mother and some lurid books had pictured for me.

In that case, death had no more terror. Dying, perhaps yes, for I had already learned from the death by cancer of one of my aunts that there might be terrible as well as quick and easy ways of dying. But the morbid fear of the coffin and the grave where one might be buried alive, and the fearful punishments that might come thereafter, fears that my mother had instilled in me, vanished suddenly and completely. When you're dead, I told myself, you don't miss life. You are nothing as you join the countless millions and billions that have dissolved into dust, you miss nothing, you want nothing, you are nothing, once you join the legions of the dead. Many years later, I was to convince myself by actual experience of the danger of sudden death both in Spain during the Civil War and in turbulent Mexico, where a high official tried to frighten me into leaving the country by suggesting the prospect of "the .30-30 and the Ley Fuga," that there were kinds of death I might fear, but that the fear of sudden death itself had really left me completely at the moment when, as a 12-year-old apprentice philosopher, I convinced myself that the terminal event called death, as distinct from modes of dying, had no longer any terror for me—the moment when I convinced myself that "when you're dead, you don't miss life."

THE BEWILDERMENT OF THE BOOKS

As these problems grew harder and more puzzling, I finally gave up the long walks and lonely dialogue, and returned to the library for more light. But the light threw uncertain shadows, and the books in the library spoke with many voices.

The Hebrew calendar told me that the universe had been created exactly 5,669 years ago come next Rosh Hashanah. Books of ancient history pushed back the epoch of recorded time for a few additional millennia. I discovered the vast sweep of archaeological and geological time, and a cozier, more comprehensible, technological time, with stone ages, an age of bronze, and one of iron. There were books that assured me that the earth had existed for millions of years, with life interrupted repeatedly by great sheets of ice descending from the poles. I found out that my beloved tramping grounds on Long Island had been laid there for me as the terminal moraine of a great glacier, which accounted for its sandy soil and huge boulders and its lack of a bedrock outcropping such as one found across the East River in Manhattan.

I succeeded in imagining an unknown world covered with giant fern forests, through which tramped monsters that dwarfed the dragons of my fairy tales. These had ceased to exist long before Jehovah created Adam and Eve and Eden, yet there were their fossil bones, and little heaps of the bones of their feastings, to prove that they had existed, while in the Brooklyn Museum was a dinosaur skeleton, tall enough for its head and its arched back to touch the ceiling, and long enough to fill the length of one of the halls of the museum. As for the fern forests that preceded the Garden of Eden, they too had left fossil fern-leaf branches behind and fossil oil and coal pockets, to prove that they had once covered the earth long ages before the God of Abraham, Isaac, and Jacob created Adam and Eve, and the serpent, and the to me totally desirable yet inexplicably forbidden Tree of Knowledge. It seemed clear to me, as I read on, that man must have walked the earth, perhaps stoop-shouldered, perhaps erect, perhaps only recently ceasing to dwell in trees, long before the God of the Old Testament created Adam and Eve. Each book I read brought fresh bewilderment and wonder, but also a growing intellectual joy that made me lose all fear of the conclusions that were being forced upon me.

I found many contending faiths with so many gods and goddesses and demigods and spirits, and in some religions, such as those of India, even single gods who presented themselves to men in many different guises, names, powers, and manifestations. Some creeds were dismissed in the books I read as myths or legends (those that had died out), but others were treated with respect even if presented with less beauty because millions of living persons believed in them. With so many creeds to choose from, no one of them seemed sufficient to impose acceptance as the unquestioned and unquestionable Gospel or divine revelation. Freed from the compulsion to believe, I rejoiced; yet still there were aspects of my freedom that troubled me.

There was nothing in the children's room of the library to answer my questions. However, the librarians had long become accustomed to my ranging through the entire library and reading and drawing out books for adults. When some new librarian questioned the presence of such a young and physically still smallish boy among grown-up books, I had two excuses, both of which were true. I told them that I had read all the red, yellow, green, blue, and vari-colored fairy tales, all the books by Horatio Alger and Ralph Henry Barbour, and G. A. Henty, and Rider Haggard . . . and I kept on rattling off names until they were convinced. My second argument was that I had to pick out books for my mother and take them out on her card, which was also true. Her guidelines for me were comparatively simple. She had a poor memory for the names of books she had read and the names of authors, so my first duty was to browse through a given book to see if she had read it before. Next, I had to see that there was plenty of plot and action and "not too much boring description to skip." Finally, she was incredibly prudish, much more prudish than she had managed to make her adolescent son, so I carefully ran through the pages of a book to see if it contained any passages that might offend her excessive modesty. Young as I was and perhaps unduly modest for a boy of my age, it was I who acted as the censor to see that the books I brought my mother were suitably pure, and not she who censored my reading.

Hence the librarians were not surprised when their precocious little visitor would ask for help in tracking down a reference to the grief and struggle and sense of unbearable loss that some nineteenth-century literary, religious, or even scientific man had felt when he found himself no longer able to believe in a single act of creation or in a personal and transcendental God who controlled and ordered and watched over the universe. I found others who could not bear the thought that man was not the lord of creation, that the universe was not created for man's benefit, and indeed was not at all concerned with his fate. And yet others who could not bear to think that when they died, their ability to think and feel and know and remember might die with them and their remains might simply dissolve into dust.

I was bewildered that I should not feel this sense of loss, but rather a sense of relief. I laid it then to the fact that they had lost a loving God, an assurance of immortality, a sense of purpose in the universe, that I did not possess. Later I added a knowledge of the shock that came in the nineteenth century from Darwin's evidence concerning the origin and evolution of species, while the twentieth century had lived with this knowledge for a long time and gotten quite used to it. When I read Matthew Arnold's grief and Julian Huxley's joy at the loss of the belief in God, I could understand the feelings of both of them. I felt cool agreement with Huxley's sense of release and gain, but it was for Matthew Arnold that I felt compassion—and pride for his stoical wounded courage and for the beauty with which he expressed it in "Dover Beach":

> The Sea of Faith
> Was once, too, at the full, and round earth's shore
> Lay like the folds of a bright girdle furled.
> But now I only hear
> Its melancholy, long, withdrawing roar,
> Retreating, to the breath
> Of the night-wind, down the vast edges drear
> And naked shingles of the world.
>
> Ah, love, let us be true
> To one another. . . .

During this long debate and reading of so many and variegated books, I learned that there were countless millions of human beings who believed in many different gods and theories of creation and of the nature of the universe. They needed to believe, I felt, and were comforted thereby. Some were made better men by their creeds and gentler in their treatment of fellow men who did not share their beliefs. But in others I found that their faith instilled a fierce and brutal intolerance and added one more irrational reason why men kill each other.

Many years later, when I was chatting with a colleague in the field of Russian studies, he said, flushing in sudden anger: "All the evils in this world are caused by religious fanaticism."

"Not so fast, Professor," I said. "Can it be that you don't know of all the cruelties practiced in Russia and her satellites by antireligious and militant atheistic intolerance?" The colleague in question bore an unexpected anger toward me for several days for that irrefutable rejoinder. In any case, whatever the balance sheet of kindness and cruelty might show, these several years of boyhood reading and thinking gave me an open-minded and courteous respect for the religious feelings I did not share, except where these feelings manifested themselves in intolerance and cruelty, in religious wars and brutal persecution.

This disorderly course in comparative religion that I had devised for myself during several years of reading and thinking left a permanent mark on my spirit that went beyond the question of what I was to believe. I developed a tolerance for and an understanding of others who needed and cherished their belief in God and immortality. So much was this true that when I became educational director (agitprop director they called it) of the Communist movement that I had helped to found, I found it impossible to accept the cruel and intolerant, militant, punitive, and persecutory atheism that the leaders of the Communist International sought to impose upon me as a bounden duty.

When I went to work for the Voice of America in the period from 1950 to 1954, religious leaders and believers were being framed, tortured, and sent to concentration camps in all the countries under Communist rule in Eastern Europe. After trying to get my script writers to write effective radio broadcasts to defend the religious freedom of the churchmen and devout believers who were being thus persecuted, I found that I had to write the scripts myself to get the requisite feeling into them. I did not believe what the persecuted believed, but I did believe in their right to freedom to harbor and practice their beliefs without interference. One day, the director of religious programming, Roger Lyons, told me that he had been chatting over the lunch table with Ed Kretzman, a minister's son and the political director of the Voice. "Who do you think is the most deeply religious man in the Voice?" Lyons asked Kretzman. And Kretzman replied, "Unquestionably, I should say, Bert Wolfe." "And you agreed with him?" I asked Lyons. "Yes, I agreed."

"But, Roger," I said, "there are more than nineteen hundred people working for the Voice, and you and Ed have picked on the one who is probably the least religious! I have neither church nor creed, nor belief in the existence of a personal God, nor any of the other things you would expect when you call a man religious. What you and Kretz have mistaken for religious feeling must be my compassion for the persecuted, my readiness to understand their feeling for their religion, and quite simply my deep concern with freedom, their freedom to believe, to practice their creed, to worship openly, to teach their children their beliefs and moral code."

"Maybe so," said Lyons after a pause, "but your concern and the earnestness of your moving scripts seemed to us, and still seem to me, religious." Similarly, when I began to teach in the Institute for the Study of Comparative Politics and Ideologies at the University of Colorado and found many teaching nuns among those teachers of the social sciences who alone are eligible to take the course, I learned that the sisters took me to be deeply religious although they never asked me what I believed. I had to touch on many delicate questions in the course of my lectures on Communist ideology, but always they seemed to feel the compassion and empathy for their faith which they mistook for acceptance of their religion.

BY WHAT SHALL MEN LIVE?

While I struggled with these large problems, again and again I was confronted with the dread question, Can I live without a God, a church, a creed? In this disenchanted, desanctified world, existing mysteriously without beginning and without end, without Creator and without any purpose, beyond its own internal laws and the purposes we give it, without God or Devil, Lawgiver or Sacred Law, without shalt or shalt-not, what was I to live by? From the books I read, from my thoughts and feelings, from the traditions I inherited or absorbed, from fragments of the creeds I had been studying, from the sense of good and evil and right and wrong that seemed to surround me and penetrate my spirit, could I devise a code of my own and follow it without any external compulsion, with no Celestial Bookkeeper watching me and recording my sins? Even as I took pride in my new freedom from prescription, I discovered the perplexities and responsibilities that went with freedom. Could man—not only me personally but man in general—live without a more authoritative code and without the dread of punishment for his wayward impulses? What would those without a transcendental faith and divinely revealed code teach their children? How would we nonbelievers decide what was good and bad, right and wrong? Was I entering into the kingdom where nothing is prohibited and all things are permitted? In the name of what would we curb the strong and the ruthless and defend the weak and defenseless? All my life, I must admit, I have continued to work on my own code of conduct, sometimes by habit and sometimes situation by situation and case by case. Insofar as I have been able to work out a code, it comes close to that Natural Law so haughtily rejected by some of my philosophical friends: the feelings that man has certain rights natural to him as a human being, rights to be granted, legislated, recognized, and protected simply because he is human. And with this, despite the philosophical pundits, I have had to make do, and I think it has done well enough to guide me and even to give me persuasiveness and eloquence at times to convince others.

THE UNANSWERED QUESTION

There was one large problem I tackled that I could not solve at 11 or 12 or 13, and have not solved yet, nor do I expect to: Why does the universe exist at all, and why is there life on the earth and perhaps elsewhere? I tried to imagine what would be if the universe did not exist, what the chaos was like that was supposed to precede the existence of the cosmos and out of which the God of the Old Testament created the universe? Could I imagine space without matter and movement? Could I conjure away in my imagination matter and energy? Could I conjure away space itself? Could I imagine empty space with nothing filling it or moving in it or occupying some part of it? And how could I conceive of abolishing space itself or think of a time before space existed? The more I wrestled with such problems the less I could explain to myself, until at last I was driven to the question of questions: Why is there something? Why is there anything? Why is there not nothing? How did it all come to be and what is its meaning?

And there my mind stopped as a boy, and there my mind stops now in the closing years of my life. The old man is no wiser in this than the little boy. These are the questions which I know I can never answer. When I came to that conclusion, I decided that these were the questions that I should cease to ask. This is the sum of my agnosticism, this is what I do not and cannot know. Hence, at the bottom of it all is a mystery. Feeling the existence of that mystery, which is the mystery of existence itself, I cannot adopt a militant atheism nor be intolerant of those who are comforted to believe that they have the answer to the question, Why is there something? Why is there anything? Why is there not nothing? And as I contemplate those last three question marks, I can understand what Albert Einstein meant, agnostic as he was, rejecting all churches and creeds and religious authorities, yet able to write: "I am a deeply religious unbeliever." If to be perpetually puzzled and in awe at this insoluble mystery of the existence of the universe and all that is in it, is to be religious, then I too can say, "I am a deeply religious unbeliever," or at least a deeply mystified one, aware of the insoluble mystery of the fact of facts—the fact of the existence and the ever-changing complexity of all that exists.

6

THE CITY'S CROWN

O youngest of the giant brood
Of cities far renowned,
In glory's race thou hast outrun
Thy rivals at a bound.
Thou art a mighty queen, New York,
And how wilt thou be crowned?
She bowed herself
And spent herself
And worked her will, forsooth,
And set upon her island heights
A citadel of truth. . . .

The song was written for the College of the City of New York by Henry Van Dyke, and set to music by the school's shy and gifted organist, Samuel Baldwin. Except for the word *forsooth,* put in for the sake of rhyme and meter, a license which must be permitted to minor poets since it is so often assumed by major ones, the words seemed right and moving to me when I entered the college, for it was then and still is to me truly the city's crown. For over a century and a quarter the great city bowed itself and spent itself to maintain for all its qualified young men, and later women, rich or poor, a tuition-free higher education. Without that enlightened generosity the city would have been much poorer than it is, and I, and thousands and tens of thousands like me, would never have gotten a higher education at all. Since 1847, when Townsend Harris, crockery merchant, tamer of the Democratic party in the tough old Ninth Ward, president of the Board of Education, Democrat with a small and a big *D,* subsequently a distinguished American diplomat, first proposed that a "free academy be founded," and overcame the bitter opposition of Whig journals, the city never wavered until America's two hundredth anniversary (a fine year to choose!) in its determination to provide a good higher education to even the poorest of its citizens. Until 1976, as from the outset, it was still tuition-free to all eligible inhabitants of the city, still a magnet for the less affluent, bright and eager young. And its standard of excellence rose steadily until it came to be known, in jest and in earnest, as a "sort of proletarian Harvard." Until 1976 twice as many of its students came from low-income families as are enrolled in the average four-year college. Until 1976 it was the great subway-circuit college, adding to the economy of free tuition the freedom from dormitory charges while its young men and women lived in their parental homes. They came from almost every square block in the city. In my own case the subway circuit involved running about a mile from Berriman Street and Glenmore Avenue to the Long Island Rail Road station at Warwick Street and paying a fare to the end of the line at Flatbush Avenue, where I took the Broadway subway train to 137th Street. Others traveled even farther than I to get their education.

Its poor have come from Irishtowns, Little Italies, and Jewish ghettos, according to the changing makeup of those whose parents had sought refuge on our shores. When I enrolled, the college was overwhelmingly Jewish, but today the boys and girls of Jewish origin (there are girls now, too) have sunk to a little less than half the thirteen or fourteen thousand full-time regular students. There are three to four thousand blacks (more than most of the country's Negro colleges have on their rolls), over a thousand Chinese-Americans, some eight hundred students of Puerto Rican origin, a sizable number of Italian and Irish Americans, besides an always-substantial group of others from poor and middle-income families. (These figures are taken from a report of the year 1973, but I doubt that they have altered greatly since, except for an increase in the proportion of students of Hispanic and West Indian origin.)

From the start there has always been opposition to the idea of a free institution of higher education. When the Townsend Harris proposal was being considered in a referendum ordered by the state legislature, a correspondent of the Whiggish *Journal of Commerce* warned that the Roman Republic had fallen because of "similar measures" and characterized the Harris proposal as "an attempt on the part of the pauper class to levy upon the active, industrious, and affluent portion of the community the expense of furnishing to their sons a college education." The referendum was passed by the people of the city by a vote of better than four to one, supported not only by the poor but by the middle class, and by many farsighted men of substance. Townsend Harris, too, was a man of substance. And so were the men who began the Northwest Ordinance with the words "Knowledge being necessary to good government and the happiness of mankind. . . ." Thus the idea is written into the very foundations of the city, and of the country whose greatest metropolis it is.

All of which makes it so puzzling to me that men in high place have so far forgotten the hopes that lie in our democratic origins as to press and nag the city of New York to abandon one of its proudest achievements. In 1960 Governor Rockefeller began pressing the city to end its tuition-free higher-educational system. He appointed two commissions to study the question, commissions so constituted that he knew and even publicized the "findings" of one of them before it really had done its work. Each year the New York State Board of Regents echoed the governor and issued a call for the imposition of tuition charges. And each year the city rejected the proposal and reminded the state officials that it is not the state but the city that "bows itself and spends itself" to give its poor and needy a chance at a free higher education.

Perhaps I should not have expected a Nelson Rockefeller to understand what it means for a poor boy with a love of books and learning to find the doors of a great college open to him by the city's bounty. Or what it means to be a boy in a family that not only does not have the money for tuition and fees for library, laboratory or textbooks, but also needs its sons and daughters to go to work as soon as the law allows, and turn in their wages to help keep the family housed and clothed and nourished and cared for medically.

As a boy at the turn of the last century, I was imbued with a distrust of the very rich who, behind the scenes, seemed to be running our country. Our President, Teddy Roosevelt, spoke of "malefactors of great wealth." The newspapers which occasionally got into our home, the *Journal* and the *American*, both Hearst papers, and Pulitzer's *Evening World*, and the popular magazines of the day, all denounced the "trusts" and their secret control of our government. William Jennings Bryan and his Populist supporters conducted a powerful presidential campaign on this issue, although Bryan muddled it somewhat by his famous "Crown of Thorns and Cross of Gold" speech. Trust-busting was fashionable although in the end it was to prove meaningless.

In time, the men of wealth seemed to become less ruthless, and their children won acclaim as philanthropists and founders of institutes, supporters of museums, builders of medical schools and hospitals, with large sums of money, albeit a minor portion of their gains. So when Nelson Rockefeller became governor of the State of New York, although I did not vote for him, I was not too disturbed, for I figured, like many another man, that "being so overwhelmingly rich, he at least will not have any motive for adding to the sums he cannot even count up, by graft and corruption. He has too much, he will not want to take more out of the state's treasury."

But as I watched our state budget climb, then vault, from year to year, and contemplated some of the senseless projects on which he spent our taxes to make his reelections easier, I had new cause to wonder at the advisability of putting such infinitely rich men into high office.

It is Thomas Jefferson, a man of substance, who has been generally recognized as the chief prophet of public education in the early years of our country. He felt that wise and honest government required the training of an elite to lead the republic, and the best possible education of our citizens would serve as an antidote to the tendency to tyranny inherent in power. In the preamble to the Virginia education law he wrote, "The general objects of this law are to provide an education adapted to the years, the capacity, and the condition of everyone, and directed to freedom and happiness." To his friend and law teacher, George Wythe, he wrote from Paris shortly after the country gained its independence: "Preach, my dear Sir, a crusade against ignorance; establish and improve the law for educating the common people."

Now Nelson Rockefeller and those who stood with him can contemplate the fact that they have undone the work of Thomas Jefferson and the other Founding Fathers. Taking advantage of the financial difficulties of the City of New York, and the not so remote bankruptcy of the State of New York as Nelson Rockefeller left it, the great city has lost its crown, and, of all years, in 1976, America lost its noblest example of free education for the children of the poor and the middle class.

I do not wish to put all the blame upon the overly rich who can no longer stop their wealth from growing, unless, like an Andrew Carnegie, they try to die poor—and even he failed in that attempt.

A large share of the blame falls upon the unthinking common man who cast his vote for men who were literally unable to understand his needs. Is it any accident that in a moment of urban difficulty the first attacks are upon the libraries and upon higher education in general? I myself must take my share of the blame for the calm with which I took Rockefeller's repeated elections "because he was too rich to want to add to his wealth by pillaging the state treasury."

Perhaps some may think that the city of New York is unique in its free higher education? Not a bit of it. There are state colleges throughout much of the country. Moreover, to the shame of rich, democratic America, the richest country in the world, be it noted that all the leading countries of Western Europe have free university education for all who want it, regardless of the income of their families, taking account only of their ability to do university work. And there are four European countries that also give all students lodgings and a stipend while they are acquiring the higher education that should make them an asset to their country, and to mankind.

To those who have always known that they would go to college, it is hard to convey the excitement and joy with which I climbed the gentle slopes of St. Nicholas Heights and beheld the Gothic towers and arches of the college that had just notified me of my admission. The complex of buildings of rough-hewn Manhattan granite bedrock trimmed with borders of shining white stone, designed by one of the best architects of my day, Stanford White, shone resplendent in a bright morning sun, built in beauty and bright with promise.

After the long discussion with my mother, after all the uncertainty, unbelievably, I was going to college! My father had run away from home and formal education at 13. My mother had been taken out of grammar school before she got her diploma because her family doctor, following the medical fashion of the 1870s, had warned her parents that too much schooling and reading was hard on girls and, being sickly, she would get "brain fever" if she didn't leave school. The lifelong pleasure she got from reading novels and the liveliness of her untutored mind suggest that she might have done well indeed in high school and college had they been open to her.

If we were a little less poor than in my younger days, it was because I was turning in what money I earned at various jobs, and because my older sister and brother had gone to work at fourteen, immediately after graduating from elementary school. For days my mother and I discussed the problem. The idea of going to college was without precedent in our family, even among all my cousins. Of course, I would have to continue to work after school and during summer vacations and would have to turn in my earnings except for the barest necessities of a college student. I had over an hour to ride on the subway, not counting the brief preliminary trip on the Long Island Rail Road, and I learned to do all my homework and reading of much else besides to the racket and roar of the subway train, where still today I can read undisturbed at high speed and even make legible notes or the outline of a talk, provided I get a seat. To help earn money for the household I worked, as I have said, at a succession of occupations: messenger boy, newsstand clerk, candy butcher, and newspaper vendor on the Long Island Rail Road, salesman for my father, private tutor, college odd jobs during study periods, and post-office clerk, all of which shielded me from the cloistered ignorance of the real world outside the confines of the academy, which permits so many of our intellectuals to pronounce unfounded judgments on a world they have not gotten to know.

Of course, my mother did not fail to remind me, "If ever you flunk a single course, out you go. . . ." But I knew there was no danger of that. I would not flunk, I would do well in my studies, I would get all I could out of the chance at a higher education, I would choose my profession promptly and plan my electives accordingly, and I would penetrate as deeply as I could into a world of wonder and intellectual delight of which several thousand library books read helter-skelter without any guidance had given me a foretaste.

To be sure, working after school and during vacations while trying to keep up with my studies and pursue the excellence to which I never ceased to aspire made things hard for me at times. But youth is youth, and on the whole I did well both as student and breadwinner. When I was appointed at the age of eighteen to the post of regular substitute post-office clerk (a device used to fill full-time clerkships with substitutes, who would not have to be given increases or paid vacations), I worked out a wonderful compromise between my employment and my studies. When the going got too hard at school, I would get a certificate of illness from a friendly physician (sick leave was without pay for a substitute), and astonishingly get well come exam time, since I was always managing to get exempted from exams, and during the Christmas rush in December, and well on into the new year until the going got too hard again. Then I would happily reappear once more when the super, who knew and approved of the careful timing of my illnesses and recovering, needed me to take the place of some clerk on vacation. The free time during my "illnesses" enabled me to complete term papers, and to know some of the pleasures and excitements of extracurricular activities such as the Clionia Literary Society, of which I became vice-president and member of its debating team; the Deutscher Verein, of which I became secretary and then president; the Philosophical Society; the Varsity Debating Team, which I helped materially to lose a debate with Fordham University. I found time, too, to participate in the exciting life of the student alcoves, where I consorted with the literary crowd, with those active in the then fashionable debate in biology and philosophy between mechanism and vitalism, and where I learned much unusual lore concerning the literatures and social movements of Eastern Europe from older special students such as Leo Pasvolsky, who became an expert on the Russian economy, Avrahm Yarmolinsky, who became curator of the Slavonic Division of the Fifth Avenue Library, and Alexander Tendler, who introduced me to my future wife, intending to show her off to me as his own sweetheart, and to Freud and Jung and other founders of modern psychoanalysis. Tendler was to become a psychiatrist himself.

Life in the alcoves (one to a class, though I frequented those of the class above me and the class below me as well as my own) gave me as much perhaps as the regular curriculum. It was there that we opened our brown paper bags with lunch brought from home and discussed and sought to settle all the problems that beset us and the world. It was in the alcoves, not in the classrooms, that I got interested in the works of Darwin, Spenser, Schopenhauer, and Nietzsche, participated in the great battles between mechanism and vitalism, first got started on Dostoyevsky and Turgenev and Tolstoy, on the plays of Ibsen and Shaw and Strindberg and the Irish dramatists, discussed sex, still taboo in the classroom, psychiatry, evolution and revolution, instrumentalism and transcendentalism, and all the host of isms that haunted and stirred the minds of the rising generation of the early twentieth century. It was in the alcoves that I received my first serious and informative treatise on sexology, a copy stenciled, bootlegged, and unsigned, which I was told had been written by Dean Kirchwey, father of the *Nation* editor, Frieda Kirchwey. It was in the alcoves that I got to meet the members of the Emersonian Society who gathered regularly in the University Settlement on New York's East Side. The Emersonians drew me and my sweetheart in as a species of honorary heathen adepts from more somnolent Brooklyn. At the University Settlement we first heard the music of the *Peer Gynt Suite* and attended dramatic readings of Ibsen's *Peer Gynt*, which remains for me today my favorite and most durable of Ibsen's plays. It was in the alcoves that we found kindred spirits, advanced and examined our half-baked solutions of insoluble problems, read our poetry to each other, shared our experiences. The first two operas I heard were the result of tickets given me by more affluent holders of season tickets which, on certain occasions, they could not use. I shall always be grateful to two *cognoscenti* who made possible a luxury I could not otherwise afford, and, more important, being good singers both, patiently explained to me the structure of these operas. Harry Schachter, Emersonian, later to become the manager of the largest department store in Louisville, Kentucky, sang all the arias and much of the rest of *Aida* to me and some eavesdroppers in our alçove, while Joe Levine, later to join the chorus of the Aborn Opera Company, sang *Carmen* using a supple falsetto for the feminine arias. The combination of the ticket and so much of the music and theme of the two operas was overflowing generosity to a boy whose prior contact with music was limited to an occasional German brass band playing with more will than skill before a neighboring corner saloon, along with the songs I was taught in elementary school, and the sentimental ballads sung by my mother when the mood and the occasion warranted. Since there was no radio and no television then, nor viable phonographs either, folks made their own entertainment, my mother being in great demand at parties because she could recite with skill narrative poems such as *The Polish Boy*, or a mournful tragedy which as a little child I called *Nellie Hist* which I besought her to recite because it contained the stirring line " 'Be still or I will kill you, Nell,' he hissed!"

Another form of musical education that began in extracurricular fashion (I took no course in music at City College) came from Professor Samuel Baldwin, whose memory I cherish. Every Wednesday afternoon at four, he would step shyly through a stage door in the Great Hall, seat himself at the organ, and begin to play. Girls from Hunter College, including of course my own, and City College boys who were lacking in pocket money, or loved music, or both, made up his audience. Baldwin had been an organist since he got the post as a boy at the age of fifteen in the most important church in St. Paul, Minnesota. He played after that at churches in Chicago and the Church of the Holy Trinity in Brooklyn Heights, then studied at the Royal Conservatory of Music in Dresden under the Saxon court organist Gustav Merkel, thereafter coming to City College as a professor of music, composer of church, choral, and orchestral music, director of the college glee club and orchestra. Though it took many more years, a good music station, and a good radio in my car to make me more conversant with and appreciative of Bach, it was Baldwin's Wednesday afternoon organ recitals that first introduced me to this his favorite composer.

Good teachers are rare in any institution, as I learned in City College, known though it was for its able teachers. Especially since the Great Depression of the 30s, when our educational system began to expand at a faster rate than that of any other country in the world, there have never been enough men and women of high teaching and scholarly quality to fill the fantastically multiplying vacancies. Many mediocre persons have therefore had to be placed in the gaps where men and women of wide culture, profound scholarship, and genuine teaching ability were lacking. Some graduate schools are a reassuring exception to this observation, for there often great scholar-teacher-inspirers have earned their posts and produced in turn disciples who sometimes equal and sometimes surpass them. It has been my experience that the good teachers and masters to whom one is indebted can be counted on one's fingers without taking off one's shoes to complete the count. The mediocrities fade from memory along with what they taught, unless they were especially memorable for the outstanding height or depth of their ineptness. Still I realize with gratitude that my college and university education have given me more than I dreamed when a college education still seemed unattainable to me.

Since I early decided to be a writer, though I had no clear idea what it was I might write, I remember best those teachers in elementary and high school and college who inspired in me the confidence that I might be able to write. They were the ones who wrote a few encouraging words on my compositions, along with their caustic comments on the sloppy appearance of my work.

I have already mentioned a Miss Rentum, who unknowingly encouraged me as early as elementary school. Then there was the high-school English teacher, Abraham Brill, who when he met my sister socially said to her, "When your brother Bertram hands in a composition, first I put an A on it, then I read it for pleasure." There was Fisher, the head of the English department in Boys' High School who would never give me more than a C or a C+, but when I expostulated that all other English teachers gave me A's, he responded, "Only a Shakespeare could get an A from *me*, but my C+ means that you have done the best that could be expected of a high-school student. I hope you are planning to teach English when you complete your education." And indeed I was, for I thought that a poor boy could not afford to become a writer unless he had some good-paying employment besides, and that teaching English was about as close as one could get to writing. When I began to teach, it was at Boys' High with Fisher as my chairman.

At college there was Lewis Freeman Mott, professor of English language and literature and department head, an unexciting classroom teacher but a learned specialist in Dante and Shakespeare and the poetry of Provence, who, when he discovered that you wrote well and loved English literature, would take you into his study, pour some sherry for himself and you, then prove himself a brilliant conversationalist and a man of great learning and love of letters. I took Shakespeare's histories, comedies, and tragedies with him. He weaned me from overvaluation of the then fashionable Ibsen, Shaw, Strindberg, and the Irish lyric dramatists, and made Shakespeare a priceless treasure to me for the rest of my life, and a pleasure to teach as well. In the final exam in Shakespeare's histories, I chose for a free composition a topic combining history and literature: "The Age of Henry IV as Portrayed in Shakespeare's History Plays, in Chaucer's *Canterbury Tales*, and in *The Vision of Piers Plowman*." He began reading Part I of my examination book over my shoulder before I had finished Part II, then said, in jest I thought, "If such and such a word"—I don't remember which—"is in the dictionary, you will get both the Ward medals in English literature and English composition." I got both. Medals were bronze in those days, not gold, nor accompanied by prize money, but they pronounced me, as all the Ward medals do quite recklessly, "The student of *greatest proficiency* in English Literature" and the student of "*greatest proficiency* in English Composition." In my senior year I had the honor of being listed again as *hors concours* for both medals. The honors gave me what I needed most, encouragement to believe that I could write.

When I graduated, Professor Mott invited me into his study, poured sherry for us, then offered me an immediate appointment as assistant tutor. I was, of course, to do graduate work for higher degrees and promotion. But an assistant tutor's salary then was only $500 a year, out of which I should have had to find funds to study at Columbia for a master's degree. Only with a master's would I become eligible to receive $1700 a year as a tutor, and then there would be the expenses of a doctorate. I considered the financial state of our family exchequer, and my younger brother's need to get a higher education too (he was to go to Cooper Union, where he studied civil engineering). Sadly and gratefully I declined the honor of a college teaching career since an English teacher in high school started at five or six times that of a college tutor. I had already taken and passed the high-school teachers' exam in English and done a year's practice teaching at Townsend Harris Hall High. With the backing of Dr. Fisher, the head of the English department, who had never given my themes higher than a C+, I got an immediate full-time substitute appointment to teach in his department, and my career as a high-school English teacher, at least so I thought, was well begun.

The teacher who contributed most to the development of my personal style as a writer was the professor of rhetoric, Earl Fenton Palmer. He was a shy and sensitive little man, a student of the Bible and the Semitic languages, and especially of the Book of Job. His favorite contemporary author was John Ruskin, whose writings on art, on morals, on society, on the ways in which the workingman might make more beautiful his life and improve his lot, Professor Palmer accepted reverently and *in toto*. From him I derived a respect for Ruskin's sometimes splendid prose style, a longing to see the "stones of Venice," the works of Gothic architecture and Florentine art, and a feeling for the light and color and mist and smoke in the romantic, pre-impressionistic landscapes of Turner, for whom Ruskin wrote his *Modern Painters* with the purpose of exalting him above all other landscape painters. My course with Palmer on English prose was at eight o'clock. Autumn and winter mornings Professor Palmer would come into the classroom, his face shining with joy, and shyly say to us: "Gentlemen, did you notice the mists on the Hudson, the ships looming out of the mist, the blood-red sun rising over the waters? A perfect painting by Turner!"

I took two courses with Professor Palmer, one in English poetry and the other in English prose. My most vivid memory from the poetry course will help the reader to understand the character of this shy teacher. Our work for the week consisted of Milton's minor poems, and he was reading aloud from "L'Allegro" the passage on Milton's two alternative versions of the birth of the Goddess of Joy. I followed the lines:

> Zephyr, with Aurora playing,
> As he met her once a-Maying,
> There, on beds of violets blue,
> And fresh-blown roses washed in dew,
> Filled her with thee, a daughter fair,
> So buxom, blithe, and debonair.

"Lovely," I thought, "and a relief after the rather heavy beginning. But doesn't the poet ever get close enough to roses to know that a bed of roses is a bed of thorns? And why should a great poet permit himself such a pedestrian, doggerel last line, just to fill out the meter and find a rhyme?"

My thoughts as critic were interrupted by a cry from Professor Palmer, a cry of agony and wrath. "My father married my mother," he thundered, "and I married the girl I love! Now what's there funny about that?"

I looked up from my book. The good professor was blushing furiously, some of the students seemed embarrassed, some astonished, some amused. Professor Palmer thought that he detected a smirk on the faces of some at the words "filled her with thee" and his shout expressed a mixture of shame and anger. He was so upset by the tumult of his own emotions that he could not continue. After a painful silence, he dismissed us with the hour scarcely begun.

How could this prudish man be a professor of English literature, I wondered, of a literature robust, often rowdy, and not infrequently bawdy? Surely one cannot find his like in the English departments of the present day. Yet this sensitive, modest, inordinately shy man was a good teacher, and moreover, my greatest teacher in the appreciation of prose style, and in the formation of a prose style of my own.

His method was as simple as it was effective. Our textbook was an anthology of short works by the great masters of English prose. Each week, or in some cases, as with Addison and Steele, each half week, was devoted to a single author. The first, as I remember, was devoted to Francis Bacon. Our professor discussed with us the social and historical setting in which Bacon wrote and sought his audience, sketched the biography of Bacon and his influence on the formation of English prose, read with us specimens of Bacon's essays, commenting as he read on the characteristics of the writer's style—such qualities as his conciseness, use of aphorism, love of balanced structure, the cumulative impact of his compound sentences consisting often of short, sharp phrases of three words each, subject, predicate, object, succeeding each other with only semicolons between, and with not a single adjective or adverb to weaken the impact. After Professor Palmer had read us a few of Bacon's essays with running commentary, and after I had read some more of them on my own, I felt I could imitate Francis Bacon's style rather closely, and that was exactly the task Palmer asked us to perform. "Select a topic that you think would have been congenial to Sir Francis, and write on it in a style which imitates the style of Bacon as closely as you can." I picked a suitable topic—I no longer remember what—and wrote an essay that looked, to me at least, as if Sir Francis himself might have written it. This was easy enough with Bacon, for his rhythms, his mannerisms, his tone, his themes, were so different from those of any other writer who has written in our language. Next we did the same thing with Milton's more majestic, more ragged and irregular prose. When it came to Swift, my power of imitation failed me, but Addison proved easy and Defoe not too hard. Week after week we got a fresh insight into the thought and mood and style of another master of English prose, ending finally, inevitably, with Ruskin. With each such exercise, I got a fresh insight into the nature of the personal style toward which I was groping. It helped me to develop an inner ear that listens critically to the sound, the precision, and the appropriateness of what I had written. And all my life I have felt a debt to Earl Fenton Palmer for that experimental laboratory for the study of English prose which he seems to have invented, for those difficult and remarkable exercises through which he put us, and for the deepened understanding he gave me of the art of writing. Often I have thought what a pity it is that in our age of academese, journalese, bureaucratese, and plain sloppy speech and writing, the whole question of style is so much neglected and misprized, and that English departments, as far as I have been able to ascertain, no longer offer so useful a course.

Two other episodes in my youthful study of English literature may put Professor Palmer's prudery into a broader perspective. The first is my experience with the study of the history of the novel under Professor Charles F. Horne, who took the robustness and bawdiness to be found in literature to be a natural part of the works that narrate or imagine the varied ways of men's expression of their vitality. When I studied under him he had already shown his proper piety by a book done in collaboration with the Reverend Julius A. Brewer, *The Bible and Its Story*. And he had demonstrated his expertise for teaching the history of the novel by one book on the birth and another on the technique of the novel. (It is a sad commentary on the mortality of books of literature that only the Bible story survives in the Stanford Library catalogue while the two other, far better books have been displaced by later and less able works.) Professor Horne's course began with the first fragmentary tale surviving on an Egyptian papyrus, took us through the novellas of Greece and Rome, such medieval folk tales as are gathered in *The Hundred Merry Tales* which supplied inspiration to Rabelais, Boccaccio, and Balzac, then on to the novels of

Richardson and Fielding, Balzac, Austen, the Brontës, Thackeray, Dickens, and Thomas Hardy, with whose *Return of the Native* and *Tess of the d'Urbervilles* the course ended. His course was a continuing feast in which we read at home at least one work a week, and not mere synopses or digests of them, then heard them brilliantly discussed in class. I got the books in the college library or the libraries of New York and Brooklyn, or read them in their reading rooms. But I was a youth of sixteen, and when I could not find Longus's *Daphnis and Chloë* in those libraries and presented myself at the Pratt Institute Free Library, I found that the relevant index card had a red star stamped on its upper left hand corner, which meant that the librarians thought me too young to be trusted to read this Greek pastoral novella of young love between a goatherd and a shepherdess, so innocent that they had to be taught the art of making love to each other, he getting his first instruction from a good-hearted courtesan, and she from her lover on their wedding night. Their union is delayed by his scruples and by suitable adventures and muted pastoral terrors in which Chloë is abducted and threatened with rape and Daphnis is carried off by pirates from whom he is rescued in comic fashion by all the cattle on the boat running to one side and capsizing their ship. Their union is delayed to the end of the final chapter when a suitable wedding ceremony takes place and the rustic guests play flutes and pipes of Pan beneath their wedding chamber. They live happily ever after, their male children being nursed by a she-goat, since goats are sacred to the great god Pan, and, their daughters nursed by a ewe. I went to Professor Horne with my sad tale that library prudery prevented me from doing my homework. He wrote a dignified letter on departmental stationery assuring the Pratt Library that Bertram Wolfe was a serious student of the history of the English novel and could safely be entrusted to read any book he was assigned to. The reader can imagine my pride when, armed with this attestation, I returned to the Pratt Library to get not only *Daphnis and Chloë*, but thereafter every book he assigned. But the reader may find it harder to imagine the age in which such books were treated as moral poison, for today *Daphnis and Chloë* is a Penguin Classic available to young lovers or would-be lovers, and literature students of any age, and can be found in a number of other translations on the open shelves of any university library. Moreover, Longus is bent on emphasizing the idyllic nature of his shepherdess and goatherd, and though he is fully aware of the wilder and more violent and even crueler side of the cults of Pan, Eros, and Dionysius, he softens and mutes this aspect at every point in his gentle tale, while so many of our contemporary novelists fill the foreground and often the whole tale with those aspects of sex dear to the heart of the Marquis de Sade, to the virtual exclusion of the warmth, the considerateness, the mutuality, and loyalty of love. This, too, makes me feel the immense difference between the age in which I grew up and the age in which the reader is reading my account. Even now they seem like two different countries.

A similar episode took place on the tennis courts of Prospect Park.

Between matches I talked with a Hunter College girl named Dorothy Miller, whose ambition, like mine, was to become a teacher of English literature and a writer. Our discussion was of *Lady Chatterley's Lover,* which had been prohibited by His Majesty's censor in England. Said Dorothy, "The great writers never need pornography or obscenity to sell their works. Look at Shakespeare's plays. You'll never find an obscene expression or thought or suggestion in any of them." "Dorothy," I cried, "they must be giving you the same expurgated texts in your Shakespeare course at Hunter College that I got in elementary and high school." I lent her my Shakespeare plays, pointing out and explaining to her the numerous bawdy puns which delighted the groundlings of Shakespeare's day, only to be Bowdlerized by pedants in future editions. As the reader may imagine, this changed her view of English letters. But the reader will find it hard to imagine that a college like Hunter was actually giving expurgated Shakespeare texts even to its specialists in English literature.

CERTAINLY NOT A HISTORIAN

The faculty at City College when I was a student there was an especially mixed assortment. Some of its older men had acquired their peak professorships by sheer longevity, surviving from a time when City College was just changing from the Free Academy to the College of the City of New York and standards of appointment were quite different from those prevailing later. Others were able young men who had attracted attention by their achievements, or by their teaching skill in the New York City high-school system or their work as students at the college itself. A prejudice against permitting Jews to teach such subjects as English or philosophy or history was still strong in many of our universities in the first decade of the twentieth century, but in City College being a Jew was becoming less and less of an obstacle to appointment. (Professor Mott, when he offered me an assistant tutorship in his department, tactfully hinted that many university English departments still felt that only pure Anglo-Saxons were capable of imparting a proper understanding of English literature, Irishmen and Jews being somewhat lacking in their innate understanding of Shakespeare and Chaucer and, no doubt, the Celtic and Hebraic elements in English literature.) Morris Raphael Cohen, the most brilliant teacher of philosophy at the college, had, after some initial difficulty, made the ascent from math teacher at Townsend Harris Hall High to teacher of logic, the philosophy of law, and the philosophy of science, with the loyal backing of the liberal philosophy department head, Harry Allen Overstreet. A. J. Goldfarb, a graduate of City College in 1900 who had been my biology teacher in Boys' High, moved up to the post of assistant professor of natural history about the same time that I entered the college. Paul Klapper, also a graduate of CCNY, brought distinction to the department of education. I learned much from him, did some teaching assistant work under his direction, and noted with pleasure his later appointment as president of Queens College. In general, it was recent graduates who did most to elevate the standards of their own alma mater when other colleges were still unwilling to recognize the scholarly excellence of City College graduates. Still today, an unusually large proportion of its faculty are men and women who got their undergraduate training at the college in which they now teach.

We may imagine that we plan our lives, but at every moment I was to find that all kinds of events would intervene to shape my life differently from my expectations and intentions. Thus, though I expected that, difficult though it might be, I should become a writer, nothing in my college career could possibly suggest that I might ever become a historian. To be sure, I had read much history in the public libraries, particularly English history, and had liked and done well in my history courses in high school. In my study of the history and literature of England both at Boys' High and in the public libraries, I acquired a lifelong respect for British parliamentary institutions and liberties. I was fascinated by the history, literature, and legends of ancient Greece. I studied Roman history by myself one summer to pass the end-of-summer condition exam and thus skip a course, and had done well in American history. But in college the study of history lost its attractiveness.

I had three required history courses at City College: medieval, Renaissance and Reformation, and American. In general, City College in those days had two years of required subjects: for an arts student, three histories, two sciences, three math courses, mastery of three foreign languages, one philosophy course in ethics or moral philosophy (which was supposed to make us good men), elementary psychology, and economics. Only after we had completed these required courses, which were intended to make us "know something about everything," were we permitted to choose our electives, which were to start us on the road to "knowing everything about something." Taken together, the two formulae I have put into quotes gave us the then prevailing definition of "an educated man," and nothing less would do. Alas, since then life has become more complicated, fields of knowledge have multiplied, and both these aims seem to have been given up. Indeed, there is no generally accepted definition of "an educated man" today. But, having started out thus on those two related roads, I find it impossible to turn back. My wayward and roving curiosity still demands—how effectually I cannot say—to "know something about everything," often to the disapproving astonishment of the specialists to whom I venture opinions in their fields. And in the field or fields in which I specialize, I have never given up the attempt "to know everything about something." Perhaps the strivings are in vain, but there they are. I remain a stubborn ancient from another age, incurable, too old and too set in my ways to learn some other, more modern definition of an educated man. Moreover, I have not even succeeded in guessing what the prevailing definition might be.

But I must return to history, and tell what I learned or didn't learn about history in my three required courses. My first course was medieval history. My professor was William George McGuckin, who had graduated from City College three years after it became a college and four years after the end of our Civil War. He was possessed by a deep aversion to the Middle Ages, or, as he preferred to call them, the Dark Ages. "Gentlemen," he would say at the beginning of a lecture, "in the Dark Ages, people never used soap! The lovely Guinevere never used soap! The brave Sir Lancelot went around all day long in sweaty and smelly leather and harness, and he never used soap!" The statement puzzled me, for in my chemistry course I had been taught that soap was invented by the ancient Hebrews several centuries before Christ and that they made their soap on the seashore by burning wood to get potash and combining it with animal fat. Other authorities attributed the invention to the Sumerians some three thousand years before the Christian era. Had neither Hebrews nor Romans nor Celts brought soap to the English before the Dark Ages became dark? And how did those characters out of the legends of King Arthur's court get into McGuckin's Middle Ages? Of course, Professor McGuckin multiplied his evidence of the darkness with descriptions of the narrow streets of London town, made narrower by some beldame's opening the shutters of her overhanging window and, with or without a casual cry of "Look out below," emptying her nightpot on the passersby. New cause for wonder: Could that be why chivalrous gentlemen gave the ladies they escorted the place nearest the wall? Many years later I thought of Professor McGuckin when my wife and I plunged deep into the Middle Ages in the narrow sidewalk-free streets of old Ravenna, that "sweet, silent, dead town" where the poet Dante found refuge from his ungrateful Florentine fellow citizens. I began to wonder why Dante, author of the great work that is the very sum of medieval civilization and of other writings that break ground for the Renaissance, found no place in McGuckin's picture of the Dark Ages. But thoughts of Dante and of Petrarch, to whom, unwittingly, the professor owed the very term Dark Ages, were interrupted by a sudden roar of motorcycles with mufflers out hurtling down the narrow street of the "silent town," causing my wife and me to fling ourselves against the wall. The more I saw of the glorious ruins left by the Middle Ages in painting, architecture, sculpture, poetry, philosophy, music, or the encyclopedic culture of the courts of an Alfonso el Sabio or a Charlemagne, the more I realized how much my professor had left out of his Dark Ages. But for years, all I could remember from his course was that the lovely Guinevere and the brave Sir Lancelot never used soap.

My journey through the Dark Ages ended at last, and I moved forward into what promised to be the brightness of the Renaissance and the stirring turbulence of the Reformation. Here our guide was Professor Thomas Moore, who, even as he handed out our textbooks, made it clear that he would not hold us accountable for the chapters on the Reformation! What more can I say?

Having finished with him as best I could, I still looked forward to the final history course, to see what depths and fresh revelations a college course in American history might offer. The professor presented a new image to me: a neatly trimmed beard, a stiff collar that buttoned in back, a reversed vest to match. His clerical garb, and his seven years as rector of the Church of St. James the Less, seemed neither to qualify nor disqualify him as a professor of American history. His three sonorous names, however, Livingston Rowe Schuyler, were redolent of our history, for they were all three the names of patrician families that had once owned vast and pleasant estates on both banks of the Hudson. In addition to a bachelor of divinity degree, he had a B.A., and M.A., and a Ph.D., from City College and New York University, and had studied, as befits a son of three patrician families, at Oxford and the University of Paris—education enough, I thought, to make a learned man and a good teacher. But alas, Professor Schuyler had no opinions! Or, at least, no opinions of his own, on any of the moot questions that make the writing of history such a fascinating occupation. If he ever ventured a judgment, he hastened to qualify it with the saving clause "as it were." When he wanted to sound really resolute, he would change the qualifying phrase into "Very much so, as it were." Then we could surmise that he might really like to stand behind the statement.

Of course, the City College history department was beginning to get some new and younger men of a different make, Nelson Mead and Jacob Salwyn Schapiro among them, but fate willed that I should get McGuckin, Moore, and Schuyler. The three of them managed to ensure that I could not dream of becoming a historian. Anything but that!

PREPARATION FOR THE ATOMIC AGE

To make up for my dispiriting journey into the past of Europe and America, my training in the sciences, both in Boys' High and in City College, was more than an arts student could have expected. The things I learned in biology, physics, and chemistry were to carry me, undazed and undismayed, through the next half century, a period of the most rapid and unsettling change in the whole history of science.

As an arts student, I was required to take three sciences. But since my teacher in biology in Boys' High, Goldfarb, had become associate professor of natural science in City College, and my no less remarkable physics instructor, Spalding, was being looked on favorably for appointment whenever a vacancy should occur as a City College associate professor of physics, the college gave me credit for both sciences. This left me with only chemistry as a required subject.

General chemistry was required for all students of the college, so that the department head, Charles Baskerville, took it upon himself to deliver three lectures a week to each of several huge groups into which the student body was subdivided. These veritable mass meetings were then broken down into classroom quiz and laboratory practice groups of manageable size under faculty members of lesser rank and interest. My own quiz and laboratory instructor was an undistinguished and boring teacher who shall remain nameless, but Baskerville proved to be both a first-rate practicing chemist and experimenter and a truly remarkable teacher whom I remember with gratitude. He was a tall, well-built, handsome man, his face a bit too mature and too fleshy to look the part of the juvenile lead in one of the popular melodramas of the day, but with a remarkable dramatic flair for making every lecture and experiment he executed before our eyes an exciting showman's performance. Besides my appreciation of his consummate acting, I gradually became aware of the fact that we were being talked to with clarity and simplicity by a first-rate thinker and experimenter in the new field of radioactivity that was, and is still, providing some of the most exciting and startling developments in the chemistry and physics of our time.

Baskerville faced us with evident pleasure in what he was doing. He stood, or rather strode up and down, on a large stage, with a bare table covered only by the apparatus for the day's experiments as the foreground. As a backdrop, there was a huge chart of the periodic table recently devised by the great Russian chemist Dmitri Ivanovich Mendeleev, who had died only five years before I began my chemistry course. Mendeleev's periodic table was a magic chart that reintroduced the Pythagorean mystery of numbers into the physical world. Mendeleev had arranged all the known elements in serried ranks or columns with column numbers like regiments in an army, lined up according to their atomic weights, and for each such column the chief of the Imperial Russian Bureau of Weights and Measures demonstrated that there were a number of common chemical behavior attributes. He left spaces for elements of which his theory suggested the probable existence, and predicted some of the characteristics that they would likely exhibit when they were found—brilliant prophecies, many of which were fulfilled before his death by other chemists following the hints in his predictions, and others of which are still being discovered or created as I write, sometimes elements with mere brief and instantaneous lives. Baskerville enjoyed himself immensely as he made us feel the marvels of this great generalization and demonstration of mathematical order in the universe. And I for my part realized that I was not merely watching a good show, nor merely absorbing some discrete facts about individual elements and compounds, but learning as well to comprehend something of enormous theoretical importance concerning the nature of the physical universe. What Darwin and his theory of evolution had done for me in putting order and design into the world of living creatures, the periodic law now did in the world of chemical elements and compounds. I got a sudden sense that the discrete facts I had been learning in physics about energy, its conservation, and its transformation; in biology about plants and animals and man; and now in chemistry about atoms and molecules, elements and compounds—gave an exciting glimpse of a synthesis of all I was learning—a heady draught of intellectual stimulant for a young freshman or sophomore. So that was what college was about, I thought, and my joy in learning grew with each fresh bit that fell into a visibly larger pattern or design. And with this grew a new reverence for the universe into which I had been born, a new mystery and a new wonder—a feeling that there was a grand design and order, even if I could not convince myself that there was a Grand Designer.

Baskerville had a gift for making every experiment seem dramatic. He took pleasure in the simplest experiment. He could take two vessels, show us that each seemed empty, explain to us that one was twice the size of the other, and that each contained a colorless, odorless, and tasteless gas, then combine them before our eyes with a controlled flame ("Otherwise there would be an explosion") and out of *two parts of hydrogen and one part of oxygen,* he would explain as if he were saying something tremendously dramatic, *make water!*

Or he would introduce us to the element sodium. He would produce it like a magician's prop, held with calipers, explaining that he could not hold the lump with his bare fingers because it reacted so vigorously with water that it would take the moisture from his fingers and leave a sore there. "Gentlemen, a deadly substance to be handled with care." Next he passed it through a "colorless" (slightly bluish, it seemed to me) Bunsen flame, which instantly flared yellow. "The yellow flame is a simple test for the presence of sodium." Next he dropped the lump of sodium into a transparent glass vessel of ordinary water and we watched it come to life, hurtle around in the water, sputtering vigorously, spinning and spinning, until it was all dissolved. "Sodium reacts vigorously with water"—who could doubt it?—"to give off hydrogen and a solution of sodium hydroxide. And sodium hydroxide, gentlemen, is caustic soda. Obviously, sodium is a metal not to be trifled with. But if I combine sodium with this greenish, irritating, even poisonous gas, chlorine, in the proper proportions, they will react completely to form a compound which is safe to eat," and, suiting the action to his words, he picked up a pinch of a white substance and ate it. "Sodium chloride, gentlemen, common table salt, you eat it every day." Who can forget such a performance by such a showman?

On another occasion he told us the story of the cyanides, described the discovery of hydrocyanic acid, which in my childhood was called prussic acid, and which provided the smell of bitter almonds as a clue to poisoning in murder mysteries. He told of an experimenter working with hydrocyanic gas who thought he had rendered that deadly poison harmless, but, carrying an apparently empty flask out of the laboratory dropped dead from breathing a bit of it that rose from the flask. "Gentlemen, let that teach you care in your experiments, for one fifth of a whiff of the gas is sufficient to finish you off." *One fifth of a whiff* was the most inexact quantitative statement Baskerville ever made, but it impressed itself on my memory so that I was not surprised when I learned, after moving to California, that capital punishment was carried out in that state by putting the man to be executed into a sealed chamber, then dropping a pellet of cyanide by mechanical means into a container of sulphuric acid, a quick method of execution that represents one of the amenities of life and death in California.

But Baskerville's greatest service to me was the upsetting of two of the fundamental dogmas with which I had thought myself to be firmly equipped when I entered college: namely that the atom was the smallest particle of matter and could not be further subdivided, and that, since the atom was the basic constituent of all matter and fixed in its attributes, there could be no transmutation of elements. These dogmas had been sacrosanct for centuries, the concept of the atom hailing from Greek thinkers of the fifth century before Christ; and the rejection of the possibility of transmutation of elements having been decreed by chemistry and physics along with the discrediting of the earliest experimental chemistry, called alchemy, in the sixteenth century of our era. But when I entered Baskerville's class or lecture hall in 1912 or 1913, both these dogmas were being called in question by eminent scientists such as Rutherford and a growing group of ardent experimenters with radioactive substances and their electrical emanations or rays. Earlier in the century Baskerville informed us, Rutherford and Soddy had declared that radioactivity could be shown to be accompanied by electrical changes in which "new types of matter" were continually being produced. And Baskerville himself, then a young chemist in his thirties, ignoring his own instructors' denunciation of this heresy by no less an authority than Lord Kelvin, had started his own personal laboratory experiments with the emanations from radioactive substances such as thorium. Rutherford and his students distinguished three types of emanations, classified according to their degree of ionization and penetrating power in air, and had already shown that the alpha particles when they came to rest and were neutralized possessed the properties and the spectrum of helium!

The world I had brought so confidently with me to college crumbled as I listened with growing excitement. Indivisible atoms and untransmutable elements were both vanishing at once. The atom was proving to be a complex world of lesser particles, and two experimenters had already shown that they could bombard a target or screen of zinc with alpha rays and strike out of the dull and stable metal a series of flashes that must be electrical in their nature. Thus had begun the bombardment and splitting of the atom that was to give us such toys as the two-mile-long linear accelerator that wrests secrets from the atom in the foothills of Stanford University.

The energy latent in the atom, I learned, must be enormous compared to the energy made free by ordinary chemical changes such as combustion, or the violent "vitality" of a lump of sodium in water. With that there was new hope of understanding the endless energy radiated by the sun in our solar system and by distant stars. And a new possibility of questioning the dogma of entropy and of the "inevitable death" of the universe. Baskerville quoted "heresy" after "heresy" to us with evident relish, communicating his excitement to many who sat facing him, not least to me. Fermi's atomic pile was still a quarter of a century away, Einstein's famous conversion formula—or rather, its fearful application to the atomic and hydrogen bombs—a half century away, but in this field at least Baskerville's lectures and my education at City College prepared me so that only the human consequences could surprise me, not the novelties themselves. Not a bad preparation for life in the atomic age for a youth of 16 or 17 taking Chemistry 1 in 1913!

MIND-SHAKER AND MIND-SHARPENER

The year 1912 proved a lucky year for me to enter City College, a special bit of luck being that it was the same year in which Morris Raphael Cohen, having "labored for six years with the Leah of mathematics while yearning for the Rachel of philosophy," at last got an appointment as associate professor in the philosophy department. All the students in the college were required in their freshman or sophomore year to take Philosophy 1, the study of ethics or moral philosophy. The consequent mass meetings were lectured to by the department head, Harry Allen Overstreet, the only required reading being *Five Great Philosophies of Life,* the Epicurean, the Stoic, the Platonic, the Aristotelian, and the Christian. Once more my mother's God must have taken care of me, for when the vast assemblage was broken down among all the members of the philosophy department into smaller classroom quiz and discussion sections, it fell to my lot to get the newly baked Associate Professor Cohen.

As he implied in his comparison of himself with Jacob longing for Rachel, he had had a hard time getting his beloved. Although he had come from Harvard with the highest possible recommendations from his teachers, James and Royce, and although the sharpness of his mind and his longing to teach philosophy were already known, his strong Eastern European accent and his obvious Jewishness counted against him in certain administrative quarters that could not conceive of entrusting to him the sacred preserve of philosophy, which in the nineteenth century was still known as Christian philosophy or theology. And they were particularly dubious about entrusting to him an ethics course with a text culminating in "The Christian Spirit of Love." Hence they had shunted him into Townsend Harris Hall High, where he was a good but unhappy teacher of mathematics.

In his sixth year, there was a sudden leap in the demand for courses in logic, for the Board of Education had made logic an examination subject for would-be high school teachers. When they listed him as plain *Mr.* in the college catalogue to give one such course in logic, he demurred and, at least so rumor had it when I entered the college, he insisted that if he was good enough to give the logic course, then he was good enough to get an appointment in the philosophy department of the college. Overstreet, whose accent, be it said in passing, was pure Oxonian, supported Cohen firmly, and the resistance was broken. The college never regretted it, for its fame and distinction increased because of his presence. He was to become a celebrated teacher and writer in the fields of moral philosphy, logic, the philosophy of law, of history, and of science, and inspiration to some of our greatest jurists such as Felix Frankfurter, Learned Hand, Oliver Wendell Holmes, Benjamin Cardozo, Louis Brandeis, and Roscoe Pound. Indeed, Cohen's writings on law have greatly broadened and deepened our view of jurisprudence, leaving a permanent mark on the deliberations and decisions of the Supreme Court to this day. And to me, as to many of our best students and faculty members, he came to be regarded as the most important single intellectual influence in the life of our college.

At first sight he was not prepossessing. A sharp pointed nose, hazel-blue eyes, a face ravaged by the lines of hunger and scarcity that he had known all through his childhood, a poverty he did not altogether escape even after he became a not-too-well paid associate professor, his face lean and marked by his constant struggle with poor health—to us youngsters this novice philosophy teacher did not look like a philosopher at all.

He completely ignored our textbook, *Five Great Philosophies of Life*, leaving it to the lectures of Professor Overstreet to deal with the contents of a mediocre book that did not conceal its bias in favor of the superiority of Christianity over Epicureanism, Stoicism, Platonism, and Aristotelianism. Instead, he distributed at our first session some mimeographed sheets dealing with problems in ethics, bidding us consider the first problem, to decide how we would solve it.

The problem was based on the plight of the citizens of Calais, and perhaps on rabbinical responses to a much older problem of the conduct of inhabitants of a besieged city. Our problem town had 600 inhabitants. Because six of its leading citizens had led the city in defiance of what it considered unjust commands of the sovereign, he had come with a mighty army, laid siege to the city, cut off its food and water, and served an ultimatum. "Surrender your six leading citizens with ropes around their necks so that We may punish them as they deserve. If you do not, We will slay not only them, but every man, woman, and child in your city will be put to the sword." "There was no relief in sight," Cohen assured us, "no escape. What would you have proposed to your fellow citizens if you had been one of the 600 inhabitants?"

He gave us a few moments for reflection, then went down the line in the order in which we happened to be seated, had us state our names and answer in turn. No escape for any of the denizens of the crowded classroom. As each of us answered, the answers provoked additional questions intended to compel us to decide on what principle we had based our answer. In short, like all the problems he put to us, it was an exercise in ethics and an exercise in logic. I happened to be sitting in the first row, first seat, so the lightning struck me first. Unfortunately, I do not remember my answer, but he asked me a second question on my reason for answering thus, then, seemingly satisfied that I had thought out the principle on which my answer was based, he ignored me henceforth, not only for the rest of the session, but for the rest of the term! Even when I waved my hand, he pretended not to see it. I felt chagrined at first, then relieved, after I saw what torments he devised for some of my classmates by question after question, until perhaps he had led one of them far away from, and into complete contradiction to, the original answer, whereupon he would declare, "As a matter of fact you're all wrong. But if you were right, what of it? What has it to do with the question or your first answer?"

One student answered, "I would give up the six to save the other 594." "Why?" "Because human life is precious, and it is better to sacrifice six lives than 600," said the student, confident that he had found a principle to hold on to. "Suppose you had to give up ten to save 590?" "The same." "Suppose 300 to save 300?" The student saw the trap closing on him; less confident now, he stuck to his principle, until finally—"Suppose you could save yourself, one single, separate person, by opening the gate and surrendering the other 599? How would you live with yourself after you had betrayed the city to save one life, your own?"

I realized I was seeing in operation a remarkable whetstone to sharpen brains. Since I was to be ignored, I settled down to watch the spectacle of student-baiting to see what effect it was having on the minds of such diverse persons. It became clear to me that Cohen did not believe the superstition that if you give every student a good school and a good teacher, all brains would become equal. In the perennial fight between nature and nurture, between genes and environmental conditioning, Cohen found room for both factors in varying proportions in the infinite variety of human beings. He knew that there were brains that he could not sharpen. If he could not rouse or shame them into the use of reason or thought, if he could not make them into suitable material for his whetstone, he tormented them, then he gave them up, in some cases quietly urging them to drop his course and get into another quiz classroom with another teacher. His wit was quick, his tongue sharp, his questions penetrating and to the point, to many of the students provoking as well as provocative. Quick in sarcasm, reticent in praise, yet, as I was to find in time, warm in friendship and encouragement. When he felt that you were making an effort to use your God-given powers of reasoning and thinking, he became tolerant, friendly, warm, began to treat you not as a student but as an equal. Something like fifty years later, I found in an issue of *Commentary* a rabbinical response that made me wonder whether he had chosen his first problem in ethics from the story of the citizens of Calais, or from the lore of the Talmud. In *Commentary* for July 1962 I found how at least one rabbi would have answered Cohen's problem number 1:

> If an enemy besieges a city and demands the surrender of one individual on threat of decimating all, or the surrender of a certain woman on the threat of violating all women, the individual may not be surrendered—in the case of the woman, even if she be a harlot.

I realized then that in Cohen's class I had gotten some training in Talmudical sharpness and Talmudical concerns in spite of the fact that I had never done more than get lost on one holiday afternoon in the exploration of the wisdom of *Tract Rosh Hashanah.*

To one student who reproached him for his "destructive criticism," Professor Cohen replied, "One must clear the ground of useless rubbish before one can begin to build." "But you have given me nothing to put in its place." Cohen answered: "You have heard the story of how Hercules cleaned the Augean stables? He took all the dirt and manure out and left them clean. You ask me, 'What did he leave in their stead?' I answer, 'Isn't it enough to have cleaned the stables?' " The story was a parable of the essence of Cohen's method of teaching.

When complaints reached Overstreet that Cohen was using nothing but case histories in ethical problems, and teaching by provoking and provocative questions, Overstreet gently hinted that a little positive preaching was also needed. "What are you doing," he asked in some Socratic questioning of his own, "to make your students into fine fellows?"

"I'm not a fine fellow myself," Cohen answered humbly. "At least, not so much better than my students that I can venture to impose my own standard on them.

"Never having discovered for myself any royal road up the rocky and dangerous steep of philosophy, I cannot conceive it to be my function to show my students such a road. The only help I can give is to teach them to climb for themselves, or sink in the mire of conventional error. All I can do to make the climbing easier is to relieve them of needless baggage that hinders their arduous climb, and thus help them to attain intellectual independence."

The most terrifying story concerning Cohen's teaching came when he first offered a course in the philosophy of law. It filled up to overflowing but was made up of would-be lawyers who thought they would be getting a head start on their law-school training, most of them students who had no interest in philosophy at all. Cohen tormented them with his own variant of the Socratic method. By the time the semester came to an end, they were miserable and he was angry; he flunked the whole pack of nonphilosophic would-be lawyers. The dean called him in, "Professor Cohen, nobody flunks virtually his entire class. How does it look? It suggests that the professor was unable to teach them anything." "Quite right, that's why I flunked them." Stubbornly he resisted pressure to make a better showing.

The next time he offered the course, only those with a real interest in the philosophy of law registered, and the entire class passed. The lesson was not lost on those who elected his other courses. When his articles began to appear in law journals and journals of philosophy, when in 1933 his book *Law and the Social Order* was published, his reputation was such that Felix Frankfurter, Oliver Wendell Holmes, and other great jurists began to exchange letters with Cohen and, in their own way, "study" with him. Frankfurter wrote in retrospect, "His lasting significance may be that to an extraordinary degree he encouraged in others the habit of contemplation. This he did as one of the greatest teachers of his time." Cardozo said, "Steadily and gallantly this pseudo lawyer has enriched our conception of jurisprudence by the fertilizing waters of a profound and pure philosophy." And Justice Holmes, "I have read his writings with admiration and great profit . . . enjoyed his conversation with equal profit, affection, and reverence. . . . I envy the youth who sit at his feet." Thus had the number of "disciples" come to outnumber by far the class of students he flunked when he opened his first course in the philosophy of law. And Cohen himself wrote in 1935 in his Introduction to Goldberg and Levenson, *Lawless Judges:*

> The American people have been accused, not unfairly, of lacking a due respect for law. In part, our judges are responsible for this fault through their failure to correct their personal opinions by objective tests and factual information. . . . The fault is mainly with our judicial system which is intellectually the weakest part of our government. It has the least opportunity to get adequate information on the issues it has to decide. Which of us who wants to inform himself on one of the principal current issues will be satisfied with listening for a few hours to a couple of lawyers and reading their briefs? Much is said about the calm atmosphere of the courts in contrast with the passionate attitudes which exist in the legislative and executive branches of the government. The truth of this is very dubious. Certainly our courts are less in contact with the actual facts of our complicated economic and social life, have no power to initiate investigations, and, by pretending to pass only on the law and not on the facts, leave the door open to most uncritical opinions.

It was opinions such as these, clearly and bravely stated, that helped to revolutionize the practice of jurisprudence in the United States, especially at the highest levels. And as I look at some recent decisions, I cannot help but feel that another Cohen is needed in this hour.

In his classroom, Cohen never once gave his own philosophical opinion on anything. No student was ever told what to believe or what to say in order to get on the right side of the teacher. The opinions he gave were on logic, on humility, on the honesty, integrity, and clarity of one's convictions, on the life of reason, on passionate attachment to the search for truth. And even those opinions were expressed not through assertions but through searching, sometimes even humiliating questions, that spared no one's vanity and knew no scruples save the scruples that sprang from those virtues themselves. "Our reason may be a pitiful candle-light in the dark and boundless sea of being," he wrote in *Reason and Nature,* "but we have nothing better, and woe to those who wilfully try to put it out." When he ventured to speak of his faith, he called it merely "the faith of a logician." He spoke of himself as a "philosophical stray dog," to which we might add, a dog forever sniffing for the truth wherever he could find it, quite unafraid to be an eclectic, a word that is anathema to the slaves of systems. If he had a doctrine, it was to be critical of doctrines. Of course, he recognized that there were situations so urgent that one had to act with imperfect knowledge before one had finished thinking out a problem, but even then one must continue to take thought, not to justify what one had done just because one had "committed oneself," but to reexamine, perhaps to reject, and acknowledge error—acknowledge it to oneself to clarify one's thinking, to others for whatever educational value open acknowledgment and correction might have.

To those of his students accustomed to receiving canned wisdom to set down in their notebooks, memorize, and repeat, this refusal to state his own beliefs was bewildering, even infuriating; to his better students it was a help to doing their own thinking, which is all he asked of them.

"Knocking logical errors and illusions out of young people's heads," he once confessed, "is not a pleasant occupation. It is much pleasanter to preach one's own convictions. But how could I in a few weeks of contact with my students hope to build up a coherent world view that should endure throughout their subsequent lives? It seemed to me a more important service in the cause of liberal civilization to develop a spirit of genuine regard for the weight of evidence and a power to discriminate between responsible and irresponsible sources of information, to inculcate the habit of admitting ignorance when we do not know, and to nourish the critical spirit of inquiry which is inseparable from the love of truth that makes men free." He would have been delighted with the aphorism of Stanford's Albert Guerard: "Philosophy consists in asking questions; sophistry in answering them; tyranny in enforcing the answers."

Moreover, he was not one to make an unthinking cult of the catchwords *modern, new, revolutionary, the latest.* He never could have accepted the latest result of some Gallup poll to be his guide or his truth.

In his youth as a student of Hebrew lore he had been attracted by the prophets and the cult of revolution, but as was his habit, he continued thinking and found room for second thoughts, third thoughts, tenth thoughts, and nth thoughts. At first he held with the prophets against the priests of Israel until he came to realize that while prophets are necessary "to prevent the hard cake of custom from choking off all growth and adaptation, men cannot live on revolutions alone. Priests are essentially guardians of the ancient and hallowed ways of the common man's life cycle from birth to death, and reforms or revolutions can be justified only if they bring about forms more congenial to human life." If the beginning of philosophy was wonder, as Aristotle had written, it was a wonder that could never cease nor be sated, never permit one to assume that one had the whole truth in one's possession. And the end of philosophy, the purpose of the unending quest for truth, was reverence for life. Though he gave up his belief in a personal God, he did not give up his piety, which he defined, following Santayana, as "reverence for the sources of one's being." Nor did he give up the Jewish "ideal of holiness that enables us to distinguish between the good and evil in men, and thus saves us from the idolatrous worship of a humanity that is full of imperfections."

7

WHAT COLLEGE NEVER TAUGHT ME

Such was my large debt to City College. But I cannot close my story of the college without confessing how I tampered with its solemn ephebic oath—nor without saying something about the overwhelming events of the two decades following my graduation for which the college left me completely unprepared.

First a word on the ephebic oath. The world of ancient Greece gave large scope not to the nation but to the city. And it seemed fitting that our metropolis, large, populous, culturally significant enough to regard itself as a sort of city-state, should imitate the ceremony by which the Athenian *ephebus*, on completing his training, so solemnly pledged his best efforts to the city that had nurtured him. On commencement day, we graduates were to take our own ephebic oath as we received our diplomas: a series of pledges to the city, ending with the vow to "transmit this, our city, not less, but greater, better, and more beautiful than it was transmitted to us." Had I been there to receive my diploma, I should have sworn to it without hesitation.

But the fates ordained that I was neither to take my finals, nor to receive my diploma, nor to act in the varsity play that I had coauthored and in which I was to play the part of our President Mezes, nor to repeat after him the words of the solemn oath. During Christmas week I caught the Spanish flu raging in the country, went from influenza to pneumonia, and missed the exams, the class play, the commencement exercises, and the oath.

The exams would have been easy enough. The play, even without my amateur acting and monotone singing, was bad enough—something I can say without being present since I had been chosen class poet and class historian with no just claim to either title. Not being able to take the exams and to graduate were more serious matters, yet they turned out not to be too serious either, for the board of trustees voted me a degree on two conditions: that I should recover and that I should satisfy my teachers. I complied with both.

While convalescing, I had time to meditate on the ephebic oath and permit myself to tamper with it. The old city was even then showing signs of decay; the succeeding thousands of graduates who have sworn to transmit it "more beautiful than they received it" have been unable to reverse the irresistible and ceaseless flow of time. Moreover, while I lay there regaining my strength, spring was coming early that year and I felt myself seized by wanderlust. I was moved to doubt that I would spend all the rest of my days in my native city or be able to transmit it "not less but greater than I found it." I loved my city. I loved its Long Island marshes and cemeteries and wooded hills, its cultural density and cosmopolitanism, its Chinatown and Little Italy and the intense life of its Jewish East Side, its old carriage houses of Brooklyn Heights and Greenwich Village, its waterfront with ships from far-off places, the libraries and museums of mid-Manhattan, the uptown college that had meant so much to me, the restaurants and food shops catering to every taste and cuisine in the world. I still remember the old city as it was with gratitude, for it formed and shaped me in countless ways. But I knew that I would not stay in it and that it would not stay as it was in my youth. I knew, too, that, more than I loved the city, I loved my precious heritage of the great language of Shakespeare and the King James Bible and that wherever I wandered and come what might, I could be faithful to it. So in my bed of convalescence with only myself as witness, I tampered with the traditional ephebic oath and swore to "leave the English language"—I did not dare say *better* and *greater*, but at least—"no worse than I found it." To this I think I have been faithful.

I have told how City College prepared me for the "atomic age," though the atomic era was to have many surprises. It is the same age that calls itself the "space age," and the college did nothing to prepare me for the thought of ever leaving the ground, except in a gas-filled balloon. I was equally unprepared for the "Great Depression" that did so much to change our image of ourselves and the nature of our social structure. And I myself have often referred to the age into which I graduated as our "Time of Troubles" and the "Age of Total Wars." Neither for the space age, nor for the great depression, nor for total wars, nor for a time of troubles did my college prepare me. Yet these things that caught me unawares and unprepared had the profoundest influence upon the course of my life, so that its actual trajectory bore no resemblance to my expectations of a quiet and settled existence as a writer and a professor of English literature and composition. When I became, as I always hoped to become, a writer, I wrote on things that I had never expected to discuss or experience.

Let me start with the "space age." When I finished my college training, it was a crushing retort to say, "You can no more do that than you can fly." And to say of someone that he talked "a mile a minute" was to imply that he was approaching absolute speed.

Except for dreamers such as the Wright brothers, who had flown their homemade propeller-driven box-kite machine over windswept sand dunes at Kitty Hawk, as early as 1903 for a distance of 825 feet in 59 seconds before it nose-dived, we were all convinced that man would never go high nor far in the air except in lighter-than-air, gas-filled, dirigible balloons. When the newspapers reported the Wright brothers' flight, many did it with skepticism about their having flown without using "some sort of concealed gas bag." It took two total wars to teach us rocketry and to produce "the nations' airy navies" that could rain their "ghastly dew" upon our cities.

I was out of college a full eleven years before Lindbergh made his solo flight across the Atlantic. My own first four trips across our country took a minimum of four days and three nights on trains. When I had the extra fare to take the *Twentieth Century* or the *Broadway Limited,* I actually went, at times, faster than a mile a minute, but I shall never forget the tedium of that first train trip in which I looked out of my window one morning on the plains of Texas, went to sleep that night in Texas, woke up the next morning, and went to sleep again the next night, still speeding through the state of Texas. Not until the spring of 1937 did I take my first plane trip, flying over the Pyrenees during the Spanish Civil War. As for leaving the stratosphere, only writers of science fiction could dream then of man's walking on the moon or trying to shoot to Mars and beyond.

In college my love of poetry and my sense of prose style grew in intensity and range; I added to my knowledge of English and German literature, and to a lesser extent of French. But those who knew me later as a teacher and writer on Hispanic and Latin-American culture and literature, on the pre-Conquest art of Mexico, Central America, and the High Andes, and as the teacher who gave the *Don Quixote* course both in Spanish and in English at Stanford, would be surprised to know that I left college without knowing one word of Spanish. I was, moreover, ignorant, nay insensitive and blind, in the whole realm of the plastic arts, and, despite the Wednesday-afternoon organ recitals of Samuel Baldwin which my sweetheart and I attended regularly throughout my college days, I remained an ignoramus in music.

As for the self-styled social sciences, I did not know enough about them at graduation to think that perhaps they might not be sciences at all, but merely attempts at systematizing and organizing bodies of descriptive knowledge. No course had led me to the great political philosophers of the ancient world, a field all too frequently neglected today, even in the training of those who will be tomorrow's teachers of political science. Neither political philosophy nor the art of politics as practiced by politicians had been taught to me.

I did take a course in elementary economics because it was a required course for all students. We had a textbook written by Professor Seager of Columbia University which presented an untroubled picture of a stable world where everything was in natural equilibrium; where currencies had fixed equivalents in gold and fixed relationships to each other; where the gold standard was eternal and the supply of gold self-regulating and always to be counted upon to give each country the proportion of the world's gold that it needed to fix its price and interest level in relation to other countries. Though William Jennings Bryan, my father's hero, had been roundly defeated in the year I was born, my textbook was still nervously refuting his bimetalism program and tying it up with the debasement of coinage and the operation of Gresham's Law. Though my father and my family had lived through two grim depressions since the year of my birth, there was not one word of explanation of depressions, crises, or the business cycle, while the social-security drive that was to overshadow the thirties was not even mentioned as a possibility or a moot point. Some things were said on the relation between men and goods, but nothing on the relations between men and men in production, distribution, and consumption. Economics itself was defined in my textbook as "the social science of business."

If we turned from the unexciting textbook to my teacher, we found ourselves face to face with a patriotic Fourth of July orator who, at the slightest excuse, would launch into a gesture-augmented oration on "the broad rolling prairies of the West, the mighty rivers, rich resources, and wonders of this great land of opportunity." As a schoolboy my breast had swelled with boyish pride at the charts and diagrams in my geography class that showed how large a share of the world's natural resources we possessed, how much of the world's wealth we produced, and how mighty our land was in the total economy of the entire world. But to get that offered to me as fresh revelation again and again in our economics class was too much of a good thing, producing only boredom relieved by knowing glances and suppressed laughter. Our professor was a tall and stout man. When I wrote my portion of the varsity play, I persuaded my tall, stout friend Joe Levine (he of the Aborn Opera Chorus) to imitate the gestures and the oratory of William Buck Guthrie, and, when he finished his orotund lecture and drew from inside a specially-sewed-in huge pocket in his coat an enormous American flag to mop his brow, I was told that it brought the house down.

But neither the textbook nor the professor prepared me in the slightest for the fantastic billion-dollar-printing-press currencies of the First World War, nor for the mess of the Versailles reparations, nor for the Keynesian theories of fiscal policy and deliberate deficit spending to combat depression and unemployment, nor for the National Recovery Act and social security, nor for our repudiation of the sacred gold standard, nor for the floating dollar, nor indeed for a single one of the economic experiments and seemingly insoluble problems that still beset our country and the world in the seventies and beyond, as the aftermath of two total wars and their attendant lesser wars and revolutions.

In the stable years that preceded the First World War, economic theory was generalized from, and served to describe, and occasionally timidly prescribed for, a *stable world.* Since 1914, however, economic theory has been lagging helplessly behind swift and startling transformations. Today economists like other social theorists work in a world that is enormously more complex than that of the nineteenth century, so that men enter the economic arena in general possessing only bits and pieces of information about the complicated game being played there. They may know significant fragments of what goes on in their own business and what they intend by their own actions, but not the unintended results that may come out of those actions, and still less do they know about what those whom they deal with intend, and as good as nothing about what will come out of the vast interplay of forces on a social scale from which many of the actual consequences will flow. Hence economic theory itself has broken down into fragmentary studies with the added mischief that some of the masters of, or rather probers into, each fragment, may come to think that they possess a *science* which sums up the whole complex activity of economic life. And they may think, too, that from their fragmentary bits and pieces they can prescribe or suggest to our swollen government some "necessary" move which will put the whole game aright. No matter what genius had given me what master course, none of this could have been so much as guessed at in the year 1913 when I took my solitary economics course.

I was myself to teach a course in economics in Spanish in Mexico City in 1924, a course in which one of my students was Angel del Rio, later to become my professor in eighteenth-century Spanish literature at Columbia University. And I was to teach a Regents' course in economics in the early 1930s at the Eron Preparatory School. But these did not resemble in the slightest the course I myself had taken at City College in 1917. Since there were no textbooks to fit the new economics that was developing daily in a succession of novelties and surprises, I used a great deal of empirical material and had my students read with me selections from the financial pages of *The New York Times*, with a running commentary from me. But the notes of my courses would be of no use or interest today either, for after they were over, the changes in the economy kept coming thicker and faster and in ever more startling fashion.

Of adventitious interest perhaps is the fact that, using the daily empirical material in the financial section of the *Times*, I predicted to my incredulous students: "As I examine our dwindling gold reserve with you each day, I cannot for the life of me see any reason why our banks should not all close in three weeks, and not reopen again until America has made up its mind to go off the gold standard." When I went into the office after class to leave my roll book, I said to the principal's wife, "Mrs. Eron, if you want to be able to pay your teachers one month from now, you had better draw all your money out of the bank, for in three weeks our banks will close."

My students laughed, and Mrs. Eron laughed. "Heh, heh, one of Mr. Wolfe's jokes." But three weeks later the banks closed and the bank holiday was proclaimed! That morning, when I went for my roll book, a frightened Mrs. Eron approached me. "Mr. Wolfe, why didn't you tell me?" "But I did tell you, Mrs. Eron." "But why didn't you say you meant it?"

When I entered my classroom, every boy and girl was standing up, crowded around my desk, ready to shower me with questions such as: "My father has one hundred shares of U.S. Steel common, should he hold or sell?" They didn't believe me when I assured them that I knew nothing about the stock market. . . .

The economics I studied in City College in 1913 had prepared me to live in and understand a world that was to vanish forever within a year after the course ended. The "laws" I learned were generalized from the stable world of the nineteenth century, a world that was to disappear when the heavy artillery of the Austro-Hungarian Army, without leaving its own soil, began on July 29, 1914, to bombard Belgrade. On that date our civilization stumbled, all unknowing, into a world without precedent in the past of mankind. It is that world we live in now, a world still uncomprehended, changing at ever more bewildering speed during the decades after 1914, still today unforeseeable, unpredictable, never standing still long enough for our economists to comprehend or generalize it. Microeconomics and macroeconomics, econometrics, *Konjunkturforschung*—prophetic conjecture—are but impressive and magnified statistical series struggling in vain to generalize themselves into a semblance of a new systematic economic theory. And so it is likely to be during the closing quarter of our century. Nor are the extrapolations of statistical runs of the moment into futurology likely to tell us anything trustworthy or substantial concerning the year 2000 and the years succeeding it.

It was the guns of August, as they came to be called, that sounded the death knell of the "Grand Century of Peace and Progress." To be sure, the cannon's roar began on July 29, when Austria's cannon bombarded the unfortified city of Belgrade in "a nice little war that would be over in a few days." But it was August 1 when the little war sprouted like Jack's beanstalk as Germany declared war on Russia, a day later invaded neutral Luxembourg, and on August 4 began to bombard the Belgian fortress of Liège, thereby bringing England into the fray. By the end of that August, Austria-Hungary and Serbia had drawn onto their respective sides Germany, Russia, France, Great Britain, Montenegro, Japan, Turkey, and Portugal. We did not yet know the word *total* as applied to warfare, so it went down into the history books as *World* War I, but in scope, both intensive and extensive, it swiftly became as total as technology and geopolitics and the absurdity of the war "aims" and war propaganda could make it.

Nothing in my high school and college days, nor my outside reading, nor the utterances of our leaders, had prepared me for war at all in the century that had been rung in with such assurance that it would be "too civilized for war." Still less did my education prepare me for a war that was to be universal and total. On the contrary, whatever I had read and heard from my elders had instilled confidence in me that Europe, torn for so many centuries by bloody, unending strife, had seen her last universal war when Napoleon's empire shrank to the island of Elba in 1814, then to a mansion-prison on St. Helena in 1815. Only on August 1, 1914, did I begin a study of Europe's history, which would teach me that the comparatively peaceful period from Waterloo to Liège was truly exceptional in the history of Europe.

In retrospect, I realize now that when the German Kaiser and the Russian Tsar in the early 1900s each used the word *unthinkable* concerning a war between their two countries, they must have been thinking of it. And that array of books proving war impossible in the civilized twentieth century—what were they but so many unconscious variations on the theme of war's impossibility at the moment when war's shadow was beginning to creep over the landscape? In 1910, Norman Angell published his *Great Illusion* to prove that under modern conditions war would be too costly to wage. Everyone would lose and no one would win, all the participants would go bankrupt in a matter of weeks, the costs of a few days of warfare with mass mobilization and massive weapons of destruction would prove war's impossibility. Moreover, the network of interlocking international investments would doubtless be strong enough to prevent its outbreak.

Three years later the "great illusion" would become a reality. Financiers and ministers of treasuries would invent systems of flooding money markets with war loans that were never to be paid, and with paper monetary symbols that mortgaged the future as they shrank to worthlessness. The astronomical costs of the war were put upon generations yet unborn, while the war's consequences would be anything but what the participants, defeated or victorious, had dreamed. When a false peace came at the end of the first total war that had refuted everything in his book, Norman Angell was knighted, and absurdly in 1933, while the second total war was in gestation, he received the Nobel Prize for a work whose central thesis had proved to be itself the "great illusion." Yet in its time, the mere title of the book had been enough to quiet people's fears. During the first decade of the twentieth century, even as the contest in navy building grew apace, the race between armor plate and armor piercers sharpened, and networks of anxious alliances were woven, broken again, and rewoven in differing combinations, as tension mounted and mobilization plans were updated, our great illusion continued to be not war, but our certainty that it could not come to pass.

It was during this period that Andrew Carnegie spent some of his uncounted millions to build a new kind of Carnegie Library of International Law in a mansard-roofed, gingerbread-turreted "Temple of Peace" in the Hague, complete with an International Court of Justice, where judges waited to settle things peacefully, if only the great powers who were decorating the temple with shimmering festoons of noncompulsory and nonbinding arbitration treaties could be persuaded to submit their differences to the judges, and treat their "decisions" as "decisive."

The Temple of Peace had been conceived at the dawn of the century, its cornerstone had been laid in 1907, and its inauguration was set for August 1913, at the Second Hague International Peace Conference. President Theodore Roosevelt, not temperamentally a peaceful man, had called the conference, and Andrew Carnegie delivered the inaugural address. In it he affirmed that the world, all unknowing, was witnessing a sudden change "from the age of barbarous war to the age of civilized peace." All that was necessary was that "the three Teutonic nations," as he called England, Germany, and the United States, "should unite on the best means of ensuring peace." Turning in his peroration to the German Kaiser he said, "One small spark creates the flame; the German Emperor holds in his hand the torch."

In November 1910, as the reader already knows, Andrew Carnegie set up the first of his trust funds to ensure enduring peace, a fund of $10 million. In February 1914, he added another barrier to war, the Church Peace Union with an endowment of $2 million. The Church Peace Union got off to a good ecumenical start in the United States and set for August 1914 a First International Conference to be held in Europe with participants from all the continents. Like the Congress of the Socialist International, also set for August 1914, it never met.

All this may seem absurdly naïve to the reader who now has the doubtful benefit of hindsight, with two world wars and innumerable lesser wars and revolutions to look back on, yet Andrew Carnegie, then widely regarded as the world's greatest industrial leader, was not alone in his beliefs.

In 1910, the President of the United States, William Howard Taft, declared: "Personally I do not see any more reason why matters of national honor should not be referred to a Court of Arbitration than matters of property or national proprietorship. . . . I do not see why questions of honor may not be submitted to a tribunal composed of men of honor who understand questions of national honor, to abide by their decision as well as any other difference arising between nations." Our Congress followed this by passing a bill authorizing the President to name a Peace Commission to study the possibility of establishing an international naval force, drawn from the great naval powers of the world, to preserve peace on the high seas. Carnegie saw this as a step in the direction of the creation of an international league of peace as part of his dream for a peaceful new world order. The next President, Woodrow Wilson, was to adopt the idea in his note to the warring powers sent in late December 1916. And his secretary of state, William Jennings Bryan, besides the novel idea of making diplomacy more temperate by serving nothing stronger than grape juice at state banquets, busied himself with weaving a web of additional arbitration treaties including a proviso to delay war at least a year, should arbitration fail. (If Woodrow Wilson had submitted his proposal for America to enter the European War to a referendum of the American people, there is ample contemporary evidence that they would have rejected the proposal, for only five months before his war message they had reelected him on the sole slogan "He kept us out of war.")

A number of our most respected leaders gladly accepted the honor of forming part of the Board of Trustees of Carnegie's Endowment for International Peace. These included Charles Eliot, president of Harvard, Nicholas Murray Butler, president of Columbia, Senator (later secretary of state) Elihu Root, Henry Pritchett, Joseph Choate, James B. Scott, John

W. Foster, Andrew Dickson White, J. G. Schmidlapp, and Oscar Strauss, with Root as chairman and William Howard Taft as honorary chairman. David Starr Jordan, the distinguished naturalist who became the first, and in my opinion the greatest, of Stanford's presidents, gave his wholehearted support, and took time amid his duties as ichthyologist and administrator to write his book *War and Waste* published in 1913. Jordan remained Stanford's president from its foundation in 1891 until his retirement in 1916 to devote himself more completely to the cause of peace in the midst of war and to found and lead the American Peace Society. After America entered the war, he became treasurer of the People's Council of America, and with the sixth number of *Facts: The People's Peace Paper,* founded by a number of us youngsters just out of college, he volunteered to become a member of our editorial advisory board. After America entered the war, Dr. Jordan established at his suite in the Biltmore Hotel in Washington, D.C., an Extension Course for Statesmen to study the problems of maintaining civil liberties in wartime and working for a just and lasting peace. It is a sign of the esteem in which he was held that his course was attended by Senators La Follette, Norris, Hiram Johnson, Borah, Vardaman, Gronna, Smoot, Curtis, and New, and by Congressmen Kitchin, Huddleston, Crosser, Hilliard, Dill, Gordon, Little, Rankin, Randall, Dillon, Cooper (Wisconsin), Cooper (West Virginia), Bowers, Crampton, Mondell, Frear, Woods, La Follette (not to be confused with the senator), Sisson, Slayden, Ragsdale, and the Socialist Meyer London.

Even after war had broken out in Europe in 1914, and the conflict that was to have been "over by Christmas" had settled down into the hopeless stalemate of a war of position, the illusion continued to rule the minds of men that the war was but an accidental blunder which, once its causes were known, need never happen again. This, as I have said, was the origin of Herbert Hoover's great War Library at Stanford (now the Hoover Institution Library on War, Revolution and Peace). And this was the origin of Ford's Peace Ship, and of Woodrow Wilson's note proposing a league to make war forever impossible, which he sent to all the belligerents in December 1916.

Henry Ford was the most celebrated industrialist of the opening decades of the twentieth century after Andrew Carnegie. Though he had given little thought to history, he too was struck with the madness of war and the need to establish an early peace without victory. Chancing one day in the autumn of 1915 to read in the *Detroit Free Press* that 20,000 men had perished during the last 24 hours of fighting without so much as the change of a foot of ground, Ford declared in the presence of a *Free Press* newspaperman that "the fighting nations are sick of war, they want to stop, they are only waiting for some disinterested party to step in and offer mediation. . . . I would be willing to spend half my fortune to shorten the war by a single day."

The giant presses blazoned forth the story. Ford was deluged with telegrams and letters and besieged by peace advocates ranging from Louis P. Lochner of the Carnegie Peace Foundation to Jane Addams of the

Emergency Peace Foundation and Rosika Schwimmer, a Hungarian woman who claimed to have in her bag the confidential statements of their war-weariness from statesmen of all the belligerent nations. When all his peace advisers agreed that all that was needed was to bring thoughtful and rational people to Europe on a ship to confer with the leaders of the warring nations, ever the practical doer he cried, "I'll get one!" and began to phone agents of steamship lines to come to a hotel suite he had taken at the Biltmore Hotel in New York. To the surprise of the newspapers that had begun to turn his "peace mission" into a chance for comedy and satire, he promptly chartered a large steamship, the *Oscar II*, sought to gather the peace planners and peace advocates as passengers, and decided to go himself, to convince the warring heads of state that they were getting nowhere, achieving nothing but ruin and waste and death, and that it was time to meet under disinterested auspices to bring the war to a close. Given the magnitude of the passions that each war leader and propagandist had aroused and the cost in lives and treasure that had somehow to be "justified," it was a quixotic enterprise, and it attracted along with many wise men and women a number of quixotic and even ludicrous hangers-on. It was these latter that the press played up, but surely the earnest effort was worthy of better and more serious treatment than the coarse ridicule and mocking inventions with which they treated it. In retrospect, Mark Sullivan wrote nearly twenty years later, "If buffoons pirouetted across the world stage in 1915, they were not Ford and the half dozen who participated with him (like Louis Lochner, Samuel S. McClure, and Judge Ben Lindsey) in the project of halting the madness; the buffoons were the rulers and statesmen and diplomats whose inability to maintain peace among civilized nations stood as the most tragic failure in the annals of history." I tended to agree with his verdict then, and continue to now, as I contemplate the consequences of that failure of our civilization, the two total wars, the danger of a third such war, and all the turmoil and disorder and barbarization and brutality they have brought in their train. Finally, I must include Woodrow Wilson's last peace effort at the end of 1916 and early 1917 among the worthy if futile attempts to bring about an earlier and more wholesome peace.

When Andrew Carnegie told the Second Arbitration and Peace Conference in his Temple of Peace in August 1913 that, without being conscious of it, the world was entering a new age, so indeed it was. But the new age was not the age of perpetual peace, but the age of total war in which we still live.

Can the reader wonder then if the naïve young man who in 1917 was to turn 21, who was taught and indoctrinated by the mood of so much of the century into which he was born and by so many distinguished leaders in the century in which he grew up, should have believed that the twentieth century would be "even more civilized" than the nineteenth and might truly be a century "too civilized for war"? Or that the years from 1914 to 1917 were to fill that young man with indignation and lead him into the activities which I must now relate?

8

HOW WILSON KEPT US OUT OF WAR

War!

It did not seem possible.

Europe beginning to tear itself apart? All the great civilized states, hearth and home of our culture, bent on destroying each other?

Could that be the Germany I knew, the land of Goethe and Schiller and Heine, of Bach and Beethoven and Mozart, of the sentimental folk songs, of the popular ballads so like our own? Could the Germany that for centuries had known how to be a single unified home of the German spirit even while it was politically divided into innumerable kingdoms, principalities, bishoprics, and free cities, now march as a single iron unit determined to overrun France, to hold a Christmas party in Paris on December 25, and to claim dominion over Europe? Was it true that German socialist workingmen, still with red cards in their pockets, could be gaily marching to shoot French socialists and syndicalists? Were the workingmen of Russia who a few years earlier had marched on the Tsar's palace crying for justice or shouting *Down with the Tsar!* now marching to the same palace to kneel before the same Emperior and sing *God keep our Tsar*? Was the marvelous, varicolored culture of Europe so thin a veneer over such depths of barbarism? Would those nations now gone mad drag the lesser nations of Europe, then the world, into this renascent barbarism and madness? How could I believe it? Yet, with each day's war bulletins, how could I doubt it?

I thanked God for putting 3,000 miles of ocean between us and Europe. I blessed my country for having no kings, harboring no dynastic ambitions, nourishing no deep hatreds, no hunger for new possessions. I was happy to think that my adventurous father had run away to America as a 13-year old boy, and that ambition had brought my mother's parents to this land in the 1840s. I rejoiced that our nation was made up of immigrants and descendants of immigrants from all the lands at war and therefore could not be tempted to take sides in the struggle tearing Europe apart. "Thank God, this is a republic; we will never get into it," I said aloud when first I read the word *war* in a newspaper headline, for it seemed to me in my simplicity that dynastic amibitions were at the root of the evil.

"FREEDOM OF THE SEAS"

From the outset Woodrow Wilson attempted to do two things that were incompatible with each other. On the one hand, he adjured our people to be "impartial in word as in deed," forbade them to give aid to any belligerent, proscribed "every transaction that might be construed as a preference to one party to the struggle before another." On the other hand, he insisted on the right of America as a neutral to trade with both sides, the demand that wrecked Jefferson's second term as it would Wilson's.

But Great Britain had the world's greatest navy and was determined to blockade any attempt on our part to trade with Germany and its allies. The German cruisers were no match for the British navy and immediately disappeared from the high seas, taking refuge in neutral ports, principally those of the United States. Britain might stop our ships, exercise the right of search and seizure of everything she deemed contraband. Germany, for her part, had only her undersea ships, or submarines. Thus, the claim of the right to trade with both sides was to prove in practice only a right to trade with the one side that could exercise an effective blockade. If we were to obey the President's desire not to show preference to either side, we would either have to declare war on Britain, as we had done in 1812, and try to break or run the blockade, or we would have to stick to the President's original intention of not showing preference to either side by forgoing our "right" to trade as neutrals.

LOANS AND CREDITS TO ONE SIDE ONLY

Even while Wilson was proscribing "every transaction that might be construed as a preference for one party to the struggle before another," American bankers and industrialists were creating an economic link with the Allies. As early as August 5, 1914, J. P. Morgan asked the State Department what its attitude might be toward making loans to the Allies. I was reassured by the State Department's answer, that loans to any belligerent were "inconsistent with the true spirit of neutrality." But that resolve of the State Department did not stand up long.

The sudden cutting off of all European orders at the war's outbreak caused a deep depression. Robert Lansing, counselor to the State Department and strongly pro-Allies, persuaded Woodrow Wilson that the extending of "short-term credits" to former huge customers would not be an unneutral act. Then the Allies sold their large holdings in American firms and used the proceeds to place large orders for munitions, coal, steel, and oil with American companies. "If the Allies run out of cash," Lansing persuaded Wilson, "the result would be . . . industrial depression, idle capital, idle labor, numerous failures, financial demoralization, and general unrest and suffering among the laboring masses." His fears thus aroused, in September 1915 Wilson approved a long-term Anglo-French loan of a half billion dollars—the largest loan ever floated in any country up to that time. Of course, the loan was managed by J. P. Morgan & Co., aided by a consortium of bankers. Our giant factories expanded, our workingmen got well-paid jobs, the numbers who were developing an interest in an Allied victory grew apace. Moreover, it began to be increasingly important for our own economy that the allied side should win, so that it might be able to make good its bonds and its debts to us. My awareness of this growing vested economic interest became a kind of empirical demonstration of the supposed economic causation of war. Out of that experience I unwittingly adopted one of the tenets of Marxism. It took several decades of observation of the total wars of our time before I was able to write in my *Marxism: 100 Years in the Life of a Doctrine:*

ECONOMICS AND MODERN WAR

War fits even less than nationalism into the materialist interpretation of history. Monstrous and terrible, rather than sordid and calculating, kindled by feelings deeper and more powerful than computation of loss and gain, reckless of all except victory, the driving forces of modern war are fierce untamable mass passions—pride, anger, xenophobia, fear, jealousy, camaraderie, exaltation, savagery—almost anything but calculations of gain or petty market interests. . . .

The "war aims," the material motives and calculations, had hastily to be improvised after war erupted—to give the irrational explosion and sacrifices an ostensibly rational explanation, a "meaning," a "justification." Actually the "meaning" of the war was in the passions themselves that the war unleashed. . . .

It is not the "bourgeois" era, with its entrance of the masses upon the stage of history, but the era before the "democratization of war" to which the historian must look for some signs of "rational calculation" in regard to war's irrational way of settling differences between nations or rulers. Then wars were often fought "rationally" for limited objectives. Then monarchs and ministers sometimes attempted to set forth their objectives and assay potential gains against mounting costs and losses. Then soldiers themselves were drilled to suppress all emotion and initiative, so that they resembled in Clausewitz's words, clockwork figures and mechanical puppets.

But the *levée en masse* and the release of the energies of the people through the French Revolution opened a new era in warfare which the first half of the twentieth century brought to "absolute perfection"; making the well-drilled mechanical soldier who fought for a few cents a day into an anachronism, and substituting the volatile popular soldier, who might fight for principle or passion or because he was conscripted, might make the cause of his state or nation his own, might more easily yield to panic or the temptation to desert, or display more astonishing and uncalculating valor. But he was as far away from the professional soldier of the seventeenth and eighteenth centuries as limited war is from total.

It is this harking back to eighteenth-century modes of thought that gives Marxist explanations their oddly old-fashioned air, for with the coming of the French Revolution the age of rationalism and enlightened calculation in war—insofar as they ever prevailed—was completely over. (Or at least until the development by absolute war of the absolute weapon which has, let us hope, introduced a new element of rational calculation.)

When the long peace after the Napoleonic Wars drew toward its end, war was to embrace ever more completely the entire population. It was to assume a terrible dynamic, defying limited aims, not to be contained in careful balance sheets nor measured by the petty calculus of gain and loss. With mass audiences and mass sounding board, foreign policy suffered a megalophonous enlargement. Its issues underwent a terrible simplification. When a whole people must be set in motion it is well-nigh impossible to mobilize them with limited and realistic aims. Where is the accountant to draw the balance sheet, or the mathematician to make the equation, between human lives and territory in total war? or among the incommensurable magnitudes of national feeling, honor, prestige, population, surface, treasure? Civilization itself, as Bergson put it, "conceals a profound instinct for war."

It was a neat and satisfying cynicism on the part of Marxism to reduce the beast, the brute, the warrior, the passion-ruled, the irrationalist in man, to the rational, and calculating economic man. This reduction began as an "abstract model" in the economic theorists of the "nation of shopkeepers" but it remained for the philosophic German studying works in the British Museum to reduce it to absurdity by making this abstract model into the key to the soul and actions of the whole man. When war actually struck, as Henri de Man records, "my Marxism received a mortal blow, for it could not explain the behavior of the masses." And the sometime socialist, sometime communist leader, Frossard, wrote: "war devastated socialism as it devastated the world."

True, I reasoned, only a few hundred or a few thousands were interested in the loans and the munitions and armament orders. But around them were grouped many leading figures of our society. The higher one went in the social scale, in wealth and social standing, in educational administrative circles, in influence over public opinion through newspapers and books and public addresses, the more one was likely to find pro-British sentiment. Writers who loved Paris as a second home were volunteering as ambulance drivers on the French Front. When newspaper editors were polled as to whether they favored the Allies or the Central Powers, out of 367 questioned, 105 declared themselves pro-Allies and only 20 pro-German. It was reassuring to me, however, to note that 245 did not answer. I could only guess at the breakdown of those who had refused, or failed, to answer. Later study led me to believe that the majority of these were probably "neutral in thought and deed," determined to keep America out of "entangling alliances" and "Europe's bloody wars." Many of our big Eastern dailies were pro-Allies, but not those in the rest of the country.

Our universities were divided. Many scholars of that well-to-do tribe who had been able to study for their Ph.D.s in Germany were admirers of German culture, which, up to 1914, had seemed to so many Americans the very zenith of culture. Many with socialistic inclinations (socialism was an amazingly widespread belief in the first decade of our century), admired Germany's well-developed social welfare system, in which she led the prewar world, and Germany's mass Socialist party and powerful trade unions. But many more scholars who were not antiwar were inclined to admire England's culture from which our own had sprung, her comparative gentleness in the long history of great empires, British honesty in government, her parliamentary system, her respect for civil rights, her spirit of fair play.

To the vested economic interests that pushed us to the Allied side, a more powerful force was added. The German U-boats were too vulnerable to give proper warning to our vessels, and often dared not wait to pick up passengers from lifeboats. When Wilson finally armed our merchant vessels, the U-boats could not even safely give warning. Hence while the British blockade involved goods, and costs, and "national dignity and honor," the submarine torpedoing sometimes cost American lives. When the British began using American flags and American markings on her ships "as a justified ruse" (or so the British informed Wilson), American vessels lost even the protection of our flag against submarine warfare.

In vain did Germany plead that Americans should not take passage on British passenger ships, or merchant ships that might be carrying munitions and other contraband of war. The Cunard Line had all the best luxury ships afloat, and many of our pro-Allied American leaders took a special delight in using the ships of the Cunard Line. To complicate matters, the British deliberately used part of the hold of such ships to carry munitions, as was to prove the case in the *Lusitania.*

Vain, too, was Germany's protest that since we claimed the privileges of neutrality, we had no right to sell munitions to one side and not the other. Wilson answered haughtily: "It is not the duty of the United States to close its markets to the Allies, since we are open to German purchases, too." I saw with apprehension that Wilson was courting disaster and possible war with such an answer, for the Germans were rendered desperate by its implications.

On a number of occasions Germany made concessions to us. When she sank one of our ships or caused loss of life under the precarious conditions of undersea warfare, Germany offered apologies and compensation for the loss of cargo and of American lives. But how much money is a compensation for the loss of a single life?

Allied strength in munitions and supplies grew mightily with the support of the amazing productive power of American factories, and hunger and scarcity closed in on Germany, driving the German Emperor at last to decide to make their submarine blockade effective at all costs. With that, the balance of hostility swung from England to Germany.

THE CASE OF THE *LUSITANIA*

The sinking of the *Lusitania* on May 7, 1915, dramatized and enormously intensified that swing. It was the first event to bring the war home to us in all its horror. To make matters worse, a natural wave of exultation swept over Germany and over German-Americans who had been watching in impotent anger while America supplied arms and food to the Allies, and their U-boats were unable to enforce their counterblockade. This was the first victory in their effort to even the score on American supplies. Quite naturally, if tactlessly, a medal was struck off in Germany celebrating the *Lusitania* sinking, a medal filled with a figure of death as a skeleton cutting down a ship. There were some German-American circles where cheers rang out, songs were sung, and toasts were drunk. One Rudolf Kuhn published a marching song in English to be sung to the popular tune of "Upidee, Upida," of which a typical stanza ran:

> Ah! The U-boat's aim was good;
> Who doesn't choke, drowns in the flood.
> Vanderbilt was there that day,
> The only one we missed was Grey.

And the German Red Cross representative in the United States, Dr. Bernhard Dernburg, said complacently, if truthfully:

> The death of the Americans might have been avoided. . . . We put our advertisements next to the announcements of the Cunard Line's sailing dates; anybody can commit suicide if he wants to.

There had been no such popular excitement in America since the sinking of the *Maine*.

"TOO PROUD TO FIGHT"

All eyes turned to our President. What would he do? What would he say? What had he meant when, on February 15, only three months earlier, he had sent Germany a note containing the phrase "We will hold the Imperial Government to strict accountability?" Some watched with hope, some with anxiety, as all eyes turned to the President.

Theodore Roosevelt thought he had the answer and was quick to give it: "It is now inconceivable that we should refrain from action. . . . We owe it not only to humanity but to our own national self-respect."

Three days later, on May 10, the President spoke in Philadelphia at a previously scheduled meeting of four thousand recently naturalized Americans. His talk got nationwide attention. In it, he seemed to be answering Theodore Roosevelt and the rapidly growing, if still minority, "war party." With calculated restraint, he did not so much as mention Germany, or the sinking of the *Lusitania*, but spoke of the meaning of America and Americanism. America, he said, must set a "special example" to a world at war. Its citizens, coming from all the lands at war, should not think of themselves as "groupings," as British-Americans, Irish-Americans, or German-Americans, but as Americans without any qualifying adjective. An America that remained at peace in the midst of war might use its resources to bind up the wounds of war when it ended and make future wars impossible. "The example of America must be the example not merely of peace because it will not fight, but of peace because peace is the healing and elevating influence, and strife is not. There is such a thing as a nation being so right that it does not need to convince others by force that it is right. . . . There is such a thing as a man being too proud to fight."

Too proud to fight! Again the President, with that verbal skill that characterized him, had found a striking slogan, as he had in his "impartial in word and deed," his "avoiding every transaction that might be construed as a preference for one party," and his "you may count upon my heart and resolution to keep you out of war." With such slogans he held the attention of his troubled countrymen, kept the country out of the well-nigh universal war, and kept alive the hope that a neutral America might help to formulate the terms of a peace of reconciliation in a war-wearied world, give aid in the reconstruction of both sides, and persuade them to form with America a union of nations to make another war impossible.

I should have thought better of his slogans if he at last had chosen to keep our citizens off belligerent passenger and merchant ships and to forego the profits that come from selling weapons of destruction to either side. Yet, I too, more skeptical than most of words that had not been lived up to, felt reassured once more. The *New York Herald*, strongly pro-Allies, might sigh: "What a pity Theodore Roosevelt is not president!" But the "war party" contracted once more. Middle-Western papers, with nothing to go by but the news the British censors let through, had been denouncing the sinking of the *Lusitania* as "brutal" and "wanton murder." Now they were glad to return to their stand for neutrality under the slogan, "Too proud to fight." Thus the *Des Moines Register and Leader* published a cartoon in which Uncle Sam was painting a sign for a little knot of well-dressed Anglophiles to contemplate, which read: STAY IN AMERICA. Their lead editorial, which on May 9 had spoken of "wanton murder," on May 13 answered Theodore Roosevelt, the *New York Tribune*, and the war party with "Trust the President." Though we had been helping one side by selling it munitions, trucks, supplies, metals, fuel, and food, on credit at that, through the greatest war loan in the history of man, I saw no choice but to reconcile myself to trusting the President, who had so recently "pledged his heart and resolution to keep us out of war."

Years later, when I examined the first *Lusitania* note, led to reading it by Walter Millis's *Road to War* (New York, 1935), I was startled to find that in it Wilson had asked the German government to abandon the U-boat blockade altogether, because it was "impossible" to use submarines against merchant ships without an "inevitable violation of many sacred principles of justice and humanity." Germany was asked to accept the one-sided British blockade and to allow us to ship contraband to British ports unhindered, while abandoning its own attempt to blockade the Allies. The Imperial German government was formally called upon to disavow its U-boat commanders in their actions, to "take immediate steps to prevent a recurrence," and not to "expect the government of the United States to omit any word or any act necessary to the performance of its sacred duty of maintaining the rights of the United States and its citizens." Had I examined the text of the *Lusitania* note then, I should have been far less trusting of our President's ability and practical determination to keep us out of war. And I should have expected Germany in desperation sooner or later to resort to unrestricted warfare against our munitions trade with England, which, after one year and nine months of vacillation, Germany actually did.

For an entire year, a troubled exchange of notes on submarine warfare continued between the United States and Germany, notes containing demands, new protests, explanations, justifications, apologies, offers of compensation. During all this time, our nation continued to put its trust in the wisdom, skill, and determination of the President. On April 18, 1916, almost a year after the sinking of the *Lusitania,* Wilson wrote a note, the chief passages of which he read to Congress, in which he gave Germany an ultimatum. Pointing out that "the ominous toll of those who have lost their lives upon ships thus attacked has mounted into the hundreds," he concluded: "Unless the Imperial German government should now immediately declare and effect an abandonment of its present methods of submarine warfare, the government of the United States can have no other choice but to sever diplomatic relations with the German Empire altogether."

Despite the growing feeling of desperation in high German circles, Germany's answer was unexpectedly compliant. On May 4, 1916, they wrote: "Imperial German government notifies the government of the United States that all its naval forces have received the following order: *Merchant vessels . . . shall not be sunk without warning and without saving human lives, unless those ships attempt to escape or offer resistance.*"

For the next nine months no ships were sunk by Germany except under circumstances which lived up to American demands and German orders to its submarines. Wilson could walk with head high. He had not permitted America to be dragged into war over the *Lusitania,* yet he had received a pledge that Germany would abandon unrestricted submarine warfare, and Germany was living up to its promise. The President's credit rose in the land. And I for my part could not choose but trust him.

"HE KEPT US OUT OF WAR"

Thus fortified, our President turned his attention to getting reelected in November of 1916. He desired above all to be President of the United States when the war should end, so that he might further his plan for a League to Outlaw War. Moreover, he was forming ideas as to how the war should end to make such a league viable. He hoped that America as the great and powerful neutral would be able to help formulate peace terms acceptable to both sides after war had exhausted them. If he should get reelected and America should stay neutral, he hoped he might go down in history as the man who had brought peace to the world and initiated a new institution to guarantee a new era of permanent peace.

His campaign committee in its last-minute appeal to workingmen voters wrote: "You are working, not fighting; alive and happy, not cannon fodder. . . . If you want war, vote for Hughes. If you want peace with honor and continued prosperity, vote for Wilson." Speaking from his home in Shadow Lawn, New Jersey, Wilson struck the same keynote: "If the country puts the Republican party into power, they will change our foreign policy radically. There is only one choice as against peace and that is war. The certain prospect of the success of the Republican party is that we shall be drawn into the embroilments of the European war."

To me, as to the American people generally, the words of what Roosevelt had called "the Byzantine logothete in the White House" were clear. They seemed to mean, "Elect Hughes and you'll get war. Elect me and I will continue to keep you out of war." I had no vote that November, for I would not turn twenty-one until January 1917, which was nearly three months away. Moreover, I thought the only safeguard in the long run was to keep our citizens off the ships of belligerents and to cease to wax fat on the profits of selling munitions to one side. Yet, could I have voted, I should have voted for Woodrow Wilson because he *had* kept us out of war, and *seemed* determined to keep us out in the future, even though he was also determined to keep up our wartime trade to one side and our citizens' right to travel on belligerent ships. These last, he insisted in his speeches and notes to the belligerents, involved our "freedom as a neutral" and our "dignity and honor." But on January 31, 1917, three months after Wilson's reelection, the German ambassador, Bernstorff, handed our President a note which put an end to his hopes of reconciling neutrality with traffic in munitions, and threatened the President's dream of bringing peace to Europe as the Great Neutral.

One of the obstacles to Wilson's peacemaking schemes was the fact that he was addressing them to governments that had blundered into war out of fear of each other, without giving any thought to the limits of the war or to definite objectives as a stopping point. When objectives are limited, wars themselves can be limited. But the peculiarity of the twentieth-century type of total war is that it is a war of entire nations of such formlessness that no limited or compromise peace aims can possibly justify the expenditures of blood and treasure. Could Wilson have realized his dream he would indeed have gone down in history as the Great Peacemaker, but the dream itself was alien to the thought or emotions of both sides.

Before we consider the shipwreck of Wilson's dream, I ought to say something of the peace movements, some of which I have already mentioned, which his own peace activities were engendering in America. All through 1915 and 1916, peace movements kept springing up in our country like mushrooms after heavy rains. Carrie Chapman Catt, the feminist leader, and Jane Addams, our greatest social worker, united to form the Woman's Peace Party. David Starr Jordan formed the American Peace Society. The Quakers developed the Peace Section of the American Friends Service Committee, while religious groups such as the Moravian Brethren set up similar bodies. Ford organized his peace ship expedition with the tight-lipped disapproval of our President. Bryan got thirty-four nations to sign arbitration treaties including a proviso that, if arbitration failed, they would at least wait for a full year of cooling off and trying to negotiate before declaring war. When Bryan resigned as secretary of state over the sharpness of the second *Lusitania* note, he plunged into the growing galaxy of peace movements "with his coat off," adding to the confusion by lending his name to all who asked him. Newton Baker, in 1911 the progressive mayor of Cleveland, formed a body to work for a League to Outlaw War (he was later to become Woodrow Wilson's secretary of war). Funds were given by the German embassy to German-American and German sympathizer organizations to keep us out, for the embassy knew that if America went to war in the end, it would not be on Germany's side. At least one Indian organization fighting in exile for India's independence from Britain and a number of Irish-American peace movements and Irish independence movements also received German funds, Indians and Irish rebels both acting on the theory that our enemy's enemy is our friend.

Each month saw the birth of a number of new peace organizations, often competing with each other for the same members and the same sources of funds. Some people gave their names and dues or contributions to any and all peace groups that approached them. So great was the confusion that the leaders of older, more professional peace organizations undertook to pool their activities and federate the organizations into the Emergency Peace Federation (the *emergency* was preparedness and after that the evident intention of our President to join the Allies, manifested in March 1917, and to introduce universal compulsory military service). By the time I got around to expressing my feelings in some organized form, it was the Emergency Peace Federation, rebaptized the People's Council of America, that I joined.

But with all the congeries of peace movements and peace organizations, undoubtedly the greatest peace crusader of 1915 and 1916 and the first two months of 1917 was the President himself. By virtue of his high office and the largeness of his plans or dreams, his activities eclipsed completely even such spotlight figures as Henry Ford, Andrew Carnegie, and William Jennings Bryan, for, while the thoughts of these last two did not go beyond planning a net of fragile arbitration treaties in which to bind up the god of war, President Wilson dreamed of nothing less than putting an end to the seemingly unending war by a peace not of victory of one side over the other but of victory for no one.

At the moment when Wilson was systematically elaborating in his own mind the steps that should lead to the fulfillment of his dream came the first of a series of unexpected shocks. On November 12, 1916, Kaiser Wilhelm called in the press, and through this unusual device, a press conference, told the Allies and the world that he was ready to talk of peace!

"Germany has," the Kaiser told the reporters, "the military and economic strength sufficient to continue the war to the bitter end. . . . But our aims are not to shatter or annihilate our adversaries. . . . Prompted by the desire to avoid further bloodshed," Germany and her allies "propose to enter forthwith into peace negotiations."

Wilson was both startled and upset. What if these peace talks should be entered into without the participation of the Great Neutral? What if the war should end in a mere breathing-spell peace, a miserable patchwork without clear principles, without settling the fundamental matters that had made this war possible, without eliminating the rancors and hatreds? He had been thinking out his own thoughts for some time, so he reacted with surprising speed. Only six days after the Kaiser's press release, he had ready, and sent out, identical notes to each of the belligerents. Their key passage reads:

> The President suggests that an early occasion be sought to call out from all nations now at war an avowal of their respective views as to the terms upon which the war might be concluded, and the arrangements which would be deemed satisfactory as a guarantee against the kindling of any similar conflict in the future. . . . In the measures to be taken to secure the future peace of the world, the people and government of the United States are as vitally and as directly interested as the governments now at war.

But the belligerents were in no mood to let a man, or a country, that had stayed outside the carnage dictate terms of peace or intervene in the peacemaking whenever it should come. Both sides made short shrift of his note. The Germans answered within a week, and told the would-be peacemaker rather coldly that they had already made their proposal and were interested, as they had stated, in "the speedy assembly on neutral ground of the delegates of the warring states" to discuss negotiations. The Allies took a little longer for they had to consider both the Kaiser's proposal and Wilson's note. Then on January 12, 1917, they told Wilson that they desired as much as he the end of the war and the prevention of future ones, but they refused "to consider a proposal that was empty and insincere" as was the Kaiser's news release. Moreover, they held that the time had not yet come to effect a peace that they would deem just. This angered Wilson even more than the Kaiser's answer, for it implied that they were determined to fight on until victory had come. And therefore, the Central Powers, too, must fight on to the bitter end, an end not remotely in sight.

Not willing to have his cherished plan rejected so unceremoniously, Wilson startled the Senate by asking a special meeting with them to use the Senate as his sounding board for a message to both sides. Though in form he was addressing the Senate of the United States, Woodrow Wilson assumed a new role that he was to claim all through the war and the negotiating of a peace: he spoke not merely to the Senate but to the entire world, and he insisted that he was speaking "on behalf of humanity . . . for the silent masses of mankind everywhere." In their name, he told the contending parties that the war had gone on long enough and caused enough misery. It was time that the fighting stopped. It must end as soon as possible, not with victory of either camp, but with a "peace without victory." "It was not pleasant to say this," he added, but "victory would mean . . . a victor's terms imposed upon the vanquished . . . a peace accepted in humiliation, under duress. . . . it would leave a sting, a bitter memory . . . * rest upon a quicksand." That is why he was offering his striking slogan, "peace without victory [since] only a peace between equals can last."

If the contending parties were willing to arrive at such a peace, he grandly offered that the United States, though it had not fought at all, would participate in the making and the enforcing of it. Further, to make it permanent and universal, it was necessary to form a "definite concert of powers which will make it virtually impossible that any such catastrophe should ever overwhelm us again." If the belligerents would set up such a concert of powers, "it is inconceivable that the United States should play no part in that great enterprise." The United States, he said with what was to turn out to prove misplaced confidence, "would be willing to participate . . . and add their authority and their power to the authority and force of other nations to guarantee peace and justice throughout the world." Such was the thought and feeling and self-image of Woodrow Wilson as he looked upon his country as the great neutral and himself as the peacemaker and spokesman for all mankind. If the reader bears that in mind, he will understand more easily the changes Wilson underwent a few weeks later, and my own feelings and experiences narrated in the next few chapters.

Having spoken for mankind, Wilson proceeded to speak for the United States, and lay down the peace terms that would be "acceptable"

* A prophetic epitaph for the eventual Treaty of Versailles.

to the great nonbelligerent. "It is right that this government should frankly formulate the conditions upon which it would feel justified in asking our people to approve its formal and solemn adherence to a League for Peace." Besides being a "peace without victory," it must be a peace that would reconstitute "a united, independent, and autonomous Poland: for every great people . . . a direct outlet to the highways of the sea . . . freedom of the seas; self-determination for all nations and peoples."

With these conditions Woodrow Wilson, as schoolmaster and history professor, lectured the belligerents and offended all of them. To be sure, the Irish thought it was the greatest speech delivered by the ruler of a great power in a hundred years, for it spoke to them of an independent Ireland. The Poles thought the same. And so did every group fighting for national self-determination or national independence. Though the Bolsheviks were to claim credit for Lenin for the decolonization movement that has since swept the world, it is obvious that Wilson was the father of the self-determination slogan, some time before he enunciated his Fourteen Points.*

His formula would have taken territory from Germany, Austria, Russia, the British Empire, France, Italy, and indeed virtually all the participants in the war. British papers called the speech quixotic, utopian, preposterous, impudent. The *London Daily Mail* asked "whether he spoke as the head of an American university or as the chief magistrate of a flesh-and-blood republic." Our own Senate set a date for debating his proposals. Some peace leaders praised, others condemned the dangerous intervention in Europe's old historic woes. But before the rising storm of discussion could reach its climax, a new act on Germany's part stilled the debate and turned all attention to Wilson's next move, for eight days after Wilson's sounding-board address to the Senate, the German ambassador, Count von Bernstorff, on January 31, 1917, delivered a note giving only one day's notice and declaring that on February 1, Germany would begin unrestricted submarine warfare. "All sea traffic will be stopped with every available weapon and without further notice."

President Wilson was stunned. Gone was his nine-month-old triumph in the U-boat controversy. Gone his certitude that America could remain neutral and lead the world to peace. Gone his feeling of confidence. When, three days later, he faced his cabinet, he was plunged in uncertainty and gloom. He would not renounce trade with England and France. He would not keep our ships clear of contraband destined to help only one side and make desperate the other. He was not willing to keep our citizens off British ships and out of trade in means of destruction. Smashed was his dream of peace without victory for anybody. Ended was the role he had assigned himself to lead the world to permanent peace. What if ruthless

* He first enunciated some of these principles in Washington, D.C., on May 27, 1916, in an address to a body calling itself the League to Enforce Peace.

submarine warfare, sinking on sight of every ship going to the Allies, should really deprive us of our trade and our ships, and the Allies of their massive supplies of food and munitions? Would the Allies ever be able to pay their huge debt to us? Would our Congress vote him the $100 million he felt he needed to put cannon and U.S. Marines on our merchant ships, a step which manifestly courted armed conflict between our merchant ships and the German U-boats? Perhaps he hoped that arming our merchant marine would cause the German navy to cease firing on our ships, but the result was just as likely to be more nighttime sinkings without survivors and a growing fighting mood among many Americans.

That the Germans would not desist in their all-out campaign soon became manifest, and their new blockade proved devastatingly successful. With that, Wilson's anger and the nation's sense of shock grew greater, yet the sentiment of the majority of our people remained strong against our entrance into the European carnage. Rather the feeling grew greater among most Americans that we had no business sending out ships into the war zones, and that it should have been the duty of our government rather than that of Germany to warn our citizens to stay off British passenger ships. There is evidence, too, that President Wilson all through February 1917 felt reluctant to give up his dream of making peace as the leader of the great neutral power.

At the end of February two events occurred that must have made up the President's mind to abandon neutrality, at the same time polarizing the country in such fashion that both the war sentiment at one extreme and the peace sentiment at the other were enormously strengthened.

The first of these events was the reluctance of the Congress to vote the $100 million he had requested for arming our merchant ships. Congressman after congressman spoke in opposition, and there seemed to be real doubt that Congress would give Wilson the authority to arm merchant ships. The sentiment for keeping out of the war and conserving our forces to aid in bringing about peace and reconstructing a war-ruined European continent, grew in the land. A majority in the country now stood where Wilson himself had stood only yesterday. Wilson remained silent while Congress debated.

At this point the Kaiser, a neurotic war leader, committed one more of the striking blunders by which, for the past year and a half, the German government had showed how little it understood the psychology of the American people, and the real situation in the "New World"—a world still "schoolboy-new" to the Kaiser and his close confidants. The German Ministry of Foreign Affairs, with Wilhelm's approval, sent a secret message to the German minister in Mexico which read as follows:

> We intend to begin on the first of February unrestricted submarine warfare. We shall endeavor in spite of this to keep the United States of America neutral. In the event of this not succeeding, we make Mexico a proposal of alliance on the follow-

ing basis: make war together, make peace together, generous financial support, and an understanding on our part that Mexico is to reconquer her lost territory in Texas, New Mexico, and Arizona. The settlement in detail is left to you. You will inform the President [Carranza] of the above most secretly as soon as the outbreak of war with the United States of America is certain.

The message was signed by Arthur Zimmermann, secretary to the Ministry of Foreign Affairs. It was in the German code, and sent by secret channels, but the British Secret Service intercepted the message and broke the code!

The British government called in Ambassador Page, who, with alacrity transmitted the message to Wilson. It was just what the President needed to electrify Congress and the country, but it sounded so fantastic and childish that he thought it must be a hoax. Surely, the leaders of the German nation could not be so ignorant of the nature of American relations, the ambivalence of Mexico's attitude toward the United States, the negligible strength of the Mexican armed forces and equipment to "reconquer Texas, New Mexico, and Arizona." Would such a listing have omitted California? Would the Germans really be ignorant of the effect of such a message on the twentieth-century inhabitants of the above states? Certainly the note signed by Zimmermann must be a British canard, or a hoax. The State Department spent a number of days investigating and getting the original German text; then it assured Wilson that it was genuine. The President called in the Associated Press. The Senate passed by voice vote a resolution to inquire whether the message was genuine, and Wilson answered: "The note referred to is authentic." Still they doubted, until Zimmermann made matters worse for Germany by confirming its authenticity in order to explain that "the instructions were only to be carried out after a declaration of war by America." With that the Bill for the Arming of Merchant Ships passed through the House by a vote of 403 to 13. Yet those thirteen votes suggested that the bill would not have clear sailing in the Senate, where debate was unlimited, and with the adjournment of Congress only three days away.

In the Senate, eleven men stood up against the authorization and financing of armed merchant vessels. All of them were redoubtable speakers and men of progressive reputation. Their leader, one of the ablest men in Congress, was Robert M. La Follette of Wisconsin. They were ready to debate until Congress had to adjourn, and if they could not convert their colleagues, they could, and did, arouse and consolidate the hitherto formless peace forces throughout the nation.

Angered by his failure to get authorization from Congress, Wilson tried to rouse the nation against his opponents. "The Senate was unable to act," he said, "because a little group of willful men, representing no opinion but their own, had determined that it should not. They have rendered the great government of the United States helpless and contemptible." Then Wilson made the discovery that other Presidents have since utilized, namely, that your own attorney general is likely to think thoughts consonant with yours. The attorney general told him that he could arm the ships without formal congressional approval, and on March 9, five days after Wilson's second inauguration, he gave the order on his own initiative and on his own initiative found the funds.

Obviously, in the last days of February and early days of March, he had made up his mind that America must go to war and make a peace, not "a peace without victory," but a "victorious peace." Nothing remained of his old plans except a League to *Enforce* the Peace when it should come. He still believed that he spoke for all mankind, but he felt now that he must turn the war itself into a crusade. He would find appropriate slogans as he had before.

On that same March 9 on which he issued the order to arm our merchant ships, he summoned Congress to a special session set for April 16 "to receive a communication concerning grave matters." Three days later, after German U-boats had sunk the *City of Memphis*, the *Illinois*, and the *Vigilancia*, the President advanced by two weeks the special session of Congress. When he addressed both houses of Congress, the members of his cabinet, and the justices of the Supreme Court, he was newly heartened by the news that the Tsar had just fallen in Russia: he could now turn his call for war into a crusade "to make the world safe for democracy." And he began to play with the idea of revolution on his own by urging the Germans to overthrow their autocratic government. To the German people themselves he promised sympathy and friendship. It was the Autocracy that they did not control that was responsible for the war: to them he promised a "war waged without hatred," and a peace in which America would "pursue no selfish aims, seek no material compensation, no conquest, no dominion." This was to be a war, he said, to "end all war," to form a "concert for peace . . . the ultimate peace of the world . . . the liberation of peoples, the German people included."

9

I Take a Stand for Peace in "a People's War"

The night before Woodrow Wilson was to deliver his war message, he could not sleep. Never one to use ghostwriters, he sat alone in his study before the typewriter on which he had just completed the text of his address, brooding over the effect his declaration of war would have upon his countrymen. Feeling the need to talk his thoughts out with someone he could confide in, the President did not send for his Secretary of War nor any other member of his Cabinet. Nor did he send for Colonel House nor for Joseph Tumulty nor for any other member of his "Kitchen Cabinet." Instead he sent to New York for Frank Cobb, editor of the *New York World*, a Democratic paper of mass circulation, in whose columns Cobb had published many Wilson interviews, and editorials favoring major presidential moves. It took until 1 A.M. before Cobb could get from New York to the President's study in the White House. Here is his account of the President's thoughts as voiced in a virtual soliloquy:

> For nights, he said, he had been lying awake. He had tried every way he knew to avoid war. I told him that his hand had been forced by Germany. Yes, he said, but do you know what that means? It would mean that we shall lose our heads along with the rest, and stop weighing right and wrong. Germany would be beaten, and so badly beaten that there would be a dictated peace, a victorious peace.
>
> It means an attempt to reconstruct a peacetime civilization with war standards. There won't be any peace standards left to work with. . . . He had no illusions about the fashion in which we were likely to fight the war. When war got going it was just war, and there weren't two kinds. Once lead a people into war and they will forget that there ever was such a thing as tolerance. To fight you must be brutal, and the spirit of ruthless brutality will enter into the very fibre of our national life, infecting Congress, the courts, the policeman on the beat, the man in the street.*

For a challenge and defense of the authenticity of the Cobb-Wilson conversation, see the note at the end of this chapter.

If he had added, "and the attorney general and the postmaster general and the President himself," it would have been a complete as well as a truly remarkable prophecy.

As President Wilson was telling his innermost thoughts and fears to Frank Cobb, thousands of opponents of America's entrance into Europe's war were jamming the railway stations to take trains that night to Washington for a last desperate appeal to stay out. Over a thousand crowded Pennsylvania Station to take the night train to Washington, and similar thousands flooded the stations in many big cities. The New York contingent bore white tulips as an antidote to the war fever that thenceforward was each day to infect fresh segments of the population, which in its overwhelming majority had been antiwar out of its own inclination and out of confidence in the leadership of a President who for nearly three years had been its antiwar leader.

I was not among the thousand who bore white tulips in Pennsylvania Station. I was not one to believe in the efficacy of tulips as a means of keeping our country out of the war madness. But I was aware of the purpose for which the President had called together the joint session of both Houses of the Congress, and was puzzling over what measures I might take as an individual to try at least to moderate the coming war fever.

From the press and from war opponents who had gone to Washington, I got many descriptions of what happened there during the next twenty-four hours. They found the central city decked out, not with white tulips but with red, white, and blue banners. The hastily organized opponents of war grouped themselves around David Starr Jordan. In the raw, wet morning they tried to organize a peace parade, but police officials, already mentally at war, refused a permit. The unembattled hosts tried to see the President and the secretaries of state, war, and navy, but found police or armed guards blocking all the entrances. They drifted back to the Congress and the steps of the Capitol, to compel the ear of the reluctant Senator Lodge, who, after an exchange of hot words, punched one of them in the nose. "I am glad that I hit him," the dignified Henry Cabot Lodge told the press, whereupon for a brief hour he was a national hero. Guards were posted at other senatorial doors, and the police cleared the Capitol steps. Senator La Follette, rapidly emerging as our leader in the Congress, tried in vain to get the police to permit a peaceful rally, demonstration, or march, quoting to deaf ears the corresponding sections of the Bill of Rights, but he had no more influence on police officials than did David Starr Jordan. Eventually the hosts of peace gathered with wilted tulips to fill a public hall, where they listened to speeches addressed only to the convinced. All these scenes of frustration were but a foretaste of the things to come in America in accordance with the prophecy Woodrow Wilson had made to Frank Cobb.

The one thing that Wilson did not expect, despite the "eleven willful men" in the Senate who had recently blocked his bill for arming merchant ships by a filibuster, was the stubborn opposition his call for a declaration of war was to meet in both houses of the new Congress.

Wilson waited until nightfall to deliver his war message, for the new House of Representatives, assembling for the first time, took all day to organize itself. In the meanwhile, the newspapers interviewed and polled members of Congress. They reported that some congressmen expressed the idea that we were being asked to go into the war because England, France, and Russia had piled up such staggering debts to our bankers and manufacturers that they could never be collected if the Allies lost. Another survey reported that "Congressmen are beginning to look upon defense of our trade routes as merely incidental." One poll revealed 76 representatives for war, 15 definitely opposed, 25 doubtful or noncommittal. Despite the big prowar sentiment, the surveys showed—giving us some hope—that most of the representatives who were for a declaration of war thought that such a declaration meant no more than "all-out aid." The press reported an actual majority of two to one against sending any of our boys to Europe.

When the President finally appeared that night, excitement rose to fever pitch. His speech of a little over a half hour was greeted with steadily mounting emotion. In it he made two solemn promises that were accepted with unquestioning enthusiasm, though they were to make much trouble later at the peace conference. One of them stated that "we have no quarrel with the German people, no feeling towards them but that of sympathy and friendship." The other declared that "this war was one in which the world must be made safe for democracy." He ended his address to torrents of applause, cheering, and the waving of little flags, mostly torn from their buttonholes by almost every congressman. Only Senator La Follette seemed to stand out, motionless, his arms folded tight on his chest, no flag in his hand.

In New York, bulletin boards that the *Times* and the *Herald* set up that night as if for election returns had only small knots of people before them, and these appeared to receive without enthusiasm the news that it was war. In the White House, when all were gone but Wilson and his secretary Tumulty, the pacifist in Wilson, dying hard, moved him to say to his secretary as applause rose from the sidewalk below: "My message today was a message of death for our young men. How strange it seems to applaud that." Then he wept with his head on a table. Tumulty did not report this until long after the war was over, the President dead, and Tumulty writing his memoirs.

It is a fearful thing," the President had told the Congress and assembled dignitaries that night, "to lead this great and peaceful people into the most terrible and disastrous of all wars." A month and a half later, on May 18, he warned the country that few Americans could remain untouched by the existing conflict. "In the sense in which we have been wont to think of armies, there are no armies in this struggle; there are entire nations armed. . . . The whole nation must be a team in which each man shall play the part for which he is best fitted." When once such machinery should be set up as he had envisioned to determine what part "each man was best fitted to play," the age of modern large-scale bureaucracy would begin in America. "War," Randolph Bourne wrote, "war is the health of the State." Two total wars, like other total tasks affecting every man which America was to undertake during the Great Depression, were to make huge goverment, huge bureaucracies, and huge multibillion-dollar budgets permanent.

On June 14, in his Flag Day address, Wilson said, "The great fact that stands out above all the rest is that this is a people's war." A people's war, however, is a total war. It was a total war that Europe had stumbled into, and a total war, as I was dimly beginning to perceive, that we were entering into after two and a half years of thoughtful avoidance. But to want to set your face against a "people's war" for whatever reasons and with whatever scruples, as I was gradually to discover, was quite different from keeping out of a war of professional and volunteer armies.

The seventeenth- and eighteenth-century wars had been fought with professional and even with mercenary armies of trained specialists in warfare while the humble peasant and workingman and the merchant and manufacturer, the artist and the writer, quietly pursued their daily lives far from the din and concerns of battle. This tradition was shattered by the French Revolution with its *levée en masse,* its "people in arms" or "armed nation." Russia, with its autocracy and its perpetual wars, had long known something akin to conscription or impressment along with lifetime military service, but the freer West required the French Revolution and then Bismarck's *Blitzkrieg* before it developed the conscript army and the concept of the entire nation geared to war.

Even in the World War of 1914, England held out for a year and a half with a volunteer army, until in January of 1916 she, too, adopted conscription over the opposition of the Labor Party.

Wilson knew no such hesitation. His decision to conscript all suitable American males had been made more than two months before he called on Congress for a declaration of war. Generals Leonard Wood and Hugh Scott initiated the idea, in secret with the agreement of Secretary of War Newton D. Baker, Judge Advocate Enoch Crowder, Major Hugh Johnson, and, of course, the President himself.

Thus the machinery for the draft was set up long before the people or the Congress knew that there was to be a draft. The director of the Government Printing Office became a coconspirator when he was directed to print secretly more than 10 million blank forms. When he discovered that his corridors were overflowing with mounting piles of blanks, he took the Washington postmaster into the conspiracy and together they filled the cellar of the post office to the ceiling with bundles of blank forms. Next the Secretary of War took into his confidence (on April 23) every state governor and all the sheriffs of the land. Finally, the men who were to be chosen to compose the local civilian draft boards were secretly notified. Wondrous to relate, and quite unlike the way in which government secrets leak today and top-secret papers are stolen and then published without so much as consulting the government, there was no leak until after Wilson sent a message to Congress asking it to pass the Draft Act. To cap the climax, Woodrow Wilson, with his remarkable gift for subtlety of phrase, announced to the astonished country, "This is in no sense a conscription of the unwilling."

Wilson tried to soften the shock of America's abandonment of its tradition of a volunteer army by telling Congress as he called for its sanction: "The necessary men will be secured by volunteering as at present, until . . . a resort to a selective draft is desirable." But the 10 million blank forms and the elaborate preparations for universal registration said otherwise. Some congressmen asked whether it would not be better to stick to volunteering, however "inefficacious and inadequate," rather than arouse resistance to our participation in the war by so unpopular a measure.

Opponents of the draft in Congress gave leadership to those of us who were shocked by the measure and the secrecy of its preparation. The opponents in Congress spoke of "the Prussianizing of America"; of "destroying democracy at home while fighting for it abroad"; of creating by such a measure "a sulky, unwilling, and indifferent army"; of "involuntary servitude"; of the "un-American character" of the proposal; of "conscription being another name for slavery." Remembering the draft riots in New York during the latter part of the Civil War, one congressman predicted that "rioting all over the country will add joy to the German heart." Champ Clark, Speaker of the House and a leading Democrat who would have gotten the nomination and election in 1912 had not William Jennings Bryan thrown his formidable party support to Woodrow Wilson, electrified the opposition to the war and the draft act by saying, "I protest with all my mind and soul against having the slur of conscript placed upon the men of Missouri. . . . there is precious little difference between a conscript and a convict." Chairman Dent of the House Military Affairs Committee refused to introduce the draft bill, and a majority of his committee sided with him in opposing a conscript army. But by May 18 the storm of opposition had blown itself out and Congress passed the Draft Act, under which, that June 5, every male between eighteen and thirty-one, whether citizen or not, with the exception of secret holdouts, registered. Having turned twenty-one in January, I too registered, and in the blank inquiring whether I had any reason to claim exemption, I wrote: "Conscientious objection to murder." My local draft board, for reasons not clear to me, noting that I had a wife dependent upon me because she was not employed, chose to put me in the first deferred classification. If the war had lasted long enough and the pool of nearly 3 million men mustered into the army had not proved sufficient, I would have had to face once more the problem of what I would do in view of my "conscientious objections to murder." Since I belonged to no recognized religious order but consulted my own conscience, I should not have been granted the status of "conscientious objector." But the war ended, thanks to our enormous contingents of fresh manpower in a war-exhausted Europe, before I should have to face the problem again.

My first personal decision concerning my attitude toward the war we were entering was not that of registering for the draft and proclaiming my conscientious objection to murdering men unknown to me for causes which did not seem to me to justify our entrance into the war that had torn Europe apart. My need to make a crucial decision came much earlier, before the passage of the Draft Act, and even before our official entrance into the war. The scene was the peaceful halls of Boys' High School, where I had just begun to teach English. I had already done practice teaching at Townsend Harris Hall High School, then spent six months teaching English at Stuyvesant High, and now, at the age of 21, I had just been invited to my old high school to teach English as a "regular substitute."

The title of "regular substitute" was an anomaly that had been devised by the Board of Education and the City fathers to save money at the expense of young teachers just beginning their careers. As vacancies occurred, young men and women who had passed their teaching examinations were appointed to fill them as "regular substitutes" working full time at a substitute's per diem salary. This permitted the City to avoid paying the *de facto* regular teacher for holidays and for summer vacations and further evaded the prescribed annual increases. Some poor souls had been filling regular vacancies in this fashion for as many as six or seven years. To meet this situation I helped to form a Substitute Teachers' Union that finally succeeded in doing away with the illicit practice. But my first problem was not my economic status but the coming entrance of my country into the war in Europe.

The war problem hit the teachers before Wilson made his war address to Congress. The mayor of the city of New York was John Purroy Mitchel, a Wilson liberal who had won election as a reform crusader on an *ad hoc* fusion ticket running against a divided Tammany. He had followed faithfully, if sometimes impatiently, Wilson's slow evolution from neutrality to preparedness, and from preparedness to armed neutrality. When the President issued his first neutrality proclamation in August 1914, Mitchel forbade the carrying of foreign flags of any belligerent in New York City parades. When Wilson called for preparedness, the mayor had shown his zeal by volunteering for part-time military training in a businessmen's training camp at Plattsburg, New York, where most of the trainees were middle-aged men of substance whose names could be found in the *Social Register*. There Mitchel wore pack and knapsack, carried a rifle, and dug practice trenches in the peaceful rural setting of Plattsburg.

On the eve of our declaration of war in 1917, the mayor sent a directive to all principals bidding them ask their teachers to sign a "loyalty pledge," assuring the President that they would "stand behind him" in whatever action he might take. I felt that this meant support of an encouragement of a declaration of war. When the circular was brought to my classroom for signature, I refused to sign. I was summoned to the principal's office by its occupant, a former Latin teacher by the name of Janes.

"Mr. Wolfe," said the principal gently, "it may interest you to know that you are the only teacher on the fourth floor who has not signed this pledge. Surely you do not lack loyalty to your country. Surely you will stand behind the President if war is declared. Do you want to attract attention to yourself as the only holdout that prevents the fourth floor from showing a one hundred percent record of loyalty?"

"I am sorry, Mr. Janes, but I consider this an encouragement to our President to seek our entrance into the war in Europe, and I cannot sign it."

"Do you feel no loyalty to your country?"

"Yes, sir, I do."

"Do you believe in the adage, 'My country, right or wrong'?"

"Mr. Janes, right or wrong, it is my country, for I was born in it. But my concept of loyalty to it includes the duty of every citizen to try to set his country right, when he thinks it is wrong."

"Well, let me put it this way. 'My country, may she ever be right, but right or wrong, my country.'?"

"Yes, of course, it is my country. But when it is wrong, I hold it to be my duty to try to set it right."

The principal's face darkened. "Mr. Wolfe," he said, "you are unfit to teach the young!" He wheeled his swivel chair around with his back to me as a signal that the interview was over.

I went on with my teaching, waiting for the ax to fall. But the Board of Education was already planning some antiwar test cases of teachers with tenure, Schmalhausen, Schneer, and Mufson, and it wanted no more publicity until those cases had been settled. Mr. Janes, apparently under orders, did not dismiss me but on his own decided to make life uncomfortable for me.

When the midterms came I got my first inkling of what the principal had in store for me. Boys' High School in those days had extremely high standards of scholarship, and if a student flunked twice in a basic course, he was expelled. To keep those standards high, the classroom teacher did not have the right to make up the questions for his own classes in midterms or finals; they were made up centrally by the department head and special committees for each course.

In one of my classes I was teaching the *Odyssey* in the Butcher and

Lang translation. I managed to make it live, and both my boys and I enjoyed ourselves. But as the midterm approached, I had the dull task of making them review the book. I hit on the idea of a "mock trial" of Odysseus for his killing of Penelope's suitors: "*Did Odysseus have the right to kill the suitors as he did?*" I divided the class into prosecutors and defenders and bade them reexamine the story to get some idea of Greek justice, Greek honor, and the like. I even suggested some library reading for the more zealous. It worked like a charm. They searched and researched the book for relevant material, had a wonderful time at the mock trial, and made an exceptionally splendid record in the midterm exam. Dr. Fisher, the department head who had refused to give me better than C-plus on my compositions when I was his star pupil, because I did not write like Shakespeare, congratulated me for my ability as a novice teacher.

At the other extreme were the classes of a young math teacher named Wallach, who could not get order in his classes, and had had difficulty teaching them anything. In one of his algebra classes, the entire class flunked the midterms. Without consultation, I received a notice from principal Janes that I was to take Wallach's math classes and he my English classes for the rest of the semester, though my license was to teach English and his mathematics.

I examined his algebra class, all of whose members had flunked the midterm. I found them frightened that they might flunk the course, and convinced that algebra was a distasteful and inscrutable mystery. "Leave your algebra texts home," I told them, "and each of you invest ten cents in a Sam Lloyd puzzle book. We'll take a rest from algebra and do some puzzles."

We solved puzzles for a week—great fun! All the more difficult ones we solved with thinly disguised algebraic devices. At the end of a week, I explained the secret of our solutions and convinced them that algebra was a painless and useful pursuit. The entire class passed the finals.

Thereupon Dr. Janes transferred me to Latin! I received a sympathetic visit from Mr. Bishop, the head of the mathematics department, who told me that he had counted on trying to persuade me to drop English and join his department permanently.

I could have shown the principal, I think, that I could make a good Latin teacher, too, if not a particularly happy one, for in this very high school I had passed four years of Latin in three and one half years. But I took the hint and resigned to take a job as an editor of a trade paper of the Jewish Master Bakers' Federation, a disagreeable task under a mean employer, but one who at least would not persecute me for my opinions and my activities off the job.

I have run a little ahead of my story in order to tell how my refusal to sign Mayor Mitchel's loyalty pledge led to my being driven temporarily out of teaching. But actually, I remained both a teacher and a writer all my life, and though now accounted a historian with at least three of my books as standard texts in many university history departments, I still think of myself as an unreconstructed English teacher. But I must now return to the moment when Congress was considering the declaration of war with Germany.

THE PEACE MOVEMENT

The multitude of antiwar partisans that gathered in Washington during the debate proved to be from many organizations, from all regions of our country, and all layers of society. There were religious opponents of war from such sects as the Quakers, the Moravian Brethren, and the Mennonites, spokesmen for groups of religious conscientious objectors, outstanding religious leaders such as John Haynes Holmes and Judah Magnes. There were Socialists and Populists and members of the Farmers' Non-Partisan League. There were people from German-American organizations still fighting the lost cause of trying to keep America neutral. There were Irish-Americans and fighters for Irish freedom, who had come to America during the war and in especially large numbers after the failure of the Easter 1916 Rebellion in Dublin, who, convinced that England was their enemy, were determined to prevent America from lining up on England's side. There were leaders of long established pacifist organizations and of women's peace movements. There were leaders on the scene such as David Starr Jordan, who had spoken against the war in many cities as soon as Wilson broke off diplomatic relations with Germany. And there were both well-to-do and impoverished loners, who represented only themselves.

In the halls of Congress there were potential leaders such as La Follette, 6 of whom had held out to the end against a vote of 82 for approval of the declaration of war. In the lower house there were 50 such members who had voted no against 373 who had voted yes. Some of these were swept out of office as the war fever took possession of much of the country, others contracted the fever themselves, while a number remained in Congress, antiwar until the very end. Among those who were hounded from office was Charles Augustus Lindbergh, Sr., who had been congressman from his Minnesota district from 1907 to 1917. Lindbergh was defeated after an election campaign in which he was called an "agent of the Kaiser." His son, the famous aviator, seemed to have developed a lifelong hatred of war as a result of witnessing his father's defeat and denigration.

Out of this varicolored conglomerate of organizations and individuals, leaders, followers, personal protesters, and loners, there gradually emerged several large organizations: a Conscientious Objectors and War Resisters League; a Women's League for Peace and Freedom; an American Committee for Democracy and Peace Terms; the American Friends Service Committee with a special Peace Section and an advisory committee for conscientious objectors; the Brethren's Service Committee; the Mennonite Central Committee; the National (later American) Civil Liberties Union; and the Emergency Peace Federation. This was the largest and most inclusive of all the organizations and tended to develop as a federation rather than an individual membership body.

Well represented, too, was the Socialist party, which had formulated its stand in an emergency convention in St. Louis three days after Woodrow Wilson asked Congress for a declaration of war. A committee consisting of Morris Hillquit, Algernon Lee, and Charles E. Ruthenberg wrote the celebrated St. Louis Resolution. Morris Hillquit was to run for mayor of the city of New York that autumn on the slogan "A vote for socialism is a vote against war," and would get a surprisingly big vote. Algernon Lee was to continue to direct the Rand School and was elected a member of the New York Board of Aldermen. Ruthenberg, leader of the Socialist party of Ohio, was to become an outstanding leader, and the general secretary, of the still unborn Communist party of America.

The St. Louis Resolution, the culmination of the nearly three years of American neutrality that permitted a freedom to American Socialists not granted to the Socialists in countries at war since 1914, began with the declaration, "The Socialist Party of the United States reaffirms its allegiance to the principles of internationalism . . . and proclaims its unalterable opposition to the war just proclaimed by the government of the United States." It blamed the war in Europe on the "conflict of capitalist interests in the European countries." America's entrance it attributed to "instigation by the predatory capitalists in the U.S. who boast of enormous profits of seven billion dollars from the manufacture and sale of munitions and war supplies and the exportation of American foodstuffs and other necessities." A seven-point program of active opposition to the war called for demonstrations, petitions, opposition to conscription, and the like, and "a campaign of education and organization among the workers . . . to enable them by concerted and harmonious mass action to shorten this war and establish a lasting peace."

MY LIFE IN THE PEACE MOVEMENT

The year 1917 was a crowded year for me, crowded with actions, experiences, and impressions closely connected with the war we were entering. During that year, countless young men like me were making individual decisions concerning their attitude toward the war. On January 19, I turned 21. On the first of April, I publicly took my stand on the war, and in a larger sense on war in general. More than a half century later, in 1973, I began a talk to the Central Slavic Conference at Oklahoma State University with these words:

> All my life I have been, and I am now, an opponent of war as a means of settling differences between nations. I consider war the cruelest, the most barbarous, the most unsatisfactory way of settling differences between countries. Man mocks his humanity when he resorts to war if any other means are available.

After supporting two wars, the Korean War when South Korea was invaded by North Korea armed and encouraged by Russia, and the Second World War after the Japanese strike on Pearl Harbor made any further attempt to keep America out of war into a patent absurdity, that statement still expresses my position today.

After I refused to sign the mayor's war loyalty pledge, I had given up teaching for editing. In April, too, I married the girl I had been going with since she was 14 and I 16. While war destroys millions of lives, it also by some unconscious compensatory instinct draws young men and women closer together because of the uncertainties of the fortunes of war and of their own fate.

During that same year, while I watched my country entering the war, I became aware that new rulers were seizing power in Russia and proposing to take Russia out of the war. I was, I must admit, completely ignorant of who these new leaders in Russia were and what their program was beyond their opposition to the war. All I knew was that we were entering the war and they were leaving it, and this induced me to open a large credit to the new, "antiwar" Russia, a credit that was only to be exhausted twelve years later, when in 1929 I got a close-up of Russia.

In May and June of 1917, I had made up my mind to register for the draft, and to record myself as a conscientious objector without noting any religious affiliation. It was a year in which several hundred thousand did not register at all. A few thousand registered but refused to serve on religious grounds or grounds of conscience. There was a small number that publicly announced their determination, also on grounds of conscience, not to register, since registration itself seemed to them cooperation with the war. And there were a few score young men who went surreptitiously to Mexico, having heard vague reports that it was a socialistic and revolutionary land. Some of these I was to meet in Mexico six years later when I went there to teach English in the Mexican government high schools.

During the course of 1917, I found myself compelled to take a number of successive antiwar stands, the rejection of Mayor Mitchel's pledge being only the first. I cooperated with the People's Council, as the Emergency Peace Foundation was now called, in various ways; I founded and edited an antiwar paper; and, although I was not a convinced socialist, I joined the Socialist party and became active in its ranks because its whole activity was concentrated during the war on opposition thereto, and it seemed to me the most stable and firmest of bodies in its antiwar activities. When the local party leaders in Manhattan and Brooklyn discovered that I could speak, write, and teach, they tried to enlist my abilities in those fields. I began to speak in Morris Hillquit's campaign for mayor in halls and on noisy street corners. I became active in the Socialist Local of the Sixth Assembly District in Brooklyn, then a delegate to the Kings County Committee and later to the Greater City Committee. I began to study with curiosity and fascination the picturesque, strong, and self-assured characters who played a leading role in party circles, as I did the striking individuals who gave tone to the life of Greenwich Village. And I came into contact with a new and intriguing type, a handful of émigrés from Russia who appeared to be "men of confidence" of V. I. Lenin and his lieutenants in the Russian Bolshevik movement. I attended some great mass meetings of the People's Council held in Madison Square Garden. As my antiwar paper grew in influence and readership, I found myself surrounded by artists and writers eager to participate in its work. Each day brought me new experiences and new acquaintances and friends full of a fresh interest, men and women I should never have met and gotten to know intimately in the course of a normal life as a high school or university English teacher.

In short, 1917 proved to be a vivid and exciting year crowded with events, impressions, ideas and problems, a year of forced ripening, developing many capacities I did not know I possessed, fostering sides of my personality that a comparable period of peace would not have nurtured. All unknown to myself, I matured swiftly and began to act as a grown-up rather than a fledgling of 21.

My first *recorded* organizational contact was with the People's Council when it was still called the Emergency Peace Federation. I say "recorded" because the Government of the United States and the Government of the State of New York combined to record it for me; otherwise I should have forgotten this insignificant detail long ago.

No sooner was war declared than the prophecy made by President Wilson to Frank Cobb began to fulfill itself. It was a self-fulfilling prophecy because the President, his postmaster general, and his attorney general began to fulfill it without delay, though in Wilson's case perhaps not without some moments of remorse. And officials everywhere began to follow the White House example.

One of Postmaster Albert Sidney Burleson's earliest steps was to violate the privacy of the mail entrusted to our postal system by ordering all letters addressed to certain organizations to be secretly opened, photographed, then sealed again, and delivered to their destination. On April 24, 1920, when the New York Joint Legislative Committee Investigating Seditious Activities, headed by Clayton R. Lusk, filed its report to the state Senate and published it in four stout volumes of well over a thousand pages each, I found a letter of mine, written in my still schoolboyish hand, beautifully photographed and reproduced facing page 992 of volume I. It had a place of honor as the first of a series of such letters, yielding only to a single postcard signed jointly by Jane Addams, S. P. Breckinridge, and Louis P. Lochner, dated April 13, 1915, and bearing only their signatures and the horrendous message: "We don't know where we're going, but we're on our way." They were manifestly going to Europe on the Holland American S.S. *Noordam* in quest for peace in a Europe at war. Since a postcard does not have to be secretly opened and resealed, and since it was mailed in 1915, that still gives my letter dated April 17, 1917, the place of honor as the earliest letter opened and resealed on the orders of Postmaster Burleson, and reproduced by the Lusk Committee.

War was declared on April 6. The date of my letter suggests that almost immediately thereafter, certainly not later than the middle of the same month, our postmaster was already violating the privacy of our mail. In addition he was beginning to deny second-class mailing privileges to a number of newspapers because he did not like what they were printing. Within another month he was declaring a number of journals "unmailable," with no hearing and no reason given.

The question arises, What was there in my letter of April 17 that made the postmaster think it worth photographing before it was resealed? And what was there that made the New York Lusk committee think it worthy of reproduction as a halftone cut?

The letter in full reads: "*Emergency Peace Federation, Gentlemen: Enclosed please find a petition with signatures. If I can be of any service, I am always at your disposal. Yours for the cause, Bertram D. Wolfe.*" What was "the cause"? It might have been opposition to a conscript army and the maintenance of our traditional volunteer army. It might have been the cause of peace—perhaps an early peace without victory, a just and moderate and democratic peace that would be less likely to breed future wars. Given the date of my letter, it was probably the first rather than the second.

But why should the simple exercise of the right of peaceful petition seem worthy of publication in these four solid volumes on *Revolutionary Radicalism*? The reader can only begin to sense the answer if he turns to the index and glossary or dossier of "radical" characters and movements and journals that comes after page 2008 of volume II, an index which itself occupies 245 pages! There on page 240 the reader will find a nine-line entry for *Wolfe, Bertram D.* which lists him as "an editor of *New York Communist;* an organizer of Communist Party; an organizer of Left Wing in U.S. [it deliberately omits the words "of the Socialist Party of America"]; arrested, and on bail, for criminal anarchy; associate editor *Communist World;* managing council *Revolutionary Age;* member National Council Left Wing (again it should be "Left Wing of the Socialist party"); pacifist activities."

If we add the words "Socialist Party" after the two mentions of "Left Wing," the account of my activities is accurate, except for the further announcement that I had been "arrested" and was out "on bail for criminal anarchy." The truth behind this misstatement was that as a member of the National Council of the Left Wing of the Socialist party, I wrote jointly with John Reed and Louis Fraina a document called the *Manifesto of the National Council of the Left Wing of the Socialist Party.* It did not seem revolutionary enough to suit Louis Fraina, then editing the *Revolutionary Age* in Boston, so he had himself appointed to "strengthen" our manifesto. All those who signed the final document were then indicted, although my indictment was kept secret because they never succeeded in laying hands on me. But the Lusk committee wrongly assumed that I had been arrested like the others, and was out on bail.

Now it may be clear to the reader why my innocent letter was given the place of prominence in the reproductions of letters. I had written to the Emergency Peace Federation (later People's Council) a letter which said next to nothing. But my function was to make it seem that the People's Council was really Communist or Communist-controlled. Actually, the People's Council was an organization consisting of a wide assortment of pacifist organizations, led by an organizing committee of men and women of an older generation than mine, who had nothing Communist about them. The members of the organizing committee consisted of eight AFL leaders such as James Maurer, president of the Pennsylvania Federation of Labor; six professors, the most prominent of whom was David Starr Jordan; nine or ten social workers of whom the most admired was Jane Addams of Hull House; six feminists whose principal activity had been working for equal rights and votes for women; six ministers and rabbis, of whom the best known were John Haynes Holmes and Judah Magnes; six leaders of peace movements; one artist; two magazine editors, one the chairman of the board of *Pearson's Magazine*, the other Max Eastman, editor of the old *Masses;* one author; three old-line Single Taxers who had long forgotten their zeal for the Single Tax; nine or ten leading Socialists, only one of whom ever became a Communist. Many of these activities overlapped. And I, when I wrote that youthful letter, was no more Communist than the older leaders, though the difference in age was to make a difference in our future course. For lack of a better brush, however, my pacifist letter was used to paint the council red.

NOTE ON THE COBB-WILSON INTERVIEW

The authenticity of this meeting between Wilson and Cobb was challenged by Professor Jerold S. Auerbach, writing in the December 1967 issue of the *Journal of American History* (LIV, 608–17). He argues that historians should have been skeptical about every detail of the incident. He notes, for example, that the first published account of the meeting was in 1924, after both Cobb and Wilson were dead, and that the source was not any document or notes made by Cobb, but rather an interview with two men who claim that they had heard Cobb's recollections of the 1917 meeting.

Moreover, Auerbach claims that the words ascribed to Wilson were so remarkably prescient of future developments that they could hardly have been uttered *before* the events predicted. He insists that Wilson could not have spoken of a "dictated peace" before the Versailles treaty was signed. And he is certain that Wilson never expressed any concern about restrictions on civil liberties in wartime, in view of numerous well-documented utterances by Wilson which reveal his profound indifference to civil liberties and his overt hostility to any persons whose actions or beliefs challenged our entrance into Europe's war. There being no evidence of any meeting held on April 2, Auerbach concludes "that the words that presumably were spoken at a nonexistent meeting on April 2 never were spoken at all."

A year later, writing in the same journal (LV, 231–35), Professor Arthur S. Link responded to Auerbach's charges. No one has ever possessed a greater or more intimate knowledge of Woodrow Wilson's life and mind than Link—possibly not even Wilson himself. Link has devoted his life to reconstructing Wilson's. As of 1975, Link had published five huge volumes of a biography which carries Wilson only up to his reelection in November 1916, and had edited fifteen volumes of a projected series of fifty volumes of Wilson's papers and correspondence. If any scholar is qualified to assess the authenticity of the Wilson-Cobb meeting, Link is that man. He argues that the meeting did take place, that the words ascribed to Wilson by Cobb were "Wilsonian in vocabulary, phrasing, and tone . . . "; that the words "dictated peace" were not so different from Wilson's warning to the belligerents that "victory would mean force upon the loser, a victor's terms imposed upon the vanquished . . . a peace accepted under duress"; that there is every reason to believe that Wilson would have spoken freely to Cobb as he had on numerous occasions, and that the opinions and predictions ascribed to Wilson were not so extraordinary that they could only have been invented after the events predicted. Link does concede two points to Auerbach: that Auerbach was justified in doubting that Wilson expressed concern that civil liberties would be eroded in wartime; and that the meeting did not take place on April 2. There was just such an intimate meeting between Cobb and Wilson, Link proves, on March 19, when, as Link notes, "Wilson was just recovering from a severe cold."

My conclusion from the debate between these two learned historians is that Auerbach has scored a point concerning Wilson's lack of concern with civil liberties for opponents of the war. But Wilson was himself a historian who knew what war did to a country and was especially cognizant of the "Gilded Age" which followed the American Civil War. Wilson is on record as having been profoundly worried about the consequences of his plunging our country into the First World War. He is on record as having written to Josephus Daniels, "The people we have unhorsed will inevitably come into control of the country, for we shall be dependent on the steel, oil and financial magnates. They will run the nation." And to Representative William C. Adamson, Wilson predicted "disorganization of business, . . . profiteering run rampant, robbery. . . ." "It would require a generation to restore normal conditions."

It is my conclusion that Link's arguments concerning a Wilson-Cobb discussion on the consequences of the coming war stand up. However, some readers may think differently, and, in any case, the debate between these two scholars is interesting, even exciting, and illustrates the painstaking detective work that good historians engage in, in trying to reconstruct the past from the fragments that come down to them. For those interested in how history is written, I warmly recommend the reading of the two lengthy articles by Auerbach and the answer by Arthur S. Link in the *Journal of American History*.

10

THE RISE AND FALL OF AN ANTIWAR PAPER

Having faced the "loyalty" pledge and the draft, I turned to the problem of my own activities in wartime. I must speak up, I thought. But how does a lone youth, with no organization to help him, get an audience? Besides, from my disastrous debut as a member of the City College debating team, I knew that I was afraid of audiences, a victim of stage fright. I must write then, for that was where I had some skill and self-confidence. But where could I get published? Perhaps if I founded my own journal . . . And where would the money come from for that? A trusting printer? Contributions? From whom? How would I sell the paper?

As a starter I turned to my classmates who had graduated with me in 1916, and to members of City College clubs in which I had played a leading role. They could make a donation, lend me money, invest. In the latter case, I assured them that they would likely lose every last cent of their investment. They were stirred by the prospect of the draft and the consequent change in their life plans. Most of them professed to be anti-war. Nobody refused me. They gave five dollars, ten dollars, some even twenty-five. But they were vague about writing for the journal, giving technical help, selling it at meetings or on street corners, or to their neighbors.

In a few days I had enough money for a first issue. Not knowing whether I could ever get out a second, I called it "Volume I, Emergency," and baptized the journal *Facts: The People's Peace Paper.* Then the first artist friend who volunteered his services, Robert Minor, convinced me that the word *Facts* should fill the whole top of the front cover, and so it appeared as a sixteen-page magazine, dated May 31, 1917, and selling at five cents a copy. The front cover bore the table of contents in display type (The Anti-Conscription Movement/What Others Are Doing About Registration/ Exemption for Christians/ Question Box for Pacifists/ The Conscientious Objector/ American Junkerdom/ Militarism at Work/ The President's Article/ Significance of the United Peace Policy/ War-Time Wisdom/ War Poems by David Paul/ News of Pacifist Activities). The poems signed David Paul were by a poet *manqué,* David P. Berenberg, teacher of German at Boys' High School and an active member of the Socialist party. It was rather poor poetry, but at least genuinely antiwar. I got cartoons for the first issue from Robert Minor, a brilliant anarchist cartoonist who later became a silly and bumbling leader of the Communist party and refused to draw any more of his powerful cartoons, "because Lenin"—as he assured me—"never drew cartoons but devoted his full time to politics." (Jay Lovestone mortally offended him at a Politburo meeting by saying: "I move that Robert Minor be instructed to draw something else besides his salary." But still he refused.) And I got two drawings for the first issue from the Socialist cartoonist Art Young, less of an artist than Minor, but with much more humor in his drawings and captions. One of his sketches showed a stout capitalist "Doing his bit" by offering "My boy to my country." The simple-faced, wide-eyed boy bore the label "Office Boy." His other drawing was a pile of corpses labeled "Twelve Thousand Young Men Killed—Four Yards of Dirt Gained." There were a few signed articles, but I had written most of the first issue, hence decided not to sign my name at all. There was no editor apparent either. My pride was a satirical-humorous column which ran in each issue, which I did sign, romantically, with the pseudonym Elbert Lovell, the first name being made up of my name and that of Ella, the girl who had newly become my wife, and the second of "love" and "Ella." I was not trying to evade the Espionage and Sedition acts, which had not yet gone into effect, but I wonder how much time official code experts spent trying to decipher the identity of Elbert Lovell.

The first number carried paid ads from the Emergency Peace Federation, the First American Conference for Democracy and Terms of Peace, the Bureau of First Aid, and the American Legal Defense League. The back cover was fully taken up by self-advertisement of the magazine, its purposes, its program, and a dubious offer of a year's subscription for one dollar.

The issue put together by this green young editor was a startling success. With the aid of Arlene Paul of the Hoover Library and Bernice B. Nichols, curator of the Peace Collection of Swarthmore College, I have succeeded in getting all but one of the six issues that mark the life of *Facts*, and the first issue stands up well even now, to my more experienced and critical eye trained by more than half a century of subsequent writing and editing. Some of the thoughts expressed may have been naïve but none of them were childish or silly. There are no typographical errors. The table of contents was balanced. There was nothing else in the field of antiwar publication to compete with it. A number of young Hunter College girls and young Socialists and pacifists volunteered to sell it on street corners and at meetings, without any compensation except moral satisfaction. Subscriptions came by every mail in surprising numbers, along with a spate of donations, free drawings from able artists, unsolicited articles from well-known writers, offers of editorial help by editorial workers from the pacifist, socialist, and anarchist movements, and from Greenwich Village, where I was already beginning to feel at home and to have many friends. The People's Council endorsed *Facts,* as I had editorially endorsed the People's Council in the first issue. The Socialist party opened its meetings to our sales. The council made substantial financial contributions in the form of full-page ads on the inside covers, and, indeed, took over the cost of the entire third issue as the "People's Council number of *Facts.*" Both David Starr Jordan and Morris Hillquit, the Socialist antiwar candidate for mayor of New York, were so pleased with the first number that they wrote for the second. Morrie Ryskind began contributing with the third issue. In the sixth number, President Jordan lent his name as a member of an editorial advisory council. Dr. Frederick A. Blossom transferred his editorial services from Margaret Sanger's *Birth Control Review,* of which he was managing editor, to *Facts.* He was typical of a number of residents of Greenwich Village who had gone from cause to cause and now found the struggle against war more interesting and exciting than the fight for women's rights, or the legalization of birth control, or any other of the movements that had claimed their attention. They brought with them experience and excitement, and bubbling enthusiasm.

Since the letter from David Starr Jordan in our second issue was one of the prize features of *Facts* (Jordan was probably the most prominent scientist to become active full time in the peace movement and certainly the most significant academic figure to do so), and since the letter is missing from his files at Stanford, it might be a good idea to quote it here. Moreover, it expresses as well as anything that appeared in *Facts* the program and mood of those who gathered around and edited and wrote for the journal.

EDITOR OF *Facts*

Dear Sir:

I am asked my conception of "the duty of a Liberal Radical in wartime." . . . A Radical, I take it, is one who thinks for himself. . . . he is not mind or conscience-bound *by* any tyranny, whether of church or State, of caste or society* * * [*Note:* the asterisks were in the original letter by Jordan; the dots represent inconsequential omission by me.—BDW] To be liberal, I take it, is to be tolerant, to recognize that one's own freedom of thought or action involves like freedom on the part of others.

In war-time, the radical, being free from political and military superstitions as well as from superstitions of religion, recognizes a wholly abnormal and monstrous state of things. War demands hate and to secure hate properly intensified, truth and freedom must be sacrificed. For this and a multitude of other reasons war is the most degrading line of effort a nation can undertake * * * The radical will oppose so far as in him lies the encroachments war makes on democracy. He will stand for freedom of speech, under the constitutional guarantees laid down by our wise fathers, who valued liberty more than we do, because they knew what it meant to be without it. He will endeavor in no way to increase the burden of hatred war is sure to bring. He will be patient even if hatred turns against him, for it is one of war's penalties, to hate all those who will not hate. He will look forward toward the end, when no people shall be ruled by outside force, but each nationality large and small, in accordance with their own culture and customs. He will realize that a democratic form of government does not ensure rule by the people. It only gives them a chance to rule if they will. And when any force outside the man himself dictates his thoughts, his discipline, his culture, in so far democracy fails to be complete. For democracy is cooperative association for mutual advantage in which the minority, for the general good, sacrifices the direction of certain actions, but never individual mind or conscience or the right of personal guidance.

In brief, the Liberal Radical will take his stand on the words which Cromwell once wrote across the statute books of Parliament: "All just powers under God are derived from Consent of the people," and on these words of Martin Luther spoken in the hour of apparent defeat: "The force of arms must be kept far from matters of the gospel."

He will say of war as the elephant Haitha said in the Indian tale: "It will pass." But it makes a vast difference which way it passes. For the noblest duty and the highest privilege of the Liberal Radical is to do the best to the end that it can never pass this way again.

David Starr Jordan

Up to this point the letter filled one column of *Facts*. How much longer the letter was I do not know, but I replaced the remaining paragraphs with a footnote. I would give a lot now to know what I cut out, for my addendum reads: "Note: The paragraphs omitted for lack of space, are in defense of America's entrance into the war on the plea of extraordinary necessity." Was I honorably condensing, or less honorably censoring an essential part of Dr. Jordan's views? I made a thorough search of the David Starr Jordan papers, which are at Stanford, hoping to restore the lost paragraphs here, but the entire letter was missing! That led me to a further investigation. I found that the earlier correspondence of President Jordan was preserved by "letterpress," that is, by pasting or copying each letter in a scrapbook. In the second decade of our century, letterpress was abandoned for the more modern method of filing carbon copies. There was a gap, however, between the two procedures when no letters were preserved by either method, the letter to the editor of *Facts* being among the missing documents. But I did find a letter of Dr. Jordan to a friend in which he summarized his letter to *Facts*, and he too omitted any mention of the concluding paragraphs. There the matter rests, for the documents of the magazine *Facts* were not preserved at all.

Another joy for the young editor was the sudden rush of first-rate caricaturists to *Facts*, each with a powerful antiwar drawing rolled up in a cardboard tube or nesting in an oversized portfolio. Besides Robert Minor and Art Young, whom I published in the first and in subsequent issues, there were Maurice Becker, Boardman Robinson, William Gropper, Hugo

Gellert, whose brother committed suicide because of inhuman treatment as a conscientious objector, H. J. Glintenkamp, Louis Lozowick, and a number of less known but able caricaturists. They were all established artists whose regular drawings were paid for adequately, even handsomely, by the big magazines and newspapers, and who had already been drawing more freely—in both senses of the word—for the *Masses*, the self-constituted organ of Greenwich Village. The *Masses* is not to be confused with the pseudo reincarnation, the *New Masses*, which was an increasingly narrow and bitter polemical organ of the Communist party in the literary field. The old *Masses* was a joyous and impudent magazine of the sort to which you contributed not only your stories or poems or drawings, but also such cash as you could spare to keep it coming out. Perhaps its spirit can be suggested by this bit of doggerel popular in its day:

> They draw nude women for the *Masses*,
> Thick, fat, ungainly lasses—
> How does that help the working classes?

The *Masses* was founded by John Reed and Max Eastman, both of whom served, in turn, as its editor. Every cause espoused by Greenwich Villagers, from socialism to the IWW (Industrial Workers of the World) Lawrence (Mass.) textile strike, from the avant-garde armory art show of 1913 to the antiwar movement of 1917, found a place in it. The antiwar articles, poems, and drawings got its editors, including the then editor in chief, Max Eastman, indicted under the Espionage Act, from which indictment Eastman got off scot-free after two sensational trials, one of which ended in a hung jury, the second in an acquittal. The *Masses* itself died of Postmaster Burleson's denial of second-class mailing rights and his subsequent declaration of the magazine's "unmailability." As for *Facts*, thanks to the overflow of fertility of the *Masses* artists, we never lacked for striking cartoons, two, three and more to an issue, as long as our journal existed. Nor did we lack for funds, articles, friendly advertisements, editorial help, enthusiastic vendors. The new magazine seemed to be making its way in a world crowded with journals, for it performed a unique function, and many friendly organizations looked at it as a sort of official organ. And its printers, the brothers Joe and Frank Canata, proved to be sympathizers who were ready to extend unlimited credit and had the right to print a union label on "the People's Peace Paper."

While I was exulting at the warm welcome the young magazine was getting and the generous help being given its green young editor, dark clouds were gathering over all those who questioned the wisdom of our entrance into the war, who urged the earliest possible peace without victory, who opposed conscription in favor of our traditional volunteer army, who said that the war should be financed by current taxation and not by bonds to be paid by future generations, who opposed the support of the Allied war aims for the acquisition of territories in a war which we had entered only "to make the world safe for democracy," who thought that democracy required us to preserve civil liberties and freedom of speech and discussion here at home—in short, all those who advocated any of the things that *Facts* had been advocating.

The attorney general, the postmaster general, the President, and the Congress, were collaborating to draft an espionage act that promised to make the whole program of *Facts* into activities "hindering the conduct of the war," and to define such activities as "espionage"—something unprecedented in the history of loosely worded law and semantic distortion. Many states were rushing through sedition acts which would soon fuse into a federal sedition act unprecedented since the election of Jefferson. Others were passing criminal syndicalism acts, aimed principally at the Industrial Workers of the World (IWW) but also at other unions and strikes called in wartime, and at radical parties. New York State was dusting off its Criminal Anarchy Law passed after the demented anarchist Czolgosz assassinated McKinley. The intent of state officials was to use it against all who questioned anything concerning the war or "the Government of the State of New York." I myself was to be indicted before long under the Criminal Anarchy Law.

From all over the country, news began to come in concerning mob violence, supported rather than frowned upon by local authorities, tarring and feathering, riding on a rail, dragging behind a car, lynching, two-minute trials in which the magistrate outdid the fury of the prosecutor in his charge to the jury. A particularly searing piece of news was the brutal murder by hanging from a railroad trestle just outside of Butte, Montana, of the crippled metal-mine organizer of the IWW, Frank Little. I did not have space in *Facts* to tell his story, but in the issue of September I offered a reward for the best version of the letter Woodrow Wilson would have written to the governor of Montana if Frank Little had been a mine owner instead of a mineworker. It was a safe offer, for officials and most newspapers condoned the murder; the *Butte Evening Post* refused to publish the known names of the lynchers, while the *Literary Digest* "inclined to the belief that Little received his just deserts."

In the August issue of *Facts* there were signs that the clouds were beginning to darken further over the paper. But there was good news, too. Thus on page 3 there was an article, "The Triumph of the People's Council," that told of the formation of a great number of new branches and allied organizations, and a rush of labor unions to endorse the council or directly affiliate with it. And there was the news that John M. Baer, candidate of the Farmers' Non-Partisan League in Minnesota, who ran in a by-election for Congress, had won a striking victory on a platform of "absolute and determined opposition to the war and the draft . . . and a peace based on the formula of no annexations and no indemnities." Both his Democratic and his Republican opponents called for their election as supporters of the President and the war, and both called for the defeat of the "pro-German and unpatriotic Baer." Baer got a decisive plurality of 1,500.

On the same page that carried these glad tidings, J. Louis Engdahl, editor of the *American Socialist,* reported that "without a hearing, without a trial," the Post Office Department had declared his journal "unmailable" and "the prisoner," i.e., 60,000 copies of the paper, "was taken out and burned." How long could papers like ours survive the denial of second-class mailing rights, the seizure and burning of whole issues, the decree that the paper itself was henceforth "unmailable"?

On page 6 of the same issue, *Facts* told the sad story of our similar fate. "*Facts,*" my article (unsigned) began, "has been suppressed by the Post Office."

We consoled ourselves:

> Evidently, *Facts* has a real message. . . . The Government fears the circulation of that message. Then our message cannot be altogether false or ridiculous. . . . If we reached only a small number there would be nothing for them to fear. . . . *Facts* is not the only paper to be suppressed. There are seventeen others, and many more to come. . . . A BIG INCREASE IN THE CIRCULATION OF FACTS AFTER IT WAS DEBARRED FROM THE MAILS, IS THE AMERICAN PEOPLE'S ANSWER! . . . A suppressed paper is an advertised paper. . . . What cannot be done above ground will be done underground. . . . take care lest you force our movement into cellars and back rooms.

When the post office confiscated all our copies mailed to subscribers, we hastily got out an issue of only eight pages in place of the usual 16 and had our volunteers hand-deliver it in the metropolitan area. For out-of-towners, we wrapped it up in other journals and mailed it third class. The extra expense would have put us out of business were it not for the credit extended by our printers and the fact that none of us, editors, writers, artists, vendors, was paid a cent, all work being volunteer.

But the next month, September, we came out with our regular issue, 16 pages, with a powerful cover drawing by Robert Minor, all in all probably the best issue so far. After all, the editor and publisher was learning his trade, and contributions of every sort, including new subscriptions, came in in greater volume than ever. It still called for subscriptions at a dollar a year, but it carried a small box on the back cover which bore the heading WE WANT YOU!

> *Facts* is distributed and sold by volunteer workers. Their only reward is the joy of participation in a great Cause. Help spread the truth. Young men and women, yours is the task and yours the glory. We need sellers, distributors and workers of all kinds. There is a job for every one. Write to FACTS PUBLISHING ASSN. 11 West 18th Street, New York City.

Volunteers kept sending in their names in still greater numbers, and I began to wonder whether besides the editor, writers, and artists, I was not also making these bright-faced young boys and girls guilty under the vague and sweeping language of the Espionage Act, the thickets and brambles of state and city ordinances, and the Sedition Act already being prepared for early passage.

I read the Espionage Act and consulted Socialist and liberal lawyers who volunteered their opinions free. The Espionage Bill had become law on June 15, 1917. It did not occur to me at first that anything I was doing, saying, or writing could conceivably come under the purview of a law calling itself the *Espionage Act*. But the law was deliberately clothed in vagueness. It made guilty of "espionage" all "false reports or false statements made with the intent to interfere with the operation or success of the military or naval forces . . . wilfully cause or attempt to cause insubordination, disloyalty, mutiny, or refusal of duty in the military or naval forces of the United States. . . ." Whoever violated these or other equally sweeping provisions "shall be punished by a fine of not more than $10,000 or imprisonment for not more than 20 years or both." Eugene V. Debs, Victor Berger, and other prominent Socialist leaders, were promptly indicted under the act, and the sixty-three-year-old Debs was sentenced to spend what promised to be the rest of his life in prison. Berger was also given twenty years and a $10,000 fine, but his sentence was later reversed.

The Espionage Act and its complement, the Sedition Act, emboldened officials, national, state, and local, and increased the fury of police and of mobs who could now feel that they were rooting out "spies." the postmaster now not only denied the leading Socialist daily, the *Milwaukee Leader*, second-class mailing rights; he declared it unmailable and then arbitrarily ordered that no one writing to it should have his letters delivered to their destination. This ended for a time the life of the *Milwaukee Leader*.

Thus, with the Espionage Act, civil liberties and the right of free discussion vanished. Public feeling was whipped up to such an extent that a mere accusation of disloyalty often sent a man to prison. Mobs started the persecution, and "a trial," as Representative Huddleston said, "became a sort of legalized mob action" Periodicals that criticized the British Empire were also closed down. The film *The Spirit of 1776*, made while Britain was not yet our ally but shown in Los Angeles with the strongest anti-British scene deleted, after war was declared by Congress landed its producer in jail for ten years under the Espionage Act, "for questioning the good faith of our ally." Though its producer was released after two and a half years, he was bankrupted by jail and a $5,000 fine and had to give up moviemaking. The prowar *New Republic* was warned after publishing an advertisement signed by John Dewey, Thorstein Veblen, Carlton Hayes, Helen Keller, and similar notables asking for assurance of a fair trial for the IWW, that if it did such a thing again it would have to answer to the Department of Justice. Publication of the *Nation*, also prowar, was suspended for a short time for criticizing the New York Police for rough and unlawful tactics in searching for possible draft evaders in subway trains. The IWW Defense Committee was denied the right to receive its own mail, containing mostly contribution of funds, and speakers who merely appealed for funds for the IWW defense were arrested in many parts of the country, Seattle, San Francisco, and New York City among them.

Organizations were formed with government approval to spy on neighbors, break up street meetings, report utterances, and function generally as legalized and respectable mobs. They bore such names as American Defense Society, National Security League, American Protective League, Home Defense League, Liberty League, Knights of Liberty, American Rights League, All-Allied Anti-German League, Anti-Yellow Dog League, American Anti-Anarchy Association, Boy Spies of America, etc. For 75 cents or a dollar one could have the authority "with the approval of the Department of Justice to make investigations with the title of 'Secret Service.' " (These words in quotes are from a letter of the Secretary of the Treasury, William G. McAdoo, to President Wilson, urging that the American Protective League with 250,000 members in 600 towns and cities, be curbed or abolished. It continued to function!)

If such was the growing atmosphere of civil terror, and if big journals like the Milwaukee *Leader* could be thus crushed, what chance had my upstart little journal? And what would happen to the volunteer young men and women who were selling it? Was I not making them responsible for all the violations of the Espionage Act which could be construed into every article?

I have no idea now what was in the sixth and last issue except that it contained an official endorsement of *Facts* by the People's Council, and an offer by David Starr Jordan, their treasurer, and several other of their leaders, to become members of an editorial advisory board. What a time for the flourishing young magazine to die! It was the Espionage Act and the nascent Sedition Act, the attorney general and the postmaster general, that were making its life difficult. But it was its editor that determined the date of its death.

I called together the young men and women, mostly Hunter girls and City College boys, and friends and collaborators of the journal. I reported on the growing civil terror and the sweeping nature of the Espionage and Sedition acts. "Any one who distributes *Facts* is guilty of spreading views which in the opinion of the Government, the Courts, and the Mob, may 'interfere with the operation or success of the military or naval forces . . . may cause or attempt to cause insubordination, disloyalty, mutiny, or refusal of duty in the military or naval forces of the United States.' For my part, I shall continue my own activities, and support and spread and amplify the things we have said in our journal. But I do not feel that I have the right to ask you to distribute and sell the journal, thus making yourself potentially vulnerable to indictment and punishment under a measure idiotically called the *Espionage* Act."

That, as far as I can remember, was the nature of my funeral oration over the magazine. It did not die for lack of support or readership. It died in full health, the need for it not ended. I looked for new ways to continue its work.

11

SOME "MEN OF CONFIDENCE" OF LENIN

It did not seem possible to me to oppose the war and war's consequences single-handed. If I did not have a paper of my own to write in, I must write in other journals. If I had no organization, I must find one. There were only three organized forces opposing the war's intolerance and seeking to moderate its fury: the variegated pacifist movement, the Vatican, and the American Socialist party. The pacifist movement was too formless, disorganized, divided, and remote. I could not "join" the Vatican nor did I feel called upon to join the American Catholic Church. Though the Pope suffered for the faithful on both sides of the battle lines and sincerely urged a gentle and early peace of reconciliation, many Roman Catholic priests in our country supported the war from their pulpits. So my choice fell on the Socialist party.

I found that we could sell *Facts* at pacifist meetings and socialist meetings when other crowds might prove indifferent or hostile. To be sure, I was not a socialist nor did I rightly know what socialism meant. But as the war fever took possession of the average street crowd, the Socialists remained a courageous body that suffered persecution and mob violence, yet stood firm. Their main issues in their 1917 New York City mayoralty campaign were the same issues we had advanced in *Facts*; so I joined them while I was still editing that journal. Almost immediately, to my astonishment, they asked me to speak at street-corner meetings.

"How can I?" I asked. "I don't know enough about socialism to answer the questions listeners may ask."

"Oh, that's nothing. How many of us do? You're against the war, aren't you? You write well and speak well on the war. That's all any of us are talking about this year. Our mayoralty campaign is being run on the slogan 'A vote for Hillquit is a vote against war.' "

Thus I became a street-corner speaker twice a week at three dollars a night. I began to read Socialist pamphlets and little Socialist books out of the promptings of my own conscience, so that I might answer questions on socialism, if they were ever asked. After reading a lot of pamphlets by our most famous speakers, I still could not answer such questions, but they were never asked, for all thoughts were on the war.

Joining the Socialist party in 1917 was an entrance into an exciting new world. There were artists and writers and assorted radicals from every cause that had attracted the bohemians of Greenwich Village who were now entering the more stirring struggle against war and wartime intolerance and terror. There were veterans from bloody labor battles I had hitherto not heard of; picturesque Hindus and colorful Irishmen, many getting help from German funds in their struggle for independence from England, our new ally; veteran Marxists of every shade battling each other with probative quotations from Marx and Engels; hobo poets such as Harry Kemp; hobo painters and hobo philosophers of colorful and rugged speech and wide esoteric learning; ex-Wobblies and present ones who had ridden the rods and cooked and slept in the jungles and along the skidrows of America's great railway junctions; rugged worker-intellectuals who seemed to have stepped out of the pages of Jack London's novels, such as Joshua Wanhope, who had sailed the seven seas, was editing and writing lead editorials for the *Socialist Call,* and would ship before the mast once more when he got sick of desk confinement and the squabbles and splits between the left wings and right wings a year or two later; and there were philosophers who in some ways resembled that justly celebrated longshoreman Eric Hoffer of the present generation. In the party were a galaxy of luminaries whom I got to know from afar, and some of them more intimately and close up. There was Jack London, who had just died but was a name to conjure with, a Socialist and rugged individualist whose books inspired me but taught me nothing of socialism; Harry Waton, a solemn and comical high priest who proved everything, even the next step in organization, by a quotation either from Marx or from Spinoza or from Herbert Spencer; Louis B. Boudin, whose *Theoretical System of Karl Marx* was internationally respected as a learned weapon against "revisionism"; Morris Hillquit, who led the mayorality campaign into which I jumped; Upton Sinclair, whose novels I knew before I joined the party; Max Eastman, strikingly handsome and persuasive, in love with life and with himself, in love with poetry and humor, and seeming to me a veritable polymath; Scott Nearing, expelled successively from two universities for stubborn adherence to his principles; Big Bill Haywood, already expelled from the Socialist party for his open advocacy of violence and sabotage but still considered a Socialist; and scores more of sparkling, learned, and colorful figures from every walk of life. And there was a great inflow of young people into the ranks of the party. Like me, they knew nothing of socialism except that it seemed to stand solid and brave against war, and base itself on a long antiwar and internationalist tradition.

Standing a little apart from the rest, there was an intriguing handful of older men of mystery, who had known struggles and prison and exile in Russia or its borderlands. They assumed new interest because they gave us to understand that they really knew what was happening in far-off Russia, and because they seemed to enjoy the confidence of and carry out mysterious missions for the new regime in the Bolshevik land. They had inside knowledge of esoteric things; they were visited by underground couriers; they had known personally some of the men who headed the new regime; they talked about them and their government as if they knew and understood what was going on in the land of Lenin and Trotsky. They possessed a fund of doctrine from old and alien battles. Sometimes they had a fund of cash to dispense, too, impressive and mysterious. As "men of confidence" of Lenin or Trotsky, they were surrounded by an aura of revolutionary romance. What worlds of variegated types did Balzac create in his *Comédie Humaine,* I fondly asked myself, that were more richly peopled than this new world that was opening up to me?

Among the "men of confidence" of V. I. Lenin, or of his close associates, were Santeri Nuorteva, a Finn who had lived in this country for a number of years and edited the Fitchburg, Massachusetts, Finnish Socialist daily *Raivaaja,* and Ludwig C.A.K. Martens, a Russian of German descent. The former suddenly appeared as "diplomatic representative" of Red Finland (for the three months that it lasted), and both in turn produced credentials as official representatives of the Russian Federated Soviet Socialist Republic. Close in their confidence were two other members of their unusual diplomatic mission, Ferdinand Peterson and Jacob Nosovitsky, each of whom turned out in the end to be a member of the Department of Justice assigned to win the confidence of Nuorteva and Martens, and of the leading factions of the newborn Communist party into which it split at the moment of its birth.

To my astonishment, Ludwig C.A.K. Martens, this unrecognized representative of a poor country struggling with breakdown and chaos, set up a "bureau" of some 30-odd persons, many of whom were to play a role in my own life at a future date. High up on the ladder were A. A. Heller, commercial attaché, who would later "find" funds for setting up International Publishers, a covert Comintern publishing house; Professor J.M. Lomonosoff, in charge of the purchase of locomotives; Gregory Weinstein, chief of the Chancellory, and editor of *Novy Mir;* Morris Hillquit, as head of his legal department; Lieutenant Colonel Boris Leonidovich Tagueeff; and Roustam Bek as nominally a propagandist and trade agent, but potentially perhaps a military attaché. On the bureau were also Kenneth Durant, of the wealthy Durant locomotive family, who was later to set up the Tass Agency in the United States and be my nominal employer when I set up a Tass Bureau in Mexico, as well as my wife's employer for several years when she worked in the Tass Bureau; Evans Clark, husband of the *Nation* editor, Freda Kirchwey, economist, university educator, editor, public figure in many capacities; Isaac A. Hourwich, a Russian-American economist and statistician of good reputation; and William Malisoff, who was to play an important role in causing the burning by the publisher Horace B. Stokes of the entire edition of 2500 copies of the only novel I ever wrote.

In Martens' "bureau," Peterson, Nuorteva's personal "shadow," was eclipsed by the special shadow and confidential courier assigned to Martens jointly by Scotland Yard and our Department of Justice, agent F-100, Jacob Nosovitsky. I first met Nosovitsky in the summer of 1919, when he came to my office where I was the associate, and *de facto* the real, editor of the *Communist World*. He was dressed in a spick-and-span white uniform, with white officer's cap marking him as assistant surgeon and medical doctor of the Cunard liner S.S. *Mauretania*. He had an M.D. from Detroit Medical College,. an appointment on the *Mauretania* with the help of Scotland Yard, a generous expense account from the Yard, and a less generous one from our Department of Justice. He avowed himself "a man of confidence" in personal touch with V. I. Lenin and showed credentials as a trusted courier from the Soviet diplomatic mission of Ludwig Martens. He was about to undertake a delicate mission, that of smuggling Louis Fraina aboard his ship for a journey to a Comintern conference in Amsterdam. This was the more impressive because Fraina, of Italian origin, had been brought to America at the age of two and had never troubled to become an American citizen. Under indictment under the New York Criminal Anarchy Law and lacking citizenship, he could not conceivably have gotten a passport. Moreover, agent F-22 (Peterson), and possibly agent F-100 (Nosovitsky), was already casting suspicion on Fraina as the source of suspicious leaks to the American government. But how could I not trust the White Uniform, the self-confidence, the array of credentials? I gave him a set of the copies of the *Communist World* so far published, and asked him to give them to Lenin. Whether he did get to see Lenin I doubt, but he came back and duly reported to me that he had given Lenin the papers, and Lenin had said: "I am glad to see that there is a Communist paper published in far-off America, but I wish it looked more as if it were really published in America." Lenin himself could not have sent me a more instructive and crushing message! Nor one better earned, for the New York *Communist World* under my editorship did have too many slogans borrowed from the Russian press. Whether Lenin's or not—I suspect not—I never forgot F-100's impudent lesson! Indeed, when ten years later Stalin accused me of being an "American Exceptionalist," it is not unlikely that agent F-100's rebuke in Lenin's name had played a part in making me guilty as charged.

THE CASE OF LUDWIG MARTENS

On January 2, 1919, the attention of the press was attracted to a man calling himself Ludwig C.A.K. Martens. He had been working in the United States for some years as an engineer and attracting no attention to himself. When his name appeared in the press as one claiming to represent the Soviet government in our country, gossip spread concerning him, but he remained a dim and colorless figure. I had never heard of a man with so many initials, yet they were his all right and not a put-on. His full name turned out to be Ludwig Christian August Karl Martens, whether because he was named after so many saints or after so many rich and doting uncles. To Lenin he was known as Ludwig Karlovich. He seemed to be an ethnic German, with an aquiline nose, blue eyes, straw-colored blond hair, wispy mustache. He spoke Russian and German fluently and had a fair command of English. He had been born in Russia to German parents. He looked like an unusually slender German businessman, but had a Russian revolutionary history from 1893 on, as a student, as a prisoner, and as an emigré. That he enjoyed the confidence of Lenin was attested to by a document with Soviet seals and signatures, naming him ambassador to the United States. Though he had been in New York for some time, he did not announce his presence until he received that document from a courier who, as he swore before a congressional committee, was unknown to him by name or person when he presented himself. Neither the press nor I could make up our minds about how the courier got here and from where, but the document bore the authentic signature of *G. Chicherin,* Lenin's *Commissar for Foreign Affairs,* and was countersigned *S. Nuorteva, Secretary of the Russian Soviet Government Bureau in New York,* a bureau that would seem to have come into existence the very day the courier arrived. Our Congress and our Department of Justice conducted many investigations, but never did get to the bottom of the matter of the courier, or the source of Martens' funds, or the real mission and true identity of Ludwig Martens. And Martens never got recognition as Ambassador, any more than had his predecessor, John Reed, who had been Lenin's mischievous previous appointee to the same post.

Nor did Martens ever quite make up his mind whether he wanted to act as secret representative to the American Communist party, or agitator among the American masses, or representative of the Russian government to American businessmen and the American government. As a result of his rather uninspiring personal qualities and uncertainty as to his mission, he never made a good job of any of his efforts. Perhaps he should not be too much blamed for this, for neither Leon Trotsky, Russia's first foreign commissar, nor Lenin himself had yet made up their minds how their "official" and "unofficial" representatives were to act in foreign lands, whether as meddling revolutionaries, as businessmen, as diplomats, or as a mixture of all three.

In any case, the more our government investigated Martens, the more puzzled they were. They found out that he had served for two years in the German army prior to the war, on entry into America had registered as a German not a Russian alien, though he neglected to register as an enemy alien when we declared war on Germany. Instead he was now a Russian and an ambassador, making demands on the ambassador of the Provisional Government, Boris Bakhmetiev, to surrender the Washington embassy together with building, contents, papers, and funds. Yet, instead of going to Washington, he opened his own "embassy" in New York, two whole floors at 110 West 40 Street.

Where did he get so much money to pay handsome salaries regularly, rent ample headquarters, buy furniture and stationery, and set up a multiform, ambitious program? The main funds that made all this magnificence possible would seem to have come from Dr. Julius Hammer, another "man of confidence" of Lenin, whom I already knew quite well. Some attempts to add more funds by smuggling crown jewels from Russia fell through from mismanagement by inept couriers. Another source of money was A. A. Heller, whom Martens "appointed" to his bureau. I got to know A. A. Heller personally, yet never well enough to penetrate the mysteries that surrounded his existence and activities in our country. When I first met him, he was "commercial attaché to Martens and to the Soviet Bureau." He possessed great wealth, supposedly made from Russian manganese. He spent large sums on Martens' mission, and was arrested and deported to Riga, Latvia, in May 1921 for his secret activities in the United States as "head of the commercial department" of Martens' embassy. But he promptly returned to America as representative of the Soviet Supreme Council of National Economy *(Vesenkha)*, and was not again deported. Once admitted, he produced large funds for the founding and subsidizing of the crypto-Communist International Publishers, which still exists and has published most of the hard-cover Communist and pro-Soviet books issued in English in this country. He remained on its board of directors while the active editorship of the firm was carried on by his friend, the Communist official A. A. Trachtenberg, who in 1904 or 1905 had received the Cross of Saint George for bravery in the Russo-Japanese War.

On at least one occasion, Martens managed to secure a loan for his manifold activities from the Irish Republican Army in New York. Another unusual source of funds was never-to-be-repaid loans and donations from American businessmen who either sympathized with the Lenin-Trotsky regime (Freud's "death wish"?) or hoped to ingratiate themselves and then make huge profits by tapping the supposedly "inexhaustible" Russian market, a story that repeated itself during the "détente" illusions of the seventies. Martens persuaded one Emerson Jennings to campaign for American governmental credits to underwrite and insure trade with Russia, a mission in which Jennings failed. Further respectability and income was derived by Martens from the Russian-American Chamber of Commerce, formed to promote the ever elusive trade with Russia, and headed by Reeve Schley, a vice-president of the Rockefeller-controlled Chase National Bank, thus prefiguring the role played by the Chase Manhattan Bank in the détente enthusiasm of the seventies. If the reader be inclined to ask, "Don't our businessmen learn anything?" I can answer, "Yes, they do, for in the seventies they are asking the United States government (us, the taxpayers) to insure all loans and credits." As to what the government and the taxpayers have learned, I cannot be so sanguine.

Martens released a statement that he was ready to expend a minimum of $200 million in imports from America. Santeri Nuorteva, more imaginative, wrote in the American Labor Yearbook for 1920:

The people of Soviet Russia require a great quantity of manufactured goods, foodstuffs, cotton, etc. The imports prior to the war were about $700,000,000 annually. Considering the extra demand of the reconstruction period, of rebuilding the railway system, of creating new factories and workshops, Soviet Russia has need of purchases . . . of double that amount.

Except for gifts from a group of sympathizers calling themselves Technical Aid to Russia, not a penny of that flow of goods was realized. But Martens took advantage of the existence of the Chamber of Commerce to send "commercial attachés" as propagandists to American businessmen, urging trade on credit, gifts to Technical Aid, pressure on America to recognize his government and his embassy. He published a magazine called *Soviet Russia* which painted first the needs and difficulties, and later the wonders of the new regime and the new Soviet man. At the same time, he personally spoke at such Communist meetings as the one held in the Central Opera House in New York, where, within one week after sending his credentials to our State Department, he told a mass meeting: "Over the heads of those who are trying to divide the workers of Russia from the workers elsewhere in the world, your solidarity and affection will reach the workers of Russia and give them new strength. . . . the American workers will support my efforts." Finally, on January 2, 1920, a warrant for his arrest and deportation was issued by Attorney General Palmer, but, what with legal obstacles and delays, it took a year to execute. On January 22, 1921, he finally set sail with seventy-five other deportees on the liner *Stockholm,* and bobbed up in Russia as an aide to Lenin on technical and engineering matters, director of concessions to foreign capitalists, and a guide to Julius Hammer and his son Armand in investing their money and securing concessions.

THE STORY OF JULIUS HAMMER

Julius Hammer was born in Russia in 1874 and died in the United States in 1948. Though he spent nearly four years in Sing Sing Prison (from February 9, 1919, to January 24, 1923), he died full of honors, the honorary pallbearers at his funeral being Frederick Gimbel, Beardsley Ruml, James W. Gerard, Justices Hulburt and Botein, and many other of New York's notables. As this suggests, he was the most discreet and able of Lenin's "men of confidence" that I found in the Socialist party when I joined.

He had known Lenin personally since 1907, when he met the Bolshevik leader at the International Socialist Congress at Stuttgart. He it was who provided the bulk of the funds to sustain Ludwig Martens's embassy and directed Martens's moves. In addition, he was a leader of the left wing of the Socialist party in 1918 and 1919, which is how I came to know him well; a member with me of the executive committee of the left wing of

Local Greater New York; a founder of the American Communist party; the patron and provider of finances for the Communist Labor party, for whom he bought a building at 108 East 12th Street, which he gave them rent free as a national headquarters, and the financial angel of their weekly journal, *The Voice of Labor*. When two of their leaders, Benjamin Gitlow and James Larkin, were sent to the Tombs in lieu of bail, he bailed them out with his own Liberty Bonds for $10,000 each. Nor was this Russian money brought him by courier, for when Lenin wrote his first letter to his Central Committee concerning Dr. Hammer, he referred to him as "the American millionaire in Sing Sing prison."

Until his imprisonment, Dr. Hammer was elected to high posts first in the left wing, then in the Communist party. Yet, though he chaired big meetings, ruling discreetly in favor of the faction he favored at the moment, I never knew him to make a speech, or to lose an appeal against his rulings as chairman of a turbulent meeting.

He was a robust, stocky, swarthy man, always faultlessly dressed in a dark-blue or black suit. He wore, as the badge of the medical doctor at that time, a dignified black Vandyke. The Lusk committee, which seemed to find out almost everything about everybody it went after, found next to nothing to say when it investigated him. His boon companion was Sebald Justius Rutgers. The left wing of the Dutch Socialist Party in the Second International was led by Rutgers, Anton Panakoek, and Henrietta Roland-Holst, all three of whom were attracted to Lenin by his antiwar stand. Lenin eventually made them into scapegoats, Roland-Holst for her uncompromising pacifism, the other two for their "infantile leftism," when the Bolshevik leader needed targets for his polemics against the "infantile sickness of leftist communism." But Lenin had nothing but good to say of Julius Hammer.

When I first met Hammer, he was a medical doctor with a successful practice, but with too much money to have made it all merely by the practice of medicine. The main source of his funds was his position as founder, president, and principal stockholder of a drug and chemical company, plus his running of the blockade that England and France had decreed against Soviet Russia, denying her not only food and war supplies but also medicines, drugs, disinfectants, and bandages. Total war, as I have already observed, is exceptionally cruel, for it is above all war on women and children and the aged. Hence I found this source of much of Dr. Hammer's funds praiseworthy, as I still do today.

When Julius Hammer became more intimate with me and he learned that in my effort to understand socialism I was reading the works of the Socialist Labor party leader Daniel De Leon, he told me that he had joined the Socialist Labor party before he joined the Socialist party, and, since the SLP's official emblem was a workingman's arm holding a hammer, he had named his oldest son Armand Hammer. His other two sons, Victor (after Julius's mother, Victoria) and Harry, were less romantically named.

I worked with Julius Hammer on a number of leading committees of the Socialist party and then of its left wing. In February 1919, he served with me on a committee to draft the manifesto and program of the left wing previously mentioned. Hammer sat in on the Editorial Committee but I do not remember his making any suggestions. He served with me on a Press Committee, where he was also a silent participant, on the local Greater New York Central Committee, and on a Committee to Prepare a National Convention. On May 11, 1919, we of the left wing succeeded in electing him chairman of the City Committee, and in June 1919, we were both members of the Steering Committee supposed to "run" the chaotic First National Conference of the Left Wing of the Socialist Party of Greater New York. Yet, with all these party activities, Dr. Hammer continued to practice medicine in his office in the Bronx, advise Ludwig Martens, and trade under license with the Soviet Union under such rubrics as the Allied Chemical and Dye Corporation of the United States, and the Amerikanskaja Obedinënnaja Kompanija (Allied American Corporation). He also toured the country as Martens's "commercial attaché" to make contacts with American businessmen, in order to foster recognition and trade with Russia.

In the summer of 1920, Dr. Julius Hammer suddenly disappeared from his usual party haunts, his committees, meetings, and posts of honor. From sensational stories in the press we soon learned why.

On June 26, 1920, a jury in a Bronx County court had found Dr. Julius Hammer guilty of manslaughter in the first degree in an abortion case. The prosecution charged that on July 5, 1919, the defendant "feloniously caused the death of one Marie Oganessoff," the wife of a former member of the Russian embassy, who had given his consent to the operation. He brought on the death, according to the indictment, by performing a curettage to bring on an abortion in a woman who had been pregnant for over a month, carrying out the operation in his office without a nurse. In his trial he had not succeeded in establishing to the satisfaction of the jury that the operation in question "was necessary to preserve her life." The penal law of New York State at the time explicitly forbade the procuring of a miscarriage under any circumstances other than that of being "necessary to preserve the life" of the woman operated on.

Four hundred physicians presented a petition to Presiding Judge Gibbs in which they said that a sentence of "up to 20 years" such as the law provided would fill all physicians with fear, and they might let women die rather than perform a curettage, if a jury of mere laymen was to decide whether the operation was "necessary to save life." The law, they said, should have been repealed years ago, and they would start a drive to have it repealed. But the Bronx County Medical Society went on record as "upholding the laws as interpreted by the court."

The question of the legalizing of a medically induced miscarriage is, of course, much more troubled than those dealing with other forms of birth control. As I write now, well over a half century after Hammer was convicted, the issue is still not finally decided in our country. The "two centuries" of which I write run into each other in this, so that the closing decades of the present one may still be taken up with the fluctuating fortunes of the conflict. Especially in the days of Hammer's trial, the shadow of illegality and crime, the secrecy, haste and shame, the sometimes questionable go-betweens, the lack of proper medical or hospital surroundings, the fantastic prices and real physical dangers that go with outlawry, all made it seem more dangerous and questionable than it is or need be.

On September 18, 1920, Julius Hammer entered Sing Sing Prison to serve a term of from three and one-half to 15 years. *The New York Times* gloated on its editorial page: "Justice Is Proved Impartial." Dr. Hammer, the editorial said, had both money ("something like a million") and influence, but all that these had done for him was "to lengthen somewhat a trial that otherwise would have been a short one." His punishment was fully deserved, and, "if the punishment errs, it is on the side of lenience." The editors expressed the hope that he might serve "for the better part of fifteen years." Yet when Dr. Hammer died, the *Times* obit, perhaps on the principle of *nihil nisi bonum,* did not even mention his sentence, his "felony," or his jail term.

In Sing Sing, Julius Hammer did not lose his air of dignity; even in prison garb he carried himself as if he were well dressed. He did the work assigned to him, often helped out in medical matters, and when Jim Larkin and Ben Gitlow were transferred from Dannemora to Sing Sing, they were delighted to find Hammer there to guide them in the mysteries of prison life.

After a little over a year of uneventful life in prison, Dr. Hammer hit the headlines again with the startling story that "the Allied Drug and Chemical Corporation, of which Dr. Julius Hammer, serving a term in Sing Sing for criminal abortion, was President" had just received the "first concession made to an American firm by the Soviet Government to operate asbestos mines in the Ural Mountains at Alapayevsk." It was the Soviet government that released the news, for it was eager to use this concessionaire and his son and representative as bellwethers to lure other American capitalists into investing in concessions in the Soviet Union. The news caused a flurry of excitement. The Department of Justice, *The New York Times* financial section, and other agencies, began investigating the mystery of how a man in prison could get a concession in far-off Russia. These investigations, publicized largely in the financial section of *The New York Times,* gave us who were interested some additional information concerning Julius Hammer as businessman, concessionaire, and financier. "A concession in Russia when you're a jailbird in Sing Sing, New York," said one of my economist friends to me with unconcealed admiration, "that's a great trick!"

How the trick was turned is somewhat obscured by Armand Hammer, who leaves his father and his father's "million or so" quite out of the picture, and portrays himself as having done the whole thing alone. But Lenin's letters tell the story more clearly. On October 14, 1921, Lenin addressed an urgent note "To the Members of the R.C.P. (B.) C.C., Attention, all members of the C.C." The note read:

> Reinstein informed me yesterday that the American millionaire *Hammer,* who is Russian-born (he is in prison on a charge of illegally procuring an abortion; actually, it is said, in revenge for his communism), is prepared to give the Ural workers *1,000,000 poods of grain* on very easy terms (5 percent) and to take *Urals valuables* on commission for sale in America.
>
> This Hammer's son (and partner), a doctor, is in Russia, and has brought Semashko $60,000 worth of surgical instruments as a gift. The son has visited the Urals with Martens and has decided to rehabilitate the Urals industry.
>
> An official report will be made by *Martens.*
>
> Lenin *

Julius Hammer was paroled from Sing Sing on January 24, 1923, and promptly left for Russia. How his son and he divided their duties as concessionaires, I do not know, but both stayed on in the Soviet Union until their concession lapsed, as well as their concession to operate the first Soviet pen-and-pencil factory. They sold their holdings to the Soviet government at handsome prices, and, unlike less favored capitalists such as Harriman and Urquart and the Swedish SKF ball-bearing firm, were allowed to convert their rubles into tangible and valuable objects for export, such as skins and furs, caviar, and a remarkable collection of art masterpieces which the Soviet censorship was chary about exhibiting to native artists, or to a public that was having Socialist realism dinned into it. The Hammers also got possession of precious chasubles, icons, crowns, scepters, jewels, and art objects expropriated from the old royalty and nobility. These formed the nucleus of a new business for the Hammer family, the famous Hammer Galleries, in which Hammer's wife and his sons were active. It has since been used on occasion as an outlet for the Soviet government of yet other precious art objects.

When Julius Hammer and his family left Russia for America I do not

* Boris Reinstein was a former member of the American Socialist Labor Party, and a friend of Julius Hammer. Semashko was the commissar of health. A pood is about 36 pounds avoirdupois so that 1 million poods would be 36 million pounds of grain. The 5 percent would suggest 5 percent on the world price of the grain. The notes to Lenin's letters in his works indicate that Julius Hammer was chairman of the board of a U.S. concession, Almerico, for developing the Alapayevsk asbestos mines in the Urals, the first Type I concession granted to an American firm, the Allied Chemical and Dye Corporation of the United States, whose subsidiary, the Allied American Corporation, owned by the Hammers, had been operating under license in the USSR since 1918, selling pharmaceuticals to the Soviet government. Armand Hammer, Julius's son, is listed as secretary of the Allied American Corporation and managed the concession while his father, its chairman, was serving his term in Sing Sing.

know, but while I was in Moscow during the first half of 1929, Julius Hammer was still there.

About Armand Hammer I have little to say, for I never met him personally. Judging from Lenin's notes to his aides, Armand was less Lenin's "man of confidence" than he has suggested in his own press releases. Thus on October 19, 1921, Lenin wrote to Ludwig Martens raising the question of whether "Hammer is in earnest about his plan to supply 1 million poods of grain (it is my impression . . . that he is, and that the plan is not mere empty talk)." "If Hammer is in earnest . . . you must try to give the whole matter the precise juridical form of a contract or *concession*. Let it be a *concession*, even if a fictitious one (asbestos or any other Ural valuables or whatever you will). To us it is important to show and get published . . . that the Americans *have entered* into *concessions*. Politically that is what is important."

And in another note to Martens, who was in charge of concessions, Lenin gives special emphasis to the exact terms of the contract, the exact wording, the careful check on *actual* fulfillment, and he adds once more how important Armand Hammer is as the bellwether to induce other American capitalists to invest (the same role Armand tried to play in the seventies). Lenin concludes this note with the words, "We must make a special effort to *nurse* the concessionaires: we must *woo* [*ukhazhivat*] the concessionaires energetically: this is superimportant both economically and politically. . . . it is very important to publish as widely as possible the facts about concessions and contracts." In a letter to the members of the Politburo dated May 24, 1922, Lenin wrote urging "*particular* support" to this first concession given to "Dr. Julius Hammer and his son, Armand," because "this is a small path leading to the American business world and this path should be made use of *in every way*." At the same time Lenin ordered a report to the head of the Cheka, F. E. Dzerzhinsky, and to the members of the Politburo on "Dr. J. Hammer and his son Armand Hammer, and their Allied Drug and Chemical Company" which he classified as "*to be shown in strict secrecy.*"

There were a number of other mysterious and fascinating figures who to one degree or another served as "men of confidence" of the Russian Bolshevik party and its leaders. An interesting example was Michael Borodin, who became prominent in the twenties as the Russians attempted to gain preponderant influence in Republican China, then under the leadership of Sun Yat-sen. But some of these men disappeared from my view, and others, like Borodin, did not become important until later in my story. In any case, it is time for me to cease talking of these characters, and to tell something of my own activities and experiences in the Socialist party.

12

IN THE SOCIALIST PARTY

Though I became an active member of the Sixth Assembly District of the Socialist Party, took the floor at weekly meetings, got elected to the County and City Committees, and became a successful street-corner speaker, my ignorance of what socialism was continued to trouble me. Indeed, I was somewhat ashamed of the leaders who were willing to make me a party spokesman after I told them that I could not answer questions on socialism if anyone in my audiences should ask them.

I decided to read up on the subject, but what should I read? I was given a list of Socialist "theoreticians" or "intellectuals" such as John Spargo, A. M. Simons, and William English Walling. However, when America declared war on Germany, they had all left the party and declared themselves pro-Wilson, prowar and pro-Allies. If that was the strength of their socialist theory, I would have none of it.

I tried the pamphlets written and published by our best street-corner speakers, only to find them insubstantial fare. Except for George R. Kirkpatrick's *War—What for?* I couldn't even lift any phrases out of them to strengthen my street-corner speeches. I turned to Louis B. Boudin's solid *Theoretical System of Karl Marx,* my first encounter with a defense of orthodox Marxism against the efforts of Eduard Bernstein, Engels's executor, to update Marxism by taking into account economic and political developments since Marx's death, but I noted to my dismay the strong streak of pro-Allied sentiment in Boudin's latest work, *Socialism and War.*

I turned to Daniel De Leon, the dogmatic, self-confident leader of the Socialist Labor party whose chief mission in life had become that of criticizing the IWW and the American Socialist party from his sectarian sanctuary. His *Two Pages from Roman History* proved first-rate as a piece of literature but of little help in deriving from the experiences and errors of the Gracchi any directions for the tactics of a modern Socialist party directions for the tactics of a modern Socialist party. In the end I was driven to the writings of Marx and Engels, their shorter works, then the three volumes of Marx's *Kapital.* By then my purpose had become rather narrow, for by that time I was one of the young leaders of the young left wing of the Socialist Party, looking for *ipse dixit* quotations to disconcert older "right-wing" and "centrist" opponents, most of whom called themselves Marxists but had never read the Marxist classics at all and had no counter-quotations ready at hand to answer us. (They could have found plenty had they known their Marx, for in his writings there are to be found the most contrary propositions, moods, attitudes, pronouncements, unified by a single person and a single temperament rather than by any systematic logic or consistency: indeed, there are in Marx's works a Marx for Kautsky and a Marx for Bernstein, a Marx for Plekhanov and for Axelrod, a Marx for Martov, and a Marx for Lenin.) In any case, the study of Marx and Marxism that I then began as a novice in the Socialist movement was to occupy me intermittently from that day to this, its latest product being my *Marxism: 100 Years in the Life of a Doctrine,* published in 1965.

As I read and read with the aim of making myself a more knowledgeable street-corner orator, almost unconsciously I entered into the age of ideologies. The certitudes of Marx and Engels and their orthodox disciples, the certitudes of a Daniel De Leon or a Morris Hillquit, a Louis Boudin or a Harry Waton, a Bill Haywood or a Louis Fraina, were all ideological certitudes. In the Socialist party we fought each other in the name of a common ideology adhered to unquestioningly by all of us. We talked in terms of isms, each claiming to be the true heir of Marxism. Unknowingly, in my debates as a "left-winger" with "right-wing" Socialists, I was staking out a claim that I was a better Marxist and that my variant of Marxism was the only proper Marxism. Though I had not been a Socialist, I now began to feel myself a Marxist.

It was the French Revolution that opened the age of ideologies; the nineteenth century in which I was born was the century that saw the development of all the leading ideologies of the modern world: socialism, communism, anarchism, nationalism, and, for want of a better term, something that might be called *noveltyism,* or the cult of the "new," the "latest," the "most modern"—the homage paid to an idea, a procedure, an object, a style, or even a term, that might be boasted of as "new," "modern," "the latest"—a kind of *get-with-it-ism. (Il faut être absolument moderne.*—Rimbaud.)

The ideological terms that I was learning to use all had their birth dates in the nineteenth or early twentieth century. According to the Oxford English Dictionary, *industrialism* was first used in English in 1831; *socialism* in French in 1832 and in English in 1839; *communism* was used by Marx in a derogatory and hostile sense in 1843, and in a favorable sense in the *Communist Manifesto* in 1848; the term *proletariat* in its modern sense first appeared in England around 1850 and in America in 1878; *imperialism* appeared in an unfavorable context in its use by Hobson in 1902; *syndicalism* made its appearance in 1907; *communism* in its modern meaning after 1917; and *totalitarianism* was born in the lexicon of Italy in 1925.

Significantly, there is no Lockeism, Adam Smithism, Millism, Weberism, Schumpeterism, Durkheimism, Taineism, Micheletism, Rankeism, Gibbonism, or Keynesism, but everybody speaks of Marxism. "If as a science," I was to write much later, "Marxism has been stripped down to a method that has yielded only invalid or unmeaningful results, its real staying power lies in the fact that it is also an *ism,* i.e., a faith." I often wavered, but insofar as I began to accept Marxism and claim to be a Marxist, I was accepting it as a faith. Indeed, a number of American psychoanalysts have recognized and accepted it for themselves, or recommended it to certain of their patients, as a "therapeutic ideology." They see in it a cure for doubt, the provision of a purpose for living where life has seemed purposeless, an assurance of a kind of anonymous immortality, and a sublimating outlet for aggression.

And indeed as I continued reading, the faith began to take possession of me. Its appeal derived in part from the fact that it was an untried ideal and that it was learnedly propounded. It was clever of Marx to marshall all his learning into a critique of capitalism (all his leading works contain the word *critique* in their titles) and avoid as "unscientific" any attempt to picture the future society that was to replace the one he was criticizing. Clearing the ground—"creative destruction"—was all he offered. The future would take care of itself, if we but gave it a chance for free play. Hence *Das Kapital, Kritik der politischen Ökonomie,* and his *Grundrisse der Kritik der politischen Ökonomie* were studies of capitalism and not at all of socialism.

For me, as for most sensitive persons, the existing society had many obvious defects, imperfections, things that could be improved, shortcomings from our dreams of perfection. One felt superior when he noted and criticized those imperfections and offered a learned-sounding, never spelled out, untried and untested remedy that cured everything at once by a simple change in property relations.

Institutions were imperfect, leading citizens were imperfect, officials were imperfect, the elite was imperfect, and the common man was imperfect. There was ugliness, greed, vulgarity, brutality, misery, all around one. How nice to think that one had answers to all problems, cures for all ills, a simple, certain, manifest remedy backed by books of enormous learning. How easy and satisfying to criticize if one had all the solutions in a single doctrine, almost a single gimmick: the alteration of property relations. And how wonderful, when one did not understand the past or the present, to be so certain of the future. Thus Marxism provided the first constituent element of modern totalitarianism, the total rejection of the entire existing society, and all that man had developed through the uncounted millennia of his existence on the face of the earth.

To be sure, there were problems, and questions, in the back of my mind. If socialism was so near, why were we not beginning to answer some questions about the future society? How would we get there without knowing where we were going? What was meant by the terms *socialize* or *own in common*? Was everything to be owned by the state, run by the state, resolved by the state? How were we to get officials who were wise and virtuous and efficient and all-knowing? As I looked at the officials we were getting by the democratic process in New York City, or the state, or the nation, I wondered what would happen if everything were to be concentrated in their hands. A hard look at the leaders of the Socialist party made me wonder, too. Or, if the unions were to own and run industries and dicker and bargain with each other and with the nonunionized majority, would that be any better? If equality of portions of the social product was to be substituted for equality of opportunity, what would happen to the pursuit of excellence, the right and duty to strive to excel, and what would happen to individual variety and difference? But I persuaded myself that a doctrine that contained so many answers to so many questions must have answers to my uncertainties also. Moreover, the "movement" I had joined—and it was more a *movement* than a party like other parties—was giving me so many interesting tasks to perform, and taking so much of my time and energy, that it scarcely left time to question and wonder.

But clearly, I am running ahead of my story. When I entered the Socialist Party it was to fight the evils attendant upon the atmosphere of total war. I was not a Socialist, nor did I have any idea of forming a "left wing." My recent growing concern with socialism was a by-product of my effort to learn what I was talking about when I spoke on street corners. My role in forming a "left wing" was to arise out of things that occurred after I had been in the Socialist Party for the better part of a year, and I shall come to them later.

At the outset I became a member of the Sixth Assembly District of Kings County, attended its weekly meetings, accepted a post as member of its Executive Committee, as a delegate to the Kings County Executive Committee, and then to the Greater New York City Committee. At that point, Julius Gerber, the city organizer, took notice of my existence and told me that I was "good material" for a Socialist assemblyman in the New York State legislature. "You are not eligible for such a nomination until you have been two years in the party, but in the meanwhile I suggest that you study law. An assemblyman's job is not really a full-time job, nor a well-paying one, but if you are a lawyer, you have a profession to fall back on, and you are better prepared to draft legislation."

I was flattered, yet more bewildered than ever that one so ignorant of the history and nature of socialism could be thought of as a spokesman in the legislature. We elected ten assemblymen from greater New York that autumn in the Hillquit campaign, and my Sixth Assembly District was one with many socialist voters. So my wife and I both registered at the New York University Law School. We had excellent teachers, particularly Vanderbilt on contracts (he later became Chief Justice of the Supreme Court of the State of New Jersey), and Burnett on real property. My wife and I soon felt that we would not want to be lawyers, since we would be obligated to fight for whichever side hired us, whether they were right or wrong; so we dropped law after the first year. But I was to find my knowledge of the law of contracts useful when I began making contracts with publishers, and when I helped the Writers Guild to draft a model contract. As for the law of real property, it taught me more about economics than I had learned in my economics course at City College. In the thirties and forties, I was to face a number of lawsuits involving the law of literary property. Since I could not afford to hire a lawyer and found that few lawyers knew anything about the law of literary property, I boned up on the subject myself, then fought and won a libel suit and a publisher's damage suit. In any case, I found that the few hours a week spent for one school year in the New York University Law School were not wasted.

In the late autumn of the first year of my membership in the Socialist party, Bertha Mailly, Executive Secretary of the Rand School of Social Science sent for me. "Comrade Wolfe," she said, "we're having trouble with the Rand School New Year's Eve Ball. Frederick Blossom is handling our publicity, but he doesn't seem to be able to put the New Year's Eve Ball across. We've taken a big hall, the Grand Central Palace; it looks as if it will be more than half empty. Would you be willing to help us? The job pays twenty-five dollars a week, and you would work for us for the next three months."

I had just thrown up my job as editor of the *Mediator*, organ of the Jewish Master Bakers' Federation, because its owner, one Morse M. Frankel, had demanded that I write an editorial blackmailing the Fleischmann's Yeast Company as "anti-Semitic" because they had refused to take an advertisement in the Jewish Master Bakers' journal. I will look for a new job after New Year's, I thought, so I accepted the Rand School offer.

I looked at the New Year's Ball advertising budget, which seemed adequate. I called on the aid of an experienced advertising man, who was a devoted Socialist, Arthur Rosenberg. He gave me some sound advice, and helped me design a black ball with the words cut out in white: "Rand School Ball." I made the ball in two sizes. Then I put ads in all the Socialist papers in all the languages in which they were published. The advertisements ranged from one inch single-column to four inches double-column, with the ball in the right-hand corner and the simple legend: "Where else can you spend New Year's Eve with so many friends and comrades as at the Grand Central Palace? Tickets 50¢ in advance—75¢ at the door." We printed ten thousand tickets with the same little ball on them. The tickets began to sell. As the demand for tickets grew we finally shifted to Madison Square Garden, and we began to advertise it as "The Dance of the Ten Thousand." On New Year's Eve the Garden's dance floor was so crowded that there was no room to dance, the conversation so animated that one could scarcely hear the two bands we had hired. Yet everyone counted the ball a great success. And Bertha Mailly asked me whether I wouldn't become publicity director of the Rand School. I asked

Frederick Blossom how he felt. He answered that he did not like publicity work, was not good at it, and would be glad if I took over. Thus began my career as labor educator, which was to last until I became a free-lance writer.

That same autumn, Albert Pauley, organizer of Local Kings (County), sent for me. "Comrade Wolfe," he said, "I have a tough job for you, if you'll take it."

"What is it?"

"Abraham Shiplacoff—you know him? He's the assemblyman of the Twenty-third Assembly District. That's Brownsville. The district is mostly Jewish: cloakmakers, garment workers, union members, readers of the *Jewish Daily Forward.* But the Ocean Hill section of the district is Irish Catholic, and Tammany is strong there. The last time Shiplacoff tried to speak on one of the street corners in their end of the district, they shouted him down, and someone hit him over the head with a soda pop bottle. He had to have three stitches. Imagine, *their assemblyman!* We haven't held a meeting there since. Would you be willing to try to open up that corner again, so that their legally elected assemblyman may have a chance to get a hearing now that he's running for reelection?"

I thought for a moment what I would say to young Irish street-corner loafers. In my boyhood I had had my hard knocks from the Atkins Avenue Gang, gone to school with them, and thought I knew them well enough. "If you'll give me a bodyguard of a dozen or so young comrades, men and women, it doesn't matter which, I'll try."

"Good boy, Bert," said Pauley, using my first name for the first time in addressing me. We picked the following Friday night.

We left our Brownsville clubhouse in sizable numbers, put up our "soapbox"—actually a well-built speaker's stand with an inclined ladder of four steps, a small platform, and a solid railing on front and sides. We hung our American flag from the front rail, and the banner of the district on a pole. A menacing crowd gathered, shouting, hooting, but I faced them confidently for a friendly guard of socialist comrades was between them and me. And I bore in mind the advice that my pedagogy teacher, Paul Klapper, had given on how to conduct oneself as a new substitute teacher facing a new class determined to make life miserable for him. I faced the hostile crowd, erect, as dignified as I could look, acting as if I had something important to tell them as soon as they grew quiet. Gradually their curiosity got the better of them; someone hissed, "*Sh-h-h,*" they grew still.

"His Holiness the Pope and the international Socialist movement," I began, "are the only ones who are concerning themselves with the problems of an early and decent peace in the midst of this terrible, bloody, endless war." The silence grew absolute, the faces tense and watchful, as they waited to see what I was going to say next. I delivered what more or less was my usual talk on war and peace and freedom, but shuttled back and forth from the Catholic Church to the Second International, emphasizing that both organizations had followers in every country, on both sides of the battle lines, and were alike interested in an early and just peace that would leave behind it no rancor for another world war.

How long I spoke I do not know, perhaps a half hour, perhaps more. Apparently someone had left my audience to tell the Tammany leader in his clubhouse nearby what was taking place. Suddenly a new group appeared at the back of the steadily growing crowd, manifestly a group that had just been dispatched from the Democratic clubhouse to start trouble. They were mostly young men. They had been drinking, and from the pockets of their jackets or the back pockets of their pants protruded whiskey bottles. I decided on a hasty windup of my talk, thanked the audience for their close attention, and, surrounded by my bodyguard, went off to the Brownsville Labor Lyceum whence we had come. I was able to report to Albert Pauley that I had opened up Ocean Hill again, but that extreme tact and watchfulness were necessary if we were to hold further meetings there. My opening sentence at the meeting was repeated everywhere. My stock as a speaker went up. I was raised to a main speaker, which meant that I would speak last instead of trying to hold the crowd until the main speaker arrived. My compensation was raised to five dollars a night. And Assemblyman Shiplacoff became my friend.

THE RAND SCHOOL OF SOCIAL SCIENCE

My work as an official of the Rand School began pleasantly. I was given a dignified title (Publicity Director), an office, some secretarial help and the right to plan my own activities. Like everything in the Socialist movement of New York after the strikingly successful Hillquit mayorality campaign, one voter in every five having voted the Socialist ticket, the school was growing rapidly and its officials and students were full of optimism. It had begun modestly in 1906 with income derived from the Rand Fund set up by Mrs. Carrie Rand and her daughter, Mrs. Carrie Rand Herron. It was housed first in one and then in another partially sublet old brownstone front house, both of them on East 19th Street, and had run for twelve years on an operating deficit made up by contributions from individuals and socialistically inclined trade unions. Driven from these brownstone houses as they were being torn down to give way to loft buildings, at this moment of rapid growth it was suddenly offered the Y.W.C.A. building at 7 East 15th Street, constructed as if to its order and sold to it for one quarter of the half million dollars it had cost to construct it. Here it could get income by renting the upper floors to trade unions, to Socialist party offices, and kindred organizations. It could set up an auditorium, a library, a bookstore, a cafeteria, classrooms, and offices, a clubroom for students, and even a gymnasium. The number of persons registered for classes and lecture courses had grown from something like 250 in its first year to over 1,500 at the moment when I became its Publicity Director.

My duties included the interviewing of a fascinating group of teachers and lecturers, ranging from recently expelled university professors such as Scott Nearing and Henry Wadsworth Longfellow Dana to Roger Baldwin and Frank Harris, in order to prepare publicity copy on their lectures or courses for use in the press, in circulars, in advertisements, and in the school catalogue. My wife was hired to teach English to its foreign-born students. I did a little teaching myself, and sometimes served as chairman of auditorium lectures. An account of one such occasion, the most exciting, will suffice. We engaged Frank Harris to give a lecture on Shakespeare, and I was delegated to act as his chairman. To my consternation, he refused to go out on the platform unless the water pitcher on the lecture table were filled not with water but another colorless liquid that looked like water but was pure gin. Somehow, I procured a quart of gin while the audience waited, added some ice in hopes of diluting it, and watched with foreboding as he poured himself half tumbler after half tumbler, and drank each off as if it were water. His legs became a little unsteady, his speech thicker, and he held onto the lectern as he talked. But the more he drank, the more brilliant his discursive talk became. No one but Bertha Mailly and I knew the secret of the water pitcher, and the lecture proved to be a startling success. Still we decided not to take another chance: his role as a Rand School lecturer ended as it had begun, with that sparkling talk on Shakespeare.

Later my work at the Rand School became less pleasant as I became identified with the leadership of the left wing of the Socialist Party of New York, while the American Socialist Society, which nominally ran the school, voted overwhelmingly to support the right wing of the Socialist Party. As the situation became more intolerable I resigned my post, carrying off as a trophy a complete copy of the mailing list which, it seemed to me, belonged to the entire Socialist movement, and hence to the left wing as well as the right. I did not steal the official list of names and addresses but laboriously copied them one by one. Of the three-person directorial staff, Algernon Lee, educational director, Bertha Mailly, executive secretary, and Alexander Trachtenberg, director of research, the first two remained permanently with the Socialist Party, while Trachtenberg, after a few years of wavering and maneuvering, joined the Communist Party, and became the director of the Comintern publishing house, International Publishers. As for the Rand School itself, its fortunes declined along with those of the Socialist Party. Nothing remains of it today except its vacation resort, Camp Tamamint, which has become a dear and prosperous resort for well-to-do vacationers. Its valuable library was given to the nearby library of New York University, where its collection remains intact and open to scholars and students of the Socialist and labor movements that may want to consult it.

THE SOCIALIST PARTY DEVELOPS WINGS

When I deliver lectures on the Soviet Union, Marxism, Communist totalitarianism, and kindred subjects, and open the meeting to questions with "no holds barred," one of the questions asked by students is, "Why did you (or how could you have) joined the Communist Party?" My answer is: "I never did, I could not conceivably have joined the Communist Party that approved the blood purges in Russia, the forced collectivization, the concentration camps, the Stalin-Hitler Pact. I did not join a Communist Party; I was one of the founders of the Communist Party of the United States. When I helped to found it, I had no idea that it would develop into an agency of a foreign power or an instrument of the Stalin faction and the Stalintern." Now I must try to tell how I came to be one of the founders of the left wing of the Socialist Party and how it developed into the Communist Party of America.

Though I did not realize it when I joined the Socialist Party, it had always been too alien to America, too Marxist, too much tormented by factional struggles that largely reflected struggles in the European Social Democratic parties. To be sure, it always had a native American contingent or "wing," consisting predominantly of Christian Socialists, or sometimes of disillusioned Single Taxers and Populists, sometimes of large contingents of Western trade unionists or farmers, sometimes of "Okies" or "Californiacs." This American strain showed itself in such leaders as Haywood, Debs, and Norman Thomas, in the fact that Upton Sinclair was nearly swept into the governorship of California during his EPIC campaign, or that the Socialist vote in Oklahoma during much of the first decade and a half of the twentieth century was proportionately the largest Socialist vote in the nation, at times reaching one-third of the total vote in that state.

However, when the Socialists managed to get a lone congressman into the House of Representatives, it was Victor Berger from the overwhelmingly German Milwaukee, steeped in German Social Democratic tradition, or Meyer London from a predominantly Jewish district of New York City, where the leading Socialist theoreticians resided after the secession of the prowar intellectuals at the beginning of America's entrance into the First World War.

Before 1912, Socialist strength was largely concentrated in the agrarian and mining areas of the West, but by 1920 New York contributed more than one fifth of Debs's total vote of over 900,000. As the native Americans from the West and Southwest dropped away for various reasons, the foreign federations began to grow in numbers, influenced by the excitements of the war and the Socialist factional struggles in their native lands, until by 1919 over half the members of the Socialist Party of America (some 53 percent) were members of the party through membership in one of these ancillary foreign federations, particularly the Russian, the Ukrainian, the South Slavic, the Lithuanian, the Lettish, and the Finnish.

Unknown to me, who was ignorant of Socialist Party history, there had been terrific factional battles in the Socialist movement, often involving fistfights, broken heads, and police intervention, prior to the fight in which I was now to engage. The most recent and greatest of these battles had been the struggle between Daniel De Leon and Morris Hillquit and their followers that resulted in the split of the Socialist movement into the Socialist Party and the Socialist Labor Party at the turn of the century, and the fight with Bill Haywood on the question of the use of violence and sabotage as weapons in the class struggle, in 1912.

Since the Socialist Party of America had been so concerned with its purity and orthodoxy that it refused to accept American society as it actually was as a basis for its work, refused to make any reasonably practical or popular suggestions for piecemeal reforms, and even feared to contaminate itself by permitting its members to strive for election to executive posts or to accept administrative appointments "under capitalism"—in short, failed to become a part of American life as the British Labour party did of British life, it tended to live not by practical political standards but by ideological ones. This made it perpetually prey to contending orthodoxies and heresies and to a succession of "left wings" and "right wings," usually too busy fighting each other to concern themselves with the defects in American society or to propose practical improvements. Though the party did not lack native American leaders and sizable American contingents, particularly in the West and Southwest, increasingly in the first two decades of the twentieth century it attracted recent European immigrants who brought with them memories of the traditions and factional divisions in the lands of their origin. Their feet were in America, their heads and hearts in the "old country."

Thus the penultimate left wing tried to get going in a house in Brooklyn in the middle of January 1917, a few months before I joined the Socialist Party, and a year before I dreamed of helping to form a left wing. Those who started, or perhaps I should say, tried to start, this left wing, were all immigrants. The home in which this score or so of immigrants from Europe met was that of Ludwig Lore, trained in the German Social Democracy, then an immigrant to America and a leading figure in the American Socialist party and its wartime left wing, and the editor of the New York *Volkszeitung*. The two other American figures present at the meeting of the twenty "left wingers" were Louis B. Boudin, lawyer and Socialist theoretician of considerable learning, who had been born in Russia but had come to the United States as a young man and had studied law at the New York University Law School, and Louis Fraina, Italian-born, who had been brought to this country at the age of two, had risen in the Socialist Labor Party to the point of being Daniel De Leon's associate editor of the *Daily People*, then had recently switched to the Socialist Party, and was the theoretician and moving spirit of the Socialist Propaganda League of America, with headquarters in Boston. (There was also one other representative of the Socialist Propaganda League named John

D. Williams, who quite likely was American or Canadian by birth but who apparently did not open his mouth at the meetings and was never heard from again.) And there was Sen Katayama from Japan, who had become internationally famous because he had embraced and kissed Plekhanov at an International Socialist Congress during the Russo-Japanese War, an embrace which had no effect upon the war or the Socialist International. There was the Dutch leftist engineer Sebald Justius Rutgers. And there were five recently arrived Russian exiles: Gregory Chudnovsky, former Plekhanovite Menshevik, had come to America in late 1916 and had immediately burrowed into the Russian Federation here and become one of the editors of the New York Russian Socialist journal *Novy Mir (New World)*; the other four, who had landed in New York only two months before or even more recently, were Nikolai Bukharin, Alexandra Kollontay, V. Volodarsky—all of whom immediately found a home as editors or contributors to *Novy Mir*—and, finally, Leon Trotsky, who had gotten off the boat only the day before (January 13, 1917) and had been invited by Bukharin to attend the meeting on January 14 in Ludwig Lore's home. Such was the group who, knowing next to nothing about America and even less about the American Socialist Party, came together in Ludwig Lore's home and prepared with complete insouciance to tell the Socialist party what to do and what kind of "left wing" it should have. (I must make an exception of three of those present: Louis Boudin, Louis Fraina, and their host, Ludwig Lore, all three of whom knew a great deal about America, remained in it, and played important roles in the founding of the left wing which we were to organize at the end of the same year.)

It was the Russians, with their superior experience in factional fighting and their greater articulateness in political discussion, who dominated the meeting that night. Trotsky and Bukharin carried their Russian differences into the meeting, attempting to impose them upon the Socialist Party. Bukharin, faithfully following Lenin's slogan "Splits, splits, and splits," proposed not to try to win the Socialist Party for their "left-wing" position, but to split off and form a separate organization, as Lenin had done between 1903 and 1912. He did not know, nor did he ask, what the mood of the majority of American Socialists was or their attitude toward the issues raised that night. Trotsky, knowing still less from his twenty-four hours on American soil, proposed to stay in the Socialist Party to try to win it, following his own habits as sole leader of the "unity faction" in Russian affairs. With the support of Boudin and Fraina and Lore, Trotsky won out, thus talking himself into leadership of this would-be American left wing. Almost exactly two months after this meeting in Lore's home, Nicholas II abdicated. The five Russians all left their new home without leaving any impression upon it, except insofar as they did so through the success of their *coup d'état* in November. Trotsky, as elected head of the Soviet and the Military Revolutionary Committee, engineered the mechanics of the coup, and became first Commissar of Foreign Affairs and then Commissar of War. Bukharin became the editor of *Pravda* and the most important party theoretician. Alexandra Kollontay became Commissar for Social Welfare. Chudnovsky helped to lead the far from brilliantly organized attack on the Petrograd Winter Palace, became its commandant, and later was killed on the Kiev front during the civil war that followed Lenin's seizure of power. Volodarsky was assassinated in 1918. But their brief presence in America, their attempt to found a left wing, and their brief stay on the editorial board of *The Class Struggle*, edited by Lore, Boudin, and Fraina, left a romantic memory to build on when we formed a new left wing of the Socialist Party at the end of that same year.

13

WE FORM A LEFT WING

When I joined the Socialist Party I did so because it seemed unshakably antiwar. There was a close relationship between the Socialist and the pacifist movements, so I moved easily from one to the other. Both were sustained and supported by the fact that the majority of Americans had been utterly against our entering into "Europe's bloody and senseless war."

There seemed every reason for the American Socialist Party to stand firm, as the IWW actually did until it died of the wounds delivered by wartime courts and police. Unlike the European parties, the American party had not been taken by surprise. It did not feel the feverish excitement that the Socialists of the Allied lands of Europe felt at the invasion of neutral Belgium, nor the apprehension felt by the German Socialists when their country faced a two-front war.

The American Socialist Party had the advantage of geographical and political remoteness and three years during which to make up its mind to oppose our entrance, to set itself against the war fever, and be proof against the President's factitious slogans.

As Winston Churchill and Arthur Link both have written, the decision to enter or not to enter depended on "the will of one man." When it became clear to the Socialist Party that Wilson had decided on war, the Socialists still had a few weeks to formulate their attitude and plan their action. As mentioned in Chapter 9, one day after war was declared by Congress, they were able to open an emergency convention in St. Louis, where the traditional "rights" and the traditional "lefts," thanks to Hillquit's skillful maneuvering, united in their acceptance of an antiwar document known as the St. Louis Resolution. Its authors were Algernon Lee and Morris Hillquit of the "right" and C. E. Ruthenberg, leader of the "old left" that had long dominated the Socialist Party of Ohio. "We brand the declaration of war by our Government," said the St. Louis manifesto, "as a crime against the nations of the world. In all modern history, there has been no war more unjustifiable than the war in which we are about to engage. No greater dishonor has ever been forced upon a people than that which the capitalist class is forcing upon this nation against its will. . . . The workers of all countries [should] refuse to support their governments in their wars."

To be sure, the manifesto did not call for much specific and dramatic action—merely demonstrations, mass petitions, and "all other means within our power." At the same time, the St. Louis convention repealed Article II, Section 6, of their constitution, which provided that any member who advocated sabotage was to be expelled. This was an act of ineptness rather than an attempt to challenge the government on the war, but the manifesto and the repeal of the article against sabotage were enough to supply the government with the means and determination to try to crush the Socialist Party, thus victimizing the right wing as well as the left. As far as I personally was concerned, the manifesto delighted me, for it fused my half-baked socialism with my deeply rooted opposition to war and, above all, to universal or total war. With such a program, I could campaign strongly for Morris Hillquit as mayor of New York and make the halls and street corners of New York ring with my speeches. And it seemed to me right to have joined the Socialist Party even before I had become a Socialist.

Prowar and pro-Wilson sentiment did exist in the party, but it existed almost exclusively, and indeed overwhelmingly, among the party's most distinguished native intellectual spokesmen, almost all of whom resigned at once. The list of seceders was impressive: John Spargo, editor of *The Comrade;* William English Walling, leader of a traditional left; Charles Edward Russell, spokesman of a traditional right; A. M. Simons, author of *Social Forces in American History;* William J. Ghent; Allan Benson, who had run for president on the Socialist ticket the year before; George D. Herron, the Christian Socialist leader who had persuaded his mother-in-law, Carrie Rand, to set up the Rand School; Ernest Unterman, the translator of the three volumes of Marx's *Kapital;* Robert Hunter, author of *Poverty;* J. Stitt Wilson, the Socialist mayor of Berkeley; W. R. Gaylord, Socialist state senator of Wisconsin; Chester Wright, editor of the *New York Call;* Frank Bohn; J. G. Phelps Stokes, Socialist millionaire; his wife, Rose Pastor Stokes; Ernest Poole, author of the best-selling Socialist novel *The Harbor;* and Upton Sinclair. Practically no one with a nationally known name was left in the Socialist Party except Eugene V. Debs, who kept strangely silent for more than a year after America entered the war.

THE HILLQUIT CAMPAIGN

At first the party acted energetically in accordance with the St. Louis Resolution. As if to offset the score or two of intellectual leaders that had left it following the St. Louis convention, the party won more than twelve thousand new members in the first two months, for it was the only political party that opposed the war. Its strength grew swiftly in the big industrial centers. In New York City, Morris Hillquit's antiwar campaign for mayor attracted the attention of the entire country. "A vote for me," he declared in meeting hall after meeting hall, on street corner after street corner, "is a vote against war." He denounced the Liberty Loans as a taxing of the little man and a mortgaging of future generations for the mistakes of the present one. He campaigned for America's withdrawal from the war, which he said we should never have entered. He demanded an early peace in which there should be neither victor nor vanquished. Excitement grew with each meeting. The leaders of the old parties began to worry that in their city, in which four years earlier the Socialist candidate had received a mere 5 percent of the vote, Hillquit might actually win. The Democratic, Republican, and fusion candidates stopped fighting each other to turn all their guns on Hillquit as "pro-German." As a novice street speaker for such a candidate I had every warrant for my own talks. He made the Socialist Party seem everything that I had wanted it to be.

When the votes were counted, Hillquit had lost. But he had run far ahead of the Republican candidate, the Socialist vote being more than two and a third times the Republican. His 145,332 votes showed that more than one voter out of every five had voted Socialist. The party elected ten assemblymen, seven aldermen, and a municipal court judge. Thickly populated Brownsville, Williamsburg, and the Bronx ran ahead of the rest of the city in Socialist votes, in the Bronx the number of Socialist voters being almost one in every three. There was a rush of new members into the party, new subscribers to the *Call*, and new students into the Rand School. The vote in other big cities was just as encouraging: in Chicago, more than one voter in every three; in Buffalo, one in every four; in Toledo, one in every three, and in Dayton 44 percent of the total vote! The vote in the nation's big cities, as Paul Douglas projected it nationally, would have been something like 4 million, more than four times the 900,000 votes that Eugene V. Debs had registered in his presidential campaign of 1912. This, thanks to mass anger at Wilson's reversal of his "he kept us out of war" slogan, was the highest vote the Socialists were ever to get.

Before long I was to discover that things were not what they seemed. I learned that the hero of the mayoralty campaign, Morris Hillquit, had not been so clearly antiwar before his nomination. In August 1914, when the world radical movement was shocked because the German and the French Socialist deputies had voted war credits to their governments, Hillquit tended to find excuses for them. He had always had close relationships with the German social democracy and lent a benevolent if sorrowful understanding to their yielding to mass patriotism. He found excuses for the French deputies, too, whose land had been invaded. And of course for the Belgians. He limited himself to deploring the fact that the European parties had all "yielded to the inexorable necessities of the situation in which they found themselves." He did not dream of expulsions, and still less of a new international, for when peace was restored among the nations he hoped that peace would be restored in the old international as well. And, although his speech accepting the nomination for mayor called for taking America out of the war, after the campaign was over and he was interviewed by William Hard of the *New Republic*, the following colloquy took place:

QUESTION: If there were a referendum on withdrawal from the war, which way would you vote?

ANSWER: I would vote *no*.

I learned, too, that the wavering in the Socialist Party of America had begun in the first year of the war. Charles Edward Russell expressed the demand that America should join the war against Germany. Congressman Berger from Milwaukee was pro-German. Abraham Cahan, editor of the powerful *Jewish Daily Forward*, had supported Russell's pro-Allies stand in a signed editorial. The *New York Call* had rejected the referendum decision overwhelmingly adopted by the Socialist Party that stipulated that any elected official who voted for war appropriations should be expelled from the party. Eugene V. Debs, whom the prewar left regarded as its outstanding leader and spokesman, urged that Russell's attitude should be treated tolerantly. The latest Socialist to be elected to Congress, Meyer London, did not take the antiwar stand of the Socialist Party referendum too seriously: when the arms bills came up in Congress, instead of speaking and voting against them, he stayed away from the sessions. He voted against the declaration of war, but afterward declared that when America was at war, "national unity" was necessary. His stand had its logic, but it was not the stand on war that I expected of a Socialist congressman.

Even Louis Boudin, a member of the old left wing who made it his specialty to join issue with Morris Hillquit, wrote in his book *Socialism and War*: "The working class of any country is vitally interested in *preserving the freedom from alien domination* of that country. And the Socialist is ready to go to war in defense of his country in order to defend that freedom. His readiness to go to war in defense of his country is however strictly limited by his desire to preserve this national freedom." What was this if not an abstract formula for the defense of Belgium and the occupied parts of France to expel the invader?

If Boudin was a leader of the classic left, and Hillquit, Berger, and London our official spokesmen, I asked myself, how long would the Socialist Party stand firm against the war? Clearly, I had no choice but to resign from this party or try to form a genuine antiwar left wing and a new, consistently antiwar international.

The climax came for me at the end of March 1918, before we had completed our first year at war. A resolution was introduced into the New York City Board of Aldermen endorsing the Third Liberty Loan and calling upon the people of the city to subscribe to the utmost. Six of the seven Socialist aldermen, whom we had elected on the Hillquit antiwar platform, voted in favor of the resolution! Algernon Lee, spokesman for the six aldermen and director of the Rand School, declared, "We urge the people of the city to respond generously to the call of the government for subscriptions to the Third Liberty Loan." The United Hebrew Trades took a five-column full-length ad in the *Call* headed: "Buy Liberty Bonds." The joint board of the cloakmakers, also led by Socialists, subscribed for $25,000 in bonds and urged its members to buy as much as they could. The International Ladies' Garment Workers took $100,000 worth, "setting an example to the nation and showing that New York was doing its share." Other Socialist-led Jewish unions followed their example. That did more than any other single event, except the Bolshevik seizure of power, to bring into being a strong left wing, and to convince me that the official leadership of the Socialist Party had been caught up by the war fever that already possessed the majority of our countrymen.

The mood of the growing left was expressed in an editorial written by Louis Fraina in *The Class Struggle* entitled "St. Louis—One Year After." "There is only one word in the English language," it began, "which can adequately describe the state of mind of the Socialist Party with respect to the war on the anniversary of the St. Louis Convention. That word is: *Chaos*." To us who remained antiwar it was obvious that the war fever, which had taken possession of an ever larger section of the American people, was now taking possession of the party leadership and much of the party membership. It was necessary to fight for the majority in the party, to demand an emergency convention to reexamine or reaffirm our attitude toward the war, and to change the leadership of the party. But, sensing the mood of anger in the rank and file, the old guard that held the administrative posts stubbornly refused for a year to hold a wartime convention and began to look for pretexts for expelling batches of the new left-wingers in order to hold on to its power.

At first the left wing grew slowly, for the official party seemed antiwar, pro-Soviet, and Marxist in its ideology. The left began more as a mood than an organization. It thought of itself, quite properly, as more consistently antiwar, more active, more ardent, more truly Marxist, whatever that might mean, since neither left, nor right, nor center knew much about Marxism. The official party was cautious about a head-on collision with the government in wartime; the left knew no such caution. It consisted largely of green and impatient new members who had joined the party because of its public antiwar stand. They were reinforced by leftist old-timers from previous battles largely in the Middle West and Far West. Among the youth in New York were also a number of young men who had joined because their parents had been radical socialists in the "old country."

The composition of the New York left wing was rather faithfully reflected in the City Committee it elected in the middle of February, 1919, consisting of Benjamin Gitlow, son of European Socialist immigrants, aged twenty-eight; Nicholas Hourwich, son of a Russian-born economist, twenty-nine; Fanny Horowitz, born abroad, of uncertain age; Jay Lovestone, born in Lithuania, twenty-one; James Larkin, Irish labor leader, forty-three; Harry Hiltzik, born in Eastern Europe, under thirty; Edward Lindgren, an old-time left-winger of many previous battles; Milton Goodman, twenty-one; John Reed, thirty-two; Joseph Brodsky and Karl Brodsky, brothers, sons of European immigrants, both under thirty; Julius Hammer, Russian-born, forty-five; Jeannette Pearl, born in Eastern Europe, about thirty; Mrs. L. Ravitch, foreign-born, age unknown; Bertram D. Wolfe, born in Brooklyn, twenty-three. Milton Goodman, Jay Lovestone, and I were the youngest of the lot, but John Reed was perhaps the youngest in spirit. I received the highest vote in the election, in part because I was an active speaker, but much more, probably, because I was a second-generation American.

The left wing got a great upsurge of strength from the Russian Revolution of 1917. The spirit of the left wing leaped high. The foreign-language federations of the Socialist Party, particularly those from the lands of the Russian Empire, grew enormously. This increased the size of the Socialist Party, but completely changed its composition. In 1912 the Socialist Party had only 12 percent of its members in the foreign-language federations. By 1919 the party had grown to 110,000 members, but over 53 percent were in foreign-language federations. Those from the areas of our country that had been settled by immigrants from the lands of Russia and her near neighbors—Russians, Ukrainians, Lithuanians, Letts, Estonians, South Slavs, and Finns—jumped to well over 20 percent of the total membership of the party, and these were the most excited by rumors and fairy tales of what was happening in their homelands, and the most impatient in their leftism. They did not care whether the American Socialist Party was split or destroyed; in fact many of those who could read Russian had learned from Lenin that the party here should be both split and destroyed. The Finns had been predominantly moderates, but after a short-lived regime calling itself Socialist arose in Finland, many of them, too, swung leftward, strengthening the Finnish contingent in the IWW and in our left wing. The Finns did not attend our meetings—they were too clannish and too little at home in English—but they put their dailies at our disposal, gave funds from their communities of steady workingmen and their big cooperative system. Our ranks swelled from the ingress of members of all the foreign federations, and suddenly we, as well as the old officials of the Socialist Party, became aware that the left wing might carry the referendum elections for delegates to the international Socialist congresses (we actually did), and for delegates to the emergency convention on the war that we were demanding. This was one more reason for their postponing the convention and for finding excuses for expelling substantial segments of our supporters from the Socialist Party.

The Russian Federation became something of a madhouse. It seemed suddenly to develop as many would-be leaders as it had articulate Russians, for most of them wanted to go back to Russia, but only after they had won positions of leadership in America, which they devoutly believed would make them welcome as leaders also in Russia. Only yesterday their lives had been consecrated by the presence of Leon Trotsky, Nicholas Bukharin, and Alexandra Kollontay living in their midst and writing for their official organ, *Novy Mir.* Now, Trotsky, Bukharin, and Kollontay were leaders of the ruling party in their homeland. Surely these would find leading positions for other returners from America who had proved to be the leaders and the best revolutionaries in the Russian Federation in this country. Every one of them felt himself a potential Lenin, Trotsky, or Bukharin, and their battles with each other became a kind of bedlam.

Alexander Stoklitsky, a solid-looking Russian built like a wrestler, led the Russian Federation forces in the Middle West. His headquarters were in Chicago at 1221 Blue Island Avenue, which he renamed the Smolny Institute, after the elegant school for girls of the nobility which the Bolsheviks had taken over as their headquarters in Petrograd after Lenin seized power. There were so many Russian immigrants working in the stockyards and the steel mills around Chicago that Stoklitsky was a real force among Midwestern Socialists, and later in the Communist movement. His chief opponent, Nicholas Hourwich, was the leader of the Russian Federation in New York City. He had red hair, a pointed red beard, a red-hot temper which made him stammer and stutter when he became enraged. His father, an equable, highly respected economist and social democrat from Russia, frankly apologized that he had left to the American Socialist party "such a son and heir." Whether he fought with us or against us, he was always a problem child in New York. When he got into an argument with the right-wing Socialist alderman, Abraham Beckerman, who had learned to fight gangsters on the Amalgamated Clothing Workers' picket line, the argument ended in an exchange of blows, Beckerman's kicking Nick Hourwich in the groin, and Hourwich's shouting so loud that the assembly hall rang with his cries, "Give me ah revulver, give me ah revulver!"—the first time such a weapon had even been thought of in the supposedly violent left wing, which had talked of revolution but never thought of guns! When he argued with Stoklitsky, an argument that would soon lapse into irate Russian epithets, we could not understand what he and Hourwich differed about, for both of them had read enough of Lenin to acquire from that old sectarian the slogan of "Splits, splits, and splits." The decisive difference from us American left-wingers was that we wanted to go to another Socialist Party convention, either to capture it or to split off from it as many Socialists as possible, while both Stoklitsky and Hourwich wanted to split away at once and form a small, pure, Leninist-Bolshevik Communist Party, the fewer the purer, and the purer and fewer, the better. "Must we stoop so low," Stoklitsky asked us scornfully when we met, "as to beg admission [to the Socialist convention] in order that we may capture the masses? Bolsheviks never run after the masses: Communists are not satisfied to be at the tail. They are ever in the lead. To be the tail is the characteristic peculiarity of the centrists." This was an echo of

Lenin's polemic against *khvostism*, or tailism, but we could not tell the difference between Stoklitsky's words and Hourwich's exhortations on splitting as soon as possible. Our desire to spend a few months more fighting for a few thousand more left-leaning Socialists from the Middle and Far West encountered stern resistance from all the foreign federations. They had been founded by the Socialist Party with the intention of being used as educational organizations to make new immigrants more familiar with the American scene, but thanks to their clannishness and their nostalgic attachment to the old country and its revolutionary moods and organizations, they had become in practice national Socialist parties attached to the Socialist Party of America and later to the left wing, and were bent on educating us instead of learning from us about the United States.

We of the left wing hoped, as John Reed and I were to write in a manifesto for the left wing, that the jobless returning soldiers and the workingmen discharged from the shipyards and other war industries would "not endure the reactionary conditions so openly advocated by the master class . . . that strikes would develop which would verge on revolutionary action. . . ." (Actually the fight against wage cuts, unemployment, and union smashing had nothing revolutionary about it.) But the foreign federations were so convinced that the United States was on the verge of a social revolution that we were even less effective than the right wing in convincing them to the contrary.

The idea of going to the Socialist Emergency Convention, in which we would have a majority of the legally elected delegates, in order to win away a few thousand additional Socialists who had only to be wooed in order to be won, seemed intolerable to both Stoklitsky and Hourwich and the cohorts they commanded. Had not Lenin split away from the Mensheviks as early as possible? Had he not split again and again? With his tiny remnant of the pure had he not actually won power over Russia? Had he tried to capture the Second International, instead of splitting it to purify it? And would he not, through the Third International, win the World Revolution? These were the questions they asked us. They did not listen to our answers.

In short, the same flood of Russian and other foreign federationists into our ranks that made it seem possible to win control of the Socialist party at its coming convention, made it harder and harder for us to go to the Emergency Convention we had demanded and claim that we constituted a majority of the party and were entitled to win control of its press, its meeting halls, and most of its members.

We did not yet dream how much splitting would be the main business at that convention. Or that our own ranks would split into two or three or more Communist parties and splinter groups when the Emergency Convention took place in Chicago. Or that Zinoviev and Lenin would write an obligatory splitting rule into their Twenty-one Points and into the early congresses of the Communist International, and would even go so far as to order us to find "centrists" in our ranks to expel, and "centrists" in the Socialist Party to repel as they began to approach us. If I had joined the already long existent Socialist Party without knowing what it was or anything about its history, at least I felt sure that, as a founder of the Communist Party and the Communist International, I should be able to help determine their nature. But I was soon to learn that the Communist Party and the Comintern would be shaped in Moscow by such things as the Twenty-one Points. And when I got a close-up of the Comintern in 1928 and '29, I found that I had less voice in shaping it than I had had in shaping the Socialist Party. Even my own party was to have nothing American about it, but was to be something that might be stamped MADE IN MOSCOW.

THE LEFT-WING MANIFESTO

As I mentioned briefly in Chapter 9, John Reed and I were named to draft a manifesto and program for the New York left wing. Both of us were fledglings in the Socialist movement, naïve and unsophisticated, new to the perplexing controversies that rent both the left wing and the Party, hence we got along perfectly as coauthors, and everything we set down seemed novel and stirring to us. Both of us misunderstood the process by which Lenin first used the cover of the Soviets and then substituted for them the rule of his party and its leadership. We looked upon the Soviets in American syndicalist terms as a confederation of industrial unions with all power and control of industry in their hands, a misunderstanding that possessed most American sympathizers with bolshevism at the time.

We tried to be conciliatory to the Socialist Party on which the left wing had declared war. "First of all," began our manifesto, "we are not a secessionist movement, nor do we contemplate splitting the party." What we aimed at was a "calm discussion" such as had proved impossible at party meetings. We were addressing ourselves not to the outside world against the party, but exclusively to party members, whom we had not been able to reach because the official party press had been barred to us.

The war had been a shock to us, as to all Socialists. We had counted on the statesmen, on the cohesive power of Christianity, on the growing strength and solidarity of the Socialist movement. Yet in a short time both Christ and Marx had failed, and Europe was in flames. "Two things only could issue from the flames," our manifesto asserted: "either international capitalist control through a League of Nations, or social revolution and the dictatorship of the proletariat."

The American Socialist movement, our manifesto charged, was "not adjusting itself to the new conditions. . . . A radical change in party policies and tactics was necessary." The party "must throw off parliamentary opportunism," stand squarely behind the Soviet Republic of Russia, the Spartacists of Germany, and the revolutionary working class in Europe, "be ready to take the leadership of the proletariat of our country and lead it towards the dictatorship of the proletariat."

Reed and I looked at our manifesto and thought it good. The New York Left Wing Council approved it at a meeting on February 8, 1919; support for it came in from many locals in other parts of the country. But at this point Louis Fraina rushed down from Boston to tell us what was wrong with our manifesto, and to make it "more revolutionary." We had endorsed "industrial unionism," meaning the IWW. Fraina said it should be called "revolutionary unionism," by which he also meant the IWW. We had no objections.

He went over it line by line, making further changes, all of which seemed acceptable to us, some of them even improvements in formulation. The principal change he introduced was a vague but serious-sounding one, a phrase dear to his heart and destined to become a shibboleth to distinguish the true revolutionary from the false. The magic word was *mass action*. We listened as respectful pupils to Fraina's superior wisdom.

The term *mass action* was German and Dutch, not Russian. Prior to 1912, the workers of Germany and the Lowlands had staged massive demonstrations and political strikes to force the liberalization of suffrage on the continent. The Belgians and Dutch wanted universal male suffrage, the Germans wanted the abolition of plural voting for the upper classes, which prevented the Social Democrats, already in a majority in Prussia, from getting a majority of deputies in the Reichstag. Rosa Luxemburg wrote for the movement a political pamphlet called *Massenstreik*, i.e., mass political strike. The Dutchmen, Pannekoek, Gorter, and Rutgers transformed the term into the vaguer, more revolutionary-sounding, more comprehensive term *mass action*. Austin Lewis, a California Socialist attorney, and Louis Fraina under the influence of S. J. Rutgers adopted the term as an article of faith to separate the revolutionary Socialists from the left-sounding centrists. Real mass action, he explained, is outside the sphere of ordinary parliamentary action; it is all-embracing; it includes the organized and the unorganized; its objectives go beyond the economic and political strike; in it coalesce political and industrial action; it is a unity of all forms of struggle and knows no limits in its aims so that "at the proper time" it may develop into mass rebellion, revolution, and proletarian dictatorship. Reed and I listened with amazement and delight. Wasn't that what we were looking for? Didn't it include everything we dreamed of? What a simple and beautiful term! Into the manifesto it went.

Until the Russians made us adherents of Soviets and Dictatorship of the Proletariat, *mass action* was our touchstone to separate the true revolutionist from the false. Henceforth, until some of the writings of Lenin became known to us, no resolution, no manifesto, no program, was complete without *mass action*. He who ignored it, or left it out, was on the other side of the barricades. Whether the masses acted or not, it was with this incantation that we exhorted them. In every strike that occurred, whether for wages or hours or working conditions, we were to put out a leaflet which bade the unlistening masses to "broaden and deepen your strike into *mass action* and revolution." When the Socialist Convention we were demanding finally occurred in August 1919 and splintered off two contending Communist movements, one calling itself the Communist Party of America and the other the Communist Labor Party, the Communist Party to which Louis Fraina and I adhered included *mass action* as a culminating point in its program, while the rival Communist Labor Party uncomprehendingly put in "action of the masses," proving to me, though not to John Reed who joined the Communist Labor Party, that the latter consisted of leaders and followers who were only pseudo Communists since they did not pass the acid test.

At the convention of the left wing held in New York on February 16, our manifesto was changed beyond recognition. To our demands for "an immediate National Convention . . . and a New International" were added a program that represented a powerful dose of Russification. The program read:

a) the organization of Workmen's Councils;
b) workmen's control of industry;
c) repudiation of all national debts, with provision to safeguard small investors;
d) expropriation of the railways and large trust organizations of capital;
e) the nationalization of foreign trade.

All of these demands, intended for early application in America, were manifestly copied from a program just received by someone who had read them in the Russian Bolshevik press. The "provision to safeguard small investors" caused much merriment among the right-wing Socialists. One of them, James Oneal, wrote: "The contradiction between the safeguards urged for 'small investors' and the ultra-proletarian character claimed for this program was immediately detected by its opponents, who ridiculed it." Actually, although it was copied from a Russian program, it did perhaps have some sense in America, where so many workingmen had bought Liberty Bonds, yet the ridicule was effective, and the left wing in later editions dropped all concern for "small investors." Had we the courage to mention workingmen's Liberty Bonds, the subscription to which we had opposed, we would have made the program a little bit more American and more ludicrous.

THE FIGHT FOR THE SOCIALIST PARTY

As the end of 1918 approached, we began an open fight for control of the Socialist Party. To strengthen our leading forces, we introduced into each of the New York county locals a motion to consolidate Kings, Queens, Richmond, and Manhattan into a single Greater New York organization. We won the referendum on this question, and at the first meeting of Local Greater New York I was elected permanent vice-chairman by a close vote, while Abraham Shiplacoff, who had voted as assemblyman against the endorsement of compulsory military service, was elected permanent chairman by the vote of both right-wing and left-wing delegates. Both chairman and vice-chairman were Brooklynites!

The right wing was seriously hampered in their debates with us by the fact that they praised the Bolshevik revolution as Socialist and antiwar and published articles in the *Call* praising the Soviet system as the fulfillment of Socialist dreams, although neither we nor they understood the Soviet setup. Even Abraham Cahan, the redoubtable right-wing editor of the *Jewish Daily Forward,* sang a hymn of praise to the Bolsheviks because they had erected a statue of Marx in the Kremlin. The *Call* simultaneously published articles on the "liberating fruits of the Russian Revolution" and on the "moral values given to the war by President Wilson." They began the year 1919 with a hymn of praise to "free Russia." Such articles left them powerless before our more unified attacks and more consistent, if confused, beliefs. It was only when they made use, as they increasingly did, of their control of the national administrative organs that they proved more powerful and more determined than we.

We took our Manifesto and Program into each local of the party, proposing a resolution for its endorsement, and a motion to invite speakers from each side. I personally debated with Socialist Alderman Alexander Braunstein in the Bronx, and scored an easy victory. The title of our debate was "Does Socialsim Need a Left Wing?" and admission was open only to red card-holders, i.e., party members. In my own local, the debate went on for weeks, until the right wing put new locks on the doors and barred us from entry. That was a physical victory for them, a foretaste of what would happen in August at the Emergency Socialist Convention. In April 1919, Louis Fraina and I debated with Rand School director Algernon Lee, and Assemblyman William Morris Feigenbaum. There was much disorder and no vote was taken.

But the debate that I still remember in painful detail was with Abraham Shiplacoff, toward whom I had friendly feelings and admiration for his vote against the endorsement of conscription. During all the bedlam of our internal party battles, I had continued my study of Marx and Engels, which I had barely begun. But for my debates, someone had put little three-by-five cards into my hand containing quotations from Marx and Engels effective for our debate, from books that I had not yet read. For example, there was an apparent crusher from Marx's *Critique of the Gotha Program* which read: "Between capitalist and communist society lies a period of revolutionary transformation from one into the other. To this corresponds a political transition period during which the state can be nothing else than the revolutionary dictatorship of the proletariat. . . . In a democratic republic . . . the class struggle has to be fought definitely to a finish. . . . Even the most commonplace democracy which sees the millennium in the democratic republic . . . towers mountain high over the kind of democracy that moves within the boundaries of what the police allow and logic forbids." To me, to my opponent, and to our audience, such quotations seemed crushers, for which of us had read Marx and Lenin and knew the gap between what Marx meant and what Lenin meant by "dictatorship of the proletariat"? The Twenty-third Assembly District voted overwhelmingly to endorse the Left-Wing Manifesto and Program, then Shiplacoff and I went out to our usual dairy restaurant to have cake and coffee.

There was an embarrassed silence until Shiplacoff burst into tears. "I have worked so hard all my life," he said, "for our party and for the labor movement, that I have never had the time to read all those books by Marx and Engels that you have read." Then he wept on in silence. Suddenly, I felt sympathy with him, and more than a little shame, for I had not read "all those books" either. Moreover, for the first time I understood how much men like Shiplacoff had given to building the party that my colleagues and I, mostly youngsters, were now tearing apart. I did not know what to say; we both left our cake and coffee unfinished, but I never forgot the episode. I began to feel more charitable toward the old-timers whose work we were helping to destroy. Though I continued to use the quotations, I could no longer summon up the scorn with which I had read them to that Brownsville Labor Lyceum meeting. I continued my study of Marx with a keen awareness that the context of every utterance had to be examined, and that, as a young would-be Marxist, I was suffering from a disease for which I have since found a name: *authoritarian quotationitis.*

As I see it now, we were rather arrogant about the Left-Wing Manifesto and Program, for though we did not hesitate to amend it or even change it beyond recognition at each of our more solemn conclaves, yet we insisted, when we submitted it to a local or state organization for approval, that it had to be adopted intact, and could not be taken up or amended *seriatim.* There was some reason for this, to be sure, for you were either for the left or against it, and no minor retouching could alter or evade that issue. The Manifesto was promptly adopted intact by the states of Michigan, Massachusetts, and Ohio, by the foreign federations, and by cities and locals all over the country.

The bitterest fight came in the city of New York, where the right wing had its strength, an experienced bureaucracy, some veterans of battles with the physical forcists in 1912, and with the Socialist Labor party at the turn of the century. I do not remember whether Shiplacoff or I was in the Chair when the battle occurred, but probably it was I, since the minutes record that all attempts to amend the Manifesto were ruled out of order by the chairman.

The "right wing" pleaded that the party had never been "right" but "left." They attempted to prove their "leftness" by quoting the St. Louis Resolution, by citing the attacks of police and mobs upon their headquarters and journals, their unalterable rejection of the "capitalist system" and their praise of the Soviet system. They fought bitterly to take up the proposals of the Manifesto and Program *seriatim,* but in vain. A vote to sustain the chair on this issue made it clear that we had a big majority at the Greater City Central Committee.

The debate was long, and occasionally learned. A left-winger from the old German left, Moses Oppenheimer, got it into his head that it was because he had neglected to instruct the new members and the old guard that they were at loggerheads. He ended his oration dramatically with the words "*Mea culpa! Mea maxima culpa!*"—which did not get the debate one whit forward. Marx was cited by both sides. Harry Waton quoted Herbert Spencer and Spinoza with thunderous irrelevancy. Oppenheimer discussed the proposal to take up our resolution *seriatim* with the words: "There are enough explosives in this resolution as it now stands to blow the party to pieces."

Finally, in the small hours of the morning, having talked and yelled ourselves hoarse, we voted by a clear majority to endorse the Left-Wing Manifesto and Program. At this, about a hundred delegates walked out and rode up to the headquarters of the Seventh Assembly District in the Bronx to organize a new party, or to "reorganize the Socialist Party." It was the first time in the history of the party that there had been such a secession from an assemblage. They elected a leading committee of fifteen, a subcommittee of nine, including Assemblyman Braunstein, German "left-winger" Oppenheimer, city organizer Julius Gerber, and other well-known members of the old guard. They voted to appeal to the New York State Committee, of which they had control. They expelled whole locals and branches for adopting the Left-Wing Program, including Syracuse, Rochester, Buffalo, Yonkers, the Bronx, Kings, Queens, the left-wing delegates to the Central Committee of Greater New York, and some lesser locals.

The right had the old machine, the old leaders, the ancient loyalties, the *Call*, the Rand School, the sympathy of the leaders of the Jewish socialist-led trade unions. The left had the new antiwar influx, the foreign federations, some old-time left leaders in the West—which meant anything west of the Hudson River—a claim to kinship with the Spartacists and Bolsheviks, the support of a new international in the making, the enthusiasm, energy, and insouciance of youth.

THE EXPULSION OF THE MAJORITY OF THE PARTY

The closer we got to the Emergency Convention scheduled for August 30 in Chicago, the more adherents we won, and the faster came the expulsions. The old guard had complete possession of the party machine, and the support not merely of the right wing and the center, but of many who were temperamentally left, but grieved to see disrupted the party in which they had spent so much of their lives and to which they had given so much devotion. Yet, as the expulsions came thick and fast and in whole global blocks, many resigned and offered support to the left out of indignation that differences were being settled in that fashion. By January, 1919, some 1,000 a month were joining the party, but by midsummer more than ten times that number were being expelled each month, and many were dropping out or resigning.

As it became clear that the left wing had gotten a sweeping majority of the vote for the election of international delegates and delegates to the forthcoming Socialist Party convention, the *Call* closed its columns to all advertisements of left-wing meetings and pronouncements, although, absurdly, it continued to publish its own praise of, and articles contributed praising Bolshevism as well as the New Russia.

Every big city had to be purged. We had a majority in Boston, Cleveland, Toledo, Akron, Buffalo, San Francisco, Oakland, Portland, Philadelphia, Detroit, Seattle, Queens, Kings (Brooklyn), the Bronx, and many other cities. Our motion to secede from the Second International and build a Third or Communist International carried by a vote of ten to one, for most of those who opposed us on other matters voted with us on this one. Thus I became one of the founders of the Communist International.

In the vote for the National Executive Committee, we won twelve out of fifteen seats. At this, the right wing decided to charge fraud. They pointed out that only about one-fifth of the total membership had voted, while the foreign federations had voted in block on their own slate and seemed to turn in as many votes as they had dues-paying members. They probably even paid dues for, and recorded the votes of, some nonexistent members.

On May 24 (a few days after a call from the ailing Morris Hillquit to "clear the decks"), by a vote of eight to two (the two being Wagenknecht, a left-winger from Ohio, and Katterfeld, a left-winger from Kansas), the National Executive Committee revoked the charter of the organization in the state of Michigan, thus expelling some 6,000 members, then suspended seven foreign-language federations for protesting the suspension of the New York branches, thereby "clearing the decks" of some 20,000 more. Then they officially decided that the vote for new officers should be left uncounted (because of "fraud"), and set August 30 for the holding of a purified national Emergency Convention in Chicago. To complete their preparations for the convention, they expelled the state organizations of Massachusetts and Ohio (for endorsing the Left-Wing Manifesto), and went on to expel the Chicago and other city and county organizations.

In January 1919, the Socialist Party membership had reached its high point of 109,589; by July of that year, with the Emergency Convention still a month away, the membership had dropped by almost two-thirds to 39,750. At least those were the figures given by the national secretary, Adolph Germer, to the National Executive Committee on the eve of the convention. The decks had been cleared for action.

14

"SPLITS, SPLITS, AND SPLITS"

In the spring and summer of 1919, the leaders of the Russian Federation of the American Socialist Party, feeling themselves to be true Bolsheviks, adopted the above words as their motto. At the same time, the old guard and the National Executive Committee of the American Socialist Party, fighting for their life against the newly developing left wing, seemed to act as if these words of Lenin were their motto also. For the next few years, the life of both right wing and left was a rash of splits, secessions, and expulsions. Yet the more wings, factions, parties, groups, and grouplets this rash of splitting begot, the less the total number of members that remained in all of them put together.

If all the state organizations, city organizations, and foreign federations that were expelled by the National Executive Committee as it prepared for the Emergency Convention of August–September 1919 could be counted as members of the left wing or nascent Communist Party, then communism in America would be starting life with something like 70,000 members, approximately two-thirds of the Socialist Party, not a small number for a country in which the total Socialist membership had never risen above 115,000. But the Communist movement itself began splitting into large and small fragments even before a Communist Party was formed. Further segments kept moving from the Socialist to the Communist Party for the next year or two, attracted by Lenin's success in the seizing and holding of power, and by the wondrous tales that pilgrims to the New Russia kept bringing back about the things that Lenin was supposed to be doing with the power he held in his hands.

The leaders of the left wing were mostly young and their names unknown to the majority of the party. Only Jim Larkin had a nationwide reputation, yet the left-wing candidates led Morris Hillquit in the election for international delegates, Hillquit running fifth. Our speakers won debate after debate in local and statewide assemblies, as we persuaded them to adopt the Left-Wing Manifesto and Program. A report of the National Executive Committee said:

An astounding state of affairs resulted. Veterans and pioneers of the movement who had served the Party in many ways for ten, twenty and thirty years, suddenly found that they had no rights in the Party except to pay dues. Members of the Left Wing, some of them never having joined the Socialist Party, some of them having only a card of the Left Wing, some of them being members only a few weeks, usurped all rights within the party organization.

This was, to be sure, an exaggeration, for we admitted only those with party cards into our left wing—how else would they have a vote on party matters? But this tells us how the old-timers felt when they were ruled out of order by a young left-wing-elected chairman, or prevented from discussing and voting *seriatim* on our program. In any case, this was one of the reasons given by the National Executive Committee for their wholesale expulsions.

SPLITS IN THE LEFT WING

Of the expelled two-thirds of the party, a majority felt that the proper "Bolshevik" thing to do was to start a new and pure Communist Party at once, without waiting for the Socialist Emergency Convention. Everything Russian had taken on a well-nigh irresistible attraction. The Russian Federation easily took over the leadership of all the foreign federations. All it seemed to lack to take control of the whole left wing was some native-born American spokesmen. They decided that the little sect of New York left-wingers led by Harry Waton wouldn't do, for he and most of his followers had noticeable foreign accents, while his Talmudic method of proposing an immediate split and the formation of a Communist Party was faintly comical. In place of quoting Marx or Lenin, he proclaimed in his thunderous voice, "Herbert Spencer says: 'Action started in a given direction leads to further action in the same direction.'—THEREFORE, we must form a Communist Party tonight."

In their quest for English-speaking spokesmen, the Russian Federation leaders finally made a strange alliance with the leaders of the Socialist party of Michigan, who had nothing in common with them, except that both the Michigan organization and the Russian Federation had been expelled at the same time.

The Michigan Socialist Party was in a class by itself. It had no interest in Russia, nor in violence, nor in "mass action," nor in underground movements, nor in the words and deeds of V.I. Lenin. Its leaders were Dennis E. Batt, an ex-machinist, and John Keracher, a shoe-store owner. They were disciples of a former leader of the Socialist Party of Canada named King, who had made a profound impression upon those to whom he had taught his special sectarian brand of Marxism. They held that the trade-union struggle was nothing but a "bourgeois" struggle. It was a waste of time to concern oneself with unionism, because it involved bargaining about the selling price of labor power. And labor power, as Marx had said, was a commodity, a piece of merchandise, to be bought and sold on the *labor market*. Further, the Michiganites believed, quite properly, that America was not near a social revolution, that American capitalism had emerged from World War I much stronger than before, and that it would continue to grow in strength until it became the greatest capitalist power in the world. Though they had a low opinion of unions and strikes, they had a high opinion of the ballot-box and of the potential "class consciousness of the worker." To bring the Marxist revolutionary message to him, all that was needed was education and more education, with Marx's works as texts and their own special doctrine as gloss. The political struggle was to be purely educational; hence there should be no immediate demands in the program of their candidates, no demands for reforms, only education for socialism and the "social revolution," an event that would take place when the majority of workingmen were properly educated in Marx's doctrine. Nothing could be more remote from the mood of the Russian Federation than Michigan's doctrinaire, pedagogic, and pedantic brand of Marxism. But the men from Michigan needed masses, while the Russian Federation needed spokesmen who could speak good English. Furthermore, neither had any use for the "opportunists" remaining in the Socialist Party; so a strange marriage of incompatibles was arranged between them. The marriage was not one that could be consummated nor last long, but it was good enough to serve to split the left wing and force the immediate formation of a separate Communist Party, of which Batt and Keracher would be the teachers and Stoklitsky and Hourwich the bosses.

When the left wing held a national conference in New York on June 21 to "consolidate its forces" and prepare for battle in August with the old guard, at least four groups confronted each other. The Russian Federation, the Michigan group, and the Watonites had a clear majority for forming an American Communist Party as "previously as possible," but they had not yet coordinated their forces. Since the conference had been called to make plans for winning control of the Socialist Party and for changing its leadership, platform, and practices, the American and other English-speaking delegates won the first round: it was voted to send delegates to the Socialist Emergency Convention and see whom and what we could win there.

At this point, the first split occurred: Harry Waton made his speech on the physical laws of gaining momentum by starting an immediate split. When this was voted down, he shouted, "Traitors!" as he and his handful of disciples left the hall to set up a Communist Party of their own in a little room.

The Russian Federation and the Michigan delegates refused to vote. Instead, they joined forces to call for the founding of a Communist Party on September 1 in Chicago. The remainder of the left wing voted to go to the Socialist convention but simultaneously to prepare a convention hall of their own, in the event that the National Executive Committee should keep us out with the aid of the police. We set up a National Council of nine: Louis Fraina of Boston, Charles E. Ruthenberg of Cleveland, I.E. Ferguson of Chicago, John J. Ballam of Boston, and James Larkin, Eadmon MacAlpine, Benjamin Gitlow, Maximilian Cohen, and Bertram Wolfe, all from New York. The *Revolutionary Age* was adopted as our official organ with Fraina as editor. He wrote a new Manifesto and Program, three times as long as the one Reed and I had written, but bearing the same marks of the influence of the IWW and Daniel De Leon, the same *mass action,* and a noticeable expansion of the influence of the writings of Lenin and Trotsky, some of which had reached America and been translated into English by Jacob Hartmann and André Tridon and published by Fraina with his own introduction and notes. It was the first contact most of us had with any of the writings of Lenin and Trotsky, and then only with things written by them during the war and after they were in power. I did not really get to know the character and views of Lenin until I got around to reading earlier works of his such as *What's to Be Done?, Tasks of the Detachments of a Revolutionary Army,* and his *Speech in My Defense Before the Revolutionary Court of Honor*—all of which were shocking to me.

The main issue between us and the foreign federations was that we wanted such additional "masses" as we could get from the Socialist Party, while they wanted "purity," in the sense that Lenin, they thought, had taught them to seek it. For them, more numbers meant more American influence, and they held the Americans—all of us, not excluding their temporary Michigan allies—in low esteem. We wanted to prove in some measure that we were an American party; they wanted to prove that they were good Russians, i.e., good Bolsheviks.

Yet, when the Socialist old guard categorically set aside the referendum on the election of the delegates, thus disallowing all our delegates entrance to the forthcoming convention, we found it harder to insist on going to the Socialist Emergency Convention at all, and were more and more tempted to join with the "real majority of left-wingers," the foreign-born workers in the foreign federations, for the formation of an instant Communist Party. For their part, they set up a "National Organization Committee," to organize a Communist Party of America on September 1, with Dennis Batt of Michigan as secretary, Stoklitsky of the Russian Federation as organizer, and J. V. Stilson, a Lettish "Old Bolshevik," who had always maintained connections with the pro-Lenin Lettish Section of the Russian Social Democrat Party back home, as treasurer. Their headquarters were at the Chicago office of the Russian Federation, otherwise known as the Smolny Institute. The new party had seven foreign federations plus a fragment of the Jewish Federation, the Michigan organization, a left-wing group from Minnesota, and a few city organizations in cities near the Canadian border or otherwise under Michigan or Russian influence.

Our National Council began to waver. Finally, at the end of July (July

28 to be exact), five of us voted to give in to the majority and go to Chicago on August 30 in order to organize a Communist Party with their group. Two held out against "dictation by the foreign federations." The two were Gitlow and Larkin. Our five were Ruthenberg, Ferguson, Ballam, Cohen and I. Of the party editors, who had no vote, Fraina sided with us, MacAlpine with Larkin and Gitlow. Thus, two Communist parties were in the making.

We were all going to Chicago, where the split would widen and another splinter or two split off. Communism seemed doomed to multiply, like the amoeba, by multiple fission. More and more sympathizers, confused by the multiplicity of splits, simply melted away. We continued to grow more and more parties and sects, with an even smaller total of members in all of them put together.

In late August 1919, all wings of the ruffled Socialist movement converged on Chicago for the war of rival conventions. The police were forgotten and were hard put to keep up with all our divisions and subdivisions. The old-guard Socialists with their still faithful adherents dug in for an expected attack on the second floor of Machinist's Hall. Their guards made each delegate show both a red card and a special white card issued by their credentials committee. Reed and Gitlow, and some fifty-odd followers, prepared to "attend," i.e., to rush, the Socialist convention. Ruthenberg left us and joined them for the fight to keep control of his old party. The right wing was forewarned by the discovery of a copy of the minutes detailing the plan of attack, and by the fact that Wagenknecht boasted to a *Chicago Tribune* reporter, "We will take over their convention by storm." The police turned up to help the right wing, or more likely to prevent the Machinist's Hall from being torn to pieces. Following orders from the national organizer of the Socialist Party, Adolph Germer, who knew almost everybody's face, the police acted as the *de facto* credentials committee.

Personally, I missed all this, as well as the disturbing and turbulent events that followed. Although I was duly elected a delegate both to the Socialist and to our own left-wing convention, I developed an infection in an ingrown toenail on the big toe of my right foot, and my doctor could think of nothing better to do but to rip off the entire toenail. While all the splits were taking place in Chicago, I was sitting in Brooklyn with one foot up on a chair, cursing my luck that I was missing the fun. I had to depend on the reports of rival delegations, each seeking my support, on stories in rival official organs, and on such subsequent works as Theodore Draper's *The Roots of American Communism* (the best on the subject), *American Communism* by James Oneal and G. A. Werner, and *Marxian Socialism in the United States*, by Daniel Bell, to try to make some sense out of the to me senseless splits that continued and multiplied in Chicago.

How I would have reacted to the splits, had I been in Chicago, I cannot say. Although I was deeply repelled by all the rival accounts and divisions, I ultimately chose the Communist Party over the Communist

Labor Party, giving no thought to the lesser splinters. If I had been in Chicago, I would have talked my heart out to unite the Communist and the Communist Labor Parties, and failing that perhaps I, too, might have dropped out, as so many thousands did. But I was faced with a *fait accompli,* and after a little hesitation, I chose the Communist Party.

Even after the Fraina-Ruthenberg-Foreign Federation group decided to boycott the Socialist convention, and the Reed-Gitlow group walked out of it, or were expelled by Germer backed by the police, the remaining rump Socialist Party was in a sufficiently antiwar and revolutionary mood that it decided to apply to the Communist International for admission. At the same time, it made demands on the Comintern that it should admit all Socialist parties that had not supported their governments in the war.

Zinoviev, aided by Lenin, retorted to such demands by drafting the Comintern's Twenty-one Points, a net designed to admit the obedient minnows of the old European parties and keep out the potentially disobedient whales. No party was to be admitted unless its press was owned and controlled by its Central Committee; unless its propaganda was "truly Communist"; unless its "reformist" and "centralist" leaders were expelled; unless it set up an underground apparatus, even if its country allowed an open revolutionary party; unless it excluded such men as Hillquit, Hilferding, Kautsky, Longuet, MacDonald, Turati, and Modigliani from their respective parties; unless it accepted the principle of "democratic centralism" and accepted as binding all decisions of the Executive Committee and congresses of the Comintern; and unless it adopted the word *Communist* in its name—in short, was Leninist or Russian Bolshevik in its organizational structure and spirit. Lenin in his call for a new international had a kind word to say for Debs, but Debs, when he learned of the Twenty-one Points, was infuriated. When Zinoviev, their principal author, was asked, "If such men as Hilferding or Hillquit should accept your Twenty-one Points to get in, what would you do?" he answered, "I would find a twenty-second point to keep them out." Finally, in November 1920, more than a year after the Socialist Party applied, the Comintern officially rejected its application.

At this point the Socialist Party was to learn that it was still not finished with splits. When the Comintern rejected the party's formal application in November 1920, yet another "left-wing" group made up its mind to secede and seek a home among the Communists. It included J. Louis Engdahl, editor of the national organ, *The American Socialist;* William F. Kruse, chairman of the Young People's Socialist League; Alexander Trachtenberg, research director of the Rand School and editor of *The American Labor Yearbook* and of *American Labor's Who's Who;* J. B. Salutsky, also known as J. B. Hardman, editor of *The American Labor Monthly* and educational director of the Amalgamated Clothing Workers' Union; and Benjamin Glassberg, a teacher at the Rand School. When these eventually broke with the SP, many more left with them. Trachtenberg, Engdahl, and Kruse eventually became officials of the Communist Party; most of the rest got lost. While the Socialist Party was still splitting, the Communists continued to split, too. How could the handful of government secret agents possibly follow all these groups and grouplets into their meeting halls, tiny rooms, and cubbyholes?

THE TWIN PARTIES
I: THE COMMUNIST LABOR PARTY

On Sunday night, August 31, 1919, after a hectic day of caucusing and negotiating, eighty-two delegates from twenty-one states, led by Reed, Larkin, and Gitlow, assembled in the billiard room on the first floor of the Machinists' Hall (a floor below the room the old Socialist party was meeting in), and adopted the name *Communist Labor Party.* Since their only issue with the *Communist Party* had been whether or not to go to the Socialist convention, they seemed to have nothing left to split on. C. E. Ruthenberg, who had been for going to the SP convention but whose heart was with the other Communist Party still aborning, moved that the first and main order of business should be unity with their twin party.

By this time Gitlow, Larkin, and Carney, another Irishman, were so angry at the Russian Federation for its attempt to dominate the Americans, that Ruthenberg's motion was voted down—by the slender margin of thirty-seven to twenty-one, after an entire night of angry debate. During the debate, Jack Carney threatened to go back to Duluth and denounce them all "for yielding to the Russians," and John Reed said that the Russian Federation would have to "come crawling on its knees" if it wanted unity. Nevertheless, they appointed a committee of five to "negotiate for unity," while they attempted to find differences in order to form a proper "sibling" party.

They began by adopting a Manifesto and Program of their own, since every party needed at least three decorative appurtenances: a Manifesto, a Program, and an Official Organ. John Reed moved that the core of the program be "the conquest of political power by the proletariat." Louis B. Boudin denounced this formulation as "unorthodox Marxism." Reed answered by quoting from the *Communist Manifesto* itself, whereupon Boudin branded the English version a "very poor translation." Gitlow reminded Boudin that this English translation had been approved by Engels personally. By challenging the *Communist Manifesto,* Gitlow said, Boudin was challenging Marx himself and trying to "dilute revolutionary Marxism." Trembling with rage, Boudin cried out: "I did not leave the party of crooks upstairs to join a party of lunatics down here," and walked out of organized socialism forever. The cartoonist Art Young, who was present, drew for the *New York Call* a picture of Boudin walking out, nose in the air, a cane under his left arm, under his right a volume of Marx's *Kapital.* It was thus that Boudin went down in Socialist-Communist folklore—until his grandniece, Cathy Boudin, fled naked from the house on West Eleventh Street in New York where bombs exploded while being put together by her Weatherman comrades. That scene, and the activities of Cathy's father, Leonard Boudin, an attorney who has defended so many radicals and terrorists in the courtroom, supplanted the memory of Louis B. Boudin as author of the best American defense of "orthodox Marxism." No doubt the elder Boudin would have disowned both Leonard and Cathy.

Continuing its work, the Program Committee of the Communist Labor Party followed rather closely Louis Fraina's Manifesto and Program, but, perhaps for originality's sake, perhaps because theory was not their strong point, substituted for Fraina's mystic term *mass action* the words *action of the masses,* a nondescript formulation since any action of a suitable number of people could be called *action of the masses.* What a to-do there was about this verbal switch in the debates between representatives of the sibling Communist parties when we attempted to line up left-wing groups for one party or the other! I remember with a little shame that that was one of the high points in my debate with Ben Gitlow when I succeeded in taking the allegiance of his native bailiwick, the Bronx, away from him. For after all the conventions in Chicago were over, we almost dropped our battle with the Socialist Party in order to concentrate on our battle with each other. This hairsplitting about mass action and action of the masses suggests how small was the gap between the two parties. The real differences were temperamental ones between rival contenders for leadership of the new common movement, and differences in the way we sought to handle a problem that troubled both them and us, namely, how to control the foreign federations and particularly the arrogant and massive bloc voting of the Russian Federation, so as to prevent it from forcing upon us a set of purely European formulae for the solution of American problems. Both groups idolized the New Russia, but speaking for myself I can say that I was at least as interested as Gitlow and Larkin in building a genuine *American* party.

THE TWIN PARTIES
II: THE COMMUNIST PARTY OF AMERICA

On September 1, one day after the CLP was founded, the convention of its twin, the CP, opened with 128 delegates, and 9 fraternal delegates with voice but no vote, at the Russian Federation Headquarters. They put up red banners, Russian revolutionary placards, pictures of Lenin, Trotsky, and Marx. As the convention was about to open on the morning of September 1, the "Anarchist Squad" of the Chicago Police broke into the hall, tore down all the decorations, and took photographs of the entire body. When Dennis Batt of the Michigan delegation mounted the platform to open the meeting, he was arrested for having "violated the Illinois antiespionage law" in a speech delivered three days earlier! A Communist lawyer who made a verbal legal protest was beaten up. Rose Pastor Stokes, who had left her husband and become antiwar, shouted, "Three cheers for the Revolution!" whereupon a male chauvinist detective yelled, "Shut up! It's always a woman that starts the trouble!" All the while, a secret agent, Jacob Spolansky, was sitting in the gallery for the entire five days that the convention lasted, taking notes for the police and for history. Clearly it was to be the more revolutionary, or at least the more turbulent and the more closely watched, of the two conventions.

Louis Fraina took Batt's place as chairman. He began hopefully: "We now once and for all end all factional disputes . . . all bickering . . . all controversy. We are here to build a party of action." However, at more or less the same moment, in the billiard room on the ground floor of Machinists' Hall, eighty-two delegates to the same congeries of Chicago conventions were building another party, so that, far from over, the controversy was just about to begin.

There was a third party that still claimed to be Marxist and Revolutionary, the old Socialist Party of America, reduced now to some mere 10,000 members. In the Socialist *Call* Hillquit could still write that the "underground work" demanded by the Comintern might yet become necessary in America, but was not needed as long as the Constitution guaranteed the right to be a legal party. He said that the Second International had "failed" in its attitude toward the war because it had represented "a class within a class, a movement for the benefit of the better-situated strata of labor—the skilled workers [who] had certain 'vested interests' in the capitalist regimes of their respective countries."

Eugene V. Debs, the outstanding mass leader, went to jail that same year for a speech which culminated with the words: "From the crown of my head to the soles of my feet I am a Bolshevik, and proud of it." Yet, at the same time, Debs denounced the Twenty-one Points as "wanting to commit us to a policy of armed insurrection . . . ridiculous, arbitrary, and autocratic." While in prison he opposed the Bolshevik terror, denounced the murder of the Tsar, and the trial of the Socialist revolutionaries. But when he got out of prison in 1922, he declared that "Sovietism is the only good thing that came out of the war." Since, whether with Hillquit or Debs, their "trumpeters gave an uncertain sound," it was a hard thing for the Socialist Party to fight the Communists. Thus it is not wholly our fault that the Socialist Party fragmented into insignificant splinters. It is not my task to tell the story of their subsequent decline, though my debate with Shiplacoff * suggests that I had a share in it.

In the Communist Labor Party convention, the Michigan delegation sought in vain to remove the call for "mass action" from its program. Mass action was to destroy the bourgeois state and substitute the dictatorship of

* See Chapter 13. If the reader wants a thoughtful exposition of the rise and fall and fate of the Socialist Party, the best attempt is Daniel Bell's ***Marxian Socialism in the United States*** (Princeton, 1967 and 1973).

the proletariat. They rightly feared that this meant violent insurrection, hence they moved to substitute *political action* for *mass action*. Defeated, they walked out, too, and set about forming a new "Communist" party of their own, the Proletarian Party, with branches characteristically close to Canada, in Detroit, Buffalo, and Rochester. It functioned as a series of schoolrooms for proletarians, led a separate existence as a third semi-Communist or non-Communist party. In the early 1930s, these branches grew during the battles for the formation of an auto workers' union in Detroit. But their growth brought their undoing, for a number of their most active and articulate members rose to positions of leadership in the auto workers' union, then were enticed into going along with the support of the Labor Political Action Committee and the Democratic Party. Their action and the demise of the Proletarian Party were ignored by the Communist Party and by whatever workingmen America possessed who might think of themselves as proletarians.

The Communist Party and the Communist Labor Party, however, being closest to each other in outlook and vocabulary, continued to exhaust themselves in polemics with each other. The Communist Party ridiculed the Communist Labor Party because it desired to be a revolutionary proletarian party, yet was hostile to the foreign federations which "represented the foreign-born majority of the American working class." The CLP retorted by deriding the Russian Federation's penchant for splits and splits and splits to preserve its purity. What could the average American workingman make of such polemics?

From Moscow came sustenance for the self-righteous splinters in the form of a call from the First Congress of the Comintern to conduct a "merciless fight" against right-wing "social-patriots" and to "criticize pitilessly" the leaders of the center. "War against the Socialist center," declared the Comintern, "is a necessary condition for successful war against imperialism." The Communist Party looked anxiously for a center toward which to be merciless and found it in those elements who were a little slower than they in breaking with the Socialist Party and hesitantly moving toward communism, or who were uncomfortable with Russian phraseology. Thus, when Benjamin Glassberg, Louis Lochner, Scott Nearing, and Ludwig Lore offered a "basis for discussion" between Socialists and Communists, they became targets of the accumulating wrath against "centrists." When somebody wanted to substitute "industrial democracy" for "proletarian dictatorship," he became the target. The *Revolutionary Age* told the Socialists moving toward them that "the center must be smashed as a necessary means of conquering the [Socialist] Party for the Party, for revolutionary socialism."

Ludwig Lore had done more than most to bring the left wing into being. He had been the principal editor of *The Class Struggle*, to which Trotsky, Kollontay, and Bukharin briefly contributed before their return to Russia. It was a left-wing theoretical organ that concerned itself as much with American as with European issues, while Louis Fraina subtitled the *Revolutionary Age* "A Chronicle and Interpretation of Events in Europe." But when it came to splitting his beloved Socialist Party, Lore wavered and sought compromises. Moreover, he admired Leon Trotsky above all other Russian Bolsheviks at the time when Zinoviev, Stalin, and Bukharin were already beginning their "Old Bolshevik" campaign against Trotsky, who so often before 1917 had been at odds with Lenin. And when the order came from Moscow to "Bolshevize" the American Communist Party by dissolving the geographically based, all-inclusive branches in favor of factory nuclei, Lore opposed it as a way of losing many good party members who did not work in factories with Communist cells. In short, poor Lore was made to order to be a centrist target. As for Scott Nearing, he lectured enthusiastically in praise of the Russian Bolsheviks and predicted in the spring of 1919 that by autumn their revolution would have spread to Germany and other parts of Central and Western Europe. Yet he had a stubborn streak of pacifism in him along with his gently bloodthirsty injunctions to wipe out all the elites in the countries to which the revolution spread, and wrote a pamphlet entitled *Violence of Solidarity, or Will Guns Settle It?* Violence, he contended, had never benefited the labor movement. When the party leaders read this, they wrote, "There is no place for pacifists in the Social Revolution." He too was made to order to be a centrist target. All his life he continued to waver, now in, now out of the Communist Party, until in his late years he took to vegetarianism and the raising of sugar maples and "natural foods" in northern New England, where he led "the simple life" and ceased to concern himself with politics. During World War II, I had a debate with him in which he defended Stalin's annexations and protectorates in Eastern Europe. When I said, "The first thing Stalin will do, Scott, in each country will be to wipe out their elites and leave them leaderless," he answered, "The world will be better off without elites." "You know, Scott," I retorted, "that if they ever set up their system in America you will be one of the first they will go after." His part of the audience waited breathless to hear his devastating reply, but all he said was, "Yes, Bert, I do know that." If the reader wants to know what a centrist was, the best I can do is to leave him with this image of Ludwig Lore and Scott Nearing.

In 1920, the Communist International intervened firmly in the quarrel between the sibling rivals in the American Communist movement. Zinoviev sent a letter ordering the two parties to meet in secret convention and fuse into the United Communist Party. They obediently united, though the seams of their fissure were to show for several more years, and another small group was to split off from both to form yet another tiny party deep underground, where nobody could hear its sputtering.

STILL THERE ARE TWO PARTIES AND A FRACTION!

Thus, the uniting of the two sibling parties gave rise to a new split even as they were uniting. Some foreign federationists saw with displeasure the fresh access of Americans into the United Communist party, and seceded before the unity convention was over. Of course, they gave ideological reasons. They declared the new United Communist Party unworthy of the name of Communist. It was led by "charlatans and adventurers"; its program lacked theoretical clarity because it used the expression "Soviet rule under a proletarian dictatorship"; did not these bunglers know that Soviet rule *was* a proletarian dictatorship? It spoke as if the use of force were a "purely defensive measure—not an offensive measure for which Communists must consciously prepare." Its unity was a unity of the ignorant and the opportunistic.

Thus, although under orders from Moscow the twin Communist parties succeeded in burying their differences and swallowing their personal animosities, there were once more two Communist Parties by the time the unity convention ended: the United Communist Party with something under 3,500 members, and the Communist Party of the seceding foreign federationists with a membership of almost 8,000 members. And the two together made up a total of under 12,000 out of a left wing which a year earlier had counted on something like 60,000 to 70,000 members as their recruiting ground. The majority disappeared, frightened away by the ruthless Red raids, or alienated by the Byzantine controversies, the ideological hairsplitting, and the abusive fury of rival party or faction polemics, the import of which was beyond their comprehension.

Although the United Communist Party was the smaller of the two now clamoring for recognition by Moscow as the only true Communist party, Zinoviev gave the United Communist Party the seal of his approval, and bade the seceders of the foreign federations reunite with the United party they were attacking with such scorn. In 1921 agents of the Comintern arrived with fresh orders to force unity upon the secessionist CP and with instructions for the United party "immediately to establish an underground" replica of itself, even "though it is possible for the party to function legally." The underground party was to "direct revolutionary propaganda .. and in case of violent suppression of the legal party organization, to carry on the work." That made for the moment three Communist parties!

In addition there were various splinter parties such as the Proletarian party of Michigan, the Industrialist Communists of Indiana, the United Toilers of New England, a group of foreign federationists who considered it a special revolutionary virtue to bury themselves as deeply underground as possible, and a Committee for a Third International that was just seceding, a little belatedly, from the Socialist party. It took several more years for these and other splinter groups (one historian has counted twelve) to wither or to fade away, or to merge with the United party. To add to the general confusion, the Palmer Red raids seized bodies, membership cards, and documents wholesale, until they drove the United Communist Party underground.

From the underground, still fighting for its right to exist legally and openly, the Communist Party established a number of legal organizations, hiking clubs, forums, workers' schools, and the like, and yet another semi-Communist party called the Workers Party of America, whose program was modified in "Aesopian" language so that the initiated would understand but the district attorneys would find it harder to convict. The Workers' Party refrained from joining the Communist International. It published open journals while the underground published literature and a journal with no names of editors, no place of publication, no sign of affiliation with its parent body. The literature that began to reach me in California (how I got there is reserved for the next chapter) carried such mysterious labels as "Number 1" (the underground party) and "Number 2" (the Workers' Party). In all this confusion nobody knew quite what he was joining, and it is not a cause for wonder that some years later a noted intellectual who probably joined one of the legal organizations, perhaps "Number 2," startled me by asking: "Tell me the truth, Bert, was I ever a member of the Communist Party?" And I wasn't sure how to answer him!

15

WE GO UNDERGROUND

Two reasonably fair-minded Socialists, James Oneal and G. A. Werner, wrote in their book *American Communism:* "The Left Wing elements produced more Communist organizations than any other country in the world." When I read this, I realized that it was true. But *why?* To this question I found a number of answers.

First, both American socialism and American communism were importations from Europe. American socialism had modeled itself on the powerful German social democracy, leading party of the Second, or Socialist, International. The Communist movements were inspired by Lenin's seizure of power in Russia. Both were alien importations into a country with a social structure basically different from the German, the Russian, and indeed from any of the countries of Europe.*

Second, the workingmen of the United States, to whom both the Socialist and the Communist movements appealed and in whose name they professed to act, differed enormously in their origins and in their lack of the native homogeneity that characterized the British, the French, the German, the Italian, or any other working class in Europe. At least until the second and third decades of the twentieth century (the period of world wars and "100 percent Americanism"), the industrial workingmen of our big cities were largely made up of constantly changing waves of immigration from Europe, each carrying with it the quite different ideologies, traditions, and organizational and leadership patterns of their different homelands. This lack of homogeneity made for constant splits in the Socialist and Communist movements and to some extent in the general labor movement as well. And the large proportion of foreign-born workingmen made easier the Red raids that were to follow.

Third, the leaders of the European radical movements were profoundly ignorant of the quite different structure of American political, economic and social life. They were bewildered that our "most advanced capitalist country" was so "backward" socially, and from Marx and Engels

* So too were the attempts to found an American Labor Party, an importation from Great Britain without deep roots in America.

to the present, they have waited impatiently for the development of a "proper Socialist movement in America." These misunderstandings of the nature of American life did not matter so much in the Second International since, as Lenin scornfully wrote, "the Second International was a mere post-office box" that did not presume to give orders to its affiliate bodies. But Lenin and Zinoviev were resolved from the outset that the Third International was to be a single, firmly centralized, disciplined world party, of which the various national movements were to be "sections," profiting by all the lessons of Lenin's successes in splitting from the "Mensheviks" and other "opportunists," lessons ratified, he thought, by his success in seizing and holding power.

Neither Lenin nor Zinoviev, his representative as head of the Comintern, hesitated to make or unmake leaders of foreign parties. Indeed, if a leader had retained his popularity in the Socialist and labor movements during the war, when his party applied to the Comintern for admission one of the demands Lenin and Zinoviev tended to make was that he be expelled as part of the "purification" of the applicant party. The rare exceptions were the leaders of antiwar minorities who had managed to survive in leadership of some split-off faction.

Lenin personally laid the foundations of the Communist International by calling a meeting of three men: another Russian, a Finn, and an "Anglo-Russian," that is to say, a man born in Russia who had spent some time in Great Britain. The three men whom Lenin called to meet with him in the Tsar's bedchamber of the Kremlin were his foreign commissar, Chicherin; the Finnish leader Yrjö Sirola, who had been foreign minister of the short-lived Finnish Socialist government and was a veteran of the Finnish movement in America; and Joseph Fineberg, a Russian of Jewish family who had lived long enough in England to become a translator of Lenin's works into English. To these three he read his draft of a manifesto inviting thirty-nine left-wing parties, groups, and tendencies to send delegates to meet on March 15 in Moscow to found the Third, or Communist, International. That he should have included his commissar for foreign affairs, Chicherin, and should have had the commissar openly send out the invitations by mail and wire, showed that he thought of "foreign affairs" as a mere brief interlude of perhaps a year while the World Revolution was spreading to Western Europe.

The four men adopted the manifesto without serious discussion, and Chicherin dispatched it to Lenin's invitees by such means of communication—courier, cable, wireless, and the like—as he could command. The American groups and tendencies of whose attitude or supposed conduct during the war Lenin approved were:

> The Socialist Labor Party;
>
> The elements of the left wing of the American Socialist Party, tendency represented by E. V. Debs and the Socialist Propaganda League;
>
> The IWW;
>
> The Workers International Industrial Union.

How little Lenin understood the American radical movement is shown by this selection.

The Socialist Labor Party, both under Daniel De Leon's leadership until his death in 1914, and under the leadership of his heirs and successors, was categorically against violent revolution as "uncivilized." Instead, the SLP favored winning control of Congress by the ballot, then abolishing the government by congressional vote, [replacing it with] an anticipated 100 percent organization of the working class into one big union of industrial unions, which would take over industry. Hence the SLP was anti-Bolshevik. When its representative, the Russian-born Boris Reinstein, sent by the SLP to the Socialist Stockholm Peace Conference, ended up in Moscow claiming to represent the SLP in the Comintern, the Socialist Labor Party repudiated him and his claim, and expelled him from their party. The IWW, whose leaders sympathized with anarchism and anarcho-syndicalism, became anti-Bolshevik and anti-Comintern as soon as they learned how Lenin was treating his own anarchists and anarcho-syndicalists.

The Workers International Industrial Union was a miniscule imitation of the IWW which Daniel De Leon had formed to be the embryo of the future "One Big Industrial Union" after the IWW ousted him. Hence it, too, besides being a mere tenuous shadow of the SLP, was anti-Bolshevik.

As for the Socialist Propaganda League, there were two of them, one supported by Letts in New England, another dominated by Stoklitsky and the Russian Federation in Chicago. The first was about to dissolve its modest forces into the Left Wing with headquarters in New York. The second would gladly have sent a representative, but was not invited, because Lenin did not know of its existence.

As for the "tendency represented by E. V. Debs," Debs was not the leader of any organized or definable tendency, though many Socialist groupings had claimed him and acclaimed him their leader, only to be subsequently disappointed by his distaste for factional controversy. The Bolsheviks, too, were to be disappointed, for he alternately praised bolshevism and sovietism and rejected and denounced the Comintern for ignorant and arrogant attempts to dictate to the American Socialist movement.

THE UNEXPECTED REVOLUTION

At the beginning of 1917 Lenin told a young people's meeting in Zurich that he did not expect to see the Revolution in his own time. Yet, only a few months later the Tsar fell, the German general staff helped Lenin to get back to Russia and supplied him with funds; the Provisional Government allowed him freedom to form a Red Guard and to undermine their government; and he took power "as easily as lifting up a feather." Yet despite the series of totally unexpected events that occasioned this vertiginous rise to power, he was convinced that the bitch-goddess success had proved that every major step he had taken in a whole lifetime of doctrinaire feuds and splits had been correct. If his splits had done it, then all the parties approaching the Comintern must be purified by splits.

The American parties, Socialist and sibling Communist, were by no means the chief victims. The two most striking cases were two of the largest mass Socialist parties in Europe, who had entered the Comintern intact, without a "purifying" split: the Norwegian Labor Party and the Italian Socialist Party. Of the Norwegian party I knew little or nothing until much later. As to the Italian party, I did not understand what had happened until Angelica Balabanoff, first secretary of the Comintern, broke with Lenin in 1920 and, when she got to America, told me personally the story of Mussolini's rise to power.

The Norwegian Labor Party had been completely antiwar, and when it joined the Comintern in 1919, it entered with 105,000 members. After a split was ordered by Lenin, to "get rid of your Mensheviks," much of its mass following was alienated, its membership shrank to 15,000, the Norwegian Communists being stripped thereby of any serious political significance.

In the Italian party, Lenin directed his fire at the faithful but independent-minded Serrati for not wanting to expel popular leaders such as Turati and Modigliani until they violated party discipline or party instructions concerning their conduct in Parliament. Thus "they could be expelled in such a way as would not alienate the masses." But Lenin retorted, "A quite small party is sufficient to attract the masses. In certain periods there is no need for a large organization. . . . You are in such a [revolutionary] preparatory period. The first stage of that period is a break with the Mensheviks like that which we carried out in 1903." Lenin had his way with the Italian party, splitting wide open the powerful workers' front in Italy. Through the breach "marched" Mussolini triumphantly to Rome, traveling not with his Blackshirts but in a Pullman sleeping car to receive his power from the hands of his King. Later, the same pattern would be repeated by Lenin's self-styled "best disciple," Joseph Stalin, in the early thirties, enabling Hitler's storm troopers to march through the breach opened between Socialists and Communists by Stalin's dogma that "the main enemy" was not the Fascists but the "Social Fascists," the "Mensheviks" of that period. Thus the splits that the Twenty-one Points brought about among the American Communist parties were nothing compared with those in Italy and Germany.

RED RAIDS AND MOB ACTION

"Under modern conditions of warfare," wrote James Truslow Adams, "hate becomes almost as essential as ammunition, and hate is manufactured." In total war, hatred of the enemy, enthusiasm for hanging the Kaiser, hatred for everything German, despite Woodrow Wilson's famous sentence in his war message: "We are not enemies of the German people," became a part of the manufacture of total war enthusiasm on the no-less-total home front. Wilson himself moved from hatred of "the military masters under whom Germany is bleeding," to "this intolerable Thing. . . . a Thing without conscience or honor or capability for covenanted peace, must be crushed." Many of our ministers of the gospel gave a pseudo-religious exaltation to this hatred. The Reverend Doctor Henry Van Dyke, who wrote our City College song, *The City's Crown,* proposed to "hang every one who lifts his voice against entering the war." Dr. Newell Dwight Hillis of Plymouth Church in Brooklyn Heights, not far from where I spent so many years of my life, told his congregation that German soldiers are "sneaking, snivelling cowards." S. Parkes Cadman, pastor of the Central Congregational Church of Brooklyn, stated that the Lutheran Church in Germany "is not the bride of Christ, but the paramour of Kaiserism." And the evangelist, Billy Sunday, when he was invited to deliver a wartime prayer in the House of Representatives, addressed his God in these words: "Thou knowest, O Lord, that no nation so infamous, vile, greedy, sensuous, or bloodthirsty, ever disgraced the pages of history."* Thus even the Kaiser's "Gott mit uns" was eclipsed in America, less used to war than the countries of Europe.

The hatred extended itself to the German language. German disappeared from many of our high schools and colleges. One who spoke German on the streets (or what sounded like German to an untutored ear) put himself in jeopardy—anything from being compelled to kiss the flag to mob violence that occasionally ended in lynching. Much of our popular vocabulary suffered a sea change. *Hamburger* became *Salisbury steak, sauerkraut* became *liberty cabbage,* Hamburg Avenue was rebaptized Liberty Avenue, making two Liberty Avenues in Brooklyn, *frankfurters* became *hot dogs,* which they remain to this day, the German bands, which on street corners enlivened so much of my childhood, disappeared from the streets. More shocking to me, Wagner, whom I didn't miss as much as I would have Mozart or Beethoven, disappeared from concert programs. Mozart and Beethoven, and Bach and Brahms, so far as I remember, were tolerated. A number of state and local governments passed laws prohibiting church services in German, teaching the German language in schools in German communities, and public addresses in any language but English.

An example of frustrated anti-Germanism of which I was a witness was the invasion of the annual Sunday concert of the Bavarian Club in the Yorkville Casino by men from the Soldiers, Sailors, and Marines Club

* I am indebted to Mark Sullivan, the great journalistic historian of the current *History of Our Times* in six volumes, for refreshing my memory and insuring my remarkable "forgettory" against error in these quotations, as well as for his having refreshed and revived my memory of much that I have experienced.

meeting, held a mile away from predominantly German-American Yorkville. They burst in and demanded that an American flag be displayed. One was immediately and cheerfully produced. Then they demanded that the "Star-Spangled Banner" be sung. It was sung with gusto. When the invaders discovered that the concert singers were singing in a foreign tongue—some songs in Italian, some in French—they shouted, "Sing in English!" But the next song proved to be Gounod's "Ave Maria," sung in Latin, and they did not dare to interrupt it. In the intermission, a man delivered a brief address exhorting the audience to subscribe generously to the "Victory Loan." Many volunteered then and there to buy bonds, and the invaders left in disgust. I, too, left in disgust at the whole spectacle, the more so because it occurred on a Sunday in May, 1919, when the war was almost six months in the past.

Speaking of concerts, there was the case of Fritz Kreisler, an Austrian by birth and in his younger days a minor officer in the Austrian army. He was one of the greatest violinists that I had heard in my youth; indeed, I thought him the greatest of all. When the mayor of East Orange, New Jersey, a city of some culture, prevented him from giving a concert already advertised and arranged, Kreisler told Sol Hurok, then the modest impresario and manager of the Socialist party's Brownsville Labor Lyceum, that he would play without fee for the benefit of any nonprofit, antiwar organization but would give no more concerts for money as long as the war fever lasted. Hurok had already helped to build the Brownsville Labor Lyceum by running benefit concerts with well-known violin virtuosos, mostly of Russian-Jewish origin, and mostly, it seemed to me, pupils of the Hungarian-born violinist Leopold Auer, who became a professor of the St. Petersburg Conservatory of Music and director of the Imperial Music Society's concerts. It was this connection of Hurok with great virtuosos and with benefit performances of music, song, and dance, that was the start of his subsequent career. As the Socialist party declined he used these connections to become the outstanding concert impresario, in America, of Russian and occasionally other European stars, troupes and choruses, for half a century, until his death in the early seventies. While I was publicity director of the Rand School, I learned of Kreisler's offer to give a concert for the benefit of the school and looked forward to interviewing him for publicity purposes; but alas! when I set up the interview with Kreisler, in his place came Sol Hurok, whom I already knew well to be genial, but no genius. Still, the concert was an enormous success financially and morally—for we were proud of Kreisler's stand—and proud of him artistically. He spent perhaps an extra hour playing favorite short pieces, as encores, for his wildly enthusiastic audience.

"THE MANUFACTURE OF HATE"

You cannot "manufacture so much hate," to use James Truslow Adam's formulation, without its contaminating domestic life. Or, as Ralph

Barton Perry put it in 1918 in the *Yale Review,* "You cannot expect to incite people to the emotional level at which they willingly give their lives, or the lives of their sons, and have them view with cool magnanimity . . . the indifference of their neighbors." Indeed, it was not the soldiers at the front who showed this hatred—they did their job, killing in order not to be killed—but it was the people back home who tended to "do their bit" in this fashion. As Dos Passos wrote after seeing war at the front as a volunteer ambulance driver for the French in 1917, and then, at the rear in America:

> The basis of war spirit, the nature of which those of us who saw anything of the rear in 1917 and 1918 must remember, is the easy intoxication of partisan hatred.
>
> Don't forget that many people take active pleasure in the lynching spirit of wartime, with its complete suspension of inhibitions against violence, just as a few even take pleasure in the actual business of butchering their fellow man. War, whether in a good cause or bad, lets loose all the basic anti-social passions that it's the business of civilized society to keep chained up, and once it starts it follows its own laws, that have little to do with progress or democracy.
>
> Everybody who has really seen war close can recognize the difference between the matter-of-fact attitude of the actual worker in the machinery of fighting and the sadistic delirium of non-combatants screaming for blood of an enemy they have never seen.

As a historian, Woodrow Wilson knew all this, and grieved as he told it to Frank Cobb the night before he delivered his war message to Congress, for he knew his people, and he knew himself. "Once lead a people into war and they will forget that there was ever such a thing as tolerance. . . . To fight you must be brutal, and the spirit of ruthless brutality will enter into the very fibre of our national life. . . ."

Our tolerance and our personal freedom were the first casualties of our entrance into the war. In England it was different. The difference was in her gentler treatment of conscientious objectors, of cabinet ministers, her pacifists and socialists who resigned out of conscience, and other dissenters. But then, the mother country was old and had gone through so many more wars, and we, England's offspring, through so few. Our Espionage Act caused the arrest of over one thousand five hundred people, but there was not one spy among them! Yet the very word espionage was a warrant for any court, any jury, to make short shrift of those brought before them, and to give any mob, such as those who lynched the crippled IWW organizer, Frank Little, a righteous feeling as they carried out their lawless deed of terror. If the Espionage Act of June, 1917, caught no spies, and the more sweeping Sedition Act a year later caught no spies, they accomplished the purposes for which they were enacted. The chief aim of the Espionage Act was to forbid obstruction to recruiting, or opposition to conscription. The Sedition Act legalized the intolerance that I have been describing. Prepared like the Espionage Act by the President and the Department of Justice, it said all that the Espionage Act had implied and legalized all that was happening in courtrooms and on the street. Up to twenty years in prison and $20,000 in fines were to be meted out to any who might make any statements that could, or might, hinder the war effort; hurt recruiting, make harder the sale of war bonds, obstruct enlistment, or incite disloyalty. It provided that anyone who shall "willfully utter, print, write, or publish any disloyal, profane, scurrilous, or abusive language about the form of government of the United States, or the military or naval forces of the United States, or the flag of the United States, or the uniform of the Army or Navy," would face a prison term. And then, for good measure, it likewise proscribed any language intended to bring any of these institutions "into contempt, scorn, contumely, or disrepute." Against the unions, particularly those of the IWW, it repeated the litany in other words, making it illegal to utter, write, publish, print, speak, or "urge, incite, or advocate, any curtailment of production in this country of any thing, or things, product or products, necessary or essential to the prosecution of the war." And it legalized what the Postmaster General had been doing without any legal warrants. He might, without trial or hearing, merely "upon evidence satisfactory to him" stamp mail as "Undeliverable Under Espionage Act." What more warrant could officials, or police, or judges, or jurors, or mob require?

The antiwar journal I was editing, *Facts*, was declared unmailable by the Postmaster, and later suspended by me when reflection told me that the young men and women who were selling it on the streets and at meetings might be arrested as "spies" under the loosely worded Espionage Acts. Journal after journal was suspended after first being declared unmailable, then having an embargo placed on its receiving any mail, including subscriptions by mail and cash contributions to make up deficits.

The two acts encouraged mobs to "take care" of public meetings and invade and smash up Socialist and Communist and IWW headquarters and even printing plants, with the complacent complicity of the police. When there were arrests, not of the attackers but of their victims, they were usually followed by kangaroo court justice on the part of self-righteous judges and juries. Younger folk, who think that the McCarthy days were the greatest extreme of "political terror," will find the atmosphere of World War I (it was not repeated in World War II) a revelation as to what can happen to our Bill of Rights, our Constitution, and our governmental system. Besides curbing our free speech and press and civil liberties, the two Espionage Acts were aimed especially at those who thought that a volunteer army was more in accordance with American tradition than a conscript army. Those who were arrested or who had to evade the police because of this view, if they have lived long enough, will be bemused to contemplate the fact that the White House in the 1970's now favors a volunteer army and that on Thanksgiving Day, 1974, the last 2,500 or so conscripts were told that they could go home because our Army had switched to an all-volunteer force. Believing that a volunteer army is appropriate to American tradition is no longer "espionage" or "sedition"!

On September 5, 1917, there were simultaneous police raids in one dozen cities of our country, in which 166 members of the IWW were seized in their headquarters or their homes "for violation of the Espionage Act." This included virtually every leader of the IWW. Those who moved up to replace them were also seized. When defense committees were set up to raise funds for their defense in the courts, those committees were raided, too, and the Postmaster General declared an embargo on their receipt of mail, opened their letters, confiscated all checks and cash and all letters of encouragement and offers of assistance.

So, too, virtually every leader of the Socialist party of America except Morris Hillquit, who was recuperating from an attack of tuberculosis, was arrested and indicted. The aged and enfeebled Debs was given a ten year prison sentence, and even after the war was over, Woodrow Wilson stubbornly refused to pardon or give him amnesty. He had to wait for Harding to release him in 1921 to spend the last five years of his life as a free man (he died when he was 81).

In New York, where the treatment of opposition was at least somewhat more temperate than the more lawless Middle and Far West, the American Defense Society set up a vigilante patrol of more than one hundred men "to put an end to seditious street oratory." As Carlyle once wrote, "Of all forms of government, a government by busybodies is the worst," and the Department of Justice publicly encouraged the formation of large organizations of spy-hunting busybodies.

Yet it must be said that the recklessness of those who rejected freedom of discussion and ordinary civil rights in the midst of this "people's war" often had behind it high-minded motives. In his Flag Day Address the President himself had set the tone for them with his "Woe to the man or group of men that seeks to stand in our way in this day of high resolution." He called ever more sharply for the silencing of all questioners and critics, for he was angered because we were quoting against him his own words of the first two and one half years of the European war. If the metal mining companies could impudently blame the attempt of the IWW to organize their workers on "German influence," there were many Americans now who had sons or husbands in the armed forces and felt that hostility to the war was equivalent to hostility to members of their own family. There were those who felt that once we were in it, no one and nothing should be allowed to question our participation. Wilson's speeches emphasized the idealism of our motives and made many feel that the war gave a deeper meaning to their lives. To them intolerance seemed righteousness; the acts of mob terror were acts of loyalty and modes of participating in the war even if one was too old to fight in it. Their action was encouraged by the Espionage Act, by the Sedition Act, by the Department of Justice, by the Attorney General, by the press, by the utterances of well-known leaders, by clergymen. What were people to think and do when Attorney General Gregory himself said of the opponents of war, "May God have mercy on them, for they need expect none from an outraged people and an avenging government"?

THE PALMER RED RAIDS

Only when the war had safely ended and a less totally involved nation could have been expected to settle down and observe its Constitution and its traditional civil liberties, did our turn come to be hunted down in earnest. If it was Attorney General Gregory who had said in wartime, "May God have mercy on them, for they need expect none from an outraged people and an avenging government," it was his successor in office, Attorney General A. Mitchell Palmer, whose name has entered into the pages of history in "The Palmer Raids." Although the war ended on November 11, 1918, the first large-scale raids directed by the Lusk Committee of the New York Legislature and by the national Department of Justice under Attorney General Mitchell Palmer occurred in 1919. Indeed, Palmer did not become Wilson's Attorney General until the Spring of 1919, many months after Germany had surrendered. Having begun life as a Quaker, a pacifist, and Wilson Liberal, he followed and even ran ahead of his leader in the application of the war spirit to peacetime.

The first wholesale rounding up of Communists in New York consisted of the backing up of moving vans (there were not enough police wagons) to the entrances of dance halls where Communists and their sympathizers were celebrating the second anniversary of the Russian Revolution, or, more precisely, Lenin's seizure of power. The date was November 8, 1919. At the same time, over 700 policemen and special agents, some of them of the horrendous-sounding "bomb squad," invaded headquarters and meetings—including meetings that had been arranged on motion of *agents provocateurs*, carried away prisoners foreign and native born, tons of paper and records and applications for membership, placards and pictures on the walls, circulars and pamphlets, and hauled everyone and everything to the local headquarters of the Department of Justice, to police stations, prisons, and temporary concentration points.

Before the First World War, only two states had laws against "sedition" or related offenses. One of them was my native New York, which adopted a Criminal Anarchy Law after the assassination of President McKinley; the other was Tennessee, the occasion of whose law I do not know. No one was ever taken into court under either statute. But during the war, and particularly after its end, thirty-five states passed laws called sedition acts, criminal syndicalist laws, and the like. One of these was the State of Michigan, into the effects of which I was to run somewhat later.

Another state that went on a lawless binge and rushed through espionage and sedition laws of its own was California. California adopted a Red Flag law, a sedition law, and a criminal syndicalist law, under which some 500 persons were arrested and more than half convicted. These laws and arrests encouraged mob action as, perhaps, mob action encouraged the adoption of this flood of laws so uncharacteristic of America in normal times.

To give one example of extralegal action, there is the mood of generally staid and quiet Berkeley, where a mob burned the Tabernacle of the Church of the Living God when Pastor Sykes failed to lower the American flag at sundown. His service was interrupted by a reproof and a demand that he make the congregation sing the *Star-Spangled Banner*. When he refused to alter the service, they plunged the Reverend Sykes and two of his elders' heads down into a baptismal font intended for total immersion!

Especially zealous in the passage and use of such laws were those states where the IWW was strong and active in the organization of the metal workers, the lumber workers, and migratory workers of various descriptions such as fruit harvesters. Encouraged by these laws, mobs sometimes made up of well-known citizens whom the newspapers and the district attorneys refused to recognize or identify in print or in Grand Jury proceedings, ran members of the IWW out of town, sometimes on a rail, sometimes with ropes around their necks, sometimes with coats of tar and feathers. Some were arrested (their tormentors never) and thrown in jail, or if too numerous, into improvised encampments. One, Andrea Salsedo, variously accused of being an anarchist, a Communist, and a bomber, was held for a week on the fourteenth floor of the Department of Justice on Park Row in New York City, from which floor he "jumped or fell" to his mangled death on the sidewalk. Others, like Frank Little and Wesley Everest of the IWW, were lynched.

The efforts of the IWW to raise wages in order to keep up with the rising cost of living, their invasion of "company towns," and their attempts to organize the unorganized, were branded as "pro-German," though Germany lay prostrate. Finally, the Federal Department of Justice made wholesale raids on their headquarters simultaneously all over the country, arrested hundreds of them, and tried over 100 in a single trial without giving any of them a chance for separate trials in which individual guilt for some definite, single crime could be tested.

The judge selected to preside over this mass "trial" was Kenesaw Mountain Landis, who had reached national celebrity by "breaking up" the Standard Oil Trust some years earlier. He had already expressed his impartiality as a judge of such offenders as he had before him by saying, "I am sorry I cannot go to war, but since I cannot go, I can at least stay at home and fight the men who are fighting the soldiers here." He ended his career in the honorific post of America's baseball czar. The chief defendant before him in the IWW wholesale trial was Big Bill Haywood, a great battered hulk of a man with one eye missing, barely pushing fifty, a miner from the age of fifteen, once tried for alleged complicity for the murder of the Governor of Idaho and acquitted, then tried by the Socialist Party for advocating violence in labor disputes to meet the violence of the employers, and expelled by the party. He was sick with diabetes, looked as if he had been through several lifetimes of battles with company police, strikebreakers, and company gunmen in his efforts to organize the Western Federation of Miners, as indeed he had. While the other hundred-odd defendants (two had gone insane in jail and one had been murdered) all received sentences of varying length and severity, Judge Landis singled out Haywood for a sentence of twenty years in prison and a $10,000 fine, a sentence which meant that he would undoubtedly die in prison. In disguise, Haywood jumped his bail of $150,000, worked his way to Europe, and thence to what he thought was the land of freedom, the Soviet Union. I saw him in Russia in the summer of 1924, a sad, sick, and deeply disillusioned man. He had hoped to turn his fighting courage and organization experience to account in the unionization of the workingmen in Russia, but their only employer, the one-party Soviet governemnt, had no use for such talents. During his first few months in Russia, Big Bill was regarded as a picturesque celebrity, making gratulatory speeches and lending moral support to the Bolshevik regime. But when he tried to organize the Russian workers and teach them to fight for their rights—the things he knew best—he was told *Hands Off!* In November, 1921, he became involved in an American workers' colony in the Kuzbas district, which had the aim of building up the metal mining industry of Siberia, and also rebuilding the mining and metals industry of the Urals, started by Peter the Great but fallen into disrepair under Lenin. But the project got more suspicion than support, and soon failed. He returned to the dreary quarters in the Hotel Lux, worked for a time for the International Labor Defense, which defended prisoners of the "class war" and political prisoners in general everywhere, but *not* in Russia. He worked on his memoirs which revived his failing spirit with memories of his battles of long ago and far away, but the memoirs are well-nigh worthless because they were mercilessly censored after his death before being published by International Publishers, for the censors cut Big Bill to their petty pattern. Not long before his death, he married a Russian woman who acted as his nurse, and held a minor post in the government. As his loneliness, isolation, and frustration grew, he took refuge in drink and in reminiscing with old friends when chance brought them to Russia. As Elizabeth Gurley Flynn, his one-time common-law wife, wrote: "Big Bill longed for the land of baseball and picket lines . . . the Mississippi River and the Rocky Mountains, the America which was his home." And where one had at least a fighting chance to speak one's mind and organize one's fellow workers. He died on May 18, 1928, at the time of my second visit to Russia. He wanted to be buried in America. Half his ashes were sent home to be buried in the Waldheim Cemetery in Chicago; the other half lies under the Kremlin Wall, for in death the rulers of Russia did have use for him. Similarly, portions of two other Americans lie interred under the Kremlin Wall: John Reed, half of whose ashes are in Portland, Oregon, and C. E. Ruthenberg, whose American half is in a cemetery in Cleveland, Ohio.

The IWW was enfeebled and virtually destroyed by its unequal battle with the government and mob attacks; it did not survive the war as a genuine force for the organization of labor.

OUR TURN COMES

Thus the war was completely over when the spirit of wartime raids and wartime ignoring of civil liberties was turned in earnest upon us. As one commentator described both the wartime and the immediate postwar period: "It was an era of lawlessness and disorderly defense of law and order, of unconstitutional defense of the Constitution, of suspicion and civil conflict—in a very literal sense a reign of terror." But since the war was over, voices were also raised, ever more strongly, against the lawlessness. Charles Evans Hughes was one of the earliest and most distinguished to speak out for constitutional procedure and civil order. In May, 1920, with the jails crowded with Communists of every description, and with 249 "dangerous" Russians already shipped abroad on the unseaworthy old vessel, the *Buford*, twelve of our best known lawyers, all authorities on Constitutional Law, published a *Report upon the Illegal Practices of the Department of Justice*, which, though ridiculed by Attorney General Palmer, had considerable effect on the subsequent proceedings. The lawyers included such names as Felix Frankfurter, then teaching at the Harvard Law School, Zechariah Chafee, and Roscoe Pound, also at the Harvard Law School, Ernest Freund, Professor of Jurisprudence and Public Law at the University of Chicago, Francis Fisher Kane, former District Attorney of Philadelphia, Judge Alfred Niles of Baltimore, Frank P. Walsh, Joint Chairman of the War Labor Board, and Dean Tyrrell Williams of Washington University.

In the "Report of the Twelve Lawyers" can be found such verdicts on the "Practices of the Department of Justice" as the following:

> Under the guise of a campaign for the suppression of radical activities, the office of the Attorney General [they are referring to Palmer], acting by its local agents throughout the country, and giving express instructions from Washington, has committed continual illegal acts. Wholesale arrests both of aliens and citizens have been made without warrant or any process of law; men and women have been jailed and held *incommunicado* without access of friend or counsel; homes have been entered without search warrant and property seized and removed; other property has been wantonly destroyed; working men and working women suspected of radical views have been shamefully abused and maltreated.

Although the report of the righteously angry twelve prominent lawyers was gotten out in a hurry, it contained a photograph of the wrecked Russian People's House after the Department of Justice agents had seized what they pleased without search warrants, torn pictures and posters from the walls, smashed typewriters, the postal scale, desks, chairs and other furnishings; affidavits from men and women who had been arrested without warrants and subjected to third-degree tortures; accounts of the use of *agents provocateurs* who manufactured false evidence; a photostat of a forged signature to a "confession" manufactured by a department agent who wrote out the supposed confession and committed the forgery; directions from the Attorney General to the Department of Justice agents on how to conduct or misconduct themselves in raids and random arrests; revolting descriptions of conditions in sardine-box overcrowded jails in Hartford, Detroit, and other cities; copies of a propaganda sheet and even printing mats supplied to magazines and newspapers telling them how to play up the cases with scareheads and scare stories; accounts of violations of the Fourth, Fifth, Eighth, and First Amendments of our Constitution by the Attorney General and his agents; careful investigations of cases of violations of our laws and practices made separately by the various signers of the report; a decent and lawful decision by Louis F. Post, Assistant Secretary of Labor, who prevented the Department of Labor from participating in the scandalous proceedings; evidence that the Department of Justice had availed itself of "government by busybodies" or organized and officially approved snoopers, spies, and mobs, to flesh out the Department of Justice for its great raids; a propaganda letter by the Attorney General to magazine editors which contains such "information" as "Bolshevism, syndicalism, the Soviet Government, sabotage, etc. are only names for old theories of violence and criminality. . . . Its sympathizers in this country are composed chiefly of criminals, mistaken idealists, social bigots, and unfortunate men and women suffering from hyperesthesia.* This Department, as far as existing laws allow [a masterpiece of understatement], intends to keep up an unflinching war against this movement no matter how cloaked or dissembled." The leader of this rowdyism was sometimes Attorney General Palmer or, as in his Flag Day Speech, the President of the United States.

Once more, I remind the younger reader to compare this reign of terror with the much milder days of Senator Joseph McCarthy, when a man or woman felt himself a hero if he pleaded the Fifth Amendment before an orderly Court or Committee.

During all these raids and savage atrocities, I continued to go about my business, and read Marx and De Leon and what I could get in English of Lenin and Trotsky. After being driven out of, or resigning from, the school system, I earned my living by editing a trade paper, *The Mediator, Organ of the Jewish Master Bakers' Federation*, then as a reporter for the *Richmond County Advance*, a newspaper in Staten Island, then in social work as one of the field workers for the Jewish Big Brothers, in charge of Jewish juvenile delinquent boys in District 13 (Harlem), until I became *de facto* editor of the *Communist World.* I say, "*de facto*," because the journal had an official editor, Maximilian Cohen, who did no editing because he was too busy with high politics in the Communist party. It also had a business manager, named Ashkenudzi, who did no business managing because we had no business to manage. He too was engaged in "high politics." I was on the masthead as associate editor. When all the conventions and splittings described in Chapter 14 were taking place and I was tied up in Brooklyn by the operation on my ingrown toenail, whoever was not a

* *Hyperesthesia,* is defined as: "unusual or pathological sensitivity of the skin, or of a particular sense."

delegate on the scene in Chicago, possessed of a vote and able to bring some little bloc of followers to either the Communist Party or the Communist Labor Party, was not elected to any post. Though I had always vied with Jim Larkin for the highest vote in all elections of officials in the New York left wing, I got no votes at all in Chicago for I was not there to be persuaded or to make my presence felt. I now found that I had to continue editing the *Communist World* as *de facto* editor, without a title, which rather pleased me, for I did not relish the idea of being dependent on earning my living as a party official, and felt freer now to indulge my wanderlust which made me anxious to see other parts of our country.

The paper I edited, I must confess, was a poor one. Lately I found a collection of all its issues, except one, in the Hoover Library, and as I reexamined them, I wondered to whom they could have been addressed; what evidence they bore that they were issued in America, and which Americans ("the workers") would have read them and understood what they were about, or would have responded to its hailstorm of slogans and exhortations.

Thus Volume I, Number 1, carried a streamer headline in 100 point type (an inch and one half high) which read: BOYCOTT THE ELECTION! I thought the slogan silly, for it might only have been justified if we were on the eve of a revolution and felt that our legislature and Congress were about to be replaced by genuine, all-powerful Soviets. I myself was running at the moment in the Socialist primaries in the Sixth Assembly District, Brooklyn, against my old friend and well-known socialist leader, William Morris Feigenbaum. The following year I was to run for Congress in the same district. So far were we from having a popular following that I was ignominiously defeated in both elections. Here is how the *Socialist Call* reported the triumph of the Right-Wing:

> The most striking victory of all was that of William M. Feigenbaum over Bert Wolfe, the Left-Wing king-pin candidate who had the best organized Left-Wing district in the city back of him, and who waged an aggressive campaign. [Its title of "best organized" was given because, when we were locked out of the Socialist headquarters at 167 Tomkins Avenue, I rented a little undergound store on Stockton Street, the entrance to which was four steps below the sidewalk, and put in its window a sign: SIXTH A.D. SOCIALIST PARTY—LEFT-WING and later 6TH A.D. COMMUNIST PARTY]. The district showed a vote of 61-42—police figures. The correct figures are 115-42.

The total vote for both Feigenbaum and myself, a mere 157 votes in a district that only two years earlier had had a Socialist majority and elected an Assemblyman, shows how much the fortunes of both Socialists and Communists had dwindled as a result of the splits and the squabbles. Manifestly the voters of the district, whether workers or "middle class" or whatever, did not understand what we were shouting about. And here were we, calling upon them to "boycott the elections" as if we were on the eve of a revolution, had outlived parliamentary elections, and were in a position to call for them to establish something called "Soviets!"

Though the C.E:C. of the Communist Party ordered me to publish the headline, BOYCOTT THE ELECTIONS, and I dutifully published an "explanation" that I had been nominated by the Left-Wing before the Communist Party was formed, "but now I DO NOT WANT YOUR VOTES!" I continued, repeating or paraphrasing the Central Executive Committee's resolution:

There are two fundamental reasons for the Communist Party's boycott. . . . the Party's attitude towards parliamentarism and . . . elections [and] the industrial crisis prevailing in America today. The Communist Party holds that the class struggle is essentially a struggle to conquer the power of the state. . . . It keeps in the foreground its appeal for proletarian revolution . . . and the dictatorship of the proletariat. Participation in elections. . . is FOR THE PURPOSE OF REVOLUTIONARY PROPAGANDA ONLY! . . . Workers, the United States seems to be on the verge of a revolutionary crisis. The workers, through their mass strikes, are challenging the state. . . . Out of these mass struggles must issue the inspiration and the means for the conquest of power by the workers. Boycott the elections!

It is only fair to say that the year 1919 was politically a turbulent year and that such events as the Seattle General Strike had convinced Lenin, too, that America was on the verge of revolution. As I remember it, my street-corner speeches contesting this election with Feigenbaum did not make much more sense than this C.E.C. appeal, for I ended every address with the words, "All power to the workers." For their part, the workingmen themselves wanted anything but the task of running the complicated affairs of the City, the State, and the Country. As a result of my speeches, some handfuls shifted from me to Feigenbaum, but the bulk of my auditors either didn't bother to vote, or if they did, cast their votes for the Democratic party. Forty-two faithfuls in the entire Assemby district voted for me. And a few of those must have been friends and relatives, for after all, it was my own, or rather my wife's election district, and a number of my wife's relatives lived in it, as well as a number of beneficiaries of her big-hearted mother.

Looking back at the *Communist World* from this distance, much of what I have said about the young Communist movement and the paper I edited seems remote, unreal, even laughable. But if the reader will make the effort to put himself back into the year 1919, the picture becomes somewhat different. The opportunities for American radicalism of all varieties seemed immense in that year of interregnum between all-out war and what was supposed to be all-out peace. Millions of soldiers were being demobilized and hundreds of thousands of those who had risked their lives at the front were finding that there were no jobs waiting for them at home. Europe was in turmoil: crowns were tumbling and ancient empires falling; there were revolutions, still not defined in their nature, in Russia, Germany, Austria-Hungary, then a Communist revolution in Hungary itself and another in Bavaria; soldiers were carrying their arms from the front and imposing their will insofar as they knew what they willed. A strikewave unprecedented in our history swept through America: the Seattle General Strike grew out of a protest at the closing down of the shipyards; the Lawrence Textile Strike; the national coal strike; and, wonder of wonders, the Boston police strike; the great steel strike involving 365,000 workers; the battles of the workers in many industries to keep wages abreast of the high cost of living, and of the employers to end the wartime gains of the labor movement to establish or restore the open shop. Not until the Great Depression would the labor movement again show so much militancy.

However much we were inspired by Lenin's success in Russia and by the revolutionary movements that seemed to be sweeping through Central Europe, we had no thought of becoming a mere adjunct and agency of the Russian Communist party. (Indeed, the refusal to become thus an agency of a foreign power was precisely the core of my battle with Joseph Stalin in 1929.) It was still a time when nothing had taken permanent shape in our movement. To the youngsters who formed a majority of our English-speaking section, it seemed possible for us to shape the party according to our will and convince or overcome those who wished to shape it according to their European traditions and loyalties. We knew America, we thought, and would convince them and make them understand how it was, what was worthy in its traditions, and what had to be fought, purified, and reformed. We improvised from day to day; everything we did, even that which was imitative or silly, seemed to us exciting, appropriate, spontaneous, and new. Ours was an interesting game, as Theodore Draper has written, "for which the rules had not yet been invented." We—at least I speak for myself and those nearest to me—felt that we were an American party that recognized large elements in our American heritage that were precious and worthy of conserving, enlarging, and building upon. Even though we were beginning to get peremptory notes from Zinoviev and not too knowledgeable, but forceful and didactic, letters from Lenin, which aimed at fitting us into the Procrustean bed of International Communism as they saw it, I still believed that they were intended only as helpful suggestions, often exciting ones, and as successful examples to imitate, after adapting them to American conditions, but not as categorical commands. In 1926, to the horror of some of our foreign-born and foreign-inspired comrades, I could still publish a pamphlet to celebrate the Sesquicentennial of the Declaration of Independence and put on its cover, under my title *Our Heritage from 1776*, a Red Flag bearing a pine tree around which was coiled a rattlesnake and beneath the tree the words, DON'T TREAD ON ME—one of the earliest banners of the American War for Independence.

A decade later, when I got to know Arthur Koestler intimately, he asked me: "What was it, Bert, that you hated in yourself, that made you join the Communist Party?" I answered proudly, "I did not join the Communist Party. I was one of its founders, and, if we note the date of the founding of the Left-Wing and its call for a 'New International,' I can count myself one of the founders of the Communist International. Nothing that I hated in myself made me join such a party, nor could I have joined it when it became the party which approved the blood purges. What I hated was total war, and America's entrance into it."

"Oh, a pacifist, eh?" he retorted, and lost interest in pursuing our conversation further. Be that as it may, the party did not stay forever new. It got tangled in its own traditions, rules, rituals, dogmas, and clichés, and more and more fitted itself into the Procrustean bed that Lenin and Zinoviev were making for it. Had I stayed in New York for a few more of its formative years, I should have learned this fact much earlier; but going suddenly to California, as I shall narrate in the next chapter, and later to Mexico, I had much more chance to stamp my temperament and my views upon the party in those places for the freer exercise of these views, so that the party as I saw or mis-saw it, continued to seem new, malleable, fresh, spontaneous, and open.

In 1919 we understood next to nothing about the American labor movement. We supported the IWW, which was being ground to pieces, against the A.F.L., which was fighting desperately to hold such strong points as it had gained during the war. If the journal I was editing seemed remote from America, the *Revolutionary Age*, edited in Boston by the best of our editors, Louis Fraina, in its very subhead proclaimed itself "A Chronicle and Interpretation of Events in Europe." And Fraina stuck doggedly to the promise in the subhead he had thought up. When he spoke of the wave of strikes in America, it was in the general terms of his diagrammatic picture of the "revolutionary age" to which his journal was dedicated. Strikes for keeping wages in line with the cost of living were of little interest to him. "These strikes," he proclaimed didactically, "must always strive to cease being strikes and become *revolutionary mass action against Capitalism and the state*. . . . Every strike must be a small revolution, organizing, educating, and disciplining the workers for the final revolutionary goal." (What would the rank and file workingman fighting desperately to keep his wages abreast of the high cost of living think of such injunctions and such haughty dismissal of his strike?) Even the great steel strike did not waken in him, in the year 1919, a feeling for the struggles of the American labor movement. In September of that year, when we had made him editor of *The Communist*, he wrote, "In the steel industry, the A.F.L. is imposing this reactionary system upon the workers—assisted by the Syndicalist W. Z. Foster! . . . Our task is to participate in this action, to develop the general political strike that will break the power of capitalism and initiate the dictatorship of the proletariat—all power to the workers!" And in October, his journal added: "The revolution is the issue in the steel strike." I imagine that neither the syndicalist William Z. Foster, nor the workingman risking his all to unionize his industry, would be either understanding or grateful for this sort of attention to his efforts.

Vol. I, No. 3 of the *Communist World*, which I was editing, reflected the fact that not only the "class war" but the war on the radical movements was being stepped up to a new high, and that our turn had come. The streamer headline cried, LONG LIVE THE COMMUNIST PARTY! The issue was no longer filled with events in Europe, but with those in New York City. The raiders had swooped down simultaneously on the local IWW headquarters; the Russian Communist daily, *Novy Mir;* the headquarters of the Communist party in which a criminal dance was in progress and from which the "dangerous terpsichoreans" were taken *en masse* to a gymnasium at police headquarters; the Communist party headquarters of the 5th Assembly District, the Bronx; the 17th Assembly District, Harlem; the Russian branch of the C.P. in Brownsville, Brooklyn; the Hungarian Workers' Home; the King's County Right Wing Central Committee, which, however, was left undisturbed when some one had the wit to ask for search and arrest warrants; a Package Party of the Young People's Socialist League, which I had just persuaded at their Congress to break with the S.P. and adopt a clause in favor of the Dictatorship of the Proletariat; a number of branches, and the Center of the Union of Russian Workers; and several other nests of conspiracy. The raid netted 2,500 captives, of which, after questioning, only 2 women and 35 men were held for prosecution. When the newspapermen asked why so many had been seized and so few held, Senator Lusk explained lamely: "Search warrants were not obtained for the purpose of taking prisoners . . . but to obtain literature [which—I interjected— they could have had free for the asking] and records of the Communist Party." Among those held were Gitlow and Larkin, charged with publishing, in the *Revolutionary Age*, the *Manifesto and Program of the Left Wing of the Socialist Party,* for which crime they went to the Tombs, and then to Sing Sing Prison.

If the *Left Wing Manifesto* was a criminal document, I knew what to expect. But they did not catch me that night in their wholesale surprise raids, for I was working late at the printing plant, correcting page proofs for issue No. 4. Number 5 appropriately contained a list of *Legal Don'ts* for members of the Communist party who might find themselves under arrest and interrogation. Thenceforth there were articles manifestly written by me, but they were unsigned. My name, and indeed, all names, disappeared from the masthead. But the telltale humorous column, *Idiotorials,* was there as usual, for in every paper I ever had a hand in, including even *The Mediator* and the *Richmond County Advance,* there had always been a humorous column. Unlike the solemn owls among my friends and comrades, I always saw a funny side to everything in which I was engaged or which touched me closely. The police, however, were not given to style analysis or content analysis, which might not have stood up well in the courtroom. Nevertheless, they felt I was missing from the seventeen men and women they had held for indictment.

WHAT EVER HAPPENED TO BERT WOLFE?

We were in the printing plant, my wife, Ella, and I, engaged in putting the latest issue of *The Communist World* "to bed,"—that is, we were proofreading the last columns of copy that had just been, or were still being set up on the linotype machine; checking earlier galley proofs against page proofs to eliminate errors the printer had put in when he reset a line to correct an error we had caught in the galley; okaying page proofs, and getting everything ready for press. I do not remember which issue it was, nor what the main banner headline was, but I should like to think that the headline was: BRITISH EMPIRE CRACKING! for that was my favorite headline in retrospect, since it was almost the only banner head that turned out to be true, although the crack I thought I perceived as I watched the Irish and Indians struggling for independence took several more decades and a second world war before it widened to the breaking point. And now as I look at countries like Uganda, given her freedom by Britain, I am not sure that they weren't better off as colonies of, historically, the most gentle of imperial masters.

At noon we went out for lunch and a breath of air free from the smell of gas jets and molten lead. I bought a paper, attracted by the headline: SEVENTEEN REDS SEIZED! SOME ARRESTED IN THEIR HIDING PLACES. I scanned the list of names of those arrested, all familiar and friends of mine. "Ella," I said, "we'd better not go home tonight. That's a list from which one name has been withheld until they lay hands on him—that's my name."

"Where shall we go?" my wife asked.

"Let's put the paper to bed first, then we'll think about it." So we returned to our task, working as steadily and fast as the measured speed of linotyper and compositor permitted. Night came, and we arranged for overtime service of printers and pressmen. By the time I okayed the press proofs and copies were being run off, it was near midnight. We were both dead tired. "Let's get one good night's sleep," I said, "and some clean underwear. Let's take a chance that they won't look for me until tomorrow." Too weary to think of where to hide, we took the Myrtle Avenue El to the station nearest our furnished room at Doctor Katims's house at 138 Sumner Avenue in Williamsburg, Brooklyn. My wife put her head on my shoulder and we both fell asleep, but woke up automatically when the conductor called "Sumner Avenue." We stumbled down the stairs, suddenly we became aware that at the bottom of the stairway was standing Vova, one of my wife's cousins. "Don't go home," he said to me, "there are two men waiting for you, one in your room and the other across the street."

"How did you know that we would take the Myrtle Avenue El?" I asked.

"We didn't. Other people are waiting at all trolley stops and el stations where you might get off."

"Who warned you that they were waiting for me?"

"Dr. Katims' wife." Dr. Katims, Republican precinct leader in an overwhelmingly Democratic and Socialist election district, was above suspicion.

Besides being our landlord, he was our family physician and friend. His wife, upon going out to shop, warned my mother-in-law, who roused relatives and friends to watch all the approaches to our home.

"Go home with Vova," I said to my wife, "and I will go to your sister Beckie's home in Linden, where you can bring me copy and proofs when you are sure you are not being followed."

I knew the city and Staten Island well, having once been a reporter there. If they had other men waiting for me at the main terminal, and other exits from New York, I thought, then it would be safest for me to take the Staten Island Ferry, the train across Staten Island to the Jersey ferry, then the ferry to Elizabethport, thence to travel to Elizabeth and Linden. By that time it would be morning, and I wouldn't have to wake up and alarm the house. I had forgotten that I was tired, but I did doze in stations and conveyances while waiting for connections. I arrived at Beckie's home in Linden in time for an early breakfast. Beckie's husband, a metal roofer handy with his hands, had screened in their porch, and thus I had a room, a little cold, despite a gas heater, where I could sleep. My editorial work I could do inside the house, which thus became the office of the *Communist World*, until *The Communist* moved to New York near the end of the year 1919 and the *Communist World* was merged into it.

AN IDYLLIC HIDEOUT

My life was peaceful there in suburban Linden, at that time a small town with empty lots, stretches of green grass, no oil refineries or other important industries. To compensate my sister-in-law for the trouble I gave her, I ran most of her errands to butcher, baker, and grocer, which occasioned one episode involving me and a pack of dogs, that went into

Linden folklore. One frosty, snowy day, I went to the butcher, quite a distance from her home, to buy liver for the family and boarder. Clutching the butcher's package under my arm close to my overcoat, I walked back to her house, thinking of an editorial I was planning to write. "Where's the liver?" cried Beckie as I took the butcher paper from under my arm. The paper had torn from the wetness of the fresh blood, and all the liver had fallen out. Not a slice was left, while behind me trailed a nondescript pack of sniffing dogs. "The dogs got it!" she cried.

"I'll see." Back I went the whole distance, retracing my path over the snow. Lying nicely refrigerated on the icy paths, I found every slice of liver. Not a bit was missing, but if the dogs had reversed their path instead of following me and the good-smelling paper, not a bit would have remained.

One other adventure is worth recording, too. When the cold nights came, my bed, however many blankets they threw over me on the porch, was icy cold. To warm it a bit, a cloth-covered rubber gas pipe was led from the kitchen gas stove to a small gas-burning heater on the porch. It helped. But one night, someone passed me in the dark on the way into the house and knocked the pipe loose from the gas stove. So well had my brother-in-law sealed the porch, that the gas fumes stayed with me as I slept, until I was awakened by a frightful headache and a desire to urinate. I stumbled into the bathroom, and fell in a dead faint on the cold tile floor. There they found me, still unconscious, in the morning. It took a few days until the carboxy-haemoglobin was eliminated from my blood, but after that I was none the worse for being so near to death. Aside from those two adventures, my life was quiet and semirustic. When I learned that my journal was to be merged with *The Communist*, I began to grow a Vandyke beard to change my appearance, and wrote to chambers of commerce of various towns in California asking them what chance there was to open a bookstore there. They all sent me colored and colorful prospectuses, each sounding more wonderful than the other. To my surprise, although my hair was brown, my Vandyke turned out to be dark red, and a perfect disguise.

My wife found life less easy. She remained, alone in our furnished room, at Dr. Katims's house. Each morning all too early, two burly men in plain clothes arrived, to see if I had come home to sleep and if they could catch me. Each day they questioned her as to my whereabouts, of which she professed ignorance. Often they took her to be questioned by District Attorney O'Rorke. He tried to appeal to her pride. "Look at you and your husband," he said, "two such cultured, well-educated people. Do you think you should be associating with such gross and vulgar people as Winitsky?" Winitsky was neither gross nor vulgar, but being enormously fat, with his clothes always ready to burst at the seams, he looked as if he might be.

On other occasions, O'Rorke asked questions about all the members of the National Left-Wing Council who had been arrested. He particularly grilled her about our friend, Jay Lovestone. Ella professed to know nothing of significance about these characters and their goings-on. "Will this refresh your memory?" O'Rorke said suddenly, pulling out of a drawer photostats of letters in her own handwriting, written to Jay Lovestone and touching both on political and personal matters. She professed ignorance of what she had written and what the letters referred to in their rather cryptic language.

Despite this early morning harassment, she made her afternoon and evening journeys to see me at her sister's home, bringing copy for editing, proofs to correct, and other materials, always making sure that she was not being followed. And from me she brought the corrected proofs back to the printing plant. One black night she burst into her sister's home in Linden, crying. "A big dog followed me in the dark. He jumped on me and knocked me over." Aside from that, nothing serious happened, for it never occurred to the detectives to watch her all day long, and follow her circumspectly when she set out to visit me.

TO THE GOLDEN LAND

Where to go in the California wonderland? To the fast-growing southland around Santa Monica where oil derricks and orange trees marched hand in hand over the hills covered with chapparal and live oak and flowering eucalyptus, and where there was as yet no thought of smog? To Santa Barbara or Monterey and Carmel where the breakers pounded the headlands of mountains that jutted far out into the waters of Monterey Bay? To some quieter town on the Peninsula like Redwood City where the climate, its brochure assured me, was "best in the West by Government test"? To the fabulous city by the Golden Gate? I had weeks and weeks to dream and decide until the year's end, when I had to choose among the lands where felicity beckoned. It was hard to choose, but in the end I chose San Francisco and have never regretted the choice, for it was a city with which I instantly fell in love. To this day as I toil in the sleepy towns of Palo Alto and Stanford, my dream of true felicity is still to move Hoover Tower to Russian Hill, overlooking the Golden Gate.

To go west, should I ask permission of the Central Executive committee? Would they grant it, or *instruct* me otherwise? I felt I owed them nothing, for they had failed to elect me to an official post just because I was not present at a maze of meeting halls and splits while laid up with an operation on a big toe, therefore I was free from any assigned task. Besides, like the maverick I was, I did not belong to any herd nor was I one to let any Central Executive or other "higher body" decide where I was to live and what I was to do for a living or a way of life.

Most important of all, I knew there was evidence of a spy in a high place, so that the moment I told the committee, my freedom would be at an end. (Actually, I learned later, there were at least two police agents that would have been privy to my whereabouts and intentions, namely, F-22, the Finnish Swede, Ferdinand Peterson, and F-100, Jacob Nosovitsky.)

I've never been afraid to accept the idea of my own imprisonment, if it became unavoidable while doing things in which I deeply believed, but unlike Maximilian Cohen, who told me that he thought it "was romantic" to be imprisoned and that it proved that one was a "real revolutionary," I wanted to continue doing what I believed I should be doing, teaching and writing and editing and speaking, and not be hampered by the fettering routine of a "romantic" cell in Sing Sing or the Tombs. In the end, I decided that I would tell no one I was going to California, but members of my family, and to tell the committee I had gone to Switzerland, traditional home of political exiles. When I got to California, as the chamber of commerce brochures convinced me, I could have my picture taken in surroundings that would look like some sunny southern slope of Switzerland, and send it as a picture postcard, to those who wondered what had happened to me. (Actually, in a walk down the Peninsula to Palm Drive at Stanford I had a picture taken which I sent by personal messenger to friends and comrades as a testimony to my presence on the sunny Italian slopes of Switzerland.)

When the time came to go, my wife and I agreed that I should go alone, and, as soon as I got a job in San Francisco, send for her, whereupon she would come as fast as the transcontinental train and the matter of packing would permit. (We did not have much to pack.) About my journey, I was still cautious, for the mad red raids were continuing on a random massive scale. (No doubt they were as mad in their fears as we in our dreams, as inept in their searches as we in our methods of evading them.) I asked my wife to buy a ticket for me from New York to San Francisco. To avoid such closely watched terminals as the Grand Central and the Pennsylvania Station, I would get on the train at Newark, she would accompany me to the next station where she could get a train back to New York City, and I would speed on for four days and three nights to the Oakland-San Francisco Ferry, which we were to enter, train and all.

It was my first trip across the country, a bitter cold day at the beginning of February, 1920, and our train was being chased by a blizzard all across the country. The next few days thereafter, no train would be able to make it. When I got to Chicago, I decided to see my first Great Lake, Lake Michigan. I walked down gently sloping streets, and then across an ice-covered expanse with no buildings on it. Finally I asked a fellow pedestrian, "I beg your pardon, sir, can you tell me how to get to Lake Michigan?"

"You've been walking on it for nearly half a mile," he answered. It was one of those rare instances in which, even far out from the shore, the lake was frozen over. From Chicago on, the blizzard still pursued us, until we went over the high Sierras, through dark tunnels and snowsheds—then suddenly we were dropping down the last slope into a region where palm trees were growing and, in late winter, buds and flowers were visible and deciduous trees had forgotten to drop their leaves because they failed to watch the calendar. I had never seen a palm tree and could not believe my eyes. So this was the golden land! Two days later, I wrote my wife that it was February 5th and that I was sitting in the warm sun, with my jacket off, on a bench in Sutro Gardens. My wife simply did not believe me: either I had joined some chamber of commerce public relations section or I was painting the glowing picture to get her to leave wintry New York City a little earlier. A few months later, when the Communist Party central office in Chicago directed me to form a protest movement among the unemployed, I found that those without jobs had simply left San Francisco with packs on their backs, were sleeping on grassy fields or in barns or on haystacks, picking their vegetables from farmlands, getting a meal from one farmhouse or another, and enjoying their spring trips through California's gentle fields. I failed utterly to form an unemployment protest movement! I was on vacation!

But that's running ahead a bit. Coming back to Chicago, when I left Lake Michigan's frozen shore, I eyed my fellow passengers. One of them, a tall, handsome man with a chiselled face, was reading *Swann's Way* in a Modern Library edition. I opened up a conversation with him. He proved to be a German-born waiter, well-read, accustomed to work in San Francisco's best restaurants, ambitious to become a writer, Otto X. . . He gave me many suggestions concerning life in San Francisco, and when he heard that I was going there "to open a bookstore," he promised to introduce me to Leon Gelber, bookseller and expert on rare books for the *White House*, a San Francisco department store, who also wanted to go into the book business for himself. All he needed was money, and perhaps we could form a partnership. But alas, if I were to open a bookstore, all I would need, too, was money, though I did not tell Otto. He told me such things as, "If you have never seen the Pacific, the way to see it for the first time is to take the Number 1 Trolley out to The Cliff. I later took his advice, and shall never forget that first view of the Pacific shore. After four days, as we approached the end of our journey, he showed signs of increasing agitation. "Aren't you glad to get back?" I asked.

"I have just come back from a trip through Europe with a wealthy woman, who paid all my expenses. I telegraphed my wife [a waitress, but not a book reader], and I don't know whether she will meet me." She did. But their marriage must have been broken all the same, for when I spent a night with Otto in his home on the Pacific shore, drinking fine Burgundy wine all night, and at dawn walking over the sandy miles of beach, she was nowhere to be seen. Otto, and Leon Gelber, were my first friends in San Francisco, and introduced me to many other interesting persons as "Arthur Albrecht, who has come out here to open a bookstore." The bookstore was eventually opened as Gelber and Lilienthal, Lilienthal having supplied the money I did not possess, and the two set up the firm, with which I had nothing to do. As far as I know, it prospered, until Gelber, often a moody person, unexpectedly committed suicide, whereupon the firm, of which he was the expert, went out of business.

But why was I introduced as "Arthur Albrecht"? Of course, it was the name I had given to Otto X, along with the story of my dream of opening a bookstore. Since I wanted to be publicly active in the San Francisco labor and radical movement without having to face extradition proceedings to be transported back to New York for "criminal anarchism," the reddish beard was not protection enough. I thought of new names (aliases the police call them) and since I knew what a poor memory I have, I did not want to have to invent a past and then forget or change some part of what I had said concerning it. "Oh, what a tangled web we weave . . ." the poet had advised me. So I took the name of a classmate whom I knew well, and with the name, a past. Arthur Albrecht and I had spent many happy hours on the banks of the Hudson hardly a stone's throw from C.C.N.Y., arguing and chatting, and settling man's fate and that of the universe. I was in those days "unconventional," and he was respectably ultra-conservative. In the City College Yearbook I helped edit, I put next to his name the dictum, "He agrees with the majority, and has the courage of his convictions." I knew that our paths would diverge, that I could never hurt his respectable career, and of course, if I ever could, I would step forward to clear him of responsibility for my doings. Actually, he pursued the even tenor of his ways, became an Economics professor in the Baruch School of Business Administration of City College, and our paths did not cross again until the night when the college decided to honor him on his becoming a Professor Emeritus, and me by giving me one of the four annual Townsend Harris Awards. That night, I decided to tell him, but when the ceremonies were over and I stepped down from the dais to the table where sat the Emeriti, he was surrounded by so many people offering congratulations, that I will have to wait for the next appropriate occasion, when I will send him a marked copy of the present book. Anyhow, I soon changed my name to Arthur Albright at the suggestion of two Scottish workingmen who were in the class that I taught on *The History of Classes through the Ages.* "Albrecht is all right for a Scotsman to pronounce," said Potts, "but most of the Americans in your class canna' pronounce it, why don't you make it Albright?" And Albright it became.

In my modest baggage on the Westward journey were the requisite weapons for the Wild West: a fountain pen and a portable typewriter. First of all I had to find a room and a job. How I found the room I no longer remember, but the search for a job is engraved on my memory. I tramped from publisher to publisher, from private academy to academy, from bookstore to bookstore: *no help wanted* was all the answer I got. I scanned the want ads for jobs that fit or attracted. Business was booming in February, 1920, but San Francisco was a branch office city. All I found were positions for bookkeeper, accountant, cashier, ledger clerk, a field in which I knew nothing.

Despite the cheapness and excellence of the food in the city's cafeterias, and the still excellent restaurants in the Latin Quarter, my meager capital dwindled rapidly toward the vanishing point. "Very well, then," I told myself, "I shall go into bookkeeping or accounting." I went to a bookstore with a window stacked with a series of *how to* books: *Letter Writing Made Easy; Dancing Made Easy; Ice Skating Made Easy; Lovemaking Made Easy; Sign Painting Made Easy; Bookkeeping Made Easy*. . . . There it was! I put down my dollar, and was on the road to accountancy.

For the next three days I spent all day on a bench in the sun in Union Square Park, reading my new book. Before I was half through with it, I began answering ads. The principle of double entry seemed so simple that I could not understand why pupils took two or more years to study commercial bookkeeping, but I knew nothing about office machines and office routine. I typed my applications, for my handwriting, while always legible when I write for others to read, at first glance looks disorderly or illegible. I enclosed in each letter of application a three by five card asking that it be filed for possible future reference in case the job was already filled when my letter came.

To my surprise, within a day, my bookkeeping book still unfinished, I got a letter from C. P. Mathey, auditor of the National Carbon Company: "The position was filled when your letter arrived, but your letter impressed me. If you are willing to take a job as a ledger clerk, which pays only $125 a month, come in and see me."

What was there to lose? Even if I were fired the first day as being too green, I would learn how to use some business machines, and be more experienced for the next job. Would I have to give references? Well, then I would give the names and addresses of some businessmen in New York. It would take a couple of weeks or more for an inquiry to go there and back (there were no commercial airplanes then.) Maybe Mr. Mathey would not even bother to write. If he did, and an unfavorable answer came back, I would really by then be an experienced ledger clerk. I talked to Mr. Mathey and got the job as ledger clerk of the National Carbon Company, a branch of Union Carbon and Carbide—a humble job, but with a proud company. And $125, when and if I got it, would buy a lot. Two days later I pawned my typewriter and even my fountain pen, and wrote Ella to come to San Francisco.

From the auditor's office I was taken to a desk in the midst of a huge floor of desks, given a loose ledger sheet and a number of primary documents like invoices or bills of sale, and told to post them in the appropriate columns. "When you fill a column, use a Burroughs to tabulate and get the sum. If you need to multiply, use the Monroe." And with that I was left to my own devices. But, how to find out how to operate a Burroughs or a Monroe?

I went over to the man operating a Monroe Calculator, and asked him a deliberately abstract question which I knew he would find too difficult to answer, and would find it much easier to show me how to operate the machine. "I know how to use a Burroughs," I said, "but I have never used a Monroe. What is the difference between them?"

"Well, this is how you use the Monroe . . . to multiply . . . to divide . . . to add . . . to subtract." Mission accomplished!

A little later, I went to the man using the Burroughs Adding Machine. "I know how to use a Monroe Calculator," I said, "but not a Burroughs. How do they differ?"

"Simple. This is how you use the Burroughs." Once more, mission accomplished! In our harsh world, you can't get a job unless you have experience, and you can't get experience unless you get a job. Yet I had solved the first two seemingly insuperable obstacles without being suspected of never in my life having done office work. I was "experienced"! I could hold the job. And indeed, I did.

For a few days I worked placidly, posting from basic documents, totalling, multiplying, completing ledger sheets, bringing them to my immediate superior. Then I noticed that I was often posting the same basic documents twice, to two different loose leaf ledger sheets for two different ledgers. However, if they ruled three more columns on ledger sheet number I, they could eliminate ledger sheet number II, and indeed, eliminate one whole ledger, along with several operations on my part, and much of the work of the bookkeeper, or whatever the title was of the man immediately above me. It would cut my posting work down by several hours. If I revealed the secret, would I talk myself out of a job? No matter. I dislike useless makework so I went in to the auditor and told him of my discovery. He looked long and hard at the two ledgers, then, "I believe you're right," said Mr. Mathey. "Mr. Albrecht, you have a good brain for an accountant. You deserve well of this company. I have no higher position yet, but from now on, your desk will pay you $150 a month instead of $125.

"What will I do with the time I save?" I asked, a little fearful. "Whatever you please. You can read if you want to, or take a walk on the roof." What use I made of that permission will appear in the next episode. For the moment, I won the unconcealed hatred of the keeper of the ledgers immediately above me, for one of his ledgers ceased to exist and apparently he couldn't find what to do in place of keeping it. But I won the unconcealed admiration of his immediate superior, Mr. Davies, the chief bookkeeper, and of C. P. Mathey, the National Carbon Company auditor.

ACID CORRODES MACHINERY

From time to time I had to go to the manufacturing part of the big National Carbon Company plant, to get basic documents or to inquire as to the meaning of some document that had not been clearly drawn up. One day I went to the armature department: a row of girls was sitting on high stools, one shoulder bent down, the other raised, winding insulated wires swiftly by hand around tiny metal armatures. When the whistle blew for lunch, I could see that these girls' shoulders and spines were more or less permanently malformed by their work. (Today, I am sure these armatures are entirely wire-bound by machinery.)

On other occasions I had to go to the storage battery department. The door leading to it was closed and bore a sign which read:

KEEP THIS DOOR CLOSED
ACID CORRODES MACHINERY!

The storage battery room was filled with acid fumes, yet men and women were working there, without masks, in a room without blowers. Every time I saw the sign it filled me with indignation, for if the machinery in the department on the nearer side of that door was protected, what about the lungs of the workers on the acid fume side?

That, too, has doubtless been taken care of by now, but every so often, even as I write this book, I'll read a news item about asbestos filaments and their effect upon the lungs of those who worked with it; or about vinyl chloride and vinylidine chloride and their effect upon the lungs and livers of men working in the factories in which it is being made into products, presumably inert when they reach the consumer. The dragging of feet by government agencies, and the attempts of a number of manufacturers to block safety regulations in the courts continue to anger me. In the case of asbestos workers, even the members of their family who do not go near the factory can develop lung cancer from the asbestos fibers the family breadwinner brings home on his clothing. When a plant in Tyler, Texas, was dismantled in 1972, waste material was trucked to huge open dumps for the Texas winds to carry it to the entire community, while a half million used burlap bags, impregnated with asbestos dust and fiber, were sold to a plant nursery which used them for packaging plants. The dangers in working with asbestos have been known for decades, yet now that unions and the government are belatedly attempting to work out safe, sanitary standards, many of the companies concerned are in the courts trying to block, delay, or reduce the standards. I no longer believe that safety regulations are better in "Socialist" countries—in the Soviet Union they are much worse and the workingmen and women and their so-called unions completely powerless—still the greed that inspires industry officials in such cases infuriates me as much as it did in my youth. Moreover, given the enormous number of new materials that are being produced by our chemists today, my sense of the need for vigilance on the part of unions, consumers' groups, and government agencies is stronger than ever.

CALIFORNIA'S COMMUNISTS

While I was preparing myself for bookkeeping, I did not neglect trying to find my way into the local Communist Party, with a new name and without a transfer card. Discreet inquiry turned up some local Communists. I told them that I had been studying Marx's writings and would now like to join the Communist Party in California. One J. A. Ragsdale, as slow-spoken as the Negro comic character actor, Stepin Fetchit, asked me whether I could and was willing to deliver a lecture on Marxism to a Communist group in Oakland. I realized that it was an attempt to test me for fitness and security, and I immediately consented. It took them a couple of weeks to arrange a talk, and to my surprise I found as I sat on the ferry bound for the Oakland shore that I had unmistakable signs of stage fright—a dry throat, an enormous and unusual drowsiness, and other symptoms. Yet, when I wasn't working to complete that vademecum, ***Bookkeeping Made Easy***, I had been seriously studying Marx's writings and preparing the talk.

I acquitted myself to the satisfaction of the local leaders, all of whom were present, and they then and there admitted me to their branch in San Francisco and began to think of me as suitable for a higher position than mere rank and file membership. By the time I had dug in as a ledger clerk, the question was being taken up in the inner councils: "Can we use Comrade Albrecht as a lecturer to compete with Macdonald, who has been preventing all the local activists, the ex-wobblies (former members of the IWW) and ex-socialists, from joining the trade unions, by teaching them that fights on hours and wages and working conditions are mere petit-bourgeois concerns with the sale of the commodity, Labor Power, under capitalism, and have nothing to do with the social revolution?" I recognized the symptoms: he was from the Socialist Party of Canada and was peddling King's sectarian doctrine, as had the members of the Socialist Party of Michigan, also under Canadian socialist influence. When I went to hear him lecture, I recognized the Scottish accent modified by life in Canada.

I was promptly admitted, too, into the Communist underground, and at the first session, I got my inkling of the high proportion of "nuts" to be found in almost any California organization.

There were two Russians, not much different from the Russians I had met in New York. One, Victor Boff, was dreaming of using his party membership as a stepping stone toward his return to Russia (via Siberia); the other, named Fineberg, remained a party member, and later, until his retirement, ran the San Francisco Branch of Amkniga, a bookstore for the sale of Soviet originated and pro-Soviet books and pamphlets. There was only one Negro, of light complexion, and he told me as he fixed me with his eyes, that he had positive proofs that the Virgin Mary and her Son were black-skinned, and he was writing a book to prove it to the world. His name, as I remember, was Costley, and his book, as far as I know, was never completed or published. The next few I interviewed were food faddists. One, thought that man became a murderous animal when he became carnivorous, and that war could be abolished by combining the preachment of Communism with vegetarianism. Another, a woman named Slaterub, told me that man in a state of nature did not know fire and ate only raw or unfired foods. She held with Upton Sinclair, also a Californian, who had suffered from much digestive difficulty while a young man and adopted a number of food fads to combat it. Always positive and ardent in his beliefs, he wrote: "I now know to be the greatest discovery of my life the deadly nature of the cooking process, which destroys the health-growing properties of foods, incites to gluttony, and is the cause of 95 percent of the diseases of the human race. We are descended from arboreal ancestors; and whoever saw a fire in a tree?" Miss Slaterub kept strictly to a diet of raw fruits and vegetables, losing weight steadily as she consumed her "natural" foods. When doctors finally convinced her that she had to turn to cooked foods and a more varied diet, with meat, or at least eggs and cheese, she was so weak that she could no longer digest what she ate, and she died of malnutrition. I remember that she weighed only some 60 pounds before she died. The Communist Party membership was small and it did not take me long to chat with each of them and find what a strange assortment they presented. Most impressive was a typesetter, named Harwood. "I am writing a book on Communism," he told me, "which will be a sensation."

"Why?"

"Because it's being dictated to me by Bakunin."

"But Bakunin was an anarchist. And besides, he's dead."

"Of course, but in the other world he was converted to Communism, and he has chosen me to be his vehicle and communicate his conversion to the men of this generation."

"How does he communicate with you?"

"Oh, in different ways—sometimes through a Ouija board, but most times through a medium. His spirit comes and talks through her when she is in a trance. He even tells me what to read and what to quote from Marx against his old views."

"Do you pay the medium for each session?"

"Of course."

"How do you know she's not fooling you? How do you know she's genuine and really in communication with Bakunin?"

"Oh, I tested her all right. I asked her to bring back the spirit of my deceased wife . . ."

"And then . . . ?"

"I asked my wife how much money I had in the bank. And she knew exactly! My wife always knew how much money I had in the bank, or even in my billfold. And nobody else knew, for I never talk of such things to anybody."

So far as I know, the ghostwriter for Bakunin has never completed the dead anarchist-aristocrat's book on Communism. If he had, it would surely have made the front pages in our press.

Of course there were a few more serious Communists among the Californians I met, enough at least to make a proper, leading committee and a show of distinction and devotion.

For distinction we had Anita Whitney, with an ancestor who had come over on the Mayflower and ancestors who had fought in the American Revolution, hence, if she chose, a DAR. She had an uncle who was a justice of the Supreme Court. She was a progressive socialite, not an uncommon type in California. By profession she was a social worker, by avocation a leader of lost causes. When I met her she was in her early fifties, already a veteran of the Socialist Party, and then of its Left-Wing. She followed James Dolsen when he led one of the walkouts of delegates to the Socialist Convention in Chicago in August, 1919. Still following Dolsen, she joined the Communist Labor Party, and when it merged with the Communist Party found herself an underground member of the merged party, otherwise known as "Number 1," and then of the Workers' Party of America ("No. 2"). For all these terrible criminal activities she was indicted under the California Criminal Syndicalist Law. California, alternately ultraliberal and ultraconservative, had during the red raid hysteria a sedition law, a criminal syndicalist law, and a red flag law, under which some 500 people were arrested and 264 convicted during the years 1919-21. Miss Whitney was arrested in November, 1919, and after a four weeks trial, given a sentence of from one to fourteen years. Free on bail, she appealed her case from court to court, until the Supreme Court of the United States in 1927 upheld the constitutionality of the California Criminal Syndicalist Law and her sentence, whereupon Governor Clement C. Young immediately ordered her release on a freely granted pardon.

Another leading figure in the San Francisco Communist movement was James Dolsen, a specialist in party organization. He was a paid party worker who returned much of his exiguous wage as a contribution to the cause. He was deadly serious. He didn't smoke because he would be "burning up the movement's money and fattening up the tobacco magnates," nor drink because that would be a waste. Since he was not much of an orator, he got things off his chest by endless writing of letters to the newspapers, and articles in the *Daily Worker*. He began life as a school teacher in the sheep country of Utah; in Chicago he ran for alderman on the Socialist ticket; in California he became a moderate left winger, and took one extra day to lead a second walkout from the Socialist Party convention. In California he was tried for criminal syndicalism, then disappeared from my view to turn up in China as a representative in the Communist-controlled International Labor Defense. One of his prosecutors in one of the six successive indictments in California had been Earl Warren, then ultraconservative, who later became the ultraliberal Chief Justice of the "Warren Supreme Court." As far as I know Dolsen was never successfully convicted under any of his indictments until 1953, when he was sentenced in Pennsylvania to twenty years for "sedition" and five years for "violating the Smith Act." In turning down his appeal, Judge Henry Xavier O'Brien said: "James Dolsen was a paid propagandist of the Communist conspiracy. He sold and distributed literature which advocated violence in the overthrowing of the Government of the United States and the Government of Pennsylvania, he was a correspondent for the *Daily Worker* . . . He was a member of the District Committee which planned the activities of the Communist Party in Western Pennsylvania. . . ." He was 68 when he began to serve his long sentence in the Blawnox Workhouse, which is the last I heard of him. He, like Anita Whitney, had accepted the Moscow Trials, the Stalin-Hitler Pact, and whatever else their party and the Comintern did, still faithful in their own minds, I think, to their earlier socialist ideals. Dolsen got no obit in *The New York Times,* without which one is never properly dead, and the *Daily Worker* no longer existed when he died.

THE CATHOLIC COMMUNIST

I had not been in the California Communist movement very long when Jim Larkin came to San Francisco. He had been indicted as one of the seventeen criminal anarchists held responsible for the signing and publishing of the *Left-Wing Manifesto,* and was out on $25,000 bail. Being one of the most fiery and stirring of our speakers, he was being sent around the country to address meetings and raise funds for the defense of those who had been arrested. (It took me the better part of a decade to realize that in the Soviet Union no political prisoner is allowed out on bail nor permitted to raise money for his defense or that of his comrades.)

Big Jim had appeared in our midst in New York in the year 1917, accompanied by tales of his labor agitation on the English waterfront and in the Irish labor movement. Many of them were true, but the one that gave him the greatest aura of glory—that he had personally participated in the armed defense of Liberty Hall during the 1916 Easter uprising until all was lost, and then escaped disguised as an old crone—could not have been true. The legend was incompatible with his huge, well over six foot frame, his broad shoulders, his huge hands and feet, his long masculine face. Stoop as he would he could not be taken for an old crone. Yet I believed the tale until I learned that he had left Dublin for American in 1914 to get guns and money from German agents, and could not possible have been in Liberty Hall on Easter Sunday, 1916.

The last time I had heard him, it was in the New Star Casino in New York City where he shocked his ritually atheistic audience by flaunting the cross he always wore buttoned in his shirt. Some question had angered him and he had pulled out his cross glinting in the stage lights and had shouted: "A man can pray to Jesus the Carpenter and be a better Socialist for it, yes, and a better man. I stand by the cross of Jesus and I stand by the arm holding the torch of Socialist light. Both *Capital* and the *Bible* are holy books to me—and to every Irish workingman." And indeed, in

Ireland no fighting unionism would have been possible if linked with a crusade against the Church and the Cross.

And there he was, facing me again. As he roared and thundered, defying Judge Weeks, District Attorney O'Rouke, and Attorney General Palmer, he sputtered and sprayed us, including me who had seated myself in the front row to test my disguise as Vandyke-bearded Arthur Albright; and to my delight I remained unrecognized by him. After he had made his collection appeal and the dollars and silver half-dollars had poured in, he asked for questions. An inveterate meeting and forum goer, who, whenever a question period was opened, was always the first questioner and always asked the same and only panacea question, put his cure-all to Larkin: "Mr. Larkin, what about birth control?"

Big Jim, thinking that the question was asked as a deliberate insult to his Catholic faith, turned a fiery red. Then the color receded as he found his tongue for a retort: "It's a Gawd damned shame your-r-r-r mother-r-r-r didn't practice it." Great was the laughter that ended the question forever at San Francisco forums. In fact, the questioner never showed up at one of our forums again.

THE GROWTH OF THE COMMUNIST MOVEMENT

San Francisco was a fruitful place to recruit workingmen and trade unionists for our movement, for many of the workingmen were veterans of the IWW, the Socialist, Populist, California utopian, and Christian Socialist movements. There was little traffic between East and West in those days, for the distance was three thousand miles of costly train fare, or else a rough journey through all kinds of weather "riding the rods." But many of them went to work during the salmon fishing and canning season on the Columbia River, or as far north as Alaska, north-south traffic being what east-west traffic has become since the airplane entered the picture. Hence, when I decided to start a class in history and Socialist doctrine, called "Society: Its Evolution and Structure," I had little fear of discovery of my former identity, quite aside from my change in appearance. My chief problem was the Tuesday night class given by Jack Macdonald which held so many workingmen aloof from the California labor movement. I faithfully attended Macdonald's class for a number of weeks, found him well-read in the literature of the British labor movement and English history. I watched him draw a map of a lord's estate, complete with location of moat, toll bridge, mill where the peasants had to bring their grain, and many other details. I decided to brush up on my English history so that I would not be found wanting when questions were asked by any of these workingmen who were under the spell of the British Socialist Party, or, the Canadian, and Macdonald's teaching. I used my new found leisure to read on the job at the National Carbon Company when I was not posting basic documents on a ledger page. I read everything British I could lay hands on from Thorald Roger's classic *Six Centuries of Work and Wages* to the latest thing just off the press from the English Workers' Education movement.

I did not want a collision with Macdonald, so since he was lecturing on Tuesdays, I chose Wednesdays. The course was begun during the last week in January, 1921. Some of his regular students joined with former left Socialists and Communists, and members of the Socialist German Turisten Verein (hiking club) to see what the new show in town was like. Macdonald responded by putting out a circular announcing that his class was to be changed to Wednesday night, whereupon I countered by changing mine to Tuesday that he had left vacant. My class grew steadily. By autumn we were running a Sunday night forum with local speakers. Thus the San Francisco Workers' School was born. Though I never attacked him, and only by implication his teachings, Macdonald's class declined until he decided to go off to New Zealand with his talents. When he returned to San Francisco much later, he carried on his missionary work by opening a radical bookstore.

At first I sought my social life with the friends that Otto X., the waiter I met on the train, and those whom Leon Gelber, the *White House* book department expert, introduced me to. The hills in and around San Francisco suggested hiking. A newly found engineer friend taught me to use the contour lines on a geodetic survey map of the region so that I could leave the roads and marked trails for hill country, yet know whether a given slope was a gentle decline or an impossible precipice, I sent more and more pressing and tempting letters to my wife urging her to join me, but she wrote that her father was seriously ill and she could not leave until he recovered. When she came, a few months later, I found that her relatives and friends had given her a farewell party on a bus they chartered for a trip to the Orange Mountains of New Jersey, that the brakes had failed, that she was standing in the bus teasing one of her eminently teasable relatives when the brakes failed, the runaway bus crashed at the bottom of a hill, and she was thrown into the windshield, many pieces of glass from the shattered pane lodging in her breast. Bleeding profusely, she heard a doctor tell an orderly, "She won't last till we get to the hospital," for he thought her lungs were pierced. But they managed to get the glass out of her chest, and at last she was well enough to join me. She found San Francisco, its hills, its nearby lakes and mountains, all that I had told her, and I had another hiking companion. But by the time we settled in a lovely apartment with nine windows facing the bay, the Pacific, the Golden Gate, and the mountains, situated high up on Ashbury Terrace on a hill flanking twin peaks, many of those attending my class had become my friends and hers, and many had joined with us in taking membership in the now increasingly Communistic (it had always been Socialist) Turisten

Verein, "Die-Natur-Freunde." Our hikes had become miracles of many-membered comradeship, such "Germanic" names as Potts and Stewart and Andy Hogg, and Ella and Arthur Albright being added to the roster.

The hiking club had a club house in Marin County on a flank of Mount Tamalpais where we could spend Friday night, and on Saturday and Sunday we hiked vast distances until the evergrowing cry, "Ven do ve eat?" compelled us to settle down, build a fire to roast the side of beef that a devoted butcher named Conrad had carried over his shoulder all the way, while the no less devoted Comrade Fischer would forego for a while the assuaging of his hunger to descend a valley and climb an opposing hill and play German folk songs for us while we ate. We had knapsacks and blankets, and often spent the night under the stars, continuing our journey until Sunday night brought us back to the San Francisco Ferry (no bridge in those days). Those were the golden days. We knew nothing of the faction fights going on in New York, still less of Trotskyism and Stalinism in Russia, and never dreamed that the day would come when this warm and friendly hiking club would divide into Communist and Nazi sympathizers, and perish of its self-inflicted wounds.

Our personal financial affairs went well, too, for C. P. Mathey readily accepted my recommendation that my wife would make a good sales statistician, and I moved from ledger clerk to being in charge of a full set of books for a surgical instrument company and then to proofreader in a printing plant.

17

A CALIFORNIA IDYLL

My wife and I discussed the question of having children. "You are under indictment," she said. "You can't even give your child your right name, nor guarantee that you won't suddenly be taken away from him and sent to prison. Better not, as long as these red raids continue and you are always liable to arrest." What could I say? We let it go at that. Yet never for a moment did I feel insecure.

People attending my class began joining the unions, and people active in the unions began joining my class. One day William Turner, the business agent of the Waiters' Union, stayed after class. "Albright," he said, "how would you like to edit a labor paper?"

"What have you in mind?"

"The *Rank and File*, it's owned by some thirty-odd progressive trade unions, and several organizations like those for Irish freedom. We'll pay you $25 a week. You will have your own printing plant, and raise money by printing jobs for the unions and other organizations. We'll help you get ads from union shops, and if you raise enough money, we'll raise your wages."

"Sounds interesting, more interesting than proofreading. But it doesn't pay well. I'm getting $1.05 an hour now for a forty-hour week, and time and a half for overtime. Besides, what's wrong with your present editor?"

"Oh, Bill Short—he's just a pacifist sky-pilot. We're tired of the Reverend Short and he's tired of us. Besides, he doesn't strike the right note for labor, and he knows it." (When I looked at copies of the *Rank and File* that Short had gotten out, I felt that Turner's estimate of him was an understatement.)

"Do you mind if I speak to him first?" I asked.

"Not at all, that's fair and proper."

I spoke to the Reverend Short; he had no objections to leaving. "I'm tired of the job," he told me, "I knew they were going to ask you. It's a monotonous job, getting it out every week, whether you have anything interesting to print or not. It's hard work raising enough money to keep the paper going, without counting the fact that you have to raise enough to pay your own salary or else. . . ." I knew what "or else" meant. I went back to Bill Turner. "Tell your committee I'm ready to accept, but I'd like to change the name from *Rank and File* to *Labor Unity*."

"Sounds all right to me," said Turner. "I'll bring your name before the Committee." Within a week I was elected Editor of the *Rank and File* and before long changed its name to *Labor Unity*.

I entered the premises of the newspaper of which I was to be the Editor and the printing plant of which I was to be the director. It was a two-windowed store front with premises running all the way to the back of the building, a linotype machine, a composer's stone table, some fonts of type, a printing press big enough to run off circulars and posters, but not big enough to run off a newspaper, and, behind the machinery, an editorial office not large enough to contain more than a single person—the Editor. No secretary, no reporters—clearly, I was to fill the weekly myself. The rest of the help consisted of one pressman, and one compositor who was also a linotyper. There was a file of back issues which I began at once to study. The compositor was Max Slaterub, the husband of the unfired-food cultist. He explained to me that they were not just printers doing a job but men who had been attending my lectures. They were prepared, if it was kept quiet, to donate a fourth of their wages each week to help support the newspaper. "Of course, we must get the regular union wage or we'd be in trouble and your plant would be struck." I was touched. And in time I was to learn that that was the spirit not only of my two assistants but of a significant portion of the San Francisco labor movement. Not for nothing had the IWW been a force in prewar California.

The unions that had set up the weekly in their fight to make the stodgy craft union labor movement more progressive and more alive to the world in which they lived, were led principally by the culinary trades and the machine building crafts. Actually the thirty founding trade unions had risen to forty-eight and the number continued to grow after I began editing the paper. Some of the unions that sponsored it were the cooks, the waiters, the machinists, the structural ironworkers, the ornamental ironworkers, the lithographers, the photoengravers. I remember [those seven] best because each of them had an active leadership that kept in touch with me and gave the paper financial and moral support. Other sponsoring unions included the boilermakers, carpenters, carmen, millmen, jewelry workers, shipfitters, potters, sausagemakers, bakers, bakery wagon drivers, cleaners and dyers, auto mechanics, meatcutters, electrical workers, fur workers, roofers, tailors, sheetmetal workers, oil workers, barbers, coppersmiths, steam fitters, cement workers, and others, including the Contra Costa Central Labor Council, and a number of unions in nearby Oakland and San Jose. The journal thus became a livelier and more readable rival to the *Labor Clarion*, the stodgy official organ of the San Francisco Central Trades and Labor Council.

Bill Turner drove me to little, unionized restaurants, introduced me, and suggested to the owner that it would be useful to put a one-, two-, or three-inch ad in *Labor Unity,* whose readers, union workingmen in the majority, would thus be encouraged to patronize his coffee shop. Since Turner was the business agent of the Waiters' Union, and the Cooks' Union officials also spoke to them, they were easily persuaded.

But it was the Cooks' Union that took me into its fold. One day its chairman visited me, and said: "Brother Albright, we'd like to elect you a delegate from our union to the Central Trades and Labor Council where your ability to talk will be of great use to the progressive bloc."

I BECOME A COOK

"But I am not a cook. I can't do much more than boil water or fry an egg."

"We'll take care of that. Be at the Paradise Coffee Shop on Post Street at 3 o'clock, after the lunch hour rush is over. It has a union card in its window. Its owner is a Greek. We'll explain things to him; he'll give you a chef's cap and gown; get behind the counter, and promptly at three begin frying some eggs. Our membership committee will be there to certify you as qualified for membership." Thus I became a member of the Cooks' Union, Local 44, and, by fraternal association, of the Bartenders International League, on February 22, 1922.

Until I did my own cooking for an entire semester while I was teaching Russian History at the University of California and learned to make such delicacies as oxtail soup (my wife remaining in New York to take care of her ailing mother), those two fried eggs and my chef's beard were about all I could boast of to qualify me for membership in the Cooks' Union. But ironically all the Membership committe had wanted was to watch me make precisely two fried eggs. A few weeks later Local 44 of the cooks elected their new member a delegate to the Central Trades and Labor Council, and before long, I found myself the spokesman for the entire group of progressive labor unions in the council. Of course, this required special preparation in unexpected fields. I had to buy a coat and pants and hat and several other objects with Union Labels easily made visible so as to pass the inspection of the Union Label committee. And I could not even go to the men's room and return safely without being accompanied by a self-appointed bodyguard, a deeply sentimental and devoted red-haired member of the Waiters' Union named Fred Siegman. When it became clear that we were getting more than one-third of the votes on our motions at regular meetings of the council and that our proportion of the vote was growing, Brother O'Connor, member of the Teamsters' Union, secretary of the council, and editor of its official organ, *The Clarion,* opened a full scale attack upon me. "I'd like to know," he said with a slight Irish brogue, "when was the last time that Brother Albright stood behind a stove in a restaurant?" At this Hugo Ernst, president of the waiters' and chairman of the culinary trades, arose to speak in all seriousness, though he had not watched me frying the two eggs: "If the Cooks' Union thinks well enough of Brother Albright to admit him as a member, that should be enough for Brother O'Connor. Besides, I'd like to know when was the last time that Brother O'Connor sat behind a team of horses or drove a truck!" That ended the debate on my *bona fides* as a cook, and we returned to the order of the day.

MY INDIAN STOCKHOLDERS

In no other state but California would it be possible for a labor paper owned by some forty or fifty trade unions to have other owners that made it something of a fighter for the general freedom of other lands. But there they were on the list of my employers—the Irish Republican Army and the Hindu *Gadir* or Hindu Freedom Party! That was pleasing to me for I had long favored freedom for both countries, and their presence among the owners widened the scope of my journal's interests.

Of course, the Irish were no novelty since there are more Irish in New York than there are in Dublin, and there were three Irish dailies, *The Irish World, The Freeman's Journal*, and *The Gaelic-American*, that had supported Hillquit's mayoralty campaign and antiwar stand. But the Indians were something new. In New York I had known only Lajpat Ray who lectured at the Rand School, and I had eaten in a Hindu restaurant where men from India, with never a woman among them, were rumored to be whispering about freedom over their bowls of Indian food. (The restaurant, rumor had it, was founded by Indian revolutionaries with the aid of German money. This must have been so, for it closed one day after we declared war on Germany.)

The Indian word *Gadir* (freedom) took on a familiar look when the *Times* printed a letter on July 21, 1917, signed R. Chandra, editor of the California *Hindustan Gadir*, asserting that the unrest in India was "not due to outside influence or agitation." Almost two years later, on April 7, 1919, one day after we declared war on Germany, Ram Chandra, editor of the *Hindustan Gadir*, was arrested in San Francisco along with 16 other plotters. He must have jumped bail and fled the country, for he was not in California when I got there. How could I get in touch with the people in the Hindu *Gadir* party who owned stock in the newspaper I was editing? Diligent inquiry turned up the name of Santokh Singh, who as far as I know had never made *The New York Times*, although he had a truly newsworthy record. He had been in America for seven years, was 28 years old, had spent some time on McNeill Island in the State of Washington, where he was held for deportation by the Department of Labor, then had been brought back to the mainland to serve a twenty-one month term for violation of our Neutrality Act. He was now free, living in San Francisco, and was regarded by the Indian refugees who made up the Hindu Gadir Party as their leader and spokesman. I invited him to visit me in my home on Ashbury Terrace. A slender, young looking and gentle-seeming man put in an appearance, wearing a well-fitting American suit, his long black hair completely concealed in a white turban, and announced himself: "Santokh Singh." Since I have always had a poor memory for names, I decided to memorize only his last name, *Singh.* "Mr. Singh, have this seat facing the sea. Make yourself at home." He sat down, seemingly relaxed and at ease. I was tempted to ask him if he cared to remove his jacket and turban, but thought better of it. I told him something about myself, as far as I could under the name of Arthur Albright, said to him that he was now "one of my bosses," and whenever he had something of interest concerning his party or India's struggle for freedom, he should write it up for *Labor Unity.* As we conversed he became more and more trustful and friendly. At one point he said, "You should not call me Mr. Singh, for all of us are called Singh."

"All of whom?"

"All of us who are Sikhs bear the community name Singh. We are a religious community of warriors. We deem it our obligation to be warriors. We must always wear a turban, and always wear a comb, and a dagger. We cannot ever go unarmed."

"Are you armed?"

"Yes, I am wearing a dagger." Smiling, he added in response to my puzzled look, "Would you like to see it? In the Punjab from which we all come, we are better armed, and religious warriors all. But in America we wear a symbolic dagger," and from under his jacket, from a belt or sash, he extracted a diminutive dagger, no bigger than a man's thumb.

"How many are you with the name Singh?"

"Oh, about five or six million, all living in the Punjab. We are rightly-regarded as the most warlike people in India. We are members of a militant religious cult which is a variant of the Hindu religion, a fighting variant which arose in our struggle to free India from Moslem domination in the sixteenth century. In 1857 our Sikh contingent were the most able fighters for Indian freedom in what the English call the Sepoy Rebellion. Our early leaders in America were Professor Sardar Teja Singh, a Harvard graduate who in 1912 moved to Stockton, California, and established our first Gurudwara or Sikh temple, and Har Dayal Singh who came to America around the same time, taught at Berkeley, founded the weekly paper called *Gadir,* which word comes from an Arabic word meaning 'struggle' and to us meaning 'freedom,' that is, *struggle for freedom.* When we found England and Germany at war, Har Dayal went to Germany to see if he could get arms for our struggle for freedom from England. With the money we got we built a building, supported our press, sent arms to India. There are hundreds, even thousands of us who grow grain and rice and fruit in the Central Valley of California. We are good farmers as well as good warriors. The Sikhs of the Central Valley are the backbone of the Hindu *Gadir* Party. And [with a michievous smile] all of us are called Singh."

"Then how shall I call you, and how shall I remember your names when I meet more of your people?"

"You shall have to memorize our full names, two in my case, more in some other cases. Singh is a religious community name, and at the same time, an honorable title. You have already met one of our people. He told me of you, that he had spoken with you, that he has respect for you, that he has broken bread with you. But probably he did not give you all his names."

"Who is that? What are all his names?"

"He is the science editor of the Hearst newspaper chain, and very much an American, in his build, in his diet, and in his citizenship. But he has not forgotten India. He is also a Sikh and his last name, as you call it, is Singh."

"Oh, yes. You mean Gobind Lal."

His full name is Gobind Lal Bihari Singh. There are millions in India called Lal, and many millions called Bihari, for they, or some of their ancestors, came from the thickly populated province of Bihar. And your friend, Gobind Lal, got one year in jail for violating the American Neutrality Act, but he was never pro-German. In fact, he broke with us when the United States declared war on Germany because he was pro-American. Another of our people, Tarkanath Das, got two years for the same reason."

Gobind Lal has since had a distinguished career as a popularizer of science, for which in 1936 he was to get a Pulitzer Prize. I noted down Gobind Lal's full name as Santokh Singh gave it to me, and became silent as I tried to assimilate all that I had learned about the great Indian subcontinent of which I knew so little.

"Also," continued Santokh Singh, "we must all wear a comb. If you would like to see it, I will remove my turban, but do not speak of this because we do not remove our turbans before strangers," and with an easy gesture he removed his turban, and from his thick black hair a tiny tortoise-shell, silver-chased comb. "We will be friends," he said, "but as for names, it is best to call me Santokh, or Santokh Singh. Is that so hard?"

"Now that I understand it, not at all. And I shall try to remember the names of all the members of your party that I meet."

With that he stood up, returned his comb to his hair, enclosed the thick tresses in his turban, thanked me, and departed, leaving me to reflect on the fact that India was an unknown world to me, who had spoken and written so freely concerning its destiny.

San Francisco in the early twenties provided my wife and me with some of the most joyous days we have known. The city itself was built like Rome, on hills, though in place of Rome's seven hills there were nine, and yet other rising ground that would be counted as hills if they were in New York City or environs. Surrounding the City and keeping it from getting overgrown, there was the Pacific Ocean on one side and San Francisco Bay on the other, and from every bit of rising land there were magnificent views of the bay, the Pacific Ocean, the Golden Gate bridge, and yet more hills and mountains across the waters. One cannot imagine without seeing it how golden the Golden Gate can be as the sun sets behind it, and how jewel-like the nearer flank of Mount Tamalpais can become in sunset colors made translucent by the haze that surrounds it. We spent every weekend in the outdoors, even in the rainy season, for the rains were for the most part of short duration. We explored the Berkeley Hills, Mount Tamalpais, the Crystal Springs Lakes, the Santa Cruz Mountains, Carmel and Monterey, and, more ambitiously, the High Sierras and that wonder of wonders, the Yosemite Valley, where at the spring flood all the rivers make their leap, of three thousand feet, as waterfalls. Come February we would walk the trails and cowpaths and uncharted forests of the Santa Cruz Mountains and gaze down into the Santa Clara Valley, in those days one continuous vista of peach, cherry, pomegranate, almond and plum blossoms. Alas, now that beautiful valley, once the prune factory of the world, has become a continuous extension of real estate developments and pizza parlors with barely a tiny grove of fruit trees, here and there, which the bulldozers have overlooked. The valley is still beautiful when seen from the heights, but I am haunted by a Spanish saying: "Cualquier tiempo pasado fué mejor." (The old times always seem better.)

Even the misadventures were joyous and memorable, as when we were caught in the High Sierras in a hailstorm in mid-July where the hailstones fell like giant ball bearings, rattling in our tiny cups, and my wife and I had to take refuge under an overhanging granite ledge until the storm was over. Or when we hiked in the Santa Cruz Mountains where there were then neither auto roads nor marked paths nor *No Trespassing* signs, and our geodetic survey map, which must have been made before I was born, showed us a little rocky summit town with a cross for a church, and several buildings to represent a Main Street with at least one general country store. When near nightfall we got there, all the roofs had fallen in and there was neither food nor shelter in this, our first ghost town.

Whenever we wanted company there were the good friends and good companions of the *Turisten Verein*, experienced hikers all, who thought California more beautiful than the Alps, who had explored every nook and cranny, every hill and stream of northern and central California. They taught us what to take with us in our knapsacks and how to satisfy our voracious hiking appetites. Members of my class flocked into the hiking club, members of the hiking club into my class, and both into the rapidly growing Communist Party, so we never lacked for warm friends old and new, including picturesque characters who had ridden the bumpers under the freight trains, cooked stew in tin cans in the hobo jungles, sailed the Pacific and other seas as sailors and stokers, fished for salmon in the Columbia River and the rivers of Canada and Alaska, and worked in the canneries, or as longshoremen on the docks, or who, like our Scottish friends, Potts and Stewart, and their English buddy, Tallentire, good carpenters all, had taken a solemn oath not to be "exploited." They picked their vegetables from farms on hikes, added a piece of meat legitimately purchased, made themselves and their guests rich stews lasting for a week by adding more meat and more farm fresh vegetables each day, and never did a day's work except to pick up some necessary cash, for things which couldn't be picked up free, by building a bookcase or a cabinet for an acquaintance or friend. One day Johnnie Stewart discovered that it was even easier and more profitable to pick up old books for a nickel, a dime or a quarter on outside book counters in San Francisco and then sell them at a profit of many hundred percent as *Americana* and *Californiana*. After that they never made another cabinet or drove another nail into a piece of wood, having changed their trade from carpenter and cabinetmaker to antiquarian.

California had been one of the most important Socialist states, with a state party made up of utopian Socialists, Christian Socialists, pacifist Socialists, pro-IWW Socialists, hobo Socialists, literary Socialists, and left wingers, but the national party had never paid much attention to them, not merely because they were "different," but much more because the party center was always in Chicago or New York, and the trip across the country before the age of the airplane was too long and too costly. When the Communist parties were formed, the entire locals of San Francisco, Oakland, and San Jose voted in a body to join the Communist Labor Party as "the more American" of the two parties, while only the Los Angeles local, led by the redheaded Russian named M. J. Golos, joined the Communist Party in which the Russian Federation had a majority.

Thus the Communist Labor Party acquired the headquarters, the journals such as the *Western Worker*, and virtually the entire membership of the Socialist Party. But from November, 1919, the new party was subjected to a series of raids and arrests, raids by the American Legion on the C.L.P. headquarters in Oakland, the arrest of party leaders under the Criminal Syndicalist Law, the physical suppression of meetings and publications in Oakland, and the arrest even of the gentle socialite, Anita Whitney. In January, 1920, the Palmer red raids picked up those whom the California police raids had missed and seized a score of alien radicals. California secured the conviction of Anita Whitney in February, of John Weiler of the Boilermakers Union in March, lost its case against J. E. Snyder, editor of the *Western Worker*, and got only a hung jury in the Dolsen case in March. These raids caused the C.L.P. and the C.P. to shrink to a shadow of their former selves. By the time I got in touch with the Communist movement in 1920, it was the deeply buried underground movement largely of the nutty characters I have already described, and it made no distinction between C.L.P. and C.P.

The situation in San Francisco was quite different from that in Oakland and Los Angeles and other parts of the state. San Francisco dutifully took cognizance of the laws passed by the State Legislature, but did not trouble to carry them out. Its mayor and police were exceptionally tolerant in this as they were in the enforcement of the 18th Amendment intended to make America permanently dry. The motto of San Francisco seemed to be then, as it is today, the same as the motto of the most enlightened of the mayors of the City of New York, William J. Gaynor, who said that he was content if he could preserve in the City "outward order and decency." Moreover, the progressive unions, not to be ignored, were unenthusiastic about the red raids and even less enthusiastic about prohibition. The Catholic Church, a power in the City, did not favor the dry laws either, and a good part of the state's inhabitants opposed them too, for after all, California was the great American wine country. Hence when we went to an Italian restaurant in the financial district or in the Latin Quarter, great, fat, unbreakable coffee mugs were set down with our food, containing not coffee but "red ink." In those days a coffee mug of red wine in any self-respecting Italian or French restaurant came free with the dinner. The dinner was served without taking orders from any of us as we sat at long tables where good fellowship prevailed among "house guests" who might never have seen each other before and might never see each other again.

Our remoteness from the party center with its "instructions," its faction fights, its sudden about-face maneuvers on order from Zinoviev in the name of the Comintern—that very remoteness from the "center of things" was one of the pleasures of life in San Francisco. This suited me perfectly. Distance, and poor means of communication made us in practice, autonomous. If we agreed with an order from the high command, we tried to carry it out zealously and explain it carefully to our growing body of sympathizers and increasingly friendly progressive trade unions. Often we agreed with what was being demanded of us, not because of unthinking devotion or blind obedience to the instructions, but because of a genuine sense of common interests and a common mood. But if the instructions were unpalatable, poorly justified, or late in reaching us, we simply paid no attention to them and continued working as we had been working. Nor were we ever called to account for it, for the line would often change again before we had time to agree or disagree and before they could even be aware that we were not carrying out the latest order.

Our California Communist movement, particularly as it centered in San Francisco, had close linkage with the more progressive section of organized labor. The paper I edited was not so much a Communist organ as it was an organ of the more progressive section of organized labor. *Labor Unity* concerned itself with strikes, with the lessons of the great general strikes of Seattle and Winnipeg, with the organization of the unorganized, with labor unity and solidarity; and with Communist doctrine and the Soviet Union only insofar as its editor turned his attention to such subjects. My trade union employers had no objection to the latter, attended my lectures with interest and enthusiasm, while one by one the active militants, without being personally solicited, made application to join our party, and welcomed William Z. Foster's initiative in the formation of the Trade Union Educational League or TUEL.

All the book-length histories of the Communist Party that have so far been written, whether the work of Howe and Coser, based largely on unreliable newspaper clippings, or the solid and scholarly two volumes of Theodore Draper, or the judiciously critical *American Communism* of Oneal and Werner, fail to take into account the local peculiarities of the movements which developed in the West which began on the left bank of the Hudson River or west of Chicago. Certainly Communism as it developed in California, particularly Northern California, varied significantly from the description of Communism in all these national histories. Only the monograph by Ralph E. Shaffer of Pomona Polytech, so far not developed into a book, takes account of Communism in the "sticks" as it exhibited itself in Northern California in the early twenties.

In it he raises the question: "Is it possible that what seems on the surface to be an 'exceptional' brand of communism in California is actually communism as it really was in the United States in the early 1920's?" In his monograph, *The Formative Years of Communism in the West: The California Phase, 1919-1924,* Professor Shaffer calls on other local historians to do similar work on the local Communist history of their own regions. If they do so, I think it will be found that Dr. Shaffer's thesis is largely true for most of the country.

What Professor Shaffer called the "exceptional brand of California Communism" was not so exceptional in the country as a whole. This was proved when in the summer of 1922 I arrived as a delegate to the Michigan convention of the Communist Party. I found it an easy matter to form a third grouping besides the bitterly factional "Geese" and "Liquidators," who were under the influence of the factional lineups at the center. This third grouping was formed from delgates who came from areas where the membership was predominantly American and remote from the influence of the frozen factions. We found that both "Geese" and "Liquidators" decided things in their separate caucuses, were unwilling to listen to, or consider, the arguments of any but their own spokesmen, and were unwilling to vote for the best and most capable candidates for the new Central Committee, regardless of factions. Our spontaneously formed third grouping, which came to hold the balance of power before the convention was over, was known derisively as "Wolfe's Rurals." But of *Geese* and *Liquidators* and *Rurals* and the faction battles and Comintern maneuvers on the shores of Lake Michigan, more later.

Another peculiarity of the San Francisco Communists is that we stubbornly refused to fight hardest against the other radical movements that were closest to us, or to get excited about the remnants of the Socialist Party or the Socialist Labor Party. When we came to nominate candidates for state office on the Workers Party ticket early in June of 1922, we picked William Turner of the Waiters Union as our candidate for governor; N. Mattson, whose first name and antecedents I have forgotten, for senator; and for congressional representatives from California, Arthur E. Albright of the Cooks Union in San Francisco; P. C. Cowdery, business manager of the *Western Worker* in Berkeley; and David Gorman of the Electrical Workers Union in Los Angeles. We also supported William Knudsen of the Socialist Labor Party, a leader in the Machinists Union, Local 68, and a supporter of *Labor Unity*, for mayor of San Francisco. He was one of the best delegates to the Central Trades and Labor Council, a leading spokesman of the Socialist Labor Party, yet especially active and able in the TUEL campaign to amalgamate the metal trades into one industrial union. We frequently used him as a speaker on the Workers' Party platform.

Our vote in the November, 1922, elections could not have been very impressive, for even many "progressive trade unionists" voted for pro-labor candidates of the Democratic party for fear of "throwing away their votes." In any case, I do not know what the actual vote was, because, for reasons which will appear below, Arthur Albright was not in San Francisco to campaign for his own election nor to learn the size of his vote. What is noteworthy about this campaign, as about the other "exceptional" characteristics of San Francisco Communism, was the fact that in 1920 we were regarded as a legitimate part of the organized labor movement, and had already worked out for ourselves a prolabor united front, not as a maneuver, but as an expression of the way we felt, a year or two before Lenin proposed to the Comintern that it go into the organized labor movements and enter into united fronts with Socialist and Labor parties and organizations for the purpose of infiltrating and capturing them.

For our part, my wife and I had fallen in love with San Francsico, its outdoor life, its warm sunlit winters, its cool summers with the exhilarating fogwind blowing in one's face, its streets running up and down the hills, its gaily overcrowded cable cars, the tolerance with which differences were argued and discussed and the affairs of the city administered. We were not regarded as outlanders, for the city was predominantly made up of outlanders, people born anywhere but in California, and exotic settlers from the distant lands across the great Pacific. True, we missed our old friends and the cultural excitement and richness of life in New York, but we had become an integral part of San Francisco. The things we missed were largely compensated for by the new experiences we could never have had on the East Coast. We had hardly started our exploration of the wonders of Chinatown and the city's ocean shore, and the hills beyond, we were just making the friendships that promised to endure, and enlarging our place as part of San Francisco's life in the course of two idyllic years, when one day a mysterious call came to our party to elect two members to go to a very secretive convention, so secretive that we were not told in what state or in what city it was to be held. To protect the convention from observation, and from police raids, our local was merely given a name and address in the Middle West—if I remember rightly it was in Chicago—and told that our delegates were to report there, and would get further instructions there. My wife and I were elected as delegates, I arranged for Dolsen to edit *Labor Unity*, and off we went from San Francisco on the overland express for a voyage into the unknown. At the first address, we were given a second name and address which I no longer remember, and there we received two tickets to St. Joseph, Michigan. From St. Joseph we were taken to Bridgman on the shores of Lake Michigan, and then another mile to a farmhouse and summer resort on the shores of the Lake amid the sand dunes.

18

WHAT EVER HAPPENED TO ARTHUR ALBRIGHT?

What a beautiful place to hold a "picnic"! (*Picnic* was our code word for the *Convention*.) Bridgman was a little unincorporated country town, with a railroad station, a small store or two, some quiet homes with spaces between each of them and its neighbor. It had less than 800 inhabitants and was some twelve miles away from the big towns of St. Joseph and Benton Harbor, big only by comparison with Bridgman. If one wanted to leave it by night, one would have to wait until the next morning for the milk train. The same was true even of St. Joseph. Our quiet haven was the farm of one Karl Wulfskeel in a wooded valley about a mile away from Bridgman. Wulfskeel supplemented his income from truck farming by renting out some cottages in the woods behind his farmhouse to summer guests who wanted to fish and swim and sail in the waters of Lake Michigan.

Ludwig Katterfeld, an old-time Socialist, now a Communist, had made all the arrangements for what he told the farmer was a singing society on a week-long outing. Even at the height of the summer season some of the cottages often went unrented, but here we were, something like seventy of us, willing to crowd into his cottages and overflow into the bedrooms of his farmhouse, and pay not by the cottage but by the head. We ate our meals together in the outdoors on tables made of sawhorses covered with boards. Mrs. Wulfskeel, who did the cooking for all of us, was a good cook, with kitchen help to do the serving. We could have no complaint about food or sleeping arrangements or the lovely surroundings or the perfect isolation of the "singing society's" meeting place.

Yet one feature of the arrangements was disquieting: Michigan was one of 18 states with a criminal syndicalist law. When we found this out, someone made a proposal to postpone the convention and make new arrangements in a state less equipped to justify a raid and wholesale arrests, but Katterfeld was obdurate. The arrangements were foolproof, he insisted. Had he not held a small local Communist convention earlier at this same farm, without mishap? Had we not traveled there circumspectly, with even the delegates unaware of their final destination? He was told that it was especially foolhardy to hold a second secret convention where one had been held before. Perhaps townsfolk in tiny Bridgman, and the police as well, had become aware of the prior gathering of strangers. Was it not a good rule of conspiracy never to hold conventions twice in the same place?

Voices rose in anger. The quiet became less quiet as loud voices carried great distances through the quiet countryside. Katterfeld was stubborn and unshakable. Lovestone and Ruthenberg, he asserted, were trying to postpone the convention for factional reasons since they did not have a majority and wanted to gain time to win one. The majority was with him and would vote to go ahead with the convention. He had been delegated to make the arrangements: these were the arrangements he had made. The angry quarrel on this simple issue told me that I had left the friendly unity of the San Francisco movement to return once more to the atmosphere of bitter factional controversies in which the aims of the Communist Party were forgotten, or buried in splits and feuds between caucus and caucus, between Communists and Communists, between *Geese* and *Liquidators*—epithets which I heard for the first time. In the end Katterfeld had his way, for after all, here we were, delegates, fraternal delegates, and three supersecret delegates from Moscow who had been smuggled into the country and brought here with extra secret precautions. Nobody was ready with any concrete proposal on where to go or what new arrangements to make. Besides, a great sum of money, which no doubt must have come from Moscow, had already been spent in bringing us all to just this spot. The cottages seemed well-sheltered in a good patch of woodland; in its center was a hollow where we could meet and talk with no one within earshot. At the edges of the woodland there were hillocks from which lookouts could keep watch to give warning of the approach of strangers. There was only one dirt road to the farm, in poor condition, easy to watch from sheltered lookouts. From the woods, sandy paths led down grassy slopes to lovely sand dunes and the great lake, where we could swim like any other innocent society on a week-long outing. We wanted to believe that everything would be all right, for we had taken the most elaborate precautions to keep the place secret even from most of the delegates and make sure by frequent changes of destination and means of travel that none of us was followed. Our better known leaders had changed trains even more often than the rest of us so that they could scrutinize all the passengers to make sure that there were no "repeaters." Each of us was certain that he had not been shadowed; all of us wanted to believe that this place was as safe as it was attractive.

Let us follow one of the lesser known rank and file comrades as he journeyed from Camden, New Jersey, where he lived and worked in a shipyard, to the Wulfskeel farm in Berrien County, Michigan, to see what precautions had been taken to protect the convention. Francis Morrow was a short, insignificant-looking man pushing forty, with hair already growing gray. Looking at him no one would dream that he was a conspirator bound for an underground convention, or that he had an alias as *Comrade Day*. He and the two other Philadelphia-Camden delegates were told only that they should attend a District Convention of Number Two, the legal Workers' Party, in Philadelphia. There the district organizer drew them aside and told them to go to an address in Cleveland, providing them with train tickets. At the Cleveland address they were directed to take a boat to Detroit, and once more given tickets. Thus they did not even have to present themselves at a ticket office which might conceivably be watched. In Detroit the three found themselves part of a larger party, fourteen in all, who were given tickets to Grand Rapids, Michigan. At this point, in violation of the strict rules of conspiracy, Morrow was able to drop a short note to his wife in Camden, telling her that he was bound for St. Joseph. In St. Joseph they were directed to Bridgman, and in Bridgman, on the night of the third day, Comrade Day was taken to the Wulfskeel farm. The convention opened the next morning. The three delegates from Philadelphia-Camden were certain that they had not been followed from stage to stage by any suspicious looking character, and had arrived unshadowed to their final destination. Indeed, they were right. They had not been followed. But the nondescript and insignificant shipyard worker, Francis A. Morrow, alias Comrade Day, had yet another pseudonym—to the Department of Justice he was known as special agent K-97!

This modest-looking man who almost never took the floor, yet never failed to vote, had attracted little attention among the activists of his district. However, the Department of Justice had learned to take him seriously. During the great wave of shipyard strikes in 1919, he had been recruited by a department agent at the wage of $1 a day to attach himself to and report on radical movements in his area. He had joined the Socialist Party; when it split, he had attached himself, as a good agent should, to the more radical wing that became the Communist Party. His promotion to section organizer was contrived by him personally by the formation of a Camden section of only four persons: his wife, himself, and two friends who knew what he was up to. When to this he added the post of secretary of the Philadelphia-Camden district, his daily wage was doubled to $2. But when he cracked the underground code of the entire party consisting of messages made up only of common fractions, his name became known to the top men in the Department of Justice, and his daily wage jumped to $5. Actually, it had been easy, a lucky accident. One day the D.O., the top man in the district, having imbibed too freely, asked his help in decoding a slip of paper filled with common fractions, showing him the printed matter in small type on the back of an innocent money order application and explaining that each numerator in a fraction indicated a line of print on the back of the money order blank, and each denominator a letter in that line. Hence, when he let his wife know that he was headed for St. Joseph, he was highly enough esteemed so that from the office of William J.

Burns, then head of the Bureau of Investigation, an urgent message went out to the head of the F.B.I.'s Chicago office, Jacob Spolansky: "Secret convention of the Communist Party now in progress in the vicinity of St. Joseph, Michigan. Proceed at once to locate same and keep under discreet surveillance."

Once K-97 got to the Convention, it became impossible for him to communicate with his superiors either concerning the location or the plans and proceedings of the gathering, for a Ground Rules Committee was appointed to make rules for greater safety. Its rules provided that no one was allowed to leave the grounds without the permission of the grounds committee. If granted for a good reason, the one who got permission must register on leaving and on returning, and his party name and absence must be reported at each roll call. Roll calls were taken three times a day to make sure that no one was missing. Those given permission to leave were only the trusted lookouts, some of whom were on sentry duty nearby, while others were sent to Bridgman to scrutinize the faces of strangers in order to see if there were any recognizable detectives among them. No person was allowed to "mingle with strangers," nor send out letters or messages. Incriminating notes and documents could not be left in baggage or rooms. Both baggage and lodgings were searched. Notes taken and every scrap of paper must be delivered each evening to the grounds committee for safekeeping or destruction. Each delegate should use his special party name (mine was Daniel Shays), and no one might use any other name in addressing a delegate, nor inquire about nor reveal what anyone's real name was. In short, Comrade K-97 could neither leave the grounds, nor take and keep notes, nor telephone, nor send letters. He never did learn the real names of the three visitors from Moscow, nor my real name either. Later, when he gave some testimony in court, he testified that the plenipotentiary representative of the Comintern, Henryk Walecki, born Maximilian Horowitz, whose name at the Convention was Ward Brooks, was actually A. Lozovsky, head of the Profintern or Red Trade Union International. Josef Pogany, a second emissary from Moscow who at the Convention used the name of Lang, and later in the American Communist Party baptized himself John Pepper, he never figured out either. The third emissary, Boris Reinstein, whom the reader may remember as having been expelled by the Socialist Labor Party because he professed to represent it at the First Congress of the Communist International, and who at the convention was called Davidson, K-97 never mentioned at all. Nor did he mention Comrade Shays, alias Albright, for reasons that will appear later. Obviously, the galaxy of pseudonyms bewildered K-97, who was himself a constellation of aliases, Comrade Day and Francis Morrow; and at a critical moment of the Convention, he suddenly turned to Francis Morrow Ashworth. He was bewildered by the pseudonyms and also by some of the language used and the esoteric matters discussed during the sessions. Verily, as Sir William Gilbert of Gilbert and Sullivan fame proclaimed, "The policeman's lot is not a happy one"—particularly if the policeman is a part-time secret agent posing as a delegate to a convention whose other delegates are all true initiates versed in the mysterious jargon and arcane history of their fraternal order.

I, and no doubt the reader, was bewildered by finding *geese* and *liquidators* at the Michigan Convention. Only diligent inquiry clarified the terms for me. The *geese*, it appeared, were worshippers of the underground and looked with distrust upon "No. 2," the legal Workers' Party that was not affiliated with the Communist International and had not written *expressis verbis* the words "violent revolution" and "dictatorship of the proletariat" into its program. The anti-Workers' Party faction had acquired the name *geese*, because their Russian-born leader, Abraham Jakira, had a speech defect that caused him to pause and make a strange sound after almost every other word of his fiery speeches. In the course of a bitter debate, Bill Dunne, exasperated by this persistent sound devoid of meaning, interrupted him to say, "Jakira, you make me sick; you cackle like a goose." At this, Israel Amter, who had already made himself celebrated in our ranks by opening his first speech to a left-wing meeting in local Kings County with the words, "Comrade Workers and Peasants of Brooklyn," cried out, "But the geese saved Rome, and we shall yet save the Party." At this, Lovestone proclaimed, "All right, then, from now on you're the Goose Caucus." The name stuck. The Goose leaders at the Convention were Katterfeld, Wagenknecht, Minor, Jakira, Amter, Lindgren, and Gitlow. All of these men were fluent in English except for Jakira, whose speech defect turned out to be a result of throat cancer. Most of their members, however, were more at home in some language other than English. Indeed, "most" is an understatement, for their membership was drawn up to some 90 percent from the foreign federations, and it was their vote plus the vote of K-97 that gave the geese their bare majority of one, at the convention. It was thus that K-97 played an historic role.

The "liquidators" were so named by the geese in imitation of an epithet used by Lenin in the years after 1905 for those who favored a fight to remain a legal party in Russia, for which Lenin charged them with wanting to "liquidate" the true or underground party. The American "liquidators" felt that they could keep an underground apparatus alive for those things that could not be done openly but that, now that the atmosphere was changing in the country, they could win much larger numbers for the movement by giving real status and powers to No. 2, the Workers' Party. This way, they hoped they might gradually win open legality for a legal Communist Party and most of its activities. When our handful of "rurals" voted for the liquidator motions on this question, the convention shaped up as 23 to 22, the majority of one being given by the vote of Comrade Day, or K-97, who, with a true police instinct, wanted the Communist movement to stay as deep underground as possible.

The leaders of the liquidators were such people as Ruthenberg, Lovestone, Dunne, Foster, Bedacht, Cannon and Browder, a group that was shortly to break into two factions, that of Foster, Cannon, Dunne, and Browder on the one hand and that of Ruthenberg, Lovestone, and Bedacht on the other. Thus, infighting would continue to be the principal business of the Communist Party, even after the raid on the Michigan Convention, and a change in the atmosphere, had made a legal party possible. This change made obsolete the main cause of infighting at the Michigan Convention. But before we take up the raid which put an end to the Convention with much of its business still unfinished, it might be interesting to take up what looked like a minor question of the Convention's technical organization, yet was a matter which gave some inkling of the future "Bolshevization" or "Russification" of the Communist Party of America.

THE BATTLE OVER THE PRESIDIUM

Of the three delegates from Moscow, it was easy to see which was head man. It was Comrade Ward Brooks, who despite his elegant English name addressed us in German, with a slight Polish or Yiddish accent. He made all the formal addresses, gave us instructions, made decisions for us when we were deadlocked, acted as if he were the director of our "singing society." The experienced people from the center, with whom he had already had some meetings, always hastened to assent to everything he said as if his words were the wise judgments of the entire Communist International and not to be questioned.

The morning of August 17 was taken up by meetings of the Central Committee with Comrade Brooks. Then there were caucus meetings, Brooks meeting first with one caucus and then with the other. Our third miniscule caucus of the "rurals" had not yet crystallized, so we were not favored with Walecki's (Brooks') guidance. In the afternoon, L. C. Wheat (Jay Lovestone) called the convention to order as Secretary of the Central Committee. Then Comintern Delegate Brooks proposed that we should elect a *Presidium,* a word that was new to me, to our country, and indeed to the English language. In 1922 it could be found neither in the thirteen-volume Oxford Dictionary nor in the unabridged Merriam-Webster, nor in the parliamentary procedure of any American club, party body, or trade union. Today it is defined as follows in *Webster's Collegiate Dictionary:* "*presidium* (Russ. prezidium): a permanent executive committee selected esp. in Communist countries to act for a larger body." In 1922, Brooks-Walecki was the first to bring this word and institution to America.

Brooks was bewildered at our bewilderment. "We elect presidiums in every meeting," he explained. "They are the directing body of the convention and determine matters of procedure and many other things. Your presidium should contain the leading representatives of each faction; the faction that has a majority here should have a majority on the presidium.

Thus many matters may be settled between the factions without time-wasting debate by the general body of the delegates."

I demanded the floor. "Comrade Brooks," I said, "you forget that this is an American convention. Here in America we do not use a presidium to decide anything for us. In fact, I am hearing the word *presidium* for the first time. We elect a chairman. We do not give him the power to decide anything beyond the routine conduct of the meeting. The convention is the sovereign body. It decides. The chairman is only its agent to keep order and recognize speakers in their proper turn. Here in America we use a parliamentary procedure that is embodied in *Roberts' Rules of Order.* Every trade union, every party local, every organization I have ever been in on any level of society recognizes *Roberts' Rules of Order.* The labor movement would not understand us if we started using a *presidium* to act for or decide a lot of matters for our conventions or for any sovereign body.

"And another thing; I believe, and I am sure many delegates here believe, that frozen factions are an undesirable thing. Faction members are accustomed to listen only to speakers from their own factions and vote only for motions made by their own faction leaders. They close their ears when anyone speaks from the opposing faction. Many of us think that when a sovereign body meets, it should listen to everyone, and get ideas from anyone who is a proper member of the body; it should vote for measures on their merits, not make all listening and voting a factional matter. I also think that majorities and minorities can actually be changed by reasonable debate, and that freezing the factions by giving them proportional representation on a presiding and directing body is an evil thing that prevents rational debate and rational decision. In such debate members may vote differently on each matter, and factions may change in number. We came together to hear each other and not merely to hear our own faction spokesmen. We meet to decide things for ourselves on their merits, not to let some ruling or directing body decide things for us on the basis of prejudiced and frozen factions."

At this there was some applause from what I have called the rurals, the delegates from the more American units far from the factional lineups and the fanaticisms of the central body. But except for the "rurals," who obviously were a tiny minority, there were blank stares at me from the delegates, and utter astonishment on the part of the men from Moscow.

I heard Comrade Lang (Pogany-Pepper) lean over and in a deliberately audible stage whisper say to Comrade Brooks: "This man thinks he's the American Lenin!"

Knowing that everybody had heard his stage whisper, I answered him. "No, I do not think, as Comrade Lang says, that I am the American Lenin. I have no such thought. But I do know that I am an American, in an American convention of the American Communist Party, and we should conform to the rules of order that would govern any trade union meeting, and indeed any meeting held in America. I move that we proceed to the election of a chairman with the ordinary powers and duties of the chairman of any American meeting, and that we drop the idea of a presidium."

Except for manifest astonishment, there was no discussion on my motion. Only a handful voted for it, and so an American meeting got a Moscow-type presidium. Obviously, Comrade Brooks had already persuaded both factions in the Central Committee that a presidium was a must, since both geese and liquidators voted for it, after which they went into an interminable wrangle as to whether the slender majority of the geese in the convention should be reflected in a majority on that august body, a wrangle that was eventually settled by Brooks himself, who proposed that they should each choose six representatives, and that he would enter the presidium as a thirteenth member with a deciding vote. But my defense of American parliamentary procedure and my attack on "frozen caucuses" won the approval of the few uncommitted "rurals." Thus a third faction came into being without any member on the presidium.

THE RAID ON THE BRIDGMAN CONVENTION

When the head of the Chicago office of the F.B.I., Spolansky, got the urgent message to go to St. Joseph, Michigan, to look for a secret Communist convention, he took only one agent with him, Edward Shanahan, and left at once for St. Joseph. There, he asked the Sheriff where in Berrien County a large secret Communist convention could possibly meet. The Sheriff guessed, "Near Bridgman." The next day, he and Shanahan scoured the countryside and woodlands in a driving rain, coming back soaking wet with no clue. But the following morning they found Wulfskeel's farm and knew they had found their quarry.

A group of men in city clothes were standing around after finishing breakfast, talking in animated knots. Trusting to their disguise in overalls the two agents went to the big house to ask for a drink from the pump and inquire about renting a room in the farmhouse. As they talked to Mrs. Wulfskeel, Spolansky caught sight of the figure, well-known in Chicago, of the labor leader, William Z. Foster. What Spolansky didn't know is that he was recognized by Foster as well. Because of the high secrecy of his membership in the Communist Party and the danger to his trade union work, Foster left immediately for Chicago, making up his mind to deny that he had ever been at the convention.

The Presidium went into emergency session when it learned that we were being spied upon. Although I was not a member, I was "co-opted" to attend this session, perhaps as a representative of the handful of "rurals." We decided to adjourn that same night, to elect a secret Central Committee then and there to carry on the work, to strengthen our guard so that no one could leave except in the order determined by us, and to tell the delegates only that because spies had been seen in the neighborhood, we would shorten the convention and adjourn in three days. But actually, as soon as night fell, we started our evacuation. We had only one car, an old Ford belonging to the farmer and driven by his son. It could hold four people besides the driver. As none of us could drive, we had to enlist the sympathy of Wulfskeel's son. We decided that the first to be evacuated would be the men from Moscow, then the new and old Central Committees, next the members under indictment and not yet apprehended (my case), and those out on bail or fresh from prison (Ruthenberg and Gitlow), and after that noncitizens and those born abroad, and finally, the native Americans with no police record. Fortunately, that left K-97 in the last batch, the indictment-free native Americans. Those whom the Ford car could not possibly take care of during the hours of darkness but who were in some preferred classification might try it on foot following a streambed with the aid of a few flashlights, under the leadership of Charles Krumbein. My wife was put into that group. Those who were left to the last were entrusted with the task of disposing of the precious documents that had accumulated during the three days of meetings by day and night (the night meetings had been held with the farmer's lanterns hanging from trees). The amount of paper that had been collected during the proceedings was enormous and was precious—precious in some measure to us, but far more so to the police. Here, too, Comrade Brooks's Muscovite ways had caused trouble. Because in Moscow's meetings it was customary for each delegate to fill out a questionnaire giving his true name and pseudonyms, the length of time he had been in the movement, the number of times he had been arrested, the time he had spent in prison or exile, and other evidences of his *stazh* or length and degree of service as a party stalwart, Walecki insisted that we too should fill out such mimeographed questionnaires. If these should fall into unfriendly hands they would provide a complete *Who's Who* of all the party leaders who had been elected to the convention or invited as fraternal delegates. There were also theses, minutes, and notes of delegates on speeches of Walecki, Foster, Jakira, Lovestone, and others, discussions of plans and tactical intentions—a perfect police dossier. Hence the Presidium's motion to "dispose of" meant to burn. But, under the direction of Ruthenberg, who should have gone out in one of the earlier categories, yet insisted on staying behind to the end as if he courted arrest, all the papers and documents were put into two huge sugar barrels, a hole was dug in the woods behind the farmhouse, everything including typewriters and a mimeograph machine was dumped into them, and the barrels were buried beneath tar paper, over which was laid a layer of sand and over that a thick layer of woodland leaves.

Next morning (August 22nd, the fifth day of the convention), the federal agents reinforced to four, augmented by the St. Joseph Sheriff and his constabulary, plus a posse of some twenty people from Berrien County, found that most of the prize prisoners were gone. Left were only seventeen native Americans, including C. E. Ruthenberg and Francis Morrow. The latter, perhaps in order to leave room for maneuver, now gave his name as Francis Ashworth. When Spolansky was questioning the prisoners one by one, Ashworth declared to him that he was federal agent K-97 and proved his good intentions by drawing a map showing where the two barrels were buried. Fortunately, my wife and I, who had filled out our questionnaires together, had stopped our list of aliases with Albright as our "true name." My list read "Daniel Shays, alias Arthur E. Albrecht, alias Arthur Albright," and Ella's list followed the same pattern. The name Wolfe appeared nowhere in either barrel. Although a number of people from the center had recognized us and knew our true names, K-97 knew no more than was in the barrel. But it was clear to me that under the names Daniel Shays, Arthur Albrecht, and Arthur Albright, I was in for another indictment. For the rest, Walecki's silly insistence on imitation of Muscovite conventions gave the police a perfect *Who's Who.* William Z. Foster had left too soon to fill out a questionnaire, but notes on his talk, minutes, and a few roll calls testified to his brief presence.

As our little Ford sped through the darkness heading for the railway station in St. Joseph, we passed two trucks with frames covered with canvas, like old covered wagons. They were unattended, but it seemed to me that they were there to take us all to jail in St. Joseph. We arrived at our destination without incident. There was no one looking for us at the railway station as, in the early morning, we boarded the milk train for Chicago. At Bridgman some more people got on, among whom I was delighted to see my wife. She had been on the foot party that had stumbled something close to a mile in darkness through woods and farmlands to the railroad station at Bridgman. We gave each other no sign of recognition, but after some time as I walked to the men's room I dropped a little ball of paper in her lap on which I had written: "Get off at South Chicago," for I felt sure that federal agents would be waiting at the main Chicago Station. I dropped a similar note in Lovestone's lap, and he passed the word to Winestone. Actually, our delegates made up the bulk of the passengers on the unusually crowded morning train. All those who continued to the end of the line at the main Chicago terminus were apprehended there by waiting federal agents.

The four of us who had gotten off at South Chicago took a taxi into town, telling the driver to take us to one of the most elegant hotels just off Lincoln Park. We figured that the better the hotel, the less likely it would be that the police should look for us there. Moments of peace, when you know you are being hunted, are especially grateful, hence, though I no longer remember the name of the hotel at which we were stopping, I do remember with pleasure the long grassy meadows over which my wife and I strolled hand in hand in Lincoln Park. But when we returned from our relaxing walk I instantly sensed danger.

William Winestone, in violation of all the rules of conspiracy, had sent a telegram to his secretary in the New York office of which he was district organizer, and she had telegraphed an answer. Federal agents were monitoring the telegraph offices, and sure enough, there they were—two inevitable, professionally recognizable men, sitting in the lobby. The man at the desk said to me: "I have a telegram here for one of your two friends, but they checked out so fast that we didn't have time to look in their boxes to see if there were any messages. Will you take the telegram for him?"

"I don't know them well enough to take their messages," I said loudly. "We just met them on the train. I have no idea where they may have gone."

My wife and I went up to our room to reflect. "Maybe they don't know us. After all, how should they know people from California? Or maybe they're waiting to see if Lovestone and Winestone will get in touch with us, or someone from the center come to give us a message. Anyhow, let's get a good night's sleep, a shower in the morning, fresh underwear, then go down to breakfast—we'll eat out and see if they follow us or how we can shake them off."

In the morning I packed our bag, put a Gillette safety razor in my pocket in hopes of getting rid of my telltale beard, then we went down to breakfast. The two men were still, or again, in the lobby. When we went out to look for a restaurant, one of the two followed us at a discreet distance. He went into the same restaurant with us and sat a few tables away. I ordered a substantial breakfast including fruit, cereal, bacon and eggs, and coffee. Our shadow did likewise. Then I stood up suddenly, leaving my breakfast untouched, and said, so that our shadow could hear me, "I'm going out to get a newspaper." I did not return, and never did eat breakfast.

By prearrangement, my wife was to go back to the hotel, check out, ask the bellboy to carry the bag to a taxi, tell the taxi driver to go to a well-known drugstore in downtown Chicago (I believe it was Walgreen's) which had checking boxes in its basement, have the taxi driver check the bag and bring her the key, then drive her to a corner near the home of Oliver Carlson, a leader of the Communist youth, at whose house she would meet me. But first she had to go to Chicago's largest department store, enter the ladies' room, stay there as long as possible, then leave the ladies' room and the department store by another door. If detective No. 2 was following her, she might succeed in shaking him off at that point. Meanwhile, at Oliver Carlson's home, I was cutting off beard and moustache with scissors, and then making it a clean shave aided by my only piece of baggage, the pocket razor. I parted my hair in the middle (I had hair then), put on a high starched collar, and made other changes in my appearance. A few hours later, when my wife, unshadowed, rang the Carlson doorbell and I answered her ring, she asked, "Does Mr. Carlson live here?" So complete was my transformation without beard or moustache, that she did not recognize me until I spoke. I knew then that I was safe. (Beards were worn in those days almost exclusively by doctors and an occasional aging professor; the rest of American manhood was trying to preserve an appearance of youth by being clean-shaven.)

From Carlson's we took a taxi to downtown Chicago, gave the taxi driver the key to the check room compartment without ourselves leaving the taxi, then had him drive all the way to Gary, Indiana, where we knew it would be safe to board a train. From Gary we went by train to Lima, Ohio. I still remember the pleasure we felt lying in the afternoon sun on the grassy lawns of a park in Lima, visiting the animals in the little park zoo, relaxing from the sense of pursuit, and knowing that by such simple stratagems we had eluded our pursuers.

The next day we boarded a train at Lima, and made our way to New York, where we visited my wife's mother, staying with her a while to think out where we should go to live next, and what name I should now assume. Obviously, since Albright was now under indictment, I could not return to San Francisco. Reluctantly we abandoned the lovely city in which we had been so happy, left all our furniture in our home on Ashbury Terrace to a good friend, and finally decided on Boston. As for Arthur Albright, he simply disappeared without a trace, except that I had one technical, legal problem to solve with him.

When Pete Isaak, son of the well-known anarchist writer and publisher of the nineteenth century, Abe Isaak, wanted to buy a plot of ground on the top of one of the highest hills in Sausalito on which to build himself a house, the owner refused to sell him part of the tract, but insisted on selling it entire at the price of $1,000. He asked me if I would take half of it for $500, which I did. Now I wanted Albright to sell the beautiful lot to Bertram D. Wolfe. A lawyer, Austin Lewis, who knew a lot about Marxism and was very friendly to me, helped me to execute a deed in which Arthur E. Albright sold the land to Bertram Wolfe "for $1 and other valuable considerations." I still have this curious document.

I had no compunction about the changes in name, though I never gave up the idea of changing back to the name with which I was born. I felt that the postwar madness that continued as long as Woodrow Wilson remained as president had forced the pseudonyms upon me, a madness which ended only when Harding nationally, Governor Al Smith in New York, Governor Young in California, and other governors in other states, began pardoning the victims of the indiscriminate red raids. In Boston I took the name of Brill, a tribute that would have amused Abraham Brill, a high school teacher of English for whom I had great admiration. But within a few months I was able to resume the name with which I was born, and was happy not to have to depart from that name again in American public life.

Living in Boston we were much nearer to our families and made a number of family visits to New York. On one such visit, we learned that the English labor leader, Albert Purcell, who had been on the British Trade Union Commission to Russia, was to speak at the old Civic Club on West 12th Street, which unfortunately has since ceased to exist, on the subject: "What I Saw in Russia." It was the custom of the Civic Club to serve tea and cookies between the formal address and the question and discussion period. As we moved towards the tea tables, we spied Theresa Wolfson, an old friend who had gone to high school with my wife, and had played tennis with us on numerous occasions. We sat down at her table, and were introduced by her to "Roberto Haberman, chairman of the Department of Foreign Languages of the Federal District in Mexico." He was a dark-haired man in his upper thirties who spoke English well and fluently. He seemed to know a great deal about me, things that a stranger should not have known: that I had been a teacher, that I was no longer teaching, that I was a writer of sorts, and much else. Later I learned that he was of Rumanian birth and a member of the American Socialist Party, who had left suddenly and secretly for Mexico in December, 1919, when government agents wanted to question him about his connections with Agnes Smedley, and what the two of them had to do with the shipment of arms to Indian revolutionaries who were fighting for independence from England. In Mexico he had attached himself to Felipe Carrillo Puerto, the radical Governor of Yucatán, who fancied himself a Communist of sorts. (For a while the Russian Revolution was extremely popular in Mexico, which was going through a revolutionary turmoil of its own, and many politicians in high place thought of themselves as "Communists," but as their knowledge of Russia grew, their enthusiasm for things Russian disappeared.) From Yucatán, Haberman had gone to Mexico City and attached himself to Luis Morones, head of the moderate, pro-government trade unions, and through the influence of Morones had gotten his government appointment in the Federal District.

"I hear you were a teacher," Haberman said to me in his very first sentence.

"Yes, I was."

"Do you like teaching?"

"Very much."

"Are you a good teacher?"

"Oh, excellent."

"Well, then, consider it settled."

"Consider what settled?" I was about to inquire. But just then the gavel came down with a bang, and everyone got up from the tea tables to return to his seat for the period of questions and discussion. "Consider what settled?" I wondered, but did not catch sight of Haberman again as the meeting broke up, so I forgot about this strange man and his strange interrogation. So many things in my life have been the product of accident, and now once again a brief conversation with Roberto Haberman was to make an enormous change in the course of my own life and that of my wife.

The F.B.I. had interested itself in the case of Arthur Albright because he had crossed state lines to go to the Michigan Convention. They went to my apartment on Ashbury Terrace only to find somebody else living there who knew nothing about my whereabouts. They went to *Labor Unity;* it had a new editor. Brother Albright no longer attended sessions of the Central Trades and Labor Council nor meetings of Local 44 of the Cooks' Union. The labor school he had founded through his lecture courses got along without him. Beard and all, he had disappeared without a trace. No one knew what had happened to him. Other convention delegates were caught up with and tried. Foster got a hung jury; Ruthenberg was convicted and was out on appeal; the others were out on bail; in 1933 all their cases were closed, something I learned only many years later; but Albright's dossier was kept open because they couldn't find him, nor find out what he was up to. . . .

HOW THE F.B.I. "CAUGHT UP" WITH ARTHUR ALBRIGHT

In 1961 and 1962 I was teaching at the University of California, Davis Campus, under the resounding title of Distinguished Professor of Russian History, and doing research for the writing of my *Fabulous Life of Diego Rivera.* One day when I was in the Art Department building looking at colored slides of the paintings of Diego Rivera, I was called to the phone. The trembling voice of the secretary of the History Department told me, "Professor Wolfe, there's a man here from the F.B.I. and he forced me to tell him where you were. He's coming over for you."

"Don't worry," I told her, "it merely means that I'll be in good hands."

A man entered the Art library, showed me his credentials, asked politely whether I minded answering some questions. "Not at all. What's on your mind?"

"We're trying to build up a case for the deportation of Harry Bridges, and we have been told that you used to live in San Francisco. Can you tell us anything about him?"

"Nothing that will be of any use to you. It's true that I was active in the San Francisco labor movement in the early twenties, but I left there before he came. So everything I know about him I got from reading the papers. I know a lot, but it's all hearsay, and of no use to you for your purposes.

He was manifestly disappointed. Suddenly he brightened up again. "Did I hear you say that you were active in the San Francisco labor movement in the early twenties?"

"That's right."

"Then maybe you can help me with another matter—the mysterious case of one Arthur E. Albrecht, or Arthur Albright. He has disappeared completely. When men elude us, we can generally find out at least where they are and what they are doing. But on him—nothing. We can't find out where he went. We can't find out what he's doing. We can't find a trace of him. It's as if he had disappeared into thin air. Maybe you can tell us something about him?"

"Sir," I said, "you are talking to him."

He slapped his forehead. "Well, I'll be damned. Anyhow, we can now close his dossier. Thank you for your courtesy, Professor Wolfe. And good luck in your teaching." At last they knew what had happened to Arthur Albright.

19

INTO THE MEXICAN MAZE

I don't know how we happened to pick on Boston, except that there was almost no intercourse between "the capital of New England" and New York, "the capital of America." And none at all between Boston and San Francisco. I was not to discover the attractions of the Harvard Yard until a later career. True, Boston had once called itself "the Athens of America," but the glory of the age of transcendentalism had passed from it, and that autumn and winter it seemed to me that its museums and halls of culture were but empty sepulchres of an intellectual activity that had betaken itself elsewhere.

My wife and I found jobs easily enough, she as a statistician in the Harvard Bureau of Business Research and I as the head of the proof room of the Atlantic Press. We found places for gentle pleasant walks: the old waterfront; the Fenway; the banks of the Charles; the low-lying Blue Hills; the pine and lupin and blueberry covered hills of Cape Cod; the rocky coast of Gloucester. But they all looked insignificant after the High Sierras, the granite walls and rushing white waters of the Yosemite, the mountains and headlands of the California coast.

I received the substantial union scale plus time-and-a-half for the first four hours of overtime and double time for any additional hours, as well as for Saturdays and holidays. I did not have to work hard, since I had a great many proofreaders under me who did all the primary proofs. But mine was the job of okaying the final press proof before the presses started rolling. I had much overtime and doubletime pay, but no leisure time to spend it, for late at night and on weekends I always found myself waiting for the pressmen to bring me the final press proof. We found that first autumn and winter in Boston, cold and damp, and dull besides, for we had not sunk any roots into the life of the city.

As soon as the Central Committee learned that I was living in Boston, they appointed me district organizer of the New England District. I did not like administrative work, for I knew that I was better suited for writing, teaching, and editing. I thought of what life would be like trying to work with all those Letts and Lithuanians and Poles and Finns who thought that it was the revolutionary duty of the party to burrow as deeply underground as possible. Unlike the San Francisco movement, they knew nothing of the New England trade unions, which also knew nothing of them. And they knew nothing of American history and traditions which I felt were my heritage and on which I was determined to build. Like the maverick I was, I turned down the offer, remaining unmoved when they sent Will Winestone up to Boston to convince me that I had to accept as "a matter of discipline." Discipline did not go so far with me that I was going to permit any august body to determine what I was fitted for, or how my wife and I should live our personal lives. Anyhow, we did not feel at home there in Boston, nor like its damp, raw, and chilly winter. What they would have done to me for my lack of "discipline" I never found out, for suddenly, unbelievably, there came a cable from Mexico City which read:

> YOU AND YOUR WIFE HAVE BEEN APPOINTED TEACHERS OF ENGLISH IN THE MEXICO CITY HIGH SCHOOL SYSTEM STOP YOUR APPOINTMENT BEGINS JANUARY FIRST YOUR TEACHING DUTIES BEGIN FEBRUARY FIFTH.

The cable was signed, *Roberto Haberman.* So that was the solution of the mystery of the Civic Club. That was what Haberman had meant by his cryptic remark, "Then consider it settled." To be sure, neither of us knew one word of Spanish, but we could get a textbook and start studying it. Nor did we have money for the journey, but the cable was clear: our appointment began January first and our duties February fifth. There was no mention of salary in the cable, yet with more than a month elapsing between appointment and teaching duties, who knows how many pesos would be waiting for us when we got there? And who knows what exotic adventures, along with the escape to a semitropical clime from Boston's dullness, and damp, raw, and chilly winter?

I did not stop to ask permission from the Central Committee to leave the country or to be transferred to another party. They held this against me until they began to get reports on the character of the work I was doing in the Mexican party; then they gave me something more than amnesty. Nor did I stop to ask why Roberto Haberman might want two teachers who knew not one word of Spanish (before long I was to find the answer). I sent a cable accepting the appointments, and went downtown by the urban train to buy a Spanish textbook from Schoenhoff's foreign bookstore. With the turning of its pages, our new life in a Spanish-speaking land began.

We went to New York to visit with our family and friends, then left by an aged steamboat of the old Ward Line that took ten days to get to the port of Vera Cruz. The ship was not long for this world, nor was the Ward Line either. We found that our second-class cabin was shared by giant tropical roaches which emerged as soon as we got into warmer seas, to share with us the fruit and cookies in the farewell basket that someone had given us. We got rid of the roaches only by tossing the basket and its contents overboard. We left winter behind us as our ship ploughed softly through summery seas, into the deep blue of the Gulf Stream from which leaped flying fish with no visible aim except to show that they too could fly. Great schools of sharks followed us to get the leftovers of each meal as they were cast overboard. We got our first view of the Southern Cross. After my wife recovered from a brief attack of the flu, we studied Spanish together, and I tried out my pitiful but growing stock of phrases on whomever could stand my painful efforts.

Fellow passengers advised us on how to conduct ourselves in Mexico City. One of them gave us the name and address of an immigrant Jewish pianist who had a vacant room for some paying guests. "He lives in the Colonia Roma," the passenger told us. "That's not far from the railway station. Our taxis have no clocks on them to tell you the fare, so you must make an agreement as to price before you get into a cab, or you're in for it. I could get to the address I've given you for one peso fifty; being foreigners, you'll probably have to give him two fifty. But not one centavo more! And no tipping! You Americans spoil all our service people with your habit of tipping."

From Vera Cruz we took a diminutive train—seeming more diminutive against the towering mountains—that climbed all day into the highest country of our continent, puffing and straining, over heights of more than twelve thousand feet, to drop down at last to Mexico City, still more than seven thousand five hundred feet above the level of the sea.

What a glorious land, we thought, as we prepared the bargain with the taxi driver who was to take us to the address we had been given in the Colonia Roma. "How much?" I asked in the best Spanish I could command.

"Ten pesos," came the reply.

"No, señor," said I, remembering the lesson I had been given on the boat, "two pesos, fifty, and not a centavo more." He glowered. How could a *gringo*, newly arrived from wealthy Yanquilandia, know what the proper fare to the Colonia Roma was? We argued back and forth, yet he did not reject the prospect of taking us to our destination. Finally he asked us to get in and he put our bags beside us. When we got on to a dark shaded street in the Colonia Roma, he drew out a big knife. "The fare, señor," he said, "is as I told you, ten pesos." Without a word, I took out the ten peso bill, glad that he did not ask for every cent I had. Then he prepared to drive us on to our destination, but I grabbed our luggage and my wife and we got out on an unknown street in an unknown city, to wait for someone to pass by to whom we might repeat the name and number of our destination.

The first to pass was a man carrying a heavy sack of lemons. Somehow I made myself understood. He took my wife's bag with his free hand and led us the few necessary blocks with great courtesy and concern for our helplessness. When I attempted to show my gratitude by giving him a tip of two silver pesos, he refused to accept them. "It was nothing," he said.

When I poured out my words of thanks, he repeated, "No hay de qué" (there's nothing to thank me for).

These were our first two Mexicans—one who pulled a knife on us yet demanded no more than he thought an uninformed and wealthy *gringo* should give, the other with his bag of lemons held over his shoulder with one hand, carrying one of our bags with the other, refusing a tip, and responding graciously to my words of thanks. Yes, indeed, we were in a new world and face to face with new adventures.

When we presented ourselves to the paymaster in the Secretariat of Education on February first and signed the payroll, he began to pile up little stacks of silver pesos, then each worth fifty cents American. He piled up so many stacks, ten to a stack, that I had to leave them standing there to go out and buy a canvas bag. We found that we had each been given two appointments of one hour each, five days a week, at five pesos per appointment. Paid every ten days we each earned 300 or more pesos per month, equivalent to $150, for that light teaching load. A peso was worth fifty cents American, but if we did not insist on imported, packaged foods or toothpaste or such from north of the border, the purchasing power in Mexican foods and domestically produced articles was quite substantial, enough to live on decently and pay the rent. We immediately discovered that this was an artistically endowed people we had come to live among, seemingly born with a sense of color and form, and that dishes and other handmade objects of great beauty sold for a song.

Both of us were appointed to teach two classes in English five days a week at the girls' high school named after Miguel Lerdo de Tejada, a former President of Mexico and a hero to the taste of the new revolutionary era, because he had been a *liberalista* and *federalista* in a country that in the nineteenth century had oscillated between conservative centralists and liberal federalists.

Our colleagues in the English Department were almost all from the United States, people who had rebelled against some aspect of American life. One woman, who spoke execrably bad, ungrammatical Spanish, was a rebel against our dry laws and had vowed never to return until our country was "once more free." Another, a Californian, believed in earthquakes, in astrology, theosophy, vegetarianism, and natural foods, which she kept in complicated balance, on a weekly basis ("If at the end of the week I find I have been short of proteins, I eat a couple of nuts"); a number of them were draft evaders who had left the United States secretly in 1917, knocked around Mexico earning a precarious, marginal living while they picked up the Spanish tongue and Mexican ways; yet others had sought refuge in Mexico because the pace of life was slower and easier, and the ways of life more attractive.

We found that our American colleagues were too much thrown together in each other's company, remaining for the most part a clannish foreign enclave of strangers in a strange land. Though they were pleasant to associate with, my wife and I decided that we would not become denizens of the American colony, but would seek to study, and if possible become an accepted part of the life of this colorful land.

Our pupils were bright and eager adolescent girls, grateful to be taught English, which was the most useful foreign language for a Mexican. There were at that time almost no native Mexicans who could teach English, so that our little enclave was welcome. Many of those we taught have since become the first native teachers of the English tongue in Mexico; now it would be almost impossible for an American to get such a position as we had, since the native-born teachers are ample in number and quite capable.

Though we did not know much Spanish at the beginning, my wife and I conscientiously prepared each lesson by looking up the Mexican equivalents of every word and phrase we intended to teach in the next day's lesson. Our lack of Spanish did not handicap us, because we employed the then fashionable "natural method" of using as far as possible only English in the classroom, yet we were always prepared to explain any difficult point in the day's lesson in Spanish. I think I won the hearts of my girls on the very first day, when I discovered that they could not say, "Mr. Wolfe," because there is no *W* in the Spanish alphabet. The best they could do in their efforts to pronounce my name was to say *Guoolf* (pronounced *Gwulf*). After several vain attempts to get them to imitate my pronunciation of my own name I said: "Señoritas, prepárense para un beso" (prepare yourselves for a kiss). I pursed my lips and said *oooo* or *uuuu* and added *ulf*. That was easy and amusing; they were delighted that they had mastered such an unpronounceable sound, and that their teacher had a sense of humor. Henceforth they would no longer say *Guasington* for America's capital, but *Wasington*.

The directora or principal of the high school was Dolores Salcedo, a woman of considerable culture and mannerly and courteous bearing. Especially notable were the graceful gestures of her hands. She attended our classes once, and decided that we knew how to teach, thereafter leaving us to our own devices. After we had been teaching for a few weeks, or rather *decenas*, for our pay and work were measured in ten day periods, Roberto Haberman sent for me to visit him at his office in the Secretariat of Education. "Bertram," he said, "I know that you are a writer as well as a teacher. Have you seen the articles written jointly by me and Carleton Beals, and published in the *Nation*, the *New Republic*, and other liberal and radical newspapers in the United States?"

"Yes, I have read some of them."

"What did you think of them?"

"I was more impressed by them before I got here."

"Well, Carleton has refused to write any more articles jointly with me. He is ill-tempered and we have quarrelled too much about what is to go into them. That's why I appointed you and your wife as teachers here. I should like you to collaborate with me on articles on Mexico." I realized then that I had gotten the unexpected cable because he needed a ghostwriter.

"No, Roberto," I said, "I don't think I can collaborate with you."

"Why not?"

"Well, you and Carleton have been picturing Mexico as a socialist paradise. I do not know too much about the country yet, but when I see the homeless boys, orphaned by all the rebellions, begging and picking pockets by day, and tearing down billboards after nine o'clock at night when the second night show has begun, sleeping on the sidewalks with nothing but the billboards to lie on, and perhaps a flea-covered little dog to wrap in their torn shirts to keep them warm, I can hardly think of Mexico as either socialist or a paradise."

Haberman's face darkened into a scowl. "That's all, señor Wolfe," he said, signifying that the interview was over. At the end of the next *decena,* my wife and I each found a dismissal slip attached to our place on the payroll. Our appointments as teachers of English were over! Here we were, strangers in a strange land, with still only a fragmentary command of the language of the country. There was no such thing as tenure, no union to appeal to. What would we do now to earn a living? Or, if we acknowledged defeat at the very beginning of our initiation into this fascinating Mexican maze, how would we scrape together the funds to get back to the United States?

We went to señorita Salcedo, our directora, to bid her good-bye. "I am sorry," she said. "You are both good teachers. None better. I'll see whether I can get you reappointed. Don't give up teaching yet. Meet your classes as usual. I will go to Licenciado* Vasconcelos (the Minister of Education) and see what I can do."

One of the features of the Mexican Government that is surprising to Americans is the fact that it is so easy for an ordinary citizen to meet with or take a plaint or plea to a high member of the Government. It was nothing for our directora to go to see the Minister of Education. (I too have entered the office of Licenciado José Vasconcelos without any elaborate ceremony or red tape, and had a long talk with him, though I was nothing but an ordinary teacher in one of his high schools.) Here is Dolores Salcedo's account to my wife and me concerning her visit on our behalf:

"I said to him, 'Mr. Minister, señor Roberto Haberman has just dismissed from my school two of my most valuable teachers of English Bertram and Ella Wolfe. Perhaps he had his reasons; I know nothing about politics and do not know what differences he may have had with Mr. Wolfe. In any case, he did not dismiss them for any reason connected with their teaching. The Wolfes are two of the best teachers I have in my

* *Licenciado* means "attorney." Almost everybody who gets a higher degree is either a *licenciado* or an *ingeniero.* Most of them do not practice law, but *licenciado* is a courtesy title, like "Doctor" for the Ph.D. in the United States.

school. They are not only teaching my girls English; they are also teaching them to be ladies, not by lecturing them, but by the example of their natural conduct toward them. After more than ten years of civil wars and rebellions, you know señor Licenciado, how harsh and hard our customs and manners have become. I think that there is nothing more important than a teacher who can teach my girls good manners and proper behavior. I have come to you, señor Vasconcelos, to ask you to reappoint Mr. and Mrs. Wolfe as teachers in Miguel Lerdo, and to inform Mr. Haberman that they can be dismissed only for reasons connected with their conduct and work as teachers, and that, if he has such complaints against them, he must discuss them with me as the directora of the high school.'

"And the Minister answered, 'I shall do as you request. I shall order their reappointment retroactive to the date of their dismissal, and inform Mr. Haberman that he has no right to dismiss them again without your consent.' "

Thus our ill fortune was remedied. Henceforth we would not be beholden to Roberto Haberman, and our stay in Mexico seemed to have been prolonged indefinitely. It was something to have become inviolate and have the Minister of Education himself behind us. The directora followed this up by appointing me head of the Foreign Language Department (one teacher of German and approximately a dozen teachers of English), and she cut my teaching load from ten hours to eight per week so that I might visit the classes of the members of my department. I proved a relaxed and gentle department head to the satisfaction of the entire department. When Haberman met me again at a social gathering, he acted as if nothing untoward had happened. As long as I was in Mexico he never found another ghostwriter nor published another article in the American press.

For us Mexico was an incredible land. For a long time, Mexico meant to us Mexico City, the capital and the largest Latin city on the North American continent. But it was a comfortable size, only some 625,000 inhabitants then as against its over 7,000,000 now. It had no tourists, for they were afraid of the unending succession of civil wars and rebellions. And it had no traffic snarls and no smog. During the winter, the dry season when there are no rains, there were only rare dust storms from the old, imperfectly filled-in Lago de Texcoco. But, winter and summer alike, especially in the magnificent mornings, the tropical sun beat down with brilliant intensity upon ancient palaces and flat-roofed houses, filling with purple darkness the windows and doorways, giving bulk to all solid forms, drawing clean lines that separated the lava and granite mountains from the light-drenched sky. A good part of the city's inhabitants were living in adobe huts with primitive, often stone-age utensils: a basin and rolling pin made of volcanic lava, a charcoal brazier, woven straw mats on the ground for beds, clay jugs, or perhaps an empty gasoline can, in which to carry water from the nearest fountain.

Many years later I was to return to Mexico and witness an electricians' strike. The tourists fled in panic from the hotels on the beautiful and broad Paseo de la Reforma (a statue and tree adorned boulevard 200 feet wide), for their elevators ran by electricity, their water was pumped up by electricity, toilets and showers no longer functioned, their food had been kept cold by electricity, and cooked and baked and roasted by electricity, so that the electricians' strike seemed to them the end of everything. But if one walked a few blocks from the magnificent Paseo de la Reforma, one found adobe huts, charcoal braziers, lamp or candle lights, water carried on the shoulders in great jugs or cans, life going on as usual, no one even knowing that there was an electricians' strike. One was forced to reflect that the more we become dependent on machinery and labor-saving devices for our daily living, the more readily life can be cut off by an electricians' strike, and the less we are likely to know how to help ourselves in an emergency.

My wife and I have been to Mexico a number of times since those days, but we both agree that the Mexico City of 625,000 inhabitants represented the golden days of our experience with Mexico.

It was winter when we came. The nights were cold, but cold is a relative term. The city lies in the tropical zone somewhere around 19 degrees north of the equator. When the wind blew from the more open north, the city, being surrounded by mountains on the east, south, and west, native Indians who had to be out at night would wrap their woolen *sarapes* or *rebozos* around nose and mouth to keep out the malevolent *aigre,* the "evil" night air which educated Mexicans call *aire.* But we found a light topcoat sufficient and the night air exhilarating, while the mornings in Mexico with their incredibly bright and warming winter sunshine had a splendor that is simply impossible to convey.

The floor of the valley in which Mexico City lies, climbs from some 7,500 feet to some 8,000 feet about the level of the sea. Above and around the city on three sides the mountains rise to heights of from eight to twelve thousand feet, and above them, sharply chiseled and glittering in their perpetual shining snow, rise the volcanic peaks of Popocatepetl to 17,800-odd feet and Ixtacihuatl, only a few hundred feet lower. How many great cities can give one such a panorama in the mistless splendor of the morning sun? We explored the city, its environs, its palaces and ruins, its pyramids and *vecindades* of adobe, sometimes in the company of the *Club de Exploradores,* founded and led by an overgrown "boy scout" over six feet tall and well into his forties, named McAllister, sometimes by ourselves, and sometimes in the company of Diego Rivera, seeing through his artist's eyes as he stopped to make a momentary sketchbook note, "the inexpressible beauty of that rich and severe, wretched and exuberant land."

THE AGE OF REVOLUTIONS

The early 1920s was an exciting time for us to live in Mexico. A series of uprisings, each with its *caudillo* or strong man, and each with some brief but sweeping "plan" for the remaking of Mexico, was moving toward its end in exhaustion, reaching out for a stability that had not existed since the overthrow of Porfirio Diaz in the "Revolution of 1910." The successive "plans," little more than attractive slogans, were so designed that such an impoverished country could never bring them to fulfillment. The land had grown poor in the uprisings, battles, and pillage, and Mexico City was filled with orphans, living as best they might, by begging and thieving, and sleeping all night on the sidewalks and in the doorways. The land was weary at last of the sport of perpetual strife and filled with hope that a new and better world was soon to be established on a firm foundation. Yet my wife and I were to witness close-up one more uprising, perhaps the most dramatic of all, with literally all the new-baked generals on one side save only one, and that one a military genius trying to hold out alone in the presidential palace. The latter had already proved himself to be the ablest military strategist in Mexico, perhaps the ablest in all its history, yet, all the same, at heart a civilian: President Alvaro Obregón. He had won the respect of the entire army, or all the armies, for they were almost as numerous as the generals, and the respect of the Mexican people, by defeating the redoubtable Pancho Villa in the Battle of Celaya, a legendary victory over a legendary folk-hero. In the battle, Obregón had lost his right arm (I have seen the crudity with which the arm was severed from the stump in battlefield surgery, photographed in *Alvaro Obregón: Su Vida y su Obra)*, but he went right on to direct and win the battle that was decisive in making Venustiano Carranza the president of Mexico.

President Carranza took power, not under a brief slogan plan, but under the Constitution of 1917, drawn up by all the leading intellectual dreamers of Mexico, and shining with brilliant promises to the folk, most of which could never be fulfilled. Yet, under his successor, Obregón, more of these promises were to be fulfilled than were those made in the Soviet Constitution of the same period, to which the Mexican Constitution has often been compared.

Carranza was a stiff-necked conservative. He reluctantly accepted the Constitution of 1917 as one more "plan," but showed no intention of fulfilling its promises. Moreover, as the next electoral period rolled around, he selected an obedient nonentity as his intended successor. His neglectful attitude towards the new Constitution, like his choice of a subservient nobody as his successor, gave his minister of war, General Obregón, his excuse for resigning, going back like a latter-day Cincinnatus to his ranch in Sonora to raise *garbanzos* (chick-peas), plus a band of Yaqui Indian supporters for yet another rebellion to overthrow Carranza in the name of the constitution of 1917. Of course, he won easily, and when we reached Mexico City, he was the country's president. As far as I could tell, the revolution was still promises, yet Obregón and his cabinet and state governors were making imaginative, if modest, steps towards the implementation of some of them.

Since Mexico was developing a one-party system, though without the totalitarian suppression and control of all other aspects of life in the country, Obregón played a large part in the selection of the state governors. Under the influence of the radical constitution of 1917, and the first vague exciting reports concerning the Russian Revolution of the same year, a number of governors cooperated with the Communist party in the matter of agrarian reform and the formation of *Ligas de Comunidades Agrarias.* General Múgica, governor of Michoacán, joined the Communist Party for a brief period. Felipe Carrillo Puerto, governor of Yucatán, regarded himself as a Socialist and earnestly attempted to establish cooperatives of the raisers of henequen, asking the advice of the American Socialist, Roberto Haberman, during the latter's stay in Yucatán. When Haberman often quoted Marx and Engels in answer, the Governor said to him: "¿Dónde están esos jóvenes? Dígales que vengan aquí y les daré puestos como consejeros." ("Where are those young fellows? Tell them to come here and I'll give them jobs as advisors.") This naive Socialist Governor continued firm in his faith until he was assassinated in the uprising of 1923.

The relation of certain members of Obregón's Cabinet to the Mexican Communist Party was more sophisticated and more complicated. Thus Adolfo de la Huerta, the minister of the Treasury, attempted to get the support of the Communists and the anarcho-syndicalists and their so-called "red unions" by subsidizing them from the state treasury, while Plutarco Elías Calles, de la Huerta's chief rival for the presidential succession and Obregón's secretario de gobernación (the word *gobernación* is untranslatable in this context since our cabinet has no such ministry), the principal determiner of governmental appointments, won the support of the so-called "yellow trade unions," the CROM or Confederación Obrera Regional Mexicana, and of the Partido Laborista, by handing out *chambas,* soft jobs with a title and salary but no duties, to the leaders of those two organizations. Similarly, Tejeda, governor of the state of Vera Cruz, supported the Communist Party and the League of Agrarian Communities of Vera Cruz with funds and ammunition when it became clear to him that they would support his faction and candidate for President in 1923. Many other established politicians gravitated briefly to the Communist Party under the impress of their own constitution and the legendary tales coming from Russia concerning the wonders of the Russian Revolution. But as the Obregón regime consolidated itself and the realities of the harshness of the new Russian regime became clear to them, the flirtation with the Communist Party ceased. When we got to Mexico, not professional politicians, but painters, formed the elite of the Mexican Communist Party. Of the *politicos,* only Senator Monzón from the state of Michoacán remained a faithful member of the Communist Party until the purges of the 1930's repelled him.

THE WORK OF JOSE VASCONCELOS

The most interesting member of Obregón's Cabinet was the Minister of Education, José Vasconcelos. There was nothing Indian about his comparatively light skin, or his black, bristly, crew-cut hair. He had been a leader of youth in 1910; in the 1920s he was still young, still filled with the hopes and illusions of youth, summed up in two mottoes, two dreams: *forjar patria*, to forge a fatherland; and *por mi raza habla el espíritu*, for my race, the spirit speaks. To forge a fatherland, he must make Mexico aware of its cultural heritage, particularly its heritage from Spain, and from the classics of the Greek and Latin lands. The race for which the spirit would speak was not the combined Latin and Anglo-Saxon peoples of the entire American continent, but only the Indio-Latin part which began below the Rio Grande and ran down to the Tierra del Fuego. He did not idealize the Indian heritage with its cult of human sacrifice, its fierce and fiery images, its adoration of death, its aspect of a "meek panther," its resignation in the face of corruption and cruelty, its senseless civil wars. His idea of race gave large room for the Spaniard and the Christian conversion. Never for a moment did he accept the black legend of the conquest. He thought of the Spanish-Christian conquest as civilizing, and, as conquests go, singularly humane. This view made it all the more remarkable that he tolerated and patronized the mural art of Diego Rivera, Alfaro Siqueiros, José Clemente Orozco, and their associates, practically all of whom were to paint on the walls he gave them an exaggerated version of the black legend. He would walk through the lower court of the Secretariat of Education where Diego painted, muttering *sandeces* (nonsense), yet he defended Rivera's frescoes against legislators grumbling at their cost and against activists of the gilded youth who sought to destroy them as "ugly." He thought of Cortez as one of the most humane conquerors in history. The latter's impetuous violence against the gods and customs of the Aztecs while the very fate of his tiny band of men was still at stake, he credited to the Christian idealism of the *Conquistador*, the work of a civilized European against barbarism, tribal backwardness, and the cruelty of the worship of a God who demanded human sacrifices and expected them to be carried out with splendor. He was proud of the fact that the Spaniards had not exterminated the conquered, nor reduced them to abject slavery, but mated with them, and, where "civilized" or of high estate, accepted them as equals.

Indeed, he once wrote that this process of civilization and integration had "terminated prematurely by the untimely separation of Mexico from Spain. If independence had come 50 years later, or even a hundred," Mexico might have separated peacefully, and fully grown, as Brazil had separated from Portugal, "achieving its independence . . . in the fullness of time and by agreement, without war," and without the warlike imprint, the internal division and conflict, the clashing *caudillismos* which had still not ended, and which left Mexico poor and brutalized, with the bulk of its

Indians still illiterate and still living on the margins of the land and its civilization. As the richest colony of Spain, he maintained, Mexico had had no need to import necessities, was able to nourish its entire people, and to give the world its standard of value in the Mexican peso, "accepted in Europe and the Far East as the best of coins." When Spain declined, the peso too declined as the standard of value, yielding first to the English pound sterling, then in turn to the America dollar. He attributed the Christianization, the civilization, and the Hispanization of the New World (always excluding the United States and Canada) to the Franciscans and the Jesuits.* "When we broke with Spain," he held, "we lost the pattern of the counter-reformation" before its work was completed. "Thereafter, our liberators from Spain were inspired by the English Masonic lodges," a force much inferior to the Franciscan-Jesuit civilizing influence. Cortez, he reminded those who would listen, had founded a municipal government with civil rights and the right of *amparo* (injunction) in the landing place at Vera Cruz, while the battle for Mexico City was still unsettled.

Later, France had added to Masonic culture the confusions of Voltaire and Rousseau, and then of Anglo-French positivism, along with the "myth of time," the superstition that time, by its mere elapse, automatically brings progress. Porfirio Diaz and his *científicos* had substituted positivism for philosophy, and to date, "our revolution has substituted no philosophy of its own." The only new thing Mexico has borrowed from Spain in its time of decay and degeneration has been *caudillismo* (bossism), with its accompanying miseries of "*motín, levantamiento, cuartelazo, pronunciamento* (riot, uprising, garrison coup, revolutionary manifesto). Mexico cannot organize itself until it wins a unity of creed and thought and spiritual understanding, for philosophy is the nerve center of a civilization."

I wish I could stop my exposition of Vasconcelos' interesting views at this point, but I must add that his "philosophical creed" was a compound of confusion. On the temple whose pillars were Greco-Roman and Catholic Christian culture, he set a capstone of vague oriental theosophy that would cause any oriental thinker to grimace to hear him expound it.

Be that as it may, this was the man to whom President Obregón unquestioningly entrusted the task of educating, or reeducating, Mexico, giving him free rein in his pronouncements and activities, and an ample budget for their purposes. For the first time in Mexican history, the sums granted for education were not inferior to the military budget. And because of, or despite his philosophy, Vasconcelos went to work with a will, and I can say without reservation that he was the greatest Minister of Education that Mexico has ever had.

* The Jesuits were the bearers of the culture of the Enlightenment to the Catholic countries of the Counter-Reformation. The bad name they were given, particularly in Northern Europe, Vasconcelos no doubt regarded as part of the "Black Legend."

The first act of the new minister was to take the major classics of Greco-Roman culture, have them translated into Spanish, then printed and bound in cheap, serviceable green cloth and sent to every school in the country to form a nucleus for its library. To tell the truth, while I lived in Mexico, no one seemed to be reading the works of Homer, Virgil, Lucretius, Cicero, Caesar, Ovid, and the like, thus made available, though many intellectuals carried off for free complete sets of them to make a shelf in their personal libraries.

Undaunted by the cool reception of his edition of the classics, Vasconcelos turned to the two huge tasks that awaited him: 1) to build schools and libraries, for the few libraries were in chaos and the schoolhouses inadequate in number and largely in ruins from neglect or from being used as redoubts in the civil wars; and 2) to restore and universalize literacy.

Before Vasconcelos finished his term in office in 1924, he had built a network of little schoolhouses all over the country, had found teachers for urban and rural schools, and founded a few people's schools for adults; had strengthened and enlarged the system of *escuelas preparatorias* (something between our senior high schools and our junior colleges), and had breathed new life into the moribund university system.

To help him in this work of construction and reconstruction, and to give refuge to intellectuals exiled from, or unwelcome, in those Latin American countries where there were military dictatorships, he offered refuge and a teaching post to men of learning, or of intellectual and political courage. From Santo Domingo he invited Pedro Henríquez Ureña, disciple of the great Spanish literary scholar, Ramón Menéndez Pidal, and son of a former president of Santo Domingo. Henríquez Ureña became the greatest of our teachers when Ella and I registered for an M.A. in Hispanic literature and culture at the Graduate School of the University of Mexico. From Chile, the Secretary of Education imported the poet, Gabriela Mistral, a poet a bit too sentimental for my taste, but a Nobel Laureate, and a warm human being. She helped Vasconcelos in his campaign for the development of general literacy, arousing many idealistic young men and women to go to the villages on the secretary's "Missionary Crusade for Universal Literacy," among adults as well as among children. The literacy of the populace had been rather limited under the Diaz regime, and even more so under his predecessors. Then the uprisings had claimed schoolhouses, teachers, and their pupils, and the degree of literacy, despite the simplicity of a highly phonetic language, had fallen below one-fifth of the population, so that more than 80 percent did not know how to read. By a forced march system Vasconcelos, aided by such devoted persons as Gabriela Mistral and those she recruited, made long strides towards the general education and reeducation of the Mexican people.

The life of Mexico became much richer and more cosmopolitan as Dr. Vasconcelos opened the gates to refugees from every Latin American land where a tyrranical government was in power. From Venezuela came Carlos León, leader of the Opposition; from Cuba, the handsome and personable

Julio Antonio Mella, who eventually died in Mexico as the target of *pistoleras* sent by the Cuban President to get him; from Peru came Victor Raúl Haya de la Torre, founder of the APRA, the American Popular Revolutionary Alliance which had its center in Lima, or wherever Haya de la Torre was at any given moment, but which also possessed a lesser following in Colombia and several other Latin-American countries. Haya led first the student movement and then an indigenous revolt of Peru's poverty-stricken millions, most of them speaking not Spanish, but Quechua. When he escaped from Peru and received refuge in Mexico, he was already writing a book critical of Marxism. Nevertheless, he accepted the opportunity to go with me to Russia to visit as a fraternal delegate (with a voice but no vote) the Fifth Congress of the Communist International. Instead of listening to his "voice," the members of the Latin-American delegation tried to tell him what was what and how he was to act in Peru; he returned to Mexico, quite properly more anti-Communist than before. My wife and I have kept in touch with him for a number of decades, and listened all night on many an occasion to his amazing gifts as a conversationalist—Latin-American intellectuals seem much more gifted, fluent and eloquent than our own intelligentsia. At least three times he won an undoubted majority of the vote for the presidency of his native land, but the military dictators always had the guns, were quicker on the draw, and more decisive in action. Once he was counted out because the ballots cast in his favor were "in the wrong color of ink." Once, after listening to him all night, in our Brooklyn Heights apartment, discoursing on "Historical Space and Time," my wife and I decided: "Haya will never be president of Peru—he loves to talk too much to act with the requisite speed and energy, and, at the right moment, to enforce his victory at the polls." *

Yet it must be said that he would have given Peru a much better government and social order, than either of those "liberals" whom his support, and that of his party, helped bring to power; or of the harsh, reactionary regimes that have alternated with them. And Latin America, too, would have had a more wholesome model and a much better outlook on its problems and their solutions if he had become the president of his country. But it is hard to say whether after his death his views and example will leave any trace behind, beyond a memory in his own country.

THE INFLUENCE OF MEXICO UPON TWO ENGLISH TEACHERS

My wife and I took a solemn pledge to one another, that we would steer clear of the American colony, stop reading *The New York Times*, and content ourselves with the outrageously bad Mexican dailies for news (at least they were in the Spanish tongue and their journalese and bu-

* Haya died in the summer of 1979.

reaucratese were but degenerate examples of the language and culture we were bent on assimilating). We would register for Masters' Degrees in Spanish literature when the next semester began, then sit in the front row, keep our eyes glued on the lips of the lecturers, and perhaps understand enough by the year's end to pass the examinations. We had Julio Jiménez Rueda for the Mexican Literature of the Colonial Period, Fernando Gamboa for Mexican Literature of the Nineteenth Century, and Pedro Henríquez Ureña for the Literature of Spain and for Spanish Philology. The first two were earnest and competent lecturers; Henríquez Ureña was a great teacher, as were all the disciples of Ramón Menéndez Pidal under whom we studied, whether in the United States or in Mexico (we continued our studies of Spanish literature, history and culture at Columbia University after we got back to the United States, and had the good fortune of apprenticing ourselves to Federico de Onís). Learning Spanish proved easy—even the signboards talked to us in Spanish. Mexican, Latin-American, and Spanish literature and history proved exciting, and first Henríquez Ureña and later Federico de Onís became our personal friends and sources of the brilliant conversation that seems to characterize all Spanish intellectuals. We not only passed our courses by dint of faithful reading and watching our teachers' lips, but Federico Gamboa published my term paper on *La novela picaresca* in the university journal. And Henríquez Ureña honored me by putting under our joint names my Master's thesis on *El romance tradicional en Méjico* in the *Homenaje ofrecido a Menéndez Pidal con motivo de cumplirse los veinticinco años de su actividad docente en la Universidad de Madrid* ("The Traditional Ballad of Spain as It Lives in Mexican Oral Tradition" *). It was quite proper for my teacher to put his name in as coauthor, for he directed my work on my thesis, and even helped me to gather a few of the ballads or fragments by having his sister and his kitchen help sing those fragments that they knew. And of course it was a great honor to me as a student who only a year or two earlier knew no Spanish whatsoever, to have my thesis published in the second of three fat volumes in honor of the great master of all the teachers of literature of my day, under the names of Henríquez Ureña, Pedro, and Wolfe, Bertram D. (Madrid, 1925). When I applied to Federico de Onís for the admission of myself and my wife into the graduate studies in Spanish Literature directed by him, he said, "I know you. Yours is the only Anglo-Saxon name in our tribute to Menéndez Pidal." That was all the entrance exam to Altos Estudios that either of us had. And as for my wife, she spent the next thirty years or so of her life after our return to New York as probably the best and the best-loved teacher of Spanish language and literature in Thomas Jefferson, and then in Bay Ridge High School.

* Published in the three-volume *Homage Offered Menéndez Pidal on His Completing Twenty-Five Years of His Activities as a Teacher in the University of Madrid.*

LAND OF FIESTAS

To one born and brought up in the United States, to live in Mexico is like doubling one's personality. The land of my birth is predominantly white, Anglo-Saxon, Protestant, and has a highly developed pecuniary, mercantile, and industrial civilization. Large areas of Mexico were still living with stone-age utensils, producing corn and beans principally for self-sustenance, engaged in sporadic local trade and barter, partly prepecuniary, producing clothing and utensils by hand labor, endowed with an instinctive plastic sense that makes the cheapest clay vessels things of beauty. Catholic and pagan Indian in its culture, Mexico secreted idols behind its altars. The attitude towards life and death is so different from ours that we felt we were truly in another world, much more remote from ours than the civilization of any of the countries of Western Europe.

The United States, except for its coastal ranges, is a vast elevated plain and plateau. Mexico, except for its rich, semitropical plain, is a land of mighty mountains and volcanoes that dwarf even Colorado, with its fifty-five peaks over 12,000 feet above the sea. Charcoal burners have burned off Mexico's sparse forests; during the short rainy season the rains simply run off in torrents into the sea; during the dry season its short rivers dwindle into creeks and its creeks into parched ravines. How could so beautiful and terrible a landscape feed its swiftly growing population, especially when the civil wars and revolutions had tapered off and modern sanitation had begun to lower the death rate? How could life be taken too seriously when it was so short and death so ready at hand? How could plans be carried out and promises fulfilled when they were so easy to make and so hard to implement?

On another note—one of the most vivid and distinctive features of Mexico's slowly disappearing folk life is the fiesta. When we got to Mexico it was the center of communal life, even in the big cities. In the smaller towns and villages it is still a truly collective expression. Indeed, though we have forgotten it, the very word *convivial* comes from the Latin *convivere,* to live together, implying the communal fiesta. A good part of each calendar year was made up of fiestas, some pagan Indian in origin, some involving remembered historical events, French and Mexican uniforms and mock battles, and the high fiestas like Christmas and Twelfth Night and Easter with its gay Saturday of Glory, when life-size clay figures lined with fireworks are suspended from wires over the streets of the city (sometimes the figures are recognizable *políticos* who have earned popular dislike), and a light touched to the little rockets causes the figures to dance and then go up in smoke. Greatest fiesta of all is the day—or rather the week—celebrating our Halloween and All Saints' Day, the week being collectively known in Mexico as the Day of the Dead. In these celebrations entire towns and villages participate, every man, woman, and child taking an active part, or making up the convivial multitude. The costs of the fiestas are met collectively. The principal participants are sometimes chosen by democratic election, sometimes by hereditary tradition. The fiesta belongs not to the *políticos* or the *caudillo*, but to the community.

No two villages have identical fiestas; sometimes they may even be held on different dates and dedicated to different patron saints or local heroes. Only this do they have in common—that the whole village is atingle for weeks before its fiesta, and that corporate conviviality and folk joyousness reach their culminating point in the two or three days or the whole week of celebration. Of course, all of them celebrate Christmas, Easter, and the Day of the Dead. All the arts and collective memories of the race contribute: music and dance and song and drama and humor and imagination. In the accompanying *puestos*, or fair booths, which sell appropriate wares often a whole year in the making, all the local and regional handicrafts offer their handmade, hand painted, or homebaked and hand-colored products.

The fiesta with its true remembering and feasting and celebrating together has disappeared from modern industrialized countries, leaving scarcely a trace. The *coup de grace* was delivered in our own land when we decided by legislative fiat and popular demand that the few great occasions in our common life which we had thought worthy of remembering were switched to the Monday nearest the actual anniversary. Then in place of drawing closer to each other and remembering and celebrating together, we may each jump into his own auto or mount his motorcycle and see how far we can drive away from home and from each other. The long weekend remains communal only in the sense that we can all say "Gee whiz" together when we hear the boxscore over the radio of the number of fatalities, which extra speed, extra distance, extra weariness, and extra drunkenness are responsible for in the triune "Holy Day" thus created. It was Mexico that made me realize that something valuable and humane has gone out of our lives along with the fiestas we have lost.

In the Mexican year there seemed to be more holidays than workdays, so many more things to remember than the mere making of a living. However, the coming of big industries to the urban centers has led employers and government to join hands to diminish the number of fiestas. The most notable result so far has been the creating of a special weekly fiesta occurring not in its season but regularly every Monday. It is popularly known as *San Lunes*, Holy Monday, the day which the industrial workingman seems to need for sobering up after the grind of regular daily fiesta-less labor followed by a Saturday pay envelope spent on an all-day Sunday convivial celebration in a *cantina*.

THE COLOR IN MEXICAN LIFE

These *cantinas* and *pulquerías*, for their part, add their own gay color to Mexican life. Each has its painted front with a background of deep blue or pastel colors on which a folk artist has painted an appropriate mural. Many of these murals are *cursi* or crude, but a number are lighted by imagination, and a few are real works of art. I found one pulquería named *La Judía,* the Jewess, which the proprietor explained to me as expressive of the boast that his pulque had never been "baptized," the unwatered Jewess figuring on the façade of his shop as a sign of the purity of his pulque. Another was called *Hombres Sabios sin Estudio;* its pulque had made them "Wise Without Study." Yet another bore the name, *Memorias del Porvenir,* Memories of the Future, a name I never fully comprehended until I learned that in the Soviet Union the future is known, and the present is known; only the past is uncertain and subject to continual change. In Mexico, all these colorful cantina fronts added to the brightness of their town walls. And some of them were painted by no less an artist than José Clemente Orozco, who began his career not by studying in Paris or Rome or Florence, but by painting murals on the walls of pulquerías.

Not only fiestas and walls of shops added their color to Mexican life. To us it seemed that almost everything this folk created had its touch of beauty. In a flea-plagued market place, a vendor whose total capital consists of a *sarape* spread out on the ground and a few peanuts and radishes and beets and spinach to sell, instinctively groups his peanuts into little pyramidal mounds so placed as to create a pleasing design, and uses the color of the radishes and spinach to make the whole display of his wares into a pattern attractive in form and color. Should you disturb his pattern by buying a little pile or two of peanuts or beets, he will promptly rearrange what is left into a fresh, pleasing pattern, almost as unconsciously as a kaleidoscope might rearrange its patterns of colored glass.

Once, when we were hiking near Oaxaca, we came upon a hillock, to the top of which a weaver had attached the warp of his loom; on the bottom of the hill he was weaving brightly colored woolen threads of all the brightest, seemingly incompatible colors into patterns in which their gaiety somehow did not clash. Gradually he climbed the hill, weaving and weaving as he climbed, until he had produced a number of attractive sarapes. In Taxco my wife and I watched silversmiths and tinsmiths beating and twisting and cutting their bright metals into lovely jewels and house furnishings. In other villages we have seen men and women spinning clay on their potters' wheels, then painting and baking them into lovely shapes, lovingly colored. From Puebla we got dishes baked or vitrified in blue and white and harmonizing colors a little cruder, but in beauty able to hold their own alongside of Meissen ware from Germany, or Talavera ware from Spain. We furnished our home with chairs from Toluca, woven of reeds, seats and backs made of cowhide, framed and supported by palm or bamboo or wood, and curved to fit the human back much better than chairs machine made in Michigan. I took pictures in churches where a lifelike monk knelt in prayer and a Jesus fell under the burden of a heavier cross, bloodier, with a bloodier crown of thorns, suffering more than all the images of Jesus Christ to be found in any other country in which we have been. The Mexicans seem to revel in their tortured Christs. The baroque of the Mexican churches is richer and more marvellous than the baroque of the churches of Austria or Spain. There is a village called San Pedro de Tlaquepaque where every artisan seems to be able to sculpt and color a trotting, curvetting horse; we have many of these horses, all good to look upon, yet among all these skilled craftsmen there is one supreme artist who added to his lightfooted, slender-limbed, flower-flanked steed an extra touch of poetry—for it stands among all our other brightly-colored gracefully curvetting steeds yet alone among them seems to be Pegasus ready to leap from the mantlepiece into the air.

THE MEXICAN MURAL RENAISSANCE

With such a sense of color, such feeling for plastic form, such fantasy inherent in the Mexican people, all that was needed was a little extra impulse—a dash of social excitement arising from dreams concerning the succession of Mexican Revolutions from 1910 to the 1920's, some buildings with fresh clean wall spaces to cover, a little research into the pigments and materials of fresco, and a handful of sophisticated artists knowledgeable in the history of art, yet no less sensitive to their Mexican folk heritage—and the walls and ceilings of Mexico's new buildings would burst into that great explosion of painting known as the Mexican Mural Renaissance.

When we got to Mexico, Diego Rivera was painting a huge encaustic mural on the front wall of the auditorium of the National Preparatory School, a sturdy baroque colonial structure completed in 1749, with close to a thousand square feet of wall. He was covering the arched wall with huge, superhuman allegorical figures over twelve feet high, making experiments with blowpipe and spatula in fusing the colors he wanted, with the melted wax used in encaustic painting. The mural is a blaze of color: deep greens, brick reds, ochers, violets, shining gold spilling over from a golden center, where a semicircle of deep blue sky studded with golden stars stands out against a shining background of the same bright gold, assimilating the pipe organ into the decorative scheme. I know of no painter in Mexico or elsewhere with the same strong sense of color as Diego Rivera.

On the stairways of the same building, Jean Charlot, Fernando Leal, and Ramon Alva de la Canal were experimenting with the revival of the lost art of true fresco, Charlot's fresco dealing with a scene from the Conquest of Mexico, Alva's with the Landing of the Spaniards, and Leal's with a Mexican Fiesta. Siqueiros was talking good painting but painting little, hesitantly, and indecisively. He was working endlessly on an angel surrounded by seashells. Orozco was moving away from his pulquería walls, his portrayals of prostitutes, and other figures from the underworld, and was now painting in the patio of the Preparatoria a fresco of Christ chopping down his own cross, and a Trinity of a bruised and handless worker and an anguished peasant kneeling beside a Mexican Revolutionary, gun in hand, who is blinded by the folds of the Red Banner under which he marches.

Even before they had finished what they were doing, Vasconcelos was offering them fresh walls to cover in the newly constructed Secretariat of Education, where there were stairway walls and three tiers of double patio walls to cover with paint. Each of the artists, and a half dozen more, were experimenting with techniques, seeking to find themselves as mural painters and as glorifiers or satirizers of the Mexican Revolution. Thus our entrance into this new world was happily timed to coincide with the Mexican Mural Renaissance.

The revolution could not give much to lowly Mexicans, for the land was too poor, and it was easier for "the men of the revolution" to enrich themselves than to enrich the people. In this there was not too much irony for a people never far from hunger, who have always used part of their meager substance for a bright succession of fiestas, eaten their humble fare from dishes shaped and colored in beauty, clothed their poverty in bright-colored raiment, carried their skimpy rations from the market in gay bags and baskets. In any case, Obregón and Vasconcelos were agreed that the Revolution could give the people literacy, and as the Minister of Education built schools and schools and gave the artists walls and walls, at least the walls in *buon fresco* could last, could glorify the folk, attract tourists and art lovers, and celebrate the Revolution.

Alfaro Siqueiros, who had not yet struck his stride as a painter, wrote a flaming manifesto for the Union of Painters, Sculptors and Allied Trades, which even those painters with the most unlikely styles or views hastened to join. Here is the attitude of Vasconcelos towards the *Sindicato*, as recorded in his memoirs:

> Siqueiros communicated to me the formation of the union. Three assistants accompanied him . . . dressed in overalls. For two years I had been patient with Siqueiros who . . . never seemed to finish some mysterious snails which he was painting on the stairway of the Preparatoria. Meanwhile the newspapers were overwhelming me with accusations that I was maintaining drones. I endured all the criticism as long as I could count on the loyalty of those I was protecting . . . and from them I demanded hard work. . . . On one occasion I had defined my esthetics: "Surface and speed is what I demand . . . I desire that they paint well and quickly because the day I go, the artists will not paint, or, will paint propaganda. . . .
>
> To Rivera, to Orozco, to Montenegro, it never occurred to create unions; it has always seemed to me that the intellectual who has recourse to such methods does so because he is intellectually weak. Art is individual and only the mediocre support themselves in gregariousness to defend . . . the worker, who can be easily replaced, never the unsubstitutable work of the artist. Therefore, when they presented themselves, I answered: "Very well. I will not deal with your union nor with

you. The money which has been going to your murals we will employ on primary school teachers. . . ."

They withdrew in confusion. But they counted on my friendship and did not have anything to be sorry for. On leaving they begged one of my secretaries: "Tell the Licenciado not to fire us; we will continue working as before."

. . . .It is proper to state at this point that each of the artists earned an almost wretched wage with employment as clerks, because I dared not enter into the budget an appropriation for painters, for they would have defeated me in the Chamber. Public opinion had not yet become accustomed to consider the encouragement of art as an obligation of the state.

The Sindicato did not long withstand this humiliating blow. Siqueiros, Rivera, Guerrero, and a number of other painters turned their excess energy into a weekly newspaper called *El Machete* for which they did free drawings and woodcuts, and joined the Communist Party, making their journal its official organ. As my wife and I joined the Communist Party there at about the same time, I got to know them all. The one with whom I had closest relationship was Diego Rivera, so accessible as he painted wall after wall in the Secretariat of Education, and who was soon elected, like me, to the Central Committee of the party.

Family portrait: Bertram D. Wolfe on his mother's lap, his father standing, his sister Lilian on the left, his brother Paul on the right.

Bertram D. Wolfe, age 3

At City College

Alias Arthur E. Albright in San Francisco

Bertram D. Wolfe as an unable seaman on the *SS Polonia* on his first trip to Moscow

Bertram D. Wolfe at the Fifth Congress.

Two members of the Italian delegation and Acevedo (rt.) on the way to the Fifth Congress of the Comintern in Moscow, 1924

A drawing made of Bertram D. Wolfe at the Fifth Congress and sold as a post card

Bertram D. Wolfe watching Diego Rivera paint the murals in the New Workers School in New York.

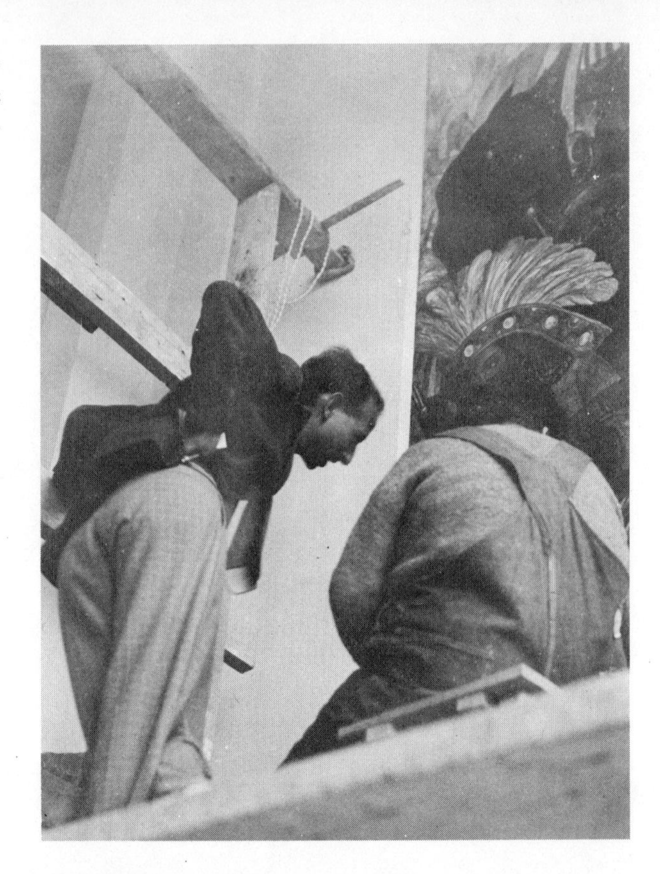

Freda Kahlo and Diego Rivera in their home in Mexico

Bertram D. Wolfe's favorite photograph of his wife Ella

Bertram D. Wolfe at an anti-war meeting, March 6, 1938. Senator Robert M. La Follette, Jr. is on his left.

At the State Department, 1954

At the Hoover Institution, 1975

20

SOME MYSTERIES OF MEXICAN POLITICS

Our self-denying ordinance, to speak to each other only in Spanish, to avoid the American colony, to read only Mexican papers and books, to count, to think, even to argue in Spanish, advanced our knowledge of the new language rapidly. Soon after I joined the Mexican Communist Party, I was able to write for *El Machete,* become an active editor of the paper, and open a course in history in the Spanish tongue. To give me the requisite vocabulary in Marxian economics, I purchased an abbreviated Spanish edition of *Das Kapital,* published in Barcelona. The very first sentence shocked me into speechlessness.

The English reads: "The wealth of those societies in which the capitalist mode of production prevails presents itself as an immense accumulation of *commodities.*" The Barcelona *traductor* or *traidor* made this read: ". . . presents itself as an immense accumulation of *comodididadas* (comforts)." I tramped through old bookshops until I found a translation of *Das Kapital* by Juan B. Justo which began ". . . . una imensa accumulación de *mercancías,*" and breathed easier again.

My course was a mixture of history, sociology, economics, and political thought, called "The Class Struggle through the Ages." The lessons were given by invitation in the headquarters of the Union of Railway Carpenters. Gradually, railway workers of other crafts began to attend, and I came to be considered the educational director of the railwaymen's unions. When in 1925 sixteen of the seventeen railway crafts set up a strike committee, they insisted that I should serve on it in an advisory capacity. Only the Locomotive Engineers, the seventeenth craft, with better wages and considering themselves more aristocratic than the others, paid no attention to the course, nor did they join the strike committee.

Many who were not railway men also attended my class. One whom I particularly remember was a cultured young newspaperman of the Spanish colony daily, *La Prensa,* named Angel del Río. A few years later, when my wife and I registered at the Graduate School of Spanish Literature of Columbia University, Angel del Río was there as our teacher of eighteenth-century Spanish Literature. Thus pupil became teacher, and teacher became pupil. He and his wife Amelia, who taught Spanish Literature at Barnard, became our intimate friends, as did Federico and Harriet de Onís.

THE OBREGON PATTERN

Obregón came to power in the name of the "revindicating revolution," the slogan of his electoral campaign to succeed Carranza. From his peaceful retreat in Sonora he began his campaign against the handpicked successor who would have been Carranza's obedient tool. His two chief lieutenants were also men of Sonora, Plutarco Elías Calles and Adolfo de la Huerta. We shall hear more of these two. Obregón's slogans were moderate. Having already defeated both Villa and Zapata on the field of battle, and having gathered around himself all those discontented with Carranza's stiff-necked conservatism, he needed no radical program. In his "Plan de Agua Prieta" (Agua Prieta is also in Sonora, in the far North near the frontier with the United States) he promised protection for all citizens and foreigners; development of industry and commerce; the resignation of Carranza in favor of de la Huerta as provisional president; elections under the supervision of the provisional government; effective suffrage and no reelection; and the revindicating revolution. As a wise old prophet, Francisco Bulnes, wrote: "National and foreign opinion looks to the Obregón coup as [an end] to the present anarchistic situation in Mexico." And Thomas Lamont of the House of Morgan wrote after a visit with President Obregón, "The attitude of the present Mexican government is satisfactory to American interests." Obregón would have to blow both hot and cold to satisfy Bulnes and Lamont on the one hand, and the workers and peasants and radical dreamers who had written Articles 27 and 123 of the Constitution of 1917 on the other. Article 27 dealt with the mineral wealth of Mexico which had been developed by foreign concessionaires under Diaz. Article 123 dealt with the rights of labor. The touchy words in Article 27 read: "All contracts and concessions made by former governments from and after the year 1876 . . . are declared subject to revision. . . ." What the oil men wanted was the "non-retroactivity" of Article 27 so that concessions made prior to the 1917 Constitution should not be subject to "revision." As to Article 123 and Obregón's handling of the labor movement, we shall consider this later at some length, for it is the key to how Obregón and his successors got along with the labor movement.

Alvaro Obregón was the most civilian of military men and militarily the most able of civilians. A military genius, as he had proved to be on the field of battle and was to prove again before I left Mexico; he was a born leader of men, and under Mexican conditions, a statesman of the first rank. He was to strive for the welfare of his people, encourage his Minister of Education to promote the people's education, encourage his Secretary of Agriculture to begin the slow and difficult work of agrarian reorganization in a country in which the landowners were strong and there was not enough arable land to satisfy the needs of the landless. In the course of his term he was to work out a pattern for stability, turn as many generals as possible into civilians with landed estates or governorships, and become master of the contradictory devices for keeping afloat on the stormy sea of Mexican political life. His successors to the present day have only to follow the pattern he had laid out, some botching it, others carrying it out faithfully. It is this system of statecraft that has ruled Mexico with minor modifications, and often with less straightforward honesty, since he was felled by an assassin's bullet when, after a discreet term of retirement, he made the mistake of trying for reelection. After all, was it not he who had coined the slogan: "SUFRAGIO EFECTIVO, NO REELECCIÓN," which in capital letters ended every official letter sent out by state officials during his first term in office? In a land where Porfirio Diaz had ruled from 1876 to 1910, and nearly everyone wore a pistol, it was dangerous to ignore it. But I am running far ahead of my story.

For internal support, every candidate for the presidency since 1910 has had to choose between the backing of the workers and peasants and that of the landowners and the Catholic clergy. The peasants are the most numerous class, though large sections of them follow the leadership of the landowners and the church. The workers were so immature and lacking in independent organization and feeling that they had not formed an important independent force and could be kept in leash by concession and purchase. Thus the two camps are nearly equal in balance and strength, and men pass over readily from one camp to the other. What the landowners and nascent industrial groups lack in numbers they make up with their economic power, easily buying generals and politicians and able at times to put large numbers of armed men into the field. The military-bureaucratic apparatus is relatively independent of both camps. From its control of the armed forces and political machinery it is capable of creating, out of its own ranks ("men of the revolution," they call themselves) new industrialists, with government subsidies and contracts and legal monopolies, and new landowners. Thus the opposing camps are constantly in unstable equilibrium and easily upset by some shift of internal support or of foreign pressure.

The First World War prepared the basis for a more stable regime by ending the counter-pulls of British and American interests. There was a definite growth in the influence of the United States and a definite recession in the power and active intervention of England. Moreover, the people of Mexico were weary of internal warfare. Germany had foolishly tried to line up Carranza against the United States, by setting up radio stations and by offering Mexico an "equal alliance"(!) in the inept Zimmermann note.

A master in understanding this complex of forces, Obregón struck out boldly on the basis of what seemed to him the strongest combination: the worker-peasant bloc as the internal support, American capital as the external support of his regime. At least, so the situation seemed to me after I had had an opportunity to study the land, its people, and its problems. A bareback rider with one foot on each of two high-spirited horses would have had an easy time in comparison, for Obregón's two high-spirited steeds were not trained to run together. He would have to make solid concessions to American capital without alienating the nationalist-minded, anti-Yankee intellectuals, and make important concessions to the masses without alienating suspicious American capital. He would have to blow hot and cold, if not in a single breath, then at least in quick succession. Only a man of audacious vision would have attempted it; only a major statesman would have gotten away with it.

Therein lies the explanation of the constant tacking and veering of the Mexican ship of state, therein the unstated background to reconcile the apparently contradictory policies that have left observers so bewildered and helpless in making up their minds as to the nature of the Mexican regime. Thus Echeverría in the seventies may send his wife with a huge performing arts troup to Cuba and urge the O.A.S. to recognize Castro, at the very moment when he is bravely resisting kidnappers and bank robbers who invoke radical phrases in his own country, even as in the twenties the Calles-Obregón regime deported simultaneously the papal delegate and a foreign-born leader of the Mexican Communist Party as "pernicious foreigners."

The Mexican government's attitude towards the labor movement is characteristically bewildering, now to the ordinary workingman and again to the foreign investor or owner of mineral lands in Mexico. Carranza, when he was seeking popular support, used as his labor agent Gerardo Murillo, better known under his pseudonym, *Dr. Atl,* as painter of landscapes, mountains, and volcanoes. The little bearded painter appeared suddenly as a labor leader in 1915, armed with vast quantities of the paper pesos rolling off of Carranza's printing presses. Thereby Dr. Atl acquired enough influence to organize anarcho-syndicalist "red battalions" for Carranza. Undoubtedly the idea was that of the then president's war minister, General Obregón, who endowed the new labor movement with palatial headquarters in the beautiful *Casa de Azulejos* (House of Tiles), formerly the Jockey Club, and today occupied by Sanborn's Restaurant and Drug Store. But when Carranza acquired absolute power, he prohibited and broke strikes and dispossessed the "red battalions" from their elegant headquarters. Dr. Atl went back to his not-too-striking landscape painting and was lost to politics until in the late thirties he reappeared as a not very successful propagandist for Germany.

However, Obregón was already working on the development of another, more serious and less "artistic" labor movement. His agent and chieftain in the new movement was Luís N. Morones, gross, fleshy, thick-lipped, heavy jowled, soft, and redolent of perfume, looking more like a journalistic cartoon of a capitalist than a labor leader. But inside this sybaritic exterior was a man ruthless, power-hungry, and hard. Obregón had first met him when he occupied Mexico City in 1915 and found Morones leading an electrical strike against a British-owned telegraph and telephone company. Obregón settled the strike by seizing the properties and "giving them" to the strikers under the management of the company foreman, Morones. Like many of the Mexican "seizures" of plants and properties, the arrangement was only temporary. But Morones knew power when he saw it, and became the labor link with the fortunes of General Obregón.

In 1918, the *Obregonista* Governor of Coahuila, Espinosa, issued a call to labor unions and workers' groups to unite in a single nationwide labor organization so that "the worker himself can study and determine the points on which his well-being can be based . . . and provide a solution of his needs. . . ." The costs of transportation, lodging, wages lost, and meeting halls, was to be paid by the State of Coahuila. Of course, Morones was there to give leadership to the new-born Confederación Regional Obrera Mexicana, or *CROM*. Morones became their head, as he did of the simultaneously formed *Partido Laborista Mexicana.* The unions that accepted this leadership found that the government was ready to provide palatial buildings for meetings and headquarters, print their journals on government printing presses, take care of the salaries of their leaders by soft jobs, in which they had only to sign in for work, then go to their union headquarters or attend to union affairs. Both the *CROM* and the Labor Party supported Obregón's candidacy for president in 1920. Morones was made Director of the Government Munitions Factory, and his comrade-in-arms, General Gasca, was made Governor of the Federal District, with a number of patronage posts to hand out to labor leaders. To get rid of obstreperous labor opponents or too-public critics, Morones formed a less known, secret band, officially named the *Grupo Acción,* and more popularly referred to as *La Palanca* (the crowbar). In Mexico if one is active in political life, he must expect to shoot and be shot at.

After Scott Nearing visited Mexico, he told a New York audience, one of whose members reported the fact to me, "The only man I saw in Mexico who didn't wear a pistol was Bert Wolfe." He was right, but if I didn't wear a pistol, it was to feel safer, for any Mexican would be faster on the draw than I, and I was safer going about unarmed. Morones himself was shot at more than once, and on occasion wounded. The *Palanca* acted as his bodyguard and the executor of his will.

One day when my friend Carleton Beals was interviewing him, Carleton heard Morones say to the chief of his *Palanca,* "Senator Field Jurado is going to attack me in the Senate tomorrow. He must not leave the Senate alive." Carleton shortened his interview and went to warn Senator Field Jurado, "Do not go to the Senate tomorrow or you will be shot."

"But I must," said the Senator. "It would be unmanly not to go. And I have a speech to deliver." He went to the Senate, delivered his speech, and as he walked down the steps to his car, was shot in the heart.

THE DE LA HUERTA REBELLION

The Obregón regime had three men from the State of Sonora, the President himself, his Secretary of *Gobernación*, Plutarco Elías Calles, and his Secretary of the Treasury, Adolfo de la Huerta. Since the slogan with which all official letters ended during his regime was: "SUFRAGIO EFECTIVO, NO REELECCION," he could not run for reelection, at least until he had let one term elapse. He would continue to be the *caudillo*, the strong man, but he had to choose from between his two Sonoran lieutenants the man who would be his successor. That was not exactly "sufragio efectivo," but that was the way things were run, and are still run, in Mexico—the president picks his successor, who is then nominated and elected by the official party, unless a rival candidate who has been counted out chooses to appeal from ballots to bullets. There is no use appealing to congress that the ballot boxes have been stuffed or the count falsified, for the ultra-democratic process while I was there consisted in letting the majority who gathered around each ballot box at daybreak on election day elect the people who would count the ballots. Invariably the defeated candidates for inspectors, with their partisans, would then withdraw, set up their own district ballot box, and thus, two sets of returns would go to the Chamber of Deputies. Since the Chamber had an overwhelming majority of the official party, the official party's candidate would invariably turn out to have been elected. Then the opposing candidate would calculate his chances in a possible uprising. It was a question of an uprising before or after election day, or silent and grumbling acceptance of a *fait accompli*, that settled the electoral process.

In 1923 General Obregón made it clear that his candidate for the succession was General Calles. But de la Huerta was Secretario de Hacienda, in charge of the National Treasury. And Obregón had ruled so well that there was a substantial surplus in its coffers. De la Huerta charged fraud, retired from the capital with the treasury and used it to buy generals, governors, leaders of social and political organizations. The generals of the Army, one after another, succumbed to his advances until he had bought all of them except one, the general in charge of the army in the capital under Obregón's watchful eye. Then, since de la Huerta could not bribe the "yellow" unions led by Morones, he turned to the "red" unions of the C.G.T. (Confederación General de Trabajadores, or General Federation of Workers) and also offered a huge sum to Manuel Ramírez, Secretary of the Communist Party, to subsidize his party. Ramírez, seeing all the military and all the funds on what must be the winning side, and with "red" support also on the more radical side, proposed that we should give our support to what looked like the winners. I led the opposition to the acceptance of the subsidy and urged that Obregón and Calles, and the larger of the two trade union bodies and the Laborista Party, represented the lesser evil. "I have been fighting," I said, "to make the unions and labor organizations independent of government subsidy. Since Obregón has lost the generals, we can get him to arm the workers and peasants, and in states like Michoacán and Vera Cruz, the Comunidades Agrarias are under our leadership. This is our chance to make the Communist Party independent of all subsidies and a power in its own right." My viewpoint carried in the Central Committee; we removed Ramírez and substituted Rafael Carrillo, leader of the youth movement, as the new Secretary of the Party.

All the other generals having "turned," that is, gone over to the side of the rebellion, President Obregón was left alone in the capital with one general and one army. Obregón gave his last general whatever money he could scrape together, and bade him go with his army over the mountains to smash the rebel front near Guadalajara. But as soon as he was safely over the mountains surrounding the capital, he too "turned," declaring himself for de la Huerta. Obregón had been staying in a hospital, playing sick while he waited to see whom he could count on. Now he could count only on himself, the last military man left to him. The characteristically Mexican story that was told everywhere was that when he returned to the Presidential Palace and went to bed, his wife murmured, "Alvaro, I'm going to turn." To which he replied in astonishment, "You too, Martha?" General Obregón, a rough master of his native tongue, coined the aphorism, "No hay general quien resiste un cañonazo de cien mil pesos (There is no general who can withstand a bombardment of 100,000 pesos)."

That same night, to my astonishment, Roberto Haberman appeared at my home and said: "All is lost. The last general turned just as soon as he got over the mountains. In a day or two, de la Huerta will be in the capital at the head of his forces. The last train that will get to Texas from here will leave at midnight tonight, with General Calles on board. Obregón refuses to leave, but all the rest of the supporters of General Calles will be on board the special train. The general has authorized me to invite you and your wife, since he is sure that you will be on the list that de la Huerta has proscribed for execution."

"Why should I be on his list?"

"De la Huerta knows, just as General Calles does, that you prevented the Communist Party and the Comunidades Agrarias which it leads from supporting the rebellion."

I reflected for a moment. "So there must be one or more government agents in high place in our party." Then I said, "Thank you, Roberto, and thank General Calles on my behalf. I have written about revolution, yet I have never seen a revolution close up. I shall stay to watch this one."

Next morning, Obregón commandeered all buses and taxis in the capital city. Then he enlisted the entire police force, took all the weapons to be found in *Fabriles*, the Government munitions factory, armed the members of the *CROM* trade unions, and sent to his native state of Sonora for the entire tribe of Yaqui Indians. He took their leader, a man named Amaro, who still wore an earring in one ear, and made him commanding general. With lightning speed, this scraped together, motorized army, the first in Mexico's history, appeared at the Guadalajara front.

The rebel army was bivouacking at its ease, certain that there were no troops left to oppose it, enjoying the smell of victory and the dream of plundering the capital. The Yaqui taxicab army had one river to cross, on the farther side of which were men with machine guns. At General Amaro's command, his Indians leaped into the river, swam against the hail of machine gun bullets, and with naked hands, by sheer numbers, took the machine guns. The army on the Western front was broken. Then the bus-and-taxicab army turned round and drove to the Eastern front and took it even more easily. The brave General Calles sheepishly returned from Mexico's Northern frontier and assumed the presidency.

I PERSUADE DIEGO RIVERA TO RESIGN FROM THE COMMUNIST PARTY

Diego Rivera's person and bulk were fabulous. His life was fabulous, his accounts of it more fabulous still. His fecundity as an artist was fabulous, too. His talk, his theories, his anecdotes, his adventures, and his successful magnifications in each retelling of them were an endless labyrinth of fables. His paintings on the walls of Mexico's public buildings are one long, beguiling fable concerning his world, his time, his country, its past, its present, its future. The tall tales for which he was famous, improvised as effortlessly as a spider spins its web, were woven so skillfully out of truth and fantasy, told with such artistry, that they compelled the momentary suspension of disbelief. If Diego had never touched brush to wall or canvas, merely talked and set his talk down, Baron Münchausen would have had to look to his reputation. That is why I called his biography a "fabulous life," and warned the reader with the words, *caveat lector*. The simple men who served on the Communist Party's Central Committee, a baker, a textile worker, a carpenter, an agrarian leader among them, were all too often taken in by Diego's vivid, picture-making fantasies.

One day in 1924 I climbed his scaffold and waited in silence for Diego to ask, "¿Qué hay?—What's up?"

"Diego," I said with embarrassment, "I think you should resign from the Party."

He stopped painting in the middle of a stroke. When he saw I was not jesting, he put down his brush, left the wet plaster to dry beyond painting, and with accustomed courtesy motioned me to precede him down the scaffold. We paced up and down the courtyard, then along crowded streets, and talked. How many hours I do not know, but the first half hour seemed a fair slice of eternity.

From the first he had seemed to me a great painter, and as a celebrity, a great publicity asset for the Communist Party. As I became aware of his amazing passion for painting and his animal strength for labor, I began to begrudge for his sake, for art's sake, and for the movement's sake every moment he spent attending committee meetings, drafting preposterous manifestoes, waiting for subcommittees that with Mexican insensitivity to time would start three or four hours late or never get started at all. Even before I felt the necessity of his resigning because of his convincing inventions, it had become increasingly clear to me that the best service he could give was with his brush. I used this argument for all it was worth, and then explained as far as I dared and as tactfully as I could, the dangers to an inexperienced committee of his overpowering mind and imagination.

"Look, Diego," I pleaded in summary, for he was manifestly hurt and shocked, "you are one of the greatest revolutionary painters in the world. It is a shame for you to waste a day or an hour of such an exceptional talent as yours. The best thing you can do for the movement is paint. As a sympathizer you are more valuable than any member. As a member who forgets what day it is, what time it is while the wall is wet and the image in your mind, you are constantly being threatened with expulsion for missing meetings."

We walked for a long time without either of us saying a word. Then Diego pressed my hand warmly to show that there was no ill will, and we went to his home to draft together his letter of resignation. As soon as I left Mexico, both Diego and the Central Committee hastened to undo my efforts. In 1926 he was readmitted into the Party, and in 1929 expelled, because the Party had been ordered by Stalin to find a "Right Danger" and expel it, and chose him to be the goat. Since his sense of dignity prevented him from accepting such an ignominious fate and reason for expulsion, he declared himself a Trotskyite. And when Trotsky could find no place in Europe that would give him admission against Russia's pressure, it was Diego who, to his own surprise, succeeded in getting the President of Mexico to give Leon Trotsky refuge.

MY DELUXE JOURNEY TO RUSSIA

When I went to Mexico, I had read only three works of Lenin, all in English translation: *The Soviets at Work; State and Revolution; The Proletarian Revolution and the Renegade Kautsky*. And I was just reading and pondering Lenin's *Imperialism: The Highest Stage of Capitalism* (or *Latest*, or *Final Stage of Capitalism*—all three titles are used in different editions). I read it with great enthusiasm. It did not occur to me that the great age of empire was in the remote past: the Babylonian, the Persian, the Egyptian, the Roman, the Mongol, then the Spanish, the Portuguese, the British, and the Napoleonic empires, all far older than the period Lenin was singling out. Nor had I read enough to find out how great was Lenin's debt to Hobson and Hilferding, nor to realize that the Russian empire was and still is today the giant of the modern world, though somewhere I had read that Russian revolutionaries had called Russia the "prison house of peoples." The little red spots all over my schoolboy map of the world had impressed me with the greatness of the British Empire, and I had supported Ireland's and India's struggles to be free. Now that I was in Mexico and in touch with refugees from so many Latin American countries to whom Vasconcelos had given refuge, I began a study of American investments in Latin America. I did not think of asking whether the American companies paid higher wages to their native workers than the native industrialists did, though the hostility of indigenous businessmen towards American investment was largely due to this fact. Nor did I ask myself whether foreign companies developed deep mining and oil extraction which native business had left undeveloped. I simply assumed that every investment of American capital in Latin America was an oppressive mark of "American Imperialism." Country by country, I compiled these investments, thereby making a great impression on the American Communist Party, the Mexican Communist Party, and the Communist International. The chief result of my studies was my election by the Communist Party of Mexico as their delegate to the Fifth Congress of the Comintern held in Moscow in 1924. I was going to Mecca at last to form part of "the General Staff of the World Revolution."

I asked for an audience with the Secretary of Education, Vasconcelos. It was granted without fuss or delay. He greeted me cordially and seemed to know who I was. "Señor Licenciado," I said, "I have just been chosen by the Communist Party as their delegate to a Congress of the Communist International. I have come to ask you whether you will grant me a leave of absence without pay for a maximum of four months. My wife can take my classes."

"Your request is granted. Your wife need not take your classes; we will find a substitute. Is this your first trip to Moscow?"

I said it was. "Well, that should be interesting. You can tell them that as far as their plans involve a struggle against American Imperialism, I am with them. I wish you a good trip." And with that he accompanied me to the door of his office.

That had been easy, but next I had business with another minister, the Secretary of Foreign Affairs. As I descended the stairs of the Secretariat of Education, I found Diego Rivera painting his murals in the courtyard. "Diego," I said, "I need your help. I cannot possibly get a passport from my government. You know the Secretary of Foreign Affairs. Do you think you can persuade him to grant me a Mexican passport?"

"Do you want to renounce your American citizenship and become a Mexican citizen?"

"Certainly not. All I want is a Mexican passport for this trip. I have gotten from Vargas Rea a copy of his birth certificate. Can I use that with *my* passport pictures?"

"We'll see. The Secretariat of Foreign Affairs is right near here. Let's go there."

We found the Foreign Minister, whose name, if I remember rightly, was Genaro Estrada, lying back in a barber's chair in an anteroom of his office, getting a shave. I had not met him before. He was big, fat, and puffy, with a pallid skin and blond hair. Without rising, he greeted Diego familiarly, extended to me a limp hand, and listened to Diego as he explained my problem.

"Have you a birth certificate? And three passport photos?"

I answered in the affirmative, whereupon he bade me go to a particular office, talk to the man at the window, and say that the minister wanted him to issue me a passport at once *sin tramites,* that is, without delays or the customary red tape.

I chose the name, Luís Vargas y Braun. The last name would cover my faint foreign accent. And I decided then and there that I was the *natural* i.e., illegitimate, son of a Mexican father and a German mother. As soon as I was old enough, they shipped me off to a boarding school in the United States where I learned English and could speak it as well as my native tongue. The passport clerk asked me no questions beyond telling me to fill out a form. Then I was equipped with a passport in such quick time that Diego was able to return to his painting with the fresco surface still wet enough to absorb the pigments.

Next I went to the office of *El Democrata,* a daily whose editor I had met in the newspapermen's union. "Señor Valenzuela," I said, "I am going to the Soviet Union. I will be glad to send you reports on what I see there. I shall give each article a separate title, but I should like to call the series of reports, *La Unión Soviètica en 1924.* I shall write under the pseudonym, Luís Vargas y Braun. Later you can sign my name to them. How much can I expect per article?"

Benigno Valenzuela was delighted at his scoop over the two larger dailies. He offered me twelve pesos per article, ten pesos to be sent to my wife as each article appeared, and an additional two pesos for each article when I returned and the whole series was completed. I reserved copyright to make the series into a book, and promised him that I would take and send him pictures where they were appropriate. He gave me credentials accrediting me both as photographer and reporter for *El Democrata.* Despite my appearance, my new personality was acquiring substance, for in the modern bureaucratic world it is documents that make the man.

A maverick, as always, it did not occur to me to ask the Comintern, or the Russian people, to tax themselves to send me in state to Moscow. I borrowed money and went into debt to get as far as New York. Diego Rivera contributed 50 pesos, a stamp collector advanced 10 pesos on condition that I would bring back to him a complete set of the memorial stamps commemorating Lenin's death—he had died in January of that year. The rest I borrowed as best I could, promising to pay back the loans on my return. In New York I secreted myself on the S. S. *Polonia* of the Polish-American Line, persuaded by Lovestone that they would treat me generously because the American Society for Technical Aid to Russia had shipped a great deal of machinery on the Polish-American Line.

I waited until they had dropped the pilot, then came out of my hiding place and presented myself to the purser. He was visibly angry, and my talk of American Communist shipments on his line made no impression on him. But the pilot's boat having departed, there was no way that he could put me off. "What can you do?" he asked finally. "Oh, anything that needs to be done," I answered boldly. So I was signed on as a workaway, an unable seaman, prone to seasickness, that would have to do anything that no one else wanted to do, anything I was ordered to perform. The S.S. *Polonia* proved to be a dirty old tub that lost only a half hour each night on our eastward journey (the faster ships lost an hour a night), and I was in for it for ten to twelve days dependent on whether we had a headwind or a tailwind and whether I could wangle permission to go ashore at Copenhagen or would have to make the complete trip to Danzig for which I had signed up.

I was given a light tan waiter's jacket (the real waiters dressed in white jackets, but I did have brass buttons), and I was set to polishing brass, brass runways that held down the carpets, brass portholes, and whatever other brass the ship could boast. Next, I was told to help the waiters in first class. The kitchen floor was thick with grease, cut occasionally by sprinkling some white powder on it which I took to be washing soda. I was instructed by the first class steward that I was to eat on the run, selecting my food from what the passengers left on their plates and that had been sufficiently maltreated so that it could not be returned intact to the icebox, for instance, an egg that had had its shell broken or a piece of meat that had been partially cut.

I had already lost my appetite to the roll of the sea, yet I was angered by the indignity implied by the steward's order. Next I was told to dry the dishes with the dirty tablecloths that had just been removed after the passengers left the dining room. Then the steward took me down below decks into some stuffy hole of a room. At one end of it was a wooden closet not much larger than a coffin. On one wall of the closet was a machine with two rotary brushes touching each other, and on the floor was a great pile of dirty knives that reached nearly to my elbow. "You are to clean these knives by putting the blades in between the rotary brushes like this," and he grasped a knife, threw a switch, and plunged the knife blade in between the swiftly revolving brushes. It came out looking clean and polished. "But be careful," he said, his slight German accent becoming more marked, "hold the handle tight while the brushes turn, until you pull out the blade, or there will be trouble." With that, he slammed shut the door of the closet so that the pile of knives should not begin to roll out as I picked them up one by one out of the pile. The "clean" knives were to be dropped into a circular woven straw basket. And outside the closet there were other similar baskets.

With the door shut, the coffin-like closet became completely airless. There was nothing but the smell of stale food, and I knew I would never complete that mountain of knives without vomiting all over the airless place. The steward was gone, so I had time to think. I must get up in the fresh air. What would happen, I wondered, if I disregarded his warning and let go of a knife handle while the brushes were whirling around a blade? I relaxed my grip on the handle. There was a loud report like a pistol shot, the knife blade broke between the brushes, and the brushes themselves stopped whirling. My hand was slightly lacerated and bled a little; I held it with a handkerchief in my left hand and waited quietly for the stroke of doom, for the loud report must have been heard throughout the ship.

The steward burst in, aflame with anger. "Louee, you Mexikaner schweinehund!" he cried, "You are too dumb even to hold on to a knife handle. Get out. I'll find somebody else to do the knives. There's not another man on the ship too dumb to hold tight to a knife handle. Get upstairs and serve tea. Someone in the kitchen will show you how to do it."

I went up willingly to carry trays of cakes to the passengers who had already gotten cups of tea or coffee. I held the tray under their noses, but they took so long to decide what kind of cake they wanted that I got sicker and sicker. Suddenly I put down the tray on the serving table and ran out to the railing. Vomiting, and feeling a fresh wind in my face, relieved me sufficiently to go back to the dining room and resume serving tea and coffee and cakes and muffins. I must have looked green in the face, but the passengers looked at the tray, not at me. Next, I was ordered to help set the tables for dinner, wiping each dish with yesterday's tablecloth, setting each place with the dirty knives that had somehow gotten polished, and with other utensils, and, as a touch of added luxury, some refrigerated flowers in the center of each table. Then I walked unsteadily in and out of the kitchen over the slippery, greasy floor to bring out rolls and butter and other accessories.

If only I could hide somewhere and get a moment's rest! But the steward was after me again. "Polish the brass rails on the floor and sweep the carpets. Everything must be spick and span in the dining room." Next it was clear the tables, wipe the dishes with the latest tablecloth, set the tables for breakfast, answer stateroom calls, and I don't know what else. By the time I had washed up and shaved for the next morning and climbed into my bunk between greasy, gray blankets without sheets, and fallen into a merciful sleep, it was midnight. It seemed only a moment of time when I heard the steward's voice shouting, "Louee, git oop. It's half past six o'clock (actually he meant ***halb sechs*** or half past five). Moreover, the ship had lost half an hour because we were going eastward, so that my watch said five o'clock. I had gotten only five hours' sleep, had eaten nothing, and was sick as a poisoned pup.

The second day went faster. I did more or less the same things, except no "cleaning" of knives in a closet. I still felt seasick, with no desire to eat of the passengers' leavings, but my mind was busy with plans to make my situation more bearable. I would play seriously sick, and maybe they would send me to the ship's doctor if there was one on board. I would bungle some of the other tasks as I had the knife-polishing, and they would lighten my burden, or put me in irons (what were "irons" like anyhow, and did they have them on the ship?), or they would set me to tasks that would keep me out of doors, or at least away from the greasy kitchen and the handling of foods. By midnight I had my plans fully laid. I would not shave, I would put on my brown khaki shirt instead of a white one, leave off my tie, tear all the buttons off my tan uniform coat except the top one, which would make me look ridiculous; my sick face as I saw it in the mirror would do the rest. Then I would present myself to the steward, and see what he would do with such a scarecrow. I would take my chances, for I really didn't care. It couldn't be much worse than my first two days as an unable seaman and man of all work that nobody else wanted to do. Without fear, I walked into the dining room, thus accoutred, and presented myself to the steward to help with breakfast.

"What the hell do you think you're doing coming into the first class dining room looking like that? Get out! Get out!"

"Where to?"

"You're out of first class. Go to the tourist steward. Report to him. Do whatever he tells you to. Tell him I sent you. Tell him you're a dumb Mexican, too dumb to work in first class."

I reported to the second class steward. He was, as I learned later, a former captain of a ship. But as the big liners took over, many of the captains of smaller ships had to take inferior jobs. The experience had humbled him and made him compassionate.

He took one look at my ashen face, then said gently, "You need some sleep. I won't need you until eleven o'clock. This sailor will show you your bunk, give you a white coat, and, if you need it, a white shirt, if he can find one small enough at the neck."

"I have a white shirt, sir."

"Good! Now get some sleep. I'll wake you at 11. How long will it take you to shave?"

"Five or ten minutes."

"Fine. Eleven fifteen will be fine. Now get a good rest." "From hell to heaven," I thought, half asleep on my feet. The "sailor" proved to be a workaway like me, except that he was an able seaman who had not wanted to sign up for a round trip because he wanted to visit his folks in Norway. "Here's your bunk. Here's a coat that will fit you since you are built like me. Let's be buddies."

"Good, let's be buddies. What do we do for each other?"

"I'll explain it after lunch. Now get some sleep."

He left me, and without undressing, I left the world and fell into a deep and tranquil sleep. When the steward came to shake me gently, I was fully refreshed, free from nausea, and felt the first pangs of hunger.

ON BEING BUDDIES

Waiting on the tourist class was easy. The tables were covered with oilcloth. They were sponged when the meal was over, and we got real dish towels to wipe the dishes. Nothing was "first class," but everything seemed cleaner. No one was seasick, as far as I could tell. They didn't pick at their food, but had real appetites, and ate everything on their plates, even mopping up the gravy with a piece of bread. In a half hour we were free, and had the right to eat our own lunch, taking what we pleased from the icebox. At this point, Arne (I think that was his name), gave me my first explanation of what it meant to be his buddy. He said; "I don't have to wait at table. I only did it this time to help you out, but as I am an A.B. (able seaman), they gave me the top job. I have to feed the officers, make their beds, polish their portholes, and that's all. Now let's eat together. You raid your icebox for oranges and apples and whatever looks good, and I'll raid the officers' icebox. Together we should make ourselves a good meal."

"We can sit down to eat?"

"Sure, we have nothing to do now until tea time except a few dishes." He came back with some first-rate food, and I added my gleanings from our icebox. We had a good meal at our leisure.

"Now," said Arne, "I'm going to show you how to hide on the ship." He took me to little used storerooms where I would likely never be discovered, then to a room containing United States Post Office mailbags in which they took our mail to Europe. They returned the empty mailbags only when they had accumulated a goodly number. "Here," my buddy said, "you can always take a snooze and not be found." Next he told me about the Seamen's Union, and about Andy Furuseth, who had been its president since some remote time like 1908 and was likely to be reelected until he died or retired. "The Union really protects you if you bring them a complaint. I belonged to the IWW, too, but it doesn't have much organization among the seamen, and can't do very much."

We went up on deck and lay on some canvas in the sun and talked. Arne decided to tell me about shore leave and how to use it profitably. "Never go after a virgin," he said. "They're hard to get and you generally have to ship off to sea again, out of cash, before you can lay one. Go after widows or divorcées. They know what it's about, know what you want, and are generally glad to meet you halfway. Of course, some of them want marriage, and you can tell them by the way they ask you personal questions, but most of them are glad you're going to ship off again before their friends and neighbors get to notice how often you're coming up and taking them out." Gratefully and humbly I saw that being buddies was something of a one-way street. I couldn't tell him nearly as much as he was telling me. After we served dinner we had the evening off and went up on deck to watch a movie. My workaway job was becoming something like a cruise, with just enough work to keep from getting bored.

The rest of the journey passed like a dream. I had gotten my sea legs, the wind seemed balmier, the sea gentler, I found pleasant the old tub's roll. Everything was simpler and cleaner in tourist or second class or whatever they called it. The steward was decent and kindly, and we did our little bit of work willingly and well. What with Arne's contributions from the officers' mess and my careful selections of the best from our icebox, we ate like lords. The passengers felt that they were our equals and not our superiors and treated us accordingly. One, who was going to a commune in Kemorovo armed with a sewing machine and intending to establish a tailoring shop or clothing factory, did his best to convert me to Communism and told me what was wrong with the Mexican labor movement, from which teachings I learned nothing.

My buddy and I spent long hours in the sun and breeze, lying on canvas or vacant deck chairs or standing at the rails, watching the waves go by. Each night we had time for a movie and a good night's sleep. We had no sheets, but the blankets were kept cleaner than those I had had when I worked in first class. It would have been a perfect journey had I not known that I had signed up to go to Danzig, but wanted to get off at the first stop, Copenhagen, where we would anchor out to sea, get no shore leave, and no one would be allowed on the lighter except those who had a ticket marked *Copenhagen.* Yet I had to get out at Copenhagen because my Comintern contact was to be met at an address in Berlin. Besides, time was running out on this slow boat, and if I went to Danzig, I would be late for the opening of the Congress in Moscow. There was no help for it. I would have to go to the ill-tempered purser again and see if I could talk him into letting me off on the lighter in the Copenhagen harbor.

I went up to the purser. He looked at me with disfavor or contempt. "Sir," I said, "I should like to get off at Copenhagen."

"You signed up as a workaway to Danzig. We don't dock at Copenhagen. There's no shore leave. You're going to continue your work until Danzig."

"When I first spoke to you, I told you that our company, Technical Aid to Russia, gave your line a lot of business, and that I had an understanding with the Polish-American Line that it would give a first-class pass on your ship. It didn't arrive on time, so I had to go as a workaway because I have an important business engagement in Berlin the day after we reach Copenhagen. I can't go to Danzig, or I'll miss my appointment. The steward had enough help before the first class steward sent me down. He can get along without me from Copenhagen. Besides, he will lose a lot of his passengers there."

His face darkened. "You signed ship's papers to Danzig, and to Danzig you go."

"I must tell you, you'll get no more work out of me after we leave Copenhagen. If you don't let me off at Copenhagen, I won't work. . . ."

His face turned fiery red, and for a moment he was speechless with anger at my impudence. That gave me time to beat him to it. As he opened his mouth to tell me off, I added quietly: "And I won't eat." That took him by surprise, his mouth remained open, but I had taken his next words away from him, and he didn't know what to say. For a long minute or two he remained silent. Then he said unexpectedly, "They don't take beggars into Denmark. You'll have to prove that you have a ticket to Berlin, or they'll suspect you of being a public charge. We'll see. Now get back there where you belong."

I was given a pass to the lighter that carried people to Copenhagen. The purser whispered something to one of his subordinates, who took charge of me on shore. He got me through customs and immigration by assuring the immigration official that he was authorized by his company to buy me a railroad ticket to Berlin. He conducted me with dignity to the railroad ticket office, then said, "Now you buy yourself a ticket to Berlin and take the next train out. We've guaranteed that you'll get out at once, but I'll be damned if we will pay one cent for your trip." As I paid for the journey, he turned on his heel and walked off.

I sought out my buddy, for he had been on the lighter, but we had avoided each other because I had a ship's officer with me. Now I found him walking along the waterfront, and together we walked into a photographer's shop, sat ourselves upon a crescent moon to be photographed, signed each other's copies, and bade each other a fond good-bye. Then I began to explore Copenhagen until train time, when Denmark got rid of its indigent immigrant. As the train whirled through the Danish countryside, I was astonished at the trimness of the landscape. Everybody was on a bicycle, the lawyer holding his handlebar with right hand and holding his briefcase in his left; the baker's boy using his left hand to hold level a tray of pastries; the schoolboy holding his bag of books. The streets were levelled cobblestones or red bricks with no dirt in the ruts. Every house had clean red gables. And as we reached more sylvan scenes, they were just as orderly—each cow, though it was late spring, clad in a blanket overcoat, standing along the tracks to watch the train go by. I was hungry, but the train had no diner.

At last we completed our journey through the diminutive land that has kept its independence and neutrality through so many of Europe's wars and demonstrated that a land does not have to industrialize in order to be prosperous, for it remains an agricultural land that lives by exporting butter and cheese and eggs and pastries to the lands that have industrialized.

A few hours after we had begun our journey from Copenhagen, the entire train slid onto a huge ferry boat and began its journey over an inlet from the Baltic Sea that would bring us to Germany. On the ferry boat there was a diner below decks but it was only for first-class passengers, and I had a second-class ticket. Nevertheless I descended the steps and had a marvelous lunch of some of the best rye bread, best butter, and best cheese I had tasted for years, then some excellent Danish pastry and coffee with first-rate heavy cream. While I was eating, a man in uniform came by and checked each ticket. He explained to me, first in Danish, then in German, that I had no right to be there on my ticket, and he levied a fine of an insignificant number of *kroner,* then let me finish my repast. When I got up on deck again we were landing in a harbor of the grimmer looking, highly industrialized German land. I caught the first train to Berlin, where a new set of adventures began.

21

A FEW MONTHS IN THE HOLY LAND

In New York, they had given me an address in Berlin where I was to meet a Comintern agent: it was in Neukölln, a strongly Communist district of the capital. I was to say: "Is Comrade Fuchs here?" It turned out to be a tobacconist's shop, poor and humble in appearance. The owner seemed to be a simple workingman who had gotten blacklisted after some strike and had managed to borrow or scrape together a sufficient sum to open this poor-looking shop in a poor district. Comrade Fuchs had not yet arrived, so he invited me into a back room, and for hospitality's sake sent one of his children out to get a *Berliner Weisse* mit *Hinbeersaft*. The boy brought back a huge glass of foaming all white beer, made from wheat, naturally bitter and therefore sweetened and foamed up with raspberry juice. The glass was big enough to wash one's head in. A woman and numerous children appeared from another back room and seated themselves at a round table with us; then the huge glass passed from hand to hand and mouth to mouth. I had never tasted *Berliner Weisse* before, and I don't care if I never taste it again, but I appreciated the unusual experience and the hospitality. By the time we had drunk it all up Comrade Fuchs appeared, plump and looking like a functionary or bureaucrat.

"Genosse Wolf-eh," he said, turning my last name into two syllables, "you speak Spanish?" I assented. "Then I have a favor to ask you: I should like you to take care of a Spanish delegate, Comrade Acevedo; see that he gets safely to Moscow. He is an old man, very old. He joined the Spanish Socialist Party, God knows how many years ago, while Engels was still alive and Pablo Iglesias was translating *Das Kapital* into Spanish, but this is the first time he has been out of his native land. I'm putting you up at the same hotel he is in."

"Is the hotel dear?" I asked.

"Don't worry, all your expenses from here on will be taken care of. Take good care of him, and don't let him out of your sight. Old as he is, Acevedo is still a child. He thinks he is going to heaven; if he could speak German he would tell everybody about it. Here are two tickets to Stettin, two tickets for the next ship to Leningrad, and two tickets from Leningrad to Moscow. Don't lose them; don't give him his. Watch over him as if he were a child, keep him out of trouble."

"By ship to Leningrad?"

"Yes, in that way you'll avoid the immigration officials and the *cordon sanitaire*. You won't have to pass through any countries hostile to the Soviet Union."

That was the end of the interview between Comrade *Fox* and Comrade Wolfe, though what Fuchs' real name was I never learned, nor did I ever see him again.

Acevedo had a big head and a big beard—black streaked with gray—large black eyes, and a face of utter candor and innocence. He really had known Pablo Iglesias and had been in the Socialist Party all his life until a section of it split off to join the Communist International. He was as childlike as Fuchs had said. Although Spain at that time was under the dictatorship of Primo de Rivera, one of Spain's gentler dictators, and the Party led an underground existence, he spoke freely and loudly of its most intimate secrets. He seemed to know but one word of German, the work *Bock*. For him, every mug of beer, whether *Bockbier* or the common, light, year-round beer, was *un Bock*. Whenever we sat down at a table his first words were "un Bock." The foam whitened his moustache and the beer ran down his beard. Somehow he reminded me of the picture of the *Wild West Wind* personified in an illustrated edition of Ruskin's children's story, *The King of the Golden River*. If more people in Northern Europe had understood Spanish, I might indeed have had difficulty getting him to Moscow. This journey was the crowning of his career, a journey to that heaven where socialism had been victorious and all his dreams fulfilled. As we sat at a table in a sidewalk cafe, he would watch the passersby, and if a streetwalker looked our way, he would ask, "Why is that girl looking at me? What does she mean by those gestures?" To which my only answer was, "Acevedo, have another Bock." And he never said no to that.

When we got to Hamburg, Fuchs had arranged an overnight stay in a hotel. I left Acevedo to his own devices, and saw a splendid performance of *Volpone*. Next morning we went to Stettin, got on a shining white steamship, found ourselves with first-class tickets, each in a separate stateroom. I slept between snow-white sheets, the more luxurious because they made me remember the greasy sheetless bunks on the *Polonia*. Acevedo retired to his stateroom to rest, and I paced the deck as we waited for the ship to weigh anchor. Seated on a deck chair was an Englishman in a blazer (blazers were peculiarly English then), reading *War and Peace* in Russian.

"How come you can read Russian?" I asked a little enviously.

"My family owned a textile company in Old Russia. It has been nationalized. I am going back on a journey of piety to see what they have done with it and how it looks now."

"What other languages do you speak?"

"French, German, Italian."

"Do you speak Spanish?"

"No, I don't know any Spanish."

"What a pity, that's my native tongue," I said, to establish my identity corresponding with my name and passport. "No matter, I was educated in the United States and speak English freely."

"Yes, I noticed two Spanish names in first class on the passenger list. You must be one of them." I thought it strange that he had already studied the passenger list.

I resumed my walk around the ship.

SPIES AND SPIES AND SPIES

At dinner we found ourselves seated at the captain's table. The Russians must have bought into this line, I thought. Still, why are we at the captain's table? There must be other, more important delegates to Moscow on this ship. Maybe Fuchs arranged this as the safest place for Acevedo. Maybe the captain, too, has been asked to watch over him. The food and service and beautiful gold-ringed plates and snowy white linen tablecloth and napkins reminded me once more of the *Polonia*.

After dinner we went to a smoking room, where Acevedo regaled himself with beer and talked loudly of Spanish Communist affairs. "Acevedo," I said, "why do you talk so loud about confidential matters?"

"Oh, who on the Northern Baltic except you and me can possibly understand Spanish?" That's an idea, I thought, and looked around the smoking room. There was the Englishman whom I had spoken to on deck, sitting alone only two or three tables away from us, with the intent look on his face of someone who was listening to something. Whom could he be listening to?

"Acevedo, will you have another Bock?" He handed me his empty glass. As I walked to the bar with the glasses, I spoke casually to the Englishman in Spanish.

"Pleasant trip we're having, isn't it?"

"Yes, very pleasant," he replied in the same language. So he was listening and must have been thinking in Spanish. So he did know Spanish! I returned with two glasses of beer and encouraged Acevedo to finish his beer fast by drinking with him. Meanwhile, I studied other faces in the smoking room, and wondered who else might understand Spanish? That tall handsome Hindu, perhaps. Could he be M. N. Roy? "Acevedo, with so much beer in you, aren't you sleepy? It's time for you to go to bed."

"Go to bed so early, with a white night on the Northern Baltic? If I were your age, I would stay up all night on such a night."

"Anyhow, you aren't looking at it in here. And you aren't my age. Go out and look at the white night. Then go to bed." And I walked him to the door.

I walked over to the tall, handsome Indian, at least three inches taller than my six feet, and well built. A Brahman, I thought, no one else would be so well fed in India that he could grow to be so tall—Roy, too, was a Brahman, maybe it *was* M. N. Roy. "I beg your pardon, sir, do you speak Spanish?"

He stared at me in astonishment. Then, after a pause, "Yes, I do."

"Then I know who you are."

"How could that be?"

"I come from Mexico City. There were five Hindus there in 1919. I know Gupta, Sen, Khankhoji, and Basra. You must be the fifth."

"Well, I guess you do know who I am," he laughed. "But who are you?"

"Do you play chess?" I parried. "Would you like to play a game with me?"

"It will be a pleasure."

I went to the steward for a chessboard and chess set. In the choice for color I got black, an advantage for Roy. We played our first few moves mechanically, as if we were playing from a book. Then, without intending to use it unfairly, I sprang my secret weapon: "Do you know there's a Scotland Yard man on board?"

"How do you know?"

I told him my circumstantial evidence. Though he seemed to me a better chess player than I, his game began to deteriorate. Suddenly, he swept the pieces off the board, forfeiting the game, and said, "I must introduce you to somebody. I want you to tell him your story." He took me to a broad-faced, kindly-looking German named Felix Wolf, and the three of us went out on deck. We were far north now; the dying afterglow in the West was being met by the predawn light in the Eastern sky. I was seeing my first white night. Obviously, Felix Wolf, though a German, was a Russian agent watching over the safety of the Comintern delegates on the boat. He seemed to know who I was and so I told him my story without introducing myself. All he said was what Roy had said: "I must introduce you to someone else. You must tell him your story."

The "someone else" remained anonymous. He spoke to me in German, but I could see that he was Russian, and in all probability Jewish, a small, slight figure of a man next to Roy, Felix Wolf, and me. When I had finished my account, he said: "We knew there was a Scotland Yard man on board, but we didn't know which one it was. You seem to have solved the problem."

I thought to myself, "So, they must have a man in Scotland Yard, but not high enough up to know the name of the man assigned to the job."

I began to worry about the fate of the Englishman. I suppose I shouldn't have minded what the fate of a "class enemy" would be, but I was concerned. "If it proves that I am right, what will you do to him?"

"Oh, nothing," the Russian secret agent replied. "Our relations with

England at present are such that all we can do is keep him on the ship until it goes back to Stettin, and then send him back where he came from." I felt relieved. At the same time, I added one more to the secret proofs that were unconsciously piling up in my own mind, that perhaps I was not a "good" Communist. I stayed up a good part of the night, wondering how many delegates to the Congress were on board, and how many secret agents; watching the afterglow die in the West and the dawn kindle in the East; noting how clearly I could see the lines on the palm of my hand (one could read by this light); enjoying the wonder of the white night on the Northern Baltic.

A RUSSIAN SPY

I had one more experience with the maze of spy rings while I was in Moscow, attending the Fifth Congress of the Communist International. The *lingua franca* of the Congress delegates was German, and those who could speak German, regardless of their country of origin, delivered their talks in that tongue. Russian had just been adopted as an official language, but most Russians spoke in German. For that reason I seated myself among the Latin American and Spanish delegations and tried to give them a running translation into Spanish of the German-language reports of Zinoviev and Radek and other Russian leaders. A rosy-cheeked young man with a red kerchief around his neck approached me, leaned over, and whispered in German, "Sprechen Sie Deutsch?" I asked him whether he couldn't speak English. He said *no.* "Do you know Tim Buck and Malcolm Bruce well?" he asked. I replied that I did, for they were two delegates from Canada whom I had known for some time, and whom I had just met again in Berlin when they were carrying a loaf of German rye bread and an entire liverwurst. I had been looking for a restaurant at the moment, but they invited me to share their repast on a park bench. It tasted so good that I imagine I took more than my share. At any rate, having broken bread and leberwurst together, we were more than comrades, we were friends.

"Will you come out into the hall?" the young man asked me. In the hall he said, "Will you tell Buck and Bruce that Scotland Yard knows both their party names and their passport names, and tell them that they should not go to the Wembley fair on their way back as they are planning to?" When I told them, they were chagrined. But they went straight back to Canada. And I thought to myself, "So the Russians do have spies in Scotland Yard. And they must have a good opinion of me for them to pick me to tell this to the Canadians. Perhaps the young man didn't tell it to them himself, because they are afraid it might be noticed by counterspies among the congress delegates." Next day, I saw the same rosy-cheeked young man walking down the street with two English delegates and talking fluently in English. So he had lied to me about not speaking English, because he thought the Spanish-speaking delegates might more easily understand English than German. Such precautions made my head spin.

When we got to Leningrad, somebody else relieved me of the job of taking care of Acevedo, so I was on my own. Leningrad was beautiful, bright, and busy, but I was not bent on sight-seeing, so I took the morning train to Moscow, intending to eat on the train. There was no diner, no people selling sandwiches at the station shops, only now and then a station with a *kipiatok*, a boiler with water at a perpetual boil, to which people rushed to fill their little tin kettles in which they had already put tea leaves, and then they unpacked their lunch. Finally somebody took mercy on me, lent me a little kettle, and gave me a tiny pinch of tea leaves. That unsweetened tea was all I had on the long journey from Leningrad to Moscow. In Moscow there was a waiting bus that took the delegates to the Hotel Lux on Tverskaya, now called Gorky Street. There the period of hunger ended, for they gave me meal tickets for three meals a day, a big stack of boxes of Russian *papirosy*, cigarettes with such long, empty, cardboard mouthpieces and such a small amount of tobacco in front, that they were named after the paper that was their principal constituent, and a substantial sum of pocket money. The *papirosy* I gave to another delegate, for I am not a smoker, and I won his eternal gratitude, which lasted until he had smoked his stack of cigarettes and mine, but since they gave us another stack of similar height each week, the eternal gratitude revived periodically.

I DISCOVER THE QUEUE

After trying the food for one day, and the waits for waiters to wait on me (now I know why they're called waiters!), and after taking into consideration the fact that I would have a debt to pay when I got back to Mexico, I asked some factotum whether it was not possible to return my breakfast and supper tickets for cash and make those meals myself. The dinner I would eat with my meal tickets. They gave me what seemed an adequate amount of cash, and I figured, correctly it turned out, that by laundering my own shirts and handkerchiefs and underwear (everything went unironed—what do you expect from a delegate from Mexico?), and by making my own breakfast and supper, I could accumulate something toward the discharge of my debt, and toward the buying of a few gifts. As they had just gone on the gold standard, or perhaps because I, being a Comintern delegate, was a privileged character, I had no trouble changing my saved rubles into dollars.

More important, I learned something of the lot of the common citizen. I discovered that the *xvost*, or queue, the waiting in line after line, first to find out the price and pick out what you wanted to buy, then in another line to pay that price and get a little paper receipt, then in a third line to exchange your receipt for your purchase, was to be an inseparable feature of socialism wherever the Russians or their disciples like Castro, or their satellites, managed to establish it. There were queues in Russia in 1924, there were longer queues in Russia in 1928, and much, much longer queues when my wife and I spent six months there in 1929. There were queues in the seventies, and, if the same regime continues, there will be queues in 1984. After they had had socialism, by their own reckoning, for more than half a century, in *Voprosy Ekonomiki* of May, 1969, economist Orlov wrote: "The Soviet people waste approximately 30 billion man-hours a year on this kind of shopping . . . the equivalent of a year's work of 15,000,000 men." "And," Orlov continued, "a recent scientific study showed that in Moscow an average purchaser wasted 5-6 times as much time in waiting as in the purchase itself. And each shopper had to visit from three to five stores to buy the necessities."

"Maybe I should have waited for the waiter," I thought. Yet my shopping needs were simple. For breakfast, an egg and some bread and butter, which didn't have to be shopped for every day. Coffee I had in the form of a five-pound can of George Washington coffee I had brought with me, a whole lot tastier than all the powdered and freeze-dried coffees the supermarkets sell today. I managed to borrow a little tin kettle, put in an egg or two, and a measured amount of coffee, went down one flight of stairs to the *kipjatok,* which had water boiling 24 hours a day, put in two cups of water, and by the time I got back to my room, both eggs and coffee were done. And for supper, some cheese, or some red caviar, or some smoked sturgeon, all of which could be purchased fresh in small quantities at a reasonable price (there were no refrigerators), and bread and butter and a pickle or an apple, made the meal. Fine wooden barrel-aged, salted dill pickles of giant size were always available, while fresh fruits could rarely be found, unless they were bought from pushcart "speculators" on the street. It was the time of the New Economic Policy, and most of the "speculators" were farmers or their wives who had brought their own fresh produce into the city.

Waiting in the lines gave me another interesting experience. Some petty *činovnik* (bureaucrat) recognized me from a picture of me which had accompanied an article I wrote on Mexico for one of the Russian papers, the article netting me fifteen or twenty rubles. "Comrades," said the chinovnik to the line as if he were addressing a mass meeting, "this comrade is a delegate to the congress of the Communist International. His time is too important for us to keep him here at the foot of the line," and with a flourish he conducted me personally to the head of the line—then took his place beside me! A mean trick, I felt. But it did not occur to me to think that this was a sign of what Djilas called "the new class." A petty bureaucrat, I thought! Surely the big men wouldn't do a thing like that.

And how right I was. The leaders had no lines to wait in. They had servants. They had special stores. And they had special delivery to their homes. But this I would learn only much later.

The Fifth Congress itself staged elaborate dramas, a display of emotional fireworks with an occasional pinwheel or Roman candle that fizzled instead of going off as it should. This was the fifth time that a World Congress had assembled in Moscow so that they had learned well the art of staging. Our first duty was a solemn one, to go to the Red Square, to form a line and enter one by one into the silence of the underground crypt where the corpse of Lenin lay carefully embalmed, to look upon the waxen face, and then ascend the opposite stairway into the noisy, workaday world. Police in the uniform of the Cheka stood as honor guards, and as guardians of the delegates. Afterwards there were ritual greetings by delegates from the leading parties from the top of the wooden tomb in which Lenin's body lay.

Our first formal session took place in the late afternoon at half past six in the Great Moscow Theater, its balconies decked with red streamers bearing revolutionary slogans. In general, all meetings started late. Delegates and leaders got up late, ate a post-midday dinner late, started their meetings late, and carried them on late into the night. Often we returned to the Hotel Lux when dawn was breaking in the sky, and the Italian delegation in particular sang their revolutionary choruses loud enough to wake up all the sleeping inhabitants for blocks around. I noted with a pang that they had changed the chorus of *Bandiera Rossa* (Red Flag) from "E viva il comunismo e la libertà" to "E viva il comunismo e la Vecheka" (And long live communism and the secret police). But they sang magnificently in chorus. Living with the strains of Italian opera since childhood had made great singers in chorus of the lot of them. The Russians sang well in chorus, too, as we learned when each morning Red Army soldiers marched singing through the streets. The Americans sang poorly and feebly, and the English couldn't even keep time with each other as they sang at our festive banquets such silly and tuneless ditties as "Tonight we will merry, merry be, and tomorrow we'll be sober." Obviously, moving to the cities had destroyed the ancient British art of ballad singing. But the Italians had lived in municipalities since Roman times, and still the grand prize for group singing went to them.

The central group of the Congress was the Russian delegation, and whenever a vexing question came up, everybody asked anxiously, "What do the Russians think?" Once that was answered clearly, they themselves knew what they thought. After the Russians, the most attention was claimed by the Germans. Listening to the other delegations, if the huge Congress listened at all, was a matter of politeness.

The star of the congress was Zinoviev. He delivered the Report on the Activity of the Executive; discussed the World Situation, Political and Economic; the Tactics of the United Front; the Tasks of the Leading Parties; dealt out praise and blame to various parties and to various individual leaders, their theories, and their actions, delivered the Closing Address. Applause for him was always tremendous, everybody stood up when he finished a speech, applauded him with energy, then sang *The International.* If the address had been an important one, a military band crashed forth with the strains of *The International* (actually unexciting music, but they had had Russian composers alter it somehow to make it sound more belligerent and more exciting), after which the applause rang out yet again. Still, there was something about Zinoviev which disappointed me. I had seen pictures of him, chiefly on postcards, showing only head, thick wavy hair, broad shoulders and chest. But as I listened I heard a thin, reedy voice, and saw a face that was soft and fleshy and looked as if he never had to shave.

If Zinoviev was the hero of the carefully staged drama, it had a villain, too, also a member of the Russian delegation—Karl Radek. Hitherto I had known him only as a writer and a jokesmith, one of the most brilliant pamphleteers and the best raconteur the Russian party or the Comintern had produced. Zinoviev castigated him without mercy, using sarcasm that was not particularly effective. When Radek tried to defend himself, his remarks were far wittier, his sarcasm more devastating, but there was a claque of Germans and Russians who shouted, heckled, and tried to drown him out.

I was shocked to see that the Russian leaders whom I had thought of as a solid phalanx of infallibles were having faction fights just like the American party, fights more bitter, in fact, and, I was to learn, far more dangerous when armed with the fearful implements of absolute power. I was bewildered, but I must admit that I did not understand what the fighting was about and what was really going on behind the scenes of this dramatic and magnificently staged Congress.

I had looked forward to seeing the great Trotsky who had directed the military coup in November, 1917, which put the Bolsheviks in power, and then had directed the Red Army which defeated all the enemies of the new power. But where was Trotsky? Nowhere to be seen at the Congress. Nowhere to be seen at Lenin's tomb when the leaders spoke there. Where was Trotsky, I asked, but got what seemed only evasive answers. "He's ill," I was told, "and recovering in the Caucasus." But why had he not sent a message to the Congress? Why not a written report? Why did no one express regret that he was ill and could not be present? Why was his name not even mentioned? Not attacked? Not defended? Not praised? Not remembered by so much as a word or a greeting from the Congress? How was a "rustic" from Mexico to know that when the *Pravda* of March 14, 1923, published a special issue celebrating the twenty-fifth anniversary of the founding of the Russian Social Democratic Labor Party, and on page after page Bukharin, Zinoviev, Stalin, and other leading Bolsheviks all wrote in praise of Lenin as the founder of the Bolshevik faction and its leader to victory, Radek chose as the title of his article, "Leon Trotsky—the Organizer of Victory"? And how was I to guess that when Zinoviev was attacking Radek for failing to bring off a revolution in Germany in 1923 when Germany was not ripe for a Communist seizure of power, through his savage attack on Radek he was really attacking the sick and absent Trotsky?

The German Revolution that didn't take place in 1923 was a mystery to me, anyhow. I had been solemnly guided to a Red Army headquarters, on the wall of which was a huge relief map of Germany, and I was told that the leadership of the Russian party and the Comintern had been so sure of a successful German Communist revolution in early November, 1923, that they had put such maps in every barracks, so that if foreign armies invaded Germany and tried to suppress the German Soviet Government, the Red Army would know how to march to its defense. It seemed thrilling. But when the German party, under Comintern orders, had called upon the German workingmen to overthrow the Weimar Republic and establish a Soviet government, the German workingmen had not responded. The leaders of the German Communist Party at that time had prophesied that this would happen, but Comintern orders were orders, and they had tried. The German party had tried to get arms for the proletariat from the United Front government of Saxony, but the Reichswehr marched in and removed the government of Socialists and Communists, and once again the workers had not responded.

The whole Politburo had been responsible, but could not admit that the Russian Politburo could be mistaken. The Comintern Executive was responsible, but could it be mistaken? Zinoviev had been responsible as head of the Comintern. But could he admit that he had been mistaken? Trotsky, too, had been sure of victory, but they could not attack Trotsky for what all of them had voted for. So a scapegoat had to be found, and what I was watching was the baiting of the scapegoat. When the Fifth Congress of the Comintern ended, Karl Radek was not reelected to the Executive Committee of the Communist International. The Thirteenth Congress of the Russian party removed him from the party Central Committee. He was reduced to a mere journalist and pamphleteer, after having been a leading figure in the Comintern and the Party since the war. But Lenin was dead, and Radek's services forgotten. Two things solaced this homely, impish-looking man. He remained one of the most interesting and lively of writers in a literature that was to become increasingly dull and more and more filled with clichés. And he had won the love of Larissa Reissner, one of the most beautiful and talented women in the Bolshevik party. Their love lasted for something like four years, until Larissa died of a sudden and rapid development of terminal cancer. To see these two devoted people together was a startling experience. Larissa was a true Russian beauty, and Radek a gnome or imp with a high, bald forehead, bulging nearsighted eyes, thick glasses, a thin upper lip and a thick lower lip, around which played a shadow of laughter. To add to his homeliness and impishness, he shaved his face clean down to the chin bone and grew a thick fringe of hair under his chin, around his neck and up to his sideburns. When he engaged in jest or swift repartee, he did not seem homely, but impish. When you heard him speak, you forgot his homeliness for his wit and sharpness of intellect.

All in all, I learned little at the Fifth Congress of the Communist International, understood nothing of what was going on behind the scenes, spoke twice, only briefly and modestly each time, attracting attention only when I told how we in Mexico had supported the Obregón government against the rebellion of de la Huerta, and as a result had gotten arms for the peasant Leagues of the Agrarian Communities of Vera Cruz and Michoacán, had obtained for Ursulo Galván, one of our central committee members, an appointment as colonel, and were now urging the peasants to hide their rifles and not return them to the regular army. They had never suspected that such complicated things, more complicated in their way than the United Front government in Saxony, could be going on in far off, "uncivilized" Mexico.

In fact, this was an example of the "united front" that the Fifth Congress was mulling over. The idea of a united front with Social Democrats was developed by Radek in Germany after the Communist party had been cut to pieces in the ill-prepared and untimely attempt of the Spartacists to seize power. His fertile imagination had included the German Reichswehr, on the theory that the burdens of the Versailles Treaty were intolerable, and that the German army could circumvent its prohibition of heavy armament by secretly manufacturing arms in the Soviet Union and selling to the Red Army a proper share of their product. After France invaded the Ruhr to collect the fantastic, uncollectible indemnities of the Versailles Treaty, after the workers of the iron, steel, and coal industries of the Ruhr refused to work for the invaders, and after their folded arms strike received the support of the Weimar government and the German nationalist movement, Radek even dreamed of a united front with the nationalists, a dream bubble that burst when the nationalists and Ruhr workingmen began fighting with each other.

Lenin, for his part, had generalized the idea of a United Front with the Social Democrats on a world scale, when he realized that the world revolution he had expected had not been touched off by the Russian Revolution, and would be a long time in coming. But now Lenin was dead, and Zinoviev, as spokesman for the Comintern, turned the United Front ideas of Lenin and Radek into something more to his own liking. As it passed through his mind and temperament it became "the United Front from below," that is, an attempt to unite with the German Social Democratic rank and file and then engage in maneuvers to overthrow the Social Democratic leadership. That was the only additional idea I derived from the Fifth Congress of the Comintern, but of course I carried it back to Mexico, modifying it to take into account the entirely distinct and exceptional conditions of Mexico. If I have been accused, as I was destined to be, of being an "American exceptionalist," I was also a Mexican exceptionalist, for the Mexican setup was entirely different from that of the United States, and neither of them resembled the labor movements of Europe. When I was accused of being an "American exceptionalist," I answered proudly that I was "an exceptionalist for every country in the world," by which I meant that each land moved toward its own future in terms of its own past, its own traditions, and its own conditions. I could not see, and do not see now, how it could have been otherwise. One has only to compare the two neighbors, France and Germany, to see that this is so.

A JOURNEY UP THE VOLGA

One Sunday morning during the Comintern Congress, a man knocked at my door in the Hotel Lux. "Could you go on a short journey to Orekhovo?" he asked. "We were planning a small meeting there of four Comintern delegates to talk to the citizens, but our principal speaker got sick, and we need a substitute." "Is it far?" I asked. "No, not far, the train gets there in two or three hours." I accepted, put on a jacket, and offered to bring Haya de la Torre from Peru with me, for I knew that he was ill at ease in Moscow and did not know what to do with himself on a Sunday.

In front of the Hotel Luxe stood a small bus. My companions were Victorio Codavila from Argentina, two years older than I and destined to become a Comintern bureaucrat and work in various Latin countries; Ho Chi Minh, then using the name of Nguyen Ai Quoc, six years my senior, destined to work for the Comintern in France, China, Thailand, and finally in Vietnam; Coutinho, a Brazilian, who stuck to his native land; Haya de la Torre, from Peru; and myself from Mexico. Our trip to Orekhovo-Zuyevo was indeed a short one. When we got there, some hansom cabs were waiting, each seating two persons plus the cabby in the driver's box. The horses were old nags that looked as if they were a heritage from tsarist times, and the cab drivers also seemed an anachronism, for they wore jackets with bright red plush sleeves and high cylindrical fur hats which curved outwards towards their flat tops. Down the cobblestoned main street the horses clattered, watched by curious and mostly silent bystanders. "Viva la Revolución Rusa," I shouted, whereupon the bystanders applauded. And Haya, amused by the red plush sleeves and fur top hats, shouted, "Viva la novia" (Long live the bride). There was no bride visible, but the bystanders were just as enthusiastic about his slogan as mine.

When we got to the Central Plaza, we entered a two-story building and gave brief speeches in Spanish, Portuguese, and, in Ho Chi Minh's case, in French. Our addresses were translated into Russian by a strangely unqualified translator, who was also our guide on the journey. He knew no French, no Spanish, no Portuguese, the three languages in which we spoke.

And he knew no English. Except for Ho Chi Minh, we knew no Russian. Our "translator" could, however, speak German and knew some Italian. Hence I told him in German approximately what I intended to say, and then he used his Italian to get a bit of the flavor of the Spanish in which I made my extemporary remarks. Undoubtedly he filled in the gaps with some Communist slogans and clichés. When we had finished this performance, he declared to me in German that I was the best of the five speakers, and for the rest of the journey I alone would do the speaking. "What rest of the journey?" I asked. "I thought I was to speak only in Orekhovo. I am taking the next train back to Moscow. I have committee meetings tomorrow morning, and a Comintern plenary session tomorrow afternoon."

"There are no more trains from Orekhovo to Moscow this afternoon," he replied. I was dumbfounded. "You mean I have to wait here in Orekhovo until tomorrow morning? What will I do here? Where are the rest of you going?"

"To Nizhni Novgorod. You might as well go with us. You can get back by train tomorrow morning from Nizhni."

Nizhni Novgorod!—how many romances were built around that name by my youthful reading! I was sorely tempted. Besides, what would I do in Orekhovo all alone until the next morning? "Is it far to Nizhni?"

"It's on the Volga. In a few minutes there will be a fast train from here." I decided to go, though I had no overnight baggage, not even an extra handkerchief.

In Nizhni Novgorod (renamed *Gorky* in 1932 after its most distinguished son), we found a great multitude waiting for us in the Central Plaza. Our guide marched us through the crowd amidst cheers, and into a public building facing the Plaza.

"Now," said my translator to me, "you go out on that balcony and address the crowd. Tell me what you are going to say, and I'll translate.

"I don't go out on that balcony," I said, "until you get me a clean handkerchief." But now even our German broke down as a means of communication, for in my mind I translated hand-kerchief as *Hand-tuch,* handcloth. But Hand-tuch in German means *towel*—the German word for *handkerchief* is *Taschentuch,* pocketcloth. *What a caprice!* my translator must have thought. "How can I get you a *Handtuch* on Sunday when all the stores are closed?"

"I don't care, I must have a clean handkerchief, or I can't go out there and speak." My guide left me with a despairing look on his face, and was gone for a long, long time, then returned with a bathtowel big enough to wrap my whole body twice around from top to toe. I then told him in a brief German resumé what I intended to say, blew my nose twice into that giant bathtowel, and stepped out on the platform to be introduced as the *Delegat iz Meksiki.* Somehow I got through my speech and stood alongside my translator without using the giant bathtowel again, but he remained sure that Mexicans make strange use of their bathtowels.

KIDNAPPED BY THE KOMSOMOLS

God knows what a delegate from Mexico could have said to a multitude in Nizhni Novgorod, and what the translator may have made of my Spanish, but the applause was tremendous. As we stepped out into the crowd, great numbers of young people surrounded me and one of them said in Russian: "We Konsomols of Kostroma are here on an excursion. We have an entire ship to ourselves. Kostroma has never seen a Mexican. We have never seen a Comintern delegate. Come with us on our steamer to Kostroma." After this was translated, I said, "I am not a Mexican. I am an American who lives in Mexico and I am here as a representative of the Mexican Communist Party."

"We have never seen an American, either."

"I'm sorry. I must get back to Moscow. I have an important committee meeting Monday morning, and a Comintern session Monday afternoon."

"You're a Communist," the youth replied. "Here in Nizhni you are under the discipline of the Nizhni Committee. The entire Secretariat is here on the Plaza. We will get them to instruct you to go to Kostroma."

"But I am a Comintern delegate, and I am under the discipline of the Executive Committee of the Comintern."

"If I call up Moscow, and they say yes, will you go?"

"How will you get anybody with authority now?"

The spokesman for the Communist youth ran into the party building from which I had spoken, and came out triumphant. "I got the Secretary of the EKKI (ECCI, Executive Committee of the Comintern), and he said, 'Yes, if Comrade Wolfe has no objections, he is so instructed.' " I did not need urging. It would be an interesting experience to travel with a boatload of young boy and girl Communists up the Northern Volga. I spent the night in Nizhni, as the guest of the local party, and next morning found myself on an old paddlewheel steamer sailing slowly up the mighty Volga River.

They were a good-looking, joyous group of passengers. At every town or village they came to, the steamer would stop and they would parade their captive up the main street, singing as they marched. At every little crescent of sandy beach, they would stop for a swim.

At the first strip of beach I noticed that the boys sat at one end of the crescent and the girls at the other, and began unlacing their shoes. I followed suit but asked myself, "What do I do for a bathing suit?" Then I glanced sideways, first at the boys, then at the girls, and asked myself, "What do they do for bathing suits?" Quite apparently, they hadn't any. We had a pleasant swim, swimming freely past each other in the water. There were no signs of embarrassment. Finally, the boys got out at their end and the girls at their end of the little crescent beach, we sun dried and dressed, and resumed our journey. I had ground for reflection. Was this a sign of a new morality? a new attitude towards the body? a goods shortage? Later, when I got back to America, I found that Will Rogers had made the same discovery as I, and had written a book entitled, *There's Not a Bathing Suit in Russia.* But by that time, by dint of inquiry, I had learned that along the rivers and in the areas remote from the Western frontier there had never been a bathing suit in Russia.

By the time we reached Kostroma on a moonlit night, I was pretty well worn out by keeping up with all the youthful activity. They put me up in a comfortable bed in some party building, where during the night all my clothes disappeared. When I woke up next morning, everything was back, washed and starched and ironed. Even my handkerchiefs had been cleaned and ironed. It was touching and unexpected hospitality. I stayed for a couple of days free from the cares and concerns of politics, except that my ubiquitous translator made me make one formal address and a farewell talk. I told them how moved I had been by their kindness and hospitality, and how completely at home among them I felt. I would always remember this textile town that had been so hospitable to me.

When this was translated, the local party secretary responded in such a way as to remind me that I was going back to Mexico not to remember Kostroma, but to carry on the class war and the struggle for the world revolution. Then I found myself on a train bound by a different route to Moscow. We stopped at Sormovo, a town whose principal industry was the building and repair of locomotives. I was taken to a great locomotive factory building, into a dingy soot-covered great hall with an arched ceiling and a platform at one end. The locomotive workers crowded into the hall where there were standing room only, so I made my talk brief after a short colloquy with my translator. I ended with a slogan in Russian which I later came to think false, but because it was in Russian, it got great applause. I remembered how enthusiastic Zinoviev was in his report describing the onward march of the world revolution (a false enthusiasm after the failure to evoke a revolution in the war with Poland, after the failure of the Spartacist Putsch, after the debacle of the German March Action of 1921, and after the failure of the uprising ordered by the Comintern in Germany in 1923), Zinoviev's optimism was false, but all this was still a closed book to me, so my Russian ending was: "*Dajte nam lokomotivy, i my vam dadim mirovuju revoljuciju.*" (Give us locomotives and we will give you the world revolution). As the applause broke out, an old man with brawny arms and an enormous beard and moustache covering his whole face rushed up to the platform and gave me a resounding kiss, prickly with beard and moustache, then men seized me and threw me high up into the air, caught me as I came down, and repeated this tossing action again and again. Apparently, there were party members well schooled in such actions, but I am sure that many in that huge audience found my slogan fatuous. It was a slogan that I had time to repent at leisure, and did not try a Russian ending slogan again.

The journey to Moscow took us through Yaroslavl, where I was mercifully spared from speaking, perhaps because of an earlier unexpected episode which made my translator more cautious about my speeches. Our train was going through a barren plateau when, on a railroad siding, I saw a number of surly-looking peasants standing in the middle of nowhere without grass to sit on, nor benches, nor shelter from the sun. "What is that?" I asked my guide. "Who are those men standing there, all dressed like peasants?"

"They are muzhiks [peasants]," he said to me, "returning to their home village."

"Why are they so far from home? Why aren't they waiting at a railroad station?"

"They are waiting here for a boxcar."

"Why a boxcar? That means no seats on the train, either. What are they doing here in the middle of nowhere?"

"They were digging peat, brown coal. Now it is harvest time and they are going back to their village."

"Corvée [conscript] labor in the new Russia?" I thought, as a shadow of doubt crossed my mind.

"I have an idea," he said, as he pulled an emergency brake rope. "Why don't you speak to them? It will be a new experience for them. Perhaps it will do them some good."

"But what can I say to them? What do they know of the outside world or of foreign affairs? Have they ever heard of Mexico?"

"Speak on whatever you please. You've done well so far. Only tell me first what you are going to say." I thought for a long while. Then I said: "I will talk to them about the agrarian reform in Mexico, about the agrarian leader, Emiliano Zapata, how much more thorough the agrarian reform is here than it has been in Mexico. Maybe that will interest them and touch on something they know."

"Fine. Outline your talk to me."

I did so hastily. Then I was conducted to a slight rise in the ground supporting the railway ties on the siding track, and that was all the platform that I had.

I spoke in Spanish. Of course they understood nothing, but they looked at me curiously. Then my guide translated. Their faces remained grim. There was no applause.

I was puzzled at their total lack of reaction, and curious to know what, if anything, they had understood. "Tell them," I said to the translator, "that I am ready to answer questions."

"No! That is impossible."

"Why, tell them," I urged. "Don't you think I know how to handle questions?"

Then, seeing how his face got set, I said aloud in my broken Russian, "*Skažite im, čto ja gotov otvevcat' na voprosy.*"

There was no escape for him, so he repeated: "The Comrade Delegate from Mexico is ready to answer a few questions. But make them short, and ask questions only about what he said."

There was a moment's pause. Then a peasant stepped forward, bowed to me, and asked: "Are you really a Mexican? Or are you a Russian dressed up like a Mexican to make us think that somewhere in the world people are concerned with what happens to us here in Russia?"

"No, I am not a Mexican," I replied. "I am an American who lives in Mexico, and I am a member of the Mexican Communist Party. I am the delegate they chose to represent Mexico at the Congress of the Communist International, at the Profintern, and, if it meets while I am in Moscow, at the Krestintern."

Their faces brightened up slightly. I was apparently a man who told the truth.

Another questioner asked, "Did the translator really translate what you said?"

"I don't understand Russian. Only a few words. I suppose he translated me correctly, but I don't know enough Russian to know whether he did or not."

The surly frowns, the look of indifference, had left their faces. They were all alive now. One of them stepped forward and said, holding towards me the right side of his coat, "You see this coat, how torn it is? I work hard. I bend over the soil. I plow and harvest. And look at me. In rags. And look at the commissar who is translating for you, he does no heavy labor, but he wears a fine leather coat."

Another man stepped forward and said to me: "He drinks. That's why he wears rags. If he would stay sober . . ."

But the torn-coat-muzhik broke in: "He is *our* commissar, our local apparatchik. He wears a leather coat, too. Don't listen to him." Murmurs of approval from the group.

I kept pressing my translator to keep translating what they said. But he was getting too upset. "Stop answering their questions. Get back on the train. Let's get out of here."

That was my first contact with peasants, and I could not forget it . . . digging peat . . . corvée labor . . . grateful to one who told them the truth . . . dislike of all "commissars" . . . our Mexican peasants are happier, I thought, and less hostile to those in authority . . . how could that be?

TALKING TO THE MEXICAN "MOUZHIK"

One of my mandates to the Soviet Union came from the Comunidades Agrarias de Vera Cruz. I was to represent them "before the Russian peasants," and if the Peasant International, of which we had heard rumors, was to meet while I was in Russia, I was to be their representative at the Krestintern. When I got back to Mexico, in the autumn of 1924, a general convention of the Leagues of Agrarian Communities of the State of Vera Cruz was held in a central theater of the town of Jalapa (actually Jalapa-Enriquez), capital of the State of Vera Cruz. From the stage of the theater, I gave a report on *The Agrarian Revolution in Russia.* I was introduced by Ursulo Galván, Chairman of the League, newly named colonel of the army, member of the Central Committee of the Communist Party. In the box on my right sat Adalberto Tejeda, governor of the State of Vera Cruz, known as a friend of the *campesinos* and of the League.

I did not tell them of the peasants I had seen on the railroad siding. I described the superior crops I had seen on some showplace cooperative farms, stressed the fact that in Vera Cruz, one of the best of the Mexican states, only 1,320 square kilometers of land had been given to the peasants as *ejidos* (communal property) as against 70,896 square kilometers that remained undistributed, while in the Soviet Union all the land had been given to the peasants as individual property (this was before Stalin's forced collectivization of the early thirties). My critique of the pitiful incompleteness of the Mexican agrarian revolution was aimed particularly at such demagogue politicians as Governor Tejeda who sat in the box on my right. When I finished my address, there was a burst of applause. Governor Tejeda leaped from his box and rushed over to embrace me. The applause grew louder still and some of his henchmen shouted, *Viva el Gobernador Bolchevique!* With that, my whole address was reduced to ashes! And there was no question period to set things straight.

As I descended the steps from the stage, a peasant clad in the snowy, sun-bleached white of the Mexican pyjama-like peasant garb came up the aisle. Taking off his huge hat in a graceful sweep and bowing before me, he asked: "Dónde dijo usted, señor, que usted vió todo eso?" (Where did you say, sir, that you saw all that?).

"En Rusia." (He looked puzzled.) "En la Union Soviética." (He continued to look puzzled.)

"Is it far?" he asked gravely. "Did you go on foot?"

I gave up. From those two experiences I concluded that I did not know how to talk to peasants.

When I returned from my trip through the Russian countryside and examined the list of committees (commissions, as they called them) of the Fifth Congress to which I had been appointed, I found that I had been put on the Organization Committee, the Trade Union Committee, the Peasant Committee, the Propaganda Committee, and the Committee on the English Party and England. But they had left me off the Committee on National and Colonial Problems. I was shocked by this omission. Since the machinery of the huge Congress was too big and mysterious for me to know where these appointments had been decided, I went directly to Dmitri Manuilski, Chairman of the Commission, and demanded that I be appointed to serve on it. I was startled by Manuilski's response, and even more so by the ignorance of the Americas displayed by this man, one of the Bolshevik "Greats" and a spokesman on many questions for the Russian delegation and the Russian party. "Let's see," he said frowning, "what has Mexico to do with the colonial and national questions and the problem of imperialism? Mexico is in South America, a backward and primitive country, far from any great power." I found in further conversation that all the Russian Communists I spoke to thought that Mexico was in South America. How could they be so ignorant of our world if they wanted to give us guidance and if we looked to them for help?

"Mexico borders on the United States," I told him. "The United States and Great Britain have competed for influence over our governments and for the right to drill for oil, to mine metals, and to help the victory in rebellions of pro-British or pro-American chieftains. America doesn't seize lands any more after victory in war, but she holds the Philippines as colonies [they have since been granted their freedom], has pursued Villa into Mexico, Sandino into Nicaragua, holds the right of intervention in Cuba through the Platt Amendment to the Cuban Constitution. . . ."

Manuilski stared at me as if I were talking Greek, then said, "All right. I will have you appointed to our commission."

In the Profintern, the Trade Union International, I continued my work as teacher of the geography, history, and economics of the Americas, but had an easier time because at the first session I took the floor to announce that Mexico had just recognized the Soviet Union!

Next day a courier came to my room in the Hotel Luxe. "Comrade Wolfe," he said, "Comrade Georgi Vasilievich Chicherin would like to have a talk with you."

"Chicherin! When? Where?"

"In his office in the Commissariat of Foreign Affairs, tomorrow morning at 3 A.M."

"At 3 A.M."—I could not believe my ears.

"Yes, at 3 A.M. You don't need a *propusk* (a pass without which you could not get admitted even to a candy factory). Just give your name to the guard at the front gate, and you will be conducted to Comrade Chicherin's office."

I was pleased and flattered. When I commented on the unusual hour for my meeting with the commissar, I was told of his nocturnal habits, and that that was his usual hour for meeting foreign diplomats.

Chicherin was world famous. He had been in the Tsar's diplomatic service, had resigned in 1904, and in 1905 had joined the Russian Social Democratic Labor Party. He had frequently opposed Lenin, but in 1917, as an internationalist in wartime, he had sided with the Bolsheviks. He was expelled from England in January, 1918, and in March of that year Lenin named him Commissar for Foreign Affairs, a position which he employed at once, to convoke by wireless the First World Congress of the Communist International and to use Russian funds to subsidize Communist parties and attempted revolutions. But in 1920 he became more diplomatic in his activities and even tried to persuade Lenin and Trotsky to abandon their posts and activities in the Communist International, in order to make the diplomatic recognition of the Soviet Government easier and more plausible. It was he who secured most of the early recognitions granted to this subversive government that wanted simultaneously to secure diplomatic recognition, trade, and credits, and to spread world revolution. Increasingly he confined himself to formal diplomacy and let others take care of the revolution. But they made his life difficult by insisting that he accept agitators and secret police agents as members of the diplomatic staff sent to countries that granted recognition.

When I got to Russia in 1924, during the period of the New Economic Policy and the stabilization of the Russian currency, the jest was current that the Soviet government had been saved by three *ches* (our sound of *ch* is represented in the Russian alphabet by a single letter, y, called *če*. The three *ches* were Chicherin, Cheka, and *Chervonets*. (*Chervonets* was the name of the stabilized ten-ruble bill, then readily redeemed for ten silver rubles, worth $5.)

Promptly at 3 A.M. I presented myself at the iron gate of the Commissariat of Foreign Affairs, gave my name, showed my Comintern credential, and was conducted directly to Chicherin's office. He was a tall, slender man with a long face made longer by a wispy goatee. He rose to shake hands with me and invited me to sit opposite him at a table where he was drinking a cup of chocolate. Other cups which showed that they had contained chocolate, none of which had been washed, were scattered around the table. They did not make for diplomatic elegance.

"What language would you like to speak?" I asked. "I cannot speak Russian, but can speak fluently in English or Spanish, fairly well in German, and less well in French."

"Any one of them," he answered.

"Then let's speak English."

"Comrade Wolfe, Mexico has just accorded the Soviet Union diplomatic recognition. How do you explain that?"

"That's easy, Comrade Chicherin. Whenever the Mexican government deals a hard blow to the Mexican labor or peasant movement, or to the Communist Party, they make up for it by a radical action in foreign affairs. I don't know what they have just done domestically, but they have silenced criticism of it from the left, or at least muted it, by recognizing your government. What does that cost them? Nothing. What weight do they carry in world affairs? None. It is an easy *quid pro quo*."

The commissar looked greatly impressed by my explanation.

"What advantage can the Soviet Union derive from recognition?"

"Not much, Comrade Chicherin. It's the first country in the Americas to give you recognition, but that won't influence other countries. As for trade—you produce grains and they produce grains; you produce gold, silver, copper, and other metals, they produce gold, silver, copper, and other metals; you produce petroleum, they produce petroleum; you can't do much trading with each other. Of course, if you are trying to get a Comintern representative into the United States, something like half of the Mexican-American border is unguarded, much of it level high plateau, sparsely populated."

"Thank you very much, Comrade Wolfe. This talk has been most interesting and most illuminating, and you seem to know your country very well." With that, he rose and conducted me to the door. Chicherin soon sent a Minister and a tiny legation to Mexico, and advised the new diplomat Stanislas Pestkowski: "If you want to understand the complicated politics of Mexico, or need help on some problem or the estimate of some personality, consult with Comrade Wolfe; he is well informed."

Many of the sessions of our congress and of its sub-committees were held in the palace inside the Kremlin. I marvelled at the sunken marble bathtubs, the red and gold decorations, the vastness of the halls, the comfort of the red and gold covered bed that I was told had been slept in by Catherine the Great—probably a fable, but I readily believed it. In it, or rather on its ornate cover, I spread out and dozed when I was weary or resting between sessions. As I contemplated the ornateness and actual beauty of the palace, I thought of Maxim Gorky's struggles to preserve the cultural beauties of Old Russia and the bitter words he had written after attending in the Winter Palace a Congress of the Peasant Poor, the landless and shiftless, whom Lenin in one of his more delirious Utopian fantasies had thought to use as rulers of the countryside. Gorky wrote:

> From the northern provinces came several thousands of peasants. Of these, hundreds were lodged in the Winter Palace of the Romanovs. When the Congress was over and these people gone, it turned out that they had polluted not only all the bathtubs of the palace, but an enormous number of precious vases as well—Sèvres, Saxon, and Oriental—which they had used as nightpots. This was not done out of necessity—all the toilets were in good order and the waterpipes functioning properly. No, this hooliganism was an expression of the desire to spoil, to deface, to sully beautiful things. During two revolutions and wars, hundreds of times I have observed this dark, vengeful striving of the people to break, corrupt, mock, shame whatever is beautiful. . . . The evil urge to spoil things of exceptional beauty comes from the same source as the shameful striving to vilify any exceptional human being.

In 1924, more than a decade before Stalin killed so many generals, factory managers, and members and leaders of the Communist Party and developed his worldwide espionage system, the spy mania had not yet developed in the Soviet Union. Hence I was able to wear a camera on a strap slung across my shoulder and climb onto the roofs of buildings in the Kremlin to get close-up shots of the onion domes covered with beaten gold that formed the tops of churches inside the Kremlin wall. No sharpshooter finished me off on a roof, and no chekist spoiled my films in order to "examine them."

Another experience worth recording is that of the entertainment offered to the "true prolets" who made up the delegations to the Profintern or Red Trade Union International. If the discussion, at its sessions, was on a much lower level than that of the Comintern sessions, the level of entertainment suitable for true workingmen was lower still. I attended one evening a banquet for the Profintern. We rode in a flotilla of motor launches up the Moscow River to a palace on a cliff that had belonged to some former nobleman. After experiencing the meager fare available to the average Muscovite waiting in the innumerable queues, I was shocked to see the profusion of fish and fowl and meats and drinks and delicacies of every description served to the proletarian delegates. Of course, many of them got drunk on the strong drink served in such profusion at every table, and they were soon bombarding each other with chicken legs and breasts, then with whole chickens, and finally with creamy cakes and other such delectable missiles. I began to feel sick at heart and then sick in the stomach at the sight of so much waste in a half-hungry country, and sicker still when I realized what a low opinion the organizers of the feast must have had of the leaders of the proletariat, the class from which the world was to expect salvation. I left the banquet hall, stumbled down the precipitous cliff, and demanded from the pilot of one of the smallest motorboats waiting to take us all back to Moscow that he take me back at once. He demurred, then found someone among the pilots who had been in a German prison camp during the First World War and who could speak German. I told him I was deathly sick and couldn't wait all night for the party to end. He found a still smaller launch which took me back to Moscow, where I walked to my hotel.

In general, I received much more attention at the Profintern sessions than I had at the Comintern. In large measure this was due to my two sensational talks, one explaining why Mexico had recognized the Soviet Union, and the other surprising the assemblage by the news that the Mexican government was paying all the expenses of the trade unions, and that I was devoting all my energies to trying to get the unions to reject the government subsidies and pay their own way. After these two talks on my part, the Moscow dailies became much more eager for me to write articles for them on the situation in Mexico, cameramen came to photograph me, and an artist (not a very good one) drew likenesses both smiling and serious. The serious one was printed on a postcard which was put on sale in Moscow, though I don't know that anyone bought it. Yet all this attention failed to make me warm to the Profintern, for it could not seem to make up its mind whether it wanted its members to split the existing trade unions of their respective countries and form little Communist-controlled revolutionary unions, or whether it preferred them to stay in the big organized union movements and try to win control of them. Consequently, all the discussion was ambiguous and amorphous. Moreover, the Russian Communist Party had manifestly assigned much less capable men to the leadership of the Profintern than to the Comintern, and the delegates had less of interest to report, so that the sessions were far less absorbing. Despite my distaste for the leadership, the entertainment, and the business sessions of the Profintern, I was selected a candidate member of the Executive Bureau of the Red Trade Union International, an honor I immediately and completely forgot until I dug up, as material for the present chapter, the picture postcard their artist had drawn of me with the title printed on the reverse side. I was not surprised that the Profintern led a more colorless life than the Comintern and died long before the Comintern was officially dissolved.

Before I left Moscow, I was invited to attend a session of a highly secret subdivision of the *Seniorenkonvent,* the Council of the Elders, itself a secret body in which conspiracies, projected revolutions, Comintern financial subsidies, and other such delicate matters were taken up. Only the most important parties were allowed to appoint their most trusted member to the Seniorenkonvent, and it in turn had yet more secret subcommittees. It was to the Subcommittee on the Budget that I was invited. "Comrade Wolfe," said Comrade Piatnitski, Organization Secretary and Treasurer of the Comintern, "what financial request has the Mexican Communist party to make of the Budget Commission?"

"Not much," I responded. "Our main problem that we are unable to meet by ourselves is the problem of the poverty and illiteracy of the average peasant. You see, our journal, *El Machete,* costs ten centavos, and the average peasant doesn't earn more than thirty to fifty centavos a day. To buy a copy of *El Machete* he would have to spend from one-third to one-fifth of his day's wages. And then, in many of the villages, most of the peasants cannot read, so we would have to send a copy free to each village to have one of our literate members read it aloud to the peasants and explain whatever they do not understand. We would like your help to send copies to such villages. I should say, $250 would cover this for a year."

The members of the budget commission stared at me in disbelief, then stared at each other, then at me again. "Did you say $250?" asked Piatnitsky incredulously. For days they had been listening to requests for hundreds of thousands of dollars, and had voted to grant considerable portions of what was requested. And here was a delegate asking for chicken feed! "I move that the Budget Commission grant the request of the Mexican Communist Party," he said finally. "Any objections? So ordered." And it was exactly $250 that I carried in my money belt across several frontiers and safely back to Mexico. In 1925 the Mexican government was to charge me with having brought $50,000 in Russian gold back to Mexico "to foment a railroad strike." But I still have the receipt issued to me by Rafael Carrillo, Secretary of the Mexican Communist Party. It reads:

Art ---- 4″ wide x 2-5/16″ high

22

I BECOME "UN VENDEDOR DE DROGAS HEROICAS"

My trip home to Mexico was comparatively uneventful. My way was paid by the Comintern, which gave me enough money to stop at the American Communist party headquarters in Chicago to report on what I knew about American imperialism in Latin America. I left Moscow by train, crossing the frontier into Poland at Negoreliye. I was startled by the clean white table cloths, clean menu cards, and first-rate food in the first Polish station after I crossed the line. Did Poland live so much better than Russia? Or was this frontier station and restaurant a show place to emphasize the difference between Poland and the Soviet Union? I didn't stay long enough in Poland to find out.

When I bought my berth on a sleeping car to Berlin I got my second surprise. The sleeping car was all compartments, each of them locked by its occupants at night. The Polish railway line made no segregation of males and females, so that I found myself in the same compartment with a strikingly beautiful young woman. Who was she? What was she doing travelling thus alone? Was she a spy? Was my passport safe? Was my money safe, including the $250 in my money belt destined for the Mexican Communist party? What did we do about undressing in the intimacy of a locked compartment? This last problem I solved by going out into the corridor when she said it was time to go to bed, and letting her undress in privacy. Then I came in and disrobed after she was in her berth, taking the precaution of sleeping on my money belt and my passport. In the morning I found them in place and intact.

When I got to Berlin I found that early September was the height of the tourist season; so many teachers and students were returning to America that I couldn't get a second-class passage on any steamship line. I walked the length of Friedrichstrasse, where all the steamship companies had offices. In each of them I got the answer, "Sorry, all sold out. You will have to go first class or come back in two or three weeks when the rush is over." At last I came to the Scandinavian-American line, a Norwegian company. Yes, they had second-class tickets, but I would have to go up to Oslo in Norway to board their flagship, the *Stavangerfjord.* They would pay my railway fare, my hotel bill for two or three days in Oslo, and any other expenses, yet charge me no more than any other line for a second-class ticket. The trip would take ten days, for the *Stavangerfjord* passed through all the beautiful fjords of the Norwegian coast before it crossed the Atlantic. That same day found me bound for Oslo and a fine hotel, in which I swear even the snow-white sheets seemed to smell of fish. Perhaps their soap was made of fish oil? The fjords were as beautiful as I had heard they were, the coastal cliffs stern and rocky. Perhaps that hard granite helps to explain the sternness of Ibsen's plays, though how he achieved the tender, lyrical beauty of the scene in which Peer Gynt takes his dying mother on an imaginary ride to a banquet in Soria Moria Castle, remains unexplained by the hard Norwegian coast.

The *Stavangerfjord* was filled with Norwegian workingmen returning to America, all solemn and dour, without a jest or a bit of lyrical speech in the lot of them. Only four of us in second class were not Scandinavians, so we changed our names to Wardson, Baumson, Cohnsen, and Wolfson to fit the fashion of the rest of them. My entire vocabulary in their language consisted of something like three or four words picked up during my brief stay in Denmark, but they went far. In the dining room of the ship, a table running its entire length carried the most marvelous *smörgasbord.* The few days going around the fjords had given me my sea legs and sea appetite, so that I would heap my plate twice with delicacies, then demand from the waiter only *kokte poteter med smör* (buttered boiled potato) and coffee, and with a *tusen tak* (a thousand thanks), my meal was complete. But the Norwegians at my table were serious eaters. For them the *smörgasbord,* two or three platefuls of it, was nothing but an appetizer, after which they would order soup, beef, potatoes, vegetables, pudding, cake, and coffee. That left me plenty of time to talk with my table mates and to jest with them. Finally one of them paused in the serious business of eating long enough to ask, "You bane komiker?" "No." "Well, you make yokes." That little dialogue was the liveliest moment of the whole trip.

In Chicago I found that my disobedience in turning down the district organizership of New England and going to Mexico without permission was completely forgiven. In fact, all members of the Central Committee of both factions had developed a high opinion of me because of my study of American investments in Latin America, my success in getting myself elected by the newspapermen's union as a delegate to the Central Labor Council, my reports on the de la Huerta rebellion, and my articles on the Mexican labor movement and the Mexican artistic renaissance. Several members of the Central Committee expressed their satisfaction at my having gone to Mexico. They listened to my report with an awareness that this was the first time they had gotten any notion of the nature of Mexican life. But I myself felt that my report was woefully inadequate, and that it would take a whole book to give them some feeling for a life so different from that of the United States. A common frontier, I realized, was not a membrane through which knowledge passes by osmosis.

A RUSSIAN MINISTER COMES TO MEXICO

For the night after my return to Mexico my wife prepared a big party to welcome her husband home. To her surprise none of the Mexican caballeros who had visited her so frequently during my absence showed up. It was the knowledge that she was a wife whose husband was six or seven thousand miles away that had been the attraction. They had listened attentively to all her stories about my adventures, but their interest was not in me—quite the contrary.

The principal event to which we now looked forward was the arrival of the Soviet diplomatic mission. Because Mexico was not important to the Soviet government at that time, they sent only a small mission. It consisted of a minister, Stanislas Pestkowski; a deputy minister, Leon Haykis (or, since the Russian alphabet has no *h*: Gaykis); a press secretary, Volinski; and a translator, named Zeitlin. We had a small delegation of party leaders at the railway station when their train arrived, and there was a brief exchange of more or less formal greetings. Pestkowski spoke in English (from 1914 to 1917 he had lived in London), and I welcomed him briefly in Spanish followed by an English translation. Later we held a formal meeting of welcome for the legation in the largest theater in Mexico City, with all seats filled and a number of standees. I delivered the address of welcome in Spanish (no translation this time), and made the startling discovery that I could speak more eloquently in Spanish than in English. Somehow the Spanish language lends itself to eloquence as the Italian does to opera, but as I have listened to the eloquence of Mexican political figures, I have often wished for the more exacting clarity and precision of English.

The legation staff was patently a small one, as if they did not expect to have much work to do, and indeed, time hung heavy on their hands. Today the Soviet legation in Mexico has absurdly over 100 members, but they do not conduct much Mexican business of any sort. Most of them are agents of the Cheka reporting on all twenty countries of Latin America and looking for opportunities to stir up antagonism to the United States. They stirred up some trouble in Mexico, too, arousing some students to engage in violent tactics, and recruiting a few of them to go to a school in the Soviet Union that trained its students in revolutionary tactics and violent actions, so that in the early seventies President Echeverría found it necessary to deport a number of these Chekist "diplomats."

The legation was a strange one. Pestkowski was a Pole who had supported Rosa Luxemburg against Lenin in the disputes in the Second International. After the February, 1917, revolution in Russia he went to Petrograd, where he took part in Lenin's seizure of power in October.

Lenin appointed him as a high official of the Telegraph Office, then he worked under Stalin as Assistant Commissar of Nationalities. However, when he, and Haykis along with him, joined the opposition group known as the Democratic Centralism Faction, both of them were shipped off to Kirghizia, where they lived in a tent among the nomadic Kirghiz. He proved more useful in work among Polish prisoners in Russia and in the negotiations that went on with the Polish government. Both he and Haykis were recalled and given various tasks until they were appointed to lead the diplomatic mission to Mexico. Pestkowski was a solemn owl of a man, kindhearted in friendships and personal relations; he wore a Russian-type beard and looked as dignified as his position required. Haykis was a better linguist, already knew quite a bit of Spanish, had an irrepressible, mischievous sense of humor, and small, bright, sparkling eyes.

Both Pestkowski and Haykis became masters of the Spanish language and served as experts on things Hispanic after their return to the Soviet Union. Haykis was sent by Stalin as Ambassador to Spain during the Spanish Civil War. He served his country faithfully, but in the course of the Civil War learned too much—about the purge of dissident Communists, Socialists, and Anarchists, and about the shipment of the entire Spanish gold reserve to the Soviet Union, from which it was never to be returned to Spain. When he got back to Russia, Stalin rewarded him by a bullet in the base of the brain, a sure cure for knowing too much.

Pestkowski, who had always been interested in history, had studied under Pokrovsky and written on Polish history and on the Polish part in the revolutionary movement of 1905. When he was recalled to Russia he was put in cold storage in *MOPR* (The International Organization for Aid to Revolutionary Fighters), then reappeared under the pseudonym of Banderas as an expert on the agrarian movements of the Hispanic lands. He, too, was arrested during the purges of 1937 and executed. He was later rehabilitated after Stalin's death, and his memoirs were published posthumously in Polish. But in 1924, both Pestkowski and Haykis looked forward with excitement to their Mexican experiences.

The press attaché, Volinsky, did not stay with us long. As his first task in the new land he set for himself the mission of getting the American newspapermen in Mexico City drunk. While in that condition he hoped they would reveal important American secrets which he could send in code to Moscow, thus advancing his fortunes. But the American newspapermen were old soaks who got their "news" from each other or from Mexican newspapermen, whom they got drunk, or from the bartender, as they gathered their news while keeping one foot on the brass rail at the Regis Bar. It was they who got Volinsky drunk, and it was Volinsky who blabbed while under the influence of a succession of Margaritas, a drink more innocent-seeming, but more insidious than vodka. He was almost immediately recalled after the American newspapermen reported Russian stories from Mexico. That reduced the mission to three.

The remaining member of the mission was Zeitlin, the translator, who got his appointment to the diplomatic service because he knew an enormous number of languages, ancient and modern Greek, Latin, German, and all the Latin tongues, including Spanish, which caused Chicherin to pluck him out of the Athens embassy. He was a Jew by birth, but a Russian novelesque type by character. Indeed, Dostoevsky and Gogol working together could not have produced such a personage. He was nothing but skin and bones, with sunken, cavernous cheeks which seemed to need a shave just after the razor had shaved them clean. He apparently hated all bodily functions. At any rate, he had a deep aversion to eating. He would subsist on nothing but tea with lemon or lime (it was limes in Mexico) and sugar for at least forty-eight hours at a stretch until he could hold out no longer. And then he would permit himself a few morsels, a bare minimum. He had an aversion to women, especially those on the prowl. He felt safe only in the presence of my wife and Pestkowski's. His one solace was music; since he had almost no translation to do, for the legation had almost no business, he spent endless hours at the piano, which he played beautifully. Many years later, in 1929 to be exact, my wife and I found him sitting on a park bench in Moscow, looking starved, miserable, and exhausted. "Zeitlin," we said, after we had exchanged greetings, "what are you doing on this bench?"

"I am waiting until I am exhausted, until I get so tired that I will fall asleep the minute I get into bed."

"Why? Isn't your room comfortable?"

"No, not now. When I left for Athens and Mexico, I gave my room to my mother. I have only one room, but it is much better than the one my mother was living in. She died while I was abroad, and the room being empty, a girl moved in. She got some kind of order, permitting her to move in."

"Well, whose room is it?"

"It's mine. I'm sure it's mine. But she thinks it is hers. And we are both afraid to take the case to court for fear we'll lose. Whoever loses will have no room at all. So I have to live with her. I have put up a curtain between her bed and mine to try to make two rooms of it. But still it's uncomfortable. So when I finish work I come to this bench, and sit here as long as I can. In really warm weather, sometimes I sleep on the bench all night. When the weather is bad, I find places."

Poor Zeitlin! He had been better off in Mexico. No matter how overpopulated Mexico City is, people somehow find more than one room, even if one has to sleep near a charcoal brazier on a *petate* (woven straw mat). We were so taken aback at his plight that we forgot to ask him where he was working and how he got to a piano.

LA LIGA ANTI-IMPERIALISTA DE LAS AMERICAS

In the course of my convincing the Comintern and the Profintern and then the American Communist Party of the value of mobilizing the Latin-American lands for a struggle against American imperialism, increasingly I convinced myself. True, except in the Spanish-American War when we annexed the Philippines and forced the Platt Amendment into the Cuban Constitution, we had shown a singular lack of desire to annex territories in our recent wars. But I had just read Lenin's *Imperialism* and had not yet had time to reflect on it. He seemed to say that if a country was rich enough to invest in other countries, it was imperialist and the recipients of the invested funds were victims.* It came to me much later that England had built many of our railroads and our waterfront warehouses, and then our railroads had gone bankrupt, and it was not we, but England, that was the victim! And most of our industries had been built either by British or French, sometimes even by German, Dutch, and Belgian capital. And America, far from becoming a subservient colony, waxed great with the aid of this foreign investment in industrialization. Today, when many underdeveloped countries are nationalizing our plants and wells, we are becoming the victims of the export of our capital and the founding of new industries in underindustrialized lands. Be that as it may, under the influence of my first uncritical reading of Lenin's *Imperialism,* I was for arousing and uniting the twenty countries of Latin America in the struggle against "American imperialism."

As I began to study the history of the lands on which I was to write, I made one startling discovery after another. My first discovery was that the countries south of the Rio Grande or Rio Bravo needed no rousing from me. For it was only natural and consoling for these countries to blame their backwardness, their military *coups,* their brutal dictatorships and their velvet-gloved dictatorships, not on their heritage from Spain, not on their separate tribes and the mountainous terrain of the Andes and the Sierra Madre, not on their barren mountains and deserts and overluxuriant jungles, not on any faults in themselves, but on their powerful, envy-inspiring neighbor to the North. As I began to look into the subject, I found that there was an entire literature, or rather two types of literature on this problem—the sensational, yellow-journal exposés, and the serious writings of intellectuals who wrote on the North American Caliban and the Latin American Ariel, on *El Coloso del Norte, El Materialismo Yanqui,* and many similar themes.

So, too, it had been easy for me to believe that American imperialist interests habitually made and unmade governments in the Latin lands, until I began to study the history of each one of them separately. Then I found that it was almost a routine expectation that whomever a given president made commander-in-chief of his armies would soon lead them in a coup d'état against him. Between 1823, the year of Peru's nefarious "Balcony Insurrection" of the military commander against his president,

* This is the basis of the term, *neo-imperialism,* applied to America, which refuses to seize lands after a war and is generous in its aid to suffering and impoverished countries.

and May, 1969, exactly 87 military men and 23 civilians passed through the House of Pizarro, the official capital of Peru—that is 110 Presidents in 146 years! Similarly, Bolivia had seen more than 180 governments in 140 years, giving an average lifespan of nine months for each government. The discovery I was making in the 1920s, the great liberator Bolivar made in his own lifetime. When his armies first freed Gran Colombia from Spain, the land he had freed included Venezuela, Ecuador, and Panama, as well as present day Colombia. And he dreamed of uniting the other Spanish-American countries land by land to Gran Colombia, to make a United States of Hispanic America comparable to, indeed greater than, the thirteen English colonies that founded the United States of America. But as one by one the military chieftains of each separate province made their separate *coups*, he wrote sadly: "America is ungovernable. He who serves the revolution ploughs the sea." These sad words have been quoted by hundreds of Latin American intellectuals. Everybody knows them by heart. But how many understand their meaning? And how many of these "R.P.M." revolutions every nine months or every year or two can conceivably be blamed on American investments in Latin America?

Yet it took a full two centuries of the existence of the United States before a Brazilian newspaperman, Carlos Lacerda, Editor of *Correo de Manhã*, could write in January, 1975:

> It is necessary to say clearly that at the moment there is only one hope for peace on earth; it is that Russia does not become stronger than the United States and that the balance of forces may be favorable to those who desire peace . . . because they love life and their creator.
>
> Any attempt to make Brazil neutral would not only weaken world peace, it would give an advantage to the totalitarian governments in their war against the freedom-loving nations. . . . To neutralize Brazil is to weaken the alliance and the resistance of America.

When he wrote that, the greatest imperialist power in the world, in fact the only one that had seized lands—a whole new empire—in World War II, was the Soviet Union.

But I had come back from my stay in the Soviet Union full of the enthusiasm I aroused in the delegates and in myself for the struggle against American imperialism. Of course, I would study the situation in Latin America and the history of its various countries, but only, I thought, to confirm and strengthen the picture I had already formed of the role of my own country in shaping or misshaping the history of Latin America. In the meantime there was so much at hand to start with that I couldn't wait. I knew the Latin-American refugees Vasconcelos had invited to teach in his schools and universities, and they all confirmed my feelings. All, that is, except Haya de la Torre. He said, to my astonishment, "I think the influence of the United States in Latin America is good, and that all our countries could learn something from yours." I was too surprised to argue with him or to ask how he had come to that strange conclusion. He assured me he would cooperate in spite of it. All the others expressed themselves as willing to lend their names to any league I might form, as members, or on an advisory board or executive committee. I turned to the Mexican artists. Would they do drawings for a journal I was planning to be called *El Libertador?* Of course they would, and for nothing. It was the same luck as I had had with the antiwar journal, *Facts.* Nay more. They were all good craftsmen and offered to save me the expense of getting printing cuts made. As they had done for *El Machete,* they would carve their own linoleum, or etch their own zinc or copper, do their etching directly on the metal, and then tack it onto blocks of wood. They would provide a distinguished cover, done by a different artist for each issue, block out the letters, illustrate the articles, do full-page caricatures and little filler and tailpiece cuts—it would be the best-looking journal circulating in Latin America, for what other country could match the artists that had sprung up in the Mexican artistic renaissance? Actually, the covers of the first four issues were drawn by Xavier Guerrero under the pseudonym of Indio.

I went to the Soviet legation to tell Pestkowski and Haykis of my wonderful plans and good luck in getting off to a strong start in literary and artistic contributors. Pestkowski had hardly heard me out before he said, "I shall be glad to donate some funds to you so that you can start at once, as soon as you have the copy and the drawings or cuts for the first issue." I realized that Moscow must have provided the funds, perhaps Chicherin himself had been convinced or instructed by the Comintern. What good fortune! I knew that I had much to learn about Latin America, but with the help of the refugees I could write or have written a concrete study or series for each country. And why wait? Like many another man, I adopted the motto, "I know nothing about it, therefore I can speak freely." Except I had an advantage over others who used that motto in that I didn't know I knew nothing about it. Thus was born *El Libertador: Organo de la Liga Anti-Imperialista Panamericana,* a monthly of which Volume I, Number 1, appeared in March, 1925. Though I was the actual editor, our agrarian leader, Ursulo Galván, appeared as its Director Gerente, and the artist Xavier Guerrero, was its administrador, while my name was nowhere to be found. The price was 10 centavos oro Americano and its annual subscription rate $1.00 oro Americano, with a note stating that "the equivalent in the coin of the various countries is acceptable."

From the very first issue *El Libertador* showed itself to be a fighting organ that attracted attention from veteran writers against American imperialism in many Latin-American countries. The first issue carried reports from Cuba, Guatemala, other countries of Central America and the Caribbean, articles critical of the Pan-American Union of Labor, news from Chile, some of it written by a Chilean refugee in Mexico, a manifesto directed to the Congress of the Marine Transport Workers of the Continent then in progress in New Orleans, a promise of the cooperation of the American Communist Party, and—what hurt Mexican officials most—an article attacking the president of Mexico, Plutarco Elías Calles, for having made Article 27 of the Constitution of 1917 non-retroactive (the article provided that the oil lands that had been granted to foreign companies under Diaz from 1887 to 1910 were to be returned to the sovereignty of Mexico. By making article 27 non-retroactive prior to 1917, Calles simply nullified it and made it meaningless). The *Libertador* article was entitled "Adios, 'Socialismo' !" and President Calles neither forgave nor forgot it, as the reader will see. I had several articles in the first issue, some unsigned, as in the case of "Adios, 'Socialismo' !" and others signed with a brand new pseudonym, *Audifaz*. Why I chose anonymity and a new pseudonym will become clear further on in the present chapter.

How well the first issue was distributed and how much attention it attracted in Latin America was shown by the appearance, beginning with Issue Number 2, of the names of battle-scarred veterans of many Latin-American countries and of liberals in the United States. It must be remembered that this was an epoch in which the United States had its marines in a number of Central American countries, and our ambassadors were quite openly engaged in what was known as "dollar diplomacy." Henríquez y Carbajal, the father of Pedro and Max Henríquez Ureña, had left the presidency of Santo Domingo and the country itself in protest against the marines sent by Woodrow Wilson into the Dominican Republic to "restore order." Haiti had been occupied, the port of Vera Cruz in Mexico seized by our marines, and expeditions of American troops to Caribbean countries had become commonplace, always to "restore order," or, as Wilson said, "to serve mankind." It was only after Herbert Hoover had quietly withdrawn our marines from the various countries and abolished the Wilson policy that it became possible for Franklin Roosevelt to proclaim the "Good Neighbor Policy" without the Latins laughing in his face.

The Argentine writer, Manuel Ugarte, born in 1874 and known in his country as one of the initiators of modernism in his *Gardens of Illusion*, and known as a fighter "checking United States advance in Latin America" in such works as *The Future of Latin America* and *The Destiny of a Continent*, sent in a promise to write for the new journal. And José Vasconcelos wrote a *Saludo Cordial*, in which he declared that "the race that produced Lincoln and Franklin cannot reject the legitimate aspirations of Latin America." There were articles from the United States, too—by Samuel Guy Inman, Scott Nearing, Ernest Gruening, and in the fifth issue appeared a drawing by Robert Minor as the cover and the first half of an article by Jay Lovestone, the second half of which was destined never to be printed.

The second issue audaciously called for an all-continental anti-imperialist congress of the countries of North and South America, laying down specific conditions for the election of delegates with voice and vote and delegates with voice but no vote. Such a congress would have been costly, for we would have had to find funds to finance the trips of delegates from distant countries. I can only imagine that we would not have made such a call had we not had some promise of funds forthcoming from the Russian legation, that is, from Moscow. But I must digress at this point to say something about the offer of funds from another source and about the diplomatic parties that were being held by Minister Pestkowski.

His parties were unique in the history of diplomacy. In formal and properly engraved notes he invited all members of the diplomatic corps represented in Mexico. Nothing was said of black tie or white tie, but it was automatically expected that the ambassadors and their deputies would appear in white tie and their wives in their best evening wear. However, to show that he represented a proletarian country, Pestkowski would invite, as well, some Communist leaders, some leaders of the pro-Communist trade unions, and such painters as Diego Rivera, Alfaro Siqueiros, and Xavier Guerrero, as well as foreign Communist leaders who were refugees in Mexico. The workingmen would come in their humble best, but painters like Diego Rivera, whether he was working late on a fresco or hoped to ***épater le bourgeois,*** might come in overalls spattered with paint, accompanied by his wife, Guadalupe, dressed in a black dress with a black silk scarf. Strange to relate, since they were customarily bored stiff by all the dull diplomatic parties that they had to give each other, to which everybody came in formal wear and engaged in evasive small talk, the members of the diplomatic corps looked forward to and enjoyed Pestkowski's unusual, mixed parties, where they could talk to undiplomatic guests about undiplomatic things, and the entertainment might be full of surprises.

Thus, at one such party Diego's wife, Guadalupe, having imbibed freely of vodka and tequila, got into a dispute with a Spanish Communist. Since she knew nothing about Communism and was accustomed to speak cynically of the way it "exploited" Diego, they soon got into an argument. Suddenly she shouted in a loud voice, "Oye, Diego, this man has insulted your wife. I want you to shoot him." Diego reached for his pistol. People pinioned his arms to his side. The party broke up in disorder. It was the talk of the diplomatic corps for days.

At another party, which I attended in ordinary street clothes as was my wont, the Japanese ambassador managed to get himself seated beside me. He spoke good English and began in a soft voice to express his interest in and enthusiasm for the journal our Liga Anti-Imperialista was publishing. "I like your magazine so much," he said, "that I would be happy to help you in whatever way I can. I should be glad to contribute funds to enlarge its circulation, or to help meet the costs of the congress you are planning to convoke. Come up to my embassy tomorrow, and we'll talk about it."

He spoke so easily and naturally, as if he were offering to pour some more wine from the bottle near him into my glass, so courteously that I felt I had to be courteous. It hadn't seemed wrong to me to accept money from the Russian legation, but the Japanese—that was different! They both seemed to want the same thing—the stirring up of Latin America against the United States. But their motives, I felt sure, were different. In any case there was no point in being discourteous at Pestkowski's dinner at which we were both guests.

"Thank you," I said, "we don't need money. Subscriptions are pouring in. Here is a letter I have just received from the famous old writer, Isidro Fabela, sending us his subscription and promising to draw up a list of those who will be glad to get the magazine."

"One dollar a year is not much for fifty-two issues of a magazine that size and so well printed and edited. You are the real editor, aren't you?"

What an embarrassing question! And what a shrewd one! "No, Ursulo Galván is the editor."

"Why is he not here tonight? I should like to have him visit me, too. But seriously, why don't you come up to see me?"

"I'm afraid, sir, I haven't got the time."

"I haven't seen any articles from you in the first three numbers of *El Libertador*. Why not? You are their best writer. I see you have a new man writing good articles for you—*Audifaz*—who is he?"

I was beginning to lose my temper in spite of my determination to keep cool. His questions were searching and impertinent. What should I say about *Audifaz?* . . . But just then, Pestkowski jumped up from his seat, his face red with too much drink. "I have written a poem," he said loudly, "in English, which I know best. It is to honor all of you at this party. I will read it, and then I will ask Mr. Bertram Wolfe to translate it into Spanish." He began to read. It was poor poetry and didn't make much sense. Under the pretense of translating I began desperately to extemporize in Spanish. My poem made more sense than his, but still it was a poor piece of verse, made of worn phrases loosely hung together. Our host led in the applause for my translation which he had sense enough to realize was better than his "poem." With that, the party broke up. The Japanese ambassador moved discreetly away from me, and my embarrassment was at an end.

SHARPENING RELATIONS BETWEEN MEXICO AND RUSSIA

Issue Number 3 of *El Libertador*, sent to the printer in May, 1925, but dated June, betrayed that relations between Mexico and Russia were growing more tense. The recognition of the Soviet Union by President Calles had been little more than a platonic gesture. As I had explained to Foreign Commissar Chicherin, whenever the government of Mexico did something reactionary in the domestic field where it had real power, it tended to offset it by a radical move in international affairs where its power was nugatory. The *quid pro quo* in this case was quite apparent by the time the first issue of *El Libertador* appeared. President Calles had made Article 27 of the 1917 Constitution non-retroactive. There was yet another part of this action, which concerned the railroads of Mexico and their future. This part was still secret, and all I had been able to do in some articles in *El Machete* and some talks to railwaymen, was to make conjectures concerning its probable or possible provisions.

In the very first issue of *El Libertador,* I had taken up both the oil land provisions and the conjectural railway provisions in an unsigned article sharply entitled, "Adios, 'Socialismo' !" It was, as I have already written, an article that President Calles had neither forgotten nor forgiven. In the second issue there was an unsigned article equally unpalatable to the president, entitled *Subvencionitis,* accusing the CROM, the official Mexican labor movement, of being kept in subservience to the government by a system of government subsidies: confiscated palaces as meeting halls; payment of its labor leaders by soft jobs with no duties except to sign the payroll; printing of its journals gratis in government-owned printing plants, etc. The article began with the words, "The principal sickness of the Mexican labor organizations is subvencionitis." Moreover, to make matters worse, the second issue contained a serious call for a continent-side, anti-imperialist congress.

The third issue contained a lead article with the ominous title: *Calles, Chicherin, Pestkowski, and Uncle Sam.* The very title suggested that President Calles was striking back—at the Anti-Imperialist League and at the Soviet government, as represented by the Russian Commissar of Foreign Affairs and the minister representing the Soviet government in Mexico.

The president chose one of the two greatest Mexican national holidays, the Fifth of May, to take exception to a comparatively innocent declaration of Commissar Chicherin. While reviewing the foreign relations of the Soviet Government, Chicherin had said: "In America we find ourselves before a question mark; but with a neighbor of the United States, Mexico, we have succeeded in reestablishing the development of our relations in the New World."

Probably all that Chicherin meant was that Mexico's example might be followed by other Latin American countries, and eventually by the United States. But President Calles preferred to interpret it to mean that Chicherin was planning to use Mexico as a "base" for developing its foreign policy in the New World. Another portion of Calles's Fifth of May Address seemed to refer not only to the remark of Chicherin, but to the activities of Minister Pestkowski in Mexico and to the Anti-Imperialist League, which was clearly attempting to rouse all of Latin America, not excluding Mexico itself, for a struggle against the advances or encroachments of North American imperialism. The key passage in the President's address said sternly: "Mexico has always taken especial care not to mix into matters that are not its business (no lo *competan*) . . . and it will not tolerate that it be taken as an instrument for the carrying out of maneuvers or combinations of international politics."

I do not know whether Chicherin took any note of Calles's criticism or whether Pestkowski engaged in any diplomatic action. But the only public response was a sharp article printed both in *El Machete* and *El Liber-*

tador. It sought to demonstrate and underscore the innocence of Commissar Chicherin's remarks. It quoted the American ambassador, Sheffield, to the effect that "The relations between Mexico and the United States are better than ever; the statements of Calles caused a magnificent impression," a remark that suggests that perhaps Ambassador Sheffield had protested to Mexican Foreign Relations Secretary Saenz at the anti-imperialist and anti-American activities being carried on in Mexico. And our article said of the president: "Calles has declared his 'independence' from Russia. Why does he not declare his independence from the United States!"

THE IMPENDING RAILWAY STRIKE

There was a sense of growing unrest among the railwaymen of Mexico. It leaked out that the Calles decision concerning Article 27 contained some understanding on the future of the railways, but the government said nothing, which explained the growing restlessness among the railwaymen. Was there an agreement that the railways would be returned to private hands after they had been made more profitable by reducing the wages of the railwaymen who were on the whole the best paid workingmen in the country? Or would the nationalization of the railways perhaps be made more complete by putting the whole system into the annual budget, which might mean that collective bargaining of the individual crafts would give way to budgetary determination of all railway expenses, including wages?

After all, we who were teaching knew that our wages had stopped completely during the de la Huerta rebellion, because President Obregón needed every centavo to pay and equip the makeshift army that he raised to fight the uprising. True, we got the back pay afterwards, but until the treasury was replenished we hungered, we borrowed, we skimped, and we dined at other people's tables. That is, all of us did except Carleton Beals, whose hot temper prompted him to secure a revolver, present himself to the paymaster with weapon pointed at the latter's head, state the number of pesos due him, demand that they be counted out on the counter in front of him and then put into a canvas bag, after which he backed out of the door still aiming the gun at the paymaster, lest the latter attempt to draw his own. Having your salary depend on the budget was sometimes a precarious thing.

I did not know what the Calles decision provided, but I speculated freely on its possible provisions both in the columns of *El Machete* and in talks to the railwaymen. Starting with my modest class for the railway carpenters, I had gradually extended my teachings to railwaymen of virtually every craft except the locomotive engineers. Men and women also came into the class from other unions, from the party membership, and from intellectual circles.

The point on which I placed the greatest emphasis when talking to any union group was that the unions must learn to pay their own way, and not depend upon the government. "Down with subvencionitis! Instead of letting your officials take soft jobs *(chambas)* from the government, pay your dues regularly, and pay their salaries yourselves, however poorly. Only then will you control your union officials and not have the government control them. You must not accept palaces from the government to meet in, but hire your own meeting places the way the bakers, the textile workers, and the C.G.T. unions do. Only then will you be free from government control. You must pay for printing your own journals, not have them done on government presses. They won't look so nice, but then you and not the government will control every word that is said in them." These were sensible things I was saying, but the Mexican labor movement was not used to paying its own way, and Mexican workingmen were not accustomed to paying dues, so for the most part they reacted lukewarmly. However, many comfortably fixed trade union functionaries were indignant, yet speechless, while some government officials were growing to feel that this active foreigner was a nuisance.

I do not wish to imply that I was making only enemies. On the contrary, my wife and I had made many friends among the artists and intellectuals; party members and union members; teachers in the school system and our fellow students; our teachers in the graduate school of the University of Mexico, students in the classes I taught; and *porteros* and their amazingly dignified, courteous children, beautiful to look at, well-behaved, and never seeming to cry or throw a tantrum. I do not know how the humble in Mexico bring up their children, but they are a pleasure to behold.

We gave parties, in our home, on Friday nights, which became so popular that there was often standing room only. Many of the intellectuals who came brought their girls with them, but singularly, never their wives. When we said, "Next time, bring your wife," they invariably answered, "Si, como no," which seemed to signify, "Yes, certainly," but the next week again they would appear with lovely girls, but never with their wives. There is no country that I have been in where courtship before marriage is more elaborate and more persistent, or where there is as big a fuss made over Mother's Day as in Mexico. When a neighboring girl was being courted, the ardent wooer would serenade her every night to keep her and us awake, but the serenading was done by *Mariachis*, hired bands that played and sang love songs through the night, while the ardent wooer remained at home to get a decent night's sleep.

But once the girl is won and has begotten children, it is quite common that she is taken out by her husband only on visits to relatives, or only if the caballero is invited to the president's reception of the Fifth of May or the Sixteenth of September. Then it is obligatory to bring your lawful wedded wife. But on other occasions the wife and mother is usually left at home with the children, and the visitor brings his girl. *La casa chica* for the mistress and *la casa grande* for the wife and mother of one's children, is a fairly common feature of Mexican middle-class life.

"COMRADE WOLFE, YOU ARE IN DANGER"

As the railwaymen prepared for a strike, the unions formed a strike committee. To my surprise, I was invited by them to form part of the committee. I felt honored, but embarrassed. I knew that a railway strike meant a head-on collision with the government, and I felt that as a foreigner and not a railway worker I had no place on a railwaymen's strike committee. I urged these objections, but those who came to invite me answered, "You come from the United States. There the unions have more experience with strikes. There are many questions to which we do not know the answers, and your advice will be of help to us." I finally agreed to sit on the committee, but not as one of its members, only in an advisory capacity. That was trouble enough.

Among the problems they put to me, the hardest was that of the locomotive engineers. There were seventeen craft unions (we in the United States have only sixteen), each with its own executive and its own autonomy. But all the crafts had adopted a common rule that if the seventeen all agreed to a strike, then a general strike committee with representatives of each craft would take over and replace the seventeen separate executives. "How can we get the locomotive engineers to agree to a strike?" they asked. "Without them there will be no general strike committee."

"I have no idea. I have no contact with them, no influence with them, no experience with them. That is your task to persuade them."

"If we start a strike without them, how can we stop them from hauling trains with strikebreakers? Ordinarily the Government recognizes the legality of a strike, and then strikebreakers are forbidden, but in this case the Government may not recognize the legality of a strike if all seventeen unions do not sanction it."

I hesitated for a long time. Then I said, "I am not a railwayman. I have no special knowledge of railways, but I have heard that those who want to stop a locomotive can do so by dropping a bar of soap into the boiler." As I said this, I knew that it was likely to cause trouble for me. Surely, among the members of this large strike committee, there was one or more who would inform some government official. If even the Japanese ambassador had been able to purchase or ferret out information on the identity of *Audifaz,* this government, so accustomed to purchasing labor leaders and the subservience of unions, must have some informers on this strike committee. But I had made my decision and must be prepared for whatever might come of it.

One night during the following week, our home on Cinco de Febrero

47, only three or four blocks from the Zócalo, the Central Plaza where all the main government buildings were, had an unexpected and uninvited guest, Enrique Delhumeau, Governor of the Federal District. I knew him only remotely, having sat with him on one or two committees, but he called me *compañero,* comrade. This did not seem as absurd as it may sound to the reader, for he had been elected on the ticket of the Laborista or Labor Party, and I was of the Communist Party which, having supported Calles against de la Huerta, had also supported his candidacy. Both parties used the term, *comrade.* I was, as well, a delegate to the Central Trades Council of the CROM from the Newspapermen's Union, and it was the CROM that had conducted the campaign of the Laborista Party for his election.

Though we were greatly puzzled, we offered him liquor and things to nibble on. He was courteous, but not of a mind to socialize at any length. In a few minutes he came to the point of his visit. "Comrade Wolfe," he said, "I have come to warn you that you are in danger."

"In danger of what?" I asked.

"I don't rightly know—in danger either of the 33 or the 30-30."

I reflected for a few moments. I knew the meaning of both numbers. "The 33" was Article 33 of the Constitution, which gave the president the right to deport "a pernicious foreigner" without the necessity of a hearing, and without the right of *amparo* for the victim, that is, without the right to apply to a court for an injunction. As for the 30-30, it was the small bore rifle that had been used so much by all sides in the civil wars of the past decade. I knew very well how it was used, for I had recently lost a friend, Mauricio Tobón, a leader of the textile workers, to the 30-30. Mexico, as I had so often been told, was a civilized country, therefore it had abolished capital punishment. Hence, when they wanted to get rid of an inconvenient person, they would arrest him, question him, apologize, and release him. As he walked away, they would shoot him in the back as a "prisoner trying to escape." Since no Mexican male would ever fail to face the enemy, he could never conceivably be shot in the back, unless he was trying to escape. The logic was unassailable. The procedure has a special name: it was called *la ley fuga,* the law of flight. So they were trying to frighten me into leaving the country of my own accord, without any scandal to them.

"Señor Delhumeau," I said finally, addressing him now not as "compañero," but as the high official that he was, "I do not frighten easily. I will never leave Mexico out of fear. Long ago, as a youth of eleven or twelve, I lost my fear of death, for I reasoned that once you are dead, you do not miss life. So if it is the 30-30, you Mexicans are good marksmen. Death will be certain and swift. That is the best of deaths. What difference then whether my body lies on a Mexican field or a field in the United States?

"But if it is the 33, Señor Delhumeau, you are the governor of the Federal District. No order for an arrest in the Federal District can possibly be executed without passing through your hands. Since you have been kind enough to warn me, will you be so good as to call me up the minute you receive it? I will drop everything and go to your office. When I see the order, with the signature of the president, I shall go home at once to pack, and will leave on the night train that same night, without any scandal for you or for me."

"Perfectamente, Compañero. Se lo prometo." (Certainly, Comrade, I give you my promise.)

At that, we shook hands, and he left.

After this "fraternal" warning, I went about my work as usual. I taught my girls in Miguel Lerdo High School, I continued my evening classes, I continued to urge trade unionists to pay their own way and make themselves independent of government subsidy, I wrote my articles in *El Machete,* and continued the unsigned and *Audifaz* articles in *El Libertador* and even piled up a backlog for succeeding issues. I signed some articles *Audifaz* which I wrote for North American liberal and radical journals, I got a certificate from Pedro Henríquez Ureña that I had completed my residence requirements for the master's degree and had passed all my courses, I handed in to him my master's thesis on *El romance tradicional en México* (The Spanish Traditional Ballad as It Survives in the Oral Tradition of Mexico), and I continued writing for Tass and for the Federated Press, for both of which I had set up an office in Mexico of which I was the sole occupant. When Kenneth Durant, who directed the New York office of Tass, learned from me that I was in danger of deportation or *la ley fuga,* he asked me to send in to him a formal resignation, so that Tass should not be involved in any scandal in connection with its one-man Mexican bureau. I talked over matters with the Soviet minister in Mexico, so that he might take any protective measures that he deemed fit. And we continued to give our Friday night parties which were as well attended as ever. I told the Central Committee of the Mexican party of the "33 or 30-30" warning, but said nothing about it to friends or acquaintances.

I continued to watch the frescoes grow on the walls of the public buildings in Mexico. In 1923 I had written, I don't remember where, what was most likely the first article on the Mexican artistic awakening to be published north of the Rio Grande, and in the August 27, 1924 issue of the *Nation* I published an article entitled, "Art and Revolution in Mexico." Now, with time running out, I began to think of writing a book on Diego Rivera.

Since life had become more uncertain and we did not know when our Mexican journey which had lasted three and one half years might come to an end, Ella and I spent more time examining the wonder of beautiful baroque churches and incredibly bloody and suffering images of Christ. I made repeated visits to the publishing house of Vanegas Arroyo, who printed the flimsy vari-colored tissue paper broadsheet ballads that were sung and sold for a few centavos in the market places and plazas, and that bore as illustrations many of the marvelous drawings of one of the world's greatest popular artists, José Guadalupe Posada. The flimsy sheet ballads I purchased from Vanegas Arroyo were to form the foundation of my Master's thesis for Federico de Onís at Columbia University. In short, life went on even more richly than usual for us in the City of Palaces, and we continued our weekend hikes over the lava beds and in the rugged and beautiful mountains surrounding it. Our explorations were enriched now by the company of Diego Rivera, who would abandon his scaffold on Sundays to accompany Ella and me, with soft lead pencil and sketch book in his pockets, stopping briefly to make abbreviated sketches to jog his memory for future easel paintings and backgrounds for frescoes. I cannot tell how much it meant to us to see the countryside through an artist's eyes and to see "Riveras" down every mountainside and every stretch of road.

PREPARING FOR ARTICLE 33

If life seemed to go on as usual, only with greater intensity of feeling, we did not neglect preparation for whatever might be coming. For the 30-30 there was no way of preparing. Moreover, not only was I unafraid, but I did not believe they would use the 30-30 when the use of Article 33 of the progressive yet dictatorial or *caudillista* Constitution of 1917 was likely to cause less scandal. Two Americans I knew had been deported under Article 33 by Carranza—Linn Gale and Charles Philips. They had been seized and unceremoniously dumped over the border to Guatemala. If I were deported to the United States, I would need no transfer to the American party. But what if I should be deported to Guatemala? There I might need identification if I could find anyone to present it to, for I knew nothing of Guatemala, nor whether it had a Communist Party. Hence Ella took a piece of silk, typed on it a "To Whom it May Concern" transfer, which was signed by Rafael Carrillo and authenticated with the rubber stamp seal of the Mexican party. This Ella sewed into the lining of my jacket, along with some ten-dollar bills. Then, at the belt line, under the lining of my trousers, she sewed some Mexican ten-peso gold pieces. Henceforth I must be sure that I never left the house with any but that particular jacket and that particular pair of pants. Thus armed with document and *dinero*, I felt more secure. These were the only preparations we could make for a possible unexpected departure.

One morning—it was the 29th of June—I left our home on Cinco de Febrero, as usual on the verge of lateness for my 10 o'clock class at the Miguel Lerdo High School. I had to run the few blocks from our home to the Zócalo if I wanted to catch the bus that would get me to the school on time. But as I ran, I became aware that two men were running behind me. I was light and swift of foot and outrunning them, and grown-up Mexican men do not run on the street. Though they were in plain clothes I was sure that they were armed. I bethought myself of *la ley fuga* and slowed up to let my pursuers catch up with me, which, puffing and panting, they did.

"Excuse me, sir," said one of them with grave politeness after he had caught sufficient breath, "we have orders to take you to the Police Commissioner."

I did not ask for a show of credentials, for I knew they must be plainclothes men and what their orders signified. "There is a class of something like forty young ladies waiting for me at the Miguel Lerdo High School where I teach. May I not telephone the Directora of the school that I shall not be able to meet my class, so that she can dismiss them or send in a substitute teacher? I was due there at 10 o'clock and it is almost ten now. And may I not call my wife and tell her not to expect me for lunch?"

"I am very sorry, sir. Our orders say that you must be permitted to communicate with no one, but be taken directly to the commissariat. There are plenty of telephones there. No doubt the commissioner will permit you to telephone the Directora and your wife."

"What am I charged with? On whose orders? Why are you taking me to the commissariat?"

"I regret it greatly, sir, but they did not tell us why. All our orders say is that we were not to break into your home, but wait outside until you appeared and then apprehend you."

"Are we going by foot or have you a car?"

"Neither, sir. We go by *tranvía* (trolley car)." And with that they hailed a trolley, sat one on each side of me, and paid my fare. Did I have some names and addresses of party members in my pockets? I wondered. Cautiously, I transferred every scrap of paper into a single pocket, and then, when the trolleybus was going at full speed, ripped them up and dropped them as unobtrusively as I could out of the open window. They looked surprised, but made no attempt to stop me or to recover the scraps of paper. Apparently they had not been ordered to search me.

So it was "the 33" and not "the 30-30." Although the press always used the term "pernicious foreigner," Article 33 was even more sweeping than that term implied. Its actual text reads:

> . . . the Executive shall have the exclusive right to expel from the Republic forthwith, and without judicial process, any foreigner whose presence he may deem inexpedient.

Does the president of any democratic country have a more absolute right than this?

When we got to the commissariat, I was registered, photographed both full face and in profile, with a number held up before me so that it would appear in the pictures. Despite my indictments in the United States, this was the first and only time that I have been arrested, photographed, and fingerprinted. Since Article 33 does not allow an *amparo* or appeal to the courts, I knew there was no sense in asking for a lawyer. Moreover, though I knew many *licenciados*, none of them was a practicing lawyer. But couldn't I at least talk to my wife? I was told that I could telephone to no one and communicate with no one, and was sent with a jailer to an underground cell in the basement of the commissariat. I heard them tell my jailer that I was to be held incommunicado. He let me walk down the stone steps in front of him, unlocked the door of a large, empty cell (there was no other prisoner in the dungeon cellar within sight or earshot), held the door open for me with the familiar Mexican courtesy, then followed me into the cell and locked the door on both of us. Good! At least I would not be without company!

Since neither of us had anything to do, I engaged him in conversation. Did he know what I was charged with? He was sorry, he did not. How long would I be there? He had no idea. Then I talked to him of his personal life. How long had he been working at his present job? Did he have a family? How many children? What ages? I did not ask him whether they were well-behaved, for all the Mexican children of the poor and lowly seemed to me well-behaved and well brought up. Was he going out to lunch? I told him that my wife was expecting me home to lunch at twelve o'clock, and that she would be worried if I didn't show up. Could he take a message to her telling her only that I would not be home for lunch? I gave him the address, which was not too far off, and with it one of my ten-peso gold pieces, an enormous tip for which he was surprised and grateful, and I wrote a note in Spanish, so that he could not think it was anything mysterious, telling Ella where I was as far as I knew, that it was cold in the cellar, that it was fixing to rain in the afternoon—the summer is the Mexican rainy season—and that I would appreciate a warm flannel shirt and a woolen *sarape* or blanket, for I would probably have to sleep on the stone floor.

He went out to lunch rather late, and left me there without a substitute custodian. After his brief lunch, he really did deliver the note to Cinco de Febrero 47. It was long past my lunch hour, and my wife had guessed what might have happened. She went to Diego Rivero, and he called up Senator Monzón to try to get information as to where I might be in detention. While the senator was questioning people in authority, Diego and my wife had been driving in a hansom cab from prison to prison inquiring about me. The afternoon rains began, my wife was driven home to get a raincoat, and she found my note which the kind jailer had really delivered. She and Diego set out again, with a beautiful Mexican *sarape* in which was contained my flannel shirt and some fruit, such as the *ahuacate* or avocado.

My jailer returned just as it began to rain hard, and water began to fall in a torrent through the tiny slit of a window at the top of one wall, which opened on the street and served for ventilation. There was a drain in the middle of the cell, but it was probably clogged, and at any rate inadequate to take care of the water that was pouring in. On the three stone sides of the cell there was an elevated curb or step wide enough for us to stand on, so as water filled the floor we both stood on the elevation against the wall. But the water kept rising until finally my jailer said, "Stay here while I go to the office and see if I can get the two of us moved up to the third floor. There are many prisoners up there. The floors are of wood there and it is dry." His determination to try to get us both moved was sharpened when a rat emerged from a hole in the corner and began swimming about in the water.

In a few minutes he returned with the news that we were going up to the third floor. He walked ahead and I followed him up the stairs. By a miracle of luck, at that moment Diego and my wife entered the main floor as I reached it. They had not yet gone to the office to ask for permission to see me. Without a word, so as not to attract the attention of anyone, my wife thrust the sarape-wrapped bundle into my hand, and I silently followed my jailer up two flights of stairs. Then he caught sight of the bundle I had in my hand. "Where did that come from?"

"I had it with me," I said brazenly. He did not know what to say, so he said nothing. He brought me into a large guarded place with wooden benches around the walls, and a number of prisoners, all males, were seated on the benches. I put the bundle under me without examining it, and felt safer if I should have to spend a cold wet night on the stone floor of the underground dungeon.

My jailer got permission to leave me, for there were plenty of guards there. I began to examine and talk with my fellow cellmates in these new, dry, warm quarters. They were there, some told me, under charges of smuggling, of trafficking in narcotics, of conducting houses of prostitution. All of them were foreigners and spoke Spanish haltingly and with marked accents. Some expected to be deported as "pernicious foreigners" under Article 33. How long would their hearings take? Some had been there for weeks, some even for months. My fate, I supposed, would be like theirs.

In the meantime Senator Monzón, because he was a senator, had succeeded in learning through gossip and from people in authority, including the minister of *Gobernación*, that I was to be deported that same night on the seven o'clock train for the border. Because a railroad strike was brewing and because of my connections with the railwaymen, they were afraid to delay my departure, lest the strike date be advanced a few days and my departure made impossible. Moreover, they wanted nothing in the press until I was safely on my way, so that *Gobernación* would not make a statement on my deportation and the reasons for it until my journey had begun.

I don't remember now whether I was fed or not during that solitary day of detention, but neither do I remember leaving hungry. That same night I was taken in a government automobile to the railway station, with a chauffeur in uniform and two plainclothesmen, one on each side of me. Obviously they were to accompany me to the frontier. The only immediate problems were two nights of sleep and two days of food on the train.

To my surprise, I got a grand send-off. Monzón, Diego, my wife, the party secretary, Rafael Carrillo, Central Committee members, and others went from house to house. The heavy downpours rain themselves out early, and they had to go on foot, for few members had phones or could afford *coches.* There was a large gathering of friends on the platform to see me off, to wish me well, to cheer, and to sing revolutionary songs and folk songs, and there was even a red banner with a white hammer and sickle. I asked my two "fellow travellers" whether I could go out on the back platform of the observation car, and they agreed, provided I did not make any speeches but stood silently between them. For all the other passengers on the train could see, the three of us were getting a grand send-off, but only one of us threw a kiss to someone on the platform and waved good-bye to the crowd.

23

THE RETURN OF THE NATIVE

I soon lost sight of my wife and comrades and friends as the train roared and whistled into the darkness. A second engine was attached behind, for we were now to climb up to 10 or 12,000 feet to get out of the valley of Mexico. I went to the men's room, accompanied by one of my two fellow travelers whose mission was to see that I got back to my native land without escaping somewhere in Mexico. I looked at myself in the mirror. I had not shaved that morning. I had no razor with me, and it would be at least two more days before I could buy one in Texas. I was a sight to behold, trying to enter at the beginning of July into hot, southern Texas, unshaven, wearing a thick flannel shirt with long sleeves, and a heavy woolen suit donned against the rainy season. What would my reception by the immigration authorites be like, a man incongrously dressed for July weather in Texas, carrying all his effects tied up in a brightly colored Mexican *sarape,* a man being deported by "revolutionary" Mexico as "too revolutionary"? Would they throw me into a hot cell in a Texas prison while they telegraphed to Washington for orders concerning me? I had two indictments against me, one in California under the name of Albright, one in New York for "Criminal anarchy" under my own name of Wolfe. Would they discover that New York indictment while they held me in a prison in southern Texas, perhaps in Laredo, and for how long would I be held? Would the Mexican press have carried a story "explaining" why I was a pernicious foreigner deported personally by the "revolutionary" President Calles, before my train got to the frontier? Would the American reporters have taken their right foot off the brass rail at the Regis Bar long enough to file a story about me, telling why the Mexican president considered me dangerous? What would the president or the secretary of *Gobernación* say about me, and would they wait until I was safely over the border?

I returned to my seat between my two unknown companions, too tired by the day's experiences to wash up, and eager to find out what kind of men these two were, how much they knew about why I was being deported, and what miniscule privileges I could get from them by proper talk and a ten-peso gold piece for each of them.

"Señores," I said, "what orders do you have concerning me?"

"We have no orders," one of them answered, apparently the head of my guard, for he did all the talking. "No orders, sir, except not to let you out of our sight, to get you safely to the border."

"And what will you do with me at the border?"

"Deliver you to our chief inspector of immigration and get a signed receipt from him."

"And what will he do with me?"

"He will deliver you, I suppose, sir, to the chief inspector of immigration of Nuevo Laredo."

"And what does he do with deportees from Mexico?"

"We don't know, sir."

"Why are you taking me to the border?"

"I have no idea. We have no orders concerning you, except what I have told you. Oh yes, I have a sealed envelope to deliver to you. I have no knowledge of what it contains, but if you sign this receipt, sir, I will give it to you now." I took the envelope without opening it, because I thought it might be a discourtesy to open it in their presence and then not satisfy their natural curiosity concerning its contents. When I read it later in the men's room, I found that I was banished from Mexico "in perpetuity," and that if I attempted to return I would be punished by five years in prison and then deported again.

I decided that I must impress my two keepers properly before I tried the influence of gold upon them. Since they didn't know that my deportation was by presidential order, and since they showed by their courtesy that they felt they were not dealing with a common criminal, I told them that I was being deported by someone high in the government who disliked me, and he was taking advantage of the fact that my friend in the cabinet was out of the city of Mexico. When my friend returned and learned of it, I would soon be returning. This impressed them properly, for they obviously had no idea of what went on in high government circles. They were carrying out orders apparently with dispassion and disinterest. The conductor passed, and looked at me curiously, but did not ask them or me for tickets. Apparently he had his orders. I asked him whether the diner was still open, and he said it was.

"Would you like to go into the *comedor* and eat with me?"

"We have had our dinner," their spokesman answered, "but one of us will go in and sit with you if you wish to eat something."

After a snack, I asked, "Would you mind if I bought a sleeper? I will buy a whole section. You two can use the lower berth and I will take the upper. So we will all rest better, and you can watch me properly."

"Perfectamente, señor, we will take turns sleeping in the lower berth, and one of us will always be sitting up while you sleep." Thus I had a sound night's sleep which I badly needed.

The next day I took some proper occasion to thank my two companions for the courtesies they were showing me, and I asked them to accept a small token of my appreciation. The token was a ten-peso gold piece for each. They were genuinely surprised and grateful, for the police in Mexico, even the plainclothes detectives, were very poorly paid. Then after a suitable interval of random conversation I told them I should like to see the chief of immigration alone in his office. They agreed that this could be arranged, and they gave me his name so that I could address him properly. I was sure that they would tell him that this was an unusual deportee who handed out ten-peso gold pieces.

During the course of the day we stopped at Saltillo, capital of the state of Coahuila, a large railway junction where we took on water and coal, changed crews, and made a comparatively long stop. I asked if I could get off the train to buy a picture postcard and a stamp and write a brief note to my wife. They greatly regretted it, but their orders were that I could not get off the train until we reached Nuevo Laredo at the frontier. However, if I gave one of them the money, he would buy me a postcard and a stamp, and then he would mail it for me. He came back with the ugliest or most *cursi* picture postcard of a little girl, framed in spots of gold, with a gold ribbon on her hat, gold borders on her sleeves, a golden belt round her waist, two rings of gold spots on the bottom of her short skirt, and gold laces on her shoes. One of them lent me a pencil, and I scrawled the brief note: "Greetings and love from Santillo. Everything very pleasant. Tomorrow the border. B." One of them jumped off the train, found a post box and mailed it, and got back on the train just as it started to move. To Ella the note with the words, "everything very pleasant," was reassuring. And indeed, everything was pleasanter than I had expected, for my two guardians were courteous.

PROBLEMS OF BEING DEPORTED TO ONE'S OWN COUNTRY

As our train got nearer and nearer to the border at Nuevo Laredo, all my attention was concentrated on the problem of my outlandish attire, appearance, and baggage.

This was the second time I was entering my native land under peculiar and difficult circumstances. The first such occasion had occurred when I was approaching the port of New York on the *Stavangerfjord* with a Mexican passport and the Mexican name of Vargas Rea y Braun. I could not boldly allege my native birth and lifelong citizenship, for in this age of paper documents, one cannot enter nor leave one's country without showing a passport. There was no help for it; I must stand on the immigrant line and show my Mexican document. Would such an un-Mexican looking person be believed? Which would win out, my face or my passport? I had already gotten a foretaste of possible trouble on the *Stavangerfjord*. A little group of passengers from the first class had taken a liking to me and sometimes descended into second class to talk with me, sometimes invited me to their upper deck for a drink. One day a girl from that group came down alone and said to me, "Mr. Solomon says, 'Aw, he's no Mexican. He's only kidding. His English is too good. I know his type. He's probably a New York businessman, a Jew like me, returning from a trip, and he is kidding us.' "

I realized that that alarming rumor had to be squelched at once. "Do you want to make some money, Miss? Bet with him that I am a Mexican and can prove it to his own satisfaction."

"How much should I bet?" she asked, wide-eyed.

"Don't bet any money. It will be like taking candy from a kid. Bet him a box of cigars—the best you can buy on the boat—against a box of candy."

She left and soon returned. "Well, we made the bet. Now what?"

I went up with her to the little group gathered in the first-class bar, opened my jacket, and took out my Mexican passport, with seal and photo.

"Well, I'll be darned!" he said, and he agreed to pay his bet.

When our boat got to the port of New York, there was the usual early September crush, and there was a long line of immigrants from other ships, at the back of which I took my place. A woman was trying to answer the inspector's questions in Spanish, and he was having trouble. I stepped forward. "I can translate," I said. Then I translated for another passenger, from German. And then even managed with Italian. The inspector took me out of the line, glanced at my passport, and said, "You're O.K. You're a Mexican. You've got a Hungarian name (he mistook Vargas for *Farkas,* which, by a weird coincidence, is the Hungarian for *wolf*), and you speak a dozen languages. You're a good one. Go to the doctor and tell him Pete says you're O.K., and if he wants, you can translate for him." The doctor talked with me for two seconds, then without examing my eyelids for trachoma, nor making me walk to see if I could walk steadily, nor giving me any of the other tests he was giving to the rest of the immigrants, waved me on into another room where my meager baggage was examined, and I entered New York City a free man.

But the problem as we approached the Mexican border was quite different. I needed no passport, but I did need an explanation of my outlandish appearnace and my "immigrant" baggage wrapped in a peasant blanket. In Texas, I knew, they would all be wearing Palm Beach suits, short-sleeved shirts, light jackets or none at all. In Laredo or San Antonio one did not go to a hotel to register with all one's belongings wrapped in a Mexican blanket, and with a three-day's beard growth on one's unshaven face. Nor did anyone claiming to be a natural-born American present himself to our immigration inspectors in such garb and with such baggage. I thought of various explanations for my weird attire and appearance in an effort to find a plausible one which would not arouse suspicion, nor call undue attention to my bizarre getup. It was the first day of July; in southern Texas no one would conceivably don the attire I was wearing, much less carry such baggage. In my mind I formulated various alternative explanations and decided to let the circumstances as they developed determine which of them I should try.

We got to Nuevo Laredo, a smallish suburb of Laredo, Texas, with a borderline and a bridge between the two of them. Instead of waiting in the line of emigrants or immigrants, I was taken directly to the office of the Chief Inspector. The talkative guard went in and handed over a piece of paper for official signature, then whispered a few words about the strange sort of deportee they had been transporting to the border. I bade my two companions of the journey a friendly good-bye, for they had truly been courteous to me, and I was ushered into the presence of the chief inspector. I slipped him two of my gold pieces (higher rank, higher *mordida* was the rule in Mexico), and explained to him that I did not wish to be delivered personally into the hands of the American chief inspector of immigration, but would like to cross the International Bridge with as much propriety and dignity as possible. He said, "I will have one of our best border guards walk with you to the center of the International Bridge, where he will put you into the hands of an American soldier from their border guard. He will conduct you to his chief."

He called a Mexican soldier by his first name and gave him a few words of explanation which I could not hear. I brazenly handed the soldier my blanket bag. "Will you please carry this for me?" I asked. He did not object. Thus disencumbered, I marched in step with as much dignity as I could assume halfway across the International Bridge, where he switched the blanket bag from his right hand to his left, gravely saluted the American soldier on guard there, and with a flourish said: "An American gentleman returning to his country. Will you have the kindness to accompany him to the chief inspector of immigration?" I took the bundle from him, thanked him, and handed him a five-peso bill. Though I knew I could not tip an American soldier in the same way as a Mexican, I saw that my new guard was impressed by the respect that had been shown me. "Would you mind carrying this *sarape* for me? I have a sprained wrist." Without a word he took the bag and conducted me to the chief of immigration, where he set it on the floor before the chief's desk.

"What nationality?" he asked.

"American."

"Where were you born?"

"In Brooklyn."

"What's an American doing in Nuevo Laredo?"

I drew out of my pocket the credential of the *Federated Press* and the credential of *El Democrata* as reporter, which Benigno Valenzuela had issued to me when I went to Russia, and put them down in front of him, giving him time to read them. "I'm a newspaperman. There's a new rebellion brewing in Mexico, and I was sleeping up in the hills beyond

Saltillo among the rebel bands, trying to find out what I could about them, their numbers, leaders, and objectives."

"O.K." he said. "If you go out that door, you won't have to wait in the line for immigrants or the line for citizens. It leads right to the platform, and you can get on the train for San Antonio and points North."

I settled down on a seat in the train. When it began to puff and shake and move, I heaved a great sigh of relief. At last, my troubles were over; I was home in my native land. The train gathered speed, covered a substantial stretch of that great land mass called Texas, then came to a stop at a station where people got off and people got on. Among the latter was an plainclothes immigration inspector or detective looking for immigrants that had been smuggled into the country. He stopped dead before me, took in my outlandish attire and baggage, and roared, "Hey, you! Get off the train." I got off, silently cursing my luck. "Who are you? Where do you come from? In what country were you born? Where yuh goin'?"

"My name is Wolfe, Bert Wolfe. I'm a native-born American. I was born in Brooklyn, at 260 Ellery Street, in Williamsburg. I'm going to Chicago, then home. My home is still in Brooklyn. Lived there all my life."

My accent and fluency in my native tongue was enough to convince him. "O.K. Sorry I dragged you off the train. Get back on. It's beginning to move." I had sold newspapers and candy on the trains of the Long Island Railroad in my youth, so it was easy for me to take a flying leap onto the accelerating train.

I had barely caught my breath and relaxed when we hit another station. Another inspector! This time I was prepared. "Where were you born?" asked the plainclothes inspector. "Who wants to know? What business is it of yours?" I retorted.

"O.K., O.K.," he said. No one but an American would be so impudent, so he passed on, scrutinizing other passengers. At every stop from Laredo to San Antonio on this local train seeming to make all stops, it was the same story. But each time I became more self-confident and more impudent. I was not made to get off the train again.

In San Antonio I used the American money my wife had sewed into my coat to buy a light summer suit for something like ten dollars, a short-sleeved cotton shirt, a safety razor, some shaving soap, and a cheap suitcase which was made of heavy cardboard and covered with a thin layer of imitation leather cloth, and I dumped into it my heavy clothes, my blanket, and its contents to give it proper weight as baggage, locking it with the little key that went with it. Then I went back to the railroad station. In the men's room, for a quarter, I got into a cabinet with a shower, a mirror, a sink, a towel, and a bar of soap. I showered, shaved, put on my new summer clothes, took my new bag out of the baggage check, then marched to the nearest big and good-looking hotel, went to the registry desk and signed in, handed my bag to a bellboy, was ushered to a comfortable and quiet room, and went to the hotel's dining room to eat on credit by signing my name and room number on the check. I sent a wire to my wife telling her of my safe arrival and my address in San Antonio, and asking her to telegraph me money. I ate three meals a day at the hotel on credit until money arrived from her. Except for a haircut and a few tips I spent not a cent, for I was nearly penniless. Since I had baggage, the hotel clerk asked no questions. I settled down to wait for the replenishment of my purse and saw the sights of San Antonio on foot, for shoe leather, until it wears out, costs nothing. I formed an impression of San Antonio more favorable than that of any other town in Texas in which I have ever been. It had trees on many of its streets. It was a town full of energy and liveliness. I was particularly impressed by the fact that although the Alamo was in the very heart of the downtown skyscraper area, the citizens of San Antonio remembered their historical monument enough not to give in to the realtors who would have given many millions of dollars to move the Alamo to the outskirts of the town and build more skyscrapers on the little downtown park or square on which it stands.

A LESSON FOR HISTORIANS

While I was exploring San Antonio, the newspapers began to arrive from Mexico City with the accounts of my deportation. *Gobernación* waited until I had actually crossed the border before letting their people, and particularly the railwaymen, know of my deportation. Then the front-page headline in *Excelsior* let it be known that President Calles under Article 33 had deported a pernicious foreigner as a vendor of narcotics. It sounded more romantic in Spanish: "como Vendedor de Drogas Heróicas," *heróico* coming from the narcotic, heroin.

The next day's paper reported that Senator Monzón, senator from the state of Michoacán, had delivered an address in the senate which said: "Bertram Wolfe is well known in the city of Mexico and in our country. He has taught in our schools and in our union halls, he has written in our papers. Everybody knows what he does. Who will believe that he is a vendor of narcotics? It does not hurt him; it hurts our government to propagate such falsehoods. It makes us ridiculous. The government should withdraw its charge and tell the truth about him."

A day later *Gobernación* did drop the charge of "vendedor de drogas heróicas" and substituted the charge that "Señor Wolfe returned from Russia with $50,000 in Russian gold to foment a railroad strike."

Often I have teased fellow historians when we were discussing the question of "documentation," by pointing out the puzzle inherent in documenting this, my own case. If they read the official government statement of July 2nd, they seem perfectly justified in saying, "the Communist leader, Bertram Wolfe, was expelled from Mexico because he engaged in the sale of narcotics." But if they take instead the Mexican government statement of July 4th or 5th, they can write, as Stanley Ross, the author of a *History of Communism in Latin America,* wrote: "Bertram Wolfe was expelled from Mexico because he returned from Russia in 1924 with $50,000 in Russian gold to foment a railroad strike." Both are official statements of the Mexican Government, therefore, any historian seems justified in citing whichever one he finds as proper documentation. Yet one statement is as false as the other, a typical example of the problems of our craft when we try to rely on official government statements as sound documentation. Truly, Clio is a difficult Muse to serve. Not for nothing have historians themselves composed the aphorism: "God, though He is omnipotent, cannot change the past. Therefore He has created historians."

Realizing what expenses I would be put to by my deportation, the Russian legation in Mexico offered to pay for my trip to Chicago and New York. Leon Haykis came to my wife with $500 and an offer of whatever further funds were needed, but she decided not to accept a penny. From our meager savings she sent me the money I asked for. My hotel bill paid, I left for Chicago to meet with the Central Committee. Since I wanted to live in New York, they offered me the post of district organizer of the New York district, the largest and most important district in the country, to which they themselves were preparing to move. "I do not like organization or administrative work," I told them. "If you insist that I take up some full-time party work, I should prefer a post that will require writing, editing, and teaching, work for which I am better suited by temperament and ability." This led to my being appointed director of the Workers' School of New York, and subsequently overseer of all the party's educational and editorial work. I called the post *Educational Director,* but I found that while I had been in San Francisco and Mexico, the party center had become increasingly Russianized or "Bolshevized," and they designated me in Russian fashion, *Agitprop Director,* that is, *Director of Agitation and Propaganda.* The term stuck in my craw; I continued to think of myself as educational director, but got used to seeing my signature at times followed by the term, *Agitprop Director.*

At the Fifth Congress of the Comintern I had heard Zinoviev proclaim it as the duty of all parties to "Bolshevize" themselves, which meant to become more and more like the Russian party. Now, only a year later, I found the American Party, under Comintern orders, abolishing the old neighborhood branches customary for the old Socialist Party and indeed for all American political parties, and substituting a system of shop committees, in which each member met in a "shop nucleus." By this arbitrary order we not only lost our American aspect, but we lost countless members who did not work in a shop where there were enough members to form a shop nucleus, or who did not work in a shop at all. Too late we attempted to take care of them by rebuilding neighborhood, precinct, and district organizations. But these were proclaimed as inferior to the shop nuclei, less "Bolshevik" and less "revolutionary," and those who put emphasis on neighborhood organization were in some cases being expelled as a "Right Danger," another direct import from Russia. I felt the same uneasy feeling about the word *Agitprop* as I did at the Michigan convention about the substitution of an authoritative *Presidium* for our American-type *Chairman.* But I held my peace, for I first had to find out what had been going on in the American Communist Party during my three-and-one-half-year stay in Mexico. Moreover, I found that the American Party was once more tied up in factional knots, and that it was virtually impossible to work in it without knowing what the factions were fighting about, and deciding with which faction to line up.

While I was in Mexico, in the early Spring of 1925, an old Bolshevik, a contemporary of Lenin and his supporter from the outset, was presented to my wife and me by Pestkowski. "This comrade wants to get into the United States as the Comintern representative to the American Communist Party. Can you two help him?" We sized him up. He was a short man with a little potbelly, a fleshy face, looking for all the world like a certain type of American-Jewish businessman. My wife volunteered to teach him English and slaved with him day after day—he was a good linguist—until he could speak English fluently. I sent to the American Party for identity cards; he was given the name on the identity cards and later assumed the name of P. Green. I decorated his button hole with a little American flag and his lapel with an Elk's button, and, dressed in an American-type suit, he was quite ready to cross the border as an American businessman returning from a visit to Mexico.

Meanwhile, I learned a great deal about him. His real name was Yakov Davidovich Drabkin, but for years he had used the name Sergei Ivanovich Gusev (pronounced, *Gusiev*). In the faction fight going on in the Russian party he was a supporter of Stalin, and, because of certain experiences in the Red Army during the civil war, a bitter enemy of Trotsky.

Gusev asked me what I thought of the situation in the American Communist Party. "It is torn by factionalism," I told him (which was no news to him). "Coming in with the authority of a Comintern representative, you can do a great deal of good if you can break down the faction walls and unify it. The leader of one group, the Ruthenberg-Lovestone Group, is Jay Lovestone. He is the Party's best political leader. The other faction is headed by William Z. Foster, a veteran trade union leader who led the stockyard strike and the steel workers' strike, and headed the Trade Union Educational League. The Party needs both experienced trade union leaders and experienced political leaders. If you can force them to work together and can unite the party and end the faction war which takes up all their energy, you will be performing the best possible service."

What I did not know was that Gusev was an early Stalinist, sent to spread the Russian faction fight to the American Party and to weaken the Foster faction because it contained a number of people, including one of its leaders, James P. Cannon, who were inclined to Trotsky. He was going to the American Party to deepen the fight, strengthen the Lovestone-Ruthenberg faction, and weaken, even destroy, the strength of the Foster-Cannon faction. When he got into the United States—without difficulty—he said to Lovestone, "Your friend, Bertram Wolfe, in Mexico, is very naive." Lovestone later repeated his verdict to me.

If to oppose factionalism, to deplore the exhaustion of all the Party's strength in inner warfare so that it has almost no energy left to carry on the fight for its declared programmatic objectives was naive, then I was naive indeed. The fact that the official representative of the Comintern considered my view naive showed what the American Party was in for. Such representatives were going to all the parties, ultimately to turn the Comintern into the Stalintern. But this was still concealed by the fact that Stalin remained in the background, while Bukharin, who also opposed Trotsky, still seemed to be the leading figure in the Communist International. Stalin had used Zinoviev against Trotsky and was now using Bukharin against Zinoviev and Trotsky; and it was to be my fate to be in Russia when Stalin turned on Bukharin, too, and stepped forth as the sole leader of the Communist International.

When I reached the Central Committee headquarters in Chicago, my first thought was to find out what was happening in Mexico. There was a letter from my wife, copies of *El Machete,* issue Number 4 of *El Libertador,* and a report from the Secretary of the Party, Rafael Carrillo. My sudden deportation had caused a certain amount of demoralization, and the things that had depended largely upon my personal activity were coming to a standstill.

I had been giving a class in economics in the railway carpenters' hall; I tried to keep it up and bring it to a decent close by sending notes for a few forthcoming sessions, in Spanish and in considerable detail, with the hope that the party secretary, Rafael Carrillo, would carry on the class in my name. But he did not have the age, the experience in teaching, or the authority and self-confidence needed. My wife's letter said: "Your *apuntes* (notes) for the class arrived in good time, but alas no class was given. Two weeks have gone by without a class, things are badly demoralized. . . . The railway unification [for the formation of a strike committee] is not going as it should be . . . our railway 'communists' instead of sticking together are fighting among themselves right out in open meetings, and last night the electricians got up and said that they would walk out, that the work done did not seem to them to be of a unifying type." (Actually, the railway strike broke out as scheduled, but the locomotive engineers never did join, and the government easily crushed the strike.)

The same letter, dated July 10, 1925, continued: "Last night Monzón, Alfaro Siqueiros, and Rafael went out on a binge *(paranda)*, and all became dead drunk, there was *balazos* (shooting) y quien sabe que más . . . that's the stuff we have to build with. . . . I've been sad all day, and Rafael, after confessing to me some of the things that had happened, was as quiet as a puppy dog, he looked whipped although I did not say a word to him." The Soviet minister and his wife had taken Ella to a movie she had already seen with me and were inviting her to share their box at a puppet show in the theater *Esperanza Iris* on the following evening. On evenings when the Pestkowskis did not visit her, the first secretary, Leon Haykis, did.

"The Directora of the school thought your expulsion was quite terrible, and she said that she would be glad to see another revolution coming soon just to show this government that it could not be so arbitrary. . . . She also offered me her home, really very sincerely, she wants me to finish up the year, but I guess not, what say?"

All in all, not a very cheering letter. A look at Number 4 of *El Libertador* was more cheering. They had succeeded in getting out an issue of 20 pages. There were some new contributors—one signing himself *Espartaco*, another *Atahualpa*—the announcement of the formation of a branch of the Liga Anti-Imperialista in Cuba, an article by Haya de la Torre, a letter from Isidro Fabela, and an article by *Audifaz*, the name under which I continued to write in Mexican papers for a long time after my expulsion.

The surprise for me was that they had pulled out the material we had prepared for page 3 and substituted an article entitled "La Deportación de Bertram D. Wolfe." There was a warm and flattering description of me, a denunciation of President Calles for having declared himself antiimperialist in words, but, at the first suggestion from the Yankee ambassador, having deported "like a common criminal a true friend of the Mexican people and one of the most active fighters against *el imperialismo estadounidense*." They expressed their confidence that my deportation would not lessen my activities on behalf of the Mexican people. Through me they sent fraternal greetings to the people of the United States.

Perhaps if I had made a *cause célèbre* of my deportation instead of trying to reenter my native land as quietly as possible, the American people might have listened for a day or two. At any rate I was pleased at my comrades' journalistic sense in putting out an article, and gratified by their kind words. I was glad to see, too, that *El Libertador*, Number 5, prepared in July and dated August, appeared on time without my help, except for another article signed *Audifaz*. But then, unexpectedly, *El Libertador* ceased its brief five months of existence. Was it because I was gone and there was no one else with similar editorial experience to take my place? Or was it that Minister Pestkowski, or Commissar Chicherin, after carefully considering President Calles' sharp rebuke of those who would use Mexico as a staging ground for international political aims, had thought better of making up *El Libertador*'s considerable deficits? I think that it was probably the latter.

Perhaps one more remark is in order concerning Mexico's attitude towards the pernicious foreigner whose right to live and teach in Mexico, President Calles had considered "inexpedient." In September of that same year, only two months after my expulsion under police escort, I received a beautifully engraved invitation from the Mexican ambassador in Washington to join him in the embassy's annual celebration of the 16th of September, Mexico's Independence Day, "as a life-long friend of Mexico." And, despite my "perpetual banishment," I have been back to Mexico at least five times, the last time directly invited by President Echeverría, both to his palace and to a festive breakfast in the Inner Court of the Anthropological Museum.

I soon learned that I could not keep up my work in Mexico once I was caught up in work in the United States. For a while I kept writing articles in Spanish for *El Machete* to show Calles that he couldn't silence me by deportation. But one cannot keep on writing for a country if one is not in the midst of its daily life: in time my voice grew still. When I returned to Mexico in the thirties it was to do other things in another context.

Before I close the present chapter of my life, I should say a word about the fate of Alvaro Obregón, for whose ability as general and as statesman I have the highest praise. When he finished his first term, which coincided with most of my stay in Mexico, he rightly felt that his work in reconstructing the battle-scarred country was still incomplete. The army had too many generals, and he had begun to remove them. He was carrying out, yet toning down—who knows how far he would have gone?—the Constitution of 1917. He was working out a rapprochement with the United States with more dignity and pride than General Calles showed. He seemed to be fighting that growing corruption of the "men of the revolution in power," which was to enrich Calles and the Callistas. He would like to have run for reelection, i.e., succeed himself for a second term, but the slogan, "Sufragio Efectivo—No Reelección" had become a fetish since the overthrow of Diaz who had ruled from 1887 to 1911. During Obregón's term of office, every official letter had ended with that slogan. So he put Calles into the presidency for an interim term of four years, after which he planned to run again. This was to be looked on not as reelection, but as a fresh election after four years of retirement to his farm in Sonora.

He easily got nominated without a murmur by the Government party and was automatically elected. Then, since a new rebellion seemed impossible after his chastening of the deserting generals, attempts were made to assassinate him. First an attempt at assassination was made in the woods of Chapultepec Park, near the presidential palace. Then on November 13, 1927, a car passed him on the road, and from it men hurled two bombs and fired ten or twelve pistol shots. He seemed to live a charmed life, for all he suffered was some small wounds in his back and face from flying glass. With characteristic bravado he went to a bullfight that same afternoon.

On July 17, 1928, a large party was given in honor of his second election in the *Restaurant La Bombilla* near San Angel, a fashionable suburb of Mexico City. There was music, feasting, drinking, and no speeches. An artist accredited to one of the two big dailies approached him with a sketchbook and soft lead pencil, and a bandaged left hand, asked if he might draw a caricature of the President, and began to show him other caricatures in his sketchbook. Suddenly he drew a tiny repeating pistol from the bandaged hand and fired six shots. It was for Mexico an unprecedented form of assassination; the charmed life of Alvaro Obregón was at an end. Plutarco Elías Calles, until then a front man for Obregón, became the boss of Mexico and determined the nomination and election of each president, until he named Cárdenas, with disastrous results for himself. It was under the Cárdenas regime, in 1936, that I decided to try a return to Mexico.

24

THE FACTIONAL WAR IN THE AMERICAN PARTY AND THE COMINTERN

The Communist Party into which President Calles' deportation order catapulted me was a party that had changed so much that it was unrecognizable to me. Although I had received its journals and its confidential documents while I lived in San Francisco and in Mexico, documents alone could not tell me how much the party had changed during my absence from New York, the largest and most important district in the United States. Though for a few years the party Central Committee was kept in Chicago to locate it "nearer to the center of the United States," the real center remained in New York. When I left for San Francisco, I was cut off from all genuine news of what was going on there. Still more remote was my life in Mexico and the Mexican Communist Party. No reading of the *Daily Worker* (published at first in Chicago, too), nor of confidential and secret party bulletins, nor of mysterious letters from Lovestone, written at first in secret code language in which the Central Committee was called the "board of directors" and the members were called "stockholders," could possibly inform me as to what was going on in the life and work of the American Communist Party. Now I had to learn what had happened and what changes had occurred during the five years or so of my life in San Francisco and Mexico, both "foreign countries" as far as knowledge of the inner life of the American Communist Party was concerned.

A SINGLE WORLD PARTY

The first notable change was that by the summer of 1925 all important decisions for the American Communist Party were being made in Moscow. If there were differences in the American party, both sides (or if there were more than two, all sides) would make their appeals to Moscow. More often than not, Moscow would send back ambiguous decisions which all sides could claim as victories for themselves. Then the Comintern might send over a representative to settle the matter, a representative already armed with secret instructions from the Russian Faction or Russian delegation to the Executive Committee of the Comintern (ECCI). Or Moscow would order each contestant to send a representative, or even a small delegation, to present its views. While Moscow was considering the matter and preparing its decision on the controversy, the whole question had to be held in abeyance in America, and the American party was kept stalled concerning it.

A conundrum was already current in the party:

"Why is the Communist Party like the Brooklyn Bridge?"

"Because it is suspended by cables."

This phenomenon was something new in the history of international socialism. All through the nineteenth century, and until the Leninist seizure of power and the formation of the Comintern in the first quarter of the twentieth century, no American Socialist, anarchist, syndicalist, or trade unionist could ever have imagined that his decisions might be made for him and his controversies settled for him in Berlin, in Paris, in London, in Rome, or still less, in Moscow. The Communists were the first organized body to belong to a centralized, disciplined, international organization, attached to, glorying in, commanded and financed by a party that had power over a great country—the greatest land empire in the world, and in all history. Because of the persuasiveness of power and the wonder of success after a century of failures and sacrifices of the radical movements, most members of the American party gloried in being "the American section" of a single, unified, worldwide International which had its seat of power and privilege in Moscow.

And indeed, though I found this Russianization or "Bolshevization" of an American party distasteful, I was forced to recognize that the first decisions made in Moscow were salutary and beneficial. When I left the Michigan convention to go to Boston and thence to Mexico, the Goose Caucus had a majority in the party and favored keeping the American party permanently "revolutionary" by keeping it permanently underground. The Communist International, having first healed the split between the two rival Communist parties—the Communist Party of America and the Communist Labor Party—and then between the American Communist Party and the United Communist Party, next turned its attention to forcing the incurable undergrounders of the Goose Caucus to dissolve their faction under pain of expulsion if they refused. After the Michigan convention was over, the plenipotentiary representative of the Comintern, Valetski (Waletski or Brooks) bullied the Communist United Toilers into dissolving their underground organization and uniting with the officially recognized Communist Party, which was already living a legal life in the changing atmosphere of America in the shape of the legal Workers' Party of America. Then there were still two parties, working together in unison and common consensus, the reluctantly illegal party known as "No. 1," and its legal reflection, the Workers' Party, known as "No. 2." If the reader finds this confusing, so did many of the members. In any event, the illegal and legal American parties merged under cabled orders from Moscow in 1923. Though there were a few holdouts who dug yet deeper underground in Boston among the Letts (for all I know they may be deep down there still), by the time I got back to the United States, the Workers' Party had changed its name to the Workers' (Communist) Party and had openly affiliated with the Communist International, while the underground party, known in code as "No. 1," had merged with it and disappeared.

Though I had originally joined the Socialist Party only because it seemed to stand steadfast in keeping America out of Europe's wars and opposing the unwholesome wartime hysteria that developed in the United States and had found myself imperceptibly stampeded into a Communist Party without rightly knowing what Communism was, and though I had tried to make it a party which was American in its ways and aims and that did not reject our heritage, I too was gradually being "Bolshevized," and I too rejoiced that the Communist International had pressured us to end our factionalism and set up an open, legal, unified party.

But almost immediately I became aware of the fact that a new factional struggle was developing in the party, more bitter, more causeless, and more absurd than the struggle between "Geese" and "Liquidators" that had just ended so fortunately.

As soon as Lenin died in 1924, and even while he lay mute and bedridden in late 1922 and throughout 1923, a bitter fight began in the Russian Communist Party over the question: Who will be Lenin's successor? A struggle over the succession is the penalty that total revolutions pay for rupturing the legitimacy of the old regime that they overthrew. The American Revolution is an exception, for we had a continuing system of government; as free-born Englishmen; with our colonial or provincial legislatures; our governors; our Continental Congress; our Articles of Confederation; our Constitution and Bill of Rights, and the good sense to elect a President who had the grace to recognize that to accept more than two terms as President might make him into a dictator or a monarch. Our revolution lacked, too, the blood purges and the terror characteristic of other revolutions. Hence we developed neither a Bonaparte, nor a Hitler, nor a Stalin. One of the greatest of the achievements of our Revolution, in contrast with the French and the Russian, is that all our leaders, save only Alexander Hamilton, died in bed. And Daniel Shays and the leader of the Whiskey Rebellion, and Jefferson Davis and Robert E. Lee, too, died in bed, Lee revered by North and South alike and the president of a university at the time of his death. Only totalitarian revolutions end by the revolution's devouring its own children.

The Russian Revolution ruptured the legitimacy of inheritance by royal blood. For a moment they had a chance and prospect of developing a new democratic legitimacy to take its place in the form of the Constituent Assembly, chosen by the first universal (i.e., male) democratic suffrage in the history of Russia and assigned the task of creating a new constitution and thus a new democratic legitimacy. But Lenin dispersed the Constituent Assembly by force of arms. It was not the Tsar that the Bolsheviks overthrew, as so many believe, but the nascent democracy of the Constituent Assembly and the Provisional Government. Thus the rupture of royal legitimacy was followed by the rupture of democratic legitimacy, and from that day to this no legitimacy has existed in Russia, nor have the Bolsheviks ever been willing to submit their actions to the judgment of their people in free, democratic, multiparty elections. If a Kennedy is shot, or a Franklin Roosevelt dies in office, we know instantly who is to succeed him. But if a Lenin or a Stalin dies, there is a temporary "collective leadership" followed by a struggle for succession. It was such a struggle for the succession after Lenin's death that began a terrific and brutal factional fight in Russia, in the Russian Communist Party, and in the Comintern. First Zinoviev, Stalin, Kamenev, and Bukharin began a merciless struggle (no holds barred) against Trotsky. Then Stalin and Bukharin began a struggle against Zinoviev, or, after they united, against Zinoviev and Trotsky. Then Stalin began a struggle against Bukharin. And how this ended with the killing of more Communists under Stalin than in any anti-Communist regime in the rest of the world, is common knowledge. Each of these struggles in turn was carried into the Comintern and poisoned the life of every Communist party in the world.

As I have said, there were two factional groupings in America, the Ruthenberg group, which favored our support of the building of an American Farmer-Labor Party, and the Foster group, which opposed giving support to such a party. The leaders of the Communist International had messed up this situation at a great distance from the American scene. Just before I was deported from Mexico, they had first given the American Communists instructions to support a Farmer-Labor Party, then to support the candidacy of La Follette, then, just as suddenly, they had ordered the American party to withdraw all support from the Farmer-Labor Party and the La Follette movement, and to run their own ticket with Foster for president and Gitlow (of the Ruthenberg group) for vice-president. When the ballots were counted, La Follette had won five million votes out of 30,000,000 cast, and the Communist ticket had polled only 33,000 votes. When Sergei Gusev, the Comintern rep, arrived in the United States, that was what the Foster group and the Ruthenberg group were quarreling about. Had the 33,000 votes been a victory or a defeat? Was the idea of a Farmer-Labor Party still viable? Should the Communists continue to work for such a party? Without Comintern interference, this issue would sooner or later have died a natural death, for La Follette was returning to the Republican Party, and the labor movement was beginning to lose interest in the idea of forming a labor party.

But as with most factional feuds in the Communist Party, behind the issues and masked by them was a personal struggle for power in the party. In this struggle William Z. Foster had built up a slight majority for the forthcoming party convention to be held in Chicago beginning August 21,

1925. He built it by amalgamating some totally disparate groups, including the Lore group, which had always opposed the labor party tactic, and the powerful Finnish Federation, which if all its members voted, had a membership in Finnish clubs and cooperatives and the like of some seven thousand, close to half the membership of the party. Actually, most of these 7,000 took no part in Communist Party activity and never attended a regular party meeting. They were a clannish folk, rich in cooperatives, in gymnastic clubs, singing societies, excursion or hiking clubs, printing plants, three daily Finnish newspapers, club houses where they met each other. But if they paid their dues, or if their leaders paid dues and purchased dues stamps for them, they were entitled to vote for convention delegates in the states where they had their settlements, and they voted *en bloc* as their leaders told them to. The Comintern rep, Gusev, who did not go out into the field at all to see what American party life down below was like, ruled that all the votes of these club and cooperative members, who were totally inactive in party life, had to be counted for the Foster group, and that the Foster group therefore was entitled to 60 percent of the delegates to the August convention, and the Ruthenberg group to forty percent.

Yet mundane party activity and issues such as the labor party question were of no interest to Gusev. What we did not know was that Gusev had instructions in his pocket to break up the disparate Foster group into its multiple components, and to drive out of it all those who still had, or were even now in 1925 acquiring, an interest in the fate of Leon Trotsky and an admiration for his role in the seizure of power in 1917 and in the organization and victory of the Red Army in the civil war. For Gusev and the Comintern and Russian party leaders, the Foster group was the worse of the two because it was corroded by the presence of "Trotskyites" within it.

Among the "Trotskyites" was Ludwig Lore, the loyal, old-fashioned, left-wing Socialist, the editor of the New York *Volkszeitung*, the oldest Socialist newspaper in the United States. He had joined, and had brought his newspaper into, the Communist movement, but he disapproved of many of the examples of Communist maneuvering. He had disapproved of the Farmer-Labor party maneuver, of the support of the La Follette maneuver, and of the "Bolshevizing" of the American party by breaking up its assembly district organizations into shop nuclei. And in the columns of his paper he had praised the services of Leon Trotsky to the victory of Bolshevism in Russia. What was worse, when the Comintern had denounced "Loreism" as a "right danger" and declared Ludwig Lore unfit for leadership or even membership in the Communist Party, he had had the nerve to defend himself in the columns of the *Volkszeitung* against the infallible pronouncements and infallible verdicts of the Communist International's Executive Committee. He was ordered to Moscow to listen to their strictures. He refused to go. He was ordered to come to our convention to listen to the strictures we were ordered to level against him. Again he refused. Then the Comintern ordered the American party to wage a campaign against "Loreism." This was the first blow against the Foster group. More serious—although this would not become manifest until our convention was over—James P. Cannon, second in command in the Foster group, was acquiring an admiration for Leon Trotsky which would lead him, for the rest of his life, to be the leader of the American Trotskyite movement.

HOW I BECAME A DELEGATE TO THE CONVENTION

I was a delegate to the August, 1925, convention (The Fourth Convention) of the Workers' Communist Party in Chicago and was an eyewitness to the dramatic scene that I am about to narrate. But first I must tell how a man who was deported from Mexico at the beginning of July, 1925, could be elected a delegate to an American party convention which began on August 21, i.e., only a little over a month and a half after I entered Texas. As soon as I got the money from my wife at my San Antonio hotel, I left San Antonio for Chicago and presented myself at the headquarters of the Central Committee of the American party. I was given a warm welcome by everybody there, as the first man ever to be deported from a foreign country to the United States because he was an active Communist. All other deportations had gone the other way, from the United States to some other country.

As soon as I asked anybody how things were going in the Workers' Party, each man began telling me of the bitter fight for party control being waged between the Foster group and the Ruthenberg group. At first I couldn't make head or tail out of their explanations of what the fight was about. I decided that I had to get my explanation from the top faction leaders of each group. I went to Lovestone, who, I knew, was the faction organizer of the Ruthenberg group. I must admit that I was bewildered by what I heard. Since both groups had zealously accepted the orders of the Comintern—for a Farmer-Labor Party then against a Farmer-Labor Party; for La Follette then against La Follette; unanimously for a Communist ticket of their own then splitting again between pro and anti views of the need and possibility of forming a labor party in the United States—each explanation, filled with factional bitterness, left me more bewildered than before. I told Lovestone, an old friend of mine since the days in which I joined the Socialist Party and helped form its Left Wing, that I was going to Foster's office to get his version of the fight. "Go ahead," said Lovestone, "by all means. Listen to both sides and then make up your mind which faction you agree with. But I must tell you that the party is so divided, that if you want to be really active in it, you will have to join one side or the other. There are no free floaters. Or if there are, they never get anywhere, and nobody ever hears of them."

"I'll make up my mind when I'm ready, Jay."

"O.K. Good luck!"

I went to Foster's office. "Bill," I said, "I've come to find out from you what all the shooting is about. I've been in Mexico, and I know nothing about what's going on here—what you stand for or what Ruthenberg stands for."

I could see the suspicion in his eyes. Knowing that I had long been intimate with Lovestone, he did not believe that I was not lined up. Manifestly he thought that I had come to spy on his group and its plans for the coming convention. "Bill," I said to disarm him, "I want you to know that I am an old admirer of yours and of the TUEL. In San Francisco I was one of the founders of the TUEL, a member of the Cooks' Union, and its delegate to the Central Trades and Labor Council. At heart I am an opponent of factionalism and believe that in the party there is a place for you in the leadership and for Lovestone and Ruthenberg in the leadership. You are the Party's most experienced trade union leader, and Lovestone, I think, is its best political leader. You ought to be working together, but since there is such a bitter fight on, and everybody seems to be lined up in one faction or the other, I should like to know what each group stands for if I have to choose between them."

I did not succeed in disarming him. He got more suspicious, more surly, more taciturn, as I tried to draw him out. I got nowhere. Finally I gave up. Next I returned to Lovestone. He talked freely. He explained the complexities of the fight on the Labor Party, and I understood what I could of the explanation. He talked about a newcomer in the party leadership and in the Ruthenberg group, one John Pepper, who had written a pamphlet called *For a Labor Party.* John Pepper turned out to be a pseudonym for Pogany, War Commissar in the short-lived Hungarian government of Bela Kun. He claimed that he was born in San Francisco, because all the birth records there had been burned in the San Francisco earthquake. Actually, he had been sent to the Michigan congress along with Valetski-Brooks and had been permitted to stay in the American party, where he quickly assumed a position of leadership in the Ruthenberg group because of his great skill in discovering differences between the European and the American scene.

After much talk with Lovestone and with other party leaders of both factions, I finally threw in my lot with the Ruthenberg group. My chief reason was that they were still in favor of the party's trying to encourage the development of a Farmer-Labor party movement. There was sentiment for it in a number of mid-Western states. The Farmer-Labor party of Minnesota was a going concern that managed to win a senator, Senator Lundeen, and a governor, Governor Olson. There was a strong sentiment for a Farmer-Labor party in the states of Washington, Oregon, and California. The workingmen in many industries were indignant that the wartime high cost of living continued into peacetime, but the wartime jobs in shipyards, in uniform-making, in transportation, etc., were being cut back, and those working in them were being thrown into the pool of the underpaid and the unemployed. The courts were granting injunctions wholesale against strikes. There had been an amazing general strike in Seattle. Wages were being cut, and the wartime fever continued for a while in the use of the term, "un-American," for strikes and attempts to organize the unorganized. The Conference for Labor Political Action of the railway workers had been on the edge of forming a labor party. So, for a variety of such reasons it seemed to me that there was still a chance in America of building a Labor party something like that in Britain. Of course, I proved wrong. All these were temporary signs of discontent which vanished during the period of Harding "normalcy," but for the moment the current swept me into the pro-Labor party, Ruthenberg, Lovestone, Pepper group. Moreover, I found it pitiful and absurd for Foster to call it a great victory that 33,000 votes had been counted for him and Gitlow, out of a total of 30,000,000 votes cast. Indeed, his eyes shifted away from mine as he told me of this "great Communist victory" with its own ticket.

For its part, the Ruthenberg group welcomed me and showed enough confidence in me to send me to represent their viewpoint in Pittsburgh at the general membership meeting that was to elect delegates to the convention. I do not remember whom the Fosterites sent to hold up their side, but when the vote took place, I had not only swept the Pittsburgh membership into the Ruthenberg camp, but they actually chose me as one of the three delegates to represent Pittsburgh at the convention. Thus I represented a town that I had never seen before in my life, and found myself one of its three delegates. That is how I came to witness, close up, the most dramatic scene that occurred in the Fourth Convention of the Workers' (Communist) Party of America.

THE COMINTERN PICKS OUR LEADERSHIP

There was a bitter fight over every point on the order of business. The fighting began with the battle in the Credentials Committee. From each district but Pittsburgh came two delegations, each claiming to have been elected. It reminded me of a Mexican election. Each side claimed that nonmembers, or members not in good standing because they had not paid their dues, were permitted to vote, distorting the election returns. Finally, Comintern rep Gusev had to intervene. He set up a Parity Commission Presidium with three members from each group and with him as the arbitrator having a deciding vote on all questions that were deadlocked. He would not listen to our contention that only a handful of Finns were entitled to vote by being active party members, but insisted that the Finnish leaders had paid dues for every Finn who belonged to a club or cooperative, thus permitting those who had never come to a party meeting to have their votes counted as genuine. In retrospect I cannot blame him, for the circumstances of extreme illegality in which he lived prevented him from going out to the countryside to see how a few score Finnish votes became seven thousand. In the end, as mentioned previously, he awarded Foster 60 percent of the delegates and Ruthenberg 40 percent, and since he spoke with the master's voice, the voice of the Comintern, there was nothing we could do about it. There was no higher court to appeal to, unless and until we went to Moscow, and there they would understand less about the voting in America and in our party and about the bloc voting of foreign federations than Gusev did.

We were in despair, but Foster exulted and began to use his majority with the ruthlessness practiced in the trade unions with which he was so familiar. On every topic there were coreports. On the question of the American party's fight against imperialism, for instance, because of my Mexican experience, I was made coreporter for the minority. Strange to relate, the reporter for the majority was Manuel Gomez, who had been deported from Mexico a few years earlier than I, by being thrown over the Guatemalan border.

In the meantime, the Ruthenberg group made all the secret arrangements concerning the living quarters of Gusev and spent social evenings with him, during which he gave us suggestions on how to fight "Loreism" as a sort of semi-Trotskyism in the Foster group. He warned us not to press Foster too hard lest we lose him. He told us stories of his contempt for Trotsky and his admiration for Stalin.

Did he give Foster, to whom his decisions had given a 60 to 40 majority of the Convention delegates, similar warnings, not to oust Ruthenberg and Lovestone from their posts? He hinted that he had done so, and went so far as to suggest that it might be possible to make a rift between Cannon and Foster, who both aspired to the leadership of the Foster group. His conversations with us kept us on edge, yet hinted that Foster might yet be blocked from using his majority to oust Ruthenberg and Lovestone from the leadership. Gusev himself became alarmed at the bitterness of the faction fight, at the danger of a split, at the devoted bands of strong-arm trade unionists used to fight hired gangsters on their picket lines, who had been mobilized to defend the leaders of each side.

The Chicago membership meeting, held just before the convention, ended in a riot in which Foster himself could not get the floor. In the biggest district, New York, the membership meeting ended in what was practically two conventions with two sets of returns. Yet the resolution to expel Lore got a unanimous vote from both sides. Foster did not dare defend Lore, knowing that the Comintern leaders had selected him as a scapegoat, but the loss of Lore and those who followed or admired him greatly weakened the Foster forces. No one except Gusev seemed to know how the bitter fighting would end. When he spoke in the parity commission (he could not appear in the open convention), he spoke slowly, quietly, preserved an appearance of actual impartiality, restrained now one side, now the other, as their bitterness got the better of them. He reminded the Foster caucus that they had gotten 60 percent of the delegates because time and his special position did not permit him to go to every district and investigate all the appeals. He reminded the Ruthenberg group that they were in the minority, but he never suggested that they give up the fight for their position or yield on any matter of principle. Then, when the deadlock seemed unbreakable, and Foster reiterated his intention of using his majority to prevent the reelection of Ruthenberg and Lovestone to their posts, this calm, reserved parity arbitrator cabled a report to his comrades in Russia, telling them exactly what instructions they should cable back to him. He enjoyed the absolute confidence of Bukharin and Stalin and the other top leaders, and they cabled back to him verbatim what he had suggested. On August 28, the eighth hot, sweltering day of the Chicago Convention, he once more called together the parity commission in his secluded hideout, pulled a cable out of his pocket, and handed it to Ruthenberg who, as secretary of the party, read it aloud to the Parity Commission with suppressed excitement:

Communist International decided under no circumstances should it be allowed that majority suppresses the Ruthenberg group, because: 1st—It has finally become clear that the Ruthenberg group is more loyal to decisions of the Communist International, and stands closer to its views.

2nd—Because it has received in more important districts the majority or an important minority.

3rd—Because Foster group employs excessively mechanical and ultra-factional methods.

Demand as minimum:

1st—Ruthenberg group must get not less than 40 percent of central executive committee.

2nd—Demand as ultimatum from majority that Ruthenberg retains post of secretary.

3rd—Categorically insist upon Lovestone's central executive committee membership.

4th—Demand as ultimatum from majority refraining removals, replacements, dispersions against factional opponents.

5th—Demand retention by Ruthenberg group of coeditorship on central organ.

6th—Demand maximum application of parity on all executive organs of party. If majority does not accept these demands then declare that, in view of circumstances of elections, unclear who has the real majority, and that methods of majority raise danger of split, therefore Communist International proposes that now only a temporary parity central executive committee be elected with neutral chairman to call new convention after passions have died down. Those who refuse to submit will be expelled.

A more dramatic scene could not have been arranged. Ruthenberg, Lovestone, and Bedacht, the representatives of the minority, could not conceal their rejoicing. Foster's jaw set; his eyes shifted back and forth from Gusev to Ruthenberg, to Cannon and Bittelman. Cannon's eyes narrowed; this was the last thing he had expected from the encouragement that Gusev had been giving him in secret. Bittelman, who had attained a position of authority in the Foster group because he could read Russian—"our theoretician" the Fosterites called him; "the Rabbi" was the nickname Lovestone had given him—could think of nothing in the columns of *Pravda* that had forewarned him of this decision. He simply collapsed into an aspect of abject despair. Foster aksed time to confer with the members of his trio, or perhaps with his whole caucus. No one objected. He and Cannon and Bittelman withdrew into another room. Somehow, a few of us from each side had attended this particular meeting of the Parity Commission, under what circumstances and for what reasons I do not remember. When Foster, Cannon, and Bittelman withdrew, a few of their lieutenants who were, as an exception, present, withdrew along with them.

How long they were gone, I do not know. While they were out the three members of the Ruthenberg caucus engaged in happy small talk with Ballam, Gitlow, and a few others of the Ruthenberg group, also present under unusual circumstances. When Foster returned, he spoke with intense bitterness. It was unheard of for him to hear his opponents characterized by the exalted leaders of the Comintern as "more loyal and closer to the views of the Communist International." It was crushing to have your majority thus snatched away from you, and see the minority protected from removal from its posts by a whole series of protective rules. When the Comintern thus gave its endorsement and ordered expulsions (the Lore group) and set up protective fences, one could only obey. Or if one rebelled, he would find himself outside the party and outside the Communist International. Yet instinctively Foster rebelled, and he determined to go to Moscow to see such patrons as Losovsky of the Profintern and appeal the entire decision.

He would not hold onto his slender majority under such humiliating conditions. He offered those who, only a few minutes ago, had seemed to be the minority, a majority in the new Executive Committee. He stated that he himself could not serve on the Central Executive Committee under such circumstances. With such a decision questioning his loyalty, it was impossible for him to take responsibility for a leading part in the work of the Party.

Gusev answered calmly that the Comintern could not accept such a decision of abdication of his leading position: he was an indispensable part of the Party's true leadership and must continue to fulfill that function. Cannon, still dreaming of Gusev's hint or promise that he, not Foster, was regarded as the best leader of the Foster caucus, suggested that a more workable Central Committee under the circumstances would be one in which the C.C. would be made up on a fifty-fifty basis. Foster and Cannon glared at each other in a way that implied that they had been fighting inside their own caucus on how to react to the new Comintern decision. As for Bittelman, he was mute and in collapse. He had no "theory" for his group in the moment of defeat.

Next Foster broke the bad news to a meeting of his entire caucus. They were stunned. He made matters worse by reopening his fight against the decision and promising to go to Moscow to appeal it, while Cannon and Dunne urged that the decision must be accepted. Cannon and Dunne proposed that the new Central Committee should be constituted on a fifty-fifty basis or it would be impossible to work. But Foster and Bittelman urged that a majority and full responsibility for actions and errors be given to the Ruthenberg group. The delegates in the caucus began to choose sides, and the caucus, yesterday a jubilant fighting unity, was split wide open into Fosterites and Cannonites, both plunged into despair. They voted with Cannon to accept the Comintern decision, but voted that their candidates to the small Political Committee or politburo should be Foster and Bittelman. The mood in the Foster caucus was so bitter, and the confusion and demoralization so great, that the caucus session lasted thirty-four hours, with delegates falling asleep in their chairs, waking up again, and resuming their bewildering discussion.

The Ruthenberg caucus was a joyous affair. The diminutive and pudgy Gusev sat at the front table among the caucus leaders as if he were one of them and a member of our group. He had a satisfied look on his face, a look of benevolent well-being, like a man who had done his duty and done it well. He had always seemed more at home in our caucus anyway. We seemed to speak a language in politics closer to his than was the talk of Foster and Cannon and Dunne and Browder. Lovestone he knew very well, for Lovestone had found him a safe residence and had visited him frequently to gossip about party affairs and personalities. My wife he knew intimately because she had taught him English, working with him for hours on end every single day while he was in Mexico. Me he knew well, too, for I had gotten him his identity card, drilled him in his identity as an American merchant returning from a visit to Mexico, and prepared him to talk if necessary of which merchants and manufacturers he had visited, what he intended to purchase in Mexico, and what difficulties he had encountered in the Mexican way of courteously bribing officials to smooth the paths of commerce, so that he could have passed muster with the keenest of interlocutors. If he thought me naive, as he had told Lovestone, he still had a liking for me and a feeling that he could trust me to speak my mind frankly and without evasion or deception. With Bedacht he spoke German, in which he was fluent. If he was less close to Ruthenberg, there had been no friction between them. In short, he felt at home in our caucus and felt a benevolent sense of having done what was right with us. He gave Ruthenberg the C.I. cable to read to the exulting crowd, then made no comment, for none was necessary. There is a little anecdote in Gitlow's memoirs which showed how at ease he was. It reads: "Wolfe's wife comes dancing into the room, and the parity man wittily remarks: 'Why are you dancing? Do you think this is a love affair? This is a Lovestone affair.' " Thus he showed that he knew Lovestone was the real organizer of the Ruthenberg caucus.

Everybody in the hall rejoiced, I along with the rest. Yet the thought crossed my mind, "This is no way to win a majority. If we get a majority because the Comintern says we are more loyal to the Communist International and closer to its views, some day it might send the same message concerning another group, call it more loyal, etc., and then our majority would be lost. The only majority that counts is the one you get by winning the conviction of every individual member on the merits of your arguments, your actions, and your views." But I soon erased that thought from my mind, telling myself that now it might be possible for us to end factionalism in the Party by winning every single member to support the group that the Comintern called "more loyal and closer to its views." And when we got back to our districts and reported on the Fourth Convention of our party, that is exactly how we reported, and what we attempted to do. And as we spread the news of the cable, the Foster group began to melt away.

When the Parity Commission met again the day after the convention (August 30), Cannon's victory in the Foster Caucus enabled Gusev to get a unanimous decision in favor of accepting the cabled instructions. Gusev put through, perhaps on Cannon's motion, a decision that the new executive should be organized on a fifty-fifty basis, with a neutral chairman—himself. A further motion was carried that in the principal districts such as New York, Philadelphia, and Cleveland, the district committees should be organized on a parity basis. And then it was moved and carried "that the representative of the C.I. (Gusev) shall be given the power to participate in the C.E.C. meetings, to cast a deciding vote, and to act as chairman." The entire Parity Commission signed the motions, Gusev signing with the name P. Green. It was the first time that the name of a Comintern rep had appeared thus openly (even though it was a pseudonym) under a resolution adopted by a convention of the American Communist Party.

Gusev had yet one more surprise for the leaders of the American party. At the first meeting of the new Parity Central Executive Committee, Gusev took the chair and then quietly announced what the new order of affairs would really be:

> Of course, we now have a parity C.E.C., but it is not exactly a parity C.E.C. With the decision of the Communist International on the question of the groups in the American Party there go parallel instructions to the C.I. representative to support that group which was the former minority. If the C.I. continued this policy, that will always be the case, that is, the C. I. representative will be supporting that group, and therefore, although we have nearly a parity C.E.C., we have a majority and a minority in the C.E.C.

In his heart Foster was furious, and he determined when next he got to Moscow to use his influence with people like Losovsky, head of the Red Trade Union International, to see if he could get the decision reversed. Too late he had realized that Gusev really had had two sets of instructions in his pocket—one to declare that in appearance and despite all credential challenges, Foster had gotten 60 percent of the delegates and Ruthenberg only 40 percent, and a second instruction to work from 60-40 to parity, and from parity to support of the Ruthenberg group. The spin of the wheel of fortune from 60-40 to a minority was all the harder to bear because it came so suddenly, at what was to all practical purposes the end of the convention. Foster insisted on his right to appeal to the Comintern the decision it had already taken, and he could not, or would not, altogether conceal this intention. But when he tried to get branches that he had carried to endorse his appeal, from within his own caucus Cannon rose to object that to endorse an appeal was to consider that the Comintern was mistaken and had made a wrong decision. "This in itself," Cannon was quoted as saying, "has an inevitable tendency to discredit the Communist International before the party comrades." What could Foster say against that with a Comintern representative still present in America and watching his every step? So far as we could tell, moreover, Foster did not even suspect that Gusev had been coaching Foster's second in command.

Yet the diehard Fosterites sensed Foster's mood. When the convention report was being discussed at a general New York membership meeting, Zack, Krumbein, and Aronberg, hard-core Fosterites all three, speaking in their own names, openly attacked the Comintern's interference with the will of the American Communists as expressed in their preconvention vote. Gusev had gone up to Montreal to take a look at the Canadian Communist Party. When he got the news of the Fosterites' defiance in New York, he wrote an article in the *Daily Worker* signed P. Green, in which he reviewed the entire story of the internal struggle in the American Communist Party, before, during, and after the convention. When he came to the postconvention discussion in New York he blamed Foster for the stand of his close followers. He wrote:

> Foster and Bittelman are actually following a line against the Comintern, although they declare that they are for the Comintern. (Such declarations are very cheap.) They are gathering the right wing of the party around them.

Foster's anger knew no bounds when he read those words. Yet he realized that a trap was being set for him and hastened to seek an escape by publishing these words:

> I am for the Comintern from start to finish. I want to work with the Comintern, and if the Comintern finds itself criss-cross with my opinions, there is only one thing to do, and that is to change my opinions to fit the policy of the Comintern.

Yet, when he got to Moscow, he made his appeal just the same.

Another penalty that Foster had to pay was the insistence of Gusev, using his parity vote, that Bittelman should not become a member of the new Political Committee, or Politburo, as it came to be called in Russian fashion. It was made up of Ruthenberg, Lovestone, and Bedacht for the new majority, and Foster and Cannon for the new minority. With that,

Cannon's treachery to Foster came out in the open. To make matters worse, a smaller Secretariat that was to settle matters between Politburo meetings did not include Foster at all: it was made up of Ruthenberg, Lovestone, and Cannon. And Cannon agreed to make a tour of the country together with Lovestone, ostensibly representing the two groups, to put across and explain the convention and Comintern decisions, and the new leadership of the party. Now Foster's enmity towards Cannon became, if anything, greater than his hatred of Lovestone, but he could not take his revenge until Cannon became a Trotskyite and carried with him such close followers as Max Schachtman, who had been editor of the *Young Worker*, and who was the most brilliant, most humorous, and most wicked-tongued member of the Youth Movement that was just beginning to grow up, and into, the party.

As for Ludwig Lore, who had supported Foster, but whom Foster now rejected as a Comintern scapegoat and "the Right Danger," it did not prove so easy to get rid of this old war-horse and veteran of the German Left-Wing Social Democracy. Lore was Secretary of the German Bureau of the Workers' Party in addition to being editor of the *Volkszeitung*. When the Central Executive Committee, including Foster, voted unanimously to remove him, the German Bureau voted 7 to 3 against his removal. The C.E.C. found it necessary to suspend the pro-Lore members of the German organization and name "loyal party members" in their place, before they could carry out their decision.

WE GLORIFY THE COMINTERN

The Communist International had intervened in the life of our party before this, and on the whole we had had reason to be grateful for their firm intervention. They had forced unity upon our warring, fragmented party. They had ended the confusion of Communist Party, Communist Labor Party, and United Communist Party. They had ended, happily I thought, the squabble between Geese and Liquidators and compelled the seemingly incurable worshipers of the underground to come up for air and join the legal, open Workers' Party under penalty of expulsion from the Communist International if they did not. What could be wrong, we thought, in such salutary intervention into the life of the American Communist party by these great Russians, who had had their wisdom certified by their success in seizing and holding power? We were getting used to appealing to them and heeding and profiting from their instructions.

But this time their intervention went much further. This time they had not sent us a Latvian like Jansen or Johnson, alias Scott. Nor a Pole like Waletski, alias Brooks, accompanied by a Hungarian named Pogany, alias John Pepper. This time they had sent us an Old Bolshevik, who was a Lenin follower since 1902, one of the twenty-four Russian Social Democrats who had helped Lenin to found the Bolshevik faction, now the Communist Party of Russia, that ruled over the largest continuous land area in the world, one-sixth of the earth. They had sent us Drabkin, alias Gusev, alias P. Green, an intimate of Zinoviev, Bukharin, Stalin, Lenin, and Trotsky (the last he hated because while he, Gusev, was serving in a leading position in the Red Army during the civil war, Trotsky had ordered him and some other Old Bolsheviks shot for indiscipline real or alleged, from which death sentence Stalin had saved him by appealing directly to Lenin). Hitherto we had thought of all these great Russian names *en bloc* as "the Russians," whose wisdom had been certified by their victory. Only now were we beginning to learn that these Old Bolsheviks were not so unified as they had seemed to us, and that they had their factions also.

Only now did it become clear to us that, while Lenin lay paralyzed and dying, all these old Bolsheviks had united to diminish the stature and standing of Leon Trotsky, who until then had seemed to be "Number 2" after Lenin. They had all alleged that Trotsky was not a true "Old Bolshevik" nor a true Leninist. Though Trotsky had still been the main reporter at the Fourth Congress of the Comintern in 1922 while Lenin on his sickbed was still alive, at the Fifth Congress in 1924, the first I attended, Trotsky was already in eclipse, nowhere mentioned and nowhere to be seen. Moreover, at our congress, some of our own members, like Ludwig Lore, were being attacked as "Trotskyites" and were being driven out of our ranks.

One of the things that was new, then, in the intervention of the Comintern at our Fifth Congress was that the same Communist International which had settled a number of our native factional struggles was beginning to export into our party (and, as it turned out, into all Communist parties) a struggle alien to the issues and interests of the country concerned, a factional struggle of their own in the Russian Communist Party.

But the cable of the Comintern read to us by P. Green, or Gusev, was so favorable and complimentary to the Ruthenberg group that we hardly gave a second thought to the sinister potential in the fact that a Russian faction fight irrelevant to America was being imported into our country.

And there was something else that was new in the intervention of the Comintern at our Fifth Congress. For the first time, that august body had stepped into the picture to "make" an American Communist leadership and to "unmake" its rivals and check their bid for power. It was not our party that decided this, but the Comintern that decided who the leadership would be that should emerge from our convention.

The circumstances of this intervention were startling, too. First we learned that a decision had been made for us in Moscow on our credentials contests, the Foster group getting 60 percent and the Ruthenberg group 40 percent of the disputed delegations. Foster had naturally concluded that the leadership of the party was being handed to him. With the ruthlessness characteristic of a trade union leader when he finds he has a majority, Foster openly stated that he would use his power to remove

Ruthenberg from the post of secretary and Lovestone from membership in the Central Executive Committee.

Then overnight, the picture was reversed. The 60-40 majority became a small 50-50 Parity Commission with an "impartial arbitrator," Gusev, who had the deciding vote. Wielding the authority of the Comintern, he could make the decision of any question go either way. Another two or three days passed, and then, in the Parity Commission, Gusev had pulled out of his pocket and had had read to us a startling cable from the Comintern in Moscow, telling us all that "it has finally become clear that the Ruthenberg group is more loyal to the decisions of the Comintern and closer to its views." With this verdict, they broke the Foster group's bid for power and made the Ruthenberg group the leadership of the party. As lesser corollaries they protected the positions of the Ruthenberg group with safeguards such as barricades, demoted Bittelman, and condemned Lore to removal from his post (and in fact from membership in the Party).

The decision was so sweeping that our unthinking, self-centered or faction-centered gratitude knew no bounds. What a glorious organ seemed the Executive Committee of the Communist International! By glorifying the Comintern we would be glorifying ourselves. By reading to the membership the decision that we were "more loyal and closer to the views of the Comintern," we might easily unite virtually the whole membership behind us, and with this weapon put an end to the bitter faction fight.

But who, we forgot to ask, was the Comintern? When a voice thundered Comintern, was it really only one voice, or at most two voices we were hearing? Was it Zinoviev, as it had appeared to me at the Fifth Congress? No, he was already under fire and on his way out. Was it Trotsky? No, for Trotsky had already been downgraded before the Fifth Congress by a merciless attack upon him by all the Old Bolsheviks, including Zinoviev, Kamenev, Bukharin, and Stalin. Was Bukharin then the main voice in the Comintern? So it had seemed to Lovestone when he visited Moscow earlier in that same year, 1925. And so it would seem clear, too, to our entire delegation to the Sixth Congress of the Comintern, including me, in the year 1928. Bukharin was not so bad, but behind him stood the enigmatic figure of the Georgian, Dzugashvili, or Stalin. What would he be like if he took sole power?

Indeed, there was something strange about Bukharin's undisputed supremacy at the Sixth Congress, for in the corridors of the congress there were already scandalous whispers about him coming from young Stalinists, as I shall relate in a succeeding chapter. What we did not yet fully realize was that the Russian Communist Party was being torn asunder by factional quarrels which were being carried into other delegations and other parties. Nor did we realize that "the Russians" or "Old Bolsheviks," whom we had always thought of as a single, unified group of Lenin's closest associates, the joint architects of victory for socialism and the incarnation of wisdom and experience, were now denouncing each other, discrediting each other, and one by one succeeding each other as the single spokesman or leader. Now each emerging leader in turn might spread his brand of factionalism to all the parties in quest for international support, and each in turn might oust those in other countries that seemed less loyal to him and less trustworthy, and might designate that group in other parties that seemed more loyal and closer to his views. One by one, a succession of Russian leaders was appearing at the front of the stage, as spokesman for the Russian party and the weighty voice of the Comintern.

We were so taken with the joys and fruits of victory—all of us, myself included—that we forgot to tell ourselves that what can be made in Moscow can as easily be unmade in Moscow.

We, who now found ourselves in seemingly unquestioned and unquestionable power, glorified the Comintern as it had never been glorified before. I, too, the maverick of what would come to be called "American exceptionalism," stilled my doubts and took advantage of our victory and the spoils of appointment of our own people to all the key posts in the party. At every membership meeting at which I reported on the Convention, I quoted the Comintern cable with unction, as if it were perpetual endorsement and holy writ. I made it explicit that to challenge this cable was to question the authority of the Comintern. In every city to which I was sent I made it clear that to challenge our group was to challenge the Communist International which had spoken its word. And the membership, weary of long factional struggle, voted overwhelmingly—in many towns unanimously, with but a few abstentions—to support the Comintern and with it our leadership of the party. No longer did I look at the Comintern as a union or confederation of like-minded yet autonomous parties, each with problems of its own that it understood best and with solutions of its own that it had to find itself. No, it was indeed a single, world party of which we were the proud American section. Sometimes, to be sure, I thought of how different the problems and tactics of the San Francisco local were from those of New York. And when I received, as I continued to receive, reports from Rafael Carrillo, Secretary of the Mexican Communist Party, I could not help but think how different the problems of Mexico and their solutions were from the problems of the United States. But I sought to push those thoughts out of my mind, and I succeeded, after a fashion, at least until the following year, 1926, the year of the Sesquicentennial celebration of the Declaration of Independence, when I wrote on *The American Revolution: Whose Revolution Is It?* and *Our Heritage from 1776*.

For the moment I honored the Comintern the more for the honor that it had conferred on us. The clearest and most explicit summary of this our view for the immediate postconvention period was written by Jay Lovestone in the *Workers' Monthly* of December, 1925:

The Communist International is . . . the real form of the international unity of our Communist movement. Decisions of the Communist International are the expression of one international experience on the problems of the different national parties. The value of this experience lies not only in the fact that in the form of Comintern decisions it corrects wrong policies, but also, and most important, it conveys this international experience in the form of theoretical and practical lessons to the party concerned. When a Comintern decision reverses a policy of a national party it is done on the basis of an experience that was not at the disposal of the body which decided the original policy. The decision of the Communist International makes available such international experience to the leadership of the national party . . .

But what if a decision of the Comintern were wrong? It couldn't be, for the working class is the most advanced class of a people—by definition, the vanguard. The Communist party of each country in turn is the vanguard of the working class—by definition. The Communist International is the union of the Communist parties of all countries, the vanguard of all the vanguards, the single united army of the working class of all countries, the union of all the wisdom of all the parties that compose it. Thus by internationalizing every national decision, even the choice of a national leadership for every party, unknowingly we were removing in advance the very basis for any correction of a faulty Comintern decision, every basis for an appeal against any decision on policy or personnel. We were ceding to a more or less small handful of men in Russia a supposed knowledge of all the persons in each party that might be considered for a particular post. A manifest absurdity, I thought to myself. But in public I spoke only of the wisdom of the world working class, the wisdom of the experienced Russian leaders, the wisdom of the Communist International. Whenever I spoke, nobody questioned, nobody challenged me. And I did not for a while dare to doubt or challenge myself. For half a year I did little thinking on special American problems. For a few more years, three to be exact, I was not to know what "a Russian" was like. I had not seen enough of them close-up. A Russian was a mythical man, a kind of class noun or common noun to conjure with. Had not "*the* Russians" under Lenin's leadership left the World War, while the Americans under Wilson's leadership were entering it? Did they not represent a New World of which I could believe almost anything, because I knew almost nothing of this New World that was yet to come? Why should I not open a large, unlimited credit to those men who had taken Russia out of the war and were building that glorious new world?

True, there was a doubting Thomas within me that told me at times, when the whirl of party work left me time to think, that the Comintern could not have been right both when it was against La Follette and then for La Follette and then once more against La Follette. Or when it was for a Labor party in America, then against a Labor party, then for a Labor party. I resolved to think things out for myself when the rush and excitement of party work permitted. But it never seemed to give me the time to think things out. With the new duties that were thrust upon me as director of the Workers' School, editor of the *Communist*, lecturer, teacher, campaigner, Educational Director or Agitprop Director of the American Communist Party, I never had time to think, except to think how to prepare each lesson and each lecture, engage lecturers and teachers, prepare the *Workers' School Bulletin,* write articles, get articles written for the *Communist,* and puzzle over the contradictions I found in Marx's *Capital,* but never did I find enough time to solve the puzzles which surely must have their answers.

25

LIFE IN THE PARTY

The first task given to me after my return to the United States was that of director of the Workers' School. When I looked for the school, I found neither workers nor teachers nor a school. A loft in a backstairs section of an old building had been subdivided by a few thin walls, so thin that people seated in any room could hear two classes at once. The school had been run first by Juliet Stuart Poyntz, a tall, stately, handsome woman, college trained, and an accepted member of the Daughters of the American Revolution. She was a good orator, with a reputation as a good Hunter College teacher, but she did not seem adapted to the teaching of our kind of students or capable of attracting good teachers, so she recruited minor party functionaries who recited theses and clichés; hence the school was not a gathering place for adults eager to continue their education. She was then replaced by Rebecca Grecht, a dynamic little, red-haired Fosterite, also innocent of the art of teaching or organizing a school for adults. When I interviewed her, she reported that there were "about 90 students in all, and a half dozen teachers," but when I attended the classes to see what was going on, I did not find anywhere near ninety students. Possibly that many had registered, but, bored, a good number had dropped out.

I immediately borrowed a large sum of money on my own personal credit, hired a secretary with as good a salary as mine (I believe mine was $25 a week, which I was paid when there was enough money in the till to pay it; hers was paid regularly). Then I wrote to scores of well-known teachers and lecturers who were sympathetic to the radical or liberal movements, and I called together the Communist fraction of the Teachers' Union and asked them to undertake teaching courses ranging from their specialties, or subjects assigned by me, to courses in "The ABC of Communism" and "English for Foreigners," for which we provided textbooks. For their safety, they were permitted to use pseudonyms; only I, who was then the organizer of the Teachers' Fraction, knew all the real names and pseudonyms of the hundreds of our members who were also members of the party Teachers' Fraction. I do not now remember for certain, but I imagine the teachers who were members of the party gave their services without pay, while outsiders were paid a fee for a lecture at our Sunday forum or for the series of lectures or courses they gave on weekday evenings. I did not have a narrow political criterion as to who might teach; I asked only that a teacher have something interesting to teach and know how to present it. The responses to my letters were more than encouraging. Some teachers agreed because they were attracted by the idea of adult education for workingmen, some because I tactfully suggested a popularization of courses they were already teaching, others because it was still fashionable for liberals to be attracted to "the great human experiment" being conducted in the Soviet Union, and yet others because of their friendliness towards me as their former student or close acquaintance.

A few agreed to give single lectures at our Sunday night forum, others to give short courses of three related talks, yet others to give twelve weekly sessions, which was the normal length that I aimed at. A number of teachers wrote bibliographies and outlines of topics, a few even suggesting an easily acquired and easily mastered textbook. Morris Rafael Cohen, my old teacher of moral philosophy and logic, gave a three week (once a week) course which was a critique of Marxist philosophy, particularly as it was expounded in detail by Engels. Lectures were given by well-known professors who had been expelled or who had resigned in protest at the freezing of dogma or the persecution of dissent during the Great War, like Scott Nearing from the Wharton School of Economics of the University of Pennsylvania, Henry Wadsworth Longfellow Dana from the Literature Department of Columbia, and the redoubtable Charles A. Beard. We got prominent advocates of racial equality, both black and white; opponents of the incursions of our marines into most of the countries of Central America; leading organizers in the trade unions that were friendly to us; pro-Communist teachers in our public high schools (under pseudonyms) who taught such subjects as the "Theory of Evolution," the "Elements of Communism," "History of the American Labor Movement," and "Social Forces in American History," with the books of James Oneal and A. M. Simons as texts. We got Roger Baldwin to give a course concerning "Civil Liberties and the Constitution." I myself gave a course on Marx's *Capital,* much travail and struggles of conscience did it occasion in me, until I determined to include such criticisms of Marxian economics as Boehm-Bawerk's *Karl Marx and the Close of His System.* I gave such replies to Boehm-Bawerk as I could figure out, but tried to make it clear that my answers were not overwhelming refutations of his contention that Volume III of *Capital* tended to substitute demand and supply as the determinant of price rather than the "labor theory of value," its determinant in Volume I.

When I had gotten together an interesting and, in part, distinguished list of lecturers and teachers and a list of attractive courses, I wrote a brief description of each course, included relevant material concerning the teachers, and persuaded two sympathetic printers, Joe and Frank Canata, to give me partial credit and to use good paper and legible type, so that we got out a first-rate catalog that was the talk of all the circles we could reach.

Then we recruited students in the party units, in the unions, through the *Daily Worker*, in the press of the Foreign Language Federations, and through small ads in liberal journals. I had acted on the principle that if your institution takes itself seriously, others take it seriously too. Moreover, the experience I had gained as publicity director of the Rand School had not been in vain. Until the New School for Social Research got its battery of exiled German professors and its authorization to grant degrees, ours was the largest school for adult evening education in lower New York. Though our fees were modest—if memory serves me, something like $2.50 or possibly $3.50 for a course, and 25 cents for a single lecture—things were humming, the classrooms were filled, and money was coming in.

I got a big school going, was able to pay off my personal debt, hire an associate director, Ben Davidson, and set up a drive for a $10,000 fund (we raised somewhere between $8,000 and $9,000 in the drive). We pooled that fund with one the party was raising for suitable downtown headquarters in the Union Square area, and thereafter the school was adequately housed. With the C.E.C.'s approval my salary was raised to $40 a week and was paid regularly from school funds.

Next we started a full-time summer school for party functionaries, bringing them in from all over the country for something like an eight or ten week course in party theoretical and organizational matters, thus strengthening our whole national setup. The students for the full-time summer school were principally recruited from district and local leaders. At this point my innate Americanism got me into trouble with the functionaries of the Communist International.

That same year, while I had been building up a large Workers' School, Bela Kun, head of the Comintern Agitprop Department at the time, reported that the Comintern itself was founding an international school in Moscow for the training of something like sixty or seventy students (functionaries from the various parties) in theoretical and practical matters. That was the origin of a school given enormous prestige by being christened the Lenin School. It opened officially in May, 1926, with the express purpose of educating Western European and American students in a three-year course, for more effective service in their respective parties, and it had the further unstated purpose of strengthening the leading faction of the Russian Party in the ranks of all other parties.

The first contingent of seven Americans included three leading Fosterites, Hathaway, Krumbein, and Kruse, and others of lesser note. They were candidates from the defeated Fosterite opposition who were there either because of their disgust at their defeat and demotion, or because they thought they could do more effective lobbying for a reversal of the Comintern cable to Gusev by being in Moscow. American blacks were incongruously assigned to the Far Eastern University, and some other Americans were recruited for schools with less prestigious names. During the next three years there were something like eleven Americans at the Lenin School, eight at the Far Eastern University, and four at the Central European School. They were from both factions and were generally of district leadership capacity. Since the Comintern insisted that it was a single world party of which the various national parties were but sections, and since it was highly centralized, and since Moscow was the center of the Communist World, these schools took precedence over any institutions that the national sections might set up.

But whenever American functionaries applied to me as the National Agitprop Director and asked for a favorable recommendation, I, all unknowing of this supreme primacy of the Lenin School, would tell them: "You would do better if you stayed in America and studied at our party school for functionaries, for you would learn much more about America, studying and working here, than if you went to Moscow for such long periods, where they are quite unfamiliar with American institutions and American ways of thinking." One or more of the applicants hastened to report this grievous heresy to the Agitprop in Moscow, or to whatever other Moscow institution they had contact with. I was not reproved for this "heresy" at the time, but when Joseph Stalin wanted to loose the lightning on me, it turned out that this was one of the things he was saving against me in my dossier. (He seemed to be keeping a dossier on everybody whose name reached his ears!)

The success of the Workers' School and the attractiveness of its catalog caused me to be named Agitprop Director, or Educational Director as I preferred to call it, on the national scene, and then to be elected to the Central Committee. Officially I was put on the national payroll, which was modest enough. In October, 1927, the complete payroll of the National Office as reported by Theodore Draper, using the minutes of the National Office as source, was as follows:

Executive Secretary: Lovestone, $40; stenographer, $25.

Agit-Prop: Wolfe [$40], paid by the New York Workers' School; Bedacht, $40; Bittelman, $40; stenographer, $25.

Organization: Stachel, $30; stenographer, $25.

Industrial: Johnstone, $30; Foster, $40; Gitlow, $40; stenographer, $25.

Anti-Imperialist: Gomez, $30.

Agricultural: Knutson, $25.

Negro: Moore, $40.

Accounts and Supplies: A. Thompson, $25.

Students (Lenin School): Hathaway, $12.50; Bell, $10 (for dependents).

A. Thompson, who was paid so poorly, was treated as a secretary or stenographer, for she was a woman, the wife of Will Herberg, then a leader in the Communist Youth. The figures are a bit misleading, since often the party treasury was empty, and then the top figures in particular had to go without pay for a while. Ben Gitlow has written, "When I got paid, I got paid $40 a week."

However, those who went without pay at times had other sources of income, for they travelled about a great deal on speaking tours and visits to units or unions, in which case they had train fare, sleeper fare if required, hotel bills, meal expenses, taxis, etc., paid on expense accounts. Moreover, those who had wives, legal or common law, generally had their income supplemented by the salaries, party or nonparty, of their mates. When the party treasury was empty, it could not declare itself bankrupt but raised funds by appeals to the members, special assessments, contributions from well-to-do sympathizers, and brazenly milked defense funds, support for strikers funds, union treasuries of Communist controlled unions, and the like. Except for the fusion of building funds, the Workers' School was on the whole exempt from such raids, for we spent money generously on catalogs and fees to lecturers and received generous support. One of our biggest supporters was the Garland Fund, an early radical foundation.

There was one great accumulation of funds that we never attempted to get money from, and that was the huge apparatus of Finnish Cooperatives with its main headquarters at Duluth and Superior at the head of Lake Superior. I was appointed the representative of the C.E.C. to the Finnish Federation, which brought me many pleasant trips to Minneapolis, St. Paul, Duluth, Superior, and other Finnish parts of the Midwest. Though the only Finnish word I knew was *Suomi,* to my surprise I soon won their confidence by plain simple talks about America and about the issues dividing the party, and the big Finnish movement became a support to the leading group and to the center. But after all my close associates and I broke with the Communist Party, the Foster-Browder leadership attempted to get a portion of the big Finnish cooperative treasury, whereupon the entire Finnish Federation seceded from the party in the name of honesty to the worker and farmer investors who had trusted them and bought shares in the Finnish cooperatives. Several decades later when I moved to Menlo Park to work at the Hoover Library, I found George Halonen, one-time leader of the Foster Caucus Finns, living next door and was pleased to note the warmth with which he greeted me and talked about old times.

FUNDS FROM RUSSIA

I was not greatly interested in the administrative and organizational side of party life, hence I asked no questions about what sums of money were coming from Russia as a contribution to the needs of the American Party, although I knew that some money came for various kinds of work. Moreover, at the outset of what he thought was to be a world revolution, Lenin made no secret of his expenditure of Russian funds to spread the revolution to other lands. On December 24, 1917, he had the Council of People's Commissars openly vote two million rubles "to the foreign representatives of the Commissariat of Foreign Affairs [that is, the new Government's 'diplomatic' department] for the needs of the international revolutionary movement." Two days later the Government's official organ, *Izvestia*, published a statement signed by Lenin, Trotsky, Bonch-Bruevich, and Gorbunov declaring that the Council of People's Commissars considered it necessary "to come to the aid of the left internationalist wing of the working class movements of all countries with all possible resources, including money. . . ." One of the aims of the invasion of the Ukraine was to make possible the sending of red Russian troops into Soviet Hungary to defend it. The call for the founding of the Third International was sent out by wireless, and invitations were issued by Foreign Commissar Chicherin. When Angelica Balabanoff, writing from Stockholm, complained to Lenin about irregularities in the distribution of the Bolshevik News (or Propaganda) Service, Lenin wrote to encourage her activities, saying, "Do not consider the cost of the work you are doing. Spend millions, tens of millions if necessary. There is plenty of money at our disposal. I understand from your letters that some of the couriers do not deliver our paper on time. Please send me their names. These saboteurs shall be shot."

But by the time I returned to America from Mexico, all these matters were highly secret. Money was sent through couriers, through trading agencies, to private addresses with one envelope sealed within another and the name of the intended recipient, or, as often as not, a pseudonym, written on the inner envelope. Then, it was no longer easy to learn what sums were given to the American party and for what purposes. My own home was used at the request of our Executive Secretary as one of these "drop-boxes," and I delivered the inner envelope without dreaming of opening it or asking whether it contained a message in code or a message in dollars. Later, when I went to Chicago to live in Lovestone's home at 5252 Broadway and "take charge of the party" for him while he went to Moscow for a stay of a few months and a faction feud, I discovered that his private address, too, was such a "drop-box," so that I was once more receiving the same kind of secret mail. And again, "taking charge" did not suggest to me that I was to open the inner envelopes and see what they contained.

Nevertheless, an examination of the testimony given, sometimes freely, sometimes reluctantly, before the House Un-American Activities Committee and other such Congressional bodies and the reading of such works as Gitlow's *I Confess* and Theodore Draper's *American Communism and Soviet Russia* have given me a reasonable, if still uncertain, notion of what the Soviet Government contributed in the way of funds to the American Communist Party during the period 1926 to 1929, when I was active as a member of the Central Executive Committee and continued as well my specialized educational, editorial, and agitprop work.

In fact, some of my information goes back as far as the Bridgman convention, when the stupid burying of documents in two barrels instead of consuming them in a bonfire enabled the government's raiding party to seize accounts that revealed that the party spent over $185,000 in one year, when its membership of under ten thousand was paying only 60 cents a month each in dues and only about half of them were paid up. Moreover, even that membership was inflated by the fact that when a man who was married paid his own dues, it was considered that his wife was also a member—the so-called dual stamp system.

Gitlow has estimated both in writing and in testimony before congressional committees that the party, plus its various auxiliary and front organizations, spent as much as $1,250,000 a year, although its constantly fluctuating membership never averaged more than 10,000 and in many years much less, during the period in question.

In its early days the Soviet government sent out confiscated jewels that had belonged to the royal family, aristocracy, and people of wealth to be sold, though the perils involved caused the bearers of the jewels at difficult inspection points to entrust the wealth to others who sometimes disappeared with it. The most notorious jewel cases are those of Louis Fraina, Ludwig Martens, and Michael Borodin, all of which have been written about a number of times. Later, actual American dollars (and in at least one celebrated case, counterfeit American twenty-dollar bills) were sent. The counterfeit bills were caught during attempts to "pass" them, but so far as I know, the other "consignments of goods," as Lovestone was accustomed to write in code, reached their intended destinations. Benjamin Gitlow, who as organization secretary at one time and occasional traveler to Moscow was in a position to know, gives the following sums, some of which are merely conjectural and possibly overstated:

The Profintern gave Foster $25,000 in 1921 for use in building the T.U.E.L.

The Comintern gave large sums for the Communist activities in the Farmer-Labor movement (amount unstated).

The Comintern gave $35,000 to start the *Daily Worker* in 1924, and $50,000 to elect Foster and Gitlow as President and Vice-President in the same year.

It contributed $100,000 in two installments for the campaign against John L. Lewis, which nearly succeeded, but was blocked by Lewis's establishment of receiverships over a number of hostile locals. When the Party broke later with the Progressive Miners to form a largely Communist opposition, their second campaign fizzled and no money would have helped.

Gitlow personally carried in his money belt $3,500 as the first installment of an intended $35,000 for the presidential campaign for Foster and Ford in 1928.

Jay Lovestone testified before the Subversive Activities Control Board under oath: "I occasionally brought some funds with me [from Moscow], others did the same." But he insisted that Gitlow was exaggerating the amounts and that his statements, a couple of which I know to be true, were "romantic."

In 1927 the British police (presumably Scotland Yard agents) raided the Soviet trading agency, Arcos, in London. (It corresponds in its public functions to Amtorg in the United States.) The police found many incriminating documents carelessly kept there, not even in code. There were semilegal cables, telegrams in code, money shipment records (never revealed by Scotland Yard), and lists of "confidential addresses." The addresses included the genial Communist lawyer, Joseph Brodsky, who received money sent by bank draft, as well as a few names and addresses of people who received confidential letters, among which was Bertram D. Wolfe, 632 Throop Avenue, Brooklyn, New York, and the same name at 5252 Broadway, Chicago, Illinois.

In 1937, long after I had broken with Joseph Stalin and the Communist movement, my own government was quite willing to grant me a passport, although they stamped it "Not Valid for Spain." Then I applied for a fortnight visa to visit England from Paris. The British consulate collected a lot of passports that day, for there was a fair going on in England, and then they returned all of them with visa stamps except one, my own. "We're sorry, Mr. Wolfe, we can't grant you a fortnight visa."

"Do you think I will overthrow the British Empire in two weeks?"

"No, sir," (gravely, without a smile) "but for reasons I do not know and cannot explain to you, we cannot grant you a visa."

"Will you telegraph to England, tell them it's for two weeks only, and ask why?"

"Yes, sir, if you will pay for the telegram both ways, we will wire the Home Office."

I went back to my hotel and wrote to Member of Parliament Fenner Brockway, who had been secretary of the Independent Labor Party since 1923, and to Lord John Hastings, a radical painter I had met at the home of Diego Rivera in Mexico, telling them of my plight. Fenner Brockway raised the question of the refusal of a visa as an interpellation to the representative of the Home Office in Parliament, but the Home Office spokesman refused to give him any explanation. Fenner Brockway rose again to call that refusal an insult to the Independent Labor Party, to which the Home Office responded: "We mean no offense to the Independent Labor Party nor to its leader in the House of Commons, but reasons of state, which we cannot divulge, prevent us from granting a visa to Mr. Bertram Wolfe." Nor were the unofficial interventions of Lord John Hastings any more effective. I did not get the visa. Some time later my brother-in-law, Harry Goldberg, who lived in the same building as I on an upper floor of 632 Throop Avenue, Brooklyn, was granted a visa, only to be followed for a week by Scotland Yard operatives to see with whom he might make contact. Then, at the end of the week, while he was seated peacefully on a park bench reading a British newspaper, a man approached him, showed a credential, inquired if his name were Harry Goldberg, then told him that it had been decided by the Home Office that he was to leave England's shores. He went.

Twenty years after my visa refusal I went by ship to England with a passport, but with no request for a visa and no British visa stamped on it. (I think visas were no longer required of Americans because of some mutual agreement between the two countries, neither of whose foundations were shaken by the change.) I got into the line for visiting foreigners; when I reached the Inspector, he asked how long I intended to stay in England.

"A fortnight or less."

"For business or pleasure?"

"Well, sir, I'll leave that up to you. Do you consider an invitation to St. Antony's College, Oxford, to deliver a talk on 'The Durability of Despotism in the Soviet System' business or pleasure?"

"O.K., Mr. Wolfe," he said in good American English, "Pass on." And he stamped an entry notice in my passport. The spell cast upon me by the Arcos raid had been broken.

During the years from 1926 to 1928 I made a number of trips through the United States, stopping at all the cities where we had a fair number of members, to give reports to membership meetings and public addresses to mass meetings. At the public meetings my main theme was generally the corruption in high government, financial, and business circles that prevailed during the Harding and Coolidge Administrations.

I would conclude my talk with a number of rhetorical questions:

"Do you like that kind of America?" The audience would shout *No!*

"Would you like to change our country into an America worthy of our past and the dreams and hopes of the Founding Fathers of this country?" They would shout *Yes!*

"Then how many of you would like to join the Communist Party and help us to make our country into one worthy of its history? Those who would, raise your hands." A fair number of hands would go up and ushers, prepared in advance, would go to each of them and give them an application blank for membership, then collect the filled-out cards. The local unit was instructed on how to follow up these applications and draw the applicants into the actual life of the party. Without realizing it, I was following a technique which I later found to be used by traveling evangelists.

When I got back to the national office I was told that I was getting more members on a single trip than any other speaker. But Jay Lovestone said to me morosely, "Bert, you're proving a good recruiter, but I want you to know that out of every ten who join our organization, we find after a few months eight have dropped out and only two remain. I don't want to discourage you, but despite our best efforts, the turnover in our organization is terribly high."

I turned my attention to this problem of high turnover. I found the chief cause to be the dullness of the average unit meeting. Life in our upper circle was absorbing. Even our faction wars involved questions of principle and theory. And when we went "down" to the units and membership meetings, we had exciting reports to give, often followed by exciting discussions. Though our permanent membership did not seem to grow much and fluctuated discouragingly, it seemed to me that we in the leadership were dealing with big things, moving whole "masses," bringing exciting news from that fount of wisdom, Moscow and the Comintern. But in the units they were discussing humdrum and unexciting questions: a collection for the International Labor Defense League; a collection for the party press; volunteers to sell the *Daily Worker* on streetcorners; sale of tickets for a dance, or a picnic, or some other device to raise money for the party's organs, the party's crises, the party's needs; the collection of dues; the discussion of faint echoes of the faction strife being carried on in another and higher sphere; and so on *ad infinitum*. Things became worse in the few shop nuclei we were able to organize under the order for "Bolshevization." At least in the assembly district branches one had met one's own friends and neighbors and sometimes discussed problems that were of general or neighborhood interest. And the members forgot the daily strain of their work. Moreover, they all spoke the same language. But a shop nucleus had two or three or perhaps five members, taken from different language federations because they worked in the same shop. And instead of escaping from their long day's work, they continued discussing it, ineffectually.

It seemed to me that the dullness in the life of the lower units might be overcome if the education I had begun, to enliven, deepen, and enlarge in the Workers' School, were spread to the lower units; if the shop nuclei, which were manifestly a compounding of weakness and dullness, were given up; if the members of the higher committees were compelled to attend the meetings of their units and enliven their sessions; if district and local leaders were brought into the center for training, including training in teaching in their own localities; if classes in writing were developed so that the "Workers' Correspondence," which was officially recognized, could make our journals and magazines more interesting, and our members more interested in the publications to which they themselves were contributing. The classes in composition were easily established, for after all I was an old and incurable English teacher, and there were many teacher-volunteers to be used, some of them quite good. But the number of members who had even the most elementary raw material for developing some talent as writers proved to be very few. The good teachers of composition were also few, while the editors of our publications, despite all the official hullabaloo concerning "Workers' Correspondence," showed little or no interest in accepting, taking the time to edit, and finding the space to publish what was turned in. My dream of a Workers' School in every city where we had a sufficient number of members and sympathizers was another bubble that soon burst. However, the ten-week summer school for local and district leaders was readily accepted and well financed. For it I built up a good curriculum, and we recruited from our leadership some good and eager teachers, or at least lecturers. The leaders we thus trained brought more understanding to their work in the various districts but showed no courage or capacity for starting other Workers' Schools even on a miniature scale. My proposal to abolish the rachitic shop nuclei brought only the threat that I would really be in hot water if I opposed "Bolshevization," which was an especial order from on high, and which, having worked in Russia, ought to work in America, too. It was only in the thirties that it was at last recognized that neighborhood branches were the natural way for political organization in America, and the shop nucleus shibboleth was abandoned after a decade of failure.

In retrospect I must admit that nothing much came out of my proposals for enlivening the work of the units through workers' education, except that a greater number of members got a theoretical underpinning for the dream they had about the ways in which socialism might improve American life. In addition, a greater number of our members got the keen and subtle pleasure of thinking that they had the answers to all the problems that beset our complex society and could "explain" these answers to the uninitiated. Moreover, through all the vicissitudes of my subsequent life, many of those who taught and studied at the Workers' School, or who took the various courses I gave there, are still my friends and show obvious pleasure when the accidents of life enable us to get in touch with each other. But all that is hardly what I had hoped for and expected when I built up the Workers' School with the belief that it would be the enlivener and enricher of the dull life and enormous turnover in our basic units.

Besides, the Party has always spent more than it has had and has felt impelled to undertake more than it was able to accomplish, so that only if the lower units and rank and file members gave their energies primarily to raising funds to meet party crises and huge party aims could the party continue to exist and function in the way it did. Hence the life of the local units would always be taken up with these same dull but ineluctable tasks. And the local party meetings remained little more than a machine to raise funds to sustain the party's ambitions.

THREE YOUNG MEN WHO WANTED TO BE WRITERS

One day three young men came to my office in the Workers' School—Michael Intrator, Whittaker Chambers, and Sender Garlin. Intrator was the most readily articulate of the three and the one I knew best, for he was taking my course in Marxian Economics. "We want to do work for the party," he said, "and we want to become good writers with a clear and decent style. Have you any suggestions?"

"Well, Mike, one learns to write by writing as one learns to swim by swimming, always striving for excellence in whatever one is writing. If you can stand working under a pompous fool, the *Daily Worker* is about to move to New York. It will have a bigger circulation and a bigger staff here, and I feel sure there will be some vacancies. But the editor is Bob Minor." Robert Minor had been a brilliant caricaturist, one of the best in the whole radical movement. But latterly he had been bitten by the bug of political ambition, had developed the idea that his bald dome resembled Lenin's, and had declared to us one day in a C.E.C. meeting, "Lenin never drew cartoons. He devoted the whole of his life to politics, and henceforth I shall do the same." With this stepping out of character began the age of his foolishness, though there is no point in my recounting the trivial and nonsensical evidences thereof. Suffice it to say that he was capable of writing such first-page banner heads as "THERE IS NO GOD"—BIMBA, Bimba being one of the leaders of our Lithuanian Federation. The sharp-tongued Lovestone once went so far in a Central Committee meeting as to say, "I move that Robert Minor be instructed to draw something else besides his salary." Minor never forgave him, but the motion, if sharp, was nevertheless a wise one, for only as a caricaturist could Minor render useful service instead of making unbelievably silly proposals. Nevertheless, despite my warning reinforced by political anecdotes, the three young men decided to go to work for the *Daily Worker,* write their best, serve the movement, and, learn the art of writing.

In the end, not one of the three could stand having Bob Minor as their boss. They all resigned, and each went his separate way in his efforts to serve the movement. Sender Garlin became a second-string careerist attaching himself now to one faction, now to another as the political seesaw suggested, remaining a middle-rank party functionary to the end of his working days. Michael Intrator, young and vigorous, was adopted by the leaders of the Furriers' Union of which the Communist Party had just won control, was taught their lucrative, seasonal craft, married Grace Lumpkin, the novelist, who took care of the striving to learn how to write, for him, and spent much of each year, after the fur making season was over, fishing for tuna and other big game fish off the Florida coast. Until a heart attack ended his days, he kept in close touch with me, with Whittaker Chambers, and with the Lovestone group, but he broke off his friendship with Sender Garlin after it became clear that he was a petty careerist.

As for Whittaker Chambers, his story is too well known for me to tell it here. He wrote uncomfortably for the *Daily Worker* for a while. He had just joined the Communist Party, shortly after I was deported from Mexico, and was made Agitprop Director. He was shy and stayed away from unit meetings, taking advantage of the "Bolshevization" which attempted only to concern itself with the shop nuclei. Nobody knew who was left to attend the branches containing the residue who were neither shop workers nor dropouts, so he stuck to his work on the *Daily* and never went to the branch to which he was assigned. At most I saw him once during all the time he was in the party. He writes that he had come to see some superior official ("party brass") who was, "if I remember rightly, its national chief of propaganda and agitation, Bertram D. Wolfe," who "in the party's name sternly informed me that the petition to get some higher incompetent removed was impermissible."

He returns to my person again only in his *Odyssey of a Friend: Letters to William F. Buckley, Jr.*, where he says that the one who understood him best was Bert Wolfe. Concerning my review of *Witness*, he writes: "Bert made the prime point—the lengths I went to to save Alger (Hiss); for that is the heart of *Witness*. Then he clinched the public points, clearly, briefly." This statement was followed by a personal letter, the only communication I ever remember having received from him. In the letter he writes:

Dear Bert,

. . . I want to thank you . . . not only because it made the necessary points so tidily. What moved me was that you noted my efforts to spare Alger. I do not remember anybody else's ever having noticed this. Yet this lies at the heart of the meaning of the whole business. The west that I meant to stand for was one of a humanity that, above all, understands, forgives, spares; and whose reality lives precisely in proportion to the courage that is required for the effort. In the contrast of that spirit with a Communism that hates, reviles, kills, in the name of an implacable *Zweckmässigkeit*, lies the crux. Thus the night in which I tried to kill myself so that, having disclosed the conspiracy for all our sakes, I might spare the conspirators by eliminating myself as a witness against them, was the high point of the case. . . . If these things are worth remembering at all, I think that, one day, when grosser aspects of this affair have sunk from sight, some few may grasp this central meaning. You have understood it in advance; and I am deeply grateful to you. . . .

That letter goes to the heart of the feelings of Whittaker Chambers toward his once intimate friend, Hiss, and the Chambers-Hiss case. If Alger Hiss should ever come to that understanding of the duty of men to their fellow humans, he would drop his attempt to impugn our court and jury system, to lower men's opinion of what he has called on occasion "the best system in the world" (in a lecture calculated to undermine our democracy), and would cease the extravagant effort to get typewriter experts to manufacture a Woodstock of 1928 that can write letters with typeprints, letter for letter, exactly like the dispatches on microfilm that Whittaker Chambers hid in the pumpkin on his farm so that the Cheka, searching his mattress, walls, and floors, could not steal them before the libel suit that Hiss had brought against him could be tried; typeprints, too, exactly like the letters that Priscilla Hiss sent to her friends and which were introduced as evidence in the libel trial and in the Hiss perjury trial. A true espionage trial, of course, could not take place, because according to the American system of justice the lapse of time had outlawed the charge to be tried. Only the perjury fell within the legal time limit, but if the perjury was true, then the espionage—outlawed or not—was true also.

The papers turned in as evidence against Hiss at his trial were partly in his own handwriting and partly typed on the 1928 Woodstock typewriter that Priscilla's father gave him, and on which Priscilla Hiss also wrote letters to friends and to women's groups. Some 200 pages of typescript were offered in evidence, all typed on the old Woodstock. Hiss's first answer in court concerning his machine was: "I am amazed, and until the day I die, I shall wonder how Whittaker Chambers got into my house to use my typewriter." It is this same typewriter that Alger Hiss has since claimed was perfectly imitated, worn letter for letter, by one specially manufactured for that purpose by the F.B.I. An attempt was made by him to get typewriter experts to duplicate this feat, but it failed. Professional experts whose lives are devoted to identifying the typewriters on which challenged documents were typed have declared that no two typewriters are exactly the same and that no other Woodstock made in that year would produce identical letters, just as no two fingerprints are identical. Moreover, by concentrating on the typewriter, Hiss has obscured the fact that a number of the documents introduced were in what he acknowledged in his perjury trial as his own handwriting.

Those of us who lived through and watched this drama cannot be fooled. However, not one, but two whole generations have grown up, in whom an attitude can perhaps be instilled by Hiss without the slightest knowledge on their part of the facts, nor where to look for them, in what books, or in what court records; nor do they even feel the suspicion that something is being put over on them. What emerged from Hiss's addresses to college audiences in the seventies is not that he is innocent, but that our courts, our jury system, our security system are corrupt and our country unjust and rotten to the core. This makes all the more shocking the decision of the Massachusetts Supreme Judicial Court in August of 1975 ordering the Massachusetts Bar Association to readmit Alger Hiss to the Bar, although it had never attempted before to tell the Bar Association what the qualifications of a member of the Bar should be, nor ever attempted to reverse a disbarment. The court found that Hiss was "presently of a good moral character," a verdict which *The New York Times* endorsed editorially by saying, "After so many years of decent behavior, Mr. Hiss should be permitted to practice his profession." Yet the court found the unreversed criminal judgment on Hiss "conclusive on the issue of guilt" and found Hiss to be "a convicted perjurer." Moreover, the court examined the testimony at the trial which made it clear that the perjury involved the handing to Chambers of espionage documents, a betrayal of trust in connection with Hiss's high office, which evidence was no longer subject to indictment only because of the Statute of Limitations. Hence, the "decent behavior" consisted in his spending much of the last quarter century in continuing to assert his innocence of the perjury charge.

THE STORY OF LENIN'S TESTAMENT

One of the most exciting episodes of the year 1926 was the result of a rumor that had reached my ears that autumn. New York is a vast whispering gallery; by keeping one's ears open one can learn many things—some of which are so, and some not so. Our national office was still in Chicago; so I was its ear to that whispering gallery in New York. Somehow I heard that Max Eastman, was getting ready to release to *The New York Times* an alleged Last Will and Testament of the dying Lenin, a hitherto secret document, the very existence of which was unknown to our party and even to the Russian Bolshevik party, except for a handful of men at its summit. Why was it not known? Was it genuine or a figment of Max Eastman's imagination? Could it be that the party that Lenin had founded and led was censoring his dying words? What had he said and to whom? What was going on in the leading party of the Comintern that such things could happen? How should we treat the story when it broke in *The New York Times?*

The last of four letters from me to Jay Lovestone on the Eastman matter was dated October 16, 1926. Two days later, on October 18, *The New York Times* published the text of the Lenin *Testament,* as the document has come to be known. It was a front page story, with an entire inside page by Max Eastman explaining its background and how he had gotten it. His translation and explanation were also carried by the *Chicago Tribune* and then by the United Press to all its members or subscriber papers, including Tass.

In my last letter to Lovestone I wrote:

> My informant was not able to see the *Times* text . . . but did see the cabled U.P. text which is reduced in the ratio of about 2 to 5. . . . I can therefore give you the following description:
>
> The "will" begins with a discussion of the stability of the Central Committee and a possible danger of a split in the RCP. It cautions against the possibility of fights and splits due to temperamental differences of such people as Trotsky and Stalin. It proposes to increase the size of the Central Committee. It describes the personal characteristics of various Committee members including Stalin, who is not too kindly dealt with; Trotsky for whom there is a mixture of praise and blame . . . ; Bukharin; Zinoviev and others. It is dated December 25, 1922, and has a postscript dated January 4, 1923. . . .

Then I advised Lovestone, in a paragraph of which I have some reason to be proud:

> Caution the *Daily* to use great care about denying the authenticity of the documents in its own name, or in refuting anything in them, for they may be ***the actual words of Lenin.***

If the *Daily Worker* wanted to attack Eastman's release, I explained, its only recourse was to quote the attacks of Leon Trotsky and Lenin's wife, Nadezhda Krupskaya, upon a book of Max Eastman's entitled *Since Lenin Died,* published a year earlier, in which there was some reference to a "Lenin Testament" and to other important documents of Lenin that had been "concealed" from the Party after his death. The book was an encomium of Trotsky, yet for reasons which I was later to decipher, both Trotsky and Krupskaya had denied the authenticity of the documents to which Eastman referred.

Though I left it to Trotsky and Krupskaya to do the denouncing of Max Eastman, thenceforward I returned many times to the problem of the authenticity, and then the completeness of Eastman's release. It was only in 1956, partly with the help of Boris Souvarine, and partly with the help of Nikita Krushchev, that I got to the bottom of the mystery and justified my instinctive feeling that the "Testament" Eastman had released 30 years earlier was indeed authentic, except for the fact that its worst words against Stalin had been unwittingly omitted by him.

"In his unconscious," Freud has written in one of his wisest observations, "no man believes in his own death." It is this fact that enables men on a field of battle in which two-thirds or more will be dead at the battle's end to nevertheless say, "My number isn't up," and to continue courageously to fight. But if it is hard for a vigorous man, though he consciously knows that all men are mortal, to believe in his own death, how much harder it is for a dictator who lives so much more fully than other persons and extends his life over the lives of so many others, to believe that he too must die! Yet in Lenin's case—the succession of strokes, including three or four major ones with their succession of miraculous recoveries, each less complete than the one before—it is as if the Angel of Death were knocking again and again on his aching skull and giving him foreknowledge that his end was near.

At the Eighth, Ninth, and Tenth Congresses of his party he had guided everything, done everything of importance from the delivery of programmatic addresses to the writing of resolutions and the judging of men. At the Eleventh Congress, held from March 27th to April 2nd, 1922, his waning powers still permitted him to deliver the opening and closing addresses; draft, but not to give final form to, two or three resolutions; and deliver the Political Report of the Central Committee. The Twelfth Congress of his party he was unable to attend at all. It was for this Congress that he dictated what he himself called a *Letter to the Congress.* On December 13 and on December 16, 1922, he had several severe attacks. It was then that Krupskaya telephoned to Stalin that her husband would not be able to attend the Twelfth Congress in person. But the doctors wrote in his medical record (he had something like twenty-five doctors, six of them specialists imported from Germany), "It was very difficult to prevail on Lenin not to speak at any sessions and to stop work for the time being." When they forbade him to do any work whatsoever, he went on strike, threatening to refuse all medical treatment unless they permitted him to dictate for brief intervals of from five to fifteen minutes at a time. It was in pain and suffering and paralysis of the arm that his strong will prevailed, and he dictated now to Krupskaya, now to Volodicheva and Fotieva, his two secretaries.

The General Secretary Stalin and the Politburo committees gave instructions to the doctors and the three recipients of Lenin's dictation that "Vladimir Ilyich may dictate daily for from five to ten minutes, but what he dictates should not be correspondence, and he should not expect any replies. Visitors are forbidden. . . . Neither his friends nor members of his family shall tell Vladimir Ilyich any political news." Under a totalitarian regime such is the way in which even the supreme leader and dictator dies!

But they reckoned without Lenin's iron will. He gradually extended his working time to some 30 or 40 minutes a day. For six weeks he continued dictating and managed to make Krupskaya tell him something of what was going on. His articles included an attack on the bureaucratic mismanagement of the Workers and Peasants Inspection (Rabkrin) of which Stalin was the head and a critique of the oppressive "great Russian chauvinism" of Stalin, Orjonikidze, and Djerzhinski [two Georgians and a Pole], whom Lenin found more chauvinistic in their great-Russianism than the actual great-Russians themselves.*

On December, 24, 1922, Lenin warned his secretary, Volodicheva, to put into the Secretaries' Log a warning that what he was now dictating was "absolutely secret," should be put under special care in a special place, should be considered strictly confidential—or, in bureaucratic terms, *soveršenno sekretno* (top secret)—and should be kept in an envelope sealed with a waxen seal and marked "not to be opened except by V. I. Lenin or, in the event of his death, by Nadezhda Krupskaya." Volodicheva confessed to Krupskaya in 1929 that she had omitted from this superscription the words, "in the event of his death"—no doubt a natural reluctance, as if death could be kept from the door by not pronouncing his name. She otherwise carried out his dictates exactly. But alas, the poor dying man, was already unable to enforce his will: Joseph Stalin as General Secretary had already given categorical instructions to his secretaries to report in detail on everything Lenin was dictating to them. Stalin had convinced himself, and then his coconspirators against Trotsky, who seemed the most likely successor, that Lenin was "a goner" and would not recover. Needless to say, since he knew what it was that Lenin was dictating in his last days of articulate speech, Stalin took a sardonic satisfaction in the fact that he would not again have to face Lenin's wrath. But Lenin's doctors continued to give optimistic reports on Lenin's chances of recovering once more, and Lenin himself, through his secretaries, let Trotsky know that he was pre-

* Lenin found these newly-converted great-Russians to be "scoundrelly and brutal bureaucrats, riff-raff drowning in a sea of great-Russian chauvinism like a fly in milk." While Stalin was alive this whole discussion of great-Russian chauvinism was omitted completely from the *Complete Works* of Lenin. But the fifth edition, edited under Khrushchev, included this part of Lenin's "Testament," and it takes up pp. 356-62 of Volume 45 of this *Complete Works*. But both Khrushchev and Brezhnev have remained silent on Lenin's stress in his "Testament" on the "right of self-determination even to the point of separation."

paring "a bombshell" against Stalin at the coming Twelfth Congress of his Party, to be held in April.

In March, 1923, it became clear to Lenin that he would not be able to attend, much less speak, at the Twelfth Congress. He dictated a note to Trotsky asking him to take up the Georgian Case in his behalf, and he released for publication that part of his "Last Will" that dealt with Stalin's mismanagement of the Workers and Peasants Inspection and the "survival of the former bureaucracy with only a superficial new coat of paint" in the state, in the Rabkrin (Inspection), and in the party.

For all of Lenin's struggle with his growing paralysis, which made it harder and harder for him to utter articulate dictation, Krupskaya abstained from delivering his *Testament* to be read to the Twelfth Congress, still hoping against hope that he would make one more miraculous recovery and deliver the message himself. At 6 A.M. on January 21st, 1924, Lenin died. Now, she thought, when the Thirteenth Congress met on May 23, 1924, it was high time that this document be read to the Congress, published in its records and in the press as Lenin's last words. But she reckoned without the wiles of the General Secretary or of the triumvirate, Zinoviev, Kamenev, Stalin, who found many uncomfortable things in these last words of their erstwhile leader. Zinoviev fondly imagined that together the three would destroy Trotsky, Lenin's most likely successor in point of popularity, and then Zinoviev would use Stalin, the "faithful wheelhorse, the unambitious party secretary," to ease Zinoviev's way to power. But they, too, reckoned without the wiles of the General Secretary. Stalin had had foreknowledge through Lenin's secretaries acting as his informants and had had plenty of time to maneuver. Just before the opening of the Thirteenth Congress Stalin read selected parts of the text to the Central Committee, hinted that the "old man" had no longer been himself when he dictated it, offered his own resignation which was promptly rejected by a decisive majority, then proposed not to read the text to the Congress at all, but only to communicate its contents to small delegations of chosen delegates, each meeting separately. Krupskaya objected indignantly, but when the matter was put to a vote, the Central Committee, all Lenin's creatures and disciples, voted 30 to 10 to ignore Lenin's request, indicated by his calling the document *Letter to the Congress.*

Lenin's *Testament* was a remarkable document, showing that he was in complete possession of his powers of thought when he formulated it in his own mind, then painfully dictated it to Volodicheva on December 24th and 25th, 1922. His postscript on Stalin's rudeness, on his accumulation of power as General Secretary, on the need to remove him from that post, and his breaking off of all personal relations with Stalin, were dictated ten days later to his other secretary, Fotieva, on January 4, 1923.

In his text Lenin took up the virtues and defects of each of the persons closest to him. His purpose? His purpose in listing an important virtue in each man was to suggest that each of them had contributed something valuable to the collectivity while it was under his guiding hand, and that none of them could or should be dispensed with or eliminated, much less—

as was to happen later—destroyed. And his purpose in listing some defect for each one of them was to suggest that none of them was fit to wield such power and authority as he had. In short, he was urging on his closest lieutenants a collective leadership.

His one other purpose was to establish "stability against a split" in the leadership:

I think the fundametal factor in the matter of stability—from this point of view—is the relationship between such members of the Central Committee as Stalin and Trotsky. The relation between them constitutes, in my opinion, a big half of the danger of that split. . . . Comrade Stalin, having become General Secretary [he had just been elected General Secretary that same year, at the beginning of April, 1922, at the Eleventh Congress of the Party, and the ailing Lenin had had only nine months to observe him in the use of his new powers], has concentrated boundless power in his hand; I am not sure that he always knows how to use that power with sufficient caution.

On the other hand, Comrade Trotsky, as he showed in his struggle with the Central Committee on the question of the People's Commissariat of Communications, is distinguished not only by his outstanding abilities—personally he is to be sure the most able man in the present Central Committee—but also by his too excessive self-confidence and an excessive attraction to the purely administrative side of affairs.

. . . I will not further characterize the other members of the Central Committee. I will only remind you that the October episode of Zinoviev and Kamenev was not, of course, accidental, but that it ought as little be used against them as the non-Bolshevism of Trotsky against him.

Of the younger members of the Central Committee I want to say a few words about Bukharin and Piatakov. They are in my opinion the most able forces (among the younger ones), and in regard to them it is necessary to bear in mind the following: Bukharin is not only the most valuable and the strongest theoretician of the party, he is also legitimately regarded as the darling *(ljubimec)* of the entire party, but his theoretical views can only with great reserve be considered as duly Marxist, for in them there is something scholastic (he has never studied, and I think never fully understood, dialectics).

Then there is Piatakov—undoubtedly a man of outstanding will and ability, but too much attracted to administration and the administrative side of things to be relied on in serious political questions.

Of course these latter remarks are made by me as applying to the present time in the assumption that both these able and loyal workers will find occasion to increase their knowledge and correct their one-sidedness.

Lenin

For the next few days Lenin kept worrying about Joseph Stalin, his powers, his empire building, his character. On the 4th of January, 1923, he dictated a postscript to his *Letter to the Congress* which reads:

Stalin is too rude *(grub* 'coarse, rough, crude'), and this fault, quite bearable in relations among us Communists, becomes intolerable in the office of General

Secretary. Therefore, I propose to the comrades to find a way to remove Stalin from that post and appoint to it another man who in all respects differs from Stalin in one point of superiority—namely, that he be more tolerant, more loyal, more courteous, and more considerate of comrades, that he be less capricious, etc. This matter may seem an insignificant trifle. But I think that from the point of view of averting a split, and from the point of view of the relationship between Trotsky and Stalin which I discussed above, this is no trifle, or such a trifle as may acquire a decisive significance.

It took many years of examination of all the available evidence for me to reconstruct the full story of the *Testament*, for all the close witnesses were under intense strain. Each one tells the story differently; all secondary accounts have some error or omission; Stalin did his best to destroy the evidence and those who knew too much about it; and even Khrushchev, in his secret speech to a closed night session of the Twentieth Congress, omitted the full story of Lenin's last quarrel with Stalin.

Stalin as General Secretary had permitted himself to order Krupskaya not to tell Lenin anything about what was happening in the Party, but from Lenin's strictures against him he could see that Krupskaya was telling her husband what she deemed necessary or what he asked questions about. Stalin called her to the phone and denounced her in crude and obscene language and threatened her with a trial by the Central Control Commission. She complained of this to Kamenev. "What one can and what one cannot discuss with Ilyich I know better than any doctor. . . . in any case, I know better than Stalin. . . . I beg you to protect me from interference with my private life and from vile invectives and threats . . . I am human . . . and my nerves are stretched to the utmost."

For his part, Lenin, who had already broken with Stalin politically by calling for his removal from the post of General Secretary, on March 5th dictated a letter to Stalin saying: ". . . I consider anything done against my wife as done against me. I am therefore asking you . . . whether you agree to retract your words and apologize, or whether you prefer the severance of all personal relations between us." Stalin hastened to write an apology, but it was never read to Lenin because that same evening he had another massive stroke and lost all power of speech.

So ends the story as I have pieced it together from all the available evidence. It justifies my feeling in 1926 that Max Eastman's release to *The New York Times* was genuine. To be sure, the last words of Lenin to Stalin were not included in Eastman's release because it was Krupskaya, as I learned, who had sent Eastman the *Testament*, and she was too modest to tell him this final story because it dealt with her personally. Moreover, I had guessed rightly in warning our *Daily Worker* not to question the authenticity of the words of the dying Lenin. And the whole episode reminds the thoughtful historian that personality, accident, and luck play large roles in the making of history. Stalin had good luck and the Russian people bad luck in that just before Lenin completed his efforts to have Stalin removed from the seat of power, his voice was stilled.

THE SACCO-VANZETTI CASE

It is well over half a century since Nicola Sacco and Bartolomeo Vanzetti were tried for a payroll robbery and murder in Braintree, Massachusetts, and a half century or more since the night of August 22nd, 1927, when at midnight something like 20,000 volts of electricity leaped through their bodies as they sat in turn in the electric chair in Charlestown Prison, yet each year books continue to come out concerning them, and the case will not die.

When it became clear that the last appeals were failing and that the two men would die sometime during the week of August 22nd, I considered it my duty to go up to Boston and make one more effort at mass pressure upon the governor to make the electrocution come at the end of the week of the 22nd instead of at the beginning (the sentence said, "the week of . . ."), while one by one the justices of the Supreme Court of the United States might be appealed to to issue one more writ of stay of execution, so that the bitter prejudice of Judge Thayer, the concealment of evidence by the district attorney, and the revaling of new evidence might be considered in order to get the two men a fresh and fairer trial. The governor had ordered the jailer to send the current through their bodies on the first possible day so that the excitement might diminish and the pressure cease. Someone else pleaded with the jailer to wait out the week, but the jailer said he didn't dare, unless the governor ordered it.

Crowds were converging on Boston from all over the country to picket the state house, in silence, with placards telling the story, but the police had taken care of that, too. They had gotten a new crime act passed called "sauntering and loitering," which enabled a police chief to read "the riot act," after which in precisely seven minutes "sauntering and loitering" would become "rioting," and all of us picketing the State House on Boston Common could be thrown into cells strategically situated under the State House itself. Seeing the confusion in the crowds on the last fatal day, without giving it a second thought I took charge and put some order into the chaos.

I do not remember how many days I stayed there, for they were days filled with passion and excitement, and we did not notice the passing of time except the nearing of the dread hour of midnight on August 22nd. Each day new groups and individuals arrived by every conceivable means of locomotion and took their places on the picket line. The Boston Common was large and always had been open to free speech by anyone who thought he had something to say. But not this time! Now "sauntering and loitering" had become "rioting," and after seven minutes we were marched or even driven to jail in droves. Some well-to-do woman, or maybe several, kept bailing us out as fast as we were thrown into cells. Then we would gather at an adjacent church opened to us, or at the nearby Socialist headquarters on Essex Street, march out with our signs and back to the Commons, and then back to the cells. But now the police (some on horseback to break up the column) began tearing up our signs. Back in our two headquarters people kept painting signs for us. We put them on flexible white wrapping paper now and concealed them under our shirts. Then we would go in little groups, or singly, to the grass of the Common and lie down, and when I stood up and took my sign out of my shirt, everyone else did likewise, marched for a few minutes, and then went back to the cells. In all the excitement, I remember one incident with special clarity. A policeman was holding me by the shoulder of my shirt, but in his other hand he was holding an Italian with his arm behind his back, pushing it up so that the captive winced with pain. "Why are you holding that man like that?" I ventured to ask.

"Those damn wops, they're causing all the trouble."

"Why, don't you know he's a labor man? He supported the police during the big police strike here." Instead of a crack over my head, I had the satisfaction of seeing the Irish policeman relax his grasp on my fellow prisoner's arm and take him by the shoulder of his shirt as he was doing with me. Then he pushed me, rather gently, into a small cell with one man already in it, and the Italian he pushed into another cell. My fellow prisoner turned out to be John Dos Passos—my first meeting with him thus took place in a police cell and proved the beginning of a warm and pleasant friendship that deepened during the many summers that I spent in Provincetown. Two such memorable events in one arrest is a high score.

That night one of the most difficult moments in my life occurred. A hall was filled with hundreds of us who had been arrested repeatedly, were out on bail, and were duty bound to appear in a Boston magistrate's courtroom the next morning for trial. We were all under a shadow, for we knew that despite the last-minute efforts of our volunteers lawyers, it was almost certain that at midnight Sacco and Vanzetti would die. Bulletins came in to us every few minutes about the failure of one or another of our emissaries to reach or convince a Supreme Court Justice or some other high legal authority. With each piece of news our gloom and anxiety deepened, as did our sense of helplessness. Messages, too, kept coming in from intellectuals from all over Europe and parts of Asia—copies of messages to the governor and the judge in the case. Three million Frenchmen had signed one of the petitions and threatened a general strike if the two men died. The names of individuals were impressive: Mahatma Gandhi, Anatole France, Bertrand Russell, Hjalmar Branting, Ramsay MacDonald, George Bernard Shaw, Maximilian Harden, Romain Rolland, Albert Einstein, John Galsworthy, H. G. Wells, Fritz Kreisler, Madame Curie, the Marquis de Lasteye (grandson of Lafayette), British and French and German labor leaders, well-known names from every land—they were still coming in to us, and still being delivered to the secretaries of the governors and the judge, who consigned them to their constantly filling waste baskets and thence to the flames—but what good were they doing? They bespoke world protest and more protest to come, but at midnight a "good shoemaker and a poor fish peddler" were to be executed just the same.

An interview was read aloud from Bartolomeo Vanzetti:

> If it had not been for these thing, I might have live out my life talking at street corners to scorning men. I might have die, unmarked, unknown, a failure. Now we are not a failure. This is our career and our triumph. Never in our full life can we hope to do such work for tolerance, for joostice, for man's onderstanding of man, as we do now by an accident.
>
> Our words—our lives—our pains—nothing! The taking of our lives—lives of a good shoemaker and a poor fishpeddler—all that last moment belong to us—that agony is our triumph!

Some of us knew the words already, but men and women wept as they heard them again.

One of our people was still cruising helplessly in a dense fog on Penobscott Bay in Maine looking for a little island called *Isle au Haut*, where Justice Harlan was supposed to be vacationing, with a petition of a stay of execution, or a writ of *certiorari*, but he never found the island in the dark and fog. Someone had gotten Justice Brandeis on the phone, but he declared that he couldn't act because his wife, out of sympathy, had lent Rosina Sacco their empty house in Dedham for the summer. Someone repeated once more that he had interviewed Justice Oliver Wendell Holmes and all the answer he got was that the national Supreme Court could not intervene in the decision of state courts unless it had grounds to declare their proceedings void or there was a chance that the entire Supreme Court or a majority of it was likely to reverse the decision. "Maybe some other justice might think differently." Yet, he wished the emissary well and openly declared without reservation that "the two men were tried in a hostile atmosphere."

The hall had workingmen of many nationalities, though the majority were of Italian origin; and many well known intellectuals or press celebrities: Edna St. Vincent Millay, John Dos Passos, Heywood Broun, Dorothy Parker, and the like, and there were messages from David Starr Jordan, John Haynes Holmes, Glenn Frank, Paul Kellogg, Oswald Garrison Villard, etc., but what good did all the signatures and adherences do? They were as impotent as the rest of us.

Someone rose from his seat to make a motion.: "I move that we all march on Charlestown jail and set these innocent men free. We can pick up others at the other hall and on the streets along the way."

There was a dead silence as I took the floor to discuss the motion. Was the man a physical force anarchist? A member of some group that wanted bloodshed for its "propaganda value"? A man driven to desperation by our impotence and the moving hands of the clock that marched ever closer to the fatal hour?

I spoke slowly, trying to gather my thoughts and find the exact words to express them. "I understand, and share the feelings of the mover of the motion. I think we all do. That is why we are here.

"But what good will it do Sacco and Vanzetti? I have not seen the Charlestown Prison, but I am sure it has thick and high walls with barbed wire or broken glass at the top. And tonight it must be guarded by seven or eight hundred troopers with guns at the ready for just such an occasion. And the Boston police, all 2,200 of whom have been on twenty-four hour alert for the last two days, are bitter and tired and hostile. We will not storm the impregnable walls of a great prison successfully, nor open cell doors, nor get Sacco and Vanzetti out. I am sure Sacco and Vanzetti would not want the useless bloodshed. Nor would they escape execution at midnight. Vanzetti's statement read to us tonight shows how he feels. I propose that we vote down this motion and spend our time discussing, or at least thinking, how we can make this injustice live in men's memories and make such injustices impossible in the future in our land."

In silence those present voted, and the peril passed. Moreover, no one said to me what had been said to Fred Beal, a young Communist who came there a few days earlier than I. When he said that he represented the Sacco-Vanzetti Defense Committee of the International Labor Defense, a known Communist organization, Joseph Moro, Secretary of the General Defense Committee had asked him bitterly, "Why can't you leave Sacco and Vanzetti alone? You people don't care about Sacco and Vanzetti; let them burn; it will be better for the cause." His indignation had some justification. The International Labor Defense had its own separate committee, collected its own funds, and had not accounted for them publicly. Undoubtedly, some of the funds had gone to pay I.L.D. salaries and perhaps other party expenses, and the martyrdom of these two men had been used more to emphasize the Communist attitude towards the American Government than to save their lives.

When I got to Boston in August, 1927, I did not know about this intense antagonism. The I.L.D. and its doings were not in the field of my interests or activities. I felt that these two men had been unfairly tried and were entitled to a fairer trial with a change of venue and other protections. I knew that they might be electrocuted in a matter of days and felt that this execution should be postponed while new legal measures were tried and new evidence examined. My help was accepted without question.

When I got back to the national office, one of our leaders rebuked me for wasting so much of my time on "those two Italian anarchists in Boston. It would have been enough to put in an appearance," he said, "to show where the Communist party stood on Sacco and Vanzetti, and then come back to your duties in New York."

I thought swiftly of many answers I might give him to the effect that I had patched up the hostility between the Anarchists' Defense Committee and the International Labor Defense, that I had assumed the leadership of the proceedings since no one else seemed to know what to do in an organized manner, and that I was the best judge of how I should spend my time in party work, especially since I was there in the field. But I knew that this would start a fight, first with the party leader and then with the leader of the International Labor Defense, Jim Cannon. And so I changed my mind and said simply, "Why, don't you care about the lives of these two anarchist workingmen who have been framed?" The one who had rebuked me was totally unprepared for this simple human question, and so he changed the subject.

WHAT IF SACCO WAS GUILTY?

Many years later Eugene Lyons told me at a private party that he believed that Sacco was guilty but Vanzetti innocent. I told him that it was his duty to write this up for some magazine, but he answered: "How can I? I was the publicity man of the Sacco-Vanzetti Defense Committee."

"Then how did you get this information?"

"I heard it from Carlo Tresca, who ought to know." Alas, Carlo was dead, having been shot as he left his newspaper, *Il Martello*, at night in a blackout during World War II. However, in due course I found that Carlo had gotten the statement from the first lawyer in the Sacco-Vanzetti case, Fred H. Moore, a lawyer with whose conduct of the case Sacco had disagreed so bitterly from the first that he finally got Moore dismissed. Moore's former wife who had worked with him all through the period said that she thought that "bitterness had poisoned his mind."

In any case, whether a bitterly prejudiced judge, a district attorney, and an anarchist-hating governor of the Commonwealth of Massachusetts contrived to kill one innocent man or two, they were both certainly entitled to a new and fairer trial and a change of venue. And all our picket line was asking for was a new trial.

I was an "Agitprop Director," but I thought neither of agitation nor of propaganda. Whether they were saved and vindicated or electrocuted without all fair rights being observed, Massachusetts justice would be called into question. If they were saved and exonerated, its reputation would rise. But our mission here was to make things better, not to prove that they required improvement. Propaganda was a by-product of a simple fight for justice and the lives of two men. As David Felix wrote in 1965 in his book, *Protest: Sacco-Vanzetti and the Intellectuals* (Indiana University Press), "Led by the Communist, Bertram D. Wolfe, who had attached himself to the Defense Committee rather than the party organization, some 125 persons paraded just above the Commons on Beacon Street before the State House." If I had known of the fight between the I.L.D. and the general Defense Committee, I would not have acted otherwise, for there were two lives to be saved and justice to be done. For me there was no "they and us" in such a matter. And the Defense Committee recognized this, and treated me accordingly.

As Upton Sinclair put it in *Boston*, his documentary novel on the Sacco-Vanzetti case, "With them walked Alfred Baker Lewis representing the Socialists, Bertram Wolfe and Harry J. Cantor [a local Boston party functionary] representing the Communists, and Grace Hutchins representing Beacon Hill and the Back Bay." Sinclair was not present, but he got the information from those who were.

This sentence, appearing in his two-volume novel first published in 1928, had a strange history. In 1929 the novel was translated into German and published by the German Communist party publishing house. It was the year in which I had my fight with Stalin, hence my name disappeared from the translation. I had become an *unperson*. I no longer existed, and never had existed. Since I had gotten safely back to America before I made my break public, they could not execute me, but they could make me disappear from all texts they published in all lands. However, in 1965 and again in 1971, Cedric Chivers, Ltd. of Bath, England, published Sinclair's novel under a new title, *August 22nd*. There I reappear on page 164 of a one-volume complete version. Am I then a person or an unperson?

The next morning I presented myself at the court to which I had repeatedly been summoned, prepared to plead my case against the state of justice in the Commonwealth of Massachusetts. I found more than a hundred others in the courtroom on the same business, which involved not only answering summons but also redeeming our bail. When the judge entered, we did not have to be asked to stand up, for it was a case of standing room only, and still more were trying to squeeze their way in. The judge took one look at the crowded space before him, asked the clerk of the court whether we were all there for the same reason, then in severe tones declared: "Case dismissed." I forced my way to the front of the diminishing crowd and said: "Your Honor, I wish to plead guilty to the charges of sauntering and loitering on Boston Commons and refusing to leave when the police chief read the riot act. I desire a trial, and I wish to make a statement on why I was there and why I refused to leave until put under arrest and into jail." (In those days no Communist, and no other radical, would dream of pleading the Fifth Amendment. That was for crooks, gangsters, and embezzlers who did not wish to testify against themselves or incriminate themselves. We believed in what we were doing, were proud of what we had said, and were glad to use the courtroom and the presence of reporters to make our statement afresh, more carefully thought out.) I had spent much of the night preparing my statement. I had dug up declarations of Judge Thayer and Governor Fuller's speech as a Congressman in which he said that he favored "Crucifixion of disloyalty—the nailing of sedition to the cross of free government" and teaching a lesson to "the whole brood of anarchists, Bolshevists, and IWWs." I had found these things and much evidence of a prejudiced jury, and a concealment of exonerating testimony known to the district attorney, in the files of the defense committee and had notes on little 3 by 5 cards. But the Judge repeated angrily: "I said, your case is dismissed. Clerk, show him the door." And the court clerk and various uniformed men unceremoniously showed me the door. All I could do was resolve that Massachusetts and America had not heard the last of the execution of Sacco and Vanzetti. Indeed, it was noteworthy that more intellectuals were aroused and radicalized by the Sacco-Vanzetti execution than by anything else that had happened in our day. As John Adams wrote in the Constitution of this same state of Massachusetts: "Every citizen is entitled to be tried by a judge as free, impartial, and independent as the lot of humanity will permit."

OUR HERITAGE

The struggle on behalf of Sacco and Vanzetti shows me to be a persistent and stubborn fighter against injustice wherever I found it in our country. Even so was I active in the Mooney cause, in the case of the Scottsboro Boys, in the fight for equal rights for blacks (I founded and edited the magazine *Race*), and in many another cause, beginning with my opposition to America's entrance into the First World War and its dreadful aftermath that has made our present century so grim. But it does not show me rejecting, as so many radicals and ritual liberals have done, America itself and my precious heritage as an American. Indeed, it took an Englishman to remind our ritual liberals that:

> the Americans themselves in the last few years have indulged in a degree of national self-denigration without parallel, and it has become increasingly difficult to respect, much less to admire, a country subject to so much vilification by its own citizens. (G. F. Hudson in *Survey*, London, Autumn, 1972.)

I had been active in so many fights of the kind of which the Sacco-Vanzetti case was one culminating point, that I had not yet had time to conclusively think out my views on my heritage as a native American. But even as I was grieving over such evils as the Mooney case and the Sacco-Vanzetti case, the ferocity and lawlessness of the Red raids, the brutality of the company-controlled police and officials in some of the company towns when we tried to enter to unionize them, and the prevailing habit of our governments, local and national, to break strikes by injunction against picket lines and the use of police and national guard to break them up, I was thinking out my attitude towards the country, its basic documents and institutions, and my heritage as an American.

Sacco and Vanzetti were executed in August, 1927, but even as their repeated attempts to get a new trial were going on, in 1926 I wrote for the *Workers' Monthly* the lead article entitled, *Whose Revolution Is It?* And in 1928 I published it as a pamphlet entitled, *Our Heritage from 1776*, Volume I, No. 1 of the Workers' School Library. Its cover contained a beautiful, multi-colored reproduction of one of the first flags of the American Revolution, a red flag with a green pine tree around which is coiled a rattlesnake, and on the flag in white, above and below the snake and pine tree, appears the motto, "Don't Tread On Me." The article and the pamphlet created a scandal in our party.

The occasion seized upon as a moment for writing the pamphlet was the Sesquicentennial of the year 1776. I knew the article would be a shock to many of our members, and that the Foster faction would try to use it against the party majority leadership. Since I was breaking new ground, I moved forward under a cautious umbrella of quotations from Lenin, whose works I was just beginning to read. I had found an article written by him in 1897, and revised during the World War, entitled, "What Inheritance Do We Reject?" But I quoted only two sentences from Lenin to make the pamphlet more palatable to our comrades in America and Moscow. For the rest, I was on my own. Alexander Bittelman sent it to Moscow with an analysis tending to prove that I was an "American chauvinist" and therefore unfit to be Agitprop Director of the American Communist Party. A brief summary is in order:

When a child comes of age [it began] he has the right to claim his inheritance. . . .

Judged by this test, the American working class is still immature—still infantile Leftist. . . . "It was a bourgeois revolution," the infantile Leftist will declare. "It created our present capitalist government. The Constitution is a capitalist constitution. The Declaration of Independence is bunk. The revolutionary fathers represented the interests of landowners, merchants and capitalists. *It is not our revolution.* It gave the workers nothing but exploitation. We have nothing to commemorate. . . ."

But the American working class must outgrow these reactions if it is to grow up. Hence, in the year 1926, on the occasion of the 150th anniversary of the first American Revolution, it is appropriate . . . to throw away the chaff of chauvinism, mystification, and reaction and keep and use the wheat of revolutionary traditions and methods and lessons.

[The latter part of the article took up the achievements of the American Revolution]:

I can only briefly list a few of the results [of the revolution] in an article that is already too long. The revolution freed the colonies from England, freed the western lands for settlement and thereby raised the standard of living of the colonials, broke the fetters upon the expansion of production and released the gigantic productive forces that are now at hand for social use . . . it also lessened to a limited extent the area of slavery, made the first weak steps in lightening the laws against debtors, disestablished the church and introduced greater religious toleration in many of the colonies, effected a much wider and more democratic distribution of the land than had existed previously, extended the suffrage slightly although the property qualification for voting was not finally abolished in all states until after 1840, forced the Bill of Rights into the American Constitution, set up a republican form of government which for its day was most advanced, and served as a revolutionary inspiration to the European bourgeoisie in the French Revolution.

Under the influence presumably of Bukharin, who was then the intellectual and spiritual leader of the Comintern and who was most likely to understand and agree with what I was driving at, the Communist International rejected the accusation of Bittelman and the Fosterites against me. But once more Stalin, that "genius of dosing" who bided his time and kept dossiers on everybody, put Bittelman's accusation in *dossier Wolfe,* so that if ever he wanted to hurl the lightning at this particular person, he would have it in readiness. When Jove is wrathful, he must not hesitate with his thunder or his lightning.

26

THE SIXTH CONGRESS "UNIFIES" OUR PARTY

The First Congress of the Comintern was a mere sham or charade. Lenin was so sure that the Russian Revolution (his seizure of power) was going to spread to Poland and Germany and become a world revolution, that, never scrupulous as to means so long as they served his sacred end, he did not mind how he scraped together the 34 or 35 persons who made up the simulacrum of a founding congress. Of these people, with the exclusion of the Russians, only three represented embryonic or genuine mass parties, two of which were left Social-Democratic organizations with no instructions on founding a new International. The third, the German Hugo Eberlein, carried genuine instructions, to oppose unyieldingly, the formation of a new International at that time. All the others were either Russian Bolsheviks or residents in Russia, mostly as prisoners of war or by accident. America was "represented" by Boris Reinstein and Siebald Justius Rutgers. Reinstein had been delegated by the Socialist Labor party of America to go not to Moscow, but to Stockholm for an all-Socialist conference on peace terms. He was promptly expelled by the S.L.P. for having permitted his name and the name of their party to be used in the Bolshevik charade. S. J. Rutgers was a member of the Dutch Left Socialist minority party who "represented" not only America, because he had been living there during the war, but also Holland and Japan, in which last country he had lived only a few months without mastering the Japanese tongue. France was represented for three days by Captain Jacques Sadoul who had been sent to the Tsar's army as a liaison officer and while there had become pro-Bolshevik. But on the fourth and last day of the founding Congress he had been stripped of his mandate because of the arrival of the antiwar Henri Guilbeaux, and all five French votes were given to Guilbeaux. Angelica Balabanoff, whom Lenin was to select, to her surprise, as Secretary of the Communist International and who put morals above politics, tried in vain to warn Lenin that Guilbeaux was an untrustworthy person. She broke with Lenin in 1920 on moral grounds and received from him a generous credential praising her work and person, to carry her safely out of Russia.

Guilbeaux ended up pro-Nazi. England was represented only by a Russian Jew named Joseph Fineberg, who had lived for some time in England, had been a member of the British Socialist Party, and was working as British expert and translator in Chicherin's Commissariat of Foreign Affairs. He remained faithful to the Comintern, became a translator of Lenin's works, was tortured under Stalin, having all his teeth knocked out during "interrogations," and was then rehabilitated and given a new set of stainless steel teeth, after which he returned to the translation of Lenin.

Other delegates were picked by Lenin (officially, by the Russian Central Committee) from small nations in the Russian Empire, such as Estonia, Latvia, Lithuania, and Finland. All of them were personally known to Lenin and had supported the Bolsheviks in the internecine feuds in the Russian Social-Democratic Labor Party. For the Swiss, Lenin appointed Fritz Platten, one of the important intermediaries between him and the German general staff during his trip through the German lines to Russia. Platten died in prison under Stalin, but was rehabilitated on what would have been his eightieth birthday. Angelica Balabanoff received a note from Lenin during the first or second session reading: "Please take the floor and announce the affiliation of the Italian Socialist Party of the Third International," but on the same scrap of paper she wrote back: "I cannot do it. . . . they must speak for themselves."

From Sweden and Norway there were real delegates, but they came from pacifist, left-leaning Socialist parties, with instructions to discuss only the Stockholm conference and an early "Socialist" peace. Most of the others were war prisoners who were delighted to be elevated into "delegates" from their lands. When Angelica Balabanoff refused to pretend to represent the Italian party, Lenin selected two Italian war prisoners and gave them each the title of delegate, personal credentials, and large sums of money, in order for them to go back to Italy and split the mass Socialist Party. Again Angelica protested, pointing out that the two men were ignorant and unscrupulous and didn't even know the vocabulary of Socialism. "For the destruction of Turati's party," he answered, "they are good enough." However, she was right. They kept the huge sums for themselves and squandered most of the money in the bars and brothels of Milan.

But the land and party and delegate to which Lenin devoted all his attention was Germany. If he and Trotsky had sent the Red Army into the Ukraine, it was not merely to reconquer that rich grain and heavy industry portion of the Tsar's empire, but no less to have the army near to Germany for a flank attack on the Allied armies that would, he was sure, invade Germany to crush the Communist revolution there. So later, against Trotsky's better judgment, Lenin would send his army against Poland. As late as 1924, when I got to the Fifth Congress of the Comintern, I could still see strong and precise three-dimensional relief maps of Germany in every barracks I visited.

In Germany there was the Spartacan group under the leadership of Rosa Luxemburg, Karl Liebknecht, Leo Jogiches, and Paul Levi. If Lenin could get them, against Rosa Luxemburg's will and judgment, to form a Communist party without waiting to win the mass of the German working class, and if he could get them to start an uprising, he was sure that the élan of his party and power would make them victorious. With that victory and the union of German industry and technology with the Russian revolution, his revolution would become irresistibly a world revolution. But all four leaders, under the influence of Rosa Luxemburg's respect for the will of the masses, had opposed an immediate break with the Socialist-minded German working class. Indeed, in the elections for a Constituent Assembly and Workers' and Soldiers' *Räte* (Councils or "Soviets") the Spartacists had not won a single delegate in all Germany. All four of the Spartacists' outstanding leaders were agreed that it was premature to form a German Communist Party or a new International. They must first win the support and understanding of the masses that figured so centrally in Luxemburg's writings and in her polemics with Lenin. That was the principal difference between a mass party in a country where one could recruit and convert freely, and a little conspiratorial party of professional revolutionaries such as Lenin had formed.

When a fresh group of young men flooded into the Spartacan movement, however, inexperienced in the ways of socialism and not imbued with Luxemburg's respect for the will of the masses and the *Massenstreik*, they outvoted their leaders in favor of an impatient, immediate uprising, which the Spartacan leaders knew in their hearts would be a mere unsuccessful *Putsch*, a disaster. But being outvoted, they felt it their duty to put themselves at the head of the forlorn uprising. Therefore, they could not go to Moscow to oppose Lenin's attempt to form a Communist International prematurely. But Lenin knew in his heart that without the Germans, his International would be no true International but only a Russian affair.

The Spartacist leaders selected the young man, Eberlein, and gave him an imperative mandate (a binding instruction) to oppose unswervingly Lenin's plan for the immediate founding of a new International. Jogiches told Paul Levi that a good reason for choosing the inexperienced Eberlein was that he was "known to be narrow-minded—indeed, obtuse—but stubborn and tenacious," which made Jogiches "feel sure that the people in Moscow would not succeed in swaying him."

When Eberlein left for Moscow, Rosa Luxemburg and Karl Liebknecht had just been assassinated while being taken to jail after the unsuccessful *Putsch*. And Jogiches was caught and assassinated shortly after the congress closed. With the deaths of these leaders and the expulsion of Levi, forced by Lenin, the last chance of a German counterweight to Bolshevik domination of the International was lost. Lenin tried many ways of pressing the young delegate and putting him off guard, then went so far as to promise that without the Germans, the meeting would be called an "International Communist Conference" to adopt a rallying appeal to all parties and groups to form a new International. Lenin's chief aim was to prevent Eberlein from walking out if the International were formed before the Germans felt the time was ripe. By various forms of pressure and persuasion they got Eberlein to express what his mandate directed, but not to walk out. In the official document the German-speaking part of Austria-Hungary was absurdly substituted for Germany, since Eberlein would not change his mind nor violate his mandate. Hence the final document began:

> The representatives of the Communist Party of German Austria, the left-wing Social Democratic Party of Sweden, the Balkan Social Democratic Revolutionary Federation of the Balkans [all the Balkan countries being represented by Christian Rakovsky, who was shortly to be named Prime Minister of the Ukraine], and the Communist Party of Hungary propose the foundation of the Communist International.

Lenin put the best face he could on the matter by declaring:

> For only a short time, naturally, hegemony within the revolutionary proletarian International has passed to the Russians, just as at different periods during the nineteenth century it belonged to the British, then to the French, and then to the Germans.

The "short time" of which Lenin spoke has lasted up till now!

A RUSSIAN INTERNATIONAL

Lenin had set the Russian seal upon the International from the outset: by the manner of selecting the so-called delegates, most of them members of his party and all but a handful residents in Russia or in its war prisoner camps; by sending out the call for the conference as a public message from Chicherin, Minister or Commissar of Foreign Affairs; by Lenin's role in opening the first session of the congress and presiding over all the sessions, making all the important chess moves and playing the role of *kibbitzer* to the minor ones; by having Trotsky write the *Manifesto* of the Congress; by having Bukharin make the first rough draft of a *Program*, while he (Lenin) wrote the resolution on "Bourgeois Democracy and the Dictatorship of the Proletariat"; by making the closing address; by having his wartime lieutenant, Zinoviev, elected Chairman of the Executive Committee of the Communist International (ECCI). Lenin's closing address ended with the words: "The hour for the founding of an international Soviet Republic is near." And in a report to the leading comrades in Moscow that same evening he closed with the prophecy, "The comrades present in this room . . . will all see the establishment of a World Federative Republic of Soviets."

Lenin believed this was so, and proceeded to act accordingly. We have noted how two million rubles were publicly voted for the spread of the world revolution, how from the two capitals of Russia couriers brought out crown jewels and other treasures for the purposes of the various "sections" of the World Communist Party. When governments recognized the Soviet Government, members of the Russian diplomatic staff, even Ministers and Ambassadors, openly subsidized the parties in the lands to which they were accredited. Joffe, the first Ambassador to Germany, did so until he was expelled, whereupon he boasted in the press of the huge sums he had given to the German Communist party. And we have seen how Minister to Mexico, Pestkowski, as late as 1924, on his own initiative gaved me funds to publish *El Libertador*.

When the world revolution did not spread as Lenin had hoped and it became expedient to make distinctions between the government and the party, secret emissaries and secret instructions were sent to each party or "section" from the "General Staff of the World Revolution." At first Lenin sent emissaries of various nationalities, always provided that they enjoyed his confidence. But increasingly the "General Staff" depended on Russians. John Reed wrote in the American journal, *The Liberator,* "By September, 1918, the Ministry of Foreign Affairs had on its payroll 68 agents in Austria-Hungary, and more than that in Germany, as well as others in France, Switzerland, and Italy." To the bewildered Angelica Balabanoff when she was in Stockholm, Lenin wrote: "Do not consider the cost. Spend millions, tens of millions if necessary. There is plenty of money at our disposal." Angelica did not know what to do with such sums, for she did not understand the uses of bribery, the purchase of supporters, nor the creation of movements and journals by foreign funds rather than by winning the support of workingmen and winning coreligionists by eloquence and persuasion.

As the Soviet government got diplomatic recognition from more and more governments, its leaders discovered yet another device—that of using diplomatic immunity as a cover for spies, whereupon they added to their couriers, their emissaries, and their Comintern reps an ever greater number of "diplomatic" spies and secret agents. When Pestkowski came to Mexico in 1924, he brought with him only three men, a deputy minister, a journalist or public relations man, and a translator. That was more than enough for the genuine diplomatic business of the Soviet government in Mexico and would quite suffice today, too. But by the 1970s the number of Soviet "diplomats" in Mexico has increased to over 100. Of the 100 at least 96 are superfluous except for espionage in the twenty countries of Latin America. Every Soviet embassy today has a number of agents whose secret rank and business outrank those of the ambassadors, and the United Nations organization is similarly honeycombed, which doesn't prevent their sending yet other agents more secretively without benefit of diplomatic immunity. Nor does it prevent their using appropriate recruits from the various Communist parties, provided either that their membership has remained secret or that they can engage in some striking action which seems to prove that they are anti-Communists. Thus, in one of the most sensational cases in this country, a man who was a secret Communist operating in a government agency made himself eligible for advancement in the government by "fingering" the other secret Communists in his department.*

SIX CONGRESSES OF THE COMINTERN

If the First Congress of the Comintern was a sham, the second and third were not. Lenin led them as he had the first, but as he began to perceive that his world revolution had not spread beyond the borders of the old Tsarist Empire, and that his "world party" had sustained defeats in Germany, in Hungary, and in Poland, his mania for splitting and splitting and splitting and for voluntaristic offensives gave way to a more healing gospel.

The sections or parties began to grow because of the persuasiveness of power and success; the war weariness of millions; and the sense of shame that the Socialist parties in the various belligerent countries had succumbed to the war fever. In vain did Lenin strive to prevent the revival of the Second International and the Amsterdam Trade Union International, yet the Communist parties grew as well, although they might have grown much faster were it not for the effects of his splitting tactics. In due course he realized that the majority of the Socialist-minded and trade union-minded workingmen were not in his camp, whereupon he turned his mind to the question of how to reach them. He wrote a special programmatic and tactical pamphlet to guide his not inconsiderable following, often much against their will, back into the trade unions which he had been trying to destroy, and into various forms of "united front" with the big Socialist parties which he had indicted as social-patriots, social-traitors, and agents of the bourgeoisie. The pamphlet, *Left-Wing Communism: An Infantile Disorder,* became the gospel of the Comintern. The "leftism" which he now treated as an infantile disorder was the will to continue the tactics he himself had been preaching all through the Great War and the first period of postwar Communism. Those who could not make the about-face with him he excoriated, then drove out of their parties.

Yet on the whole it was a healing gospel: in place of split, split, split—a united front; in place of ridiculing parliamentarism—taking more seriously parliamentary elections; in place of dual unionism—a return to the old mass unions or their "infiltration" He had to fight a serious struggle with

* If the reader wishes to learn more about the founding of the Communist International and Lenin's role therein, the best book is *Lenin and the Comintern,* by Branko Lazitch and Milorad M. Drachkovitch (Stanford: Hoover Institute, 1972). So, too, for the characters that figure in this part of my story, the reader cannot find anything else to equal the *Biographical Dictionary of the Comintern,* by the same authors (Stanford: Hoover Institute, 1973). For a thorough study of the work of Soviet agents and spies in foreign countries, the best book is John Barron's *KGB* (paperback, New York: Bantam, 1974).

the British Communists when he demanded that they return to the British Labor Party. And he faced another difficult struggle in his own party when he asked it to recognize the failure of his policy of universal socialization, of the reckless debasing of the currency, and of the prohibition of all trade as "criminal speculation." He proposed instead the New Economic Policy or NEP, under which the Russian economy began to recover.

At the Fourth Congress of the Comintern in November, 1922, Lenin, not feeling well enough to participate actively, asked Leon Trotsky to make the main report in his place. Trotsky's report was entitled, "On the New Soviet Economic Policy and the Perspectives of the Soviet Revolution." At the Fifth Congress, Trotsky was ill. He was not allowed even to put in an appearance, nor was he sent any message of greeting, nor was any asked of him. But the reader has already learned how the Fifth Congress appeared to the inexperienced eyes of the delegate from Mexico (in Chapter 21).

After three years of lively activity in the American Communist Party, I was chosen as one of its delegates to the Sixth Congress, which met in Moscow from July 11th to September lst, 1928. It was on the whole the most important Congress since the Second. It was notable for the numbers attending, 558 delegates from 58 parties; for the able theoretical leadership of all its most important matters by Nikolai Bukharin; and for the adoption at last of *The Program of the Communist International,* which the participants estimated to be the most important document since the *Communist Manifesto.* It was even held to be an improvement on that classic work of prophecy, in that the new *Program* dealt with an international party that actually held power, was "building socialism" on one-sixth of the earth, and had "sections" in more than fifty other countries through which it hoped to extend its revolution and its power to all the countries of the world.

TO MECCA ONCE MORE

I went to the Sixth Congress not as a workaway, but as a second-class passenger on a Cunard Line ship with all expenses paid by the Communist International. I duly applied for a passport under my own name, paid my $10 fee, then received $9 back (they charged a dollar for saying *No!*) together with a letter saying;

> Acting under the authority given to me by act of Congress, I have decided not to grant you a passport.
>
> Faithfully yours,
> *(Signed)* Frank B. Kellogg
> Secretary of State.

I was prepared for the possibility of such a reply, though I had not expected the irony of the "Faithfully yours," nor the $1 charge for the "service." Since I believed, and continue to believe, in the right of people freely to enter and leave their native lands, I had gotten a friend in Canada to get me a Canadian passport under the name of Albert Ward. In my application for an American passport I had given the name of the ship on which I intended to leave and the date of my sailing. Unhesitatingly I took the same ship on the same date indicated, and sailed to Portsmouth, thence to Le Havre, and then went by train to Paris, Berlin, and Moscow, keeping an account of my expenditures which were recompensed by the Comintern. It was a smooth trip with no adventures worthy of note, except for two problems that unexpectedly faced me on the British steamer.

The first came before the giant ship left the harbor of New York. I was pacing the deck with an engineer from the north of England, who was slightly drunk from a farewell party. A man passed us as the first call came up, "All ashore that's going ashore."

Why, hallo, comrade Wolfe," he cried. "Where are you going?"

I paused for an imperceptible second then said, "My name isn't Conrad, and I don't believe I know you."

"Why, don't you come from New York?"

"I'm from Montreal."

Just then came the second cry of "All ashore," and my puzzled questioner left me. My tipsy companion said nothing. He never referred to the episode on the five or six days of the trip, but when he was leaving at Portsmouth, he was drunk once more, and the liquor seemed to revive his memory of our first walk on the deck. "There'sh somethin' funny about you," he said. "I heard what that fellow said to you. Anyhow, good-bye and good luck," and he lurched toward the gangplank.

The second episode was also due to the way in which ships throw their passengers together. Someone asked me, "By the way, what's the name of that lovely park in Montreal?" I know now that it is *Mount Royal,* but I had never been in Montreal at that time, so I fended that one off by answering, "Oh, we natives just call it *The Park,*" and I changed the subject.

The moral, if there is a moral to the verse that begins, "Oh, what a tangled web we weave . . . ," is not to go by steamship but by air, but in 1928 Lindbergh's famous solo flight across the Atlantic to Le Bourget Airfield was only one year behind us, and there was no means for any but a Lindbergh to cross the ocean by plane. Incidentally, sometime in late May or early June of 1927 I had written a signed article in the *Daily Worker* praising Lindbergh for his heroic deed, and had spoken of the adventurous spirit of American youth. The ever watchful Bittelman had immediately attacked me in the Politburo and had sent a cable to Moscow about my "American chauvinism," but that seems to have been one complaint that Stalin did not find worthy of putting in my *dossier.* If he had, I think I would have known how to defend myself.

On the surface, the Sixth Congress of the Communist International seemed to run like an engineer's dream of a frictionless machine. If not every one of the 558 delegates spoke, at least every one of the 58 parties had its say. If there were differences in these parties, every faction had its spokesman. The congress had 46 sessions, and the stenographic account appeared in Russian and German in six hefty volumes. The program we adopted and the resolutions that were passed took up an entire volume by themselves.

Nikolai Ivanovich Bukharin delivered the opening address, the *Report on the International Situation,* and the opening and closing addresses on the *program* which he had been engaged in writing since the First Congress of the Comintern, sat on the platform during all 46 sessions, only occasionally asking a cochairman to take the chair, kept a pad and pencil busy, apparently taking copious notes on what every speaker said, delivered the closing address, and was unanimously elected chairman of the incoming Executive Committee of the Comintern. He was a brilliant, eloquent, gay, and humorous speaker and a subtle master of the Russian tongue. He could also speak German, French, and English as occasion required. His addresses were delivered in German, the *lingua franca* of the Comintern. His leadership of the debates gave them an intellectual and theoretical quality that made it a pleasure to listen when he took the floor.

When I asked for and got the floor at the thirty-sixth session to discuss the problems of industrialization of the colonial lands by their respective "mother countries" and the state of affairs in Latin America, I took advantage of my nearness to Bukharin's place at the Presidium table to see what kind of notes he was taking on my speech. I discovered that his notebook had not a word in it, only a series of skillful caricature portraits of each of the speakers. He had been an artist in his youth before he met Lenin and became an active Leninist. A glance told me that his drawing of me was much better than the one a professional artist had done of me at the Fifth Congress, which the Russians had then printed as a picture postcard.

There were, however, a few things that bothered me in Bukharin's report on the international situation. One of them was the insistence that a new world war was imminent. Of course, in our century of heavily armed nations, war could break out at any moment and could swell into a world war. But I knew that my country was not preparing for immediate war and that England and France were still weary and weakened by the First World War, which had ended with the impossible Versailles treaty. They suffered, too, from a shortage of recruitable young men. They had lost an entire generation in the four years of wholesale slaughter. When my friend, Walter Pach, an art critic, went to Paris after World War I and asked what was doing in the field of painting, Picasso, Leger, Matisse, and other prewar painters told him what *they* were doing. But when Pach asked, "*Et les jeunes?*" They answered, "*Nous sommes les jeunes.*" Most of the young men who might have become the great painters of the next generation had been killed on the fields of battle defending France against the German invasion. Only old men remained to carry on the arts. How could France then dream of starting another world war before a new generation had reached manhood?

The Comintern, however, informed us that there was danger of an immediate outbreak of war. Russia would be invaded by the combined capitalist powers and their satellites. The signs? The collapse of the British General Strike of 1926; the breaking off of Britain's diplomatic relations with the Soviet Union; the raid on *Arcos;* the break of the British trade unions with the pseudo trade unions of Russia; Chiang Kai-shek's break with the Chinese Communists that were infiltrating the Kuomintang and the expulsion of Borodin for interfering in Chinese internal affairs. But did these disparate phenomena amount to an imminent danger of war?

Dutifully, in 1926, 1927, and 1928 we tried to find an immediate danger of a new world war, with America, which had emerged from World War I as the great creditor nation and the strongest world power, as the leader of a new war. Was it to be a war against England and Japan for control of the world, or a war against the Soviet Union in which all capitalist powers united? Not seeing striking signs of either—we said both. In 1928 Lovestone wrote a twenty-page pamphlet called *America Prepares the Next War.* And in *The Communist,* of which I was now the editor, I returned to my old theme of the horrors of total war. I got an able chemist, whose name doesn't matter here, to write a series on poison gases and chemical warfare. But suddenly my chemist disappeared from the scene of public life. Apparently, the Soviet Secret Police (the G.P.U.) had taken an interest in such a specialist, perhaps with the favorable recommendation of the Central Committee or its executive secretary, and he disappeared from my view. I did not hear from him again until some time during World War II when he had broken with his secret employers, and, finding the journal *Foreign Affairs* during the grand alliance too full of illusions concerning Stalin as our glorious ally, he tried to persuade me to write for the journal and "cure" its editor of his grand alliance illusions.

When I returned from the Sixth Congress of the Communist International, I wrote in a report: ". . . the whole work of the Sixth Congress on every question leads to the same conclusion—that the war danger is the decisive factor in the present situation. The keynote of the message of the congress to the various sections of the Comintern may be summed up with two slogans as follows: We are in a war period, and Prepare the parties for war."

Did I believe this? It still seemed improbable to me that such a war would break out in the 1920s. Not until 1939, when Stalin and Hitler signed a pact for the division of the world, did a general world war begin. And then the issues and the protagonists were quite different. Why then did I silence my doubts on the presence of a war situation at the end of the twenties? It is a question that it is hard for me to answer. While in Moscow I tried to get hold of Bukharin to argue with him and question him on this matter, but as the factotum of the Congress, he never had a spare moment, so I returned to America with my doubts, although I stilled them, because taking the line of the Communist International as gospel was becoming a habit with me as with everybody else in our party.

Coupled with this fixation on the imminent war danger was a declaration that in all parties everywhere in the world "the Right danger has become the main danger." Why? Why in all parties everywhere in the world? Was not each party in a different stage of development? Did they not have different components and differing histories?

Added to that was the categorical declaration that all parties were now entering into a "Third Period." Why the periodization? And why for all parties? Had not some of these 58 parties barely been formed before the Sixth Congress? Were they, too, already in their "Third Period"? I was answered that the Comintern was a single world party dealing with a single world situation, and that all its parties, new or old, were but sections of this one world party dealing with a single world situation.

I examined Bukharin's report, The World Situation. "The third period," it said, "is the period in which the economy of capitalism and at the same time the economy of the Soviet Union surpass the pre-war level . . . This third period, in which the antagonisms between the growth of productive forces and the restriction of markets have greatly intensified, inevitably leads to a fresh epoch of wars among the imperialist states, of wars against imperialism . . . of gigantic class struggles." I was back to the imminent war danger, plus a new element: "gigantic class struggles."

Since I could not get ten or fifteen minutes alone with Bukharin, I tried another member of the Russian delegation, Dmitri Manuilski. Our discussion was short and sharp. It ended something like this:

"Comrade Manuilski, do you not see that the world consists of an infinite variety of countries in enormously different stages of development, with different social structures and different concerns?"

"No, we see one world. We are a world party, every section of which faces the same world situation. The little powers will be dragged in the wake of the great powers, as they were in the last world war. Maybe you think America is an exception to our analysis? I think America is now in its 1905, and will soon be in its 1917."

I looked at him in amazement. The America of Warren Harding and Calvin Coolidge in its 1905! In the thirties America was to go through the greatest depression in its history without a 1905 or a 1917 occurring. It might have done Manuilski some good to live in America for a while before he dogmatized so simply. I could get nothing from him, and I felt I could give nothing to him. That ended our discussion.

THE CORRIDOR CONGRESS

On the surface, the Congress going on in the Great Hall of the Columns proceeded with complete unanimity. In little rooms and cubicles around the Great Hall, where the resolutions on the work of the separate parties were discussed, there might be differences, often sharp differences, but sooner or later what the Russian delegation wanted to be adopted there was also adopted unanimously—or else the days of the few holdouts in the ranks of the Comintern were numbered.

Bukharin, as we have seen, delivered all the reports in the Great Hall, and all of his reports were adopted unanimously. At the final 46th session of the Congress he was unanimously elected Chairman of the incoming Executive Committee of the Communist International. The hall rang with cheers for him; the delegates rose to their feet and sang *The International* in his honor in their various languages.

But on every side of the Great Hall, as in any well-built theater or opera house, there were exits leading to corridors which surrounded the meeting place. And in these corridors there were a number of young men from the Russian Communist Party led by the Georgian, Vissarion (or Besso) Lominadze, and his inseparable associate, Lazar Abramovich Shatskin, two leaders of the Russian Communist Youth Movement. They hardly troubled to attend the Congress itself or to listen to Bukharin's addresses and reports, but seemed to spend all their time in the corridors, buttonholing delegates as they went out into the corridors for a rest or a smoke, and retailing gossip against Bukharin. "Yes, his report on the world situation is all right now, but only after the Politburo amended it and eliminated its errors." They said the same of his Program and his report thereon, and of every other address or report he delivered. "We corrected him . . . we put in or sharpened the formulation of the idea of the Third Period and the idea that the Right Danger was the main danger in every party." When a delegate would ask who "we" was, he learned that "we" was the Stalinists, or Joseph Stalin himself, or one of his close adherents and spokesmen.

Why, then, was Bukharin reporting on everything? Why was he getting such stormy applause? Why was he unanimously elected Chairman of the ECCI? Why was Stalin so silent at the Congress? Why did there appear to be two "congresses,"—one in the Great Hall luxuriating in its enthusiasm and unanimity, and another going on in the corridors, full of gossip, carping criticism, and hints of Bukharin's unworthiness to lead the Communist International? Was it because Joseph Stalin was still virtually unknown in the Communist International and Bukharin the most popular figure in all the parties, except where some faction remembered Trotsky's role in the conquest of power in November, 1917, and in directing the Red Army in the years of the civil war? Was a fight brewing in the Russian Communist Party? If so, why were their differences not ventilated in the Congress itself or in one of its subcommittees? After all, the World Congress was the supreme body of the Communist International, and it was settling all the problems and differences within each of its subordinate sections or parties. What else but a World Congress such as this with its 58 parties represented would have the authority to settle differences in the most important of its parties? Would all our parties not feel the blow if a fight should break out in the Russian Communist Party?

We of the American delegation held a meeting with the German delegation to discuss this question. We instructed our spokesmen in the most confidential and most important of the subcommittees of the Congress, the *Seniorenkonvent*, or Council of the Elders, to ask point blank whether there was a fight brewing in the Russian Communist Party. And if so, why shouldn't all the parties of the Comintern help to settle it, since it concerned all of them and since they were now present in a World Congress, the supreme body of the International?

It was our delegate to the *Seniorenkonvent*, Jay Lovestone, who asked the question: "Is there a fight brewing in the Russian Communist Party? If so, isn't a World Congress with a special Russian subcommission the place to settle it?"

Stalin took it upon himself to answer. "There are no differences in the leadership of the Russian party," he said gruffly. "All the reports of Comrade Bukharin to the Congress were considered by our Central Committee and approved unanimously." The answer seemed simple and reassuring, yet it left unsolved the mystery of the "Corridor Congress." And, though we did not fully realize it when Lovestone reported to us, Stalin had several reasons for being furious. He was getting ready to fight Bukharin as soon as the congress safely adjourned. But take it up at the Sixth Congress? Never! For he had as yet no standing in the Communist International; he had never delivered a report to a Congress, nor played a leading role in any of them. He knew how to wait. He was waiting now for the delegates from the 58 parties to return to their homelands. When the Congress which cheered Bukharin until the rafters rang was safely adjourned, then would be the time to begin his attack, first on Bukharin's followers and then on the leaders of all the parties that showed admiration for the one whom the dying Lenin had called the "darling of the party." Yet here was Lovestone, and Ewert for the German delegation, asking that a Russian Commission be set up by the Congress to settle differences in the Russian party. And who were all these nobodies that filled the hall of the Sixth Congress? It was all right for the Russians to judge all the other parties and their problems, but what gave the other parties the impudence to believe that they could judge the Russians? Stalin would never forgive Lovestone's attempt to call the Russian party to account for its internal affairs before the Congress.

And Joseph Stalin had yet another special reason for harboring suspicions concerning Lovestone. When the Budget Commission of the *Seniorenkonvent* met to consider the requests of the American Communist party for funds, Lovestone said: "For our campaigns on issues that spring from American life, we ask no assistance. If our issues are properly chosen, we should be able to raise money to support our campaigns from the masses to whom we are appealing. But whenever the American party is asked to carry on some campaign by the Comintern on some international issue affecting all lands, then we may make a request for funds to cover the costs of such a campaign." This dignified statement, one would think, would arouse enthusiasm in the Russian party, for the American party was offering to finance the campaigns that rose directly out of the issues of American life, the campaign for funds being part of the campaign on the issues. Yet Stalin's insight told him that this was a "Declaration of Independence" on the part of the American party, and Stalin wanted the parties to be dependent as completely as possible on the Russian party and thus more subservient to it.

Perhaps the difference might be illustrated by a story just then current in our movement. The First World War had swallowed up all efforts and all materials, so that new homes were not built and there was a shortage of living space. There followed a period of prosperity and high interest rates; rents for apartments skyrocketed. Our party formed tenants' leagues, called rent strikes, set up picket lines to prevent the ousting of tenants and the dumping of their household goods on the streets for failure to pay the rent on time.

As the story goes, the picket line of one of the apartment houses chose to carry signs concerning both rents and the worldwide campaign ordered by the Comintern under the slogan, "Hands Off China." Whereupon the landlord approached a woman tenant leading the line with a placard reading "HANDS OFF CHINA!"

"Sarah," said the landlord, "I have a bargain to make with you. I'll keep my hands off China; you keep your hands off my apartment house."

The "Hands Off China" campaign seemed a proper one on a world scale at the moment, but America's attitude toward China, still conditioned by the "Open Door" policy, was quite different from that of the powers that had seized extraterritorial treaty ports and seemed to be trying to extend their areas of extraterritorial control. The rent issue was close to the feelings of the tenant pickets, while "Hands Off China" seemed remote to tenants striking in the Bronx. For the rent issue Lovestone believed he could raise funds from those who suffered from high rents. For *Hands Off China!* we would conduct a campaign, too, but might ask help with funds if the campaign proved costly and collections meager. Stalin rightly recognized in Lovestone's distinction a "declaration of independence" and yet other heresies.

And heresies were easy to find when one was looking for them and had the authority to declare what was orthodoxy and what was heresy. Thus from 1925 to 1928 it was official doctrine in the Comintern that "American capitalism is still healthy," though it might be good insurance policy to add "but not for long." The words, "still healthy," were first used by Eugene Varga, a Hungarian who had been People's Commissar for Finance and Chairman of the Supreme Economic Council of the short-lived Hungarian Soviet Republic of 1919, and then, fleeing to Russia, had become the official oracle of the Communist International on the state of the economy of the world. Having pronounced American capitalism still healthy in 1925, in 1926 he enlarged his formula by adding, "as opposed to

European capitalism . . . it is certainly on the upgrade." The American Commissions set up by the Comintern at various times played variations on this theme, such as "American finance capitalism is now more powerful than ever . . . but will get ever more deeply entangled in the contradictions and crises of European capitalism." Absurdly enough, the reverse of this "but" clause proved to be true in the 1930s when it was the European economy that got ever more entangled in the great crisis which started on the American farms in 1926, spread to the cities, industry, and the stock market in 1929, and then to Europe.

When Bukharin succeeded Zinoviev as the leader of the Comintern, he broadened the formula to read "the United States, to some extent Japan, and some British dominions are still countries of upward capitalist development." Later he added that "American capitalism is the stronghold of the entire capitalist system, the most powerful capitalism in the world."

Thus, Jay Lovestone seemed to be saying nothing unusual when he declared in July, 1928, "We have an economic depression . . . but the American national economy, as such, is not declining fundamentally."

By the end of 1927 Stalin, having safely disposed of Zinoviev and Trotsky with Bukharin's aid, decided to turn on Bukharin and rule the world alone. Lovestone, Stalin reckoned, was the leader of an American faction to which the Comintern, under Bukharin's leadership, had given full support. The Comintern had found Lovestone's faction "more loyal" to it and "closer to its views." What was needed now was an issue to prove that the majority leadership of the American party was less loyal and infinitely distant from the Comintern's views. Stalin decided that Lovestone was an American exceptionalist, a believer that America was an exception to the newly proclaimed dogma of the Third Period, the period of fierce and decisive class battles and the universal decay of capitalism.

At the Fifteenth Congress of the Russian party, which prepared the party's stand for the Sixth Congress of the Comintern, Stalin decided that the period of "partial and temporary stabilization of capitalism" had come to an end, that capitalism was in a new state of "collapsing stabilization" and was on "the eve of a new revolutionary upsurge." This was the Third Period that Bukharin, under Stalin's pressure, had announced in his report on the world situation.

According to Stalin this new period of "revolutionary upsurge" applied to America just as well as to Europe. His proof? The American and worldwide Sacco-Vanzetti demonstrations! But Bukharin, in his report, still fenced with Stalin's new analysis. Yes, he said, we are "at the beginning of a new period . . . a period of active struggle . . . But I do not wish to say that we are now on the eve of an immediate revolutionary situation in Europe." Still less, he cautioned, was there a revolutionary situation in the United States. Yet that is just what Stalin was trying to force upon him with the formula of a new "Third Period." And Manuilsky, as spokesman for Stalin, pointed up the disagreement in the Russian delegation by warning us that we should not "draw pessimistic conclusions concerning the prospects of the American Communist and labor movements." Those prospects were for "the revolutionization of America" in the near future. That is what he had meant by telling me, as he later did Lovestone in the American Commission, that America had reached its "period of 1905."

There we sat in the Sixth Congress like dummies, for Bukharin did not, nor did he dare to, tell us of the losing battle he was fighting in the Russian Stalin-packed Politburo and Central Committee. So we left for America satisfied, for the new oracle had spoken with Delphic clarity, and indeed we could take heart when we saw that Bukharin was *unanimously* elected Chairman of the incoming Executive Committee of the Comintern, all the Russians voting for him like the rest of us, and joining in the final demonstration in his honor. How could we know that a week before the Congress opened, Bukharin in despair secretly visited Kamenev and told him with trembling lips that Stalin "is an unprincipled intriguer who subordinates everything to the preservation of his power. In order to get rid of someone, at any given moment he will change his theories . . . He has spoiled the program for me in many places . . . He will slay me with chess moves."

Stalin was not quite ready for the kill, and he knew that he could not stake his exiguous world reputation against Bukharin's at the Sixth World Congress of the Communist International. But as soon as the delegates had left for their homes, Stalin opened fire on Bukharin. Even then the battle was waged for some time behind the scenes. It took us several months to realize that there was something wrong in Moscow.

I TRY TO ELECT FOSTER AS PRESIDENT OF THE UNITED STATES

When we got back to America in September, we found a presidential election on our hands. We had already nominated our most popular trade union leader, William Z. Foster, as our candidate for president, and Benjamin Gitlow, prominent in the New York trade union movement, as vice-president, and had imitated the absurd prolonged cheering and marching with state delegation banners through the hall that characterized the Democratic and Republican conventions. I think that both the older parties outdistanced us in the number of carefully counted minutes in which they could not contain their carefully organized marching through the hall. Undaunted by our inferior noise-making capacity, I as Agitprop Director, like the two candidates who headed our ticket, toured the country from end to end, trying to bring out the vote in support of our nominees. For me it was a wonderful chance to see our country, and wherever I went, we managed to fill a hall with our supporters, many of them, however, foreign-born workers who had not even troubled to become citizens and potential voters.

Somewhere in the middle of the campaign our candidate for vice-president, Benjamin Gitlow, disappeared for a few days and failed to notify the national office that he was taking a rest, or to give the reasons for the break in his energetic campaign. The fertile mind of John Pepper got the bright idea of having the national office release a story that our candidate for vice-president had been kidnapped in the middle of the Arizona desert and sequestered by sinister persons unknown to us. This melodrama was featured for several days in the *Daily Worker* and released to "the capitalist press." Then suddenly Gitlow reappeared to meet his next speaking date. The fact behind this weird tale was that the Communist organizers in Arizona had cancelled Gitlow's speaking date in Phoenix, owing to rumors that a vigilante committee had been formed to drive Gitlow out of the state and cast him loose somewhere in the midst of the desert. When the organizers informed Gitlow, he did not stop over in Phoenix. Eventually he did speak there with not a sign of a vigilante committee, except that some group had made sure that no hall could be secured and our candidate for vice-president had to speak in the central plaza. Orating in his powerful voice, Ben Gitlow could just as well have spoken in the noisiest plaza in Rome and been heard by everybody. Of course, the irresponsible fiction backfired and surely added nothing to our total vote. In the end, despite the best efforts of our campaigners (Foster campaigned in Moscow until he got back from the Sixth Congress; Gitlow stayed home and spent the entire summer campaigning), our Agitprop Director, and many other speakers; our candidates got 48,228 votes in the 33 states where we managed to get on the ballot, the Socialist candidate Norman Thomas got something like 268,000 votes, Alfred E. Smith received some fifteen million, and Herbert Hoover twenty-one million. For the first time the Communist Party outdistanced the Socialist Labor Party nationally, but it received something like one-sixth of the vote of the Socialist Party. Foster professed to see in his own vote and in that of the pro-labor Catholic, Alfred Smith, a sign of the radicalization of America.

WE DISPOSE OF THE OPPOSITION

As soon as we were convinced that we had not elected a president of the United States, we turned to the more esoteric business of our internal party life. The delegates to the Sixth Congress of the Comintern, both those of the party majority and those of the opposition, reported to membership meetings everywhere on the results of the Congress. During the course of this discussion, candidates were nominated for the forthcoming Sixth Congress of the American Communist Party. In our reports we discussed the strength or weakness of American capitalism, the degree of radicalization of the American working class, the Right Danger, the War Danger, the new Program on which the Comintern, or rather Bukharin, had been working since the First Congress, and the need, underscored by the instructions of the Comintern, to abolish factionalism in our party and create a unified party.

We won an overwhelming victory over our opposition and might have wiped it out completely had it not been for the fact that some of its leaders took comfort from the "Corridor Congress," which seemed to tell a different story from the Congress that met and made unanimous decisions in the Hall of Columns.

"The voting for convention delegates," I wrote in *International Press Correspondence (Inprecorr)*, "completely wiped out the party opposition as a political force in all industrial centers. The opposition received no votes among the miners, steelworkers, or textile workers. The vote on the Iron Range was 107 against 1. . . on the Copper Range 115 to 0. . . . in the Ohio Coal Fields 115-0. The Anthracite and Soft Coal Regions voted unanimously for the Central Committee. . . . The opposition received some support only in California and in New York, in which city the opposition carried 5 units and the Central Committee 72."

In the article in *Inprecorr* I offered some reasons for the resounding defeat of the opposition:

First, they campaigned for support on the basis of having reservations about the decisions of the Sixth World Congress. This aroused the indignation of our members who had had dinned into them loyalty to the Comintern and its decisions—but it must have been pleasing to Joseph Stalin, for the Sixth World Congress was to be Bukharin's last public performance, while the Corridor Congress about which the opposition voiced its reservations was nothing less than embryonic Stalinism, the wave of the future.

Second, the opposition rejected, but the membership favored, the Central Committee's proposal for unity "on the basis of the acceptance of the Comintern's decisions, all other matters to be adjusted by mutual agreement."

Third, in the course of the discussion part of the opposition bloc, Cannon and his followers, went over to Trotskyism, and were expelled from the party by unanimous vote of the Central Committee, including the minority members.

Fourth, "the most capable leader of the party opposition, Comrade Foster, was defeated for leadership of the opposition by Comrade Bittelman." The secret reason behind the Bittelman rebellion was that Lovestone and Pepper had at last come to accept my view suggested to Gusev in Mexico, which Gusev had called "naive"—namely, that Foster should be recognized as the ablest and most experienced trade union leader in the party and Lovestone as the ablest political leader, and on the basis of this mutual recognition and division of labor, unity should be established in a party that needed the experience and insights of both of them.

This, it seemed to us, is what the Comintern had been demanding and what the party needed—the end of the long factional struggle between Fosterites and Lovestonites. Dutifully, we discussed the "War Danger," the "Right Danger as the main danger," the "radicalization of the American working class," the expected "upsurge of new and fierce class battles," and all the unanimous decisions of the Sixth World Congress. We rejoiced, I perhaps more than others, at the sound basis that seemed to have been laid for unity between the Fosterite trade union specialists and the Lovestonite political specialists and experts in matters of theory.

To be sure, I was sceptical about the imminence of the "War Danger." Was it anything more than a device to stir greater loyalty to the Soviet government and its leaders? But, as I have already told the reader, I contented myself with the congenial task of emphasizing the horrors of modern total war and its technology, particularly the use of chemical warfare.

As for the Right Danger, I did not know what it was meant to signify, nor did Lovestone. Had we suspected that Stalin was sharpening this slogan as a deadly weapon against Bukharin, we might have thought twice about mechanically repeating it.

In late 1928, as he sharpened this new and deadly weapon, anointing its tip with poison, Stalin still publicly declared: "In the Political Bureau there are neither 'Right' nor 'Left' deviations nor conciliators towards these deviations. This must be said quite categorically. It is time to put a stop to the tittletattle spread by enemies of the party and by oppositionists of all kinds about there being a Right deviation, or a conciliatory attitude toward the Right deviation, in the Political Bureau of our Central Committee" (from Stalin's speech, *The Right Danger in the CPSU*, delivered on October 19, 1920). Since we did not know the real situation in the Russian Party, we looked a little foolishly for representatives of the Right Danger in our own Party.

And as for the prophesied upsurge of huge class battles in America, neither Lovestone, nor Foster, nor I myself, nor any perceptive leader of the American party believed in its immediacy. We all agreed that Manuilsky's *bon mot* about America having reached its 1905 was utter nonsense. And the behavior of our workingmen during the long depression of the 1930s was to prove that we were right. But we had been so used to repeating formulae adopted by the Communist International that we imbedded these dubious formulations concerning huge class battles into the documents we put out.

For the rest, we faced our forthcoming convention with unwonted confidence, for we had won almost all the delegates and had to adopt the generous and healing decision to freely grant Foster and his followers a number of additional delegates that they had not won from the membership during the discussion and voting period.

We faced the Communist International, too, with confidence. We had put an end to the long factional struggle, as they had so often routinely demanded, even while their often ambiguous decisions had worked to keep the warring factions alive so that the men in Moscow might choose among them. For the first time, moreover, there was a majority approaching unanimity that might act as a leading force should. And for the first time in our history, the overwhelming majority of the delegates to the convention had been workers in industry, mostly heavy industry, and not party functionaries who might perhaps have once been industrial workingmen.

Finally, the Comintern's Sixth Congress had pleased us. Despite the residue of doubts just cited, we incorporated all the decisions adopted unanimously by the Congress into our own convention resolutions. Whomever we next sent to Moscow should be able to go, not in the company of a bitterly fighting, dissenting minority, but as the real representative of over 90% of his party. Even if we had used proportional representation, which was not customary in trade unions or in our party, and if we had added together all the votes the opposition had won in New York City and California and in small towns of light industry and trade elsewhere, the Central Committee's majority would still have been something like 75% of the total vote cast. Following our usual procedure, we had won our ninety-odd percentage of the delegates after a full and free discussion of two months in all units, with representatives appearing from all factions, and with fair and free elections in which no administrative or mechanical measures had been used to secure this overwhelming vote, and no fight had occurred in the purely formal Credentials Committee.

Yet, without knowing it, we had crossed the Rubicon. Nothing could so anger Stalin as the awareness that the American party was now at last united and free from significant factions or factionalism, and that it was united behind men like Lovestone, whom he suspected of sympathizing with Bukharin. What he needed for his next moves on a world scale was not united parties, byt parties divided into warring factions from which he could pick and choose the most pliant and subservient. Only thus could he turn the Comintern into the Stalintern.

27

ARMED WITH A SLINGSHOT

The opposition's position seemed so hopeless and Bittelman's leadership so inferior to Foster's, that Fosterites of long standing began to desert. Thus Ella Reeve Bloor, a veteran of the Socialist and Communist movements, wrote to Foster from California, "There would be no real opposition *without you.* No one through the country knows Aronberg or Bittelman. Out here, the opposition is called the 'Foster group' and things are done in your name that would make you gasp for breath." Cannon and his intimates had gone over to Trotskyism. Foster wavered between fighting on with secret encouragement from Lozovsky who considered the TUEL to be the American branch of the Profintern, or taking seriously the prospect for a dignified unification of the party with himself as the outstanding trade union leader. We were in, it seemed, for a blessed period of peace, or at least a long breathing spell from factionalism, and a chance, as I had written in my 1926 pamphlet, *Our Heritage from 1776,* "to begin to discover America," its native peculiarities, and our heritage from them.

Then suddenly out of a clear sky, there were several flashes of heat lighting. The premonitory signs of a storm were coming from Moscow.

TWO MORE LETTERS ON THE AMERICAN QUESTION

On September 7, 1928, one short week after the Sixth Congress adjourned, a letter was dispatched to the American party from the Executive Committee of the Communist International. It was a trifle ambiguous, but on the whole favorable to the Central Committee majority. It declared that both factions had made some Right Errors, but "the charge against the majority of the Central Committee of the Party as representing a Right line is unfounded."

What were our "Right Errors"? They were not spelled out and the term was not given clear meaning. Moreover, though Lovestone was diligently seeking out "Right-Errors" as per orders, neither Foster nor Lovestone nor I really believed that there was a serious "Right-Danger" in the American party. Nevertheless, as an editor of *The Communist*, in December, 1928, I dutifully wrote the lead article entitled, "The Right-Danger in the Comintern," largely a collection of abstract clichés, parroting the phrases used in *Inprecorr* and Communist resolutions. There was little substance or concreteness to my article, either.

"The Sixth Congress," Lovestone wrote, "examined and hunted for Right-Dangers with a microscope and telescope, and wherever it found these [dangers], it hunted them down with heavy artillery and machine-gun fire."

Though we hunted with whatever "scopes" we possessed, about all we could find were such miniscule pecadillos as the fact that the California Communists, in challenging the California Socialists to a preelection debate had addressed their challenge, "Dear Comrades." It seemed to me that this hardly warranted the use of either heavy artillery or machine-gun fire against the district organizer and Executive Committee, who were severely condemned for the "grave error" of sending a letter "independent of its contents," in which the "ever more fascist" Socialist leadership was addressed as "comrades." Had I been in that Political Committee meeting, I feel sure I should have voted against the reproof.* Yet before long I was to learn that Stalin was to call the Socialists "Social-Fascists" and pronounce them, rather than the Nazis, the main danger in Germany. This was a concept that none of us could accept.

In any case, Lovestone found the letter of September 7th on the whole favorable since it categorically declared that the "charge against the Central Committee of representing a Right line was unfounded." The Party majority published this letter and, on Lovestone's motion, gave its own reasonable interpretation that "the Comintern is continuing its policy of supporting the present party leadership."

Such was the letter of September 7th. But scarcely two months later came a second letter of different tenor. It was dated November 21, 1928. One could not think that it came from the same body. Its tone was critical, even menacing. It reprimanded the majority leadership for "too much self-praise and too little self-criticism." It rebuked the majority for interpreting the letter of two months earlier as "continuing the Comintern's support politically, of the present party leadership." The letter commented severely: "This formulation could easily lead to the interpretation that the congress has expressly declared its confidence in the majority, in contrast to the minority. But this is not so."

* Some time after I wrote the above, Ludmila Sidoroff discovered in the Hoover Archives a circular showing that I was to be our debater with the California Socialists and therefore must have been an accomplice in the making of this fearful right error.

What was this but a call to arms to the minority to reopen the faction fight? And to give time for more mischief, the letter specifically instructed the American leadership to postpone their intended convention until February, 1929. That meant time for another two months' discussion period and implied that the ECCI, some subcommittee of the Comintern, or somebody in high place in it had in mind the preparation of yet another letter to add fuel to the fire it was rekindling.

Lovestone kept this November letter to himself for an entire week so that he could puzzle out its meaning and decide what to do about it. Then he turned it over to the Politburo together with an answer he had drafted.

When the Executive Committee of the Communist International speaks with such sharpness, there is little a "section" can do beyond accepting it. In gingerly fashion one may put it into the context of the more favorable decisions made at the Sixth Congress and immediately after. And perhaps by careful lobbying and seeing the "right people," one might later come to the decision to offset it in tone and content. But the draft Lovestone presented to the Central Executive Committee of the party was essentially one of humble agreement, containing such statements as:

> The Central Executive Committee accepts and endorses without reservations the criticism of the Communist International contained in the letter. The Political Secretariat of the Comintern is correct in stating that the Central Executive Committee declaration of October 2 . . . did not place with sufficient emphasis the criticism of the Right-mistakes in the Party [a vague and rather wooly phrase]. . . . The Central Executive Committee regrets the impression of self-praise given in its decision of October 2. . . .

Then it quoted as a judgment, not of the majority leadership alone but of *the whole party,* the undoubted praise that the Sixth Congress gave to the improvement of the work of the American Communist Party; agreed to postpone its convention until February as directed; and ended with four slogans, of which one consisted of the cheerless and humble words, "For merciless self-criticism of errors of the Central Executive Committee and the Party as a whole!" Such was the rhetoric being forced upon the American party, and doubtless upon other parties, by some mysterious changes that were going on.

The change of tone was so great between the September letter and the November letter that we realized something mysterious was happening. Obviously, we were not being properly informed by our own representative there. "Bert," Lovestone said to me, "something is happening is Moscow that I do not understand. Our representative, Engdahl, doesn't seem to notice any change. He hasn't told us a thing. Neither has anyone else. This unfriendly letter comes as a complete surprise. Some stronger man must replace Engdahl. While everything is in flux here and we are trying to negotiate party unity with Bill Foster, I can't leave. We need a first-rate man there, so you'll have to go. You will sit on the Executive Committee (ECCI) and Presidium. But more important, you will see the top Russians and find out what's happening and how you can influence things."

"How long will I have to stay there?"

"Your stay will be indefinite, until you are recalled or replaced. You had better take Ella with you. You're in for a long stay."

The idea was attractive, but I stalled while I thought it over. To sit on what unctuously called itself "The General Staff of the World Revolution," to get to know the top men of the Russian Communist party, to see what life in Russia was really like—it all sounded exciting. Mexico had made great changes in my way of looking at life. What would Russia do to me?

"Why didn't Engdahl tell us something about what is really happening?" I asked.

"Oh, him! He's a lightweight, a dimwit. He spends his time chasing the girls—they're easily caught by an American, and they can always hope to snare one for good and get taken to America. But politically, he doesn't know what's happening under his nose."

"Then why did you send him?"

"Oh, all the parties do that. They elect their top leaders to the ECCI, but they're needed at home, so they send substitutes. But now something important is happening there, something puzzling. We need a top man to inform us and represent us and inform the Russians, too. Bert, you've simply got to go."

"When do I leave?"

"I can't tell you yet. A change of reps has to go through the Politburo, maybe even the Central Committee. We'll have to find reasons for recalling Engdahl without spelling everything out too clearly."

"O.K. I'll go." I knocked off work to go home and tell Ella to get ready for the big move to a new land. The news was quite upsetting to my wife. Not that she didn't look forward to the adventure, but she was upset that I couldn't give her a fixed date. It was the uncertainty that upset her. A man can set off on a journey in a day, with a few hours to pack—many more hours in my case to think what to take with me in books and documents for the making of possible reports—and some special thought concerning Russia's wintry cold at the Moscow latitude—things like mufflers, lined gloves, earmuffs, heavy overcoat, flannel shirts. And some thought about taking things you couldn't buy in Moscow, like a five-pound can of Washington coffee (what they called coffee in Moscow was an undrinkable concoction), bandaids, disinfectants, and other ordinary medicaments that were almost impossible to get in Russia after more than a decade of the new social order.* I gathered the things together that I thought necessary and therefore didn't mind in the least the uncertainty as to the date of departure. But on Ella the uncertainty seemed to cause considerable

* After six decades this is still true, because Russia invests most of her capital on things for power and war and only the bare minimum on consumer goods for the masses. After five or six decades Russia is still both a developing country and a superpower, the second country in the world in military might and crowding us closely, but the twentieth in production per capita.

strain. Credentials, typed on silk and signed by Lovestone, were sewed into the lining of my jacket. I secured a passport from Canada once more, for I knew our own Government would not give us a passport for such a journey. At last we got steamship tickets and our date of departure was settled.

The trip was uneventful. When we got to our first frontier and were standing in line waiting for the Immigration Inspector, I thought it best to remind my wife that she was traveling as a Canadian. "Ella," I said, "which do you like better, living in New York or in Montreal?"

"Why I was never in Montreal in my life!"

The look on my face was enough to tell her that she had better have been in Montreal. In any case, when husband and wife travel on one passport, the Inspector normally addresses all questions to the husband, so there were no problems.

When we got to Berlin it was New Year's Eve. We were invited to a party at the home of M. N. Roy, at which all the girls seemed to be German blondes, including technical secretaries of the large German delegation in Moscow, and virtually all the men were Indians. The party lasted all night—first at Roy's home, and then we marched arm in arm through the crowds of Germans who were marching rather more with determination than with joy along Unter den Linden and Friedrichstrasse. We got back to our hotel at dawn on the first day of 1929, the year, as Stalin was to call it, of the *Great Turn.* In America, the stock market was to reach its feverish heights and then, that autumn, the Great Depression would begin. In Germany, the Nazi movement, that same autumn, would begin to attain a mass character. In the countries and regions that lived largely by the sale of raw materials, prices would plummet abruptly and stay down for years. In Russia, Stalin would arrogate to himself absolute personal power and begin the forced collectivization of agriculture, the helter-skelter planless plan, and forced-tempo industrialization. It was indeed to be the year of the *Velikij Perelom,* the Great Turn. I do not know whether the determined, solid dancing and marching on the boulevards of Berlin was a sign of the feeling of uncertainty, even depression, among the Germans who filled the streets from side to side, or whether that was the way they always celebrated the fact that an old year was dying and a new one coming in. The following night, when we took the train eastward, Ella had developed a severe cold which turned into influenza. I was her nurse, and by the time we got to Moscow she was recovering and I had gotten it.

Despite my influenza I began at once to make the rounds of those I thought I had to see, trying to protect them from infection by keeping a decent distance away from those I spoke to. The first man I went to see was J. Louis Engdahl. To my consternation, before I could open my mouth, he said to me, "Bert, tell me, what's happening here?"

"You've been here two years, while I haven't been here two days. It's up to you to tell me what's happening."

"Well, I don't know what's going on. They don't seem as friendly as they used to be. They just adopted a nasty letter to the American party."

"Did you vote against it?"

"How could I? Everybody else voted for it without discussion. It was full of good, old-time radical formulations. I couldn't be the only one to vote against it, could I?"

"Of course you could. It's your party. You could have spoken against what you didn't like. You could have offered amendments. You could have voted against it."

"Oh, it wasn't that bad."

I felt a sense of hopelessness. Anyhow, he was going home. Now it was my job. "Have you got a copy? Let's see it."

Engdahl handed me his copy, headed: OPEN LETTER TO THE CENTRAL COMMITTEE OF THE AMERICAN COMMUNIST PARTY.

I read the letter with utter dismay. Its authors seemed completely ignorant of the realities of American life, the internal life of the American Communist Party, the American labor movement, the nature of the American government, the place of America in the world of the twenties. It began with two or three paragraphs of praise, then cancelled them out with twenty or thirty paragraphs of condemnation, the praise being as irrelevant as the censure. It talked of right-errors and left-errors as if they were counters in a word game, without once spelling out concretely what the errors were or why they were errors. It justly denounced the factionalism which for six years had eaten at the vitals of the American party without taking into account the fact that the party had finally unified itself behind the Central Committee, and that, unless the Comintern now intervened, the faction war was over. Clearly, the *Open Letter* did intervene for the express purpose of rekindling that struggle, even as it denounced it.

The letter denounced both factions for having failed to mention, of all things, a textile strike in Lodz, Poland. "In the theses of both groups," it complained, "the Lodz strike is not even mentioned!" Why in God's name should either group think of mentioning a textile strike in Poland when writing theses on America? Undoubtedly Stalin was planning to use one or two events—in this case the Lodz strike and a workers' struggle in the Ruhr—as symbols or proofs of a supposed worldwide Third Period of "fierce class struggles" and a new time of "world revolution" everywhere. Whoever wrote the letter could just as well have said that both sides had failed to mention the uprising in Canton that ended in failure, or the great wave of textile and railway strikes in Bombay, or with better right the struggles of Sandino and his guerilla bands against the American marines in Nicaragua. If they wanted to make an indictment of our leadership on the basis of what we had "left out" of our theses, they could have filled a book.

When the *Open Letter* did try to touch on an American theme, its author, or authors, wrote that "the election of Herbert Hoover means that American imperialism is resolutely embarked upon a course which leads to colonial wars of occupation . . ." This in view of the fact that Herbert Hoover was beginning to reverse the process started by Woodrow Wilson of sending marines to country after country in Central America in vain attempts to "stabilize governments and restore order." It was only because Herbert Hoover did withdraw our marines from the various Central American lands that Franklin Roosevelt could announce the "good neighbor policy" without having observers of our foreign policy laugh in his face.

I read the letter over and over again without making any sense out of it. It was an *Open Letter* to be published in the *Daily Worker* in order to start a new faction war, and it was so confused that there could be no clarity in the controversy it would incite so that the Comintern would have to intervene to pronounce judgments on the formless issues raised and persons involved. It must have been written not by clear-thinking theoreticians like Bukharin nor willful ones like Stalin, but by some petty bureaucrats in the Comintern apparatus. Probably some old enemies of our party majority like Lozovsky and Bennet had put their heads together to concoct it. In 1906 Lozovsky had fled from arrest and exile in Russia to Paris, where he worked in the Hatters' Union and became its chairman from 1909 to 1917. Returning to Bolshevism in 1917, he had opposed Lenin on the trade union question and had been expelled from the Bolshevik party in 1918, then rehabilitated as one of the few Bolsheviks who knew something about trade unions, and made Secretary General of the rachitic Red Trade Union International or Profintern. Was it he who put into the *Open Letter* the demand that we abandon Lenin's teachings on working in the established trade unions and set up dual, revolutionary unions of our own little handfuls? Or did it come from some higher-up figure bent on having nothing but "revolutionary unions" for the *Third Period?* (Actually, Stalin's line and Lozovsky's on unions coincided.)

Bennet was the English pseudonym of Goldfarb, who had been a furious enemy of the Communists while writing for the *Jewish Daily Forward* in New York. Returning to Russia after the 1917 uprisings, he had changed his name to Petrovsky, and then, rising in the Comintern to the post of Chairman of the Anglo-American Commission, he had changed his name to Bennet. His stay in America as a Jewish Social Democrat had not helped him much to understand the United States.

No matter who had written the *Open Letter,* I had to demand that it be rejected or completely rewritten from start to finish, and preferably sent as a confidential document, not an open letter. Despite my influenza and the fever I was running, I went to Otto Kuusinen, a Finn in exile in Russia who functioned as Acting Secretary of the ECCI, and asked for an appointment with Bukharin. "Bukharin," he told me, "is not well."

"Can I visit him to inquire after his health?"

"No," said Kuusinen firmly, "he is too sick to function as chairman of the ECCI."

I got the same answer when I asked the same question of Piatnitski,

Organization Secretary of the Comintern. I returned to Kuusinen's office. "I'd like to see Comrade Stalin," I told him.

"Comrade Stalin is too busy."

"Then I should like to tell you and Comrade Piatnitski what I think of the *Open Letter* that the EECI has decided to send to the American Communist Party. I have just gotten a copy from Comrade Engdahl. I don't know who wrote it, but whoever did was quite ignorant of America and of the situation in our Party. Unless we make some drastic changes in it, it will disgrace the Comintern with any American who reads it. I have just arrived, I have all the latest information. I now make a formal request to you on behalf of the American Communist Party whose representative to the EECI I am, that a special meeting of the Executive Committee be called as soon as possible to consider changes in the letter."

Kuusinen stared at me in astonishment. "Why, why, why, uh, uh, uh," he intoned in his slightly nasal, high-pitched voice. "You are talking of an official document. It has already been adopted by the Executive Committee of the Communist International, adopted by a unanimous vote. Your own representative voted for it. It is now *an official document*. It will have to be sent off without change. Your Party will have to publish it at once as the prelude to your forthcoming convention."

"Comrade Kuunsinen," I said, "I have just come fresh from America, while Engdahl has been here two years. What does he know about the present situation in our country? The ECCI will have to listen to a report from me on what's wrong with that letter and will have to make changes in it, many changes, in tone and in substance. We would look foolish if we publish it. So would the Comintern. We need a special session to reexamine and correct that letter."

"I-i-impossible," he sputtered. "Calm down, Comrade Wolfe. This is now an official document of the Comintern. No one can change it now. You had nothing to do with it. It was adopted before you arrived, and you cannot change it."

"Comrade Kuusinen," I said solemnly, "if you refuse to call a special session of the Executive, or the Presidium, to hear a report from a delegate who is fresh from America on the changes that should be made in that letter, I shall cable my party to that effect, and advise them to reject the letter and refuse to publish it until it is properly amended." Perhaps only an American would have dreamed of talking that way to the Executive of the Communist International about one of its *unanimous* decisions.

Comrade Kuusinen stared at me in utter astonishment. Such language he had never heard in the precincts of the Comintern and he did not know what to say. "Why don't you see Comrade Piatnitski? See Comrade Gusev? See Comrade Bennet of the Anglo-American Commission? Talk to them about it."

"I shall see Piatnitski and I shall see Gusev, and I shall tell them exactly the same thing I have just told you."

We stared at each other for a long time in silence. "If you got such a meeting of the Presidium," he inquired at last, "how much time would you need to discuss the letter and report on the American situation?"

"At least an hour. And after they discuss my report, perhaps fifteen or twenty minutes for rebuttal."

Another long pause. Kuusinen was turning something over in his mind. "Comrade Wolfe," he said at last, "I shall take it up and see whether it is possible." He bent his head over his desk drawer, took out a little sheet of paper and a pencil not more than an inch long. His central drawer was filled with such Lilliputian pencils, the longest of them no more than two inches long from tip to eraser. Was there such a shortage of pencils in Russia? Or did these dwarf pencils symbolize some psychological quirk in his mind? Perhaps Freud might have an answer; at any rate, I didn't. I watched him make a note so tiny that I couldn't read it nor even tell what language it was in. I left his office without another word.

I do not remember what happened during the rest of that day. As I walked up Tverskaya to the Hotel Lux from the Comintern Building, a distance of between a quarter and a half mile, I noted that the lines were getting longer in front of the shops, longer than in 1928, longer than in 1924. In 1924 I had thought charitably of the long lines in front of food stores and other shops as part of the scaffolding of the magnificent but still unfinished edifice that the Bolsheviks were building in the New Russia. When the scaffolding was taken down, the new edifice would be seen in all its splendor. Now, in 1929, I began to wonder: how long would the *xvost*, the queue, continue to exist? And why had the lines grown longer instead of shorter, more ubiquitous instead of more rare?

But my influenza was getting worse and I had the *Open Letter* to think of. When I got into my room I tried to sort the documents I had brought with me, sort them by topics which I tried to match with passages from the fuzzy *Open Letter*. Where my wife was, I don't remember. I suppose she was taking in some of the sights on the streets of a city and world she had never visited before. I had no one else to talk things over with in all of Moscow. Gusev would have been outwardly friendly, but he had voted for the *Open Letter* and would give me the same advice if I had the energy to look for him. Piatnitski would be cold, perhaps hostile. Wicks, who had just been sent by the Central Committee of our party to the Profintern, heaven knows why, was notorious for his vituperation in polemics. Pepper had been summoned back to Moscow, but was afraid of what might await him and was hiding somewhere in America. Bukharin, I had been told, was ill; Stalin too busy. Ewart of the German delegation had been in America briefly as a Comintern rep and was friendly, but he was newly in trouble himself as an incarnation of the "Right Danger" because he had tried to remove Thaelmann, one of Stalin's favorites, from the German leadership when Thaelmann's brother-in-law, Wittdorf, was caught appropriating party funds, and Thaelmann protected him from punishment. In all Moscow there was no one I trusted to consult with, and my influenza and accompanying fever made it hard to think without talking out loud to someone. I lay down, trying to rest, and decided to postpone the battle that faced me until I felt better. But at midnight my phone rang. An unknown voice said: "Comrade Wolfe, there will be a meeting of the Presidium of the ECCI tomorrow. You will be given one hour to present a report on the American Question."

"You mean today? It's about midnight."

"Yes, today. We will send a car for you."

I knew their habits. The first meeting of the day—what would be a morning meeting in our country—would begin after dinner, the main meal of the day, taken at three in the afternoon, and the session might last most of the night. There was no time to lose. I got up, mind awake now under the stress of coming conflict, prepared a pot of boiling water on the *primus*, the single-burner, kerosene stove in my room (having taken the boiling water to start with from the 24-hour boiling *kipjatok* one floor below), opened our can of George Washington coffee and the bottle of vodka I had purchased, and with the aid of coffee and vodka and the sense of urgency, stayed up the whole night and continued next morning preparing my report until the auto came for me. When I took my temperature in the morning it was 104 degrees Fahrenheit.

THE PRESIDIUM OF THE ECCI

The Presidium of the Executive Committee of the Comintern was assembled in force, filling a fairly large meeting room, perhaps forty or fifty or more people representing all important parties, with larger delegations of Italians, Frenchmen, and Germans, and a still larger representation of Russians, including two members of the *Komsomol* or Communist Youth movement, the same two who had been most active in the "Corridor Congress," Lominadze and Shatskin. All the leading Russians seemed to be there except the two top ones, Bukharin, who should have been chairing the meeting, and Stalin, who almost never attended Comintern meetings but depended on reports from his favorites or men of confidence. Whoever was in the chair, probably either Kuusinen or Piatnitski, said simply: "Comrades, this is a special meeting of the Presidium of the ECCI to hear Comrade Wolfe, who has just arrived from America as their new representative to the ECCI. He will give a report on the situation in America, for which he has one hour."

I spoke, naturally, in English, saying that I would discuss the *Open Letter to the American Communist Party*, point out certain weaknesses and inaccuracies in it, and propose certain changes which I thought necessary to make it more in accord with the real situation in my country and in the American party. Then I paused to allow for translation of that brief statement into the various languages of the Presidium.

Practically everybody gathered around the German translator, for most of the members of the Presidium understood German. I went over to this group to listen to the German translation. I was shocked to discover that the translator was making no attempt to translate me accurately, indeed, was making a joke of what I had just said.

I strode back to the rostrum filled with anger. With such a translator, my hour would be wasted. And he knew better, for I had heard the same man translate decently, if not brilliantly, at the Sixth Congress. I had never delivered an address in German in my life, indeed, never spoken more than grammar-book and *Deutscher Verein* German. But after all, I was the honor student and Ward Medal winner in German at the College of the City of New York, and had read poems and ballads, novels and dramas, and works of Marx and Engels and Freud not yet available in English in the original German. I had long ceased using a dictionary, which meant that I had learned to think in German even if I had never spoken it. True, I was ill, and the notes and documents before me were all in English. Nevertheless, in a flash I decided that I would try to speak in German.

"Comrades," I said directly in German, "having listened to the supposed translation of my first remarks by the German translator, I see that it is better to speak bad German here than good English. I have had no practice in speaking German, so I beg those who love the German tongue to forgive me for what I am going to do to it, but I shall try to speak to you in German."

This made a big saving in the miserly hour allotted to me, for I did not pause once thereafter for translation into any other tongue. At first I was slow and hesitant, but my mind soon began working in German; speed and emphasis, and even word order, came to me, and I said what I wanted to clearly and sharply, if not elegantly. I did not look at the faces of my auditors as I was accustomed to when I spoke in English, but kept my eyes and my mind glued to my notes and focused my attention on putting my thoughts into proper and vigorous German. I could feel that the audience had become more attentive and that my speech flowed more easily.

My fever must have risen; the strain told on me—suddenly, at the end of about a half hour, to my consternation I collapsed and fell to the floor, without losing consciousness. There was a stir in the room, but only one person, the prim and elderly Elena Stasova (she was then in her sixties), came up to the platform with two aspirins and a paper cup filled with water. "You are very ill, Comrade Wolfe. I urge you to stop speaking.

"Comrade Stasova," I answered, struggling to my feet, "can you guarantee that I will get another meeting of the Presidium to give me my remaining half hour?" For some reason she shrank back from me as if I had asked for something dangerous. She did not answer, so I returned to the rostrum and resumed my address. I said that the *Open Letter* had been written by some ignorant official of the Comintern who knew nothing about America or its trade union movement and was ignorant of Lenin's *Left-Wing Communism: An Infantile Disorder* and his injunction to us, as it had been the injunction of Marx and Engels, to stay with the mainstream of the labor movement.

When I finished speaking, keeping closely to the time set, the chairman did not ask for questions or discussion as I had expected, but crisply declared that my time was up and the meeting adjourned. Then a strange thing happened. I stepped unsteadily down the steps from the platform, and all the participants rose to their feet, but did not walk out into the aisles or begin to disperse. I had seen such behavior as a tribute when some prominent leader spoke—indeed, it was to become a ritual whenever Comrade Stalin addressed a meeting. But why were they standing like that now? Surely not for me, a mere unknown from an unimportant party. Though I tottered uncertainly, out of illness and weariness, I looked at the faces of those who had been my auditors. Some seemed to me to look puzzled, some shocked, some contemptuous. No one looked at me with sympathy or a smile. People whom I had known for years looked as if they feared contact with me. Perhaps that is why they didn't step out into the aisles. I fixed my eyes on Ercoli (Togliatti), who had been a devoted admirer of Bukharin and one whom I had known, it seemed to me intimately, since the Fifth Congress of 1924. I could see him shrink back from his place on the aisle, as if he feared that I might grasp his hand and ask something like, "What did you think of my talk?"

As I saw all those I knew who had positions on the aisle shrinking slightly, imperceptibly, away from me, as if I were a leper, I suddenly realized that I had not been denouncing an *Open Letter* drafted by petty bureaucrats and malevolent or ignorant minor officials like Lozovsky and Bennet-Goldfarb, but that the real author, or at least the real commander that such a letter be written, could be none other than Joseph Stalin, who must be the new boss of the Comintern and the Russian Communist Party. So that was the man with whom I had just engaged in battle! It was more serious than I had thought, and I had my work cut out for me. But I did not know enough about him to be in awe or afraid. If this was the man who had ordered such a miserable letter to be written, then this was the man whom I would have to argue with and fight. And I would need reinforcements from America.

A BRAVE WOMAN

Then another unexpected thing happened. As I stumbled uncertainly down the long aisle, an old woman holding a cane with a hand gnarled by arthritis walked just as slowly up the aisle from the back of the hall. She met me in almost the exact center and extended her right hand, also gnarled and contracted by arthritis, to grasp mine. All eyes were on us now as if it were a spectacle that they must watch.

"Sehr gut, genosse Wolfe," she said in a deep, hoarse voice that carried through the hall. "*Sehr gut, politisch!*" And then, her wrinkled old face lighting up with a warm smile, she added, *Und sehr gut Deutsch!*" It was Klara Zetkin, the old boon companion of Rosa Luxemburg, of whom Rosa had declared to August Bebel, "There are only two men left in the German Social Democracy, Klara and I."

So I was not altogether alone in that big meeting. I never forgot that moment. And I was especially grateful for the kind words, perhaps exaggerated quite a little, "*und sehr gut Deutsch.*"

I paid dearly for my hour-long talk with a fever of 104 degrees and higher before the hour was over. The whip having been cracked and a unanimous vote taken before I got my special meeting of the Presidium, my address had no effect except to make me *persona non grata* with the Supreme Chief. The Executive Committee of the Comintern simply ignored my criticisms, my refutations, my reductions to absurdity, and sent off the letter to America with all its nonsense and malice, without a single voice against it in Moscow now, for I had developed a painful abscess in my inner ear. For several weeks I was bedridden. A woman doctor was brought to my bedside, but she could speak no language but Russian, and neither Ella nor I could speak to her in Russian about my ailment. She did not know how to drain an abscess through the eardrum, and fortunately it did not occur to her to pierce the drum which might have relieved the pain but ended the use of my left ear. When the pain became unendurable I asked her for sleeping pills, using every device from pig Latin to pantomime to make my request clear to her, but what I got was a prescription in pharmacist's Latin for some pain and fever pills containing a large proportion of caffein citrate, which could hardly put me to sleep. As my temperature continued to rise, she ordered an alcohol rub, but it turned out to be a Sunday and no drugstore was open. I was being visited that day by Leon Haykis, whose friendship I had won when he was First Secretary of Russia's Mexican legation. Half unconscious, I remember hearing him curse as he sacrificed a bottle of his own special high-proof vodka in place of rubbing alcohol. Eventually the poisons in the inner ear drained through the intact eardrum, gradually bringing relief. During all this time, the dignitaries and functionaries of the Comintern in Moscow ignored my presence, and without so much as telling me, sent a second letter as well as two delegates or Comintern reps to America—Philip Dengel of Germany, a hard-boiled leftist follower of Thaelman and Stalin, and Harry Pollitt of Great Britain—with instructions to upset the American party leadership, remove Jay Lovestone in favor of William Z. Foster as General Secretary, and make other changes. Having discovered how stubborn and effective my critique of their officially ordered *Open Letter* had been, and how ill I was, they were quite satisifed not to have me know or say anything.

As I began to recover, my first problem was the cold of an exceptionally bitter winter in Moscow. On a number of days the thermometer registered 40 below zero (the point at which Fahrenheit and Centigrade coincide), but fortunately all but one of them were windless days, days of a still cold, not hard to take. But with an abscessed ear I had to have something more than the ear muffs I had brought from America. Some kind soul went from store to store trying to find me an *ušanka,* a cap of stout leather lined with fur, with a visor that sinks low on your forehead and a backpiece that covers the back of your neck and your ears and ties around your chin, or, in warmer weather, over your head, something like an American hunter's cap. But alas, all Russian heads seem to be round, and mine is long, so that every winter cap brought to me was too tight in length, constricting my forehead but covering my ears. All winter I went around with a tight, roundhead Russian cap.

One warmer, sunny day I decided to go down once more to the Comintern, about a half mile from the Hotel Lux, in order to make another attempt to find out if I could see Bukharin and learn from him what was happening in the Russian party. As I was leaving the hotel, I saw Bukharin himself stepping out of a chauffeur-driven limousine which had just stopped in front of the Lux. His cheeks were rosy, his countenance serene; he looked in the best of health. I hurried over to him. "How do you feel, Comrade Bukharin? I hear you have not been well. You look fine now."

"Oh, I feel all right physically, but the Politburo has decided that I am too ill to function as Chairman of the ECCI."

"What was the vote?"

"Five to four."

"And how did you vote?"

"I was one of the four."

So that was it! The man named Nikolai Ivanovich Bukharin was in the best of health. But the Communist leader, Bukharin, elected unanimously by the highest body of the Communist International, the World Congress, sovereign over all other bodies and sections and Politburos of the International, by a vote of five to four was too sick to function as the Comintern's chairman.*

THE AMERICAN PARTY DEFIES THE BOSS

During my illness I was unable to communicate to the leadership of the American party the fragments of what I was learning of the situation in Moscow. In fact, until I met Bukharin when he was on a visit to someone in the Hotel Lux, I did not realize the magnitude and overwhelming character of the *coup d'état* that was taking place in the Russian party. Even when I began to understand it, I did not know how the secret code I had worked out with Jay Lovestone could serve for such a huge and unexpected turn of affairs. Nor did I know how, with the aid of his meager code

* The same fact of his political illness had earlier been communicated by Bukharin to Kamenev in secret conversation, and Kamenev had written it "in confidence" to Zinoviev, whose mail was being opened by the G.P.U. As a result the news was all over Moscow.

of fifty secret (and we were sure, undecipherable equivalents), I could tell them of the removal of Bukharin, without implying that I felt they could also adopt a resolution favoring such a removal, especially because I was gradually learning from the whispering gallery surrounding the Comintern about the bitter, if chivalrous battle that Bukharin was waging against Stalin's procedures in the party and mounting policy of pressure and terror against the peasants, and even against workers. Our code, which when we devised it seemed to foresee every possible or probable eventuality, proved hopelessly inadequate for the communication of these large events.

For their part, the leaders of the American party were overwhelmed by the two insolent and hostile letters, and the two hostile Comintern representatives who suddenly arrived in America on the eve of a convention in which they had won over 90% of the delegates. In the confusion and turmoil that followed, they did not succeed (perhaps did not even remember) to inform their solitary, bedridden representative in Moscow of what was happening in America.

The situation in the American party so far as Bukharin was concerned was a complicated and difficult one. He had been the theoretical leader of the Comintern in the ouster of Zinoviev and the denigration of Trotsky, in the exposition of the NEP, and in the propagation of Lenin's last thoughts and utterances during the prolonged period when Lenin lay paralyzed and dying, with time to reflect on what he had done and what he had left undone in his impulsive leadership of the new State and the Party with its monopoly of power. The crafty and cautious Stalin had accepted Bukharin as spokesman—during the fights with Zinoviev and Trotsky; the entire period of Stalin's so-called reconstruction of Russia's industries, which had been ruined by war, civil war, and errors in Lenin's primitive application of Marx's formulae concerning the abolition of money and the free market; "socialization" (i.e., nationalization) down to the last inkwell and ream of paper; the establishment of barter and distribution according to "labor-spent" credits; and the "dictatorship of the proletariat" exercised in ways that Marx would never have recognized. Bukharin had been speaking for Stalin as well as for himself when he urged that centralized planning must have as a major aim the well-being of the masses in whose name the seizure of power had been accomplished and in whose name the party ruled.

After Bukharin replaced Zinoviev as the chairman of the Comintern's Executive in 1926, Bukharin's brochure, *The Building of Socialism,* had been advertised for over a year in *The Communist International,* official organ of the Comintern published in three languages. And the advertisement had said in plain English (or German or French or Russian), "Nikolai Bukharin is now acknowledged as the most outstanding theorist of the Communist International." This advertisement continued in every issue until April 1, 1928. Then it sank to a place in a mere list of books published and advertised, while a month and a half later, in the issue of May 15, 1928, the feature advertisement was a new brochure by a new "most outstanding" theoretician. Its author was Joseph Stalin. It was called *Leninism* and was the first of a series of such works, each written in the same dogmatic. catechetical style, of which the best known is probably *Problems of Leninism.* The featured advertisement did not hail Stalin as the outstanding theoretician, but described the book as "A Complete Up-to-Date, and Authoritative Book on the Communist Theory and Practice." The key word was not "complete" or "up-to-date," but *Authoritative.*" But which of us knew then how to read such Byzantine signs? Or to know why, or even notice that, two months later, on the eve of the Sixth Congress, Bukharin's brochure, *The Building of Socialism,* disappeared altogether? It wasn't until a year later that Stalin called our attention to its disappearance from officially circulated works, not because Bukharin, but because Stalin had changed his theories. Then, in his speech, *On the Right Deviation in the C.P.S.U.,* delivered to the Central Committee, Stalin charged Bukharin's pamphlet with "blindness," with "non-Marxist theories," with "failure to see the specific features of the new period." In this thunderous denunciation was spelled out who and where the focus of the "Right Danger" was, and what it was that Stalin was reading into the ambiguous term, "Third Period."

Here was I, alone in Moscow. And I had learned, from words coming from Bukharin's own mouth, that he had actually been removed by a vote of five to four from the Politburo of the Russian party. How was I to cable this to Lovestone in the meager words of the fifty-word secret code we had devised between us. How could I tell him, as I began to learn from the whispering gallery, that Bukharin was fighting for his life, that he was not without support in his party, that Stalin had the machine and was packing committee after committee and institution after institution with new appointees to outvote the Bukharinites, that compromise was still possible though not probable? How was I to tell him how I felt about what we should do to retain the leadership of our party and yet retain our self-respect in this Russian faction fight? How to tell him that some spokesmen for Stalin, and possible Stalin himself, had assured the Fosterites that if they held out, in a few months they would get support and control of the American party, provided Foster would accept wholeheartedly the new Third Period policy of splitting the existing unions and forming new revolutionary unions—in short, the policy of "dual unionism," which ran against all that Foster had stood for during more than a decade of union activity?

OUR SECRET CODE

When I left for Moscow, Lovestone and I knew only too well that the bosses of the Comintern also owned the cables and the secret police. If I wrote letters, they would be steamed open, then sealed again. In fact, one day my wife went down to the barber shop in the Lux to get a haircut (she wore bobbed hair then); she found the barber shop closed, but there in the corner between the barber's and the stairway the *dvornik,* a janitor who looked like a simple peasant but was actually a Chekist (obliged to report on everything that went on, and about who was visited by whom at the Comintern's hotel), who was sitting at a *primus* stove over a boiling teakettle and steaming open the letters to us. Hence we had decided to arrange between us a foolproof code, or so we hoped, that could be used in letter or cable and not deciphered except by us. Lovestone and I had known each other intimately since 1917, and, being possessed of two quite different types of sense of humor, we had a number of private jokes that we could turn to account without fear that those not privy to the jokes could crack the code. We devised fifty numbered expressions of such wordplay covering everything that we could foresee or even imagine might possibly happen and need confidential telling.

To give an example or two, there was the absurd name of *Schmendrick* for Robert Minor and of *Wobbly* for William W. Weinstone. Wobbly was simple enough for Weinstone, who was enormously vain and ambitious and kept changing sides in the factional divisions in our party according to which side he imagined would wield more power and might be willing to advance him to the post of General Secretary of the party, in return for the support he thought he could bring to it as the secretary of the biggest district, that of New York City. But *Schmendrick* was the result of a more complicated story. When Robert Minor was sent to Moscow to represent the American party for an indefinite length of time, he had come to Lovestone and solemnly asked, "What name should I use on my passport?" More in jest than in earnest, Lovestone had answered, "You could take the name *Schmendrick;* that's a good Russian name." Actually it was a Yiddish word which means something like a yokel or a clown. To make matters worse, Lovestone added, "Good Russian initials would be I. M." And Bob Minor took seriously the suggestion and became *I. M. Schmendrick,* and Schmendrick he was in our code.

But we had not dreamed of imagining the removal of Bukharin who seemed safe as the head of the Comintern until the next Congress. The word we had taken for him was *Bookman,* too obvious now I feared. And in all our fifty equivalents, we had set down no code word for the removal of anybody.

I went through the entire list of fifty numbered equivalents, and the only expression that seemed usable was one which was intended to report some decision of the Russian party or the Comintern Executive which it might be well for the American Central Committee to follow and endorse. We had agreed that I should report the Russian resolution and my suggestion by cabling the words, "When did the C.E.C. vote to. . . ." In this case I would have to add the words: ". . . approve, or suggest, the removal of Bookman."

Would Lovestone understand, I asked myself anxiously, that I was recommending that he had better move to remove Bukharin as Chairman of the ECCI? Or would he understand that the Russian Central Committee had removed Bukharin from his post? In the whole fifty-word list I could find no other expression that was remotely usable. With a heavy heart I sent the ambiguous message.

But if my comrades in America did not know what was happening in Moscow, I was even more completely uninformed on what was happening in the United States. While my wife and I were traveling by steamship and rail to Moscow, the American Communist Party was holding a plenary session of its Central Executive Committee in preparation for its coming convention. There it became obvious that the old opposition, despite its being virtually wiped out in the election of delegates for the Convention, had gotten some secret encouragement from the Corridor Congress, from Stalin's agents, and perhaps from Stalin personally, who had held a secret interview with William Z. Foster during the Sixth Congress of the Comintern. They had been told, in effect, that Bukharin was finished, that the parties attending the Sixth World Congress would be purged of many of their leaders, and that in a few months they would be given, not by a vote of our membership, but by orders from Moscow, the leadership of the American Communist Party. Lovestone would be removed from his post and sent on a mission to some other country.

The opposition was in complete disorder after its resounding defeat, indeed, annihilation, in the party delegate elections. Foster, whose whole trade union stock in trade for more than a decade had been the notion of penetrating the American Federation of Labor and winning leadership in union after union through the militants in the Trade Union Educational League, suddenly found himself faced with the decision that in the "Third Period" the Communists were to split and pull out of the old unions and form "revolutionary unions" for the new period of revolutions. The slowness and ambiguity of some of his statements of adaptation to the new line gave Bittelman his opportunity to displace Foster as leader of the opposition. Bittelman had an advantage over both Foster and Lovestone in that he could read Russian and knew a few days or even weeks before anybody else what new line to advocate to keep abreast of the changes Stalin was making in the Comintern. When eight leaders of the Foster group attacked Foster himself, he humbly declared that he had always gotten his theoretical guidance from Bittelman.

There was no love lost between Bittelman and Foster, and the rank and file of the old Foster caucus would never have accepted an unattractive talmudist like Bittelman as their leader. Foster had dropped the idea of complete party unity, and when the German Comintern rep, Philip Dengel, let it be known that he had orders to make Foster the new Secretary and the new leader of the American Communisty Party, Foster took heart and fought Bittelman in his caucus and Lovestone in the Plenum and convention.

In the Party Plenum, Lovestone unswervingly took the line of the Sixth Congress of the Comintern as it had been expounded by Bukharin as the reporter on everything at the Congress. But Lovestone, too, accepted the line on dual unionism as had Foster. Only I, completely out of tune with the new line aborning, had attacked dual unionism in the meager one-hour talk I had exacted from the Presidium of the Comintern, in my criticism of their *Open Letter* to our convention. My stand was partly based on Lenin's guiding pamphlet, *Left-Wing Communism: An Infantile Disorder*, and partly on my own contention that one should enroll in a Communist party only those who agree with its program, while in a trade union or in a strike "we did not ask whether a workingman was Communist or Socialist or Democrat or Republican, but only whether he worked for the same employer as the other workingmen in his industry." Lenin in his pamphlet had made his position on the established trade unions a practical matter: when he had not succeeded in destroying them, he decided that they must be joined or infiltrated. But although I invoked Lenin's name, I made it a matter of principle to distinguish between a trade union that should include all workers in a given trade or shop, and a political party that based itself on a political program and accepted only those who agreed with the program. Had Lovestone and Foster heard my talk on that occasion, they would both have felt compelled to repudiate me, whatever they may have felt in their hearts. And Lenin, if he could have split and destroyed the "yellow unions" as he called them, would have repudiated me too! But even now, facing this triple-imagined repudiation, I think I was right in my distinction between the nature of a party and the nature of a union, and I imagine Lovestone and Foster, without the overpowering pressure of the Stalinist Comintern, would have agreed with me.

Besides the trade union question, the other issues most disputed at the plenary session of our Central Committee held while I was on the high seas, or on the rails, on my way to Moscow, were the problem of the strength of American imperialism or of the American economy, and the attitude of the two factions towards the decisions of the Sixth Congress of the Comintern.

THE QUESTION OF AMERICAN "EXCEPTIONALISM"

On the strength of the American economy, Lovestone had said (as I was able to read in the January, 1929, *Communist*):

> America's aggressive imperialist role today . . . grows out of its rising strength, and not out of any present tendency to decline . . . *The Central point in the international situation is woven around the fact of the aggressive role of American imperialism growing out of its still ascending strength.*
>
> We all say, the opposition with us and we with the opposition, that the center of gravity of capitalist world economy has shifted from Europe to America . . . *Amer-*

ican imperialism is the aggressor today, precicely because of this transfer of economic hegemony, precisely because of this increase in strength . . . We say that the *aggressive role of American imperialism is based on its present strength and presisely on its tremendous, still unexhausted reserve power.*

This, and other similar statements by Lovestone, marred the picture that Stalin was forcing on the Comintern that the "Third Period" was one in which capitalist stabilization was ending, and that all countries, not excluding the United States, were in decline and ripe for a period of fierce, all-embracing class battles and a new wave of revolutions. That the American economy was still destined to ascend and take greater precedence in world power for some time can now with hindsight be declared to be clear, as the next three or four decades were to show, despite the Great Depression.

The question of America's exceptional development of a feudalism-free society lacking a strong and permanent socialist movement such as was developing in Europe, had troubled Marx and Engels, too, in their day. They wrote innumerable letters to the German Marxists who had settled in America, explaining now one, now another of America's exceptional circumstances that had prevented and would still continue to prevent the American workingmen from following the path of the workingmen of Germany. I have written a pamphlet on the question embodying all their principal statements (*Marx and America*, John Day Pamphlet No. 38, New York, 1934); I will not repeat the substance of their views here. Suffice it to say that in the 1890s, when Marx was dead for a decade and Engels nearing death, the latter was still writing to Sorge and to Florence Kelley explaining the reasons why the American working class could not be moved by attempts to instruct them in European dogmas, but only "by their own experience . . . and by defeats" in the actions they undertook, and in his last few years Engels was still consoling himself by telling the last surviving European Marxists in America that "after the first step beyond the bourgeois viewpoint had been made, things will move faster, like everything else in America," move indeed with the speed of "a prairie fire."

In 1926 and 1927 the Comintern through its chairman and spokesman, Bukharin, was still making the puzzling statement that "our party in America is quite small, but American capitalism is the strongest in the world." Thus more than three-quarters of a century after the *Communist Manifesto*, America was still the great exception to the supposed rule that the more advanced the development of capitaism, the more it became a hindrance on economic development and the greater was the growth of the Socialist, or Communist, movement. It was the recognition of this concern with the continued upward movement of the American economy that in 1928 was stigmatized as the Lovestone heresy of "American exceptionalism."

But when Stalin and his spokesmen nagged me about my own "American exceptionalism," they were speaking of something quite different, and probably from their point of view a more grievous heresy. Stalin had put in his dossier Bittelman's complaints about my "American chauvinism," my insistence that we must study America in detail to become aware of its distinctive pecularities and that we must claim our American. heritage. When Lovestone, in his article in the *Daily Worker* of July 4, 1926 (his Sesquicentennial article), also spoke of "the heritage," he made it exclusively a heritage of revolutionary methods and tactics. In the same article he wrote, "We must guard against any Americanization craze." I could never have made such a statement. I was not afraid that our party, whose overwhelming majority was foreign-born, and whose ideology was so largely made up from our study of Marx and Lenin and European socialism, could possibly push "too far" our Americanization. Moreover, unlike so many American Communists, I had never rejected my American heritage.

I had opposed our entrance into the First World War, opposed total war as I understood it, opposed conscription as being against our tradition of a volunteer army, and opposed the mad postwar fever of the Palmer Red raids, but I had done all this in the name of my American heritage as I understood it and had never rejected that heritage itself.

When Stalin and his lieutenants, after ragging me about Lovestone's "American exceptionalism," began nagging me on my own American "exceptionalism," I finally made the sweeping statement, "I am an exceptionalist for every country in the world." By this I meant that I believed that each country differs from every other country, that each country moves toward its own future in terms of its own past, its own traditions, and its own history. In America, one of our basic tasks was to "discover America." If I were a Canadian or a native of India or China or Italy, I would make the same statement concerning the history, the traditions, the problems, the possibilities, the evils, the needs of that land.

THE ATTITUDE TOWARD BUKHARIN AND THE SIXTH WORLD CONGRESS OF THE COMINTERN

The words that were fatal for Lovestone's standing with Joseph Stalin were not those stating that the American economy would be the strongest in the world, at least for several more decades. They were the words concerning the attitude of the two factions toward the Sixth Congress. At the congress itself, the opposition had had one of Foster's lesser followers, Jack Johnstone, voice reservations about the Congress' decisions and reports. These reservations had been suggested by whisperings and gossip in the so-called Corridor Congress. They were repeated verbatim by the spokesman for the opposition at the Plenary Session of our own Central Committee which I have been describing. About them Lovestone said:

The time has arrived to stop reserving for yourself the right to be wrong. This means, if persisted in, opposition to the line of the Comintern. The opposition bases its policy on the supposition that American imperialism has reached its apex.

What did Comrade Bukharin say about this? I still quote Comrade Bukharin. For me he does not represent the Right Wing of the Communist International, although for some he does. For me Comrade Bukharin represents the Communist line, the line of the C.C. of the C.P.S.U. Therefore Comrade Bukharin is an authority—of the C.I.

Years later, when Lovestone was testifying before a Congressional comittee, he himself blamed these words for his removal by Stalin. That is too simple, as I have already suggested in this chapter, but his words were a key cause, and Lovestone's own view is interesting:

Everybody was rallying to endorse Stalin. I was not only a personal friend of Bukharin, but I had fundamental agreement with him on international questions, though on Russian questions I had agreement with Stalin and not with him. [In light of what he later learned about the Russian question, this sounds shocking, but that is probably a sound statement of his mood at that moment.] In that meeting I objected to the American Communist Party's lining up. I said, "We will wear no Stalin buttons, and we will wear no Bukharin buttons, and we will not engage in gangsterism against Stalin or Bukharin." I said that Stalin was my leader as leader of the Communist Party; that I respected him, had high regard for his opinion and caliber of thinking. [On what I said on Bukharin] a cable was sent to Moscow. That cable was passed around throughout the International, and that pretty much served as . . . my political death certificate.

28

STALIN AND BUKHARIN IN CLOSE-UP

Here I was in Moscow, alone, with no one to consult, slowly recovering my fighting strength as the abscess in my inner ear, without anodynes or meaningful treatment, gradually oozed its pus through the eardrum by osmosis. Thus weakened, and ignored as "too sick," I was facing the most powerful political machine in the world. The letter I had fought so hard against was sent without change and without even letting me know.

Though I was 33 years old and had spent all my adult life since the age of 21 in the antiwar, Socialist, and Communist movements of Mexico and the United States, and though I had been a delegate to the Fifth and Sixth Congresses of the Comintern and was now a resident member of the Executive Committee of the Communist International, I was in many respects still a green youth who did not understand the workings of the Comintern or the mighty Stalinist power machine which I was opposing. In some ways this was fortunate, for I was unafraid and stubborn, and felt sure that if I presented our case fairly and convincingly and made clear the will of my party, it would be respected.

There was a time when everything had been thus new and fresh in our young Communist Party, when one could believe, as I did, that it was an American party, basing itself on American conditions as we saw them, American traditions as we inherited them, American needs as we understood them. Our early discussions and documents and decisions all came from an innocent, sometimes wise, sometimes foolish, candor.

This freshness had gone out of the movement at a comparatively early date, but I had missed the process, for first I had gone to San Francisco, where by teaching and discussion, and editing *Labor Unity*, and by speaking for the Progressive Factions of the San Francisco Labor Council, I had been able to set the impress of my own independent judgment on major matters. Then I had gone to Mexico where my influence upon a raw, young movement was even greater and where Comintern intervention was still unknown. When I was deported to the United States I busied myself with the building of the Workers' School, the development of the party's educational work that had been sorely neglected and bungled, the supervision of our publication, the commemoration, in what seemed to me good party fashion, of the Sesquicentennial Celebration of the Declaration of Independence, and a series of speaking tours. Thus I missed most of the infighting going on at our headquarters. The Comintern representative, Gusev, was not far wrong when he told Lovestone that my proposal for him to unify our party was "naive."

My first awakening as to the way in which the Comintern could intervene in American party life came when Gusev read us the cable from Moscow which declared: "It has finally become clear that the Ruthenberg group is more loyal to the decisions of the Communist International and stands closer to its views." I was astounded. The Foster group, in a hard-fought battle, had just won a majority of the delegates to our convention, but the Comintern ordered the convention to set up parity on all executive organs of the party and make Gusev the "neutral chairman" of a fifty-fifty Central Committee. The "neutral" Chairman then proceeded to vote in favor of the proposals of the Ruthenberg-Lovestone Group, thus giving it the *de facto* majority of the incoming committees.

I admit that I was not only astounded, but somewhat troubled. If the Comintern in Moscow could give us a *de facto* majority in spite of the close vote favoring the Foster Group, could it not on some other occasion reverse another convention election in contrary fashion?

But if I was astounded, I must confess that I was also delighted. Like the other leaders of the Ruthenberg group, I addressed membership meetings in various localities taking full advantage of the words, "more loyal and closer to its views." By such methods we trained the rank and file of our membership to accept unquestioningly whatever verdict came from Moscow. And by such support we gradually extended our majority in the party until, in the convention held in March, 1929, while I was in Moscow, we carried over ninety percent of the total vote and virtually one hundred percent of the convention delegates.

Now in Moscow I got a close-up of what mischief we had done in our party by inculcating in its members the idea that word from Mecca was sufficient to reverse a decision of the American Political Bureau, its Central Committee, its congresses, and the overwhelming vote of its membership during the discussion period that preceded the elections to a party congress. And judging from the reactions of the entire membership of the Executive of the Comintern, the same identical thing had been happening in every party of the Comintern. When I had been making my hour-long talk to the Presidium of the Comintern Executive, they had not been listening, for Stalin, and through him the Russian party, had already spoken, and I was urging the revocation or fundamental revision of an *Open Letter* that Stalin himself had ordered, to overturn the leadership of the American Communist Party. Or, if any delegate listened to me, it was with a sense of shock at my ignorant audacity and a sense of fear that he might seem to show friendliness or sympathy toward me after I had challenged the *Xozjain* and *Vožd* (the Boss and Leader) of the Comintern.

If the Comintern ignored me though I was the sole official representative of the American Communist Party in Moscow, so did my comrades in America. As was customary after a World Congress, they were preparing to call a convention of their own party to implement and apply its decisions. In December, while I was on my way to Moscow, the Central Committee held a plenary, i.e., an enlarged session, with district leaders and other prominent officials present. At this enlarged meeting they adopted a number of decisions of which Lovestone did not inform me. One of them was in the form of a competition between party leadership and opposition, each trying to be more zealous than the other in accepting Stalin's dictum on separate or dual unions of Communists and their close sympathizers. Neither Lovestone nor Foster liked this; in their hearts they knew that the decision was wrong and would isolate the party from such organized trade union support as we had. Foster said glumly, "We are now entering upon a prolonged period of dual unionism." Lovestone was no less glum when he attempted to compete with Foster. And the eight Fosterites led by Bittelman, who had attacked Foster, tried to go both leaders one better by calling for the formation of a "new revolutionary trade union center."

At the same plenary session they vied with each other, too, in attacking Bukharin as a manifestation of the "Right Danger"—Lovestone more reluctantly, for he was competing now for Stalin's trust and favor.

The majority then moved that the party should hold a convention in January or February, as soon as there could be a free and open discussion period and the election of delegates. The Bittelman-Foster opposition countered with a motion to postpone the convention and request the Comintern to send "guidance and advice"—which showed that Bittelman, with his ability to read the sacred texts in *Pravda*, knew exactly what the Comintern was preparing to do. The convention was not held until March 1-9, with the "guidance" of a fresh (in both senses) *Open Letter* from the Comintern, of which neither the officials in Moscow nor Lovestone in New York saw fit to inform me.

But this prolonged discussion and election period gave Lovestone and his associates an overwhelming triumph, 95 delegates out of the 104 elected, or something over 90%. Of this Lovestone did inform me, and I wrote an article in *Inprecorr* entitled "Results of Election to 6th American Party Congress," in which I said that the overwhelming support for the party leadership had "completely wiped out the opposition as a political force in all industrial centers," and thus put an end to the long factional struggle in the United States. I cannot imagine that Stalin was happy when he learned that *Inprecorr* had published this article, for his new *Open Letter to the American Communist Party* said exactly the opposite.

The one decision I learned of promptly was a decision adopted by the Congress of the American party against Bukharin. Lovestone cabled me immediately that both the Politburo and the Congress had adopted unanimous decisions denouncing Bukharin and demanding his removal as Chairman of the Executive Committee of the Comintern. This news I received promptly, for Lovestone hoped that it would disarm Stalin's hostility against him. Lovestone did not know Stalin's vengeful, suspicious, and unforgiving nature. Which of us did then?

When I received this cable from Lovestone my heart sank.

And when I realized that Lovestone expected me to communicate his news to Kuusinen, Piatnitski, and Gusev, to such Stalinist agents as Lominadze, and, if possible, to Stalin personally, I realized once more how useless our fifty-phrase code was for communicating the real situation. There was nothing in our fifty cryptograms enabling me to cable that I was now all alone, ever since my one-hour address against the Stalin-inspired *Open Letter to the American Party*. How could I tell Lovestone by our ineffectual code that no one would listen to me now, that I was an outcast, a pariah? That Stalin had no intention of agreeing to my request that I be granted a personal interview? That Lovestone's sudden, last-minute switch, *post factum*, would most likely be greeted with cynicism rather than satisfaction? And how could I urge him to wait, since Bukharin was still fighting for his life and still had a majority in many key places? Had I not seen in the case of the Politburo that Stalin, as General Secretary of the Party and head of the Secretariat, the Org Buro, and the Personnel Assignment Organs, could pack any committee where Bukharin had a majority and reverse its vote overnight?

It was a great relief to me when I learned that it was not my cable, but other secret sources arriving just before my cable that had induced Lovestone to compete with Foster and Bittelman in denouncing Bukharin. Watching Bukharin still struggling for his political life, I should have been pained to think that it was my cable that had prompted Lovestone to denounce Bukharin and call for his removal.

At this point I should say something about the widespread belief that Lovestone and his followers were Bukharinites, in the sense that Cannon and his group were Trotskyites, or Ruth Fischer of the German party a Zinovievite. Lovestone and his group (including myself) had always felt that no national party could possibly be built as a mere appendage to some faction in the Russian party. We were an American party, and the discussions and controversies that should concern us were not Russian questions—however interesting or important—but American questions. However, journalists finding that there was a Trotskyite movement in America and a Stalinite movement in America, found it easy to conclude that we, too, must be the tail of a Russian faction, Bukharinites. To be sure, Lovestone, as he has testified before the congressional committee already cited, admired Bukharin, felt friendly toward him, and agreed with him on international questions. Indeed, Bukharin was admired in all the leading parties and was far better known than Stalin in the Russian party, hence, Stalin, secretly fighting him in the Russian Politburo during the "unanimous" congress, had not dared to break with him at the Sixth Congress of the Comintern, for the still-obscure Secretary of the Russian party would have suffered an overwhelming defeat.

But immediately after the World Congress was safely adjourned, Stalin sprang his marvelous invention, to have the Politburo vote that the newly reelected Chairman was too sick to serve. Indeed, Bukharin never chaired so much as a single session of the Executive to which he had just been unanimously elected! When the Comintern Executive met in Plenary session in December, Stalin trotted out that gray, stuttering, stubornly mechanical yes-man, Molotov (*nyet* to every diplomat in international negotiation, but always *da* to Stalin). Molotov was not even elected by the Executive Committee of the Comintern; he simply took the chair by vote of the Russian Politburo.

As for myself, even before I met Bukharin personally, I was attracted by his writings: his *Imperialism and World Economy*, from which Lenin had borrowed freely for his own *Imperialism, the Highest Stage of Capitalism;* his *Economics of the Transition Period* (both of which I read in German); and his *The Economic Theory of the Leisure Class*, which I read and reread in English, for it purported to be a refutation of Boehn-Bawerk's *Karl Marx and the Close of His System*, which, as I have already told the reader, greatly troubled me. In addition, Bukharin's book was an attempt to refute the Austrian marginal utility school of economics, a refutation which I found entirely satisfactory at the time and carried triumphantly into my own courses on Marxian Economics. But something like four decades thereafter, when I wrote "Das Kapital One Hundred Years Later," * I had acquired a new respect for the uses of the marginal theory, which caused me to conclude my chapter on *Das Kapital* with these words:

> The state that was to wither away, having set out to wither by taking over everything, "planning" everything, and running everybody in every activity of life, now finds its total, centralized "planning" in profound crisis. In the Western world, despite the growth of state intervention, the market continues to perform many of the functions of determining the optimal allocation of scarce resources. But in the totally centralized, totally statized, command economy of Russia, where the "anarchy of the free market" has been duly abolished as Marx bade, the central problem has become the mathematical determination of the marginal or differential yield in alternative uses and allocations of scarce resources—capital, skills, management, labor, materials—among competing ends. . . . *Ekonomičeskaja Gazeta* on November 10, 1962, noted that the project for the Novo-Lipetsk steel mill alone comprised ninety-one volumes totalling 70,000 pages and undertook to "blueprint the

* *Antioch Review*, Winter 1966-1967, later forming Chapter III of my *An Ideology in Power: Reflections on the Russian Revolution.*

placement of each nail, lamp, washstand . . . everything except for one thing—its economic effectiveness."

Alarmed by such warnings, the party bosses delegated such outstanding economists as Birman, Liberman, mathematician Volkonski, and mathematical economist Kantorovich to propose reforms, a "transition from charismatics to mathematics in Soviet economic planning." But the Soviet bosses of today, who have neither charisma nor mathematics in their favor, rejected or deviscerated the reforms, so that I ended my chapter with the sentence: "After one hundred years, in place of a stimulus, poor Marx and his doctrine have become a fetter on the further growth of the productive forces in the land that invokes his name."

I first got to know Bukharin personally at the Sixth World Congress of the Comintern. He made the stirring, yet modest, frequently lighthearted opening address; he reported on the world situation; he presented a program for the Comintern that Lenin had designated him to write at the First World Congress that, characteristically, he took from 1919 to 1928 to complete; he opened and closed the debate on the proposed program; he delivered the closing address at the long congress's end, whereupon he was unanimously elected, as the reader knows, the chairman of the Executive Committee of the International, which meant that he was supposed to be the leader of the International until the next world congress.

As he sat at a little table in his official chair, Bukharin dutifully took the notes which turned out to be caricatures of each speaker. When I realized what sort of notes the Chairman was taking, even as he knew that Stalin had his knife sharpened ready to scalp him when the congress was over, I remembered Krupskaya's account of Bukharin's first visit to Lenin in Krakow. He had arrived on foot still carrying on his back a huge canvas bag which contained as an important part of his baggage a considerable number of paintings he had just done of lovely scenes in the mountains around Zakopane. In the same baggage, brought for that first meeting with the leader of Bolshevism, he had, according to Krupskaya, a number of "splendid reproductions of paintings by German artists, which we examined with intense interest."

From the beginning, Lenin and Bukharin differed on many things, yet the Socialist painter (then calling himself Orlov) fell in love with Lenin; he abandoned painting as his career to follow and quarrel forthrightly with Lenin and stick to him until the end. I have used the expression, *fell in love with Lenin,* but I would not use the verb, *love,* for the attitude of any other of Lenin's disciples. They admired Lenin, followed him, often accepted his pronouncements blindly without venturing to question, they were proud of his party-serving or group-serving cynicism, and after his death, they glorified, sanctified, worshipped him, made his every utterance into a sacred text, any sentence of which might have probative value, raised his mummified corpse to the level of an *ikon,* or rather to that of patron saint of Mother Russia: but they did not love him as Bukharin did. Still stranger, as Leonard Schapiro has written, "Lenin's own relations with Bukharin were a curious amalgam of irritation, indebtedness, and—something rare for Lenin—genuine affection." With, or more often without, acknowledgment, Lenin derived some of his views on imperialism from Bukharin's *Imperialism and World Economy* and wrote a highly laudatory introduction to that book, which preceded his own by a couple of months. Yet Lenin did not grasp, or did not accept, Bukharin's view that monopoly capitalism would not eliminate, but would cohabit with free competition in the advanced countries of Europe and America. Bukharin felt, too, that Lenin failed to understand state capitalism, and thus described wrongly the nature of the Soviet economy during the period of the NEP. But Bukharin did not press this point too hard, for he was an ardent supporter of the NEP regardless of terminological descriptions. Lenin was indebted, too, to Bukharin's *Economics of the Transition Period,* a book which at first infuriated Lenin because of its powerful attack upon a state foreshadowing a modern totalitarian one and resembling the oppressive, all-embracing state of Jack London's *Iron Heel.* Bukharin pictured this state not unlike the one that Stalin was to "perfect," a state of "militaristic state capitalism, . . . a monster, a modern leviathan, which ran everything and everybody and mercilessly crushes all resistance . . . the centralization of the barracks . . . brutal regimentation and the bloody repression of the proletariat." These fragments which I have put together from various places in Bukharin's anticipation of the totalitarian state were what he was fighting against when I was watching him in his last hopeless struggle against Stalin in 1929.

In 1916 Lenin had expressed his distaste for what Bukharin was saying and had written to him sharply of his "semi-anarchist position." Touchingly, Bukharin answered: "Let us argue frankly, but please do not make the attack so sharp that I cannot continue to work with you."

Lenin, for his part, had second thoughts. Bukharin's picture of the Leviathan State forced him to read once more Engels's *Origin of the Family, Private Property, and the State* where he found scriptural justification for Bukharin's "semi-anarchist" views. Thereupon he borrowed generously from Bukharin for his own totally uncharacteristic *State and Revolution.* He made no public acknowledgment of his indebtedness, but in a letter to Kollontay he said that he had learned much from Bukharin, a rare admission for him, and in 1917 he bade Krupskaya write: "V. I. asked me to tell you that he no longer has any disagreements with you on the question of the state."

Yet things did not end there, for once in power, Lenin moved back to his position on the state, and Bukharin moved toward him, consoled by the firm belief that the proletariat, through the Party, was in control of the state, and so long as this was so this special form of proletarian "Leviathan State" could be prevented from oppressing the proletariat and the peasantry. In 1929 that was what Bukharin was fighting Stalin to prevent. In any case, when Lenin was on his deathbed, in one of the last documents from his hand, his so-called *Testament,* he declared: "Bukharin is not only the party's greatest and most valuable theoretician, but he is also rightly considered the beloved *ljubimec)* of the whole party."

Theoretically Bukharin was a Marxist, but, what was unusual among Marxists in the twentieth century, he was an independent thinker and not a mere quoter and repeater of Marxist clichés. He was a believer in the blessed Utopia that would come after the existing order was cleared away, but in the meanwhile he made original studies of that order, of finance capital, of monopoly, of the continued existence of the market side by side with the giant trusts. He instantly became a Leninist at that first meeting, but as we have seen, no parrot Leninist. He continued to do his own thinking and arguing, and in important matters he taught Lenin as well as followed him. He knew that the Utopia he dreamed of would not come merely by totally rejecting and clearing the ground of the entire existing order. He found elements in that order, and in the existing culture and historical traditions of the society that mankind had developed in the course of centuries, which the proletariat would do well to use and learn from. His arguments first with Trotsky, and then with Stalin, were over the question of how to serve the worker, not merely to use him as a battering ram on the way to power. He argued, too, with both of them on the question of how to improve the lot of the peasant rather than to pillage him for the sake of "socialist industrialization." Wasn't the welfare of the masses the main aim of socialism, and would it be *Socialist* industrialization or a *Socialist* state if it didn't plan accordingly?

He did not accept Lenin without question, either. When he learned that Lenin had accepted considerable sums of German money to build the machine that seized power he was deeply shocked, and it is not unlikely that this explains the unusual bitterness of his fight against Lenin's desire to sign the Brest Treaty giving Germany so much of Russia, plus a separate peace so that they might withdraw their troops from Russia and throw them against the West. This was the only time that Bukharin organized a group or faction to fight Lenin, the left opposition. Once the separate peace issue was settled, he returned to his devotion to the Bolshevik leader.

Though some of his writings during the flush of excitement after the Bolsheviks seized power and during his brief period of "Left-Communism" were truly horrendous, his personal acts toward the people of Russia were never so. He never used the firing squad as Trotsky did on deserters from the Red Army, nor organized a planned famine against the peasants, nor ordered a bullet in the base of the brain of any of his own comrades, as Stalin did. Perhaps his most ruthless statement was the clever, shocking pronouncement, "Of course we should have two parties, one in power, the other in prison." But when it came to the test, when Lenin demanded the death penalty for the twelve long-imprisoned leaders of the Socialist Revolutionary party, and the Bolsheviks sent a delegation headed by Bukharin to treat with the Second International on the question of a united front in April, 1922, and incidentally to explain the forthcoming trial of the *Twelve Who Are to Die*,* to Lenin's disgust and indignation Bukharin gave the leaders of the Second International assurances that every facility would be given to the accused for a fair trial and proper defense—that lawyers like the distinguished Belgian Socialist leader, Emile Vandervelde, might represent the S.R. leaders, and that they would not be executed. Lenin fought in the Politburo for the repudiation of Bukharin's promises, but Bukharin defended them successfully.

Bukharin was the party's natural peacemaker. He had the naive idea that personal friendship with Trotsky could continue while he attacked Trotsky's extreme industrialization views. When Lenin became paralyzed and died, Bukharin seriously proposed a collective leadership and opposed a struggle for a personal succession. As he had tried to mediate between Trotsky and Lenin, so he tried to act as peacemaker between the anti-Trotsky triumvirate, Zinoviev, Kamenev, and Stalin, and Trotsky himself. When Kamenev and Zinoviev were being exiled by the Politburo to a remote part of Russia, Bukharin voted against the decision. And when Stalin proposed to deport Trotsky from Russia to Turkey, so that he "might discredit himself by writing for the bourgeois press and giving out interviews which would show him to be an agent of the enemies of the Soviet Union," Bukharin, Rykov, and Tomsky voted *no*, Bukharin doing so with tears in his eyes. When Stalin and his yes-men passed the resolution by a vote of 6 to 3, Bukharin wept openly.

Lenin's attitude toward Bukharin was revealed not only by calling him the *ljubimec* of the entire party, the only personal characterization in Lenin's *Testament*. There are other occasions which reveal Lenin's unusual personal affection for the "disciple" who argued most often with him. Thus there is a little known episode when Bukharin was seriously ill in 1921, and Lenin's concern was so deep that when the German government refused Bukharin a visa to go to Germany for medical treatment, Lenin wrote to the Soviet Ambassador in Germany, Krestinskii, asking him to approach Chancellor Wirth personally, with a message from Lenin which read something like this: "I am an old man and I have no children. Bukharin is like a son to me. I ask as a personal favor . . . that Bukharin be given a visa and the opportunity to receive treatment in Germany." The visa was then issued.**

Like almost everybody who came into contact with him, I found Bukharin a gentle and lovable character of singular personal charm. Nay more, for of all the leaders of the Bolshevik party that I got to know personally, he was the only one that I found to be human and gentle at

* The title of a pamphlet by Wladimir Woytinsky.

** The evidence for this, both in Bolshevik sources and in the well-informed accounts of Yurii Denike and Boris Nikolaevsky has been gathered by Stephen Cohen in his biography of Bukharin, pp. 152-53, and p. 419, n. 97.

heart. So far as I know, he alone of all the top leaders ever shed tears at a Politburo meeting; he alone ever expressed in writing, compassion for the suffering of the masses of the Russian people, knowing in his heart that his party was responsible for that suffering because of its ruthless attempts to establish "socialism" in so backward a country. He never assumed an administrative job, a fact which helped to keep his own record clean of human atrocities, and he never aspired to leadership over the Russian Communist party and the country it ruled, though many humble people wished he had. If any Bolshevik might have tried, in Dubcek's words, to establish "socialism with a human face," it might have been he. He favored a more rapid industrialization of backward Russia, but not at the expense of the working class whose well-being he believed it was the party's duty to serve. Nor at the expense of the peasantry who made up the impoverished mass of the Russian people. He was not ashamed to say in writing that the party of which he was a theoretical leader was pillaging the peasants by taking away their grain at insignificant state-fixed prices, backed by terroristic requisitions and searches and seizures, without giving the peasant a fair amount of consumers' industrial goods in return for the grain they not so much purchased as took.

Besides his compassion for the peasant and workingmen and for all the toiling poor who work so hard to produce for power and war but not for themselves, and who are unable to produce consumers' goods on such a scale as would abolish the *xvosty* (the long lines before every store that take so many millions of man-hours out of the lives of those who wait in them), Bukharin had another little-known trait: a love of animals. Just as he carried paintings in his knapsack when he went to make his first call upon Lenin, so Bukharin carried pets of every description with him when he went to live in the Kremlin: hedgehogs, garter snakes, a crippled hawk, a fox, and other strange pets. "Years later, long after he was dead," wrote Svetlana Alliluyeva in her *Twenty Letters to a Friend,* " 'Bukharin's fox' was still racing around in the Kremlin, which was empty and desolate by that time, and playing hide and seek in the Tainitsky Garden."

If I have devoted so much space to this profile of Nikolai Ivanovich Bukharin, it is not because I was a "Bukharinite" as other Americans were "Trotskyites" or "Stalinites"—there are many things he had written which I disagreed with, and in any case I could not think of our party as a tail to any faction of the Russian party—but because I considered and still consider him the most human and attractive of all the Bolshevik leaders I have met, and because his *Notes of an Economist* * make him the ghost that haunts every banquet in which the Soviet leaders celebrate the industrialization and militarization of their country, and the collectivization of agriculture. To close this friendly portrayal of Bukharin I might add a half sentence from Edward Hallett Carr with whom I have had so little occasion to agree. In his review of Stephen Cohen's *Bukharin and the Bolshe-*

* For an English translation, see my *Khrushchev and Stalin's Ghost,* pp. 295-315.

vik Revolution, Carr wrote: "It was a malign fate which cast so gentle a nature into a maelstrom of revolution." I feel the same way about him. Yet because he was led on by the will-o'-the-wisp of his Utopian vision of where the revolution might lead, it is in the context that we must judge him. And in that context, too, he still comes out as the best, the most human, the géntlest, the worthiest of the Bolsheviks I have known.

STALIN PREPARES A LITTLE TRAP FOR ME

It was a Sunday night in early February, I think February 10, 1929. Some time between 9 and 10 at night with Ella and me reading or writing in our room in the Hotel Lux, a loud knock unexpectedly sounded on our door. I opened to a courier from the Comintern. He presented several sheets of paper to me with nothing on them but the names of members of the Executive Committee of the Comintern, and two columns ruled, in which they might vote *Yes* or *No.*

"*Eine fliegende Abstimmung, Genosse Wolfe,*" he said in German. "The Politburo of the Russian Party is debating the question of whether it should expel Leon Trotsky from the Soviet Union and deprive him of his citizenship for counter-revolutionary activities. They would like to know how the delegates to ECCI (the Executive Committee of the Comintern) feel about such a deportation. You are to vote *yes* or *no.*"

I felt a sudden flush of indignation. I was not a partisan of Trotsky's. I did not like his arrogant temperament. I had written much against him, mostly, it is true, out of ignorance, as I accepted and repeated blindly what the leaders of the Russian party said against him. I had become ashamed of that pamphlet, but when I was distributing copies of my pamphlets to important libraries, I reluctantly included *What is the Trotsky Opposition?* for each library, for it was a fact of history that I had written it, and I felt I had to make it available to historians who might study the American Communist Party.

But that was not what concerned me that night when the courier was bidding me vote *yes* or *no* in a *fliegende Abstimmung,* a flying vote off the cuff without any chance to discuss such an important matter as Trotsky's deportation in a meeting of the Executive.

"Are they in such a hurry," I asked, "that they can't wait until Monday or Tuesday for a meeting of the ECCI or the Presidium?"

"*Ja, sie haben viele eile*—they're in a big hurry."

"But," I continued slowly in German, "after all, it is to our outside world that he is to be deported. It is we who will have to handle such a prominent Bolshevik living among us. Besides, the Soviet Union will be setting a dangerous example for anti-Communist governments who will be delighted to follow Russian precedent and deport Communist leaders and deprive them of citizenship. I should like to hear what other representatives to the Executive from other countries feel about the whole idea, and give my own thoughts and have them corrected or confirmed. I cannot vote just *yes* or *no* on the deportation and denaturalization of the man who was the head of the Military Revolutionary Committee that kept the soldiers passive the night the Bolsheviks seized power. And who was the organizer of the Red Army that won the civil war. It won't be easy for us to explain that the government he did so much to found and defend is depriving him of his citizenship. Your *Ja oder Nein Blatt* doesn't even have a space for comments. I am opposed to such a *fliegende Abstimmung* on a subject so important, and instead of voting, I call for a meeting of the Executive or the Presidium."

The courier followed my remarks with unconcealed astonishment. He knit his brows and I could see that he was trying to memorize what I was saying. I had seen such knit brows before on American Secret Service men (it was in the days before the tape recorder was invented). "One of Trillisser's men," I said to myself (Trillisser headed the Comintern Secret Service). "He will report everything I have said to Stalin. Well, let him. It is something Stalin should hear."

I don't remember now whether it was Tuesday or Wednesday, the 12th or the 13th. I opened my morning mail which came to me complete, but not unread by Chekists disguised as hotel porters. The Paris *Herald-Tribune* was on top of the mail, carrying the banner headline all across the first page:

LEON TROTSKY IN CONSTANTINOPLE!

So he had been on the high seas for days in an old Soviet boat and was actually pulling into the Constantinople Harbor while the hollow comedy of the *fliegende Abstimmung* was being played. And Stalin had acted to exile Trotsky to the outside world without consulting the Executive Committee of the Comintern at all. He was merely trying to trap us to see which of us might have a soft spot in our hearts for Trotsky. Or, since he had seen with scorn how Bukharin wept in the Politburo when the deportation resolution was adopted, he felt he might find out which of us were *Bukharinites.* Well, one more black mark in my dossier. And one more reason for distrusting the crafty Stalin.

29

I HELP STALIN SET A TRAP

I stood looking out of the window of our room in the Hotel Lux one morning near the end of February. My wife was fast asleep in the bed nearby, but I was wide awake, for I had just come home from one of those meetings of the Executive of the Comintern that would begin between 3 and 4 in the afternoon, and end, if there was a long-winded report by Molotov (made longer by his painful stuttering on the p's and b's and his inability to think of a synonym in the rich Russian tongue that said the same thing without beginning with a p or a b), somewhere between 3 and 4 in the morning. Then, since Molotov was regarded as spokesman for the "Russian Delegation," that is, for Stalin, a spokesman for every leading delegation, the German, the French, the Italian and the like, would make a speech of repetitive endorsement, an endorsement distinguished neither by its color or originality nor wit or brevity.

The Russian leaders got up late each morning, accustoming the rest of the Executive to do the same. We ate a nondescript breakfast of the type known as *Continental*, which was followed in the early hours of the afternoon by a heavy dinner including soup with a slab of tough meat in it, frequently horsemeat, if we ate on our meal ticket in the Arbat Restaurant, a few blocks away from the Lux. What the Russian leaders ate I never found out, but since my wife and I were staying in Moscow for an indefinite period, we acquired a simple, wholesome peasant cook named Fanya. She could make any meat seem tender and was a genius at baking apple fritters. When Lovestone came, she piled his plate high, but when the head of International Publishers, Alexander Trachtenberg, came with his wife, a pair she didn't like, they were lucky if they got three fritters apiece on their plate. Our dinner never ended until three o'clock in the afternoon or later, after which we went the short distance from the Hotel Lux to the Comintern Building at 6 Mokhavaia Street, under the Kremlin Wall, or to a large meeting hall like the Hall of Columns (once a nobles' club) also right near the Kremlin Wall, or, on more solemn occasions, to a larger hall in some palace inside the Kremlin itself. The post-prandial meeting which started between three and four P.M. was the "morning meeting," so to speak, which dragged on so long that no second meeting was possible. We were saved from exhaustion by a break around five or six o'clock for tea and lemon and red caviar (if Stalin came, it was pearl gray).

Sometime between midnight and morning we would walk home, or, if we wished to wait, we could commandeeer by phone a limousine with a chauffeur. From the Fifth and Sixth Congresses which had been great mass meetings, we had walked home in groups, singing, led by the Italians with their natural ability to make the welkin ring with their *Bandiera Rossa,* waking up all the sleeping inhabitants living near our line of march. But from the ECCI meeting most rode in limousines, and those who walked talked in low tones. As for me, I walked alone: no one would walk with me or talk with me.

What was I doing attending those big, dull, servile, and repetitious meetings? I was waiting for opportunities to get in a word edgewise presenting our position. If a German delegate, for instance, spoke enthusiastically of splitting and crushing the great German trade unions and forming separate "revolutionary unions," I would remind the Germans that they would be splitting the working class, weakening the resistance to Nazism, alienating themselves from the German workingmen who believed in their unions. Then I would apply the same idea to America until the chairman called me to order or told me time was up. Or if the Germans spoke of a "revolutionary situation" in Germany, I would tell how absurd it was to speak of America being "on the verge of its 1905," as the polished but far from bright Dmitri Manuilsky had tried to assure me. I was trying to present our position, to inspire some who I knew agreed with me in secret to speak up. But I was talking to closed ears, and the chairman made more and more pointed efforts not to see me or hear me when I rose to ask for the floor.

And the mornings? How did I spend them? I went down to the Comintern Building in the morning, too, going from official to official to ask for an interview with Stalin. I told each of them I had a message from the leadership of the American party which I was to deliver to Joseph Stalin personally. "Stalin is too busy," I was told. Or "Put it in writing."

In any case, it was unheard of that the newly enthroned leader of the Comintern should refuse the repeated requests of the sole representative to the ECCI of the American party, a party not altogether unimportant in itself, and rendered especially important now that its leadership was about to be put on trial. From the day I arrived I had sent word through proper channels to Stalin that I had a special message from the leader of the American party to communicate with him. But whether Lovestone's fate was already settled in Stalin's mind, or whether I was to be ignored and humiliated because I had spoken of the "ignorance of America" in the Stalin-decreed *Open Letter to the American Communist Party,* Stalin never had time to receive me. I was struck by the contrast with Lenin, who had received, listened to, and argued with such men as Giacinto Serrati of the Italian party and Paul Levi of the German, even when he was planning to oust them. Stalin was conducting a different kind of Court and required a different kind of courtier.

So I spent my mornings pestering the working crew of Comintern officials, such as Otto Kuusinen, the Sovietized Finn who was the key member of the Political Secretariat of the Comintern, and Iosif Piatnitsky who was one of Lenin's men of confidence and was now the Organization Secretary of the Executive Committee. They were awed and frightened by the sudden downfall of Bukharin and kept telling me: "Why don't you see Stalin? Why don't you see Gusev?"

I saw Gusev, too, and told him what I wanted to tell Stalin, knowing that he would report what I said. And I saw some of the younger Stalinists who had been the activists of the anti-Bukharinite "Corridor Congress," young men like the Georgian, Vissarion Lominadze, and the rising star among the young Germans, Heinz Neumann, and others like them who had Stalin's ear and would report my words to him.

But there I stood that morning late in February between four and five in the still starlit predawn and reviewed my work. It was clear to me that all my lone and lonely efforts to present our position to Stalin or to the servile Executive of the Comintern were getting me nowhere.

What was the powerless boy from Brooklyn doing so far from home, trying to get a half-hour interview with the most powerful man in Russia, one of the most powerful men in the world? And why couldn't I get the half hour, when all I wanted to do was deliver a message that wasn't even pleasant to me? Lovestone and I had rehearsed the message several times before I left America. He directed me to assure Stalin of the total loyalty of the American leadership to the Comintern, to explain that the leadership knew it had won its overwhelming majority in the party only through the past support of the Comintern, that it could not keep its majority against the Comintern. I was to ask why the Comintern messages were now hostile and harassing. What was behind the trouble? What could we do about it, for, I was to add, we knew we could not continue to lead the party without the Comintern's support, guidance, and approval.

In short, it was an offer of submission. The Lovestone majority had gotten along with Zinoviev, had gotten along with Bukharin, and was ready to subordinate itself to the new leadership of Joseph Stalin.

To be sure, Lovestone knew we could not have any voice in Russian policy or leadership anyhow, nor did we desire such a voice. What we wanted was not so much support as to be let alone to fight on American issues as our knowledge of America suggested to us, and not be disturbed by Moscow efforts to keep factionalism alive in our party, or start it afresh after we had won virtually the entire party in free and fair elections. "Count on our loyal endorsement on whatever you find necessary to do in Russia, and let us use our own judgment on what we have to do in America, undisturbed by the Losovskys who don't understand the American trade unions, or by the 'American' Commissions that have no Americans on them." But of course, we couldn't put it that way, for the Russians, having been successful in seizing power in their own land, were sure they could tell any party how to take power in its land. Yet that was the tenor of my message, and I couldn't even get to Stalin to deliver it.

"Getting nowhere," I repeated to myself. "I'm wasting my time and getting nowhere." Maybe I should take a rest for a while. Maybe my wife and I should see a bit of Russia, take a trip to Leningrad, or down the Volga to see how the great collectivization drive was affecting the peasants, and what they would do with the cattle which they had raised personally, now that they were being driven with all their belongings onto the collective farms . . .

As if in answer to my meditations, my eyes fell at that moment in the predawn light on a long line of women bundled up in all sorts of rags against the merciless early morning cold, standing in a long line on Tverskaya Street which ran down the boulevard and around the corner and disappeared from view. They were carrying pitchers, kettles, empty cans, any receptacle that would hold milk. Milk would run out before the long lines were satisfied by even a fraction, and I thought of the babies, the invalids, the ailing, to whom milk was essential. The same was true of butter, cheese, eggs, fruit, ready-made clothing, and cloth to make your own. Lemons and oranges were sold only on the Black Market, and then at prohibitive prices. In short, as Stalin attacked the NEP and the land owned by the individual farmer or peasant, the "scaffolding," far from coming down, was growing in the form of longer lines before every store. And the Bolsheviks had been in power for over a decade! No, this was no time to take Ella on a trip to see the wonders of the New Russia. Nor would we have been allowed inland from the Southern Volga anyhow. My ECCI credential would have been no help to me in getting to see such sights. The sight of the long, frozen milk line that had been waiting, judging from its size, from at least 4 A.M. in the cold pre-dawn, discouraged me, and I went to bed at last. In the morning, as often happens to me when I go to bed with some unsolved problem troubling me, I awoke with the solution clear in my mind of what to do about the fact that all my efforts as a lone representative of a party under a cloud were getting me nowhere.

The vote for delegates to the Sixth Convention of the American Communist party, set for February 1, had been an overwhelming triumph for the party leadership. The opposition was in disarray since Bittelman, and Browder, the latter newly returned from Shanghai under a cloud, were both attacking Foster, the real leader and most valuable member of the opposition. Up until the end of 1928, Bittelman had been no more than the "theoretician" of William Z. Foster, his "talmudist" as some called him, giving Foster advice by translating from the latest issues of *Pravda* or *Izvestia.* And Browder had been no more than Foster's protegé and office manager, or "office boy," as Bill Dunne, the most rugged and personally interesting of the Fosterites, had labelled him. Now "talmudist" and "office boy" were in revolt against the chief of their faction; the faction itself had been devastated by Jim Cannon's sudden conversion to Trotskyism and the secession or expulsion of some hundred-odd members of the opposition as "Trotskyites." Moreover, our party leadership had won something like 90% of the delegates to the convention, and the voting for delegates "had completely wiped out the opposition as a political force in all industrial centers."

Strengthened by this triumph and the disintegration of the opposition, Lovestone, Gitlow, and Bedacht, and other leaders on the home front, were showing increasing militancy in putting through their program for the American party and had informed the Comintern that the long faction fight in the American party was at an end. Why could we not, I asked myself, run the party now as seemed proper to us, and inform the Comintern, i.e., Stalin, that we were the leadership of the party and had to be recognized as such and treated accordingly? If I was getting nowhere as a lone spokesman for our views, what I needed was reinforcements. Why could not Lovestone come over to Moscow with other leaders of our party like Gitlow and Bedacht, request a meeting with Stalin, explain our program, and give Stalin the pacifying message that Lovestone had instructed me to give him? He could not refuse the whole group of us a half hour of his time, and then we could have it out with him. We could hold our convention first, and then send over a large and impressive delegation. I sat down and wrote a letter to Lovestone, not in code this time, telling him the difficulties I had been having, the ineffectualness of my efforts, the need for reinforcements, and the possibility of using them to win from Stalin some respect for, or at least grudging recognition of, our leadership and its program for America.

My suggestion fell on fertile ground. Lovestone was of the opinion that Stalin could not set aside such an overwhelming majority. "If there is one thing Stalin respects," Lovestone was wont to say, "it is power. Let us show him that we have the power in our party and he will respect that, as long as he is assured that we will not meddle in Russian matters."

Gitlow went even further. "If we have a majority in the party, and the Communist International attempts to take it away, let us break with the Communist International and maintain our hold on the party."

There was only one gloomy, negative voice: that of John Pepper (Jozef Pogany, the Commissar of War of the Bela Kun Government), whom Bukharin had permitted to go to America where he had acquired a position of high leadership in our majority. One day he received a cable ordering him to return to Moscow immediately. He was even refused permission to stay for the convention, which the Comintern had arbitrarily postponed from February 1st to March 1st so that it could send representatives and give us "guidance and advice." Pepper became panicky and profoundly depressed: he feared that the recall spelled his doom. Lovestone cabled that Pepper was leaving immediately, but because of his illegal status would have to go roundabout through Mexico and the Far East. Actually, he went into hiding (where he got into scrapes with two jealous secretaries at once, thus imperilling and eventually betraying his hiding place to the party), and he planned to stay in America to give secret guidance to the majority leaders at the convention. He insisted that his recall signified that we had already lost on the Moscow front, and that we would be fools to accept my advice and go to Moscow, which would put our leaders at Stalin's mercy. But Lovestone was sure that he could come to a satisfactory understanding with Stalin if he talked to him, face to face.

ANOTHER OPEN LETTER TELLS OUR CONVENTION WHAT IT MUST DO

At this point something happened that made the trap which, in my innocence I had helped Stalin set, seem irresistible to Jay Lovestone. A new *Open Letter* was addressed to the American Party's convention. It told the convention what it must believe about America, what it must think, what it must do, what it must say. And along with the *Open Letter* came two Comintern delegates with plenipotentiary powers to see that the convention voted on every point as it was told to vote by the superior wisdom of Moscow's expertise on everything going on elsewhere.

The letter was ostensibly adopted by the Executive Committee of the Communist International and was signed accordingly, but I attended every meeting of that Executive and its Presidium and no such letter was adopted or even discussed at any of those sessions. J. Louis Engdahl, the Representative of the American Party that preceded me, had been given a chance to hear, to discuss, to offer amendments to, and to vote on, the previous *Open Letter*. Where this new letter was concocted, in what secret commission, I never learned. Having seen and heard what I had done in my hour's talk in German on the previous *Open Letter*, they felt that this time I was to be kept in the dark about the drafting of such a letter or its dispatch to America: I was not permitted to discuss, to move amendments, to vote on, or even to know of its existence. Hence, though it was signed *Executive Committee of the Communist International*, even the ECCI was not given a chance to discuss it.

What then was this new, empty, and ignorant letter of political guidance proposing to the American Communist party convention? and through it to the American people?

It ended with four "principal conditions to transform the party," if not America. They looked impressive because each of them was numbered and had a separate paragraph. But three of the four were made up of the same hollow-sounding clichés as the rest of the document of "political guidance." Point 1, for example, demanded that the American party "transform itself" by developing "a correct perspective in the analysis of the general crisis of capitalism and American imperialism." What that "correct perspective" might be, it tactfully declined to say, possibly because Stalin himself had still not formed a "correct perspective" to prove that America was on the eve of "fierce class battles and revolutionary struggles."

Point 2 demanded that the party place, in the center of its work, the daily needs of the working class. A great discovery!

Point 3 bade us "free the party from its immigrant narrowness" and make our "wide basis the American workers . . . with due attention to the Negroes." (This, like Point 2 above, was indeed discovering America.)

Point 4, however, the last and only definite point, had the ring of a genuine command and was backed with a threat that had in it the sound of Stalin's voice and character. "4. Liquidation of factionalism . . .", a command backed by the words: "The VIth Convention of the Workers (Communist) Party must categorically prohibit any further factional struggle, under the threat of expulsion from the Party." In addition, Point 4, with its accompanying threat, demanded that we draw workers into the leadership and that we "lay the foundation of a normal Party life, especially internal democracy (sic!), self-criticism, and iron Party discipline, based on the unconditional subordination of the minority to the majority, and an unconditional recognition of the decisions of the Comintern."

Yes, there was the ring of Stalin's voice in every word of Point 4 and its method of enforcement. But the rest of the letter was a hollow shell that gave no sound if you held it to your ear. Surely, one thought as one read and reread the letter of "political guidance," there must be something else in reserve to instruct and guide and direct the Convention.

And there was. Characteristically for Stalin, it was not theoretical or political analysis, but categorical organizational commands. In Russia, Bukharin had fought with theory, and Stalin had fought with organization, and Stalin had won. And so it was intended to be now with the Sixth Convention of the American Communist Party. The convention had been ordered postponed a month, and, at the end of the month, before the delegates still rejoicing at their overwhelming victory in the discussion and election period, there stood two grim figures possessed of secret "organizational proposals." Neither was a Russian, but they carried about them the aura of command, for they were representatives of the Executive Committee of the Communist International. One of them was an Englishman, Harry Pollitt (after all, the representatives had to speak English somehow to an American convention), and the other was a German, Philipp Dengel. If two people are sent by the commanding body of the Comintern, one of them has to be supreme over the other. The Supreme Commander of this dual delegation was Dengel. He spoke for both of them and did all the talking, in secret meetings of both caucuses and in secret sessions of the Politburo, held where the police might not surprise the two foreign Communists who had smuggled themselves into the country with false documents that would not bear close scrutiny. And what they brought was not "organizational *proposals*" to a sovereign body, but "organizational *commands* to a subordinate section" of the Communist International.

Harry Pollitt was a boilermaker by trade and a militant trade unionist. In a party lacking in political and theoretical thinkers (except for Rajani Palme Dutt, who was half Indian and half Swede and an Oxford graduate in history and philosophy), Pollitt had risen to the rank of Central Committee and Politburo member and representative of his party to the ECCI. In 1929 Joseph Stalin, looking for an Englishman who wouldn't ask questions, insisted on Pollitt's elevation to the secretaryship of his party over the opposition of a great many of its members. And now he was further favored by being made the English-speaking member of the two-man delegation from the ECCI to the American party convention. In the midst of the turmoil at the convention he distinguished himself by his oracular silence.

But not so Philipp Dengel. He had begun life in the modest position of a private school teacher. Then, drafted into the German army in 1913, he proved a correct and obedient soldier who was soon made a noncommissioned officer. A good top sergeant, he was promoted to a lieutenancy, though judging from the brusque and tactless way in which he communicated to the convention the commands with which he had been entrusted, a top sergeant he remained all his life. In the German Communist movement he belonged to the confused and confusing ultra-left German Communist Labor Party (KAPD), then to the ultra-left of Ruth Fischer, and then, when Stalin assured the German party that they must accept Thaelmann as their leader, he became a Thaelmannite (all of which is beyond the scope of these memoirs and beyond the capacity of their author to elucidate). Thereafter, Dengel spent most of his time in Moscow and won the favor of Stalin because of his subalternate obedience to his superiors and his demand for similar obedience from those below him. He was sent on official missions by the Comintern to the British, the Scandinavian, the Spanish, and various Latin-American parties, and he worked for the party apparatuses of Paris and Prague. He taught in the Lenin School, and in Moscow somehow passed as an authority on all of the countries to which he had been briefly sent, which was fair enough, for he knew as much about one of them as about any other. Now here he was in the United States, bursting with importance in his zeal to communicate the organizational proposals he carried from the Comintern.

The first organizational order was to remove Jay Lovestone as executive secretary and "elect" William Z. Foster in his stead. Foster was to receive the new title which Stalin had already assumed for himself, namely, that of general secretary. He was also to be given a majority on a new Secretariat, a new Politburo, and a new Central Committee. When leaders of the convention majority informed Representative Dengel that there had just been a month-long, free, democratic discussion and election of delegates who rejected all that Foster stood for, Dengel answered haughtily that he favored the minority of the convention and was instructed by the Comintern Executive for which he spoke to make them into the majority, and to make Foster General Secretary. Delegate after delegate thereupon denounced Foster for his sins real and imaginary, chief of which was his support of the sale of War Loans ("Liberty Bonds") during World War I, and his urging of workingmen to purchase them at a time when "true revolutionaries were going to jail for their opposition to the war." Leaders and local rank and filers alike engaged in the onslaught against Foster's reputation.

On the third day of the convention, at a meeting of the Political Committee, Dengel, bursting with indignation because his voice, the voice of the Comintern incarnate at this convention in his person, was receiving such rebellious treatment, demanded the immediate acceptance and unanimous endorsement of the Comintern's order to make Foster General Secretary. Every member of the Lovestone majority on the Political Committee spoke and voted against Dengel's "proposal." Even Weinstone, who had changed allegiances so often that he had become widely known as William Wobbly Weinstone, voted against the Dengel ukase. Jay Lovestone was quiet, for the election of Foster meant the removal of Lovestone, but Gitlow, Bedacht, Minor, Stachel, and Weinstone took part in the demolition of Foster's record. Foster had to listen to much of this on the convention floor, but the General Secretaryship which had eluded him once before was something he coveted. Now for the second time it almost seemed within his grasp. Dengel, however, was beside himself with rage.

Dengel's second secret weapon was something the convention could not defy, for they could not vote on it. It was a Comintern instruction that to "end the evil of factionalism" and the six-year long faction war in the American party, the two "chief factionalists," who were officially declared to be Lovestone and Bittelman, should be withdrawn from American soil and sent to Moscow to be put at the disposal of the Comintern for "important work" in some other party or some other land.

Lovestone, however, was prepared for this, for I had long ago sent him a coded cable and letter telling him that Moscow was rife with rumors that he would be ordered to come to Moscow, and that to show impartiality, if not to make him proud, Bittelman would be ordered to come too. Lovestone had won too huge a majority in the convention elections to give up without a struggle, but this would be a struggle of trying skill and diplomacy, for the "invitation to come to Moscow to be assigned important work by the Comintern" had a categorical and peremptory tone about it. If he flatly refused to go, the Comintern would order the American party to expel him. If he went, he would fret and molder and decline into innocuous bureaucratic desuetude, or would be sent to some remote land in Africa or Asia far from the America which was the object of his knowledge and concern. But at least his first step was clear: he must have the convention assert its natural sovereignty (at least natural for any national body in any country provided it was not affiliated with the "democratic" centralized Comintern). He would not run for reelection as Executive or "General" Secretary, but his overwhelming majority emboldened him to stir up his caucus of virtually the entire convention to defy the Comintern representatives and prevent them from handing Foster the prize of General Secretary. At a faction caucus Lovestone, in subtle fashion, and all the other leaders of his majority in open fashion, whipped up a spirit of rebellion against the ukase dictating the handing over of the party to those who had just been defeated. They chose Benjamin Gitlow to fill the new office of General Secretary, thus keeping their power intact. And as the majority of the convention, they defied Dengel's orders to give "General Secretary Foster" a majority on the Central Committee, the Politburo, and the Secretariat. Instead, they decided, as was their right, to elect a majority of their people to the incoming Central Committee, Politburo, and Secretariat. The Politburo, for instance, was made up of ten Majorityites, four Fosterites.

What was Dengel to report to Stalin? What was Stalin, i.e., the Comintern, to do? How could he dictate to a determined majority that they give over their rights to a defeated, demoralized, and discredited minority? Of course, the Comintern had never hesitated to reverse convention majorities before. In fact, Gusev, backed by Bukharin and Stalin, had done just that when Foster won a majority at the Fourth Convention of our party in August, 1925, and Gusev had contrived to get the famous cable sent to the American party that declared, "It has finally become clear that the Ruthenberg Group is more loyal to the Comintern and closer to its views," and "a Parity Central Committee" must be set up with Gusev as "impartial Chairman," impartially leaning, that is, toward the Ruthenberg-Lovestone group. But there was one big difference. Foster and his caucus could not summon up the courage nor evoke in their variegated caucus the unity to defy the Comintern.

This time a rebellious convention had given the party leadership a safe majority in the Central Executive Committee, the Political Committee and the Secretariat, while Foster, having just lost the Cannon group to Trotskyism (some hundred or so members having been expelled from the party as Trotskyites), and facing fresh intrigues from Bittelman and Browder, could not even present a creditable, unified opposition. What had the American party to fear if it held firm and kept its control of such institutions as the *Daily Worker*, the Workers' School, the Fellow Traveller Organizations, the whole going machine of the party?

True, the American party, like all the parties (with the exception of the German, where Rosa Luxemberg's spirit lived on after her murder) had thoughtlessly, even cheerfully, surrendered its autonomy at the Second Congress of the Comintern in 1920, when it adopted the statute provision: "The Communist International must, in fact and in deed, be a single Communist Party of the entire world. The parties working in the various countries are but its separate sections." We had thought then that the Russian party would give guidance and understanding, but we had never dreamed that, as it had gradually accustomed itself to doing, it would get to dictating tactics, resolutions, appointments of leaders even down to trade union and section and local leaders, postponement of decisions, commands by commissions that knew nothing of America, orders as to who should come as delegates to Moscow, and the like. Only now were we truly realizing the grim nature of the joke: "How does the American Communist Party resemble the Brooklyn Bridge? They are both suspended on cables."

Undoubtedly there would be a scathing review of the decisions of the convention by the Comintern, or whoever was designated to speak for it. And another *Open Letter* excoriating the party's leaders for their lack of loyalty to the Comintern. But what could they do in Moscow if we rejected their haughty review? If we refused to publish their *Open Letter,* or published it together with a courteous but effective answer? Never before had a rebellious convention so completely defied such unreasonable Comintern orders. We could answer them in ways they would not forget, and perhaps loosen somewhat the crippling bands of Comintern dictatorship. As Theodore Draper has said in his *American Communism and Soviet Russia:*

> It is hard to say what might have happened if Lovestone's group had decided to let well enough alone and waited for the Comintern to make the next move. A policy of watchful waiting could not have been more disastrous than the one actually pursued.

For the "disastrous policy actually pursued," I was chiefly responsible.

REINFORCEMENTS OR READY-MADE PRISONERS?

I had been fighting now for over two months, and aside from the one-hour talk I had compelled them to listen to, I had not gotten a genuine hearing, nor an audience with Stalin, nor any recognition of my presence in Moscow as the accredited representative of the American party on the Executive of the Comintern. I was tired of being pointedly ignored, fighting all alone, not getting anywhere. No wonder I felt the need for reinforcements and urged Lovestone to send a strong and representative delegation to Moscow to "have it out with Stalin."

At the convention itself a number of things happened that strengthened my feeling that a strong delegation backed by an overwhelming ninety percent majority in our party would enable us to settle all our problems with Stalin. And Lovestone himself continued to be certain that once he talked face to face with Stalin, backed by a strong American delegation, he could come to a satisfactory agreement. He had weathered the storm accompanying the decline of Trotsky's fortunes, the battle of Bukharin and Stalin with Zinoviev—why could he not come to a similar arrangement recognizing the ousting of Bukharin and the new and sole leadership of Stalin, and thus get leeway to carry on a decent policy on American questions in America?

Something in Point 4 at the end of the *Open Letter to the convention* strengthened Lovestone's idea that Stalin would be amenable to "comradely discussion." Point 4 (the last point in the letter) had demanded that we draw proletarians into the leadership of the Party. This gave Lovestone a bright idea: what if the proletarian delegates at the convention—they were a large and impressive contingent—should address a letter to Stalin in their own name, listing after each signature the industry from which the signer came? The letter they drafted appealed to Stalin to use his influence on the Executive of the Comintern to reverse the Comintern's organization proposals and permit the convention to elect its own Central Executive, Politburo, Executive Secretary, and other officials, and make its own decisions on American questions, subject to the revision and approval of the Communist International.

To the astonishment of all concerned, including both factions of the convention, Stalin sent a courteous cable in reply, in which he seemed to yield in a number of important matters, and even said some kindly things about the achievement of the American party in winning to its banner genuine American proletarians. He left his representative, Dengel, in an absurd, even ridiculous position. Dengel had been insisting as part of his "confidential instructions" that William Z. Foster must be "elected" General Secretary of the party, and that the convention must "choose" to choose Fosterite majorities on all leading bodies. Now Stalin declared that the convention might choose its own Central Executive Committee as it pleased, and the Central Executive might elect the top leadership as it pleased. But on two things he insisted. Lovestone and Bittelman must be sent to Moscow for Comintern work, and John Pepper must leave for Moscow without another day's delay. And the Comintern would in due course review the decisions of the convention. Foster was as displeased as Dengel with Stalin's cable.

Lovestone was delighted at the effect the "proletarian" cable had had. It strengthened his idea that if he took with him a strong delegation made up of some of the best of our native American workingman leaders and a contingent of our top officials—Gitlow, Bedacht, and himself—to reinforce my efforts, it might be easier to get Stalin to relent on the question of his exile from America. Certainly, it would be better than going alone.

Up to the moment of Stalin's more or less courteous response to the proletarian cable, Ben Gitlow had been in favor of simply refusing to surrender the party in which his group had won the overwhelming majority. "I have spent twenty years," he had been saying again and again, "helping to build the Socialist and then the Communist Party. I have gone to jail for our movement. I have sacrificed much to help the standing of the Soviet Union in America and to defend the rights of our party. I do not propose to let anybody try to drive me out of it or take my rights as a party member and official away from me. We have won our majority. Let's sit tight and hold on to it."

But Stalin's courteous-seeming cable empowering the convention to elect its own leadership beguiled him into thinking that Stalin was relenting, and that a strong delegation, with a predominant proletarian contingent speaking in the name of a virtually united party, would set things straight.

My appeal for reinforcements being thus morally strengthened, the leadership of the party had the convention itself choose a delegation of ten: William Miller, a Detroit machinist in the auto industry; Tom Myerscough, a mine organizer popular among the bituminous coal miners; William J. White, a veteran of the steel industry; Alex Noral, a farm expert; Ella Reeve Bloor, a lifelong organizer first of the Socialist, then of the Communist Party; Otto Huiswood, a West Indian Negro; and Edward Welsh, an American-born Negro who would spend his later years as an organizer for the A.F.L.-C.I.O., trying to teach African Negro workingmen how to form unions independent of their governments. To these the convention added Lovestone, thus making him not a man going into exile but a part of a representative delegation, and they added Gitlow and Bedacht, too. As soon as they arrived in Moscow, they added me to the delegation and held their caucus meetings not in the Hotel Bristol where Lovestone, Gitlow, and Bedacht were put up, but in my room in the Hotel Lux. When Harry M. Wicks, the party's representative on the Profintern, was added, that made fifteen Yankee "guests" of Joseph Stalin. Of course, the impressive size of the delegation brought us an early interview with Stalin, the interviewers being Lovestone and myself, with a remarkable polyglot named Tivel as translator. I let Lovestone do all the talking. Stalin, too, limited himself to listening and making notes on what Lovestone was saying, notes of which he would make striking use in the hearings of the commission on the American Question.

30

SEEKING JUSTICE FROM STALIN

Thirteen leaders of the American party set sail from New York Harbor on March 23, 1929, in quest of justice from the now unchallenged voice of the Comintern, Joseph Stalin. Their hopes were high, for the delegation was the largest and most impressive that had ever gone from America to Moscow. A unique feature was its ten "proletarians," nine of whom, that is all except Huiswood from the Dutch West Indies, were native-born Americans and, in the main, leading figures from such industries as steel and coal and automobiles. With them were three top leaders of the party, and behind the delegation was something like ninety percent of the party membership. The delegation had been publicly chosen by the party convention itself. Almost anyone on the delegation knew more about America and its problems than anyone in Moscow, including Stalin, and all they were seeking was the right of a lawfully elected majority to exercise the very rights which the party had conferred upon them.

To be sure, it was an uninvited delegation: the Americans had had the nerve to choose it themselves without asking the permission and approval of the Comintern. Moreover, on the very ship on which they sailed they found Alexander Bittelman, who, unlike Lovestone, was obediently accepting the decree of his exile from America and would no doubt be permitted to speak against them at some American Commission. Moreover, the Comintern itself, i.e., Joseph Stalin, had invited both Foster and Weinstone to come to Moscow to make trouble for the delegation. Both he and Foster went with high hopes of their own, for each was consumed with the ambition to become General Secretary of the American party, now that the ousting of Lovestone had left a vacuum. Indeed, that ambition was the secret of Weinstone's wobbling. He had reluctantly played second fiddle to Lovestone; he had offered Cannon a new coalition against both Foster and Lovestone just before Cannon spoiled his dream by going all out for Leon Trotsky. And he had dickered with Foster, although their ambitions clashed too directly. In short, he had offered support to any and every faction and had experimented with building a faction of his own called "the Unity Caucus," always suggesting himself as General Secretary and assuring whomsoever would listen that as District Organizer of New York City, the largest district in the country, he could get the district to follow him into whatever camp he entered. Like most of the uninvited members of the delegation of thirteen, Bittelman, Foster, and Weinstone, too, knew more about America than anyone in Moscow. But the three who were specifically invited were quite ready to support Stalin and make trouble for the Convention's delegation. However, the delegation felt sure it could handle all three with ease if it was given fair play in a free discussion before the ECCI, or a fairly constituted American Commission. And Lovestone felt certain he could come to an understanding with Stalin as he had with Zinoviev and Bukharin when they were in turn the voice of the Comintern.

To be sure, there was one problem to which the delegation had perhaps not given sufficient thought. Here were the three top generals leaving their entire army behind them, six thousand miles away, and going into potentially hostile territory with nothing but a bodyguard of ten proletarians. Whom did they leave behind to lead their army while they were six thousand miles away? What mischief might take place in America while they were in Moscow? What real power did this "impressive delegation" wield if it failed to impress? What mischief could Stalin do in America, speaking in the name of the Comintern and blocking their means of communication? What if he should, as well he might, decide to play the role of prosecutor, judge, jury, and perhaps even jailer? His cable to the "Convention Proletarians" had seemed benign enough when he retreated on the question of making Foster General Secretary and giving him a majority in all committees; yet on one thing his voice was firm and hard: Lovestone must come to Moscow and not go back to America.

I must confess that I had not thought this problem through when I called so insistently for "reinforcements," for "a strong delegation to have it out with Stalin." I had not realized how thin was the layer of top leadership, how hard it would be to find "lieutenant generals" to fill their places if the three top generals were away at the same time.

And though I had seen Stalin's ruthlessness in action when he removed Bukharin; though I had watched Stalin's maneuvers in exiling Trotsky from Russia and in packing all the committees in which he lost to Bukharin by one vote, somehow I remained naive enough to envisage a comparatively free and fair discussion of American issues, and proper respect for a ninety-percent majority in our party and the *de facto* liquidation and demoralization of the opposition.

Lovestone was the real commander-in-chief of the delegation. He had been the organizer of the Ruthenberg group even while Ruthenberg was alive, and after his death he became the unquestioned leader, spokesman, and strategist of the party majority. Gitlow had been elected General Secretary in his place when it was decided that Lovestone should not run for the office. And Max Bedacht was the party's Agitprop Director, a post he had taken over when I left for Moscow.

Of course, Lovestone had worried about leaving the home front uncovered, but so poor was the leadership material in the American party that it was hard to think of whom to trust with the temporary command posts. Had I still been in America, perhaps Lovestone would have tried to persuade me to take the top administrative post, something I would not have relished, for my interest was in party education and not in administration. If a strong and determined leader were to have been left to cover the home front, it should of course have been Gitlow, who could have been trusted not to let Stalin take the party away from its leadership by any maneuvers at a distance. But then the delegation would have been that much poorer, for Lovestone was a representative of the American Party without an office in it any longer. To make the American delegation a strong one, both majority leader Lovestone and General Secretary Gitlow had to head it together. Bedacht could have been left to hold the fort, but he was not as strong a character as Gitlow or Lovestone.

Hence, after much searching of the roster of leading figures in the party majority, Lovestone made a choice that shocked me. He picked on Robert Minor—he whom our secret cable code not inappropriately referred to as *Schmendrick*—to become Acting General Secretary of the party. Minor was vain and foolish and in my opinion untrustworthy, and though even now in retrospect I cannot think whom I could have picked of sufficient stature to be Acting General Secretary, it would not have been Bob Minor.

I think Lovestone himself might have been a little uneasy at trusting *Schmendrick* with so important a post. Gitlow must have felt as I did about him, for he wrote of the delegation's departure that "Robert Minor was there to see us off. He was in the most jubilant spirits as if we were going on a picnic. . . . When the time came to say good-bye, he grabbed my hand and as he bade us farewell the crafty glimmer in his eyes gave me forebodings. I told Lovestone, 'Jay, that sly grin he gave me when we said good-bye worries me. . . . I have a premonition that he will double-cross us . . .' " (Of course, Gitlow wrote this ten years later in his book, *I Confess,* and there may be some wisdom of hindsight in it. But it is not, as it may seem, hindsight on my part, for Bob Minor would have been the last man in our group that I would have trusted with the key post of Acting General Secretary.)

" 'Don't worry,' Lovestone replied to Gitlow. 'After all, we have Stachel to depend upon. Bob Minor will have to wake up very early in the morning to pull any tricks against us.' "

Actually, Lovestone felt he had two more key men to rely on: Jack Stachel, the party's Organization Secretary and Lovestone's adviser on personnel in many a faction fight; and Joseph Brodsky, the jovial, competent, loyal lawyer of the Communist Party who advised the party on all legal matters and who had supported the Lovestone group through thick and thin.

I had no doubt about Joe Brodsky, but Jack Stachel was an enigma to me. Before he became a Communist, he had been a medicine man, one who earned his living by selling some quack patent medicine panacea on street-corner soapboxes, on platforms in public plazas, or on stages built in empty lots in the suburbs of New York City. These medicine men were a source of entertainment to me as a boy. (I remember one in particular who sold Diamondback Rattlesnake Oil and Rattlesnake soap, cure-alls, specimens of which he gave out as prizes in popular entertainment contests, then demonstrated their virtues in a voice that could charm, yet drown out the grinding of trolley car wheels on nearby rails that passed his speaker's stand.) The medicine man is now an extinct species, which disappeared with the invention of radio, television, and modern cure-all drug advertising. Just as the species was growing extinct, Jack Stachel appeared in our midst, an accomplished street speaker, a convinced Communist who chose the Ruthenberg-Lovestone group and was soon functioning as a faction organizer in the New York District, where he blocked Weinstone's wobbling maneuvers, and thence rose to the post of Organization Secretary of the party.

Jack Stachel was obsessed with factionalism, factional maneuvers, and faction personnel lists to the virtual exclusion of every other aspect of party life. At conventions he would stay awake all night in his hotel room making and remaking lists of names of those who should form an incoming Central Committee or State or City Committee, along with lists of alternates and other sub-committee lists. In the morning his hotel room floor would be strewn with crumpled scraps of paper, lists made and altered and remade, and he would come into the convention session ready with a carefully thought out list of names for each committee. In all my conversations with him, he never talked of anything but faction maneuvers and faction business until I began to wonder what emotion had brought him to full-time party work and what other feelings he might have. Yet, when my wife and I had dinner at his home, we found it a happy one, and learned that he had fallen love with his Bertha when she was married to someone else and had besieged her home, paraded the streets nearby to catch a glimpse of her, and persuaded her at last that he was offering a deep and intense love such as she had never known. Being at heart a romantic, my opinion of him went up, though I did not cease to wonder at his monomaniacal obsession with factionalism. In any case, Minor, Stachel, Brodsky—such were the lieutenant generals who were advanced to the command of the home front.

To these three lieutenant generals Lovestone gave a difficult and secret task. Suppose Stalin should attempt to take the party away from his group while they were in Moscow; in that case the substitute commanders were to hold on to the party's official organ, its headquarters, its fronts or auxiliary bodies, and transfer the ownership of every piece of property to absolutely reliable leading members of the Lovestone group. Stachel was to make up the list of reliables for Minor and Brodsky. Brodsky was to arrange the sale of the headquarters of the party and the Workers' School, which was held in trust by the ever-unreliable Weinstone. Brodsky was to prepare, too, the deeds of transfer of all party property that could be transferred, as well as of fellow-traveler fronts like the Workers' Defense League and the Workers' Aid. Of course, none of this should be attempted unless a special code cable from Lovestone to Stachel said it was necessary. Thus the home front was to be protected in an extreme emergency.

A COLD RECEPTION IN BERLIN

When the Delegation got to Berlin, it got a second warning which reinforced the one Pepper had given. When they applied for visas at the office that regularly took care of Comintern delegates, they were made to feel at once that the Comintern had not invited nor authorized such a delegation. It had been chosen by a rebellious convention, and the Comintern office in Berlin could do nothing for these thirteen people until it received instructions from Moscow. In the meanwhile, the delegation, whose way was being paid by the Americans and not the Comintern, had to put up in hotels at considerable expense, send telegrams, pay for meals. Five days they were kept waiting, during which time they picked up Comintern news in Berlin. They learned of the expulsion of Ewert and other leaders of the German Party because they had caught Thaelmann covering up an embezzlement of party funds by his brother-in-law, Wittdorf. Stalin was looking for lame ducks or people under a cloud. If he made them leaders of their parties, they were wholly beholden to him, and he could exalt them or destroy them without a murmur on their part. So Stalin had declared the semiliterate and guilty Thaelmann the leader of the German party and Ewert a "conciliator toward the Right Wing." Ewert was sent abroad on various missions, then sentenced to jail in Brazil for 13 years and four months. In prison he went insane, and when granted an amnesty, he lived in various medical institutions in East Germany until his death.

In Berlin, if Gitlow's memory is sound on this point, the delegation received a cable from Jack Stachel that I had cabled New York that no delegation was necessary, that only Lovestone should come to Moscow. This was, of course, if such a cable existed, a forgery either by Stachel or the Comintern, for I had been pleading since the end of February for just such reinforcements as were coming to help me in my lone struggle.

Lovestone, Gitlow, and Bedacht visited M. N. Roy in Berlin. He had never been a Bukharinite, but as soon as Stalin's fortunes began to rise, he had become a devoted Stalinist. When Stalin decided to order an uprising in Canton against Chiang Kai-shek, he sent Roy, Lominadze, and other loyal Stalinites to execute the mad maneuver. When it ended in disaster, he wanted Roy to take the blame. When the proud Roy refused the role of scapegoat, Stalin expelled him. Now Roy laughed at Lovestone for planning to put himself and his delegation in the ruthless Stalin's power. "Once you are in Russia you are like a trapped animal." But Lovestone ignored his warning, as he had Pepper's, and remained firm in his belief that he could come to an agreement with Stalin. When the delegation finally crossed the border, their baggage was searched, a new humiliation to which Comintern delegates were never subjected. Clearly, their preliminary welcome was not a warm one.

One other piece of gossip that the delegation picked up in Berlin may help to explain the kind of reception Stalin had prepared for it. The Germans were watching with excitement what was happening in the American party, a party they had hitherto ignored. The Germans our delegates spoke to all knew that the American party convention had defied the orders of the Comintern. Some of them had heard about the rebellion from Dengel or his cronies; others had heard about my attack on the Comintern's *Open Letter* of January from Klara Zetkin. Some expressed shock that the German party had yielded so easily in the Wittdorf-Thaelmann scandal while the much weaker American party was holding out. Those who sympathized with Klara Zetkin, Gitlow wrote, "cautiously expressed the opinion that perhaps the American party would end the system of vassalage to the Russian leadership on the part of other parties."

Even if the Convention had stood firm and not put its "impressive delegation" into Stalin's hands, this was too much to hope, for Stalin did not care how many leaders and parties he expelled while he was changing the Comintern into the Stalintern.

STALIN'S IDEA OF AN AMERICAN COMMISSION

Whether Stalin was shocked by the rebellion of our party convention against his Comintern orders and his Comintern reps or startled by the convention's decision, without Comintern invitation or Comintern permission, to send a thirteen-man delegation including ten proletarians to Moscow to appeal for the right to exercise its natural powers as a duly elected majority, or because Stalin realized that other parties were watching to see how the American "declaration of independence" would turn out, he had the Comintern set up a commission that was unique in the history of the Communist International, probably unique too in the history of commissions set up in one country to judge the rights of a corporate body in another country.

Obviously something more seemed at stake to him than the faction controversies of a distant, second-rate party that had hitherto always been ostentatiously loyal to the Communist International and its leading Russian party. For reasons of internal politics Stalin had christened the year 1929 the year of the *Velikij Perelom* (the year of the Great Turn). But the fact that Joseph Stalin decided that he himself would serve on the American Commission, thus being obliged to consume much time and put his own reputation at stake, showed that he had chosen the American question to symbolize a *Velikij Perelom* in the life and structure of the Comintern.

The composition of the American Commission showed that Stalin was taking no chances. It was a commission of twelve members, of which eight were Russians and three more had been so long in the Soviet Union that they might be reckoned as adoptive Russians. The eight Russians were Stalin himself; his echo chamber, Molotov; Lozovsky; Manuilsky; Gusev; Khitarov (representing the Young Communist International); Moireva; and Mikhailov, alias Williams, who served as secretary of the commission. The chairman was Otto Kuusinen, the Finn who had so long lived in Russia that after serving from 1921 to 1939, as Secretary of the Executive Committee of the Comintern, he had openly become a Soviet official, Member of the Supreme Soviet of the USSR, Chairman of the Presidium of the Supreme Soviet of the Karelian Soviet Republic, member of the Central Committee, then the Secretary of the Central Committee of the Communist Party of the Soviet Union. The other semi-naturalized Russians were Bela Kun, briefly chairman of the Hungarian Soviet Republic, then refugee in Russia where he served as emissary of the Comintern to various parties and countries; and that gray nonentity, Walter Ulbricht. When the Spartacan uprising, or rather *Putsch*, of 1919 ended in disaster, Rosa Luxemburg, Karl Liebknecht, and Ulbricht were surprised in their hideout in Berlin and while they were being taken to prison by German officers, their captors murdered two of them, Luxemburg and Liebknecht. Ulbricht they considered too insignificant to assassinate, and so he survived. Beginning in the middle twenties he spent most of his time in Comintern work under Piatnitsky in the Central European Bureau of the Communist International. When Stalin was engaged in the blood purge of most German leaders who had taken refuge in Russia, or was surrendering them to Hitler as an earnest of good faith in the Stalin-Hitler Pact, Ulbricht endorsed Stalin's purges and Stalin's pact with Hitler, thus surviving to be elevated by Stalin to a position of leadership in the East German government as Chairman of the Council of State.

The above accounts for eleven of the twelve members of the American Commission. The twelfth was an Englishman, Tom Bell, who showed so little understanding of the American question that Lovestone in our caucus gatherings changed his name to Dumb Bell. Needless to say, there was no American on the American Commission. In any case, with eight Russians out of twelve Committee members, it mattered little who the other four might be. And with Stalin in person a member of the Commission, he had only to speak, and it mattered not at all what the other eleven might be thinking.

PREPARING FOR BATTLE

The reinforcements I had been waiting for arrived on April 7, and a week later the sessions began. We devoted the intervening week to planning our appeal to the Comintern and exchanging news with each other (I telling what had been happening in Moscow that I had found impossible to send in code; Lovestone and Gitlow giving an account of Dengel's behavior when he collided with our rebellious convention). We also warned our inexperienced proletarians about the blandishments that would be used on them in an attempt to seduce them. Lozovsky had already won over Harry Wicks, our representative to the Profintern, by promising him promotion in the American leadership. And the Comintern had won over many of the students at the Lenin School whom we had sent over as a contingent supporting the party majority. The Lenin students had been overwhelmed by the anti-Bukharin propaganda, by the sudden exaltation of Stalin's name and person, and by the atmosphere of inquisition surrounding all the assaults on the leaders of the German party, the Austrian party, the Czechoslovak party, the Swedish and the Norwegian. Moreover, that spring I had seen the first public sign of the *Velikij Perelom* when Stalin's face, retouched and glorified, had blossomed forth as the front cover of every magazine in Russia, not excluding the journal devoted to modes and fashions. Many of our Lenin students had become convinced by this barrage of propaganda that all the leaders of various parties who were being expelled or removed were either Right-Wingers or conciliators. They came to the enlarged meetings of our delegation, thereby jamming the room my wife and I shared in the Hotel Lux, to warn us solemnly not to speak to one or another such discarded leader because he was guilty of the crime of Rightwingism or the more heinous one of conciliator.

We warned our ten stalwart proletarians that while we would be treated like pariahs, they would be wooed by flattery, offers of promotion to official party leadership, excursions, attractive girls, banquets, tickets to theater and opera, and the like. Thus forewarned, and guided by their own feelings, our proletarians really did prove stalwart, and nine of the ten held firm when the critical moment came.

During the week that elapsed before the American Commission began its sessions, Lovestone and Gitlow also tried visiting Kuusinen, whom they both knew well, to see if the chairman of the commission might give them some notion of what was in store for us. He was reluctant to see them, alleging that he was too busy with Comintern work, but when they insisted that they wanted to have a talk with him, he finally, in his naturally courteous way, consented. He had been a great admirer of Bukharin and quite friendly to Lovestone. He listened without rejoinder while they narrated the situation in America and pleaded that the American Party would be damaged, and the Comintern with it, if so overwhelming a majority should be overruled by fiat from Moscow and Lovestone compelled to leave the Party and the country which meant everything to him. They were pleading for the simple right to carry out the mandate that the party convention and elections had given. If this were denied, Lovestone said, our condition in the party and among its supporters would be unbearable. "But," Gitlow reported, "Kuusinen shrugged his shoulders and made a remark which explained the helplessness and dejection of the man. 'You,' said Kuusinen in German, 'You have a country to go back to, but I am an exile from my country and a refugee here. You must understand that there is nothing I can do.' "

That remark closed the interview and seemed to promise at least gentleness and parliamentary courtesy from the Chairman of the American Commission. And indeed, though his conduct of his chairmanship was scrupulously correct, when it came time for him to make an address against the obduracy of the American delegation, his words were soft but his denunciation was ruthless. So he had served Bukharin earlier, with admiration and devotion, but when the time came to make his fateful choice, he had saved himself from demotion or extinction by denouncing Bukharin with unusual energy and sharpness. That is why Otto Kuusinen, who had thrown in his lot with the Russian Bolsheviks when he became an exile from Finland, and who ended his life as Secretary of the Central Committee of the Communist Party of the Soviet Union, died on May 17, 1964, that most unnatural of deaths for an Old Bolshevik, a natural death, at the age of 83, and was given one of the biggest state funerals that the Soviet Union has ever known.

THE AMERICAN COMMISSION AT WORK

The sessions of the American Commission were more like an inquisition than a hearing or trial. Eight Russians and their four allies sat in judgment on the American delegation. And they were energetically supported by their invited agents in the American party, Foster, Bittelman, and Weinstone. The opening session consisted of a two-hour presentation of the majority delegation's appeal by Gitlow, then a denunciation of more or less equal length by William Z. Foster for the opposition.

This was followed by a number of sessions in which the judges all took turns at cross-examining the American delegates with most of the fire concentrated against Lovestone. Every charge large and small that was ever alleged against the American party majority was dug up, apparently from the detailed dossier that Stalin or his secretaries kept up on him. Every judge in turn enjoyed himself in this free and safe target practice until at last everybody got tired of this stage of the hearings.

At this point our trial was recessed because the Russian party was to hold a plenary session of its Central Committee which eight of our twelve judges had to attend. Gitlow as a member of the Presidium of the Executive of the Comintern was given an invitation to attend. Lovestone asked for one also and it was denied him on the false excuse that the number of invitations to foreign members of the Comintern was limited. Actually, he was entitled as a member of the ECCI to attend, and I, who was only taking his place while he was in America, was not. But out of curiosity, I presented my credential as an American representative and was admitted.

The Plenum was held in a large hall, the Throne Room of the Tsar's Palace in the Kremlin, and every member, important or unimportant, of the ECCI found room in it, except Jay Lovestone, so that his exclusion was a deliberate insult intended to show that the verdict had already been decided on before our appeal was heard and that Lovestone was no longer a functioning leader of the American party.

Stalin had decided that this Plenum should finish off Bukharin, change his "ill health" to official removal by the Russian party as one of its representatives in the Comintern, and make visible Molotov's place as his successor. In order to make the new Chairman of the Executive Committee shine, if it were possible for so dull a character to shine, Stalin saw to it that Molotov should make two reports such as Bukharin might have made, one on the World Situation and one on the Struggle against War. Unfortunately, the contrast between the plodding Molotov and the sparkling Bukharin, was too great; comparing what he said and how he said it with any report that Bukharin had ever given must have made many of those present feel, as I did, that the Comintern had lost its voice in the droning dullness of this unimpressive figure. On the first day, in order to elevate him and show that Bukharin would not be missed, Stalin had him report to the Plenum on the World Situation. Since Bukharin might have taken three hours on so large a topic, he spoke twice as long, and kept using the Russian word, *položenie* which came out *p-p-p-p-položenie.* It never occurred to him to substitute the word *situacija,* which would have occasioned no difficulty. On the second day he spoke at equal length on the Struggle against War. *Struggle* came out as *b-b-b-b-bor'ba,* and this time, unfortunately, the Russian language is so poor in synonyms for *struggle* that there probably was no escape for him.

As the Plenum went on its preordained way, there was one explosive episode involving the American party. Bukharin, knowing that these were his last days in the top leadership, complained that a campaign had been conducted against him, its Chairman, in every leading party of the Comintern, and as an example cited the unanimous resolution denouncing him adopted by the American party convention. He said rightly that Dengel had carried the campaign to America in the name of the Comintern, that Dengel had said that the C.I. considered Lovestone's group to be Bukharinite in character, and that it could not clear itself except by denouncing Bukharin by name. Dengel had pressed, the opposition had pressed, and Lovestone's own caucus had pressed him to yield. Finally, Lovestone and Gitlow, under all this pressure, had drafted and introduced a resolution denouncing Bukharin and suggesting that he should be formally ousted from his post of leadership in the Comintern, and Lovestone had even supplemented this by sending a cable of greetings and congratulations to the Russian party under its "Bolshevik leadership headed by Comrade Stalin."

Dengel, attempting to exonerate Stalin and himself of responsibility for these backstairs diplomatic maneuvers, made a statement to the Plenum of the Russian party denying that he had anything to do with the American resolution against Bukharin, which was merely the work of the American majority and an example of its unprincipledness. Thereupon Gitlow, infuriated, drafted a statement saying that Dengel had made the suggestion to the American party that only by such a statement against Bukharin could the party clear itself of the charge of Bukharinism with the leaders of the Comintern. The next day, when Gitlow handed in his statement and asked that it be immediately translated into Russian, Stalin was quite upset. When he got an oral translation from one of his translators, he became furious, for no doubt he himself had been behind Dengel's maneuvers. He had the Plenum adjourn for the day, and Gitlow's statement was never read to the Plenum but went instead into Stalin's file on the new General Secretary of the American party.

STALIN'S ADDRESSES ON THE AMERICAN QUESTION

Lozovsky, Bell, Gusev, Kun, and the Bulgarian Kolarov had each been permitted to deliver ritual addresses denouncing the American party and its leadership before the American Commission went into temporary adjournment to let its eight Russians attend the Plenum of their own party's Central Committee. But the speeches of Molotov and Stalin were delayed until May 6 to work up to a climax to the solemn act of judgment on America and the American party.

I will spare the reader the details of Molotov's address, if not out of kindness, then because I should have to anyhow, since I don't remember a word of it. But Stalin's speeches (there were three of them, for he found he could not finish off the stubborn Americans by one pronouncement of anathema and a single threat of excommunication) represent something unique in the history of the Comintern and in the political life of Joseph Stalin. In the small adjoining rooms of the great halls in which Communist World Congresses were held, Stalin had sometimes briefly pronounced verdicts on the leadership of the German or the Chinese party, but never before had he spoken publicly or at such length on the internal affairs of any party, nor would he ever do so again. These three addresses were immediately published in English translation in the United States with the purpose of annihilating the American party's leadership and consecrating, a little ambiguously, the Foster opposition. But almost as promptly the attempt was made to recall his words, for they revealed with dangerous clarity that Joseph Stalin, the Russian leader from Georgia, was laying down the political and tactical lines of the American Communist Party and making and unmaking the American party's General Secretaries, Secretariats, and other nominally autonomous bodies. When committees of the Congress of the United States began to use such documents to prove that the American Communist Party had its line and tactics dictated, and its leaders picked, by the leader of the Russian Communist Party, and was thus clearly an agency of a foreign power, Stalin directed that his addresses on the American Question should cease to exist, indeed that such nonexistence should be made retroactive and the speeches become unspeeches. Thereupon there was an epidemic of raids on libraries known to possess collections of documents on the history of Communism and of the Communist International. Pamphlets disappeared into the briefcases of innocent-seeming readers; sharp razors cut out pages from Communist magazines; skilled removers, unnoticed, managed to conjure away telltale copies of certain numbers of the *Daily Worker* from wrapped-up collections and even from bound volumes. Alert librarians discovered some such depredations, and agents of our Secret Service found a young sailor in the reading room of the Fifth Avenue Library in New York City, razor blade in hand, performing just such operations on innocent books, magazines, and pamphlets. They arrested him, then offered him immunity if he would tell who had ordered him to perform the political surgery, but the sailor preferred to go to jail instead. So, too, when I was working on the present chapter and tried to find such documents as the Comintern's *Open Letter to the American Convention* which had been published in the *Daily Worker* of March 4, 1929, I hopefully turned the pages of a beautifully kept and bound volume of the *Daily Worker* in the Hoover Library. The issues of March 1 to March 4 were missing, and one could not tell that they had been removed! I managed to get the letter all the same because our devoted assistant director for Western Language Library Operations, Arline Paul, by due diligence finally located, in the libraries of a university that had best remain nameless, a complete microfilm of the *Daily Worker* for that year, photographed before the excisions occurred.

Stalin's first concern in his address of May 6 was the seemingly abstract question of "American exceptionalism." His target was Jay Lovestone, but his buckshot was scattered freely on all of us.

> I do not intend to speak at great length [he began]. I shall not deal with the political position of the leaders of the majority and the minority . . . since it has become evident that both groups are guilty of the fundamental error of exaggerating the specific features of American capitalism. You know that this exaggeration lies at the root of every opportunist error committed by the majority and the minority group.
>
> It would be wrong to ignore the specific features of American capitalism. . . . But it would be still more wrong to base the activities of the Communist Party on

these specific features, since the foundation of the activities of every Communist Party, including the American, on which it must base itself, must be the general features of capitalism, which are the same for all countries, and not its specific features in any given country.*

It is on this that the internationalism of the Communist Party is founded. Specific features are only supplementary to general features. The error of both groups is that they exaggerate the significance of the specific features of American capitalism, and thereby overlook the basic features of American capitalism which are characteristic of world capitalism as a whole. . . . That is the basis for the unsteadiness of both sections of the American Communist Party in matters of principle.

Only at this point did I begin to understand why Stalin had invented the heresy of *American exceptionalism.* "*It would be wrong to ignore the specific peculiarities of American capitalism,*" but "*every Communist Party including the American must base itself . . . on the general features of capitalism, which are the same for all countries, and not on its specific features in any given country. Specific features are only supplementary. . . . It is on this that the internationalism of the Communist Party is founded . . .*"

If we accepted this dictum, he had us where he wanted us. If the Comintern declared that in the entire International the "Left-Danger is the main danger," then we had to find a grave and menacing Left-Danger in America, too. Lenin had done just that at the Second Congress of the Comintern with his programmatic pamphlet written for that purpose, *The Children's Sickness of "Leftism" in Communism (Detskaja Bolezn' "Levizmy" v Kommunizme,* better known in English as *"Left-Wing" Communism: An Infantile Disorder*). Then Lenin had found such a "Children's Complaint" in all parties. For our part, we really had the "infantile disorder" in America at that time: in our worship of dual unionism; our support of the IWW which had been crushed during the war and by the Palmer Red raids; our detestation of the American Federation of Labor; our early slogan to "Broaden and Deepen" each strike into "Mass Action and Revolution"; and many other childish imitations of what we thought had been done in Russia. And we really learned much from Lenin's pamphlet and his speeches at the Second Congress.

Now, under far different circumstances and without Lenin's occasional deep breaths of realism, Joseph Stalin in his fight to finish off his quondam ally and theoretician, Bukharin, declared the "Right-Danger" (i.e., Bukharin) the "Main Danger" in every country. He also declared that a revolutionary upsurge and ever more embittered class war was a present

* This remark seems to be the symmetrical opposite of my declaration, namely: "I am an exceptionalist for every country in the world. Each country moves towards its own future in terms of its own past, its own traditions, and its own peculiar conditions that make each land different from all the others."

feature of every country. Therefore he bade us find a menacing "Right-Danger" in America, in the organized labor movement, in the Socialist Party, in the embryonic Farmer-Labor Party movement, and above all in our own party, in its leadership and its opposition, but worst of all in "Comrades Lovestone and Pepper."

According to this solemn opening of Stalin's first address on the American question, European and American conditions could differ and the specific peculiarities of America should be "taken into account," but America like the rest of the world must suddenly take a violent left turn.

What was it then, Stalin asked, that prevented the American party from taking advantage of this sharpening class war verging on revolution? What if not the fact that both majority and minority paid too much attention to the relatively unimportant, specific American peculiarities, and thus themselves constituted the "Right-Danger" that prevented them from seeing the uniformity of the revolutionary upsurge in all countries, including America?

Yes, perhaps we Americans might know more about the specific conditions and peculiarities of America than any commission the Comintern might appoint on the American question. We might know more about peculiarly American matters than Lozovsky or Petrovsky-Bennet-Goldfarb or even Molotov. Or, oh frightful heresy and blasphemy never to be breathed or thought, than Stalin himself. Yes, we might talk them down on some specific American peculiarities. But who in America would dare to say that he knew more about the *international situation*, the *world situation*, those general features the profound knowledge of which made the Russians automatically the leaders of the Comintern and the Comintern the leader of all its sections?

Hence the question of "American exceptionalism" was for Stalin no mere abstract, theoretical question. Let the American comrades speak all they pleased of the specific features or specific peculiarities of American life that made it different from French or German or Russian or Chinese. But these specific features could never determine the American party's tactics or political policy or theory, for they were but supplementary, secondary, insignificant. They might use their American knowledge to make the Comintern line of any given moment more intelligible and acceptable to American workingmen. But it was the general features of the world situation that determined what must happen in America as in any other country. Otherwise, where was the basis of your internationalism? How do you belong in the World Communist party? Who in America, what faction, what group, what person, dares to say that he knows more about the general features of the world situation than the collective wisdom of the Communist International, guided as it is by the victory-tested wisdom of the only revolutionary party that has succeeded in seizing power and successfully builds socialism on one-sixth of the earth?

After delivering himself of this bit of "theory," Stalin went over to the more familiar field of organizational measures to crush his opponents.

Both majority and minority, he said, were guilty of "unprincipled factionalism" and based their dealings with the Comintern "on a policy of rotten diplomacy, a policy of diplomatic intrigue." How dared Foster and Bittelman call themselves "Stalinites"? That was no way to "demonstrate their loyalty to the C.P.S.U. But, my dear comrades, that is disgraceful. Do you not know that there are no 'Stalinites,' that there must be no 'Stalinites'?" (At this point I thought of how the Stalinites were using the term Bukharinite, and how every magazine in Russia had just broken out with a glorified face of Stalin as its front cover. How long would it be, I asked myself, before it would become dangerous not to call oneself a Stalinite and not to applaud one's hands sore every time a speaker mentioned his name?)

Next my attention was arrested by the fact that Stalin was condemning us for *agiotage*—clearly a French word. What did it mean? What did he mean by it? I must admit I had to go to a dictionary to find that it meant seeking profit by playing the stock market or the foreign exchange market. Stalin illustrated the term thus:

> The Foster Group wants to demonstrate its devotion to the C.P.S.U. by declaring themselves 'Stalinites.' Good! We, the Lovestonites, will go still further and demand the removal of Comrade Bukharin from the Comintern. Let the Fosterites try to beat that! Let them know over there in Moscow that we Americans know how to play the stock market. . . .
>
> But, Comrades, the Comintern is not a stock market. The Comintern is the Holy of Holies of the working class. *Either* we are Leninists, and our relations with one another must be *čisty kristal'nyj* (pure as crystal), in which case there should be no room in our ranks for rotten diplomatic intrigue; *or* we are not Leninists, in which case rotten diplomacy and unprincipled faction struggle will have full scope in our relations. One thing or the other. We must choose, Comrades.

At that a part of my mind flew off even while the rest of it strained to hear every word in Russian and in simultaneous earphone translation. *Holy of Holies!* I thought. *Pure and clean as crystal! No room in our ranks for rotten, diplomatic intrigue!* All this from the man whom I had seen raise his red card "democratically," like any other delegate to the Sixth Congress, when Bukharin was being unanimously reelected Chairman.

I first discovered that one's head can do many things at one and the same time when, as a public speaker, I became aware of the fact that I could follow a line of thought, think of effective formulations, watch to see whether those in the back row could hear me, check the timbre of my voice, and do many other things at once while I was addressing an audience. But by now my head was in a whirl, as was that of all the Americans. Most of the "bystanders," the members of the Executive from other parties, seemed to be enjoying our discomfiture, and congratulating themselves that they had jumped on the bandwagon just in time. Stalin, too, seemed to be enjoying himself, rejoicing particularly that he had us in his power (my fault!), and could harass and torment all the Americans to teach other parties what it would mean to resist the new leader of the Comintern in the slightest.

Stalin's main target was Lovestone whom he blamed, quite properly, for the American party convention's resistance to the instructions he had given Dengel. But he kept shooting at Foster, too, balancing every attack on the majority with an attack on the minority to reduce the American party to a state of disorderly collapse. Foster was particularly miserable, for Stalin baldly declared that Foster had been lying when he claimed that, in his secret interview with Stalin during the Sixth Congress, he had been promised support by the leaders of the Comintern. Foster had to keep quiet, too, and listen while both Stalin and Molotov denied that the Comintern had given their emissary, Dengel, instructions to turn the American party over to the opposition and make Foster general secretary.

Then he would denounce Pepper for deceiving the Comintern about his return to Russia, for American exceptionalism, for right wingism, and Pepper, who had just arrived in Russia during the last couple days, was not even allowed to be present, for he was under "indictment" for disobeying and deceiving the Comintern, and was soon to be put on trial for his offenses.

But always Stalin would return to Lovestone, whom he was vengefully determined to discredit for having contemplated and organized resistance, and for having lined up ten of the Party's "proletarian leaders" and brought them to Moscow to ask for the rescinding of the Comintern's orders.

After denouncing Foster for keeping his talk with Stalin secret and using it to bolster the morale of his defeated faction (it *was* secret, and was so intended by Stalin), the prosecutor, who was not supposed to be answered, turned again to the American *bête noire* who had tried to defy him:

> I refer to the talk with Comrade Lovestone that took place the other day. What did he speak about? He asked that the Presidium of the ECCI rescind its decision to withdraw him from America. . . . He promised to be a loyal soldier of the Comintern and prove it in practice. . . . He said he was not seeking for high positions in the American Communist Party, but only begged that he be tested and given the opportunity to prove his loyalty to the Comintern. . . . I told him that experiments in testing the loyalty of Comrade Lovestone have already been going on for three years, but no good has come of them. I said it would be better for the Communist Party of America and for the Comintern if Comrades Lovestone and Bittelman were kept in Moscow for a time . . . one of the surest means of curing the American Communist Party of factionalism and saving it from disintegration. I said that although this was my opinion, I agreed to submit the proposal of Comrade Lovestone to the consideration of the Russian Comrades, and undertook to inform him of the opinion of the Russian Comrades. That seems perfectly clear. Yet Comrade Lovestone . . . is spreading all kinds of rumors concerning this conversation.

What a lesson to those leaders of other parties who had come into the American Commission sessions occasionally, hoping that American resistance to Comintern orders, i.e., "the Russian comrades," i.e., Joseph Stalin, would restore some autonomy to the other parties! Clearly, the best they could get was this public humiliation and arbitrary exile from their parties as "guests" of Moscow. How many leaders had already been thus destroyed and permitted to wither, useless and inactive, far from their parties and their native lands?

STALIN'S SOLUTION TO THE AMERICAN QUESTION

Stalin's speech on the American question seemed long and wearying because of the falsehoods that we could not or dared not answer at that session, because of the calculated insults to Foster and Lovestone, because we were dying for a chance to answer almost every point in it, and because of the shameless hypocrisy of his *čistyj kristal'nyj* way of conducting the life of the *Holy of Holies* free from ***rotten diplomacy*** and ***unprincipled faction struggle*** since he had taken dominion over the Russian Politburo and the Comintern. Yet when I read the speech afterwards—it was distributed to us in English translation and in German and Russian within 24 hours—I found it was an extremely short one for a report by a leading Russian Communist. Anyhow, long-seeming or short, it was with a feeling of actual relief that we heard him come to his key organizational conclusions. There were six of them:

1. The proposals of the delegation of the E.C.C.I. [Dengel and Pollitt] must be approved with the exclusion of the proposals . . . which approximate those of Comrade Foster.

2. A [new] open letter must be sent in the name of the ECCI to the members of the American Party. ["To the members" meant a declaration of war on the leadership and an appeal over their heads to the membership to support the Comintern against the leadership which they had just elected at their own convention.]

3. The action of the leaders of the majority at the Convention, particularly on the question of Pepper, must be condemned.

4. An end must be put to the present situation in the Communist Party of America, in which the questions of positive work . . . are replaced by petty questions of the factional struggle between the Lovestone group and the Foster group.

5. The Secretariat of the Executive Committee of the American Party must be reorganized, with the inclusion of such workers therein . . . who are capable of placing the interests of the Party above the interests of individual groups and their leaders.

6. Comrades Lovestone and Bittelman must be summoned and placed at the disposal of the Comintern, in order that the members of the American Commu-

nist Party should at last understand that the Comintern intends to fight factionalism in all seriousness.

Stalin closed his address as he had opened it, with a paragraph of "theory," which was the least he could do as the Marxist-Leninist leader of the world revolution and the world proletariat. The key sentences of his peroration were:

I think the moment is not far off when a revolutionary crisis will develop in America. And when a revolutionary crisis develops in America, that will be the beginning of the end of world capitalism as a whole. It is essential that the American Communist Party should be capable of meeting that historical moment fully prepared to assume the leadership of the impending class struggle in America. For that end the Communist Party must be improved and bolshevized. . . . That is why I think, comrades, that serious attention must be paid to the proposals of the Commission . . . for the aim of these proposals is to render the Communist Party of America a healthy Party, to eradicate factionalism, to create unity, to strengthen the Party, and to bolshevize it.

As we considered Stalin's six proposals, we realized that the decisive ones were proposals five and six. Number five showed that Stalin had done some thinking since he ordered Dengel to make Foster General Secretary and give his group a majority on all committees. After all, he himself was working now through only one committee in his own party, the Secretariat of which he was the General Secretary. Through it he could pack all other committees, the Politburo, the Central Committee, the Committee on Organization and Personnel, the Control Commission, the editorial boards of journals, even Bukharin's pet committee of Red professors. Why could he not put men of his own choice, men who would owe everything to him, on an American secretariat and stop the nonsense of discussion periods, general elections of convention delegates, and election by them of central committees, politburos, and a general secretary?

Moreover, did he really want Foster as General Secretary and leader of an artificially created majority? What he wanted as leaders of each party, he was beginning to realize, were men who were nothing, preferably in trouble and with a stain on their reputations, like Thaelmann. He who was about to be reduced to nothing could be raised to everything, and if need be, reduced to nothing again without the power to resist. Foster, on the other hand, had a following in the American working class; he had led a packinghouse strike, a steel strike, a labor party movement, had founded the Trade Union Educational League and similar bodies, had a devoted following in his own party on whom he might be able to count to defend him. Moreover, John Pepper had almost persuaded Foster to make peace with Lovestone, and then where would the ECCI find leverage to fight the independent and united leadership of the American party? Furthermore, Trotskyism had arisen in the Foster group under the leadership of James P. Cannon, a co-leader with Foster of the American opposition, and Foster had concealed Cannon's Trotskyism until the presidential election campaign of 1928 was over.

Precisely while Stalin was pondering this problem, Earl Browder suddenly had to return from Shanghai where he had been working as head of the Pan-Pacific Trade Union Secretariat. He had returned in disgrace, for his secret bureau, masquerading as a commercial concern trading in the Far East, had been exposed to the police and intelligence agencies of China, Japan, and other interested secret services by an act of incredible ineptness on the part of Browder, a supposedly capable and experienced underground worker. Browder's "commercial firm" had been the headquarters to which everybody reported who went to China and other Far Eastern countries for confidential work. Large sums of money had to be sent to Browder, and his then wife, Kitty Harris, was sent to take to him $5,000 from New York. Aronberg, the New York connection and a leading and belligerent member of the Foster group, had given her a five-thousand-dollar bill and told her it would be easier to secrete on her person if she took it as a single bill. Once delivered to Browder, he decided to change it for smaller bills at a bank in Manila. The manager told him that the serial numbers of such large bills were registered by the American government, and he would have to wait for a reply before cashing it. Browder fled with his banknote, but then tried to cash it in other cities, including Tokyo. Before long every intelligence agency in the Far East was on his trail. Only the loyalty and knowledge of a subordinate Chinese employee who recognized that Chinese secret police were investigating the place enabled everybody there to flee in time, disrupting and destroying every kind of secret work going on in the region. Piatnitsky, Organization Secretary of the Comintern, was infuriated by the ineptness, by the loss of all the money that had been spent on Far Eastern work when Russia was so badly in need of foreign exchange currency, and by the disruption of so much secret work so painfully built up. He brought Browder up on charges of incompetence and criminal negligence. Once more there was a piece of "damaged goods" to be rescued and raised up from nothing to the post of general secretary and revered leader of the American Communist party. Lozovsky helped out his ertswhile appointee to the Pan-Pacific Trade Union bureau by framing two other completely innocent people who had been assigned to subordinate posts there, and who now received the blame for the breakdown of all the work in the Far East.

Stalin's point five showed, too, why he had yielded so generously to the "proletarian cable" from the American convention which petitioned him to let the convention majority elect a central committee of its own choosing. Why not, since he was to work through Browder as his new general secretary, and through a "secretariat that must be reorganized by the inclusion of workers." Why not, if the secretariat was thus packed by the inclusion of the most inexperienced who had not seen fit to line up in support of Foster or of Lovestone?

But of course, Stalin's last point was the most important of all. "Comrades Lovestone and Bittelman must be summoned" to Moscow and removed from the American party to show the party that "the Comintern intends to fight factionalism in all seriousness." Stalin's political instinct, or more narrowly his organizational instinct, told him that Lovestone was the dynamic figure who had organized the American party majority, won ninety percent of the convention, and was putting an end to the faction struggle in ways that would make the American party more independent and autonomous. Bittelman was added merely for symmetry. But Lovestone was the man who had organized the convention to resist the instructions of the Comintern's, or Stalin's, emissary. And Lovestone's illusion that he could come to an understanding with Stalin, plus my naive view that it was necessary to send a strong delegation to Moscow to reinforce our efforts to settle the "American question" with some respect for American realities, had now put Lovestone in Stalin's hands, and with him the entire top leadership of the American party.

When Stalin concluded his six points with the fateful words: "Such is the solution in my opinion," he had every reason to think that the resistance of the American leaders would cease. When he spoke, the Comintern was speaking, and the Russian party was speaking. The defiant Americans had carried on a resistance against these two highest powers, such as few Communist Parties had ever dared to engage in. But nothing in their past conduct could lead Stalin to believe that after they had carried their appeal to Moscow and had it thus rejected, they would dream of defying the Russian party on its own home battleground. Or defy the Comintern when through Stalin's authoritative pronouncements it had solemnly rendered its verdict. Greater leaders of greater parties had made such appeals and been brought to heel. The history of the Communist International was filled with the names of lost leaders: Serrati, Levi, Bordiga, Brandler, Chen Tu-hsiu, Pankhurst, Höglund—the list of the defeated or the excommunicated could be extended indefinitely. More important leaders than Lovestone from more important parties than ours had been "summoned to Moscow for work," and had withered away as useless exiles in the recesses and crevices of the Holy of Holies. We had appealed, our appeal was now rejected, the case was closed. Stalin's only problem seemed to be what to do with these hostages that Lovestone and I in our folly had put into his hands.

To be sure, there were some formalities still to be complied with. Molotov, Kuusinen, and Gusev, a subcommission of the American Commission, would have to meet to draft the same verdict in proper form. Then the Presidium of the Executive of the Comintern would have to vote on the report. We had only one vote on the Presidium, that of Benjamin Gitlow, for neither Lovestone nor I was a member of the Presidium. We had no reason to believe that the other members from all the other parties would fail to vote unanimously, save for Gitlow, to approve Stalin's "opinion." Then we would be asked to make a statement accepting the decision of the Communist International.

31

THE SHOWDOWN

Stalin delivered his first address on the American question on May 6, complete with his "opinion." Molotov, Kuusinen, and Gusev would present their "findings" to the full American Commission on May 12. Then the Presidium as a whole would meet to hear and vote on the Report of the American Commission. And we would be asked one by one, each as his name was called, to declare that, now that the Comintern had given its verdict, we as loyal members of the Communist International accepted the verdict and would carry it out and teach our party to welcome it.

We still had one trump card to play which Lovestone had been holding close to his chest: to find a way to advise our holding force in America—Minor, Stachel, and Brodsky—to transfer the ownership of the entire physical apparatus of the Party into reliable hands, and to ask the party members to wait for our imminent return to hear what had happened in Moscow. Stalin had a trump card in his hand, too, which he was holding close to his chest. We were still too naive in our belief in Communist fair play to permit ourselves to suspect that he would play that card.

Distance prevented the three "generals" who had cut themselves off from their troops from knowing precisely what their replacements, the "lieutenant generals," were doing. Since May 3rd strange and slightly ambiguous cables were coming from Minor and Stachel to Lovestone. The cable of May 3rd denied "false rumors of any differences between Minor, Lovestone, and Stachel," but urged the "quickest return of the delegation including Lovestone" to combat a campaign by "Browder, Weisbord, and Johnstone," i.e., the Fosterites. On May 9, three days after Stalin's hostile and decisive speech, another cable spoke of "sharpening factionalism . . . spreading rumors," then gave assurances of "unquestioned support" by the party rank and file. Then came a cable from the New York organization secretary, Bert Miller, alias Ben Mandel. His suspicions had been awakened by the discovery that Minor and Stachel seemed to be conferring with factional enemies. But so elaborate were Bert Miller's precautions lest the G.P.U. discover what his cable was trying to warn about, that he put the message into language that not even Jay Lovestone could decode. Moreover, he signed himself *Liver and Onions*, his favorite dish at the party cafeteria, and none of us could guess who *Liver and Onions* was, nor could the Moscow cable office spell the culinary signature correctly.

We met almost continuously, Lovestone, Gitlow, Bedacht, and I, in my room at the Lux, to debate our next move. Fortunately, electronic eavesdropping had not yet been developed, or Stalin would have known everything that we were saying. The ambiguity and alarm in the cables from America, and the certainty that Stalin had already found "the solution," drove us to the conclusion that Lovestone would have to play in America the trump card he had in reserve there, and that we had nothing to gain by waiting until Molotov, Kuusinen, and Gusev found that Stalin's "solution" was perfect. While we looked for a messenger, someone going on a journey abroad on a party mission, to carry a letter from us to Stachel and Minor, we decided to assume the offensive against Stalin's "solution." A risky thing to do, but what else was there left to us except abject submission? On May 9 we took the unprecedented step of letting the ECCI know that we were aware that an unfavorable decision had been taken by Stalin, hence by the American Commission, hence by the ECCI. We declared openly that the decision would be ruinous to Communism and the Comintern's good name in America, and therefore had still to be reconsidered. If the "solution" that Stalin and Molotov had each outlined on May 6 were adopted, the membership of our party, we said, would be forced to conclude that "the Executive Committee of the Communist International desires to destroy the American Central Executive Committee, and therefore follows the policy of legalizing the past factionalism of the opposition bloc and inviting its continuation in the future."

Stalin, for his part, being a fighter who knew how to read between the lines of any statement that threatened his solution of any problem, dropped all pretense that he was fighting equally against Bittelman and Lovestone, to concentrate his fire on Jay Lovestone and the party majority he represented. There was only one issue: "*For or against the Communist International.*" On May 11, even before the findings of the Subcommission were to be discussed or voted on, the "report of Molotov, Kuusinen, and Gusev" was distributed to all members of the Presidium of the ECCI, not as a report for discussion but as a new *Open Letter* to the members of the American party to be sent to America over the heads of the delegation that had come to Moscow to make its appeal. The report bore the title: ADDRESS BY THE EXECUTIVE COMMITTEE OF THE COMMUNIST INTERNATIONAL TO ALL MEMBERS OF THE COMMUNIST PARTY OF THE UNITED STATES.

Clearly, there were to be no amendments, no concessions, no real discussion of this "Address." They were to discuss us, not the still unadopted report. On May 12 every member of the Subcommission and every member of the Commission with its eight Russians and their four faithful followers repeated the "solution" and then warned and admonished us. The same procedure was again repeated at the solemn all-night session of May 14 by every leading party represented on the Presidium. Then they would begin, even before we got back to America, to put to the American party the question: *For or against the Communist International?*

MAY 12: KUUSINEN PUTS THE QUESTION

The *Address* was much sharper and more one-sided than Stalin's speech of May 6. The party majority (Lovestone in particular) was accused of "misleading honest proletarian members."

Kuusinen said that he had questioned Comrade Wolfe in the Subcommission about the C.C. majority and particularly about Comrade Lovestone. Comrade Wolfe "thought that the Sixth World Congress, when it said that the *American Party had shown itself a firm leader in many strenuous class fights,* was talking about the C.C. majority," declared Kuusinen. "Wolfe stated that Lovestone and other comrades leading the party were among the very best that had been produced by the American working class." Then Kuusinen continued, "Comrade Lovestone is a very able, a very gifted comrade but . . . he has not yet learned the difference between a group leader and a party leader. . . . If Comrade Lovestone should agree to our proposal to spend a certain amount of time not in the American Party but in some other work in the International . . . this would not mean his political death but his political betterment, if only he wishes to be better. . . . I consider a bad sign the threat Lovestone uttered at the close of his speech when he said:

> Whatever work is given me, I will do. But we have a deep conviction that such an organizational proposal as the one aiming to take me away from our Party is not a personal matter, but a slap in the face of our entire leadership. . . . We say to you, comrades: Criticize, condemn, but don't take any measures that will pull our party up by its roots. . . . By accepting this draft letter, we would only further the demoralization, collapse and chaos in our Party.

"What does this mean? Is this not a concealed threat?" Kuusinen asked. Thus he worked up to his final challenge to us:

> From your declaration we see plainly that it is no longer a fight of the leaders of the majority of the C.C. against the minority group . . . but a factional attitude towards the Executive of the Comintern.
>
> Do you really wish to enter upon this path of splitting? A clear answer to this question must be given *here in Moscow*. . . . Will you help the Comintern in the fight for the elimination of factionalism, or will you hinder the work of the Executive? Will you take up a fight against the Executive . . . or will you submit unconditionally without reservations? Will you urge your own supporters, the whole of the membership, to carry out unconditionally the decisions of the Comintern? Yes or no?

We wanted time to prepare our answer, so we postponed the statement demanded of us until the following day. Thereupon Molotov took the floor as the second member of the American subcommission. (So far as I remember, the third member, Gusev, did not speak, perhaps because he alone knew something—too uncomfortably much—about the American question.

For the first and only time I saw Molotov speaking in anger. He spoke faster than was his wont, did not grope for words, stuttered hardly at all. He opened his speech with a resounding scolding:

Notwithstanding the fact that the Commission and Comrade Kuusinen as the Reporter appealed to the delegates here, asking them to answer as to whether . . . they undertake unconditionally to submit to the decisions of the Comintern, . . . even to this question which is elementary for each communist, we see that the comrades give no answer, that they want to clarify for themselves first their factional position. . . . It seems to me that this is a bad sign, that it shows that the comrades do not go along the path desired by the Comintern. . . . We must get a clear and concise answer to this question *here at this session*.

Of course, Molotov was right. We knew now what the path desired by the Comintern was; we knew, too—no one better than I who had watched the process—*who* the Comintern was; we knew that we must prepare our statement carefully, since Stalin and his obedient cohorts were trying to trap us, and every careless word we uttered would be used against us and repeated again and again in every medium at the disposal of the Comintern. We knew that our statement must be carefully thought out, that it must present our position with skill and dignity, that before the week was out, the cables, which were Stalin's monopoly (one of the advantages of the stratification of everything), would be humming denunciations, insults, falsehoods against us, and that we might have difficulty getting our reply to America.

Moreover, Kuusinen as chairman of the Subcommission had already hinted at a split, at mass desertions from us in America, and deserters from our delegation even here in Moscow. He pointed out that Weinstone and Wicks had already unreservedly accepted the line of the Comintern, and that "in the United States there is a whole number of such comrades." This was no time for careless improvisation. We refused to be provoked either by Kuusinen's veiled threat or by Molotov's ultimatum that "*We must get a clear and concise answer to this question here at this session.*" The meeting adjourned perforce in the face of our stubborn silence. Immediately thereafter Lovestone, Gitlow, Bedacht, and I met in my room, not to draft an answer to the Subcommission, but to play our next card in the difficult and uneven battle, by drafting a cable to Minor and Stachel apprising them of the situation in Moscow and bidding them make final preparations for carrying out the legal measures that would take over the property of the party and its front organizations.

The cable we prepared was one of alarm. It described the new *Open Letter* that was about to be sent to America as a document aiming to discredit and destroy the present party leadership and turn the party over to the opposition. It called our leadership unprincipled factionalists and rotten diplomatists, and it falsified our political views. It was being sent over the heads of the Central Committee to the party membership, who would be asked to choose between the leadership it had selected and the Comintern, and it laid the basis for expelling thousands of members if they gave the wrong answer to this false dilemma. Key sections of our cable read:

> Draft decision means destruction Party unless firm solid front maintained. Take no action any proposals by anybody or cabled CI instruction cabling draft letter instructing publish same, until delegation arrives. Situation astounding, outrageous, can't be understood until arrival.
>
> Possibility entire delegation being forcibly detained, therefore, unless you hear from us within ten days that we are returning, start wide movement units and press for return complete convention delegation inclusive Lovestone, Wolfe, to hear report our side case. . . .
>
> Carefully check all units all property all connections all mailing lists of auxiliaries, all sublists district lists removing same from offices and unreliables. Check all checking accounts all organizations seeing that authorized signers are exclusively reliables appointing secretariat for auxiliaries and treasury disauthorizing present signature. Instantly finish preparations sell building, especially eliminating W[einstone] trusteeship. Remove Mania Reiss.
>
> Absolutely don't cable acknowledgment of cognizance this cablegram but guide thereby.

The language and style was Lovestone's, but all four of us signed it.

But how would we get the cable safely and secretly out of Russia? For that a happy accident seemed to play into our hands. On May 10, one day after Stalin's first philippic against us, Lovestone and Gitlow were invited to a farewell party given by an American who had been recommended either by Lovestone or Gitlow for employment by the G.P.U. The party was held at the Grand Hotel, where both of our people met their friend, the head of his department, and two women operatives, all of whom were engaged in espionage work in foreign countries. The two male secret service men talked freely about the "mess" in the Comintern. "Many of the best leaders are being expelled in favor of incompetents. The Comintern is in danger of collapse." The Chief of the G.P.U. Department said: "Yes, there is a great difference between Lenin's regime and Stalin's. Stalin rules by virtue of his power; Lenin ruled by virtue of his authority." A feast was served: rare wines, brandies, champagne, caviar, paté, and other luxuries and delicacies. Then the G.P.U. agent who was formerly in the American party informed Gitlow and Lovestone that he was leaving Moscow on May 12 (the very day on which the American Commission was to report), and was taking with him to Berlin a pouch under diplomatic seal which would not be opened until it reached its destination. Our two delegation leaders asked him if he could take in it a letter of the most confidential nature which we had to be sure would not be opened. He agreed. "The letter" was the cable we had prepared. Gitlow said that he would also like to have taken in the pouch and mailed in Berlin, a confidential letter to his wife, in which he would report what was happening, ask her to report it to his mother, a veteran party member, and his mother to report it to Stachel. This, too, was agreed to. Here was our chance to send our confidential messages, uncensored, from Berlin!

The letter Gitlow sent to his wife was crudely opened and crudely resealed again, from which we may conclude that our confidential messages to Stachel and Minor were also carefully examined and duly reported to Stalin. Even if they had not been, the farcical Bob Minor and the "ever dependable" Jack Stachel had decided in whom power was vested and who was and who was not the Comintern. Whether they thought that ours was a lost cause, or because they calculated that they might rise thereby to the very top of the party, they were already in secret communication with the enemy. Even while they were sending us their reassuring cables, they were revealing all our secrets to Joseph Stalin and his organization machine, and to the men of our party opposition with whom they thought they would soon be sharing power.

We for our part were not sure that we wanted to, or needed to, use the weapon of the transfer of possession of the party machinery. We were communicating, we thought, in the greatest secrecy with agents whom Lovestone trusted. As long as that cable from Berlin remained secret, we still had a choice. Moreover, we had not, even as the cable went off, accustomed ourselves to the idea that we were breaking with the Comintern. Lovestone in particular thought that with the party machinery and press in our possession we would be negotiating from a position of strength and that in the end the Comintern would have to make more favorable terms with us since we would be negotiating as a functioning party. As Theodore Draper has written of our mood at that moment, we were still "far more interested in preventing the Comintern from taking the party away from us than we were in taking the party away from the Comintern."

The third man Lovestone had put his trust in, Joseph Brodsky, also balked when the showdown came. He was not, I think, sly and treacherous as Minor and Stachel were. Nor do I regard him as one who, as Gitlow was to think, would violate his solemn promise to Lovestone in order to keep his post as the party's legal representative. Rather, I feel that when it came to the showdown, he was one of those who felt the enormity of a break with the Communist International, which Lovestone more than any other man had taught him to revere. At any rate, when he had all the transfer papers prepared, he refused to execute them or to file them with the proper legal authorities.

MAY 14: THE BREAK

On the night of May 14 we of the American delegation were summoned to hear the verdict on our appeal. The spectacle was made a gala affair. It took place, if memory serves me, in the auditorium of the old club of the nobility, the Hall of Columns. Stalin was there to take personal charge of the occasion. It was a meeting of the Presidium of the Executive Committee of the Communist International, a large enough body and theoretically a powerful enough one to decide the fate of the American party, its present leadership, and its delegation elected by our recent convention. But the whole world of the Comintern in Moscow was present to watch our discomfiture and to tell us off. The leaders of all the parties who were then in Moscow came to behold, and as far as time would permit, to take the floor against us. American Communists working on the staff of the Comintern and the Profintern, Americans studying at the Lenin School and the Far Eastern University, even Americans who were there on special missions, were specifically and personally invited. My wife, who of course had sat in at the caucus meetings in our room in the Hotel Lux but who doesn't remember being present at Stalin's first speech on the 6th (who could forget that scolding who had listened to it?), was also personally invited, not because she was my wife, but because she was working on the staff of the Comintern as a research worker on Latin America. She, too, it was hoped, would denounce us. Officials of the Profintern were present as well as officials of the Comintern who were not members of the Executive. All told there were over 150 persons present, of whom only something like 30 or 40 were voting members of the Presidium. (I don't remember the size, which was not too much smaller than the Executive Committee it replaced, for almost every party had at least one representative on it. Besides, I never troubled to count its membership, since under the reign of Stalin they always seemed to cast one unanimous vote.) This time the vote would not be unanimous, for we had one voting member on the august body, Benjamin Gitlow. But with Stalin present as insistent advocate, prosecuting attorney, and judge, it was a foregone conclusion that the vote would be n-1 versus 1. And so it was.

But of course the main feature of this unusual spectacle was not the vote of the Presidium, but the denunciation of the leadership of our party, of the uninvited delegation which Lovestone had brought to Moscow, and of Lovestone himself. Though the General Secretary of the Communist Party of the Soviet Union spoke in his usual scarcely audible voice so that people had to lean forward and cup their ears to hear every precious word, he was astounded now that we had not already yielded after his scornful indictment of May 6. A whole week had elapsed and we had not surrendered yet! Hence he began by calling our stubbornness "unique."

> Comrades, we are faced with a unique fact, worthy of the most serious attention. A month has passed since the American Delegation arrived in Moscow. For almost a whole month we have been occupied with it . . . and with indicating methods of clearing up the situation. . . . You know that Comrade Lovestone insisted that the Russian comrades should express their views. . . . The Russian comrades have already had their say on the essential aspects of the question [actually only on the exile of Lovestone to Moscow]. Accordingly, the Commission has fulfilled all the

conditions requisite for finding a solution. And what do we find? Instead of a serious attitude . . . a fresh outburst. . . . Instead of waiting until the draft decision appeared [in final form], the American Delegation broke out with the declaration of May 9, a superfactional, anti-party declaration. . . . The American Commission criticized this declaration to shreds. One would have thought that the American delegation would have given thought to this and corrected its errors. The direct contrary has occurred! No sooner had the draft decision appeared than the American delegation broke out with the new declaration of May 14, a declaration more factional and anti-party than that of May 9. . . . Comrade Gitlow read it to us here during the course of his speech. The fundamental feature is that it proclaims the thesis of *non-submission* to the decisions of the Presidium of the ECCI. That means that the extreme factionalism of the leaders of the majority has driven them into the path of insubordination, hence of warfare against the Comintern.

It cannot be denied that our American comrades have the right to disagree with the draft decision and the right to oppose it. But the trouble is that their declaration of May 14 does not stop there. . . . It considers that the fight must be continued even after the draft becomes the decision of the Presidium of the ECCI. Therefore we must put the question squarely to the members of the American delegation: When the draft assumes the force of an obligatory decision of the Comintern, do they consider themselves entitled not to submit to that decision? That is the crux of the matter, Comrades.

And that was to be the crux of the evening of May 14 and the early hours of May 15 during which was held the final session of this unique, unusually long, unusually public discussion of the fate of a Communist Party, conducted with the personal presence, the active participation, and indeed the stage direction of Joseph Stalin.

As for me, I had been conducting my fight with the newly-anointed leader of the Soviet Union and the Comintern for almost five months now, since January 2nd, when I attacked the *Open Letter* he had ordered, a struggle which (I was to learn a few years later) could have lasted that long only because Stalin was just beginning to learn the uses of his newly-acquired absolute power, and he had not yet perfected his technique for cutting short discussion. But to return to Stalin's speech, which at this point becomes increasingly insulting:

This declaration of the American delegation of May 14 was drawn up rather craftily . . . by some sly attorney, some pettifogging lawyer. On the one hand the declaration states that its authors are unable to accept this new draft letter, to assume responsibility before the party membership for its execution, to endorse the inevitable, irreparable damage that it is bound to bring to our Party. . . . And this is called loyalty to the Comintern!

Then he turned on Lovestone, who continued to be his chief target all along. Stalin accused him of being the author of the latest statement, of "needing it to deceive the membership," of resembling Prime Minister Chamberlain and Comrades Zinoviev and Trotsky. Stalin's language, still cool-seeming and "comradely," now descended to the use of such terms as "factional tricksters and manipulators, unprincipled intriguers and back-stage wire-pullers, masters of the formation of unprincipled blocs, Philistines and Babbits." Finally, his anger mounting though his voice still remained quiet, the ruler of the Comintern came to threats. The first was a threat that the Comintern would split the American party, expelling all who questioned his "solution":

You declare that you have a sure majority in the American Communist Party and that you will retain that majority. . . . That is untrue . . . absolutely untrue. You had a majority because the American Communist Party regarded you until now as the determined supporters of the Communist International. . . . But what will happen if the American workers learn that you intend to break the unity of the Comintern and are thinking of conducting a fight against its executive bodies? That is the question, dear comrades. Do you think that the American workers will follow your lead against the Comintern? . . . . Popular leaders who had greater authority than you have found themselves isolated as soon as they raised the banner against the Comintern. Do you think you will fare better? . . . At present you still have a formal majority. But tomorrow you will have no majority and will find yourselves completely isolated if you attempt to start a fight against the decisions of the Presidium of the Executive Committee of the Comintern. You may be certain of that, dear Comrades.

Next he announced what amounted to a political death warrant for Lovestone. It contrasted sharply with the words the Chairman of the Commission, Otto Kuusinen, had uttered only two days previously ("If Comrade Lovestone should agree to spend a certain amount of time not in the American Party but in some other work in the international . . . this would not mean his political death but his political betterment. . . ."). Like Kuusinen, Stalin admitted that Lovestone was "a capable and talented comrade," an admission which was cut out of his speech when it was published in America, although Stalin added:

Comrade Lovestone after all is not such a great leader. He is, of course, a capable and talented comrade. But how have his capabilities been employed? In scandalmongering, in factional intrigue. Comrade Lovestone is indisputably an adroit and talented factional wire-puller. No one can deny him that. . . . But not every factional leader has the gift of being a party leader. ***I doubt very much that at this stage Comrade Lovestone can be a Party leader.*** (emphasis mine)

The long diatribe closed with an enumeration of some other "Right-Wingers, Conciliators with Right Wings, and incorrigible factionalists" that the Comintern was getting rid of "in the ranks of the C.P.S.U., the German Communist Party, the Czechoslovakian Party, the French Party." Now the time had come for "the incorrigible factionalists in the American Communist Party. . . . It is necessary to set about at once cleaning the Communist Parties of Right and Conciliatory elements who objectively represent the agency of social democracy within the ranks of the Communist Party. . . . The merit of the draft of the Commission consists in the fact that it assists the Communist Party of America in carrying this main task into effect." So Stalin ended his second speech on the American question amidst prolonged and stormy applause, from which, as far as I could see, only our threatened delegation sitting all in one row ventured to abstain.

STALIN PUTS THE AMERICANS ON THE SPOT

Having finished his long diatribe, Stalin was sure the case was closed, and nothing remained except for the Presidium to vote to make his "solution" the official solution of the Communist International. It was long past midnight when the Presidium voted to endorse the *Address of the ECCI to All Members of the Communist Party of the United States.* The *Address* was adopted by all but one—Benjamin Gitlow.

Up to that moment, as Stalin had admitted, it was permissible for some American comrades to oppose or seek to alter the *Address.* But now that it had been changed from his proposed solution to the Comintern's, disagreement or opposition or amendment or rejection was no longer possible. It remained only to put the American delegates on the spot, one by one, and Stalin himself made the motion to make each American delegate say before we adjourned that he accepted the decision of the Comintern and would carry it out.

The members of the Presidium and the guests and onlookers were already on their feet ready to go home when Stalin rose to move that each member of the American delegation should now be called upon to state personally that he accepted and would obey the decision. Everybody sat down again, feeling that the drama was not over, as each member of the American delegation was called by name and asked to answer Stalin's question.

And indeed, the next hour was filled with drama as each of us took the floor. The members of the proletarian contingent were called on first, to prevent leaders from giving them guidance. One by one, as if we had prepared them, they said that they considered the decision harmful to our Party and the Comintern and unsuited to America, that they would accept it as a matter of discipline, judge how it worked out in practice, and review its appropriateness at our next convention. Alex Noral, a farm expert and a comparatively new party member, was under greater strain than the others. He stumbled as he spoke, and ten days later signed a statement of qualified submission. Bill White, a veteran steelworker who was fearless and had fought many battles and come out unscarred, startled all of us, especially the Europeans and the Russians, by using his excellent tenor voice to sing a little song to Stalin about a girl who had planted a seed and then kept pulling it up to see how the roots were getting on. "Comrade Stalin," he ended, "our Party is just sinking its roots into our American soil. Don't keep pulling it up to see how it is getting on, or you will destroy it. I accept your decision as a matter of discipline, but I am convinced that

that is what you are doing to the American Party. Let us alone and we'll grow until you will be proud of us." The members of the Presidium looked at each other in utter astonishment. "Sing a song to Comrade Stalin!" their faces said. "Whoever heard of a Communist doing such a thing at a Comintern Executive Session?" They could not be more astonished than the Finns and Scandinavians in Minnesota were whenever their district organizer, Norman Tallentire, a great elocutionist, would break into poetry, as he so often did, in the midst of one of his speeches or reports.

The next little drama occurred when Max Bedacht was called on. In our conferences he had been the most irate among us and the most militant in his suggestions as to the wording of our statements. He had signed the cable with Gitlow, Lovestone, and me that we sent to Jack Stachel from Berlin on May 12. But when he perceived next day that Stalin was deliberately maneuvering us into total insubordination or abject surrender, he cried all night into his pillow in the bed he shared with Ben Gitlow in the Hotel Bristol. Now his nerves cracked under the strain. With tears in his voice, he accepted the Presidium's decision. For the first time that evening there was applause for one of our delegation. But it was half-hearted, for his auditors sensed that the promise was given with reluctance and that they were witnessing not a triumph but a tragedy. It took Bedacht a few weeks to work out a better-seeming rationale for his action. Then he wrote in the *Daily Worker:* "After we have argued the matter out with the Comintern and after the argument is settled by a definite decision, we not only accept the decision as a matter of discipline, but we accept the correctness of the decision as a matter of recognizing the international and ideological superiority of the Comintern over ourselves."

Gitlow explained Bedacht's action as the result of his need to support a wife and four daughters, and his reluctance to give up the life of a party functionary to earn his living once more as a barber. Lovestone teasingly agreed with Gitlow, and started to compose a limerick which began, "Max Bedacht mit Kinder acht"—though I doubt that Lovestone's poetic prowess carried him much beyond that first line. I for my part recognized the sentimentalist in Bedacht, and thought that there were many of our supporters whom we would lose because, even as he, they could not bear to break with the Comintern, which we ourselves had begun by revering and had taught them to revere. Ten years later Lovestone told a Congressional Committee: "I reaped a harvest of my own sowing. I was largely responsible for that mechanical concept of loyalty to the Communist International, and it came home to roost with its claws in my eyes."

When Bedacht came home to America, Stachel and Minor treated him as a trophy, from their betraying of Lovestone's cable, and, to add to the confusion in the party's so-called Enlightenment Campaign, they put him on the Secretariat, which thus became Bedacht, Minor, Weinstone, and Foster. Then Mikhailov (Williams), who had been the Secretary of the American Commission during our hearings in Moscow, and whom Stalin now sent over to America to direct the overturn in the party, made a motion that Bedacht should become Acting General Secretary. In this way the members of the former majority group might be made to feel that the party was not being handed over to the former opposition. But of course Max didn't last long as Acting General Secretary and was soon shunted off to one of the party's minor auxiliary organizations, the International Workers Order, where he expended his frustrated zeal, in building it into the Party's largest and most prosperous auxiliary. Still he remained unnoticed and uninfluential on the side lines until 1948, when he was expelled from the party and the Comintern after all, for criticizing the Stalinized party's official position on the "national question," for writing that its policies toward the Negroes and the Jews were too "nationalistic" and lacking in "Socialist content." Thus poor Max, who had sacrificed the right of free discussion and party democracy in order not to break with the Comintern, was expelled for attempting to discuss two lesser issues. He had been a member of the German Social Democracy and its left-wing since he was 18. Coming to America at the age of 20, he had given the American party 29 years of devoted service. So far as I could find out from Theodore Draper's interview with him after he was expelled, his last public political act was to try to explain and defend himself in one of the obscure splinter group papers, a mimeographed bulletin entitled *Towards Socialism* briefly published by one Francis Franklin. The Bedacht whom Draper interviewed was a lonely and embittered man who in 1929 had sacrificed views that were dear to him in order to remain in the Communist International.

Lovestone was called on next. He was mulling over in his mind the problem of how he could get back to America. His statement was cautious; he suggested that he would accept any assignment the Comintern wished, but ended with the declaration that the new *Address* and the disruption of the leadership of our party would bring great harm to the party and the Comintern itself in America. However, he was accepting the decision as a matter of discipline.

When my name was called I said in essence what we had all agreed on: "I am convinced, that the line currently being forced upon the American party will hurt our party. I accept the line as a matter of discipline, but I am certain that by the time our next discussion period and convention come around, the harm the new line has done will be manifest to all. At any rate, I reserve the right that belongs to every Communist to reexamine that line and see how it has worked out, when the next preconvention discussion period permits such free discussion." (What I did not know was that there would never be another free discussion period in the new Stalintern.)

Gitlow was the last American to be called on. His temper had been rising steadily as he listened to our statements, and although he had agreed, too, to denounce the decision but accept it as a matter of discipline—how else could we get out of the trap into which Lovestone's folly and mine had brought us?—he now felt that he could not accept all the insults which Stalin had uttered and that the *Address* embodied, not even as a matter of discipline to get out of the country. He could not restrain his anger as the rest of us had done. To the astonishment of all his auditors including Joseph Stalin, who did not believe that anyone would defy him openly under such circumstances as we were in, he said:

> I cannot accept this decision. I cannot accept the demand made upon me here, to discredit myself before the American working class. If I did I would be discrediting myself and the leadership of our Party, and the Party itself that could give rise to such a leadership. Not only do I vote against the decision, but when I get back to the United States, I will *fight* against it.

STALIN'S THIRD SPEECH

Stalin had made his motion that each of us be put on the carpet, expecting that one by one we would do what other Communist dissenters had done in the past under similar circumstances. He expected us to use the word ***discipline*** as had so many before us, but then to say humbly: "Now that the Comintern has decided, I will do my best to carry out its decision."

As one by one we expressed our continued disagreement with the Comintern decision, his anger rose steadily. On May 6 he had thought that one speech by him would be enough, after which the Presidium would vote, and we would give up our opposition. Thus many comrades in the past had accepted distasteful decisions as a matter of discipline and continued their membership in their respective parties. But this was a new day. This was the year of the *Velikij Perelom,* the Great Turn. Henceforth, concealed dissent would not be permitted. That might have been all right under Lenin, Zinoviev, and Bukharin. But that was not the way he would run his party, nor the Comintern. He had chosen this unprecedented month-long discussion with the Americans and publicly participated in it himself, to show all sections of the Comintern that such "rotten diplomacy" was no longer possible where Stalin ruled.

Leaping to his feet, still striving to keep his voice quiet and calm, he could not altogether conceal his anger. Later he had to tone down or strike out some expressions. But except for one passage which I restore below from memory, and have checked with all the Americans who heard him, I shall quote from his third speech on the American question as he finally permitted it to be published:

> It seems to me, Comrades, that certain American comrades fail to understand the position that has been created now that the Draft has been adopted by the Presidium. Apparently they do not realize that to defend one's convictions when a decision has not yet been made is one thing, and to submit to the will of the Comintern after a decision has been made is another. . . . Now that the Draft of

the Commission has become the decision of the Presidium, the American Delegates should have the manhood (sic) to submit to the will of the collective, and assume responsibility for carrying out the decision of the Comintern.

We ought to value the firmness and stubbornness displayed here by eight of the ten* American Delegates in their fight against the draft of the Commission [this entire sentence was omitted from Stalin's speech when it was officially published by the new party leadership as part of their "enlightenment campaign"]. But it is impossible to approve the fact that these eight comrades, after their views have suffered complete defeat, refuse to subordinate their will to the will of the higher collective. . . . True Bolshevik courage does not consist in placing one's individual will above the will of the collective, above the will of the Comintern. True courage consists in being strong enough to master and overcome one's self and subordinate one's will to the collective, the higher party body. . . .

Comrades Gitlow and Lovestone announced here with aplomb that their conscience and convictions do not permit them to submit to the decision of the Presidium and carry it out. But only anarchists, individualists, can talk like that, not Bolsheviks, not Leninists. . . . They talk of their conscience! . . . Members of the American Delegation, do you think that the conscience and convictions of Comrade Gitlow are above the conscience and convictions of the overwhelming majority of the Presidium of the ECCI?

Next Stalin compared us to workers in a factory who "on the plea of their convictions, declare against a strike. . . . What would you say if ten or twenty workers, representing a minority in the factory, declared that they would not submit to the decision of the majority of the workers, since they were not in agreement with that decision? What would you call them, dear comrades? You know that such workers are usually called strikebreakers."

Stalin's anger rising, he saw fit later to cut out completely a passage predicting our future. From strikebreakers he reduced us to pygmies, nobodies, compared with the giants who had fought him and whom he had defeated.

And you, [he shouted, his voice suddenly rising above its usual low monotone] who are you? Who do you think you are? Trotsky defied me. Where is he? Zinoviev defied me. Where is he? Bukharin defied me. Where is he? And you! Who are you? Yes, you will get back to America. But when you get there, nobody will be with you except your wives.

But to return to the printed text of his speech. In later editing he apparently substituted for that thunderous ending the following peroration:

Finally, a few words as to the fate of the American Communist Party. . . . The Comrades of the American Delegation regard the matter too tragically. They

* Stalin's "eight out of ten" must have been put in later when he edited his speech. The other two are Max Bedacht and Alex Noral, who signed a statement of submission a week later.

declare that with the adoption of the Draft, the American party will either perish or at least will totter on the brink of a precipice. That is not so, comrades. . . . The American Party lives, and will continue to live, in spite of the prophecies of the American Delegation. . . .

No, Comrades, the American Communist Party will not perish. It will live and flourish to the dismay of the enemies of the working class. Only one small factional group will perish if it continues to be stubborn, if it does not submit to the will of the Comintern. . . . If it is inevitable that this one small factional group will perish, then let it perish, as long as the Communist Party will grow and develop. You look at the situation too pessimistically, dear Comrades of the American Delegation. My outlook is optimistic.

His third speech was finished. The exemplary show trial for which he had chosen our party was ended. At the moment of greatest anger, he had said: "Yes, you will get back to America." That at least was something. But he had not said when, only promising that we would find our party a shambles. Was he bound to keep his promise? And when and how would we get out? Should we not, could we not, find a means of racing back to present our story to our comrades? Above all, how would Lovestone get out?

But we had no time to think of these problems after three o'clock in the morning, for, having finished his third denunciation, Stalin arose abruptly from his seat on the platform without so much as a motion to adjourn. Immediately, bodyguards and secretaries surrounded him, the entire auditorium rose and stood fixed in their places facing the aisle down which the Leader and his retinue would march. There was absolute silence in the hall as he proceeded, with everybody facing him. But when he came to the row of stubborn Americans he stopped, and reached out his hand to our handsome Negro member of the delegation, Edward Welsh, who stood between Lovestone and me. Welsh put his hand behind his back and said aloud: "What the hell does this bastard single me out for?" Though he did not understand English, Stalin flushed, for he understood the tone and the gesture, and he resumed his march to his car. Then we Americans, shunned by everyone, marched out into the white night that was already tinged with the light of dawn, bought oranges from a street peddler, sucking on them in silence, too weary from the strain to discuss the problems that beset us.

32

HOW WE GOT OUT

The afternoon after the Presidium meeting, that is to say, on May 15, Ben Gitlow and Jay Lovestone began visiting friends, real or imagined, to find out how our delegation could get back to America in a hurry. One of their first calls was on Dr. Julius Hammer, whom we had all known since 1917. Gitlow's purpose was to collect some dues from him, for he still retained his membership in the American party, more comfortable and free from a hail of instructions such as he would have gotten had he transferred to the Russian party. Indeed, both he and his son were careful to keep the safeguard of their American citizenship, and Julius returned to America prior to World War II, where he died in 1948 at the age of 72, restored to membership in the county, state, and national medical associations. His honorary pallbearers included Frederic A. Gimbel, Beardsley Ruml, Charles S. McCabe, James W. Gerard, Judges Murray Hulbert, and Bernard Botein, along with a number of distinguished doctors. No mention was made in *The New York Times* obit of his membership in the Socialist Labor, Socialist, and Communist Parties, or of his conviction in the abortion case.

"He was glad to see us," Ben Gitlow reported, "for he had some very startling news for us concerning the American Party. We asked him how the news had reached him so quickly, for it was supposed to be kept secret until the Central Committee in the United States received it and had an opportunity to act on it. His son, Armand, he told us, had seen Walter Duranty of *The New York Times* that morning. Duranty informed him that he had been given the news of the decision on the American Party with the request to cable it to the United States immediately."

Obviously, the Comintern machine was already in high gear, and though Stalin had been branding Trotsky a traitor for using the "capitalist" press, and in one of his three addresses had denounced our factional controversies because they disclosed party matters to the bourgeoisie, he was manifestly not averse to using the capitalist press himself to reach the interested portion of the American public with the highest possible speed. However, Duranty found the report on American exceptionalism and other heresies and the tangled tale of Lovestone and Pepper so difficult to understand that he waited until the 18th for *Pravda*'s account to bring some intelligibility into his story. On May 19 the *Times* gave its first account to American party members and the public under the quadruple head and subheads: MOSCOW CHIEFS HIT REDS OF AMERICA / PUBLISH A FOUR-COLUMN REPROOF OF "UNPRINCIPLED INTRIGUE" / PUNITIVE STEPS TAKEN / LEADERS WHO QUESTIONED RUSSIAN CONTROL REMOVED AND SECRETARIAT REORGANIZED.

How much the average *Times* reader could make of it I cannot imagine. The story itself was still confused and confusing. But it did make clear the fact that "the Party has been soundly spanked," that "the majority group and its leader, Jay Lovestone, bear the chief responsibility for conduct which is insufferable" and "have employed the maneuvers of rotten bourgeois diplomacy." And there were cryptic statements in that special language, *Cominternish*, on "the Pepperian theory of American exceptionalism." After he reported all these mysteries and heresies as best he could, Duranty added a final mischievous paragraph of his own:

> It has happened before that a foreign Communist Party has claimed to know more about the affairs of its own country than the Kremlin, but to the best of your correspondent's knowledge this is the first time that the party linen has been washed so publicly.

Thus Walter Duranty had scored a scoop, and Joseph Stalin had gotten the jump on us. Moreover, it had become clear to me that Stalin had other weapons in his arsenal to poison the American Communist Party towards us before we could even get back to America. Lovestone, however, was convinced that out of fairness and curiosity the party comrades would wait to hear our version of the "sound spanking" administered to us at the foot of the Kremlin Wall. Besides, he was sure that Jack Stachel had already received our cable sent from Berlin and was taking all the agreed-upon measures so that we would not be shelterless when we reached our country.

WE FIND OUT THAT WE ARE PRISONERS

"They have to let me go back to America first," Lovestone said, "even if they are going to send me to Afghanistan, for the Comintern Statutes provide that a member of the ECCI, if he is sent to some other country on a special mission in some other land, has the right to return to his own country first for a maximum of two months to pack his things and arrange his personal affairs."

"Stalin won't let you back," I said, "without a statement by you denouncing yourself, our majority rule, and our Party as we ran it."

"I'll dicker with Molotov on a statement; he's not too bright."

"Jay, it's too late to discover it now, but you should never have come here."

"You asked for reinforcements for a showdown."

"I hope we're not all in a trap. But yours is a special case."

"If we don't all get out, we have asked Stachel to ring the alarm in the party and in the press. It will be difficult for a government that is trying to get recognition from the United States to keep us all here in the face of such a public campaign."

Ten years later, in a Congressional Committee to Investigate Un-American Propaganda Activities in the United States, the Committee's Research Director, J. B. Matthews, said: "I would like to ask you this question: Didn't you know any better than to go to Moscow?"

Lovestone answered Matthews with embarrassment that he had been brought up in the American tradition of fair play, even in a fight; that he was sure that our overwhelming majority would be respected, that he could come to an agreement with Stalin, or, coming back, mobilize our organization to defeat him. But he could have answered more simply for both of us: "*No, we didn't know any better, neither Bert Wolfe nor I.*" But then in 1929, even Joseph Stalin himself was only beginning to learn what he could do with absolute power.

Gitlow, too, was certain that "they can't keep me here. I am a member of the Presidium of the Executive Committee of the Comintern. Besides, I have told them that I am going back to America to fight their decision, and I have rejected it. All they can do is to expel me and let me go."

As for me, I said nothing. I counted on the fact that I had come to Russia as America's delegate on the Executive of the Comintern. But with Gitlow and Lovestone there, I should have lost my job, and had no reason to remain in the Soviet Union. All I needed was to get my passport back (they take away the passport of a Comintern delegate as soon as he enters the country) with an exit visa in it, and for my wife the same. Until I got that, I was a prisoner, for there was no crossing the heavily guarded Soviet frontier without a passport with an exit visa. I would request my own and my wife's visas at once from Piatnitsky. What could they keep me for? Why would they want to? As soon as I left Gitlow and Lovestone, I would go up to Mokhavaya 6 and see Piatnitsky.

But alas for the illusions of Lovestone and Gitlow that their membership on the ECCI, to which they were chosen by the Sixth Congress, would carry weight! The ECCI held an immediate meeting to implement by organization actions the political decisions of the *Open Letter* to our members, and, on the motion of Molotov himself, Lovestone, Gitlow, and I were removed from all our positions in the Comintern, the Profintern, and even the American party. Moreover, the Secretariat of the American party was immediately enlarged (in Moscow!) by the addition of Robert Minor and Max Bedacht, to give the illusion that the majority of our recent convention was being maintained, while Gitlow and Lovestone were removed. As a further measure for the new majority being made in Moscow, the ECCI at the same meeting voted to send a Committee of Three, headed by Boris Mikhailov, alias Williams, to form part of the American (!) Secretariat, thus raising the Secretariat to six by adding three Muscovites.

The idea of ruling through the Secretariat; of enlarging the Secretariat of the American party by adding from Moscow three agents who were not even members of the American party; of putting Bedacht and Minor on the Secretariat for a time to lull the rank and file of our members into believing that the party was not being turned over to the opposition; the giving of a Russian, Boris Mikhailov (Williams), not merely a post on the American Secretariat but plenipotentiary power over the Secretariat, over the Politburo, over the Central Committee, over the Control Commission, and over all district leaders and District Committees of the American party—all this manifestly stemmed from Stalin, through his mouthpiece, Molotov, who neither thought so swiftly or so powerfully, and who brought the motions into the Executive Committee of the Communist International which approved them by the usual submissive unanimous vote. Thus were Boris Mikhailov and his two assistants "elected" members of the American Secretariat even as they were speeding on their way to America to turn the party upside down.

Once Stalin felt himself challenged there was no means he would not use against the challengers, for he could only conceive of any challenge as a summons to total war. Once he felt that Lovestone had challenged him, it was sheer illusion on Lovestone's part that a truce was possible. In a war such as Stalin waged there was never a second prize for the loser. Already, though we did not know it, Stalin had ordered Kuusinen and Piatnitsky to pick out emissaries speaking every foreign language that foreign-born members of the American Party could speak, and shipping them at once by fast boat to America to take control of the foreign-speaking groups and federations. That was how Stalin had packed committees and consolidated his rule in Russia. He was planning to have the Secretariat, properly packed, run our party and all its organs, just as he had used his own General Secretary's post and Secretariat in Russia. He was vesting Mikhailov-Williams with dictatorial powers over every institution in our party before his emissary had touched ground on American soil. Thus, overnight, without so much as a vote of our Central Committee (why take chances with those Americans?), the machinery of the American party was remade in Stalin's image, complete with Russian control of the Secretariat. Mikhailov-Williams was the voice of the Russian party, the voice of the Comintern, and the voice of the Communist party of the United States, the moment he landed in America. Only a voice from on high in the Kremlin could overrule him.

But to make this transplanted Kremlin voice effective, Mikhailov had to make sure that every unit, every organ of the party, would get rid of those stubborn Americans who would not endorse the *Address* which the Comintern so benevolently had sent them, or who wanted to wait until Lovestone, Gitlow, and Wolfe got back to America to hear their side of the story. For this, too, Stalin had his measures ready: to keep Lovestone, Gitlow, and Wolfe out of the United States for good, or as long as possible; and to unleash on the astonished rank and file of the American party something skillfully baptized the *Enlightenment Campaign*.

The Russian triumvirs left for America two days after Stalin made his last attack on us on May 14. Three days later Bedacht, Weinstone, and Foster were called in, handed their visaed passports and funds for their trip, and told to leave for home immediately to provide an American face for the new Secretariat and the new dictatorship. Nothing loath, they left, and Max Bedacht went straight to my home in Brooklyn to live. Since his wife and daughters were in Chicago, my large-hearted mother-in-law took him in as a free boarder and lodger, as she had taken in so many relatives and near-relatives and many a needy *landsman* when they came from Russia. My wife and I also returned later to live with my wife's mother, and Bedacht's insensitivity in returning to my home after his break was to cause me much embarrassment, for he was to report daily on my speech and activities and my necessarily secret meetings with party members, until I told him, courteously, in as gentle a fashion as possible, that his presence in the same residence with me had become embarrassing for both of us.

Before he left for America, Bedacht was called in for a private conference with Comintern officials who discussed with him his role in the strategy they were planning. According to Gitlow, Bedacht was told that the Comintern was sending the American party "an initial sum of fifty thousand dollars" for the fight. (How Gitlow got wind of this I do not know, but it is certain that Stalin would spare no funds and no schemes in the battle to which we had had the impudence to challenge him.)

Despite all these swift moves and the enormity of the power behind them, we had not lost all hope. Lovestone especially was still optimistic. "Stachel must have received our Berlin cable by now, and before long they will find that we are not defenseless. Only we must get to America immediately to present our side of the story."

And indeed, Stachel did receive our cable on the 15th. He immediately decoded it, supplied it with footnotes and explanations, revealed it to our opponents, and cabled it back to Stalin and his Comintern functionaries. On May 18th the Comintern got this information. Armed with this secret for which Minor and Stachel sought to disclaim responsibility and supported by Duranty's dispatch in *The New York Times*, the startled Central Committee unanimously accepted the *Address* of the executive of the Comintern. This information, too, "the faithful Jack Stachel" cabled to Moscow on the 18th. And also on the 18th, *Pravda* published four columns with a due portion of Stalin's vituperative addresses concerning the decisions of the American Commission and the Presidium. On May 20 the *Daily Worker* gave the astounded party membership its first inkling of the downfall of Lovestone and Gitlow by publishing the *Address* and the news that the Central Committee, on the 18th, had unanimously endorsed it.

To add to the confusion, on May 24 Noral, Huiswood, Ella Reeve Bloor, and Max Bedacht published an equivocal statement declaring that they disagreed with the Comintern's organizational proposals, but had no intention of opposing a decision of the Comintern now that it was official. Only Ella Reeve Bloor had the grace to come to us to explain that all her life she had been useful only as a speaker at big mass meetings which now only the "official party" could provide. She pleaded for permission to return to the fold and solemnly promised that under no circumstances, whatever the cost to her, would she ever utter a word condemning us. Moreover, though the new party leaders and the new Secretariat pressed her and badgered her, she kept her promise. As for the faithful Stachel and Minor, as late as May 19 they still cabled to Lovestone in the name of the leaders of our caucus and themselves personally that the new Comintern decisions were "antagonistic" to their personal views, and that they were "standing by" all the decisions of the Sixth Convention of the American party including its demand for Lovestone's return to America. Thus comforted, Lovestone still placed his hope on an early return.

But how to get there without delay? Lovestone went at once to see a top Comintern functionary, I think Kuusinen, to remind the Comintern that as a member of its Executive, he, Jay Lovestone, had the right to go to America for two months to regulate his personal affairs before he was sent to some other country. "You cannot go," he was told gravely, "until you have testified concerning your role in the Pepper case. Comrade Pepper has been consigned for trial to the International Control Commission of the Comintern. Besides, we need a satisfactory statement from you accepting the Comintern decision. And we need the approval of the Central Committee of the American Party. And besides, isn't two months a long time to take to regulate your personal affairs and ship your effects?"

"I do not need two months, though the Comintern statutes give me that right; I need only two weeks. And I will see if we cannot work out a satisfactory statement concerning the Comintern decision on the American Party. And by the way, Comrade, where are you people planning to send me?"

"How would you like to be the plenipotentiary representative of the Communist International in India and Pakistan?"

"It sounds rather far, but once my affairs in the United States are wound up I will go wherever I am sent."

With that, Lovestone turned his mind to the question of making a new statement, more acceptable to the bureaucrats of the Comintern and to the Central Committee of the American Party. At the same time, he kept looking for some member or members of that species now so rare in Moscow, a friend who might help him to get back to America promptly.

Next it was Gitlow's turn to ask for the return of his passport with a visa in it permitting him to cross the frontier of that workers' paradise. When the American delegation was finished and Gitlow had no reason for remaining in Moscow, Piatnitsky said that he and Lovestone were ordered to stay in Moscow at the request of the International Control Commission to testify on the Pepper case. "Besides," Comrade Piatnitsky added, "we have an important mission for you to perform in Latin America. The Comintern would like to send you to Mexico as Plenipotentiary Representative to the Mexican party. And the G.P.U. headquarters for Latin America are in Mexico; you can work for them in any and all Latin American countries."

"Nothing doing," Gitlow exploded. "I want my passport and I want to go home to my own country to report on my mission as a member of our delegation elected at our last convention. Anyhow, what would I do in Latin America since I know no Spanish?"

"All right, then," Piatnitsky responded, "you can go as soon as your work here is finished." Thus Gitlow was kept in Moscow waiting for his passport. Each day he walked to Mokhavaya No. 6 from the Bristol Hotel. At the Comintern Building he was kept waiting in an anteroom for hours. Each day he demanded his passport and his visa. And each day he was told he would receive his passport "when the Control Commission decides that you are no longer needed on the Pepper case." In short, he was a prisoner, elegantly treated, given a room at the Bristol, allowed to walk freely from the Bristol to the Comintern Building, or anywhere else in Moscow, given three meals a day, a stack of Russian cigarettes, and even spending money—but still a prisoner. The Pepper case was mere subterfuge. They wanted to keep us away from America until they had worked their will on our party. Had he been a citizen of some Balkan or Baltic country, he might have been kept indefinitely while Stalin sought some method of breaking the will of a man who had defied him. But Stalin was a careful calculator. He wanted recognition from powerful, wealthy America, and he greatly feared that if he kept men like Gitlow too long, there might begin a campaign in America for Gitlow's—and Lovestone's and my—freedom. At last, after two weeks of the daily trek from the Bristol to the Comintern Headquarters and from the Comintern to the Bristol, one day Benjamin Gitlow was ushered into the more secretive office of Abramovitz, where passports were issued—passports visaed with the Government seal, and passports forged by careful reproduction of those they took from us. Abramovitz gave him his passport, already visaed, a letter sealed with a wax seal which he was not to break but which would give him "special treatment at the frontier," and added a friendly warning: "Comrade Gitlow, one is either with the Comintern or against it. Being in opposition on some issues, on any issue, leads down the road to becoming a renegade." Ben Gitlow left early the next morning, June 2nd, and agreed to wait for Lovestone and me in Paris, so that we could travel together on the same ship to America and use our time discussing our plan of battle for our party.

With the withdrawal of Bedacht, Mother Bloor, Huiswood, and Noral, our group of stubborn holdouts was reduced to seven: William Miller, a Detroit machinist and a member of the Auto Workers' Union; William White, the man who sang a song to Stalin, a steelworker and steel union organizer; Tom Myerscough, anthracite coal miner and organizer of the United Mine Workers; Edward Welsh, who put his hand behind his back when Stalin tried to grasp it and told Stalin in plain English what he thought of the demagogic maneuver; and Ben Gitlow, Jay Lovestone, and Bert Wolfe, It was these, the stubborn seven, who signed the *Appeal to the Comintern,* asking it to reverse itself on the American question. The *Appeal,* our first statement from America outlining our position, was originally set down in 38 mimeographed pages, then reduced to four huge pages of newspaper size, for which it got to be familiarly referred to as "The Bedsheet." We dated it July 10, 1929. As Theodore Draper notes in his *American Communism and Soviet Russia,* "It contains much valuable information not available elsewhere, and its reliability may be judged from the fact that the official reply of the Central Committee left its factual statements virtually unchallenged. ("Statement of the Central Committee of the Communist Party of the U.S.A. on the Appeal of Jay Lovestone and Others to the Communist International," *Daily Worker,* July 23 and 25, 1929"—also a "bedsheet" requiring two oversized pages of the *Daily,* with a day in between to catch your breath.)

As for Miller, Myerscough, White, and Welsh, no very serious effort was made to prevent them from going back to America, except in the case of Ed Welsh. All of them were called in for interviews, offered bribes in the form of promotion into party functionaries and leaders, a stay on some beach in the Crimea, trips to other countries as representatives of the Comintern or the Profintern. And all were admonished with threats that if they hastened back to America before the Enlightenment Campaign was over and tried to intervene in that affair, they would meet with disgrace, expulsion from the party and the labor movement, and the dread epithet of renegade. They quietly persisted in their determination to go home, and after a delay of a little over a week, they were given their passports with visas.

A word about Eddie Welsh. He was, as I have said, a tall, handsome black with a rich golden brown complexion, an enormous amount of self-possession and courage. He had some white blood in his ancestry, but no concern at all with that question. He married a white girl, also a Communist, and their marriage lasted through a long lifetime, and they never met with the question of being rejected as a mixed marriage by either whites or blacks. In our circles there were no such prejudices. Moreover, Eddie detested being thought of as a "Negro Communist" or a "Communist Negro," which helps to explain his indignation and brave outburst when

Stalin singled him out to shake his hand, after all the insults thrown at our delegation.

I could tell many interesting tales about Eddie Welsh, but will limit myself to two minor anecdotes. In the thirties I founded the magazine *Race*, for which many distinguished Negro intellectuals, men like Ralph Bunche and other Negro leaders, wrote. We held one of the first interracial conferences, in Washington, D. C. I was staying at the Statler-Hilton, which did not then admit Negroes except through the servants' entrance, and we wanted to hold an "interracial" committee meeting in my room, to which Welsh was invited. I waited in the lobby of the hotel; when he appeared, I opened the front door for him and, as he entered, I bowed low to this tall, handsome man. "A prince from Godknowswhere," the lobby attendants thought; my act of homage worked like a charm.

On another occasion, Eddie and I were sitting on a park bench in Moscow in 1929, when two young boys approached and stared with unconcealed wonder at the first Negro they had ever seen. "Do you think," asked the smaller lad in Russian, "that if I spit on my finger and rub it on his cheek, it will come off?" "*eto ne kul'turnoe*" (that's not cultured or polite), was all the response his scientific inquiry received.

Despite Welsh's public insult to Stalin—or perhaps on account of it—a special effort was made to prevent him from going back to America to tell his story of our experiences in Moscow. He was offered an extended vacation in the Crimea, to be followed by a stay in Russia to speak and write on the Negro question, and he was told that he would receive a regular salary, and in addition a special fee for every article he wrote and for every lecture he delivered on the lot of the Negro in America. He rejected the offers out of hand with unconcealed indignation and got his passport along with the other proletarian members of the delegation. When he got to America, he became a leading figure in our opposition group, where he never spoke on the Negro question. In his later years he became an organizer for the Free Trade Union Committee of the American Federation of Labor. He was sent to Africa where his rich golden brown complexion was a help, where he attempted the insurmountable task, in country after country, of teaching the African workingmen to form free trade unions independent of their respective governments.

MY INTERVIEW WITH PIATNITSKY

After the "proletarians" were sent off, my turn came next. I went to Piatnitsky and to Abramovitz and demanded my passport back with a visa in it. "My task is over," I told Piatnitsky. "I was sent here by the American party to take Lovestone's place on the ECCI. Now Lovestone is here, and my job is ended. I want to go back to my native land."

"We gave the others permission to go, but Gitlow and Lovestone are needed here to testify before the International Control Commission on the Pepper case. And you are such a capable and valuable comrade, that the Comintern desires to use your services in some important post."

"I want to go home," I answered, and the very sound of that brief sentence made tears well up within me.

"Comrade Wolfe, the Comintern needs a first-rate man in Korea. Our movement is underground there. How would you like to be sent with plenipotentiary powers, and proper business connections, to represent the Communist International in Korea?"

Korea, I thought, swarming with Japanese secret agents. Even if I put on a pointed conical straw hat, I'd stick out like a sore thumb, and the Japanese agents would be on my trail in the first week. ("A death sentence for Bert," Gitlow said when I reported my interview to him and Lovestone.) But all I answered was the same plaintive refrain, "I want to go home."

Then my sense of humor got the better of my longing for home and country, and I added, "Comrade Piatnitsky, you want to send Gitlow to Mexico because he can speak Yiddish. You want to send me to Korea because I can speak Spanish. But tell me, why are you sending Lovestone to India?"

Piatnitsky looked at me in utter amazement. When God gave him the attributes of a good Leninist professional revolutionary and then of a good organization secretary for the Comintern, He must have decided that he didn't need for that even a trace of a sense of humor. Besides, as Piatnitsky stared at me, even if it had occurred to him that that was a jest, he would have thought that nobody could joke when he is offered a high post by the Comintern. When at last he assimilated my question as a helpful organizational suggestion, he said: "We're not so sure of India for Lovestone, but he can go anywhere where they don't speak any English." Then my interlocutor returned to the task of tempting me.

"You know, Comrade Wolfe, you could have an important post in the G.P.U. They have a high opinion of you."

"Why has the G.P.U. a high opinion of me?" I asked.

"Well, Comrade Wolfe, for almost five months you have been sending letters and cables in code to Lovestone in America. They have set their best code experts to decipher your code, and despite all the letters and cables they had to work on, they never could crack your code. You must be good, they said, and they could make good use of you."

"I want to go home."

"Comrade Wolfe, you are tired. You've been fighting here all alone since the beginning of the year. You've been under a great nervous strain. You need a rest. Go down to Sochi [on the Black Sea where Stalin took his vacations], lie on a beach, and rest and swim and sun yourself until you are calm and well rested. Then come back here, and we'll work out some assignment for you that really interests you."

"I want to go home."

"We could use you anywhere but in America," said Piatnitsky wearily, his pack of tempting offers exhausted. "In America you'll only get in trouble. But go and see Abramovitz. Tell him you want to go home, and he'll see when he can get you your passport back and get you a visa."

I knew Abramovitz's desk with its roll top under which he could poke his nose when he was doing something especially confidential. I had had to see him too many times on special missions. I had seen the jewels and rings which he still occasionally gave to agents on missions abroad. I knew he had our passports in his own security files and that he himself had the *pečat'* (the seal) and the visa stamp with which he could issue a governmental visa without consulting anyone in the Commissariat of Foreign Affairs. So the *when* in Piatnitsky's promise told me that they would keep me in Russia as long as possible. ("We'll have to demand the return of Wolfe to America," said Gitlow after hearing my report. "We may have to start a public campaign for his return.")

GITLOW OUTWITS THE BORDER GUARD

At the Moscow Airport Ben Gitlow pondered the sealed letter he was supposed to deliver to the G.P.U. border guard so as to get "special treatment." Since he had been instructed not to break the seal, he was suspicious. He had no sealing wax and no official seal to reseal it, so he finally decided not to present it. Instead he presented his passport, showed his visa, and then his credential identifying him as a member of the Presidium of the E.C.C.I. Documents have a magic of their own in Russia; his high-sounding I.D. card worked like a charm. His baggage was not searched, passport and baggage were stamped with due courtesy, and a G.P.U. agent conducted him to the boarding ramp. When he got safely onto a Western plane he broke the seal of his letter and had it translated for him. It contained instructions to the customs and border guards to search him and his baggage most thoroughly, and to take away all documents, all printed matter, all papers of any sort. He was thankful for his ever-present suspicion.

ELLA CHOOSES ME INSTEAD OF THE PARTY

A few days later when the Comintern got word from Stachel and their emissaries in America that the "enlightenment campaign" was working *wie geschmiert* (as if everything had been greased), and when Piatnitsky found that I could not be detained on the excuse that I was needed to testify in the Pepper case, since I was not at our recent convention nor even in the United States when the Pepper ructions were going on (naturally, I did not dream of testifying that Pepper confessed to me on his first visit to my room in the Lux that he had never been in Mexico, and cross-questioned me on the appearance of Mexico City, what its main streets were and how they looked, what notable sights a hasty tour might have taken in)—and after Piatnitsky had convinced himself that I could not be seduced by such wonders as Sochi and Korea and a chance to serve in the G.P.U., suddenly on one of my daily pester-visits to Abramovitz, he produced my passport with visas for me and my wife, and an I.D. card, unsealed, to guarantee me "courteous special treatment at the frontier." Only one more special effort to detain me was made. Our good friend, Gusev, came to find out how my wife was reacting to my break with the Comintern. He found that she was deeply distressed, as Bedacht had been, at the idea of such a break. Thereupon he tried earnestly to persuade her that she should break with her renegade husband, instead, and remain in the Soviet Union, "working for Stalin" as a research worker on Latin America.

Gusev failed to convince her to leave me and break her marriage vow, "for better or for worse, for richer or for poorer, in sickness and in health. . . ." As we enter into the sixth decade of our married life together, she is still with me. Not until they *instructed* her, a year or so later, to "denounce me as a renegade, a traitor, and an enemy of the Soviet Union," did she break with the American party, for whose new leadership she had contempt. She joined the Communist opposition, wrote for our journal, and did research work for us on Latin America.

I GET "SPECIAL TREATMENT" AT THE BORDER

While we were still in Moscow in June, 1929, I had wanted to give her a chance to see lovely Leningrad, with its broad boulevards, its beautiful buildings and monuments, its breath of fresh air from the West (Moscow is redolent of Asia, Leningrad of Western Europe). But all she wanted then was to get back to America. She had "seen enough of Russia" and of the Comintern and the way it was run. Like me she "wanted to go home." She could not bear the thought of staying another few days to see Leningrad. She wanted to go home the shortest way possible, so once more we took the railroad to Negorelye, and there received our baggage inspection. Negorelye was an insignificant railroad station with a dirty, poorly supplied restaurant, with countless Russians lying on the station floor waiting for local trains. Still naive and trusting I confidently handed my card to the G.P.U. agent who was both customs and passenger inspector, that special card that identified me as a member of the Executive Committee of the Comintern and that was "to guarantee me special treatment." And believe me, I got it. Somewhere on the card was a tiny mark, a mere pen scratch, which the Inspector searched for with care. When he found it, he bade me open all our bags, pulled everything out in disorder, and heaped together in a pile every scrap of paper, printed or hand-or typewritten. In German, and in my pitiful scraps of broken tourist Russian, I protested. To my surprise, the G.P.U. agent was apologetic, as had been the one who searched our bags and trunk in our hotel room before I locked them. (The trunk was one we were carrying home for Elsa Bloch, an American party secretary who had just been assigned to a year's work in the Comintern.)

"I am going to put a G.P.U. seal on that trunk which goes into the baggage car, and it will not be opened at the frontier. Is there anything special you would like to put in before I seal it?"

"I have two silver rubles (they were real silver and worth a real half dollar each at that time). I know that we are forbidden to take out any Russian currency, but I should like to keep them as souvenirs."

"They will be there when you open the trunk," he said kindly, and we have them yet as souvenirs of our stay in Russia.

And in Moscow, when our bags and trunk were being taken to the chauffeur-driven car provided for us by the Comintern, the porter who had steamed open my letters, read them, and sealed them again while I was living at the Lux, manfully helped with the baggage, and then grasped my hand warmly and said in Russian, "Good-bye, Comrade Wolfe. I hope to see you here again under better circumstances." He too was a G.P.U. agent, assigned to protect us, to watch us, and to report on us. But in all these three cases, I felt genuine sympathy and realized that the great Russian *Apparat* was still divided into Bukharinites and Stalinists, and that in all three cases there was genuine sympathy and perhaps even admiration at the fight we had just put up.

Anyhow, the agent at Negorelye was genuinely sympathetic, and when he apologized for seizing all my papers, he whispered, "There was a mark on your card that bade us take every scrap of paper away from you before we let you back on the train."

"But those 3 by 5 cards with my own handwriting on them have nothing to do with Russia and nothing to do with politics or the Comintern. They are notes I am making for an article on psychology, based on this book I was reading on the train."

He glanced anxiously at the book which I had in my arm under my topcoat, saw that it was in English, and that inside on the flyleaf there was the signature of the Commissar of Education of the Karelian Soviet Republic, Yrjö Sirola. Thereupon, he said nothing about confiscating the book as part of the written and printed matter that he was to strip from me, but stuck it into my baggage where it accompanied me all the way to America.

Yrjö Sirola, like Kuusinen, was a "man without a country" who had taken refuge in the Soviet Union after the fall of the short-lived Finnish Socialist Republic. But unlike Kuusinen, he was not a careerist and sang no successive hosannas to Zinoviev, Bukharin (whose intellect and ethics he admired), or Stalin. He remained his own man in exile in Russia, thinking his own thoughts, expressing them where and when he dared. When he could not approve and dared not oppose, he kept silent. He had had an interesting career which several times crossed mine. As a student in Finland he had been one of the founders of the Young Finns. In 1903 he became a Social Democrat, in 1905 the Secretary of the Finnish Socialist Party. He spent some time in the Finnish movement in the United States where he first got to know of my existence, since the Central Committee of the C.P. frequently sent me to the big Finnish movement centering in the area of Minnesota and Wisconsin. When the Finnish Socialist government was formed in 1918, he became its Minister of Foreign Affairs. In Moscow he was one of the founders, and then the Chairman, of the Finnish Communist Party. He soon became a prominent figure in the ECCI and was sent to America under the name of Frank Miller, where he was a Comintern Rep from 1925 to 1927. There he took a liking to me and the educational activities which I engaged in, for they represented work similar to that which attracted him. He engaged in private talks with me, offering friendly and wise corrections to some of the articles I had written. By the time I got to see him again in Moscow he was a member of the International Control Commission of the Comintern, a body supposedly controlling the moral behavior of the officials of the International, and originally intended by Lenin to consist of Communists with the highest moral principles (Sirola, incidentally, was the son of a Finnish Protestant pastor.) As a member of the Control Commission, he had sat in on the sessions of my lonely fight with Stalin during early 1929 and then my activities as part of the American delegation which came as "reinforcements." As a member of the Control Commission he attended the sessions, silent—what could he say as the Stalinist juggernaut began to get under way? But his face looked now distressed, now sympathetic, now impassive, as he watched our ordeal. Never for a moment did it show contempt or hostility. When at last I got my passport and visa and my wife and I were ready to depart, he unobtrusively contrived to bid me good-bye. "Comrade Wolfe," he said as he pressed my hand, "I hope to see you back again under better circumstances." Then he handed me Watson's *Behaviorism*, as fashionable then as B. F. Skinner is now. "Here's something for you to read on your journey." It was this touching act that set me to reading Watson, and the 3 by 5 cards that I had been filling with my notes and thoughts were the most precious thing that the G.P.U. inspector at Negorelye had taken from me in his ransacking of my luggage.

"I'm sorry, Comrade Wolfe," he said. "I cannot read English."

"Isn't there anyone at this frontier station that can read English?"

"No, Comrade, but if you will put your home address on the pack of cards, and they prove to be what you say, they will be at your home in America before you get there." And so indeed they were. With them, and the book Sirola had given me, I got my mind off my grief, and the first article I wrote aside from polemics against Stalinism was "The Balance Sheet of Behaviorism." It was published in the *Virginia Quarterly Review* of October, 1930. As for Sirola, just as Stalin's wholesale purges of Lenin's other lieutenants began in 1936, Yrjö Sirola, Commissar of Education of the Karelian Autonomous Soviet Republic, died a natural death and was given a state funeral.

THE CONTRAST BETWEEN THE POLISH AND RUSSIAN FRONTIERS

The search over, we were allowed to get back on the train at last. In a few minutes we were in Stolpce, the first station on the Polish side of the frontier. The contrast was astonishing. The search of our baggage here was cursory and courteous. The station was trim and clean and new-looking. The restaurant where Ella and I went to assuage our hunger—we had waited for the Polish side after one look into the dingy restaurant in the Russian frontier station, with its meager choice of dishes scribbled on grease-stained, flyspecked menus (was the paper shortage really that bad?)—had large windows which let in the light, snow-white tablecloths, clean typed menus with an ample choice of dishes, moderate prices, courteous waiters. Of course, this was a deliberate showplace (the restaurant in the great Warsaw station was not that spotless); all the same, the contrast hit home. Even today, after Poland has been twice conquered and humiliated and economically pillaged as well as ideologically and politically subjected, the Poles manage to maintain better-supplied and cleaner and more efficient shops and restaurants; and a better standard of living than the official model of Socialism, the Soviet Union, though how and why this is so does not belong in my story. Anyhow, it was not just the shining spotlessness of Stolpce, a little railroad terminus town not much bigger than its counterpart, Negorelye, that made it memorable, but the fact that we now knew we were in the "outside world" where we could freely come and go.

We carried our grief with us after five months of disillusionment in Russia, along with the feelings of uneasiness of the last three or four weeks, when we wondered whether we would ever get out. So that we can't help but remember the little town of Stolpce. True, our government had twice denied me a passport under the detestable passport system that had been instituted as a result of the First World War and the Palmer hysteria. When in 1937 at last the government granted me a passport, it was stamped NOT VALID FOR SPAIN. I went there, to the Republican side, nonetheless, and all that happened to me was that Ray Murphy, a deputy secretary of state, called me up on the telephone to say, "Bert, I see you were in Spain. Could I ask you some questions about what's happening there? What can you tell me of the Lincoln Batallion?"

JAY LOVESTONE'S ESCAPE

By now it was getting into June, and with Gitlow and me gone and even the "proletarian bodyguard" departed, Lovestone was in Moscow alone, depressed, deprived of anything much to offer in negotiations with the All Powerful and his subservient apparatus of committees and functionaries. Jay was getting desperate. How long would they keep him? When would he get back to America? What was happening there? Would he indeed ever get out?

During the last week of May he had tried to get two weeks in America, and had been drafting statements to try to satisfy his tormentors. They acknowledged his right to take two weeks in America to arrange his personal affairs, but refused to say when; they told him that in any case he could not get the two weeks to which he was entitled until he withdrew his statement of May 14th and accepted the decision of the Comintern. On May 22 Lovestone presented a statement withdrawing his previous condemnation of the Comintern's decision, offered to accept it as a disciplined Communist, but maintained his disagreement with the instructions on organization matters which Dengel had brought to our recent convention. This was immediately rejected as insufficient.

Then Garlandi, an amiable Italian representative on the Secretariat of the ECCI, tried to break the deadlock by moving that "Comrade Jay Lovestone should be *instructed* to endorse the Comintern's new policy in the United States." If he agreed, he would be permitted to go back to America for two weeks for purely personal affairs. Lovestone eagerly agreed, while the entire Secretariat of the ECCI at which the motion was made seemed relieved that the mind-straining negotiations were over. Lovestone forthwith drafted a statement reading:

> Under instructions of the Secretariat of the Executive Committee of the Communist International, I hereby endorse the recent decision of the Presidium of the Executive.

But in the end, snail-paced Molotov, who had been mulling over the public implications of such a statement, said as if Stalin or the Comintern were speaking: "No, we cannot accept that, because the first part of it would indict us for resorting to questionable practices." It was precisely these practices they were following with us Americans, but he did not want it to be clearly stated in writing. So Lovestone's second proposal fell through.

On May 30 Jay tried again, drafting a statement similar to the submission statement of Noral, Huiswood, and Bloor. On May 31 the ECCI's Political Committee accepted and sent this cable to the new Russian-dominated Secretariat in New York:

> Lovestone requests permission to go to America for personal affairs for two weeks in America beginning June 12th after which he consents to remain at the disposal of the ECCI for work in the CI. He withdrew his declaration made in the Presidium, regarding insubordination as incorrect and impermissible in the Comintern. He declared that he submits to ECCI and in this connection he pledged

himself not to interfere in the internal affairs of the CPUSA. The Political Secretariat permitted him to go for two weeks, but the date of departure will be fixed, if you don't object to his going to America now. Communicate your opinion immediately.

Two days after the Comintern sent its cable apprising the Secretariat of the American party that it had no objections to Lovestone's going to New York for two weeks, Jay Lovestone sent a cable to the new leadership of the American party repeating the statement he had just made to the Comintern's Secretariat. It was the Comintern that had demanded it for publication in the American party press in order to strengthen the "Enlightenment Campaign" going on in the party. But by this time the new leadership in New York, made up of such people as Stachel, Minor, and Bedacht, allied with their former Fosterite opponents, was more afraid of Lovestone's reappearance in America than the Comintern was. Though the old party majority was demoralized, its members frightened, confused, or being expelled wholesale, Minor and Stachel were afraid to face him, and the still unstable new leadership was afraid of his very presence on American soil. Even if it was only for two weeks, the Comintern then sending him to India or Afghanistan, how could they destroy him utterly if he was still "valuable for important work for the Comintern" and might someday make a comeback? The timid leaders, and even the plenipotentiary potentate from the Russian party dominating the whole American party apparatus, thought it better to take no chances. They knew only too well Lovestone's gifts and strengths and felt that nothing would make them safe but to destroy him utterly and have him expelled from the C.I. and the American party, with his name made a target for the "spitting squad."

So far the *Daily Worker* had published nothing concerning Lovestone's present stance or plight. On June 4 the American Secretariat, captained by Mikhailov-Williams with such aides-de-camp as Minor and Stachel, cabled to Moscow that they doubted the honorable intentions of Jay Lovestone and the need for him to come to America at the moment to arrange his personal affairs. They pointed out that they were in possession of a "factional cable dated Moscow, May 15th, giving detailed technical instructions preparing a split," and they asked the Comintern to demand another written statement from Lovestone for American publication which would accept the decisions without any reservations whatsoever and condemn "his previous splitting tactics." They added that even if Lovestone should make such a statement, they would still not consider his visit to America possible until the completion of their own "Enlightenment Campaign" and in any case not before the beginning of July.

The caretaker leadership declared that Lovestone's statement which the Comintern had accepted was inadequate and unfit for publication in the American party press. Now what was Lovestone to do? He had gone as far as he felt he could in concessions; his statement had been accepted, his passport returned, although they refused to give him an exit visa and other necessary documents on the grounds that they were not sending him anywhere, but he was going on his own initiative and therefore he would have to get everything himself. A few days later they informed him that the American Secretariat had rejected his statement and had found his intended visit unacceptable also.

Having been thrust thus on his own initiative, he redoubled his efforts to find his way out of Russia by himself. The borders of the Soviet land were not then as hermetically sealed as they were to become a few years after the blood purges and the spy mania—Trotsky and Bukharin and the rest all being spies and agents of foreign powers. The main exits were carefully watched by the G.P.U., particularly such rail avenues of egress as the railroad to the Polish border. If he took the train as I did, he might be halted at the border no matter what visas and documents he secured. So Lovestone decided to try to get out by air.

As I have already suggested in my own case, the party was not yet a cowed and terrified monolith. Stalin had won absolute power, but not the minds and hearts and quaking spirits of all his "comrades." Lovestone searched discreetly, looked for, and found, friends. He has never told the story of how and where he found them, for, though most of them are dead by now, even to hint at their names might have hastened their demise. I have never asked him where he found them or who they were, nor do I intend to ask him now. But on June 11 he went to the airport, far less carefully watched than the railway stations, showed his passport, his card identifying him as a member of the Executive Committee of the Communist International, and was courteously conducted to the ramp that brought him into the plane for Danzig. Conveniently, Sovflot and Lufthansa had fairly recently established such a flight under the auspices of the Russo-German company, Deruluft, and mostly it was the big brass that took the plane. When he got off in Danzig he breathed more freely. The Comintern did not even know of his absence for a number of days; Stalin himself did not learn of it for at least four.

THE ENLIGHTENMENT CAMPAIGN

Not until June 22 did the Comintern recover sufficiently from its surprise that Jay Lovestone had succeeded in slipping through the tightly guarded wall that separated the workers paradise from the capitalist inferno. On June 22 the American party received a cablegram from the Communist International which read:

> Comrade Lovestone left June eleventh for United States of America despite decision Politsecretariat, Executive Committee, Communist International. Despite his promise to submit political declaration for press recognizing his mistakes, condemning his factional work and undertaking to carry out decision of ECCI, did

not submit declaration. It now became clear that notwithstanding his persistent denial in the ECCI he, together with Pepper during Sixth Convention, was factionally intriguing behind back of Convention, and whole history of Pepper's fictitious departure from U.S.A. prior convention, was invented by him with sole object of misleading ECCI, Convention, and his own faction. In view of this, Politsecretariat ECCI calls upon all members and organizations CPUSA to condemn these methods of intrigue, falsehood, and disruptive activities, methods petty bourgeois politiciandom and demoralization of party intolerable in Communist movement; all former factional supporters of Lovestone wishing sincerely carry into effect decisions ECCI must understand unconditional necessity of open repudiation of the opposition expressed by Lovestone at session of Politsecretariat ECCI June seventh that many while declaring solidarity with open letter ECCI are not sincere and that they play the saints in order to retain contact with their "factional apparatus" which according to Lovestone statement the former majority of the CEC had. Politsecretariat ECCI demands all former adherents Lovestone publicly dissociate themselves from him.

(signed)
Politsecretariat, Executive Committee,
Communist International.

The style of this cable suggests that Joseph Stalin dictated its contents personally and perhaps even supervised its composition. Yet it posed several problems for the new caretaker leadership of the American party. In the first place, in contradiction to the statement of the cable, Lovestone had submitted a political declaration for the press such as he had promised, and the Politsecretariat of the CI, with Molotov presiding, had found the declaration acceptable. It was the American caretaker regime that, out of fear of Lovestone's influence, had rejected the Lovestone declaration and decided to keep it secret from the membership.

A second problem, especially for such caretaker leaders as Stachel and Minor, was that of deciding how long Jay Lovestone had been a deceiver of the Comintern with them supposedly ignorant of his intentions, and how long he had been an American spokesman for the "international right-wing," as they were now preparing to accuse him. These and similar problems took them five days to settle, by which time Jay Lovestone, always a fast traveller although there were as yet no transatlantic airflights, was already in New York. It was this that stopped the debate and galvanized them into immediate action. Without summoning him for a hearing, without giving him a chance to tell his own side of what had happened in Moscow, on June 27 they published an entire page of the *Daily Worker*, eight columns wide (actually a column wider than *The New York Times*) headed from one end to the other in 36-point (half-inch high) type:

STATEMENT OF THE CENTRAL COMMITTEE ON
THE EXPULSION OF JAY LOVESTONE FROM THE
COMMUNIST PARTY OF THE UNITED STATES
OF AMERICA

Under that, boxed, and four columns wide, was a heading in 18-point type:

A CABLEGRAM FROM THE COMMUNIST INTERNATIONAL

while somewhere below the middle of this "bedsheet" was another 18-point headline stretching across the page:

MATERIAL FOR ENLIGHTENMENT OF PARTY MEMBERSHIP
ON THE C.I. ADDRESS TO OUR PARTY

which was largely made up of a letter from me to the American Secretariat, dated New York, June 23, at which I rejoiced, for they gave my letter verbatim without doctoring, falsifying, or omitting a single word. It was the only honest statement that ever got into the *Daily Worker* during the entire "discussion" so cunningly dubbed "The Enlightenment Campaign."

The headline concerning the expulsion of Jay Lovestone from the party of which he had been a founder, and but yesterday the outstanding leader, was so startling that the caretaker regime had difficulty explaining and justifying it. Hence they threw into the bedsheet-length explanation everything they could think of.

For the first time the party learned that Lovestone had made a new statement of "disagreement, but submission," but they did not learn that the new statement had been declared acceptable by the Comintern. The Central Committee admitted that it had been sitting on this new statement for almost three weeks, from June 9th to June 27th, only to release it now. Earlier, "the Central Committee [had deemed that] it could not permit the use of the channels of the party or its use by the press" for the "insidious purposes of Lovestone."

Now, too, the Caretaker Regime felt that it was time to use Jack Stachel's dread secret: the cable we had sent him from Berlin on May 15 bidding him prepare the final steps for the taking over of the party machinery to forestall the horde of Comintern agents Stalin was sending from Moscow to take the party out of the hands of the party majority. The text of our Berlin cable was released much as we sent it, with some convenient excisions—but there was not one word to hint that it had been sent to Stachel personally, or that Minor, Stachel, and Brodsky had given their prior agreement to the plan. "Lovestone's cable of May 15," they wrote, "was sent from Moscow to former group supporters" who remained nameless. And well they might.

The expulsion notice further states: "The mobilization of Lovestone and Pepper for a political struggle against the CI . . . places Lovestone today in the ranks of the International-right fighting against the Communist International . . . the culmination of a long line of political development." How long had the party majority, including such leaders of the majority's caucus as Minor and Stachel, followed Lovestone and Pepper on this nefarious course? To this no answer is given in the expulsion statement, nor are any names mentioned except those of Lovestone and Pepper. But the Lovestone-Pepper line is traced back to the Ninth Plenum of the ECCI. When did this Plenum take place? No rank and file reader would be likely to know, but the Ninth Plenum met in Moscow from the 9th to the 25th of February, 1928. It was at this Plenum that Joseph Stalin, that "genius of dosing," as Bukharin called him, administered one of the first doses to Bukharin and his associates and admirers from that poisonous bottle, the successive doses of which "revealed the counter-revolutionary kulak nature of the Right capitulators . . . and the necessity of concentrating fire on the Right Deviation" (from the Preface of the Marx-Engels-Lenin Institute's English Translation of J. Stalin, *Works,* Vol. XI, 1928-March 1929). But where were Minor, Stachel, and Bedacht, three leaders of the caretaker regime, when that "long line of political development" began? They were themselves leaders in the majority caucus, cheering their heads off for Lovestone and peddling the same line. Here, too, however, no names are given, and Lovestone seems a mighty giant "deviating rightwards as part of the International Right-Wing" all alone, or helped only by John Pepper, to line up 90% of the delegates to a party Convention.

In any case, this full-page "Statement of the Central Committee on the Expulsion of Jay Lovestone" is a sort of *omnium gatherum* in which Lovestone's critical remark on a "running sore" in the Comintern, his and Pepper's supposed "American exceptionalism," his "Thesis Presented to the Sixth Convention of the Party," the hocus-pocus of Pepper's nontrip to Mexico, and a number of other supposedly single-handed wonders of Lovestone as a Communist Paul Bunyan, all come to a conclusion with the words: "The Central Committee answers the challenge of Lovestone with his expulsion from the Communist party." However, the Central Committee doesn't stop with that dramatic climax, but adds yet another full double column to their tapeworm announcement.

Surely that was a startling sentence with which the entire page should have ended. But whoever drafted the Central Committee statement had so little sense of climax or drama that he added an entire double column of anticlimax after that sentence, pieced out with something like eight paragraphs on what the new regime intended to do while "enlightening" the membership of the party. Then they drew a discreet double line of one-point rules, returning to the attack on Lovestone with material that they had not managed to put into the general indictment of yesterday's leader of the Party, headlined, once more across the whole page:

MATERIAL FOR ENLIGHTENMENT OF PARTY MEMBERSHIP
ON THE CI ADDRESS TO OUR PARTY

the last double column of which ended, not with the expulsion of Jay Lovestone, but with the introduction of a lesser name, my own, and the announcement of a lesser penalty, my suspension from the Politburo. Thus what should have been the most dramatic announcement so far in the internal life of our party, tapers off with almost a half of its last double column concluding, not with Lovestone's name, but with eight mentions of the name and strange misdeed of "Comrade Wolfe."

THE GRAVE OFFENSE OF COMRADE WOLFE

Since I am at a loss to explain how my name and stance and my comparatively modest indictment got to make up the grand finale of this full page dedicated to explaining to the party's rank and file how their yesterday's outstanding leader had become today, that is on June 27, a "renegade expelled from the party," I shall leave the task to the closing double-column citation of my own misdeed and my letter of defense, and shall follow that with Robert Minor's solemn explanation of the same event as he recited it to the Tenth Plenum of the ECCI. His explanation was made in a speech delivered to a plenary session of the Executive of the Communist International on September 17, 1929. He spoke of course in English, but his talk was then translated into a number of languages and printed in English, French, German, and Russian in *Inprecorr* (the press service of the Comintern, which is issued for reprinting in all the languages of the world that are used in the world Communist press). At the head of the press release is the superscription, "Unpublished Manuscripts—Please Reprint," so that I do not know into how many languages my misdeed, thus chronicled, was translated.

First, the account in the *Daily Worker* of June 27, 1929, on page 4, which page, as we have seen, bears the sensational heading: STATEMENT OF THE CENTRAL COMMITTEE ON THE EXPULSION OF JAY LOVESTONE. On the lower third of that page, under the lesser heading of *Material for the Enlightenment of Party Membership on the CI Address,* without any further subhead or any further explanation of why it is enlightening, my letter is reprinted to fill out the page. Therefore, the page on Lovestone's expulsion ends thus:

The Political Committee in its meeting of June 25th had before it a declaration of Comrade Bertram D. Wolfe, as follows:

Secretariat, Communist Party, New York, June 23, 1929
United States of America

Dear Comrades:

I have your letter of June 21 giving me 48 hours to make a written statement of my position on the latest Comintern decisions. At the same time you instruct me what my statement "must" declare.

My convictions on the questions involved prevent me from making the declaration you dictate.

For example, I cannot honestly declare "that I recognize the complete correctness of the Comintern Address and the related Comintern decisions on the American question," since I regard that address and the accompanying decisions as INCORRECT AND INJURIOUS to the American Section of the Comintern and the Comintern as a whole. I submit to the decisions referred to, not because I agree with them, but in spite of my disagreement, as a matter of discipline and loyalty to the Comintern.

You also instruct me that I must "denounce and emphatically condemn the anti-Comintern conduct" of the delegation from our Sixth Convention to the Comintern. I emphatically do not regard the conduct of our delegation as anti-Comintern, but on the contrary, am convinced that it did its best to defend and urge what it thought, and what our convention thought, was in line with the best interests of the Comintern.

To sum up, my position is one of disagreement with the recent address, and related decisions, and my submission to it as a matter of discipline and loyalty.

With Communist Greetings.

(Signed) Bertram D. Wolfe

The Secretariat and Political Bureau regard the statement of Comrade Wolfe [as] inadequate particularly in his refusal to condemn his actions in the Presidium session of May 14th. The Secretariat also asked Comrade Wolfe for a statement of attitude on the splitting cable of Lovestone on May 15th as well as upon his attitude toward the violation of discipline on the part of Lovestone in returning to the United States. [These last two demands were made of me orally at the meeting while I was being cross-questioned, for besides sending in my letter I had made bold to attend personally the meeting of the Political Bureau of which I was a member.]

Comrade Wolfe in his answer to the questions put to him clearly showed his unwillingness to condemn Lovestone's flagrant violation of CI discipline, or to condemn the open steps taken in the cable of May 15th to split our Party. In addition to this Comrade Wolfe made it clear that he could not conscientiously defend the CI line and make himself an agent of the Central Committee and of the Political Bureau in the carrying through of the major campaign of the Party at the present moment: The Enlightenment Campaign on the CI address. The Political Committee came to the conclusion that it cannot permit the establishment of the institution of passive members of the Politbureau, members who declare either their unwillingness or their incapability to carry out the Party line as formulated in the Address of the CI. Members of leading party committees who cannot be active in leading the Party membership in the campaigns of the Party, have no place on the leading committees of the Party.

At the Political Bureau Comrade Wolfe continued to take issue with the basic political line of the CI.

The Political Committee therefore decided unanimously, against the vote of Wolfe, to suspend Comrade Wolfe from membership in the Political Committee of the Party.

Of course, according to the Statutes of the Party they had no right to remove me, for I had been elected a member of the Political Bureau by the Sixth Convention of the party while I was representing the party in Moscow, and only another convention could suspend or remove me. But what are statutes among comrades, when sitting before me as judges and overseers of the Secretariat, the Politbureau, and all the organs of the party?

At any rate, with the vote not to expel, but to suspend, Comrade Wolfe from membership in the Political Committee, ended the startling page concerning the expulsion of Jay Lovestone. As there was no such thing as a sergeant-at-arms present and no one made a move to expel me bodily from the meeting, I stayed stubbornly in my seat, facing the three from Moscow, Mikhailov and his two companions, and outstaring Stachel and Minor and Foster, who had more than once resorted to violence at our meetings. And I had the pleasure of registering my lone vote against the expulsion of Jay Lovestone from the party. Though I did not expect them to take notice of my negative vote, it was duly set down in their minutes and solemnly imparted by Robert Minor in his report to the Executive Committee of the Communist International at the Tenth Plenum in Moscow. Said Minor: "Lovestone and Gitlow were summoned to appear at our Secretariat. They failed to appear. Wolfe came to the Polcom and made a speech at that Polcom meeting which absolutely astounded us. Well, we expelled Lovestone with a unanimous decision of the Political Bureau with the exception of the vote of Wolfe. And we suspended Wolfe from the Political Bureau with only one vote in addition to his." I cannot now figure out whose that "one vote in addition to my own" might have been.

A few days later, the powers that now ruled the party came to the conclusion that they had committed a boner in merely suspending me from the Political Committee. Thereupon they sent to my home a little pink slip which informed that the Political Committee, meeting in my absence, had voted unanimously to "instruct me as the Agitprop Director of the Party to undertake a nationwide tour touching all towns or cities which have a unit of the Party, and to address all units with a talk effectively calculated to convince the members of the absolute correctness of the new Comintern *Open Letter* and all accompanying decisions on the American question." To this I replied: "Dear Comrades: I am so constituted that I am utterly unable to make a convincing speech in favor of any matter on which I am myself not convinced. Your instruction therefore makes no sense since I am firmly convinced of the incorrectness of the latest *Open Letter* of the Comintern. Since I regard the *Address* as incorrect and injurious and reserve the right when the next Convention discussion period comes, to examine how the latest Comintern decisions have injured our Party and the Comintern, I must reject your instruction as morally and psychologically impossible and must urge you to rescind it in order to avoid raising a false issue of discipline when, as my letter of June 23rd informs you, 'I submit to the decisions referred to not because I agree with them, but, in spite of my disagreement, as a matter of discipline.' "

Thereupon the Political Committee voted to expel me from the party for refusing to carry out an "official instruction," thus opening a discussion among some observers as to whether I had broken with the party or been expelled by it.

HOW THEY ENLIGHTENED THE PARTY

Apparently Stalin wanted no scandals about more-or-less-known Americans like Lovestone, Gitlow, and me being held prisoner in Russia. All he wanted to do was to have us offered "important work for the Comintern" anywhere but in our own land. And if we stubbornly refused, he would keep us as long as possible while he sent his pack of agents to America to turn our party upside down and make it impossible for us to find an audience among our comrades, to whom we could give a true account of what had happened to Moscow. And it must be said that he succeeded, for our inability to cross the Soviet frontier into a freer world without our passports and our visas gave him the power to hold us while his "enlightenment campaign" did its work.

Besides sending over a dictator armed with all the Comintern's powers, and with powers it had never dreamed of before, he had reorganized our Secretariat in Moscow and packed it with three Muscovites. But that was only a matter of restructuring a high command. The Comintern leaders knew that our party never had more than some 2,000 native-born Americans or members whose household language was English, this out of a membership that fluctuated between nine and twelve thousand. America was a land whose heavy industries like coal mining and steel smelting were largely manned by foreign-born workers, while even such light industries as the garment trades were filled with recent immigrants whose language of preference was Yiddish or Italian. Finns and Scandinavians worked at lumbering, while the textile industry was a Babel of a half dozen or more European tongues. Hence Stalin ordered the Comintern to send Communist orators at once, who knew nothing about our party, our country, or our fight, but knew by heart and could translate into their own languages the new decisions of the Comintern on the American question. The Comintern sent agitators who could speak Yiddish, Finnish, Ukrainian, German, Hungarian, Lithuanian, Estonian, Russian, Italian, Spanish, South Slavic, Scandinavian, Czech, Slovak, Slovene, Polish, and several other tongues, not forgetting English. Each speaker of whatever tongue was the voice of the Comintern, armed with plenipotentiary powers conferred upon him as a representative of the Communist International, including the power to expel from any meeting he had addressed any miscreant who did not approve of what he had said or did not want to vote for the resolution he had introduced. In addition to Stalin's, and the resolution's, insults and falsehoods concerning our views, the most preposterous things were said of us. Thus in a number of locals the members were told that we tried to arouse anti-Soviet agitation by claiming that we could not get out of Russia and by appealing to the American Consul or the American ambassador. When somebody had the sense to suggest that there was no American Consul to appeal to in Moscow, since the United States did not recognize the Soviet government, the speaker answered that we had appealed to the American Consulate in Riga, Latvia. No one had the temerity to ask how we got to Riga to appeal to him if we couldn't get out of Russia. But the one who had pointed out the absurdity was set down as a "troublemaker" or a "questioner of the Comintern line," and at the end of the evening he was expelled with the other enemies of the Comintern.

The Enlightenment Campaign procedure was simple and swift. While we fretted in Moscow, meetings were being called simultaneously all over the United States. In each meeting someone gave a report on behalf of the Comintern. Then a resolution was introduced denouncing us as "renegades, counter-revolutionaries, enemies of the Soviet Union and the Comintern." On this a vote was taken. The voters were told to hold up their hands until all the names had been written down of those who had not voted for the resolution. Next the names were called out of those who had not voted, and each of them was given a chance to vote "for or against the Comintern." Those who voted *no* on the resolution were expelled that same night. Those who abstained from voting and so stated, were also expelled that same night. Those who said that they could not vote until they had heard our side of the story were also expelled that same night. Then everybody who had voted in favor of the resolution was compelled to vote *yes* (under threat of expulsion) on the expulsion of his comrades. Thus by the end of the evening those who remained in good standing were compelled to share the guilt for the expulsion of their innocent comrades, including abstainers and those who desired to hear both sides. Anyone who remained after this great purge procedure were thenceforth the enlightened ones and constituted the legal unit of the party. The rest were cast, unenlightened, into outer darkness, and the enlightened ones were instructed to have no intercourse with their expelled comrades of yesterday.

When this process had been completed throughout our party, in every unit and in every foreign federation and in every committee of party officials, Stalin was ready, if necessary to avoid a scandal, to let Gitlow and me go home. But Lovestone he did not intend to let out of his grasp and power. Lovestone was able to join us thanks only to his ingenuity and to his secret sympathizers and connections in Moscow. That is why the first attempt to "enlighten" the party in print was the full-page spread in the *Daily Worker* of June 27 on the "Expulsion of Jay Lovestone from the Communist Party of the United States." And the first hodge-podge labelled "Material for the Enlightenment of Party Membership" was the peculiar appendix to the expulsion decree, consisting of Lovestone's statement of "disagreement but submission," hitherto suppressed, our secret cable to Jack Stachel of May 15th from Berlin, and the text of my letter to the Secretariat declaring that I was constitutionally unable to deliver a convincing talk in favor of something of which I myself was not convinced.

On the same page, near the bottom, there was a box 1¾ inches deep, which seemed to promise that there would be a real discussion with all viewpoints represented. Entitled ENLIGHTENMENT CAMPAIGN ON THE COMINTERN ADDRESS TO THE COMMUNIST PARTY, it began bravely with the words: "The Politbureau is desirous of securing the broadest possible Enlightenment Campaign on the Comintern Address." But "broadest enlightenment" did not mean the broadest discussion or even any discussion, though the next sentence read, "All Party members are invited to write their opinions for the Party press. [If anyone had escaped Enlightenment Purge Night, that would catch them!]. Resolutions of factory nuclei will be printed in this section. Send all material dealing with this campaign to Comrade Jack Stachel, care National Office." And then the national office address was given, and that was all! In a few issues of the paper, resolutions denouncing us were printed. Contrary resolutions or doubting ones were left unprinted but followed up by the expulsion of their authors. And that was all the broad discussion there was.

To be sure, there was also one other half page of "Enlightenment Campaign: Documents Bearing on the Comintern Address," the nub of which lay in the following decision of the ECCI:

> In view of the fact that Comrade Lovestone refused to undertake unconditionally to submit and to actively carry out the decisions of the Executive Committee of the Communist International of May 14th on the question of the American Communist Party, the Political Secretariat resolves:
>
> 1a. To remove Comrade Lovestone from membership in the Political Committee of the Central Committee of the Communist Party of America.
>
> 1b. With regard to the declaration of Comrade Lovestone that he intends to leave for America, whereby he will grossly violate the discipline of the Comintern; the Secretariat gives to Comrade Lovestone the most serious warning. . . .
>
> 2. In view of the fact that Comrade Gitlow had declared at the Presidium that he will resist the decisions of the Presidium on the American question;—to remove Comrade Gitlow from the Secretariat and from the Politbureau of the Communist Party of America, and to ask the Central Committee of the Communist Party of the United States to remove from the Politbureau all such members as will refuse to submit to the decisions of the ECCI.
>
> 3. To ask the Central Committee of the Communist Party of the United States to recall Comrade Wolfe and to send in his place another representative, because Comrade Wolfe refuses to carry out the decisions of the Presidium. Also, the committee is to free Comrade Wolfe from his work as Director of the Latin-American Secretariat.

This Resolution was adopted while we were still in Moscow. But it was enlightening indeed, for it told how we were to be treated regardless of our declarations—that we accepted the resolutions on the American question.

It told the American rank and filer where expulsions from office in the American party originated. And it showed him what his fate would be if he himself abstained from voting, questioned the decision to expel his comrades, or, out of a sense of fairness, wanted to wait until we got back to America and he could hear our report. The document was enlightening indeed and truly belonged under the head of: "Documents for the Enlightenment Campaign." Its message to the readers was a simple one: *caveat lector!* Let the reader beware, for this will be his fate if he questions the decisions on American matters made in Moscow, or shows any sign that he still believes that the American Party is entitled to determine its own affairs, choose its own officers, or decide anything (like splitting the unions and forming pure Communist unions, for example) that the Comintern has already decided for his party.

Aside from these two documents, and a number of resolutions, denouncing us, adopted by the purged locals or committees, a reader of the *Daily Worker* will look in vain for any "broad discussion" such as we were accustomed to before Stalin turned the Comintern into the Stalintern. By the time we got back to America we were already pariahs, while the party was reduced to a shambles in which none were left except those who were ready to condemn without a hearing. And Stalin had established the pattern of his future enlargement of Marxist-Leninist theory: *Enlightenment by Purge.* The only reason I am able to set down the story of my five-month struggle with him is that he had not yet perfected his technique for cutting short discussion.

33

WE UNDERTAKE THE MODEST TASK OF CORRECTING STALIN

By the time Stalin and his emissaries, working through the new Moscow-made "American" Secretariat and the new Political Committee, also made in Moscow, had finished enlightening the American Communist Party, the party was a shambles. Branches, locals, shop units, district committees, had been decimated and reorganized. Within a week of "Enlightenment" hundreds were expelled, and thousands had dropped out in disgust. The expelled included most of the older members, not older in years, but older in experience and included those who had founded the party, like Gitlow and Lovestone and me, and those who had stood the tests of the Palmer Red Raids, indictments, and prison terms (Gitlow was out of prison because Governor Alfred Smith had pardoned him, I because of my skill in disappearing and reappearing under a new name to be active in a new center; Lovestone had indictments pending which had lapsed because of a change of political climate and the statute of limitations). At the next plenum of the party, a report on approximate membership showed less than half the number that had been members before the "enlightenment campaign." Most of those who had dropped out or been thrown out did not come to Lovestone or Gitlow or me for an account of what had happened, but simply dropped out in disgust with Comintern politics.

When Lovestone set foot on American soil and had been in New York a mere three days, he was expelled. Thereupon the issue in those units which had not yet voted was narrowed down to: for the expulsion of Lovestone or against? for Lovestone or for the Comintern?

Here is a typical example, as nearly as I can remember it, of a unit enlightenment as told to me by a participant. The one who came to me had just been expelled for refusing to vote in favor of the expulsion of Lovestone until he should have an opportunity to hear Lovestone's account of what had happened in Moscow. "Twenty-seven were present at our special emergency meeting to hear a report. After the report, no one was permitted to speak against the motion to expel Lovestone. If we asked a question we got a rude answer from the Reporter, but no one was permitted to question the report as a whole or the justice of a motion to expel a man without giving him a hearing in his own defense. I tried that and was answered roughly that, 'Lovestone and his delegation got a month's hearing in Moscow. The time for hearings has passed. The Comintern has condemned him, after all the hearings, as a renegade, a splitter, and a right-winger. Are you ready to reject a decision of the Executive Committee of the Communist International and of your own Political Bureau and Secretariat? What kind of Communist are you?'

"Then we took a vote. *For* Lovestone's expulsion, fifteen. *Against,* twelve. The twelve were next declared by the Reporter to have lost their right of further discussion or participation in the meeting. Next a motion was made to expel the twelve. Some of those who had voted for Lovestone's expulsion were not in favor of expelling rank and file members merely for having voted against the expulsion of Lovestone. The motion to expel the twelve carried, but only by a vote of nine to six out of the fifteen who had voted for Lovestone's expulsion. The Reporter declared those six disloyal to the Comintern and made a motion for their expulsion from the Party. No discussion, but a vote of five to four in favor of the expulsion of the six. The Reporter then wanted the four who had voted against that expulsion to be expelled, but by that time we were all tired out and disgusted and it was late. Someone moved to adjourn and the motion was carried by acclamation. I guess everyone shouted *aye,* including those who had lost their right to vote. I went home filled with gloom. I'm a Communist all right, but I think I've had enough of the Comintern and its way of interfering in our party life. And I've had enough of politics if even Communist politics is such a dirty business." He was expressing the mood of many, who did not come to us to tell us how they felt. Moreover, at that moment the same mood was one of several contending for dominance in my own spirit.

The caretakers who retained their hold on the reorganized party were satisfied with their work. They had practically completed the Enlightenment Campaign before our return. If a unit had been dissolved or expelled wholesale, what did it matter? Then there would be no one left in it who could vote against the Comintern, its Secretariat, or its personal embodiment in Stalin. Those who had supported us up to then were in utter confusion, first because we had not been able to get back from Moscow to report, and second because they were shocked by the secret plot of Lovestone to transfer the party's institutions into reliable hands and to sell the largest of its buildings for cash to carry on the movement during its reorganization. All this seemed a conspiracy against the Comintern and even against our own majority caucus, for there was no Lovestone on hand to explain and justify it.

We had charged that Stalin's purpose in his new Comintern decisions had been to turn the party over to the Foster opposition. But was this really so? On the one hand there were Stalin's clever maneuvers to put Minor, Stachel, and Bedacht on the Secretariat or Politburo, and to make

Bedacht, for the moment, General Secretary. The Old Majority still seemed to have a majority! Everybody was on the leading committees except Lovestone, Gitlow, and Wolfe, who had been away for five months anyway. On the other hand, to Foster's chagrin, Stalin seemed to be showing no inclination to make Foster General Secretary of the party.

Actually, Stalin had no interest in elevating the opposition into the leadership of the party. What he wanted was to Stalinize the party, and all other parties, to turn them into monoliths, into parties of zombies, aggregations of men who would put Russia's interests first in all matters, who would execute his commands without pausing to think what they meant or whether they contradicted what he had said yesterday.

Indeed, Stalin thought that Foster had shown several undesirable characteristics and was not the kind of man he was looking for to make a good secretary general for a Stalintern party. Stalin was one who forgot nothing and forgave nothing. He remembered that Foster was the leader of a group that had included Cannon and the Cannonites, who after the Sixth Congress had become Trotskyites. Was this a defect in Foster? Whether it was or not, why had Foster taken so many months to expose Cannon, expel him from his caucus, and move to expel him from the party? Foster's excuse was that he was running for president of the United States on the Communist ticket when he discovered Cannon's Trotskyism, and did not want to hurt the election campaign by starting such a squabble before the campaign was over. Squabble indeed! Did Foster call that a squabble when it was a matter of treason to the Soviet Union? Foster's duty was to cleanse the ranks of his caucus and the party the day he discovered the "filth" in his caucus. And what importance was a Communist ticket in an American election that got less than fifty thousand votes against thirty million for the winner in a country with a population of a hundred and fifty million people?

Then Foster had postponed the exposure further because the party was engaged in the election of delegates to its convention and he feared the exposure would cause him to lose delegates. Another petty concern compared with Trotskyism! Stalin did not forgive Foster for either delay, for what were a handful of votes for a Communist candidate for president, or a handful of votes to an American party convention in which Stalin intended to call the shots and make the decisions anyway, compared with the ousting of vile traitors who supported Stalin's arch enemy, Leon Trotsky, and who were therefore enemies of the Russian Communist Party, the Soviet government, and the Communist International?

There were two other grave counts against Foster. One was that under Pepper's influence, he had almost accepted peace with Lovestone, who was the American incarnation of the International Right-Wing, i.e., a suspected Bukharinite. If there were not two factions in the American party, how could Stalin play one against the other? In fact, from Zinoviev's day on, it was the consistent practice of the Comintern to give Delphic decisions on controversies in all the parties except the Russian, *on-the-one-*

hand, on-the-other-hand decisions, so ambiguous that each faction could claim that the Comintern had supported it. This practice the German Communists cynically called *Flickenpolitik,* every decision being made up of a *Flick* for one side and then a *Flick* for the other. The Comintern, i.e., the Russian party, would not have been able to manipulate the parties so easily if any of them had developed a real solid unity based upon the situation and tactics of its own country.

The fourth count against Foster in Stalin's opinion was the most serious of all. He had a real following in the American labor movement and at some time might assume an independent stand on some question and appeal successfully to his American following, as Lovestone had done with his following in the American Communist party. What Stalin needed to turn each party into a proper section of the Stalintern was a completely obedient party that would think him the fount of all wisdom, that would have leaders whom he, Stalin, had personally made and could as easily unmake again. At this point, Earl Browder hove into view.

THE ASCENSION OF EARL BROWDER

Earl Browder was born in Wichita, Kansas, of an old America family that had come to this country before our War of Independence. He was a bookkeeper and accountant by trade, had belonged to the Socialist party until the Communist party was founded, was a pacifist during World War I, and was imprisoned in 1917 for opposing the draft and America's entrance into the European War. Until he met William Z. Foster and persuaded him to go to the First Congress of Lozovsky's Red Trade Union International (or Profintern), his principal occupation had been that of office worker. In Moscow, Foster secretly joined the American Communist Party, affiliating the Trade Union International (T.U.E.L.), which he had founded, to the Profintern. Thereupon Browder became Foster's office manager and the editor of the T.U.E.L.'s official organ, *The Workers' Monthly.* Lozovsky for his part became the patron of Foster and of Browder in the Comintern, tried to advance their fortunes, and became the chief supporter in the Comintern of the Foster opposition in our party, whereupon Lovestone, who loved to pun with people's names, took to calling him Louseovsky. Up to this time, Browder did not attract Stalin's attention.

In 1927 Browder, still an obscure figure in our party and in the Comintern, was sent by Lozovsky to the Far East and made the Director of the Pan-Pacific Secretariat of the Profintern and editor of the *Pan-Pacific Worker* in Shanghai. Still, Browder was an uninteresting figure, and of no particular interest to Stalin. But in Shanghai Earl Browder got into trouble, was precipitously recalled to Moscow while I was there in 1929, as I have already mentioned, and brought up on charges by no less a figure than Osip Piatnitsky, Organization Secretary and Head of the Section of

Secret International Relations of the Comintern, and was charged by Piatnitsky with "incompetence as an underground worker," "criminal negligence," and the "waste of large sums of foreign currency," when Moscow itself was so badly in need of good, firm cash to purchase machines and whole factories from the United States for the first Five-Year Plan. At last, Stalin's attention was attracted to the hitherto obscure person of Earl Browder.

Comrade Browder was now "damaged goods" and Stalin began to look into his misdeeds. The heads of all the other secret agencies that had had to close up because of Browder's thoughtlessness also appeared in Moscow, in good time for Piatnitsky to summon them to testify against the ineptness of and the harm done by the Director of the Pan-Pacific Secretariat of the Profintern.

But at this point, the Comintern in the person of Joseph Stalin jumped in and stayed the hand of fate. Earl Browder was exactly what he was looking for to make into an obsequious and totally obedient General Secretary for the American Communist party—damaged goods, a handful of dust, that Stalin could shape into a supreme leader, and could make crumble into dust again if ever he blew a hot breath at him. "A good man," he told the ever-obedient Piatnitsky, "one who has gone to jail for the cause, a tried and trusted revolutionary, one of the best that the American party possesses, we don't have many such and can't afford to waste him because of a mere trivial error." And because it was Stalin that had saved him, Earl Browder began to feel enormously self-important: he would strive to be in the American party what Stalin was in the Russian. Thereupon Browder launched an attack on his old leader, Foster, and was to treat him meanly thenceforward, even preventing him from answering Browder's own attacks upon him. And thus, after due preparation, did Earl Browder become the (for many years) "revered" General Secretary of the American Communist Party.

WE TRY TO GATHER OUR FORCES

If Lovestone had remained in America after his sweepingly victorious convention, if he had not had the convention elect a delegation or had sent one headed by Gitlow and Bedacht while he stayed home to take care of the home front, perhaps he might have managed the difficult maneuver of transferring the assets of the party to more reliable hands and could have broken the news gradually to his following, helped as he would have been by Stalin's arrogance and his constant sending of inept and inappropriate orders to the American party. And Minor and Stachel would not have dared betray him. But being 6,000 miles away, and with the seeming possibility that he would never be permitted to return to his own country once he had put himself, by my urging and his own conviction, into Stalin's hands, it was natural for such characterless functionaries as Minor and

Stachel to transfer their allegiance to the man whose power was beginning to make and unmake leaders in the German, Swedish, the Norwegian, the Austrian, the French, the Czech, the Italian, and many other parties. The partial exceptions were such parties as the Italian and the Chinese, in which Togliatti in the first case and Chou En-lai in the second knew when to jump from being worshippers of Bukharin to worshippers of Stalin. Knowing when to jump became an important attribute in the leadership of all Communist Parties.

If the American party convention had stayed home and left the next move to Stalin, he would have been hard put to find any devices for upsetting the solidly based American leadership. Five months later, when it became the turn of the Swedish party to be Stalinized, the Swedes profited by our example. Summoned to Moscow for the purpose of being discredited and removed, they simply refused to go, and answered all insults quietly but firmly from home territory. Stalin and his retinue of functionaries thundered against them and denounced their most popular, historically engendered leaders like Kilbom and Höglund as Right-Wingers, renegades, traitors to the Comintern, enemies of the Soviet Union and of the Swedish working class. But though they were a neighboring country, the arrows fell far short of the mark. The Swedish party went on with its work, was kept virtually intact, even gained in the respect of the Swedish working class, kept its journals alive, kept its seats in Parliament. When in 1934 it got tired of taking abuse from "comrades," it changed its name to the Swedish Socialist party, which has become far and above the largest party in Sweden. Without too much opposition from other parties, it has built a society which has ample room for private industry, small and large. The great auto plants and ballbearing plants are privately owned, as is 90% of all the industry in Sweden, while the Government has a large interest only in water power production, iron ore extraction, and railroads. At the same time they have built a unique example of the welfare state, with enormously high taxes on everyone and everything and the most complete system of social welfare from womb to tomb. Whether this is desirable or not I must leave to the reader to decide, but what is pertinent here is that today the Swedish Socialist party, having refused to go to Canossa to be enlightened and detained, has built in accordance with its own program, the most advanced, that is the most complete, of all the welfare states that any European Socialist party has constructed. This is their Socialism.

However, the American Communist Party, even if it had not put its top delegation into Stalin's power, would have had a far different fate from the Swedish. What that fate would have been is impossible to conjecture. But in retrospect, I have come to the conclusion that there was no solid, durable place in the American political scene for a Communist party, as there has been none for the much older, and much more popular, Socialist party, or indeed for any purely ideological party, or for any purely class party aimed at kindling a class war against most other Americans. The Swedish party, unlike ours, was a mass party solidly rooted in a Swedish and general European Socialist tradition. When I contemplate the massive growth of our national budget and our national bureaucracy, the enormous quantity of paper shufflers, elected by no one, and not responsible to the people, when I see how legislators, executives, and judges act, and, of their own regulations of local and state entities, of schools, colleges, universities and private enterprise of every description, I sometimes think that we, too, are marching unconsciously into a kind of state socialism, marching backwards into socialism even as we shout free markets and free enterprise.

WE FIND IT HARD TO GET A HEARING

Lovestone had counted on three things that would enable him to deal with Stalin from a position of strength as the leader of one party dealing with the leader of another. One was the 90 percent of the party that had supported all of his moves at the convention; the second was the supposed faithfulness of his lieutenants, Stachel and Minor, who would enable us to keep the party apparatus going; the third was the expectation that Stalin would play fair according to the statutes of the Communist International. There was also a fourth, unspoken: that we would return to America immediately after our appeal had been heard and judged, and be able to tell the real story of the Moscow hearings and machinations to the party members. That would have been *our* enlightenment campaign, and to our way of thinking the only valid one: for who but Americans, members of the American delegation, would have the right and duty to report to the Party on the results of their mission? But, as the reader already knows, all of these calculations miscarried.

The three to four weeks of polite imprisonment, and the terrifying, Moscow-run "Enlightenment Campaign" had done their work. By the time we got back, thousands had voted for Lovestone's expulsion, and by implication Gitlow's and mine, during their single night of terror or enlightenment, committing themselves without a hearing. They were therefore ashamed or afraid to meet us, or were working themselves up to self-righteous indignation at the very idea of meeting us, shaking hands with us, or listening to our story. They had already sullied themselves further by voting to expel those who had wanted nothing more than to hear our side of the story before voting on expulsion. In addition they had already received categorical instructions to regard us as unclean and to have no social contact with us. The Central Control Commission was enlarged with the Muscovites to make short shrift of anyone caught shaking hands with us, exchanging greetings, or listening to our sinful words. They were further instructed to break with members of their own family who refused to do as they had done, to divorce and denounce publicly husband or wife, to break with parents, to shun friends who did not shun us.

Men and women who had yesterday felt affection and admiration for us now looked down or away as they passed us on the sidewalk, even crossing the street to avoid looking into our eyes. It will suffice to cite the case of Carl Brodsky, brother of the party lawyer, Joe, who stopped to shake hands with me on Thirteenth Street and exchange no more than the time of day. "How are you, Bert?" he asked. "And how's Ella?" Fine, fine," I replied. "And how is Ada?"

Two days later he was called before the enlarged Central Control Commission with its Muscovite representative added. "You were seen two days ago near the party headquarters on Thirteenth Street stopping to shake hands and chat with Bert Wolfe. What did you talk about? What have you to say in your defense?"

"My wife and I," he answered, "have known him and his wife for over ten years. All I asked was how his wife was and he asked how my wife was. Then I walked on."

"And what will the ordinary worker think if in the *Daily* we denounce Wolfe as a traitor and a renegade and an enemy of the Soviet Union and the Comintern, and then they see you smiling and shaking hands with him?"

The following week I received a letter from Carl Brodsky marked *Confidential:* "Dear Bert, I was called before the Central Control Commission the other day for shaking hands with you and asking after Ella's health. For this I received a reprimand and a solemn warning. If I pass you on the street henceforth and do not take notice of you, please forgive me. Ada and I feel the same affection for you two that we always did, but I must obey the C.C.C. if I want to keep my membership in the party. I hope you will understand."

The Central Control Commission, or the Secretariat, for several months did not summon up enough courage, or impudence, to call upon my wife and instruct her to divorce me and publicly denounce me as a renegade, a traitor, and an enemy of the Soviet Union. When it finally did so, that was too much for her, who had been trying quietly to continue as a party member, editing a shop paper for the party workers in the Hattie Carnegie dress shop, and writing articles on Latin America for the party press. Thus, they drove my wife to join the Communist opposition.

Besides the handicaps of the guilt complex of some party members, the bewilderment of others about Lovestone's secret plan to transfer ownership of the party machinery, and the severe prohibitions against talking to or listening to us, we were handicapped by the fact that Jay Lovestone was not expelled until June 27th, and Gitlow and I not until some time in July, while the cases of Tom Myerscough, Frank Vrataric, Bill White, and Eddie Welsh, who managed to win us a following in such districts as the Anthracite Coal Mining region and the Steel Mills, took somewhat longer. By the time Lovestone, Gitlow, and I were expelled, it was full summer, and many of the comrades we had hoped to talk to were away on vacation. A few locals, a segment of industry where a Bill White could give his own report to his fellows about events in Moscow, and in the case of the West Coast, the entire Seattle District where the leaders included several who had taken courses with "A. E. Albright" in the Workers' School which I had founded in San Francisco, reacted with indignation against the wholesale expulsions and particularly the condemnation of our delegation before it had even been given a chance to report.

The letter from Seattle, because it was addressed to me rather than to Lovestone, is still in my files and reads:

Dear Comrade Bert:

Was out of town for several weeks on vacation in an inaccessible place where I could not get a *Daily* when the news came through about Jay and Gitlow and you. Later I saw Gardos [a leader of the Hungarian Federation] in S.F. and learned about it. I returned to the district where I found that the D.E.C. [District Executive Committee] had already acted as good saints and I was preparing to reopen the matter. I had previously learned that Sorenson had not taken a very good position. . . .

To my surprise, and contrary to my expectations, I found that he had changed his position and that the League Buro, too, was unanimously against expulsions, removals, and for the appeal. . . . The vote on the District Buro was Sorenson, Todes, Gray, Siro, the League D.O., and two others against expulsion, removals, for reinstatement, the Appeal, etc. Lawrie, Levitt, and two others for the C.E.C. position.

The "League D.O." mentioned in the letter is the District Organizer of the Young Communist League. Among the youth we had much more support than among the old-timers who had had loyalty to the Comintern, no matter who ran it at any given moment. Youth leaders who came to give their full time and energy to the Communist opposition we were forming included such leaders as Will Herberg and Herbert Zam. Of course, when a whole district gave us a majority in its leading committees, Muscovite Commissars immediately appeared to expel those committees and all in the district who sided with them or refused to vote for their expulsion. Yet such letters and the reports from the Anthracite and the Steel Mill districts told us that we were not entirely alone in the world.

It was noteworthy that a number of individuals who were known in the Party for their earnestness as students of the works of Marx and the few works of Lenin and Trotsky thus far translated into English, as well as their skill in bringing in new members through social evenings and study groups in their own homes, joined us now out of moral indignation at the fact that we had not been allowed to return promptly to our own country, nor to state our own case as part of a true enlightenment campaign. So, too, did trade union activists and leaders, who had never been with us in the faction fights in the party, join us. In the needle trades unions, for example, there were such men as Charles S. (Sasha) Zimmerman, a leader of Local 22 of the Dressmakers, who brought with him a number of needle trades workers who had fought the hired gangsters of the employers on picket lines and were now able to act as our bodyguards when the official party tried to break up our open meetings by physical force. Most striking were the actions of such men as Nelson (don't ask me for his first name; I think it was Louis but nobody ever called him anything but Nelson, prefixed neither by Louis nor comrade nor brother nor mister). All his life long he had been an anarchist and a quick-tempered, good-humored, pugnacious leader in the needle trades, but now he foreswore his anarchism out of moral indignation at the way Stalin had treated us. And he too brought a number of his followers into our ranks. A similar case was that of Martin Temple in Mexico, who had been a Socialist in his youth, and a pacifist all his life. Now he joined our ranks, tried to set up a durable section in Mexico, and contributed large sums of money such as fifty or a hundred dollars at a time to sustaining our headquarters and our press. Our headquarters began as a single room plus a cubbyhole at 37 East 28th Street. Later as we grew stronger and I built up the New Workers School, we moved nearer to the party headquarters, taking two whole floors in a ramshackle old building at 15 West 14th Street, where Diego Rivera painted his movable frescoes known as *Portrait of America.* The anarchist, Nelson, the pacifist, Martin Temple, and the leader of Local 22, Sasha Zimmerman, because they had joined us on moral grounds, stuck with us to the end.

Yes, it was comforting to see that we were not alone. However, we grew slowly and never attained such numbers as could seriously contend with the official party outside of the city of New York. Whenever we won ground in some industry, the party would plant its own colonizers there to dislodge us. Thus we were among the pioneers in the auto industry in Detroit, and one of our members even won the presidency in the nascent union, but then the official party rushed in in such numbers that they dislodged us.

We were not alone, yet it took us four months to gather together enough expelled or seceding party members and enough funds to begin the publication of something more than mimeographed statements and the "bedsheet" *Appeal to the Comintern againsts Its Decision on the American Question.* Dated November 1, 1929, we got out a good-looking, well edited, lively semimonthly, tabloid size, the first issue being 20 pages and the subsequent ones 16 pages, entitled *Revolutionary Age.* It had a plethora of editors and contributors. The chairman of the editorial board was Jay Lovestone; the editor, Ben Gitlow; the associate editor, B. D. Wolfe; and the editorial board included, among those already known to the reader, Will Herberg, Bert Miller, Frank Vrataric, Ed Welsh, W. J. White, Herbert Zam, and Charles S. Zimmerman, plus the editors, and other names, for a total of sixteen.

The *Revolutionary Age* had the subtitle, "Organ of the Communist Party U.S.A.—Majority Group." We did not intend to suggest that we had with us a majority of the party, but merely to remind our readers that we had been (as indeed we had) the founders of the Communist Party and the leaders of the Majority Group when we went to Moscow, where we were besmirched and detained until our majority could be smashed, frightened, demoralized, and fed false fairy stories or witch tales before we were permitted to return to America. The name of our journal was also an appeal to the traditions of the American party which we had founded in 1919, and which William Z. Foster and the bulk of his followers did not join until 1923 or later.* We reminded our Communist readers that we were purposely evoking the memory of that earlier *Revolutionary Age* that had helped to oppose America's entrance into the First World War and to build the Left-Wing of the Socialist Party. A typical example from the front page lead editorial said:

When the United States entered the World War the founders of the *Revolutionary Age* were among the most active fighters against American imperialism and its war plans. No sellers of Liberty Bonds [a reference to William Z. Foster] were to be found in their ranks. . . .

In 1919 their offices were ransacked and destroyed. Its editor, manager, and members of its National Council, were arrested and indicted. Ruthenberg, Gitlow, and Larkin were sent to prison for terms of 5 to 10 years. . . .

When Lenin sent out the call for the organization of the Communist International, he included "the group around the Revolutionary Age." To this group fell the great historic mission not only of being the organizers of the Communist Party in the United States but of being among the founders of the Communist International. . . .

The elements around the Revolutionary Age founded our Party and carried it through the most difficult periods. Around them crystallized the leadership under which the Party developed into a fighting revolutionary Party. . . . [The declaration then recited a list of what the Comintern had called "fierce class battles"—Passaic, New Bedford, miners' strikes, needle trades strikes, organization of the unorganized.]

All these achievements were made in spite of a most pernicious internal war that has been raging since 1923 . . . under the leadership of William Z. Foster, who came into the party in 1922 from the ranks of the A.F. of L. bureaucracy. . . .

Finally, under the pressure of nearly 90 percent of the membership, the bankrupt, unprincipled factional group was defeated at the Sixth Convention. . . . The Party stood united behind its historically developed leadership. . . .

Precisely at this time it became involved in the general crisis in the Communist International. Under the pretext of "fighting the Rights" the present leadership of the Communist International . . . has thrown the sections of the International into isolation, chaos, and confusion, and the best and most experienced revolutionists in all parties have been driven out and expelled, to be replaced by incapable, politically bankrupt "new leaderships."

The Communist Party of the United States could not be exempt from this

* Foster joined the Party secretly in 1922, openly in 1923. During the latter year he began building his caucus and started his fight for the leadership of the Party, which ended with his overwhelming defeat in our 1929 convention six years later.

general crisis. This crisis is characterized by the recent address of the ECCI with its revisionist line, its wild charges, its disastrous proposals . . . by the rapid decline of the Party into sectarianism and isolation . . . by the mass expulsion of hundreds of the best and oldest comrades in the Party.

Thus did the *Revolutionary Age* explain its reappearance and appeal for support in its efforts to correct the false line of the party and the Comintern, and to reunify the party on the basis of a sound Leninist line.

The *Revolutionary Age* was so much better written and edited than were the official party papers that its circulation grew rapidly. Party members bought it surreptitiously from newsstands; party leaders read it in order to see what we were up to and to figure out how to answer us; even the Soviet Union ordered a number of copies to distribute among those who had the duty of attacking us.

But our membership grew much more slowly. How many members did we have? I don't rightly know, since I did not concern myself with administrative matters, although Lovestone tried his best, and tried repeatedly, to persuade me, even to "instruct" me by a majority vote in our leading committee, to become a full time functionary. I, for my part, concerned myself with writing, teaching, doing a humorous column, and building a New Workers' School on the plan of the old one that I had earlier headed. Gitlow says that we started with a membership of some 150 out of the more than two thousands that dropped out and the many hundreds additional that were expelled. When Gitlow broke with us in 1933 for reasons which will be explained later, he wrote, "The Lovestoneites did not attain a membership in excess of 350 throughout my connection with the group." This was probably an understatement, for as I pointed out to Ben when he was resigning, the big Lithuanian Federation had just broken with the official party and was affiliating with us. Later the Finnish Federation, when the party aroused its indigation by trying to take funds from the treasury of its huge cooperative system, also made the gesture of fraternal affiliation. But in both cases, this did not mean active membership on the part of Lithuanians or Finns, but only of a handful of its leaders. All in all, however, I am fairly certain that our active membership never rose above 500. The party itself, in its zeal to show the men in Moscow how much it knew, published an article in *Inprecorr* in which it gave the absurdly precise figure of 202 for our initial membership after they had expelled, or lost in the "Enlightenment Campaign," they said, something over 2,000 members. What happened to them? Most of them dropped out of political life for good, concluding that if that was how even the Communist International behaved, then all politics must be corrupt and not worth pursuing. Others continued to drop out of the party for years, but once more only a small proportion of the dropouts actually joined our ranks, though many more contributed funds occasionally, read our press and pamphlets, took courses at the New Workers School, attended our meetings, and supported the surprisingly large proportion of our members who became spark plugs in, and even leaders of, trade unions, and helped our fight to block the party's attempts to split the unions and form dual Communist unions under instructions from Moscow.

STALIN SPLITS THE WORLD LABOR MOVEMENT

Stalin attempted to split the powerful German trade unions in the same fashion by taking out all the Communists and their sympathizers to form "Revolutionary Unions," a success which helped to paralyze the German working class when Hitler was rising to power. As Stalin and his trade union lieutenant, Lozovsky, carried these splits or attempted splits from land to land, the Communist parties isolated themselves increasingly from the working class, especially in countries with mass parties and well-nigh all-inclusive mass union movements. Finally Lozovsky himself had to give warning to the Profintern Unions:

> There was no need to shout from the housetops, "Destroy the unions," as was done in Germany. But, rather that we want to break up the reformist trade unions, that we want to weaken them, that we want to explode their discipline, that we want to wrest the workers from them, that we want to explode the trade union apparatus and destroy it; of that there cannot be the slightest doubt.

Naturally, that didn't help any.

THE SPLINTER SYNDROME

After Lenin seized power in the fall of 1917, from all lands men and women turned in the midst of the darkness of universal war toward the beacon of hope they thought they saw shining from the Kremlin towers. Men who hated war and longed for peace turned toward the false dawn in the east because they had been shocked to their inmost depths by the failure of all their institutions from the churches of the Prince of Peace to the Socialist International. Socialists looked toward Moscow for the redemption of the sullied honor of their movement. Impatient rebels who had long fretted at the slowness with which the nineteenth and early twentieth century had been realizing their dreams, and who were now shocked by the speed with which the civilized world had relapsed into brutality, thought that Lenin's success represented a short cut to the realization of their dreams of socialism and perpetual peace.

In his first decree Lenin had called to the world for peace and world revolution simultaneously. For him to call for peace was but a means to bring about revolution, but many heard it as a call for revolution to bring about peace. From all the ends of the earth, across mountains and seas, through shell-torn battlefields and past sentries, they found their way to answer Lenin's call. Each heard what he longed to hear and managed to be deaf to that which meant most to Lenin, but which did not fit his own dreams.

The lives of those who survived the first terrible years of disillusion and then broke or were expelled, tell a hopeful story. For almost as soon as they arrived, Lenin began his struggle to reshape their spirits according to his blueprint of rockhardness, ruthlessness, amoralism, unthinking obedience, and to replace their love and pity for their fellow men by hatred for "the system" and the men that in his mind embodied it. He saw these followers as cogs in his machine.

For a time it seemed as if he might really turn this variegated band of rebels and dreamers into something like identical cogs in a machine or ball bearings of equal diameter and hardness to support the wheels of his juggernaut.

But human beings are infinite in their variety, and the human spirit is a stubborn thing. Those who streamed toward Moscow were even more varied than ordinary beings, each high-spirited and unique in his own person. For a shorter or longer time they strove to preserve their illusions. They seemed to adapt themselves, to repeat the same phrases, obey the same orders, be shaped, or silenced, into an appearance of conformity with Lenin's blueprint. But one by one they questioned, measured the dream against the deed, the fantasy against reality, then spoke up, were expelled, or broke away, each for his own reasons and in his own fashion. Gradually, or suddenly and startlingly, they assumed their original shapes once more. They were profoundly changed, to be sure, by the experience they had been through, but each was changed in ways that accorded with his own nature and in ways that intensified their original qualities. The very colors that were to have been bleached out were the aspects of their spirits which the experience reinforced. Even when we faced Joseph Stalin on the prisoners' bench in the Hall of Columns, Gitlow, Lovestone, and I, and Bill White and Eddie Welch, answered the prosecutor's stern questions in different ways.

To be sure, we had a number of common grounds for our break with Stalin. Among them some of the more obvious were these:

1. We believed in party democracy at least to the extent that it existed in the statutes and customs of the Comintern, while Stalin and his lieutenants made a mockery of every concept of democracy.

2. Our position was that the Communist International should have a collective leadership, genuinely international in character, but made up of national leaders of national Communist movements. In that collective leadership, federal in character, Russia would have the first place by virtue of its experience, its success in seizing power, and its rule over a great country, but it would be no more than the first among equals, wise enough to advise the rest of us, but wiser still in knowing how to listen and let us make our own final decisions, because the least of our national leaderships knew more about its own country than the wisest of the Russians did.

3. We differed in 1929 with the Communist International, which in

actuality meant the Stalin-dominated Russian Communist Party, over a series of questions involving American conditions, American institutions, and American thinking. For this we were denounced as "American Exceptionalists." We were denounced as American Exceptionalists because we insisted that there were certain historical traditions and institutions peculiar to America. Lovestone was the most important target to Stalin and the most vulnerable of "Exceptionalists" because he wrote largely on economics, but I made matters worse by boldly saying that we (or at least I) were exceptionalists for every country in the world, each of which had its own unique and peculiar history, its own traditions, its own national temperament and psychology, and would move forward toward its own future in terms of its own national history and traditions.

4. We held, as Marx and Engels and Lenin had held, that there was less of a Socialist tradition and less radicalism in America than in the lands of Europe, for which "American backwardness" Marx and Engels and Lenin each offered a number of differing explanations at different times. We denied that America had already "reached its 1905 and was moving at top speed toward its 1917," as Manuilsky had argued in a discussion with me. We denied that the American labor movement was inherently as Socialist as the various European movements (which also differed markedly from each other). Lovestone differed with Stalin on the entire trend of American economics and politics. The position of Stalin was that the American economic system was in its final crisis and the revolution in America was just around the corner. We might have liked to believe that the prolonged crisis which we had predicted was the beginning of the progressive acceleration of our country's toboggan slide from which there would be no recovery, but as the depression deepened, Lovestone had the impudence to write that the American economy was still the strongest in the world and still growing stronger in its relative position among the advanced countries then in crisis, that the ascendancy of the United States in the world was still continuing, as indeed our marvelous retooling when World War II came and such exploits as the Marshall Plan were to prove. Even today, Gemrany, France, and England are quite ready to recognize that the United States is Number One, despite all our vicissitudes and self-criticism.

5. We differed with Stalin and hence with the Comintern and Profintern on the question of dual unionism. (Lovestone, who had been forced much against his will to accept Stalin's ukase on this question in order to avoid [or so he hoped] Stalin's interference with the leadership of the American party, swung back to his true position as soon as our break with Stalin permitted it.) Stalin & Co. developed a theory that it was necessary to split the American Federation of Labor and organize new unions and a new trade union center of "revolutionary unions" that would simply be an appendage of the Communist Party and would destroy all the influence that Communist unionists had won by their loyal activities in such unions as coal, steel, textiles, etc.

6. We differed profoundly with Stalin on his theory of "Social Fascism," which denounced the Socialists as Fascists and as the main enemy of the Communists. At the time when Hitler was stretching his hand to grasp power, Stalin developed the fatal theory that the main obstacle to the victory of the Communists in Germany was the powerful Social Democracy and mass trade unions. "Let the Nazis win," he reasoned. "They will dispose of the Social Democrats, and after that will come our turn to rule Germany." Hence, at a time when united trade unions and a common front of Social Democratic and Communist parties could easily have blocked Hitler's rise to power, Stalin compelled the German Communists, much against their will, to split off from the great trade unions and set up a Communist Union Center and ordered the Communist Party to direct all its fire not against the Nazis but against "the main enemy," the Socialists, rebaptized by him *Social Fascists.* Thus did Stalin help the Nazis to take over Germany, giving a disastrous course not only to German history but to the history of the world. In love with his theory, Stalin also ordered us to split the American trade unions and try to break up the already feeble Socialist party, which, of course, now became *Social Fascist.*

LOVESTONE, GITLOW, AND WOLFE: THREE DIFFERENT TYPES

These believers it would seem, and others like them, should have been enough to unite the new Communist opposition that we were forming, and keep it united. When Lovestone, Gitlow, and I became the three leaders of that opposition, we held the above views in common. Yet we were three unique and different persons, with three different and distinct backgrounds, and different views on a number of key questions.

Gitlow was moved mostly by resentment—resentment because after he had gone to prison for his Communist beliefs, and, as he thought, for his loyalty to the "Workers' Fatherland, the Soviet Union," and after twenty years of loyal activity first in the Socialist and then in the Communist movement since the age of 18, Stalin had presumed to insult him as an "unprincipled petty-bourgeois politician," had accused him of crimes he had not committed, and was trying to take him away from the movement into which he was born (both his father and mother were first Socialists and then Communists here) and send him to Latin America, whence he could never return in good standing, since Stalin had disgraced him by his wanton charges. Thus Gitlow's attitude towards Stalin was one of irreconcilable hatred and defiance.

Lovestone, however, being a more practical politician and one experienced in getting along with the Russians, whether it was Lenin or Trotsky or Zinoviev or Stalin who spoke for them, was unable to give up the idea that after the newly fabricated leadership of the Stalintern Parties, made up of political ineptness and "damaged goods," had demonstrated that under them their parties would lose ground and the Comintern grow weaker, and after those Stalin had driven out had demonstrated that they were better leaders, more successful in building up their parties and the Comintern, and better defenders of the Soviet Union, then Stalin would be glad to *take them back again* and a new *modus vivendi* could be arrived at within a more variegated and democratic Comintern.

"At the time of the break," Lovestone told a congressional committee, "I had a fundamental agreement with Bukharin on international questions, though on Russian questions I had agreement with Stalin, and not with him." This agreement with Stalin on what he was doing in Russia continued in Lovestone's mind for over six years, until he was cured of the illusion by the blood purges. Gitlow, on the other hand, having two Russian Jewish parents, had relatives in the southern part of the Soviet Union who were suffering from Stalin's abolition of the NEP; his forced collectivization of hundreds of thousands of small independent farms into giant kolkhozes, and his state-engineered famine meant to break the spirit of resistance of the small farmers, all of whom, if they resisted or opposed collectivization, were called *kulaks,* a species which Stalin said were to be "liquidated as a class." In 1932, while Lovestone was in Europe trying to make closer connections with the expelled Brandlerites in Germany, with other expelled leaders like Roy of India, Serra (Tasca or Rossi) of the Italian party, and similar victims of the Stalinization of the Comintern, Gitlow wrote him:

> Another point which we must be careful in considering is the question of the present economic collapse of the Soviet Union. I have been getting reports . . . of such gravity as to indicate an acute situation. Conditions today in Russia are frightful. I suppose that in Germany you are able to get some first-hand information on the same thing. To hold that the present situation there is due to a fall in export prices, in my opinion, is taking too shallow a view of the situation. There are other factors involved, including the whole line, methods, and regime of the leadership of the Communist Party of the Soviet Union.

To this Lovestone replied sharply from Berlin in a letter dated July 2, 1932:

> *Your remarks on the Russian situation:* I still believe that our resolution was correct and is correct. Yes, I have quite a bit more information, information from critical, high officials, rather than from disgruntled, declassed Jewish peasants. . . . Finally, the crop this year, through no fault of Joe, and through no virtue of Trotsky or Bukharin, happens to be a bad one. . . . Without minimizing the difficulties and certainly without excusing Joe's factionalism, we must admit that if it hadn't been for the substantial achievements of the Five-Year Plan based on a generally correct line, the situation in the USSR today in the face of the aggravating world market situation would be far worse.

Gitlow, of course, was right: that year millions of Russians starved to death.

THE LOVESTONE-GITLOW CONTROVERSY

In December 1930 Jay Lovestone went to Germany to attend the Third Conference of the German Communist Opposition, which was held on December 13 and 14, 1930. The Germans, particularly Brandler and Thalheimer, greatly strengthened Lovestone's belief that although Stalin's regime was harmful and destructive both in Russia and in the Communist International, nevertheless his General Line toward rapid Socialist industrialization and toward the rapid collectivization of agriculture was correct: first as the only possible road to Socialism; and second for the rapid development of the defense of the proletarian state against the threatening attacks of the imperialist powers." Brandler and Thalheimer had been expelled thanks to the efforts of Zinoviev and Stalin to find scapegoats for the lamentable failure of the German Comintern-ordered uprising of 1923. The Russian party had found for their successors Ruth Fischer and Arkadi Maslow, who proved to be incompetent as leaders. Stalin had then substituted Thaelmann. Then, M. N. Roy was another scapegoat of Stalin's (for the disaster of the Canton *Putsch*). He too was a supporter of Stalin's internal General Line and helped to reinforce Lovestone's feeling that Stalin would sooner or later convince himself that the Foster-Browder regime was a disaster for American Communism, and that some way would be found for reunifying us with the Comintern.

When Lovestone came back to America and proposed that we endorse the line of the Communist opposition of Germany, he was startled, and Gitlow was heartened, to find that the New York membership reacted indignantly against the proposal. They felt a deeper antagonism to Stalin than he did. Lovestone then gave up his fight for the endorsement of the German Resolution, or its essence, but he did not give up the task of educating his group in favor of the endorsement in the main, of Stalin's General Line in internal Russian agriculture and industry.

Jay Lovestone and Will Herberg, who became his chief assistant in this campaign, began inserting long and glowing articles in the *Workers' Age* * on the achievements of the General Line and the first Five-Year Plan. A specimen of Jay's enthusiasm on the subject speaks of:

> An industrial and agricultural progress the rate and volume of which are unequaled and even undreamt of in the history of mankind.

Herberg for his part, apparently more informed and more realistic about what was happening in Russia, wrote an article in which he admitted, as Lovestone did not, "a lower production in grain and light commodities for the villages," but developed a whole series of excuses for this "temporary phenomenon." I had long ceased to be associate editor of the *Workers'*

* The *Revolutionary Age*, not long after its founding, changed its name to the *Workers' Age*, while we dropped the title *Communist Opposition, Majority Group*, for the simpler, *Communist Opposition*.

Age and Lovestone had become the *de facto* editor, as he always was chairman of the editorial board. But I was shocked to find that Lovestone now began reprinting, without comment, dispatches of the mendacious, pro-Stalinist Walter Duranty, Russian correspondent of *The New York Times*. Thus on June 11, 1933, Duranty cabled an article headed: SUCCESSES OF SOVIET ECONOMY. On June 15 it was published in the *Workers' Age*. So, too, when Duranty went down the Volga and into the southern region of Russia and the Ukraine where millions were starving to death and cabled a conscienceless article from Rostov-on-Don for *The New York Times* of September 11, on September 15 the *Workers' Age* gave it a double head at the favored left side of the front page, two columns on the first page and a runover on page two, under the heading: SOVIETS SCORE IN AGRICULTURE AND BETTER LIFE IS AIM. Duranty's glowing dispatch ended with the words: "Thus with tardy but effective wisdom, the Bolsheviks were winning the agrarian war." I for my part knew Walter Duranty personally and had already concluded that he was a consummate liar, heartless about the fate of the Soviet people, and was backing Stalin either out of admiration for a ruthless strong man, or for some other reasons of his own.

A few years later Walter Duranty published a book entitled *I Write as I Please* in which he indeed boasted how early he had picked Stalin as a "winner," and "it's like a racehorse; when a man picks a winner he backs him all the way." Like many another worshipper of power and success, thus did Walter Duranty concern himself with the fate of the Russian people and the fact of the frightful famine that accompanied the forced collectivization and the "liquidation of the kulaks as a class." I am sure that Lovestone acquired contempt for Walter Duranty and his reports in the end, but for the moment the reports served to confirm his position against Gitlow's and to propagandize our membership by indirection, after the New York membership meeting had rejected his resolution to endorse the German view of "the correctness of the general line of the CPSU towards rapid Socialist industrialization and the rapid collectivization of agriculture as the only possible road to Socialism."

As for me, I was faced with a difficult decision. Had Lovestone introduced a formal resolution into our ensuing conference endorsing Stalin's line in that fashion, I should of course have voted against it and told the whole story of Stalin's brutality as I witnessed it during my five months of watching him cut the Bukharin forces to pieces. For I had seen more of Stalin-in-action in those five months than either Lovestone or Gitlow in their few weeks of pseudo-hearings. I knew we could expect nothing of Stalin but ever increasing brutality in his methods of fighting in his party, the Comintern, and throughout the Russian land; though, of course, I could not dream that it would go as far as blood purges of all of Lenin's lieutenants; the development of his concentration camp system; the slaying of more Communists than any avowed anti-Communist government in the world has ever done. But, I sensed enough to fight a formal resolution of endorsement of Stalin's line to the bitter end, and if I could not win our membership to follow me in such a controversy, I too, like Gitlow, would resign.

But now Lovestone beat a skillful parliamentary retreat as he sensed the feeling about Stalin and his General Line held by the overwhelming majority of our members, in our biggest, the New York, district. At the conference he merely introduced the original resolution, which our group had adopted at its first conference, a resolution that blurred the Gitlow issue and that had been adopted unanimously. Then Gitlow, a poor tactician at best, merely introduced an amendment which was weak in spirit and confusing in language. I could not vote against the reintroduction of the resolution we had adopted nearly two years earlier, which was still worth reaffirming. Nor could I vote for the bloodless amendment of Gitlow. All I could do was assure him of my sympathy with his feelings toward Stalin and urge him not to resign. But resign he did, particularly angry when Lovestone began a whispering campaign against his weaknesses as an "organizer." He was our organization secretary, and to tell the truth, ill fitted for the part. He knew nothing about organization, his strength lay in his powerful voice and his ability to rouse an audience to a fever pitch; yet the best organization ability in the world—Lovestone was the best among us in that—could not have made our group grow much faster.

I myself should like to have written on Stalin and on his General Line, but I was handicapped by the fact that I will not write about anything without feeling that I know it well. I could not go to the starvation areas: my one glimpse of a gang of peasant corvée laborers; my awareness that the lines in front of stores were long in 1924, longer in 1928, and still longer in 1929; my awareness that consumer goods grew scarcer and shoddier with the crushing of the NEP; and a few other such bits and pieces, were not enough to do a decent piece of writing on the then state of Russia or on Stalin's General Line. Besides, my closeup of Stalin and the real workings of the Comintern had given me a profound distaste for what I had seen in my five and a half months in Russia as a member of the ECCI. I felt that I would never write on Russia and indeed kept that silent vow until 1939 when Stalin and Hitler signed a pact.

As I observed in an earlier chapter, my feelings about Russia were initially formed by the passion and moral force of nineteenth-century Russian literature. And when in 1917 America entered the First World War and Lenin seized power with the objective of taking Russia out of the war, the contrast caused me to open a large credit to Russia and to Lenin. But I knew nothing about the Soviet Union's economic and political life, had had no opportunity to study the Russian tongue or read Lenin's works, and knew next to nothing about the life of the masses or the direction in which Russia was developing under its new rulers. So, as my temperament commanded, I wrote virtually nothing about Russia in my ten years in the

Socialist and Communist parties, but stuck to writing about the Americas which I then began to study more deeply, and to such topics as Marxism on which I gradually became learned by dint of sheer stubbornness.

MY MOTHER'S GOD SAVES ME FROM WRITING NONSENSE

Only once did I nearly fall into the error of writing a book on Russia, and that in Spanish. In 1924, when I went to the Soviet Union as a delegate from the Mexican party to the Fifth Congress of the Comintern, I made a contract with the Mexican daily, *El Demócrata,* then edited by Benigno Valenzuela, and sent him 39 articles from Moscow which he published under the general title, *La Unión Soviética en 1924*. The material was gleaned largely from handouts from the agitprop department of the Comintern concerning the wonders of the Socialism they were building. And the year 1924 was really a year of hope, for the NEP was getting under way in earnest, there was a growing abundance of consumer goods and private trade, and many who had suffered under the earlier rigors of "War Communism" were filled with cheerful expectations.

By the time my 39 articles were completed and published and I had received the sum of twelve pesos ($6) per article, I was back in Mexico. The Minister of the Soviet Legation, Stanislas Pestkovski, expressed his enormous enthusiasm for the series, and said, "Bert, write one more concluding article to make it 40, and we will find the money to publish it for you as a book."

But at this point my mother's God intervened, the one of whom she was wont to say to me, "Only God takes care of fools like you!" The Mexican Government deported me as a vendor of narcotics before I could write the 40th article! When my wife left Mexico, many months later, she brought the 39 clippings with her, along with such other effects as seemed transportable. I read them over, asked myself how I knew that all those handouts were true, told myself I was now in a land with excellent university libraries on Russia which I might consult, and use to check and improve my book. As a result I never wrote the fortieth chapter and never published the book, either in Spanish or in English. Hence I must thank God, or perhaps President Calles, for giving me time to think, and thus keeping from publishing, in good faith, much mendacious nonsense.

So too during our discussion on the Russian question, which lasted in overt form from September, 1932, to the middle of February, 1933, I alone of the leading and interested members wrote not one word on the controversy, although the *Workers' Age* was open to all who wished to write discussion articles. I knew that Lovestone was wrong about Stalin's General Line, grievously wrong, and that Gitlow in his instinctively sound but shambling way was right. I knew, too, that I did not know enough of the facts or details to make a decent contribution to the discussion. It isn't that I stopped writing; writing was my calling. But I wrote on Marxism and on Diego Rivera and his painting; I planned the courses for the New Workers School; I got out a second enlarged edition of my 52-page pamphlet *What is the Communist Opposition?*, for the first edition had proved the most popular pamphlet we had published and had already sold out; I did a review article on the American Communist Party's weak, sloppy, cliché-strewn "theoretical organ," entitled "Chewing on Straw: *The Communist* for One Year"; I edited and translated all of Diego Rivera's articles for a special *Rivera Supplement of the Workers' Age;* I wrote ads, articles, posters, a catalogue, and other forms of publicity for the New Workers School (after all, this was the third school, beginning with the Rand School of Social Science, for which I had been made or had made myself the publicity director, and the product, like the list of courses and teachers, was more than creditable for such a small organization); I did a 32-page pamphlet for the John Day Company, for which I went through all the writings of Marx and Engels, selecting and commenting on passages that had any bearing on the special problems of the American working class such as sectarianism, a labor party, the American Civil War, contempt for theory, the role and nature of the trade unions, political strategy, and tactics. All during this six-month period of our discussion I contributed not one word on Stalin's General Line or on our group's attitude toward the Russian question. Only after the discussion came to an end, and Benjamin Gitlow resigned (although our National Committee urged him not to and promised him every opportunity to express his views), did I finally write an article on Joseph Stalin. It was not on his General Line in industry and agriculture, however, but on the Stalin cult, the unsavory beginnings of which I had witnessed during my stay in Russia in 1929. By 1933 he was on the road to becoming the expert-on-everything who would soon become capable of telling composers how to compose, painters how to paint, writers how to write, tell Vavilov why he was wrong in genetics, tell linguists and etymologists that there was only one true and correct theory of language, namely, that of Nikolai Yakovlevich Marr (correct, that is, until 1950, when Stalin pronounced Marr anti-Marxist and unscientific), tell astronomers that they were guilty of "wrecking" in the stars, and in general become capable of telling anyone and everyone how to do better what he could do best. My own contribution to this Stalin cult was entitled: *"Marxism-Leninism-Stalinism"—The Birth of a New "Ism"*.

As Stalin's brutality grew with his expertise and power, as its ubiquity grew with the extension of his cult, and as the Russian Revolution under his leadership caught up with and surpassed the law propounded by the French Revolution *(Die Revolution frisst ihre eigene Kinder)*, the idea of qualifying myself to write on Russia became ever more distasteful to me. I turned to the history and culture of Latin America and Spain, until the Stalin-Hitler Pact led me to devote the rest of my life from 1939 on to studying and writing and teaching on Russia.

34

DIEGO'S ROAD TO NEW YORK

One significant difference between Jay, Ben, and me was that Lovestone and Gitlow thought of themselves as full-time party officials, or, to use the uglier word the Russians brought into the Comintern, *functionaries*. They lived thus from the time I first knew them, and both became full-time workers on the meager, uncertain, and irregular pay of the Communist opposition. But I always felt that I would work as a full-time party official, only when I thought there was no one else who could do the particular job I felt I would be skilled at. My building up and directing of the Workers' School after my deportation from Mexico was typical of a full-time post I accepted because I felt sure of my qualifications for doing that work successfully.

My five months in Russia further confirmed my determination never to be dependent on a paid party post, but to get a job once more as a high school teacher and then find some way through the thicket that blocks the path to the enchanted land of living well or ill, by free-lance writing, which had been my ambition from childhood on. I took politics seriously but did not want to make it the whole of my life.

However, I began to scan the help wanted section of *The New York Times* for a position as a teacher in a private high school or preparatory school. From there I would somehow find my road to professional writing. Within a few days I found an advertisement calling for an experienced teacher of English and asking that the applicant state what other high school subjects he could teach and the minimum salary he was willing to accept. The reply was to be sent to a box number. I made my application as brief as possible. "Graduation from the College of the City of New York, Phi Beta Kappa, cum laude; two years of experience teaching English in Boys' High School, Brooklyn; some five years as Head of the Department of Foreign Languages in the Mexico City Escuela Superior Miguel Lerdo de Tejada, fit me for the position you advertised in today's *New York Times*. I can teach any subject in high school curriculum except solid geometry, trigonometry, calculus, and qualitative or quantitative chemistry. I should expect a salary of $40 a week until I have shown what I can do." And I enclosed a 3×5 card with my name, address and telephone number, which could be filed in case the position advertised was already filled.

When I spoke to unemployed teachers whom I knew, they assured me that $40 was too high. Teachers were working in private schools for $25 a week. "You'll never get an answer to that letter." And indeed the director of the private prep school, who proved to be Joseph Eron of the Eron Preparatory School, felt the same way. He sent for teacher after teacher who had applied, but he could not get that single sentence of mine out of his mind. Three weeks I waited, hunting in vain for other possibilities, and then Mr. Eron sent for me. "Yours was the best letter," he said, "but others are willing to work for much less. Do you think you could act as my assistant principal? And you can really teach all those subjects in the high school curriculum? If you were the Head of the Department of Foreign Languages in Mexico City, why did you leave Mexico?"

"I got homesick." Apparently he had not noticed the gap in my *curriculum vitae.* I breathed easier, and got the job. Mr. Eron did not discover who I was nor the story of my ten years in the Communist party until much later, when he found an article about me in his favorite paper, the *Jewish Daily Forward.* But by that time I had made such a good record in getting my students through the Four-Year High School English Exam of the Board of Regents, that it no longer mattered. "If I had known your past," he said, "you never would have gotten the job, but now I see you are too good a teacher to let go."

When Gitlow resigned and our numbers and finances became a little more substantial, Lovestone made a number of efforts to get me into full-time work for the Communist opposition, but each time he met with instant rebuff, unargued as to my reason, except that I pointed to the pamphlets I had published, the articles I had written, the meetings I had addressed, the way I was building up the New Workers' School and teaching in it. I stayed in the Eron Preparatory School until my work with Diego Rivera showed me the way out, and during my stay with Eron taught German, French, Spanish, algebra, economics, and several other subjects, with English remaining my main subject all the while.

While I was teaching for a living at the Eron School, at the same time I founded and tried to build up a New Workers' School to resemble and to rival the old Workers' School that I had built up in the party. We did not have anything like the same size membership to draw from, but as in the case of the older school, I acted on the theory that if you take yourself seriously others are likely to do the same. Once more I printed a beautiful catalogue on credit, with not as many courses nor as many pages; but we had a goodly number of top flight teachers and top flight courses related to our field. As in the party school, I persuaded a number of non-Communist teachers to participate, along with our own standbys. My old philosophy professor, Morris Raphael Cohen, agreed to give a series of lectures, not because he was a Communist or a Communist oppositionist—quite the contrary—but out of friendship for me. His lectures brought crowds that overflowed our auditorium. So, too, David Saposs gave a course on Labor Problems; V. F. Calverton, the editor of the *Modern Monthly*, a course on Literature and Society; and Diego Rivera, nominally at that point a Trotskyite, gave a series not for them but for us, including such titles as "The Social Content of My Murals," "The Role of the Artist in Society," "The Plastic Structure of my Frescoes," "Nationalism and Art," "Art and the Worker," "The Art of the Two Americas: Mexico and the U.S.A.," "The Radio City Mural—What I Painted and Why Nelson Rockefeller Stopped Me." He lectured in Spanish, and I caught his words on the wing, translating them into English. Sometimes he chided me for how I was translating an occasionally silly statement of his, trying to make it more sensible; sometimes I chided him in Spanish, even while I was translating; all to the delight of the audience which jammed the hall and overflowed into the corridors. He was so enormous and fat and I was so tall and thin, that the performance of the two of us together in friendly and close symbiosis was promptly dubbed: "Spare Ribs and Gravy."

Strange to relate, though the official party was more than twelve times our size, their Sunday night forums dwindled as ours grew, for their officials, subbing as Sunday night speakers, chewed over the old straw of the Comintern clichés, and they could not match our range of speakers, nor the range and significance of the subjects we worked out. Thus, when the fiftieth anniversary of the death of Karl Marx occurred on March 4, 1933, the party had a routine meeting repeating the clichés of the Comintern which repeated the clichés of the Russian party which buried Marx once more by overlaying him with Lenin and Lenin with Stalin. The New Workers' School, on the other hand, had a series of five successive Sunday night lectures with the following subjects and speakers: "Marx and America," Bertram Wolfe; "Marx and Spinoza," Jim Cork; "Marxism and Modern Thought," Will Herberg; "Marxism and American Culture," V. F. Calverton; "Marxism Today," Jay Lovestone.

While the party school made us green with envy with the initial registration they could get together for a class, their attendance dropped away sharply out of the dullness of their teachers and courses and the boredom of those who had been coaxed or "instructed" into attending, while our registrants tended to stick to the end, though few of the nonmembers thus attracted were moved to join our ranks, they would try another course or another teacher. Finally, when Diego Rivera, who was at the height of his fame and the center of a cloud of controversies, became a stellar attraction by painting on our very walls movable frescoes (movable because our school was in an old rickety building), our hall filled to overflowing, including people sitting on the floors and standing in the corridors. Only the fact that the Fire Department did not seem to suspect that our little splinter group could attract such audiences saved us from a police and fire inspectors' raid, or a flat shutdown, because our floors were not much more solid than our walls and the fire laws were being multiply violated.

When I met Diego at the beginning of the 1920s, when he had just returned from a decade and a half in Europe, drawn back to his native Mexico by rumors about the meaning of Mexico's twelve turbulent years of formless uprisings, vast programs, and the nugatory fulfillment of them, a revolution that so far was naught but promises. Those programs and promises were something for Diego's gargantuan imagination to fill in according to his own dreams. He brought back with him an undigested mixture of Spanish anarchism, Russian terrorism, Soviet Marxism-Leninism, Mexican agrarianism—the redemption of the poor peasant and the Indian. All these "isms" were blended and transformed as they filtered through his homesick dreams and were assimilated to Paris art revolutions and devices for attracting attention by wild deeds, novel programs, and tall tales, among which last Diego's tales were known to be the tallest, so tall and wild that Ilya Ehrenburg made him the hero of his farcical novel, *Julio Jurenito*.

He brought back with him, too, a highly sophisticated technique and sensibility, the skills acquired by imitating scores of great painters ancient and modern, without altogether acquiring a style of his own (it took the Mexican Revolution to make him into the painter who by his work awakened fresh techniques in Mexico and the United States and contributed greatly to what has come to be called "the Mexican Renaissance"). He carried with him in his intellectual baggage the memories of thousands and thousands of great works he had seen, and had often copied, in the cathedrals, palaces, museums, plazas, market places, and painters' studios of all the art galleries of Europe.

To these gifts he added a deepened love for his native land and the determination to fuse the skills acquired in Europe with the powerful, fierce, and beautiful heritage of pre-Conquest Mexican art and the still living plastic sense of the Mexican folk, in order to paint for them on what he hoped would be accessible public walls, his idea of the meaning of the Mexican and Russian Revolutions.

Luck was with him, for he found in the capital a whole troop of like-minded young artists to share his dream with, to discuss and argue and quarrel and vie with, in trying to revive the ancient art of fresco on large and publicly visible walls. The new regime was made to order, too, to fulfill his dreams. The new President was Obregón, the best soldier and the best civic builder that the Revolution has had. And, as I have said earlier, the Minister of Education was the revolutionary youth leader, grown a little older, José Vasconcelos, the best Education Minister that Mexico had produced, a man of wide-ranging culture, determined to build schools, spread literacy, and take young artists under his wing.

Both Obregón and his Education Minister seemed to agree that one thing they could give the folk was a sense of dignity, a sense of *patria* in place of or in addition to a sense of locality and tribe, as well as the ability to read and write both in Spanish and in their native tongues. The people were to be given, too, a vision of the "meaning" of the Revolution through words, through song and dance, through missionary teachers, and through paintings on the walls of all the ruined buildings the new regime was reconstructing.

But unfortunately, that vision varied with each painter, and Vasconcelos did not agree with any of them nor altogether like their style. But with a breadth of criterion that did him credit, all he demanded of them was a serious attitude toward their own handiwork. When the newspapers attacked Diego's style and content, the minister avoided a direct discussion of esthetics, defining his attitude in the formula, "Surface and speed is what I demand. . . . I desire that they paint well and quickly because the day I go, the artists will not paint or will paint propaganda art."

Surface and speed! If that was what was wanted, Diego led the lot of them. In March, 1923, Rivera began the first of his great works—a series of 123 frescoes on the walls of a spacious courtyard three stories high, two city blocks long and one wide—the patio of the Ministry of Education. The total surface painted by him on the three floors, and on the walls of the stairways for good measure, was over 17,000 square feet of frescoes, the equivalent of a painting one foot deep and over three miles long. During the same period he was also painting thirty frescoes in the chapel of the Agricultural School in Chapingo on walls and curved ceilings, some of the finest work he has done. Though he had a squad of assistants, apprentices, and fellow painters toiling under him, they did color grinding, plastering, cementing, and tracing by dusting charcoal through little holes made by a tracing wheel on the paper on which Diego had drawn his sketch for the next day's wet plaster and cement mixture. They performed many other ancillary tasks, but Diego did all the painting on these and on the future frescoes in Cuernavaca, the National Palace, the Detroit Institute of Arts, the Radio City mural destroyed on Nelson Rockefeller's order, the New Workers' School, the Palace of Fine Arts in Mexico City, and many smaller enterprises such as the Health Building in Mexico, the Hotel Reforma banquet hall, the San Francisco Stock Exchange, the Art Insitute of San Francisco, the murals now in the lobby of the library of the San Francisco City College, the Institute of Cardiology, the Hospital of the Race, the Lerma Canal, the façade of the Teatro de los Insurgentes, the outdoor encaustics of the Mexico City stadium, two panels in the Trotskyite International Workers School, some wood carvings in Chapingo, some stained glass windows in the Health Building, and no doubt a few more that I have omitted. Indeed, Diego was a monster of nature, a tireless giant, a prodigy of fecundity, rapidity, and prodigality of creation, a painter with an insatiable appetite for walls, for themes, and for paper and canvas as well. Such sheer fecundity occurs but rarely in the history of man. He is for painting and drawing what a Lope de Vega is for drama. Such men, by the ease and volume and massiveness of their work, and by the excellence of so large a part of it, enlarge one's faith in the capacity of man.

A word should be said at this point about Diego's Communism and the propaganda in his painting. Both Diego and Picasso wished to be considered Communist painters, but there is little of real propaganda in Diego's work (or in Picasso's; unless we consider some of his early paintings sympathetic toward the poor; a sympathy which the Communists in power have not shown; there is nothing of Communism in Picasso's work). Their adherence to Communism was used as the occasional utterances of Linus Pauling have been used by the Communists because they are celebrities. Only because they remained outside the walls of the Communist-controlled totalitarian lands were Rivera and Picasso able to paint in such un-Communist fashion and create according to their own vision, which is the chief moral imperative of the artist. As I have already said, Rivera resigned once from the Central Committee of the Mexican Communist party because I persuaded him to, a delicate matter; and I did that because I thought that his overpowering imagination, and love of inventing tall tales with full supporting details, was leading the other Central Committee Members into a false vision of the realities of Mexican life. When I was deported, Diego immediately rejoined the party, only to be expelled two years later because Stalin had ordered every party to find and extirpate the "Right-Danger" and in Mexico he was tagged as "IT." To find a less ridiculous reason for being expelled, he became a Trotskyite, and from then on was under fire from the Communists until in his last years he made his peace with the party (and at the same time with the Catholic Church).* When he came to New York in 1929, the Communist drumfire against him was at its height.

Both Rivera and Picasso loved freedom and took for granted the freedom to follow their vision. They never dreamt that in the modern world direct censorship of painting was possible. But in the new Russia, to censorship by the powerful has been added total ownership and total control of all museums, all galleries, all institutions that might commission, purchase, or display one's painting. One can hide an occasional manuscript for posterity, but who can hide a stack of paintings or find a public wall? While Diego was in the Soviet Union on Lunacharsky's invitation, he could not find a wall on which to paint according to his vision, or get approval of that vision. In one of his articles on his credo in the realm of art he wrote in a Soviet journal:

> The workman, ever burdened with his daily labor, could cultivate his taste only in contact with the worst and vilest part of bourgeois art which reached him in cheap chromos and illustrated journals. This bad taste in turn stamps all the industrial products which his salary commands. . . . Popular art produced for the people has

* On this, see Chapter 33 of my ***Fabulous Life of Diego Rivera,*** entitled "Both Moscow and Rome."

been almost wiped out by an industrial product of the worst esthetic quality. . . . Only the work of art itself can raise the standard of taste. . . .

Needless to say, the censor's irate pencil cut this out and even suppressed whole articles, which he had to publish later in the *Workers' Age* or in an American art journal.

As for Picasso, who was not as concerned as Diego was with painting for the people, he lost his temper when a friend reminded him after one of his pro-Communist gestures of the fate of painters such as he in the Soviet Union. Then, growing thoughtful, he said for quotation:

If they threw me into jail, I would sever an artery in my arm, and on the floor of my cell, with my last drop of blood, I would paint one more Picasso.

Needless to say, this too was not printed in the Soviet Union.

What then induces a Picasso or a Rivera, or for that matter, a Siqueiros, to serve the party which, if it takes power in his country, would make some servile and philistine censor the arbiter of his painting? To this question Karl Marx has no answer, nor has Lenin, nor Stalin, nor Khrushchev, nor Brezhnev, nor Mao Tse-tung. Perhaps Freud does, though: he called it the death wish.

Diego strove to be a Communist painter, but there is something gentle and deeply affectionate in his painting of the humble and the lowly or even in the scenes of exploitation of the laborer. Often he resorts to a bit of text, a scroll held in the hand of one of his figures, to say what his painting does not say otherwise. Thus he paints a miner, strong and powerful and good to look at, entering into a mine. Nearby, another miner climbs out wearily, utterly exhausted by his labor, being searched for gold with outstretched arms in the gesture of a crucifixion. On the mine shaft, Diego painted a little scroll with a verse by the Communist poet, Gutierrez Cruz:

Compañero minero,	Comrade miner,
doblegado bajo el peso de la tierra,	Bowed under the weight of earth,
tu mano yerra	Thy hand does wrong
cuando saca metal para el dinero.	When it digs metal to become money.
Haz puñales	Make daggers
con todos los metales,	Of all the metals,
y así,	And thou wilt see
verás que los metales	How after that all metals
después son para tí.	Are for thee.

On the right of this is a panel showing worker and peasant in a fraternal embrace, a painting which has some of the strength and tenderness of the Italian primitives. And on the left is the fresco of a *trapiche,* a factory in which sugar is melted and refined. It conveys some notion of the rhythmic dance of the labor of the sugar workers as they grind the curved cane stalks, pour the juice, and stir it in the vats. Work here, far from exhausting toil, is a rhythmic dance, Diego's dogmas as a Communist giving ground to his vision as a painter, with results that are in proportion as propagandistically weak as they are plastically strong.

Indeed, as we go through the vast body of wall painting by Rivera, it is hard to think of any passages of real anger and hatred. One finds neither the bombastic rhetoric so frequent in Siqueiros's social painting, nor the prophetic and furious denunciation which at times moves Orozco. Rivera was not born to be a Savónarola in paint as Orozco was, nor a strident soap-boxer like Siqueiros.

"I say we have had enough of pretty pictures of grinning peons in Tehuana dress," Siqueiros told the press in his last attack on Rivera less than two years before the latter's death. "I say, to hell with ox carts—let's see more tractors and bulldozers. Mexican art suffers from primitivism and archaeologism."

But the weakest passages in Rivera's painting (for example, his panel on *The Future* in the National Palace) are precisely his tractors and bulldozers. Nor have tractors and bulldozers yielded any plastic beauty or expressiveness in the work of Siqueiros, nor those of Orozco and Tamayo. As for Rivera, the tenderest and most lyrical sections of his work are those inspired by the love of his people, by the beauty of the Mexican landscape, and by the life of the Mexican folk, a life which, for all its misery and poverty, is the expression of a civilization more passionate and esthetic than rational. In his weavers and fishermen, in invaders, climbing down the curved branches of trees and vines, led to a secret hideout by a traitor, is neither the cruelty and brutality of war nor exploitation but the arabesque or a plastic dance. In the awkward grace of his Mexican children and the simple, elegant, abstracted curve of the back of one of his burden bearers, it is not poverty and the frightful load of the burden that we see, but the tenderness of the vision of a painter who loved his country and his people. The world he truly idealized was not the grim world referred to in *The Future* panel, but the poetic world of pre-Conquest civilization as seen by his fantasy. The colors of that world are brighter, the forms more solid, the air flooded with a brighter light. Here is joy and beauty in labor, preternatural skill in primitive surgery and science, plastic and hieratic splendor in the ceremonies of human sacrifice. The terrifyingly beautiful and monstrous gods and temples are free from the feeling of terror, and full of splendor. What can tractor and bulldozer and belt conveyor offer to compete with this vision? Or with the grace and beauty which Rivera sees in the disinherited descendants of this splendid people, the simple Indians and Indian children whom Rivera portrays with such tenderness and affection, and in whose name he claims the lost inheritance? The love and glory of this legend are missing when he comes to the United States.

DIEGO TRIES TO PAINT THE ART OF A CONTINENT

Mexico was to Rivera the homeground, the base of a triangle that encompassed his dreams of contributing through his work to the understanding of the life of his time. Toward Mexico he was drawn by birth, nurture, sensibility, by the compelling voice of natural and plastic beauty, by the wonders real and imagined of its pre-Conquest life and legend, and by the promise of the latest Mexican Revolution.

Russia was, he thought, the model land of social transformation. He had dreamed that he could paint for it, and by painting there, possibly fructify its art and enrich his own. That dream had ended in a rude awakening; the Comintern's hosannas of praise and acclamation in many tongues had suddenly transformed themselves into blasts of insult and denigration. All the Communist painters had been asking for walls in government buildings, but now they denounced him as a painter of palaces (the National Palace whose walls are seen by millions of Mexicans every year) and a painter for millionaires, because Dwight Morrow had paid, not too well, for his magnificent murals of the Conquest on the outside walls of the Palace of Cortés.

> It is a hard test for any painting—wrote the sensitive critic Philip Youtz, in the *Bulletin of the Pennsylvania Museum of Art*—to be set as a rival to Nature herself. . . . The painted landscape which is the background for the figures in the story of the Conquest of Mexico has to stand against the real landscape which is one of the most striking in the world. The result . . . proves that man too can create a world.

Thus it was that Rivera was accustomed to match his frescoes to the architecture of the building, to the surrounding scene, and the meaning of the building or the uses to which it was to be put. But when he got to California, and after that Detroit, and then New York, this marvellous faculty largely escaped him, for he was in an alien land which he admired and respected but hardly understood.

DIEGO'S APPRECIATION OF THE UNITED STATES

Above all it was as an artist that the United States attracted Diego. New York's skyscrapers, first glimpsed from New York Harbor when he was bound for Russia, seemed to him amazing monuments to man's audacious powers of construction, and works of incomparable beauty. Later, when I took auto rides with him through the city, its steel bridges and express highways were to him works of enchantment. The nonstop highways, the smooth ribbon of road, the clean-lined cut-offs, the stone overpasses, with evidence of human intelligence in every detail of their design, held his bulging eyes spellbound, with scarcely a glance at the mere smidgins of nature that were left standing at the sides or factitiously set up by way of restoration. "Your engineers are your great artists," he told me. "These highways are the most beautiful thing I have seen in your beautiful country. In all the constructions of man's past—pyramids, Roman roads and aqueducts, cathedrals and palaces, there is nothing to equal these. Out of them and the machine will come the style of tomorrow." And on another occasion: "Now I understand why painters like Morse and Fulton directed their genius chiefly into mechanical construction. While some architects are stupidly copying what the ancients did better in accord with the needs of their own time, the best architects of our age are finding their esthetic and functional inspiration in American industrial buildings, machine design, and engineering, the greatest expressions of the plastic genius of this new world." To be sure, Fulton and Morse were both painters of sorts as well as inventors and were therefore, to Diego's perfervid imagination, Yankee prototypes of Leonardo da Vinci. When Diego sailed into New York Harbor from California on a foggy, wintry morning in December, 1931, and saw a red sun rising over the Brooklyn Bridge, he told an astonished reporter: "Here it is—the might, the power, the energy, the sadness, the glory, the youthfulness of our lands." In a free union of the esthetics and the world views of the two Americas, the industrial workers of the north and the peasants of the south, the factories of the United States with the raw materials of Latin America, the utilitarian and functional aesthetics of the machine with the innate plastic sense of the Amerindian peoples, the mating of the style which glass and concrete and steel were even then engendering with the spirit of the forms that pre-Conquest Mexican, Central American, Peruvian, and Colombian art had begotten, he foresaw the dawn of new splendors for the continent. And when he started his American journey in California, the first ambitious mural he undertook was a serious, if not altogether successful, attempt to paint precisely this larger theme.

FROM CALIFORNIA TO NEW YORK BY FORD

It was through California, not New York, that Diego invaded *Yanquilandia* to paint his dream of the unity of the two Americas. William Gerstle, president of the San Francisco Art Commission, Ralph Stackpole, the sculptor, Timothy Pfleuger, architect of the new Stock Exchange, and Albert Bender, insurance broker and generous patron of the arts, were the principal Californians who persuaded the exiguous world of San Francisco art patrons to get together the money for the trip and some modest mural painting projects. But when Diego tried to secure a permit to reside for six months in the United States and engage in the subversive art of beautifying some of the public walls of San Francisco, this painter "for millionaires and palaces, and agent of American imperialism," as the Communist parties of Mexico and the United States were calling him, was refused permission to visit our country!

This, as the reader has gathered by now, is one aspect of our immigration laws which I have never understood: the trembling fear of our great country that an artist, a writer, an invitee to a science seminar, or some other visiting intellectual can shake the foundations of our state through a brief residence among us. To refuse a passport for Charlie Chaplin can harm us far more, to put it mildly, than to be proud of his presence and rejoice at the tragic-comic gaiety of his films. Before we sweep away the debris of passports and visas, as I feel someday we will, we must attend as soon as possible to this damaging and senseless cowardice at having a distinguished artist or intellectual among us.

Be that as it may, the leaders of San Francisco intellectual society shared my view, and Albert Bender went to work finding out who was responsible for the disgraceful barring of an artist from his city. He found out that the original ban came from the State Department. Without raising a scandal as the Communist party would have preferred to do in similar cases, he got influential friends in the department to reconsider the matter. Then he advised Diego, "I think you can come through to California whenever you are ready." Diego came, lectured, wrote, painted, trained other painters as apprentices, left behind him some good portraits, some frescoes that are not among his best, was the center of some splendid controversies, stirred the art world, thereby putting greater life into it, gave our artists much in technique and example, sowed disciples in three of our cities and to a lesser extent throughout the land, gave our critics food for thought, then left for his native land once more without shaking our republic to its foundations, or making any perceptible record on the Richter scale of earthquakes.

When Diego arrived in San Francisco, all sorts of ultra-Americanists and native painters let loose a barrage on him and on the Stock Exchange for having hired a foreign painter, a Communist, an artist who had "carried simplicity to the point of naiveté, almost childishness." The *San Francisco Chronicle* did a montage of the stairway of the Stock Exchange Luncheon Club where he was supposed to paint, placing his *Night of the Rich* on the wall showing Rockefeller, Morgan, and Henry Ford dining on ticker tape with a Mexican capitalist (from his frescoes in the Secretariat of Education)! The *Chronicle* entitled it *The Kiss of Judas.*

At this moment Diego had the good sense to send for his divorced wife, Frida Kahlo, on the pretext that her endless succession of skeletal ailments following an auto accident which broke her pelvis in three places, could only be properly diagnosed and treated by Dr. Eloesser of San Francisco.

DIEGO CALLS FOR REINFORCEMENTS

At this point a digression is in order. Diego first got to know Frida Kahlo as a mop-haired nuisance at the *Preparatoria*, where he was painting his first wall, an encaustic, in the auditorium. She was thirteen then, a bright but neglectful student, a madcap tomboy, the ringleader of a gang of mischievous youngsters that kept the halls of the Preparatoria in turmoil: unpopular professors were drowned in waves of noise; air-filled paper bags burst in the corridors; bags of water dropped mysteriously over partitions; a home-made bomb exploded in a reverberating hall. Always the provosts would come too late to lay their hands on the disappearing ringleader, Frida. She possessed then an almost boyish beauty with bright, audacious eyes, long-lashed under thick black eyebrows, coming from a mixture of German-Jewish (her father) and Mexican blood. Her favorite companions were newsboys on the sidewalks of the city, from whom she acquired a store of street-Arab wisdom and the raciest and richest vocabulary of obscenities I have ever known anyone of her sex to possess. When she had spent a little time in the United States she got to possess an equal English vocabulary and a marvelous repertoire of comic and ribald songs.

As soon as Frida set eyes on the huge painter who had installed himself in the auditorium, she made him a butt of her pranks. She soaped the stairway he was to descend, then hopefully hid herself behind a pillar. The slow, heavy-footed, work-weary painter didn't slip. She felt compensated only in part when the rector fell down the stage stairs at assembly next morning. When the director of the Preparatoria, Lombardo Toledano, expelled her, Vasconcelos told him, "If you can't manage a little girl like that, you are not fit to be director of such an institution." She was reinstated.

Some time after finishing school, Frida met with a frightful auto accident. When Dr. Eloesser examined the x-rays of her triply fractured pelvis, and her foot and toe operations, he found it difficult to believe that they belonged to the living and laughing girl that stood before him. For an entire year after the accident her doctors had not known whether she would ever walk again. The once irrepressible Frida lay flat on her back strapped to a board and encased in a plaster cast. During this time she underwent a profound metamorphosis in character. In her boredom she called for paints, brushes, and an easel stand within reach of her arms, which alone were free to move. Like most Mexican children, and no doubt more than most, she had a sense of form and color plus a wayward imagination all her own. Out of the trying ordeal she became an artist. When she was able to walk at last, she remembered the fat painter with the frog-face she had used to tease. He was painting now on the top floor of the Secretariat of Education. "*Oiga Diego, baje usted,*" she cried. He did not remember the hoyden in this slightly bashful eighteen-year-old girl, but he came down from his scaffold. From behind her back she drew forth a little square of canvas, asking him for "an honest opinion and no compliments."

The painter's eyes flashed in recognition of talent. "Keep it up, little girl," he said. "It's good, except the background, which is too much Dr. Atl. Have you any more?"

"Sí, señor, but it is hard for me to carry them here. I live in Coyoacán, Calle de Londres 127. Would you call on me next Sunday?"

"I'd be delighted." Frida had once told a group of girl students discussing their "ambitions," "my ambition is to have a child by Diego Rivera. And I'm going to tell him so, some day." In time, after a perilous miscarriage in Detroit, followed by a compulsory abortion in Mexico—her broken pelvis was not adequate to bear a child—her girlhood desire was to become an obsession which she expressed in several of her paintings. In the fall of 1938 I was to carry some of those paintings with me on an old Ward Line ship to New York, for a one-man show of her work. At the Customs House an inspector informed me that two of her moving works dealing with this theme, one of them showing a skeleton lying on the canopy over her bed, with her below, both strewn with flowers, were pornographic, and could not be admitted into the United States. I asked to see the top customs official, who on the spot ruled that all her paintings were "a little strange, but genuine works of art," and as such they were admitted duty free. I felt proud of the Chief Customs Inspector of the Port of New York for his ability to recognize genuine works of art when he saw them, particularly since they were the work of Frida Kahlo, who, from the outset of her efforts, proved to be a truly great painter. For whatever reason, the Society for the Suppression of Vice never denounced her one-man show, which astonished the New York art critics, giving her an immediate reputation. I reviewed the show and interviewed Frida for the October, 1938, issue of *Vogue*, where it was published under the title, "The Rise of a New Rivera."

When Diego went to Russia in 1928, his then wife, Guadalupe Marín broke with Diego, charging that he had gone to live permanently in Moscow to avoid supporting her and the two daughters he had begotten with her. On his return, after a year of random affairs, he married Frida, although her father, old man Kahlo, a German photographer, had warned him, "Frida is a clever girl, but she is a *demonio oculto*—a concealed devil." "I know it," said Diego, and with that their engagement was sealed. Unlike the other women in his life, three of whom might be counted as wives, Guadalupe being so by a church wedding, Frida played the role of companion, friend, confidante, comrade, and critic, in which last role he respected her as he did no other critic who had tried to give him suggestions or advice.

For obvious reasons (her crippled state always concealed by the magnificent wide-sweeping Mexican costumes she wore), Diego never painted a nude of Frida. But when he was painting in the Health Building, she persuaded her own sister to pose in the nude. The result was an affair, reluctant on her sister's part, that caused Frida bitter anguish, unlike the casual way in which she had taken all the other affairs of Diego. A lonely, miserable time followed for both. Frida moved into a room in another part of the city, raged and wept and nursed her grief in secret, became too restless to paint, left suddenly for New York where she told her grief to my wife and me as her most intimate friends there, and vainly tried to get "even" by having "affairs" of her own.

In an earlier book on Rivera's life I had written, "In the tenth year of their marriage (I should have said seventh) Diego grows more and more dependent upon his wife's judgment and comradeship. If he should lose her now, the solitude which besets him (the party campaign against him had reached its height) would be much heavier than it is."

Shortly after the book appeared, Diego secured a divorce from Frida and with pretended gaiety gave a large party to celebrate it. To one of my best friends whom he had invited, Diego said loudly, for all to hear, "Martin, tell Bert that I have divorced Frida to prove that my biographer was wrong."

A year passed, a year of personal unhappiness for both of them. When he got to San Francisco he wrote a letter to Frida urging her to come to have her orthopedic ailments treated by Dr. Eloesser.

Frida for her part wrote a moving letter to him, beginning by making fun of all the lady admirers who were wooing him by posing or by climbing the scaffold to exclaim as they watched him paint. They were nothing to her—"mere flirtations, that have only made me understand in the end that I love you more than my own skin."

With this wise, brave letter, Frida reconciled herself both with Diego and with her younger sister whose protective guardian she was. Thus prompted, Diego remarried Frida Kahlo on his fifty-fourth birthday. When I telegraphed my congratulations, I could not resist the impulse to ask whether he had remarried Frida to prove that his biographer was right? And he was right, for they remained close to each other and inseparable until the day of her death. But at this point it is only necessary to say that with Diego and Frida together, all the hostile criticism against hiring a "foreign painter" to paint San Francisco's walls died down. As a pair, they were irresistible and took the city by storm.

Diego and Frida fell completely in love with San Francisco on their second honeymoon, and California fell in love with this novel pair. While Diego was painting there, Dr. W. R. Valentiner and Edgar P. Richardson went to San Francisco from Detroit to see what all the excitement in art circles was about. Valentiner was the director of the Detroit Institute of Arts of which Edsel Ford was patron and chairman of the board. Moreover, Edsel Ford was also a member of the board of directors of the Museum of Modern Art in New York, so that an invitation to paint the walls of the Garden Court of the Detroit Institute of Arts might also involve a chance to paint some important walls in the financial capital of the United States.

But Diego had his problems with Detroit. Its people were not so universally tolerant as those of San Francisco. The Garden Court of the Museum was singualarly inappropriate for the realization of his dream to paint, in the auto capital of the world, the art of the conveyor belt, the machine, and the worker working in series, for the courtyard was decorated, if that's the word for it, in a rather crude imitation Italian baroque, broken at frequent intervals by little windows and ventilators framed in wavy molding, by pilasters, by heads of satyrs in rounded relief, by strips of cross moldings, and by doorways, while in the midst of the Garden Court was a fountain which Diego described to me as *horrorosa*. The decoration cost him many a headache and many a fit of fury. Always Diego had done his best to make his frescoes harmonize with the architecture of the building of which they were to form an integral part, the building's uses, and the life of the city or region in the midst of which it was located. Only if architect and painter got together before the building began could conflict be totally avoided; but this time the gap was unbridgeable between Italy and the age of American imitation baroque, rather crude at that, and the age of the machine at its most modern. In the end Diego decided to sacrifice the architectural "decoration," which he considered false to the spirit of the city, and to regard the city's spirit as his "architectural" guide. Though Edsel Ford's contribution to pay the painter was not munificent, Diego seized on more and more of the walls. He would have painted the ceiling, too, if it had not been of glass and had to be left open to admit light. With the cunning of which he was master, he set to work to subordinate and assimilate the decoration to his painting in such fashion that the stone trim would be overwhelmed and seem to disappear into the painted wall. Even so, although this work, when considered as painting, and as painting inspired by machinery and modern industry, is probably the best that he did in the United States, his battle with the decoration and the architecture is not altogether successful. But since the decoration is only surface ornament, it might easily be removed and the walls simplified thereby to greater harmony with the imposing painting. Perhaps some day a bold museum curator may have the courage to do so. But I am afraid that nothing can rescue the added painting of figures and hands that he did just under the ceiling, for their incongruity is a failure of the painter, not the architect.

But it was not the incongruity of the second grade Italian baroque with the most magnificent machinery that industrial man had so far invented that made Diego a center of controversy in Detroit. He had spent three excited months wandering through miles of machinery, making sketches in the Ford, Chrysler, Michigan Alkali, Edison, Parke-Davis, and many other plants before he so much as erected his scaffold. As a man may turn over half a library to make a book, and a novelist half a town to make a character, so Diego went through all of Detroit's industrial plants to paint one single panel of the twenty-seven which were to make the plastic unity of man and machine, and through this unity give man dominion over nature, to which he had through so many ages been subservient. Putting aside the inappropriate decor and the spaces above that Diego filled with allegorical nude figures of which no one could comprehend the allegory, the panels that paint the wave that runs through electrons, mountains, water, the machine, the conveyor, man's labor, life and death and sound and light and power are well organized and successfully rendered on Detroit's museum walls. Indeed, some of his turbines possess more beauty and more of an erotic quality than his nudes in Chapingo and the Health Building in Mexico.*

Diego's trouble began when he went to Parke-Davis and beheld the orderliness, cleanliness, beauty, and instrumental magic of the laboratories of these modern alchemists, the biological-chemical experimenters. He decided to paint a panel dedicated to vaccines, and of course he found an extra panel of wall on which to do it. It was what in writing would be called a set piece. The center is a child, being tenderly held by a nurse and gently vaccinated by a doctor. The nurse has a "halo" in the form of a white cap, and the child another in the form of golden hair or a baby bonnet. In front of them are gentle-faced animals, a horse, some sheep, and a cow, from which material for vaccines is taken, while behind child, nurse, and doctor are three experimenters, working in a laboratory with microscope, flask, and retort. It was instantly obvious to the beholder that this was a modern version of the Holy Family, with animals in the "barnyard," and the three Magi bearing the gifts of science.**

For more than a year the painter labored, compressing acres of machinery into a few hundred square feet of wall, yet making them true to their form and function and movement. Mechanism was to Diego what it had been to Leonardo and not many painters in between. But all was covered with red drapes. "The work in material, manner, and enormity," wrote an art critic of the *Detroit Sunday Times,* "is beyond the conception of the people outside the red drapes. When they see it, it will hit them like a bolt." And so indeed it did.

On March 13, 1933, when the paintings were officially unveiled, people looked in vain for the statuesque female in classic drapes holding a tiny automobile in one hand and a torch of light in the other. Instead they saw "the spirit of Detroit" at work—in laboratories, sputtering flames from welding torches, writhing through the waves of belt conveyors, bending muscular and absorbed over shapes of silvery steel being shaped into auto bodies, peering through light masks, toiling in overalls, making motors that vaguely suggested flowers and clean-lined, glistening metal planes poised for flight. Nowhere was pomp and luxury, nowhere hollow allegory, only working men and women, engineers, and chemists, while even Edsel Ford, donor of the fresco to the Museum, appears in it only to be put to work on the design of an automobile.

Anathema was not slow to descend upon painter and painting. Churchmen and busybodies who had never concerned themselves with painting,

* See Plate 117 in *The Fabulous Life of Diego Rivera.*

** See Plate 116 in *The Fabulous Life of Diego Rivera.*

formed mutual-excitation societies to secure the removal of the "Holy Family" or "Vaccination" panel. One wonders as one gazes at this beautiful and tender work, redolent of early Italian painting, how anyone could regard it as blasphemy and seek its destruction. Or how the same people could have missed the more mischievous allusion to the "temptation of Saint Anthony" in the depiction of the manager of a chemical factory trying to concentrate on adding machine tapes and accounts while surrounded by the exposed knees and calves of girls working around him.

Eight days after the unveiling of the painting there was a meeting, in the office of the then curate of St. Paul's Episcopal Cathedral, of people representing several points of view but all agreeing to unite to crystallize sentiment for the removal of the murals. Councilman Bradley submitted in the council a motion to have the walls whitewashed, calling them "a travesty on the spirit of Detroit, completely ignoring the cultural and spiritual aspects of the city." To defend the frescoes, committees were set up. One was headed by Fred L. Black, President of the People's Museum Association; another was made up of Detroit labor and radical organizations.

The Museum issued a strong defense of the paintings, and, thanks in part to the controversy, clocked the greatest number of persons the Museum had ever had attending an exhibition. Dr. Valentiner pronounced the vaccination "a finely executed, rationalistic interpretation of the beautiful legend of the Holy Family." When the *Detroit News* declared editorially that the entire work should be whitewashed from the walls, the art critic, Walter Pach, wired from New York: "If these paintings are whitewashed, nothing can ever be done to whitewash America." The battle continued pro and con, enlarging the celebrity of the name of Diego Rivera. Edsel Ford chimed in with a rather feeble defense. Two years later Dr. Valentiner wrote Rivera, "Your murals are still the greatest attraction of Detroit." As I write these lines they are still on the walls, and the citizens of Detroit are eager to show them to visitors as one of the city's main attractions.

The art critic, Elie Faure, wrote Diego from Paris that "the machine has become the enemy here, all the writers, painters, and dramatists overwhelm it with bourgeois anathema. . . . Fear reigns. . . . You cannot know the pleasure I derive from seeing you use the machine as the motif of plastic emotion and decoration in your new frescoes which seem strongly beautiful to me, even though the color element which I so much admire in your work is lacking from the photographs. . . ."

Faure published a few photographs in art magazines with his commentary, then his whole letter to Diego as an article in *Art et Médicine.* His article concludes:

> The poetry of the machine which was born in the frescoes of Mexico and San Francisco dominates those of Detroit: flames escaping from drills, dazzling, crackling motors, silent and dancing rhythms of rods and pistons—all these beat the

cadences of a new march—the rehearsals of a still hesitant humanity. You see the witchery . . . of illuminating arcs over the ocean, Babel towers above the cities—from now on all this becomes a part of our inner being, and woe to those who do not feel it. The hate which you see is really love. Once more man attempts to understand man in the midst of force itself—these are the new themes. . . . Mexico can well be proud of her great painters who can give expression to this new age.

Publicity and controversy in Detroit, praise in Paris—that was all Diego needed for his continued storming of America. In Paris he had learned that publicity and controversy attract attention, purchasers, and patrons to one's painting. He had consciously or unwittingly occasioned ample controversy in his native land. But he had never foreseen how the American press could keep a controversial celebrity almost continuously on the front page, until millions who had never looked closely at a picture except on a calendar or in the "funnies" could convince themselves that they cared about a celebrated and controversial painter, cared whether his paintings stayed on, or were whitewashed off, a wall, had acquired a desire to see the painter in the flesh, to watch him paint, and even to contemplate or ponder his paintings. Of course, all this hullabaloo immediately got him an invitation to paint a "machinery and industry" mural at the Chicago World's Fair which had christened itself "a Century of Progress."

And from New York came word, together with a woman who was an art agent, art dealer, and art adviser to the Rockefellers, Frances Flynn Payne, that the moguls of the art world in the nation's financial capital were getting interested in arranging for Diego to paint a wall in Rockefeller Center, then under construction. To have the Rockefellers in New York, the Fords in Detroit, the Chicago World's Fair—probably in the General Motors Building—as his patrons, with the readiness to have him paint not in their private homes but on walls so accessible to the masses, while Moscow would not give him a wall. Had Michaelangelo, "pricked on by your popes and kings" been more favored?

35

THE BATTLE OF ROCKEFELLER CENTER

The theme offered to Diego for painting on the wall of the elevator bank facing the main entrance to the new RCA Building in Radio City was: *Man at the Crossroads Looking with Hope and High Vision to the Choosing of a New and Better Future.* It was a theme to make many a painter quail but it seemed made to order for Diego. Moreover, it was not of Diego's choosing but was proposed to him by Nelson Rockefeller, director of construction of the complex of buildings to be known as Rockefeller Center. The agreement, between one of the world's most celebrated painters and the scion of one of the world's richest financial dynasties to give the people of New York a public wall with such a theme painted on it, was the result of protracted and precarious negotiations with an impressive conclave of members from the world of finance, and some of their advisers and contacts from the world of art and culture. As early as December 9, 1930, the home of John D. Rockefeller, Jr. was the scene of the first meeting of this unusual Sanhedrin. Everyone present was supposed to know something of art, something of cultural relations, and something of financing them. They had come together to form an organization that would "promote friendship between the people of Mexico and the United States by encouraging cultural relations and the interchange of fine and applied arts." Just to get this unusual gathering together, John D. Rockefeller, Jr. had set up a promotion fund of $15,000, and Mrs. Frances Flynn Payne, adviser to the Rockefellers on art, had devoted six months of preliminary work. Diego Rivera had already been chosen, at least in the mind of Nelson Rockefeller, to be the connecting link between this group and Latin America. At its first meeting, the group christened itself the Mexican Arts Association, and to guarantee the limited liability of all the wealthy men present, arranged for its formal incorporation. Winthrop Aldrich, brother of Mrs. John D. Rockefeller, was elected president, Mrs. Emily Johnson De Forest, wife of the president of the Metropolitan Museum of Art, honorary president, and Frank Crowninshield, editor and publisher of *Vogue* and a trustee of the Museum of Modern Art, secretary. Mr. Aldrich was empowered to name all other officers, there being quite a list of the elite of finance, museology, and art patronage present to select from. The board of directors included: Mrs. Abby Rockefeller, W. W. Aldrich, Mrs. Elizabeth Morrow, the director of the Guggenheim Foundation, Henry Allen Moe, Mrs. Emily De Forest, Frank Crowninshield, Mrs. Frances Flynn Payne, and a number of other members of relevant sections of the American elite. The inquisitive reader can find a more complete list in this author's *The Fabulous Life of Diego Rivera.*

Although Nelson Rockefeller and his family had homes, land and oil wells in a number of Latin American countries, they decided to select Mexico as their first land of esthetic interest, and Diego Rivera as suitable for their first venture. He was a central figure of the much written about Mexican mural renaissance, and of a number of controversies that had made headlines in the American press, normally so little used to headline affairs of art. His was a name that would bring their venture wide publicity. Diego was still painting, on his vast walls in the National Palace court, his ambitious attempt to picture the Mexico of *yesterday* (pre-Conquest), *today* (from the Conquest through Independence to the age of Calles), and *tomorrow* (a stuffy Karl Marx pointing at a landscape of factories and a planetarium), and he was already dreaming of Detroit and a better version of the art of the age of the machine. He was surprised at this time, to receive a visit from Mrs. Frances Flynn Payne. He accepted with pleasure her offer to help sell his paintings at a good price, and a fair commission for her, in the United States, and to arrange a one-man retrospective show of his work in the Museum of Modern Art in New York. It was a step toward publicizing the new Mexican Art Association that had just been formed in the home of John D. Rockefeller, Jr., and it gave Nelson Rockefeller a chance to see what Diego Rivera would do in Detroit, and how he would get along with the Ford family there, before making him an offer of a stairway wall to paint in the main entrance to the main building in Rockefeller Center.

Diego joyfully accepted Mrs. Payne's invitation. And well he might, for more than he understood, the doors of America's financial and art centers were being opened to him. He applied for a leave of absence from his painting on the National Palace stairway. When finally he got it in November, he took the *Morro Castle* of the Ward Line to New York, with some painters' materials but without a painting in his hand or in his baggage, to present a one-man retrospective show in New York in the Museum of Modern Art.

Yet he did not arrive in New York Harbor empty-handed, for Captain Wilmot of the *Morro Castle*, as soon as he discovered what sort of passenger he had on board, fixed up for him a temporary studio on the (as I know from experience) rocking boat, and let Diego paint to his heart's content from before sunrise until 8 bells at midnight, or whenever he stumbled into his bunk, asleep from exhaustion. He made some sea sketches and paintings, but his major work was a number of movable frescoes in steel frames on full plaster and cement, backed by wood and chicken wire, each panel reproducing one of his Mexican murals and each of them weighing approximately 300 pounds. The best and most lyrical was a reproduction of his famous painting of a gentle-faced Emiliano Zapata leading a spirited, beautiful white horse, followed by members of his guerrilla band armed with what looked like hoes that had been tooled into battle axes. This reproduction, painted on board ship and exhibited by the Museum of Modern Art, which owns it, has been reproduced in full color by Alfred Barr in *Masters of Modern Art* (New York, 1945).

As soon as he landed in New York, Diego continued painting in a studio provided by the Museum in the Heckscher Building, then the home of the Museum of Modern Art. On the *Morro Castle* and in the large studio later provided, he completed in the brief space of a month and ten days, seven of the 300-pound movable frescoes, each six by eight feet in painted surface. "They are movable," he explained to reporters, "because in ancient days wall paintings lasted as long as the Cathedrals whose story they illustrated, but yours is a land where buildings do not live long; you keep tearing them down and building new ones in their place. Good frescoes should live longer than your buildings." Four of Diego's frescoes which he had completed on the boat were reproductions of details from those Mexican murals of his which pleased him most, and three were impressions of New York. In addition to that stupendous labor, he did a number of watercolors and sketches.

In the meanwhile, the Museum staff did a heroic job of assembling and borrowing works of Rivera wherever they could find them. By Christmas Eve (or to be more precise, December 23rd) the painter and the Museum had put together some 150 items: the seven frescoes; 56 oils and encaustics; 25 water-colors; and a number of drawings, sketches, and studies for frescoes. It was not the whole Diego—what show or book could embrace the massive whole of his creativity? Yet it was sufficient to give some notion of the nature of the painter and his development up to that moment. Messrs. Barr and Abbott produced an excellent catalogue to supplement the show.

For the most part the critics were warm in their praise of an art to which they were not altogether accustomed, although increasing pilgrimages to Mexico had familiarized many of them with the frescoes seen in actual scale on actual walls and with the background of Mexican life from pre-Conquest to the present day that were reflected in the paintings.

Only Diego's impressions of New York aroused controversy. Diego had done three such paintings, called *Electric Welding, Pneumatic Drilling,* and *Frozen Assets.* They were intended to show New York at work and New York in the midst of the Great Depression. The welders and the drillers were protectively masked—no faces! The drilling showed the drill bits dancing, wraiths of dust rising and curling round the workers, the men's garments curving round their muscles in lines emphasizing the rhythm of the drills, and one could almost hear the racket, the silence being due only to the fact that talkie paintings had not yet been invented.

This was not a New York to make the critics comfortable, for "surely the city had more beautiful scenes, and things, and people to paint." It was the *Frozen Assets* that they found most unattractive, always of course in esthetic terms. Diego had painted the city on three levels: at the base, a well-guarded bank vault with immobilized wealth; in the middle a municipal lodging house which Diego had visited, with men lying on the floor like corpses in a morgue; and crowning the whole, New York's skyline, the immobilized skyscrapers like monuments on a tomb of business activity that had died away.

This was the beginning of the third year of our Great Depression, and Americans were very touchy. It was impolite, even a little alarming, for an invited guest to have snapped the host when he was not dressed for a picture. What might be paint when he got to know America better? Some critics now had sober second thoughts about the frescoes they had praised. They admitted in their accustomed esthetic vocabulary that the frescoes were "closely contained . . . tonally rich . . . forcefully defined . . . significant and characteristic statements. . . ." Then came the *buts*, which narrowed down in the end to reservations about *Frozen Assets*. Here too the language was technical, but each stricture directly or indirectly betrayed the fact that the critic's unfavorable reaction was to that aspect of the painting which so many of them scorned to mention: its bitter truth and its social intention.

As usual with the controversies that circled around Diego's head, this one served only to increase the popular interest in his one-man show. In the first two weeks 31,625 persons paid admission. Before the show was over it outdid Matisse's record, and indeed broke all records in the Museum's brief history.

But there was nothing in this experience to alienate Nelson Rockefeller or put his associates in the Mexican Art Association on guard. By the early summer Rockefeller, through his architects, opened negotiations with Diego Rivera, as well as with Henri Matisse and Pablo Picasso. The written proposals from the construction engineers invited the three painters to enter into a "competition," the terms of which seemed designed to restrain these three turbulent spirits. They were to submit preliminary projects, for which they were to receive $300 each, for paintings in which no color was to be used, "only black, white, and gray." The mural itself was to be done on canvas, the painting was to cover no more than "from sixty to seventy percent of the canvas," the scale of the drawings was to be "8 foot, six inches for the human figure in the front plane." The instructions even stipulated that five coats of varnish were to cover the pigment. Clearly, Raymond Hood who headed the construction engineers and wrote the stipulations was of no mind to have bright, powerful paintings overwhelm the formal structure of the main entrance to his principal building. Visitors were to see the building, not the paintings. One would think that Nelson Rockefeller, heir of the great art collector, Abby Rockefeller, would have wanted just the opposite, else why try to engage the services of painters with such strong individual and personal styles? Otherwise housepainters who did the rest of the walls could have decorated the lobby, too, using stencils if necessary.

Matisse rejected the commission out of hand on the ground of its scale, theme, and character, which did not accord with his style. Picasso refused to receive the representative of the architects and did not so much as answer Raymond Hood's letter. Diego Rivera, too, rejected the proposal, in a letter written in French to Raymond Hood, from which I translate:

> I thank you. Ten years ago I would have accepted your kind invitation with pleasure. It would have helped me start. . . . But since then I have worked enough and am known enough to ask of each one who wants my work that he ask for it on my worth. One can always ask me to make a sketch and then take it or leave it, naturally, but no "competition"—I am beyond that point now.
>
> Permit me to tell you that I don't understand this way of dealing with me; especially when you and Mr. Nelson Rockefeller have had the amiability to indicate your interest in having my collaboration without previous solicitation on my part.

"Sorry you can't accept," telegraphed Raymond Hood tersely. But when Nelson Rockefeller saw Diego's letter he decided to accept Diego without competition.

Diego was eager to do something large and sensational on a wall highly visible to the people of the city, but when he heard that Frank Brangwyn and José María Sert, an Englishman and a Spaniard of minor talents, had been approached and had agreed to paint the walls flanking his in colorless colors, there was a fresh crisis. He did not mind so much the frippery that was being dispersed through many of the buildings of Rockefeller Center, but for his mural to be flanked by the work of two men for whose work he had contempt, was too much for him. Besides, he was not satisfied to paint without the vivid color that was one of the marks of his style, nor to do a mere canvas mural in place of a true fresco that could live as long as the building.

From May to October, 1932, the uneasy negotiations continued between him and Raymond Hood. Diego sought to convince Hood that he should use his natural colors instead of black, white, and gray, and that he should do a true fresco, without any increase in payment. He wrote huge tracts in French in an effort to give architect Hood an education in art. Here is a typical sample:

> Never have I believed that mural painting should have as its principal characteristic the conserving of the plane surface of the wall, for in that case the best mural would be a uniform coat of color. . . . Monumental painting does not have as its object ornamenting, but extending in time and space the life of the architecture. . . .
>
> We would accentuate the funereal feeling which is fatally aroused in the pub-

lic by the juxtaposition of black and white. . . . In the lower parts of a building one always has the feeling of a crypt. . . . Suppose some ill-disposed person should chance upon a nickname such as *Undertakers' Palace* . . .

Again and again, relations in these lengthy disputations between obstinate painter and obstinate architect were strained to the breaking point, but always Nelson Rockefeller would be there to head off the break, functioning as diplomat, friendly intervenor, executive vice-president of Rockefeller Center, Inc. and, without obtruding it too crassly, the real boss of the whole undertaking. Always he straightened things out, soothed Raymond Hood's feelings, and sustained Diego in his various demands as a painter. After all, he knew more about art and artists than Raymond Hood. It is not too easy for architect and painter to agree in the construction of a modernistic building, but the arbitrator between them was tactful as well as powerful, and Diego's arguments prevailed.

WHAT WAS DIEGO TO PAINT?

Diego mused over the theme that had been given him by one of the richest men in America: *Man at the Crossroads Looking with Hope and High Vision to the Choosing of a New and Better Future.* In engaging his services, Diego felt that they must have known what his vision of a "New and Better Future" would be. As if to reassure him that their tastes in art were superior to any possible prejudice against his social theme, or his vision of a "Better Future," several members of the Rockefeller family had been purchasing works of his. Thus, Mrs. John D. Rockefeller, Jr., daughter of the late Senator Nelson Aldrich, had included among her purchases his notebook of Russian sketches, a notebook of 45 sketches made on May Day, 1928, of Red Army cavalry, Red Army on trucks, in formation, on parade, all made when Diego was in Moscow, still in good standing, and expecting to paint murals in the Soviet Union for which these were preliminary sketches. The former Mary Todhunter Clark, at that time Nelson Rockefeller's wife and also a discriminating art collector, had purchased works of Diego Rivera on the basis of their artistic merit rather than their ideology, while Nelson Rockefeller himself had praised Rivera's Detroit murals and deplored the unenlightened controversy they had aroused. It was only after seeing Diego's "interpretation of Detroit industrial life" that Nelson Rockefeller had made his own offer and broached his theme.

While Diego was puzzling over the words, "Crossroads," and "Newer and Better Future," he received a second, lengthier set of instructions on the theme he was to paint. It said in part:

The philosophical or spiritual quality should dominate. . . . We want the paintings to make people pause and think and turn their minds inward and upward. . . . We hope these paintings may stimulate not only a material but above all a spiritual awakening. . . .

Our theme is NEW FRONTIERS.

To understand what we mean by "New Frontiers," look back over the development of the United States as a nation.

Today our frontiers are of a different kind. . . . Man cannot pass up his pressing problems by "moving on." He has to solve them on his own lot. The development of civilization is no longer lateral; it is inward and upward. It is the cultivation of man's soul and mind, the coming into a fuller comprehension of the meaning and mystery of life.

For the development of the paintings in this hallway, these frontiers are—

1. Man's new relation to Matter . . . and

2. Man's new relation to Man. That is man's new and more complete understanding of the real meaning of the Sermon on the Mount.

"More verbosity and less explicitness," thought Diego. "Clearly he wants more science in it, while he has reduced the 'New and Better Future' to the Sermon on the Mount. Well, I can work with that, too." Diego felt that all this vagueness would be much harder for him to paint then the Mexico of the National Palace, the Palace of Cortés, and the Secretariat of Education. He set to work to give a preliminary verbal description of what he thought he would paint. In view of the smashup which was to end the whole enterprise, it is interesting to set down Diego's own first thoughts as he expressed them in a letter to Nelson Rockefeller, accompanied by preliminary sketches.

Diego cannily left it to Brangwyn "to depict the development of the ethical relations of mankind." "My painting," he added, "will show as the culmination of this evolution, human intelligence in possession of the Forces of Nature, expressed by the lightning striking off the hand of Jupiter and being transformed into useful electricity that helps to cure, . . . unites men through radio and television, and furnishes light and motive power. Below [this] the Man of Science presents the scale of Natural Evolution . . . which replaces the Superstitions of the past. This is the frontier of Ethical Evolution." (If Rockefeller wanted "NEW FRONTIERS," Diego would give them to him.)

So too Diego left the development of technical power to Sert (unconsciously he was planning the whole triptych by time of this letter!). "My panel," he continued, "will show the Workers arriving at a true understanding of their rights regarding the means of production, which has resulted in the planning of the liquidation of Tyranny, [which will be] personified by a crumbling statue of Caesar whose head has fallen to the ground. This is expressed by the placing of the hands of the producers in gesture of possession over a map of the world resting on sheaves of wheat supported by a dynamo . . . Machinery and Scientific Technique . . . This is the Frontier of Material Development.

"The main plastic function of the central panel is to express the axis of the building, its loftiness, and the ascending echelon of its lateral masses. For this, color will be employed in the center of the composition, merging laterally with the general *clair-obscur.*

"In the center, the telescope brings to the vision and understanding of man the most distant celestial bodies, and the microscope makes visible and comprehensible infinitesimal living organisms, connecting atoms and cells with the astral system. . . . Exactly in the median line the cosmic energy received by two antennae is conducted to the machinery controlled by the Worker. . . . The Worker gives his right hand to the Peasant who is questioning him, and with his left hand takes the hand of the wounded soldier, victim of war, leading him on the New Road.*

"Above the Worker, on the right side, the Cinema shows a group of young women engaged in health-giving sports, and on the left a group of unemployed workmen in a breadline. Above this . . . is an image of War. . . .

"In the center, Man is expressed in his triple aspect—the Peasant who develops from the Earth the products which are the origin of all the riches of mankind, the Worker who transforms and distributes the raw materials given by the Earth, and the Soldier who, under the Ethical Force that produces martyrs in religions and wars, represents Sacrifice. Man, represented by these three figures, looks with uncertainty but with high hope towards a more complete future balance between the Technical and Ethical development of Mankind necessary to a New, more Humane, and Logical Order."

Both Todd, head of the construction engineers (Todd, Robertson and Todd), and Raymond Hood who had fought Diego on the question of color, carefully read Diego's verbal description and studied the sketches accompanying it. "Enough said," wrote Todd. "We are all happy and looking forward with great confidence and assurance to your larger scale details and the finished result." And Raymond Hood, after going over the whole thing with Nelson Rockefeller, wired: "Sketch approved by Mr. Rockefeller. . . . Can go right ahead with larger scale." In March, 1933, Diego moved his scaffold and other apparatus into Radio City and began to paint.

The comparatively high fee of $21,000, though nothing to boast about considering that the space to be covered was 1,071 square feet and that Diego had to pay his own plasterers, pigment grinders, and other helpers, enabled him to hire a larger number of assistants than usual to speed up

* In view of the dispute that arose later as to what Nelson Rockefeller had accepted and what he had not, it is interesting to note that neither in his descriptive text nor in the accompanying sketch is there any suggestion on Diego's part that the worker-leader would be V. I. Lenin. In Diego's accompanying sketch the worker-leader joining the hands of worker, peasant, and soldier is a lay figure wearing a cap, which might in the end have the face of an American workingman or of Lenin. . . .

the work. The assistants were on the whole a radical lot, men and women that might be described as "fellow travellers," a matter that became important at a later stage of the Battle of Rockefeller Center. These included Ben Shahn, who wanted to study fresco technique under Diego and whose Sacco and Vanzetti series Diego had admired, Lucienne Bloch, daughter of the composer Ernst Bloch, who had been a W.P.A. sculptor until she began to work for Diego in Detroit, Steve Dimitroff, Lucienne's husband, Lou Block, Hideo Noda, Arthur Nierendorf, and Antonio Sánchez Flores, Diego's chemist, whom he had brought with him from Mexico. The work progressed swiftly and soon the "crypt" in the RCA Building began to glow with color and stir with strange images in which Diego was trying to reconcile his verbiage and metaphors with those of Nelson Rockefeller.

Two great elongated ellipses crossed each other in the center of the wall, one revealing the wonders of the microscope, the other showing what the telescope brought to the gazers at the stars—cells, plasms, diseased tissues, bacteria, crossing nebulae comets, flaming suns, solar systems. Those formed "the crossroads" that Rockefeller had proposed, and where they crossed was Man—rather empty-faced but "looking," I suppose, "with hope and high vision to the choosing of a new and better future." Below him are plants, signifying agriculture, above him a complicated machine such as never was on land or sea, signifying industry. Above the ellipses and in the angles formed by them are scenes from contemporary life. To the right of man, shown as if in a motion picture or a television scene, are the evils of present-day society as Diego saw them, evils which must be overcome if man is to build a new and better future. The evils include a nightclub with music, people carousing, and women playing cards; beyond that, an unemployment demonstration about to be broken up by the police; a battlefield with searchlights playing; men in gas masks; tanks; planes flying overhead. To the left of the Great Crossroads are depicted an athletic stadium with girls engaged in sports; a May Day demonstration in a "Socialist land," its participants obviously Russians; flaming red banners; and the figure of the "worker-leader" joining in his huge hands the hands of a black and a white workingman and a soldier, in a fraternal handclasp.

The architects and directors of construction became increasingly uneasy—it was "too realistic," too full of color and life, too propagandistic.

But on April 3 Diego was reassured by another friendly note from Nelson Rockefeller who had seen "in the Sunday paper" an "extremely good photograph" of him working on the RCA mural. Obviously, the photograph, if it showed any part of the mural, showed it greatly reduced and in black and white. "Everybody is most enthusiastic about the work you are doing. As you know, the building opens on the first of May and it will be tremendously effective to have your mural there to greet the people as they come in for the opening."

"The First of May"—a suggestive date full of portent for the painter! He must make it "tremendously effective" indeed. He had been waiting for some such impetus as that. The Communist Party of the United States was hitting him harder than ever. They asked Joseph Freeman to falsify a description of the mural he was painting on the stairway of the National Palace, and Freeman complied. Freeman wrote that at first the Independence Fighter, Father Hidalgo, had been in a panel along with Mexico holding a worker and a peasant in her arms, but that Diego had "substituted harmless objects such as grapes and mangoes" in the final fresco. Only in the *Workers' Age* could Diego find space to point out that both the original sketch and the final fresco had contained no mangoes, but only grapes, which were connected with Hidalgo by the fact that the good Father Hidalgo had violated the Spanish prohibition against the cultivation of the grape for wine in Mexico, and had taught the Indians to use the forbidden fruit. After the refutation of this canard, the *Daily Worker* and the *New Masses* began bombarding Diego with charges that now that he had made his peace with capitalism and imperialism he was painting in America for the millionaires, Rockefeller and Ford.

He would show them! He had not yet painted in the figure and features of the Worker-Leader who was joining the hands of worker, peasant, and soldier in fraternal handclasp. What better Worker-Leader could he choose for a painting to be unveiled on the First of May than V. I. Lenin? Rockefeller's careless encouragement and the Communist Party's goading combined to illuminate the features of Lenin under the Worker-Leader's cap. No Joseph Freeman could misrepresent such a painting, speaking in the eloquent tongue of a fresco in full color on a public wall where all could behold it.

LENIN APPEARS IN ROCKEFELLER CENTER

It was not until April 24th that a reporter, Joseph Lilly of the *World-Telegram*, got wind of what was going up behind the red canvas and what it was that would be unveiled on the first of May. His impressions were featured in this, the leading afternoon paper, under the headline:

RIVERA PAINTS SCENES OF COMMUNIST ACTIVITY
AND JOHN D. JR. FOOTS THE BILL

Joseph Lilly's article more than justified the headline. It read in part:

> Diego Rivera is completing on the walls of the RCA Building a magnificent fresco that is likely to provoke the greatest sensation of his career . . . microbes given life by poison gases used in war . . . germs of infectious and hereditary social diseases . . . so placed as to indicate them as the results of a civilization revolving around night clubs . . . a Communist demonstration . . . iron-jawed policemen, one swinging his club. . . . The dominant color is red—red head-dress, red flags, waves of red in a victorious onsweep. . . . "Mrs. Rockefeller said she liked my painting very much . . . Mr. Rockefeller likes it too. . . ."

Diego continued painting at that inhuman speed of which he alone among the Mexican Renaissance painters was capable, wearing out all his helpers, striving to get everything spread out upon the wall by May 1st. The Worker-Leader's cap disappeared and Lenin's bald head, unmistakable, took its place. The workman's American face and vacuous gaze as he sought "with high vision . . . for a newer and better future" gave way to Lenin's familiar, slightly Mongolian eyes firmly set on *his future,* the seizure and uses of power. Just before the first of May Diego completed Lenin's portrait, standing out lifelike and dominant as the only strong face in the whole fresco, and on May Day he contemplated his creation and saw that it was good, for the two great ellipses that crossed the wall now called the attention of the beholder to Lenin, the Worker-Leader who already knew the recipe for a newer and better future.

On May 4th Diego received the following letter:

When I was in the No. 1 building at Rockefeller Center yesterday viewing the progress of your thrilling mural, I noticed that in the most recent portion of the painting you had included a portrait of Lenin. This piece is beautifully painted but it seems to me that his portrait appearing in this mural might very easily offend a great many people. If it were in a private house it would be one thing, but this mural is in a public building and the situation is therefore quite different. As much as I dislike to do so, I am afraid we must ask you to substitute the face of some unknown man where Lenin's face now appears.

You know how enthusiastic I am about the work you have been doing and that to date we have in no way restricted you either in subject or treatment. I am sure you will understand our feeling in this situation and we will greatly appreciate your making the suggested substitution.

With best wishes, I remain sincerely,
(Signed) Nelson A. Rockefeller

I was with Diego when the letter was delivered to him by personal messenger. He asked me to read it, then to translate it into Spanish so that he could get the exact meaning of every phrase. "What do you think?" he asked. "Have I not the right, as painters have always done, to paint into my mural people I know? To use any model which seems suitable for each generalized figure that was in my sketch?"

"Yes, Diego, but the great painters of the Renaissance painted either the patron or somebody related to him or friendly toward him. Do you think that if Pope Alexander VI or Lorenzo di Medici had commissioned a painting, he would expect the central figure to be Girolamo Savonarola?"

"Well, what other Worker-Leader could Rockefeller expect me to paint? Lenin is the only possible choice."

"Perhaps he could have expected Trotsky, Diego. Or, for all I know, even Stalin. But once you had put a workingman's cap on the figure in your sketch, he had no reason to expect a portrait of Lenin or Trotsky.

This bald head and Trotsky's ancient Russian Red Army cap were both excluded."

"True. But what do you want me to do? Let Nelson Rockefeller censor my painting and make me remove Lenin's face once I have painted it there? What would the party say about my being a painter for millionaires?"

I PROPOSE LINCOLN TO SAVE THE FRESCO

"Diego, I have a good idea. A compromise no one could attack and no one could object to. Why not offer to substitute the head of Abraham Lincoln? He is the symbol of the freedom of the slaves, of the preservation of the American Union, of generosity to the freed Negroes and the defeated Southern States, of general amnesty to all political prisoners. As you know, Karl Marx wrote the Address of the First International to Abraham Lincoln, in which he said:

> The workingmen of Europe feel sure that, as the American War for Independence initiated a new era of ascendancy for the middle class, so the American anti-slavery war will do for the working classes. They consider it an earnest of the epoch to come that it fell to the lot of Abraham Lincoln, the single-minded son of the working class, to lead the country through the matchless struggle for the rescue of an enchained race and the reconstruction of a social world.

"As in all his writings on the tempo of the social revolution he longed for, Marx is overly optimistic, but his attitude toward slavery was sound and there will be nothing to be ashamed of in your putting Abe Lincoln's face in the central point of your mural. Nor can Rockefeller object, nor can any visitors to the RCA Building. I shall dig up the complete text of the Address of the First International, and much more concerning Abe Lincoln, so that you will get a deeper feeling for our greatest president and make his homely-beautiful face shine as it should in the center of your mural."

"Yes, please do that," said Diego. "Your idea is a good one. I shall call together those who are working with me on the fresco and read them Rockefeller's letter. And you can bring your material on Lincoln and explain your proposal."

"Actually, Diego, it will improve your mural, which is a little too Russian now, and will make it more moving to every American beholder. Besides, it is the only way to save this huge fresco you have so nearly completed."

But when Diego called the council of war of his collaborators, all of them with their abstract, semi-fellow-traveller radicalism, were for an open break which would be "much more exciting."

"If you remove the head of Lenin," they told him, "we will go on strike and picket you and your painting and the RCA building." It was not hard for them to persuade Diego. He had been uneasy from the first with such a patron as Nelson Rockefeller. The years of merciless criticism by the Communist party had left their scars. Besides, an open break would be more sensational, and Diego was never one to flee from confrontation or sensational encounter. My proposal to save the mural by making Lincoln the central figure was buried by the hail of objections. They would show the party, they would show Rockefeller, they would carry the battle into the streets of New York and into the headlines.

I put my notes on Lincoln back into my pocket. And on May 6 Diego Rivera sent Nelson Rockefeller the following answer to his letter:

> . . . The head of Lenin was included in the original sketch now in the hands of Mr. Raymond Hood, and in the drawings made on the wall. . . . Each time it appeared as a general and abstract representation of the concept of leader. . . . Now I have merely changed the place in which the figure appears, giving it a less real physical place as if projected by a television apparatus. . . . I understand . . . the point of view concerning business affairs of a commercial public building, although I am sure that the class of person who is capable of being offended by a deceased great man would feel offended . . . by the entire conception of my painting. Therefore, rather than mutilate the conception, I would prefer the physical destruction of the conception in its entirety, but preserving at least its integrity . . . logical and plastic.
>
> I should like as far as possible to find an acceptable solution to the problem you raise, and suggest that I should change the sector which shows people playing bridge and dancing, and put in its place in perfect balance with the Lenin portion, the figure of some great American historical leader such as Lincoln, who symbolized the unification of the country and the abolition of slavery. . . .
>
> I am sure that the solution I propose will entirely clarify the historical meaning of the figure of leader as represented by Lenin and Lincoln. No one will be able to object to them without objecting to the most fundamental feelings of love and solidarity. . . . Also it will clarify the general meaning of the painting.

This letter was meant to be conciliatory and to leave the door open for further negotiations, but actually Diego had tried to straddle two horses facing in different directions, and had fallen between them. Moreover, he had made a dangerous suggestion concerning "the physical destruction of the conception in its entirety."

THE BATTLE BEGINS

For four or five days there was an ominous silence. Diego hired a photographer to take pictures of the almost finished murals, but guards appeared to prevent his taking pictures, declaring that they had just received orders to bar all photographers from the building. Lucienne Bloch thereupon concealed a tiny Leica camera in her bosom, climbed the scaffold, opened one button of her blouse and went looking at segment after segment of the mural, taking such pictures as she could. If I have reproductions now of most of that mural in our *Portrait of America* and *Fabulous Life of Diego Rivera,* it is thanks to her skill and daring.

The next stage of the battle can best be told in the language of a war communiqué which Diego recorded in his Introduction to our *Portrait of America.*

> A mysterious warlike atmosphere made itself felt from the very morning of the day that hostilities broke out [May 9]. The private police patrolling the Center had already been reinforced during the night and on that day their number was again doubled. Towards 11 o'clock in the morning, the commander-in-chief of the building issued orders to porters and detectives on duty . . . to begin occupying the important strategic positions . . . and even the space behind the little working shack which was the headquarters of the defenders. . . . The lieutenants ordered their force . . . not to permit entrance to the beleaguered fort to anyone besides the painter and his assistants (five men and two women [the other woman besides Lucienne was Diego's wife, Frida]). . . . At dinner time when the defending forces were reduced to a minimum. . . . Field Marshal Robertson of Todd, Robertson and Todd, protected by a triple line of men in uniform and in civilian clothes, invited me down from the scaffold to parley in the working shack and to deliver there an ultimatum along with the final check. The ultimatum was an order for me to stop work.
>
> In the meantime, a platoon of concealed sappers . . . charged upon the scaffold and replaced it expertly with smaller ones . . . and then began to raise into position large frames of stretched canvas with which they covered the wall. . . . Before I left the building an hour later, carpenters had already covered the mural as though they feared that the entire city, with its banks and stock exchange, great buildings and millionaires' residences, would be destroyed utterly by the mere presence of an image of Vladimir Ilyich. . . . Thus was won the glorious victory of Capital against the portrait of Lenin in the Battle of Rockefeller Center. . . .

In less than an hour after Diego was ousted, a demonstration of workingmen under the lead of our Communist opposition appeared upon the scene with signs of protest, for we too were prepared. So were the police on horseback who charged upon the demonstrators. With that the affair became one more *cause célèbre* in the stormy life of Diego Rivera.

Protests poured in from individual artists and associations of artists from all over the country. Andrew Dasburg wired the support of the artists and writers of Taos, New Mixico; Witter Bynner those of Santa Fe; John Sloan signed and collected names from the Society of Independents; Ralph Pearson lined up his art students; Walter Pach, Lewis Mumford, Carleton Beals, Alfred Stieglitz, Peggy Bacon, Suzanne La Follette, Niles Spencer, A. Baylinson, George Biddle, Van Wyck Brooks, Stuart Chase, Freda Kirchwey, Hubert Herring, George S. Counts, Helene Sardou—were a few of the names signed to telegrams addressed to Rockefeller with copy to Rivera, or to Rivera with copy to Rockefeller. Mountains of telegrams poured in giving Frida and Diego days and nights of sleepless excitement. Art was once more on the front page.

The Communist party was caught defenseless in no-man's-land. It did not want to defend, still less praise Rivera, who had committed the double Stalinist sin of helping Trotsky to get a visa to Mexico when Stalin had almost succeeded in making the entire globe seem a world without a visa, and Diego had to boot been declared guilty of the ordained crime of being Mexico's official Right-Winger. Nor did they want to take the side of Diego's millionaire patron. Nor have any "Marxist" explanation of the visible mysteries: a revolutionary painter for millionaires; a revolutionary painting in the main entrance of the RCA Building which was itself the main building of an entire complex called Rockefeller Center; the rejection by the union of millionaires of the "painter for millionaires," which rejection was not slow in coming; and a Communist Party silent and speechless on the Battle of Rockefeller Center, on the painting itself, and on all the millionaires who now rejected the painter who only yesterday had done the magnificent Cuernavaca paintings for Dwight Morrow to give as a gift to the Mexican Government, and then climaxed his trajectory by painting the mural of modern industry for Ford in Detroit and the "Lenin Mural" for Rockefeller in New York, the world's financial capital. The bewildered silence and inaction of the Communist Party climaxed this triple absurdity. When every newspaper in America was flaring its front page headlines on Rockefeller, Rivera, and Radio City, the *Daily Worker* alone could neither report, nor explain, nor explain away the battle, nor exhort anybody from the sidelines, and it alone was silent on the biggest news of the day.

THE MILLIONAIRES BOW OUT

As for America's millionaire art patrons, they were not caught gaping in no-man's-land. They instantly sensed their role in the much-touted "class struggle." Herman Black, Chicago publisher, after seeing Diego's work in San Francisco, had written him that he expected to persuade the management of the coming Chicago World's Fair, christened *The Century of Progress,* to have the painter do a "machinery and industy" mural in the General Motors Building. Further negotiations had moved Diego to prepare sketches for such a mural to be called *Forge and Foundry.* But on May 12th, three days after the architect's and constructor's shock troops had covered up the mural in Radio City, Diego received a wire from Albert Kahn, architect for the General Motors Building:

> HAVE INSTRUCTIONS FROM GENERAL MOTORS EXECUTIVES
> DISCONTINUE WITH CHICAGO MURAL. . . .

As if that were a signal from a wizard's wand all the promised walls in America vanished with that telegram. The painter was cut off from further large walls for murals in the land of modern industry and machinery which had so deeply fascinated him.

Diego took to the air to explain his side of the controversy. In a broadcast over WEVD, which he read as best he could in English after I translated and edited his script, he said:

> The case of Diego Rivera is a small matter. . . . But let us take as an example an American millionaire who buys the Sistine Chapel, which contains the great work of Michelangelo. . . . Would that millionaire have the right to destroy the Sistine Chapel . . . because it is his property? There is not a single cultured and sensitive man who would not be indignant before the destruction of the Sistine Chapel, because the Sistine Chapel is the property of all humanity. . . . Suppose that another millionaire should buy the unpublished manuscripts in which a scientist like Einstein had left the key to his mathematical theories. Would the millionaire have the right to burn those manuscripts? . . . There is not a single man of science nor a single man of common sense who would not be indignant at the idea of the destruction of an unpublished manuscript which was the key to the theories of Einstein.
>
> We all recognize then that in human creation there is something which belongs to humanity at large, and that no individual has the right to destroy it or keep it solely for his own enjoyment.

And it is this position that the world of art and intellect took concerning the murals of Diego Rivera that had just been covered up by canvas in Radio City.

So powerful was the storm let loose by the ousting of the painter and the covering up of the painting, so many were the painters and art critics and intellectuals in general who either sent telegrams or appeals, or came in person to see Nelson and John D., Jr. and plead for the preservation of the painting, even if it remained covered for future generations, that there was no gainsaying the demands made upon the Rockefeller family. One group of artists and art experts came with an offer to remove the mural intact, albeit in sections, from the wall to put it up somewhere else. The Committee that made this proposal brought proof that frescoes had been thus successfully undercut, removed, and set up on other walls. They brought, too, figures on the cost of such a transference and evidence that they themselves could raise the funds to cover that cost. They arranged to compensate the Rockefellers, or the Radio City Construction Corporation, for their outlays of money to the painter. Of course, the Rockefeller family felt that such an action would be embarrassing, for the fresco could then be viewed elsewhere, and the controversy would thus be kept alive. Within a few days the Rockefellers felt that they must yield a promise to preserve the fresco, keep it covered by a canvas, and have the canvas painted by another artist in monochrome like the companion paintings of Brangwyn and Sert that flanked the now blank canvas covering. The whole campaign to preserve Diego's fresco developed in such a whirlwind of public agitation that on May 12 Nelson Rockefeller personally pledged his word to a delegation of artists and art lovers that the painting would be preserved for future generations to decide whether they wanted it displayed or not. Of course, reporters accompanied each such delegation, so that as early as May 12th, in its afternoon editions, the *New York World-Telegram,* then the leading afternoon paper, was able to carry the pledge of the Rockefeller family, given by Nelson, that "the uncompleted fresco of Diego Rivera will not be destroyed, nor in any way mutilated . . . but will be covered, to remain hidden for an indefinite time." The generous thing would have been to let Diego finish it and permit full-color photographs to be taken (the Leica in Lucienne Bloch's magic blouse was still a secret), but considering the agitation the Rockefellers had been compelled to face, it was hard to find too much fault with their decision not to let Diego return to the wall and, in the full glare of publicity, finish his fresco.

Once the pledge was given and the small army of guards reduced in size, the agitation died down. "Let future generations decide whether this is a cultural treasure or not"—the formula worked wonders in quieting the storm over "vandalism," for since the painting was invisible and supposedly even unphotographed, who could venture to claim to speak for the judgment of that mysterious entity, "future generations?"

However, some eight months after this solemn assurance had been given to a visiting delegation and the "future generations," the Rockefellers coldly calculated that the whole affair must have been forgotten. They succeeded in getting a municipal art exhibition prepared for this prestigious new building, and chose that moment, or more precisely the hour of midnight of Saturday, February 9, 1934, to have the mural removed from the wall by their own ruthless methods, namely, the smashing of the laboriously painted surface to powder.

The Rockefellers had counted on the passage of time, the rights of private property, and the vested interest of all the artists of New York and environs to get a chance to show their paintings in the new RCA lobby. But they had grievously miscalculated. Many artists withdrew their paintings from the show that was just opening, each with a statement calculated to make Nelson Rockefeller's hair curl. Among those who withdrew, listed in alphabetical order, were Baylinson, Becker, Biddle, Gellert, Glintenkamp, Gropper, Laning, Lozowick, Pach, Sardeau, Shahn, and Sloan. Walter Pach, in his book, *Queer Thing, Painting* (Harper Brothers, 1938), wrote that those who withdrew their paintings were given to understand that they would have trouble getting invited again to show future paintings unless they withdrew their withdrawals. This may have influenced a few painters who had not felt strongly enough to issue a statement to the press, but in general the ranks of the indignant painters held firm. José Clemente Orozco added his name to the protesters, and Gaston Lachaise, who had done an important sculptural group in Rockefeller Center, not something to be easily withdrawn, refused to lower his dignity as an artist by exhibiting a fresh piece of his work in this hall haunted by the ghost of a murdered mural.

CHRIST TOO IS SCOURGED OUT OF MAMMON'S TEMPLE

A comic coda to the Rivera controversy came when the conservative painter, Frank Brangwyn, who had been commissioned to paint a mural allusive to the Sermon on the Mount, was told, when his painting arrived in December, that it was rejected because he had painted Christ as a figure in it. Diego jumped into the breach.

> I don't like Brangwyn as a painter [he told reporters], but I defend his right, like mine, to express his own feelings and ideas in his painting. . . . If the owners of the building don't want in it the figure of Christ because it is a commercial building, this means . . . that today nineteen hundred years after He scourged them from His Temple, the money changers take their revenge . . . by scourging Him from the temple of commerce. By forbidding a Christian painter to paint Christ and a Communist painter to paint Lenin, they prove that when they hire a painter, they think they are buying him body and soul. . . .

But Brangwyn was not one for fierce controversy and Nelson Rockefeller had had enough of controversy for the moment, so they patched it up by agreeing that the figure of Christ should withdraw a bit, become more shadowy, and turn His back—ironic symbol!—on what Diego had christened the temple of the money changers. Sert produced another colorless work for the other side of the colored mural. But Diego's wall remained blank for year after year as painter after painter refused to cover the telltale space. Finally Sert undertook the job. People pass his two murals without so much as a glance at them, while Diego's fresco could not have been passed unnoticed. By agreeing to cover the telltale gap, the colorless Sert has perhaps guaranteed himself a little place in the history of art he would not otherwise have won!

CAN A MILLIONAIRE BUY A WORK OF ART TO DESTROY?

When Nelson Rockefeller drove Rivera from the scaffold in the RCA Building, he had one of his messengers hand Diego to the last penny the amount stipulated in the contract. This deprived the artist of any right to appeal to our courts to protect the integrity of the painting. Our laws will recognize such rights as may be settled in money, but knows naught of the artist's right to integrity of his work. In Diego's homeland the law provides that the artist retains a right over the integrity of his work despite its sale at the highest of prices or to the richest of men. A purchaser cannot destroy it nor make the slightest alteration in the work without the express consent of its maker. Nor can a work of any importance be exported according to Mexican law, for it is considered a "national treasure." If the purchaser wishes to export it, he must either be a good smuggler, a skillful dispenser of bribes, or get the express consent of the government thus to diminish the art treasures of the land. But in the United States a billionaire could use his fortune to buy up all the art treasures that constitute the country's and mankind's cultural heritage, and enjoy himself painting a moustache on the Mona Lisa or destroying the treasures of an entire museum. It has been bought and paid for, and thereafter there is no law to stop the billionaire from doing to his hoard of treasure what he will.

HOW ROCKEFELLER BUILT UP THE NEW WORKERS' SCHOOL

However, a painter has his own way of taking revenge. Diego had been promised $21,000 for this enormous work, a sum out of which he had to pay for his materials and the wages of his assistants. The Rockefellers, not too poor but too cautious to pay it all at once, still owed him $14,000. Out of this, $6,300 of the original price (30%) was to go to Mrs. Payne as commission for having arranged the celebrated project. An additional $8,000 Diego owed for materials and the wages of his assistants. That left him almost $7,000 of the Rockefeller money, not clear profit for more than that had gone for Frida's and his living expenses. But anyhow, it was actual cash in hand.

Diego knew that his painting would be kept covered for a long time, but did not dream that it would be barbarously destroyed. However, he was determined now to speak to the people of New York through a mural on a public wall. So he gave a precise account to the press of the munificent deal with billionaires, ending with an announcement that he now had in hand almost $7,000 of "Rockefeller money," all of which he could do with as he pleased, even if the whole enterprise ended in a net loss. "So long as the remainder of this check holds out," he declared, "I will use it to paint in any suitable building that has a wall to offer, an exact reproduction of my buried mural, and will bring it to completion. If the wall is differently shaped, I will alter the structure of the mural to fit the architecture, but the theme will be the same. I will paint free of charge, meeting my own expenses and the wages of my assistants. All I ask from the owner of the building is the actual cost of physical materials used in the painting."

He was besieged with offers of walls, but in each case the dimensions were totally unsuitable, or the walls would not be accessible to the public view, or he did not like the uses to which the building was put. In the end he accepted none of the places offered, but decided upon one of his own choosing, totally unsuitable for the reproduction of the buried mural that he had in mind.

Frida and Diego had examined every building offered and considered every possibility. Then one day they sent for me, and each chiming in, they told me that I had been so helpful during the entire confrontation with the Rockefellers and with the Communist Party, and was such a willing translator in all of Diego's "Spareribs and Gravy" appearances, and that the *Workers Age* had opened its columns so generously for Diego to defend himself against party attacks and to recount his work in Radio City and his purpose as a painter, that Diego had decided to paint in the New Workers' School. I was overwhelmed with delight, but raised many and important objections.

"Diego, the New Workers' School is a ramshackle old building on West 14th Street. It is falling to pieces. It, and probably the whole block of buildings on which it stands, will soon be torn down."

"I thought of that," said Diego, "when I lectured in your school. So I will paint movable frescoes that will outlast the building, frescoes such as I painted for the Museum of Modern Art. You can move them when you move your school to another building, and if I am still here, I will help you to install them. If not, some of my assistants may help you."

DIEGO DECIDES TO PAINT THE STORY OF OUR COUNTRY

"But the structure is unsuitable for a reproduction of your buried mural."

"That's true, so I am going to put you to work without pay. I will do frescoes dealing with the history of the United States. I will tell the story of your country if you will help me with the iconography and the selection of characters good and bad that played an important role in the shaping of your great country. I will expect you to find prints and paintings and portraits of the actors in the story we are telling. And I will ask you to help me understand their characters and their roles. Your auditorium is not big enough to accommodate the crowds you are attracting (he was thinking of the overflow crowds that came to hear him with me translating). By my painting I shall make it look bigger. In the frescoes there will be personages which I will paint more or less life size. They will make the auditorium look bigger and more accommodating."

"Diego, we don't even have the money to pay for materials."

"That's nothing. I think my assistants may be willing to work for less money on such a project (they were). And Frida and I can move to cheaper quarters than the Barbizon Plaza. As for the buried RCA murals, the Mexican Government has offered me an entire wall in the Palacio de Bellas Artes (The Palace of Fine Arts), where I can paint what I please. I shall paint the Rockefeller fresco there if he doesn't uncover it soon."

And so, all my objections answered, the question was settled.

DIEGO'S PORTRAIT OF AMERICA OR A WOLFE'S EYE VIEW?

Of course, neither size, nor structure, nor use permitted the repainting of the Rockefeller mural in our building, so Diego hit on the idea of painting the history of the United States, as in the National Palace in Mexico he was painting the history of his own land.

For the first time [Diego wrote afterward in our joint book, *Portrait of America*] I painted on a wall that belonged to the workers, not because they own the building . . . but because the frescoes are painted on movable panels. . . . They all helped in the work, and there in the modest premises of a dirty old building on 14th Street . . . I found myself in what was for me the best place in the city. . . . I did all I could to make something that would be useful to the workers, and I have the technical and analytical certainty that those frescoes are the best that I have painted.

Diego's latest, while he was doing it, was always "the best that I have painted." But I, who had a hand in helping him plan this series of panels, could not share his view that it was the best, or even one of the best of his frescoes. Try as I might, and I tried hard as I shall narrate, I could not make him feel like an American or absorb into his spirit the history and traditions of our country.

Because he was painting in an auditorium usually jammed with people, he filled the foreground of each panel, just a little above the heads of the seated public, with human figures slightly larger than life size. Thus the people filling our hall seemed to be continued by the lifelike figures in the wall. As if by a miracle, our crowded auditorium acquired an extension and a feeling of amplitude, "mixing," as Rodin had sought with the "Burghers of Calais," "their heroic life with the daily life of the city." The upper, middle ground of each panel is occupied by masses of men in action, those same masses whose representative heroes fill the lower foreground. At the top rises and falls all around the hall the beautiful landscape of our vast country, while in each panel—except one in which the painter deliberately aimed to give a feeling of confusion—some solid tree trunk, or edifice, or other uprising object gives visual support to the ceiling and adds to the height, the amplitude, and the dignity of the long, narrow, low auditorium.

The frescoes, twenty-one in all, occupying 700 square feet of wall space, were painted on movable sectional panels of the painter's own design: each panel was framed in wood, fastened at the corners by metal cleats, backed by wooden crosspieces, composition board, and chicken wire, and various coats of plaster, topped off with Diego's usual fresco surface of ground marble and cement, painted swiftly both in outline and in color while the surface of the marble and cement was still wet enough to absorb the pigments, but not so wet that the pigments would run into each other. Each single panel weighed about 300 pounds. In a land where structures are built so that they shall not endure but quickly be "written off" and replaced, these panels stood the test of their designer, for the murals were moved and set in place in our new home when we moved our school and offices from 14th to 23rd Street, without suffering a single scratch or crack. And many years later when the New Workers' School and the organization behind it were dissolved, they were donated to the International Ladies Garment Workers Union and again moved without a crack to their Summer Recreation Camp (Unity House) in Forest Park, Pennyslvania, where they were set up in the dining hall.

Thus Diego proved that his technique for making movable walls for impermanent buildings was successful, but his experiment in "painting for the workers" was less so. David Dubinsky and other officials of the I.L.G.W.U. exercised a censorship of their own. They considered two small panels, criticizing some aspects of the New Deal, and one full-sized panel entitled "Communist Unity" too "Communist" or too anti-Roosevelt for their dining hall. These three panels were not put up with the rest, but by roundabout ways found their resting place on the walls of private collectors. When last I heard of them, they were hanging inappropriately on the walls of the home of Mr. and Mrs. Joseph Willen of New York.

Diego, too, became a censor of his "painting for workers," for in 1952, being on one of his humble quests for readmission into the official Communist Party of Mexico, he himself no longer wished his panel on "Communist Unity" with its cruel but faithful protrait of Joseph Stalin as the "party executioner" of all of Lenin's lieutenants, and its more favorable pictures of Trotsky, Bukharin, Lovestone, Rosa Luxemburg, Edward Welsh, and me as "the teacher of the workers," to be reproduced in a monograph for which the painter himself was supplying the photos, the monograph dealing with a fifty-year retrospective of his painting. In it he reproduced only 18 of the 21 panels. *Communist Unity* was not among them!

If Diego's *Portrait of America* lacks the internal life and magnificence of his Mexican history on the walls of the National Palace in Mexico City, this is only natural, for how could the painter have as deep a knowledge and feeling for Abe Lincoln, John Brown, Thoreau, or Emerson as for Hidalgo, Juarez, Quetzalcoatl, or Zapata? Moreover, the faults of these murals are in many points more those of the writer than of the painter, for I was the chief mediator between Diego and our history. And I still had so much to learn about our country's history when I became Diego's instructor.

Obviously, for the purposes of art, mere facts are not enough. The history of our country had to be felt as well as known, reacted to as well as apprehended, absorbed into the painter's spirit. Many of the painter's assistants and members of our faculty and student body were recruited to make the history of our country somewhat accessible to the painter. We avoided academic histories in favor of contemporary documents and contemporary iconography of the period being painted. Ben Shahn helped me enormously with iconography. We ransacked libraries, collections of old newspapers, and museums for contemporary prints, woodcuts, oils, newspaper caricatures. We brought him, in my translation, the bitter attacks and the worshipful praise of those whom he was using as personages in his story. We ran through the speeches and writings of each representative selected; we distilled bitter hatreds and fulsome examples of admiration and love. Words were checked against deeds, outcomes against gloomy or sanguine expectations, moods of the nameless masses were studied, in whom these outstanding men had inspired love or hatred; we even delved into the myths which friend or foe created. How well these methods succeeded, at their best, was thanks principally to Diego's prehensile mind—is testified alike by the beauty and vividness of such portraits as those of Franklin, Paine, Emerson, Thoreau, Walt Whitman, Lincoln, and John Brown. How Diego, and we, felt is shown, too, by the bitter power of such caricatures as that of J. P. Morgan, the first. Many may disagree with Rivera's graphic interpretation of our history, but none can deny its impact or strength, nor regard it as a mere cold exercise in learning facts by rote. Indeed, whatever its shortcomings, there is no example by one of our own painters that comes anywhere near giving so moving a portrayal of our people, our land, and our history. Though it exists today only in a book *(Portrait of America)*, * it still exists as a challenge to our own artists.

When Diego had finished his frescoes in the New Workers' School, he still had a bit of "Rockefeller money" left, so he decided to try to satisfy the New York Trotskyites who had looked with bitter envy on his painting for us. Neither Diego nor Frida had formed any personal affection with any of the local Trotskyites, but he now moved to their headquarters and did two small panels representing the Russian Revolution with Trotsky as a central figure, as he was in the Bolshevik seizure of power, and the *Fourth International*, which Trotsky had recently founded to replace the third. With that his funds were exhausted, and so he decided to go back home and finish the National Palace frescoes.

A PAINTER'S REVENGE

In the New Workers' School he had done with malicious glee two biting protraits of John D. Rockefeller, the first and second. Nelson he deemed unworthy of even a caricature. But when he got to Mexico and learned that the fresco in Radio City had been wantonly smashed to bits in violation of Nelson's solemn promise given to a committee of artists and critics, Diego applied to the Mexican government for permission to paint on a larger wall in the Palacio de Bellas Artes in order to redo the Radio City fresco so that the world might see it. They had denied him the right

* The panels were destroyed by a fire at the I.L.G.W.U. camp (Unity House) in Pennsylvania.

even to photograph his work before they broke it up, so now he was determined to bring it to life in full color and monumental scale that it might haunt them and that the world might judge between Nelson Rockefeller and him.

The building forced him to make some changes. The elevator shaft in the RCA Building had been a natural triptych, a main wall flanked by two sides, but this new wall was flat. The figures which had been on the sides he now introduced into the two sides of the flat wall, adding Trotsky and Marx to fill out some extra space. But otherwise, for the first time in his life as a mural painter, he ignored both the architecture and the uses of the building, for he was anxious to show what it was that Rockefeller had destroyed. But involuntarily there is less simplicity, less solidity of structure, less power, more delicacy and emphasis on line. Thus it is influenced by the architecture and ornamentation of the building, yet does not accord with it nor with its use. Moreover, it has lost its dramatic impact and original intention to *épater le bourgeois.*

The most interesting change from the original is structurally minor and not influenced by the architecture. It is the introduction into the nightclub scene, close to the microscope's enlargement of the germs of syphilis and other venereal diseases, of a portrait of John D. Rockefeller, Jr. "Let them be well used," said Hamlet of the players, "for they are the abstracts and brief chronicles of time; after your death you would better have a bad epitaph than their ill report while you live." And perhaps it is more dangerous to use painters ill, since bad epitaph and ill report are one.

36

THE MAKING OF A WRITER

While Diego was painting his frescoes at the New Workers' School, our auditorium was crowded day and night. Reporters came to interview him and carried off entertaining controversies. Photographers came both to photograph him at work and the work itself. People came to watch him paint, always a spectacular sight, due to his bulk and speed and the readiness with which at the end of a long, hard day he might step off the scaffold, narrow his eyes as he looked at his work, and then sometimes go back again and destroy the latest segment if it did not totally please him—or if Frida made some justifiably critical remark. Droves came to hear him lecture in Spanish on the structure and design and meaning of what he was painting, while I walked alongside of him translating into English and occasionally arguing with the painter in Spanish. They came in droves, too, to hear me lecture in English on the history that was being painted. Some American history classes came in a body, led by their instructors who gave friendly and/or critical accounts of what was on the walls. Until Diego got to the more controversial contemporary history section, a number of American history teachers hit on the idea of using the murals as a lively and exciting review lesson on the history of our country.

Diego was invited to more and more places to lecture on any and everything, sometimes with outrageous and hilarious disregard for truth. Always he dragged me along to complete the entertainment by my translations, and stubbornly refused to speak in French and utilize the interpreter that the Institutes inviting him had provided.

Only once was Diego's stubbornness unsuccessful. The Anthropological Society was meeting in New York and invited Diego, a great collector of various works of pre-Conquest art of all Mexican civilizations, to talk on the ancient art of Mexico, and they designated René d'Harnoncourt, who spoke excellent French, Spanish, and English and was one of their number, to be the translator. Diego demurred and asked them to invite me to translate for him. They said they would get a better technical translation from a professional anthropologist and rejected my services. Diego was furious. He took revenge after his fashion.

He chose to tell the astounded anthropologists that the Aztec civilization was one of the earliest mercantile and pecuniary civilizations in the world. He said, "Some people think that all these little broken pieces of idols are the results of ravages of time, but nothing of the sort is true. They used the full-sized idol as large coins, and when they had to make change, they broke up the idols into little pieces and developed a precise scale of size for the value of each coin. You will never understand the Aztec civilization if you don't know this important fact." He paused for translation. Poor d'Harnoncourt, blushing furiously, was compelled to recite with precision this amazing nonsense and give it the same emphasis as Diego had given it, as if he believed what he was saying, in English. This was only the beginning of a lecture the inventions of which kept the anthropologists in a turmoil. Should they interrupt the speaker and tell him what he was saying was nonsense, and that the Aztec civilization was based on the precise exaction of tribute from conquered tribes, supplemented by barter and the levy of captives for human sacrifice? Should they show that they felt insulted? Should they stop the farce altogether? Or should they, as some of the more imaginative souls were minded to do, sit back and enjoy one of Diego Rivera's tall stories? The evening ended in hopeless confusion and nobody so much as remembered to thank the speaker for the "light" he had shed, or the translator for his faithful reproduction of Diego's startling picture of Aztec civilization. Somehow Diego's tall story didn't make the press, although it was almost the only time that he didn't make headlines when he sought them.

More and more publishers were becoming aware that Diego Rivera was "a celebrity" and should be induced to write a book on his paintings in the New Workers' School. Finally, Pascal Covici of Covici-Friede, a Chicago publisher newly moved to New York and known principally for his pornographic publications, came to see the paintings and the painter. The publishing house was near bankruptcy, something I did not know. Covici thought: "Maybe Communism is the pornography of the depression and will pull us out." He offered an immediate advance and an immediate contract to publish Diego's paintings at the School and Diego's opinion of America, as soon as the series should be finished. They dickered. Finally, Diego said: "I will give you the pictures in suitably reproducible form but I will not write the text."

"Oh, that's all right," said Pat Covici. "We have ghostwriters who can write the text for you. All we want is your signature."

"There is only one writer fit to write such a text," Diego retorted, "and that is the man who planned the pictures with me and taught me the history of this country, Mr. Bertram Wolfe," and he introduced me with a flourish.

"Can he write?" asked Pat.

"Yes, sir, he is a great writer in both Spanish and English, none better. I will not do the book unless he is the writer."

Pat Covici looked at me askance. He would rather use a professional ghostwriter. But I rejoiced. At last, a chance to become a free-lance writer! And with a first book by Rivera and Wolfe! What more could I ask?

"We don't need much text," he said to me crisply. "All we want is the pictures, the painter's name on the jacket, and a brief explanation of the meaning of each panel on the walls of your school. As for his paintings in California and Detroit, let him tell you what he tried to do there. A thousand words for California and Detroit will do, and then one thousand words for each panel in the New Workers' School."

"A thousand words for his impressions of our country!" I exclaimed. "And then a thousand words for each period of our history, with its heroes and its villains, its dreams and what came of them? What do you think we are, phonographs?"

"The text doesn't matter," he answered callously. "What matters is Diego's pictures and Diego's name. The rest is padding, the shorter the better: an identification of the main figures in the foreground of each panel, what they wanted to accomplish, and what came of it. It takes a lot of money to print thirty or forty plates. We can't afford to add much wordage. Besides, you have only three weeks to do the whole thing. We have to get it out for the spring season or it won't sell at all. Our salesmen have to be briefed on the book, and we have to get them out on the road, and an ad or two in the papers. That's book publishing—rush, rush, rush, and if you reach the book stores too late, you have to take back all the unsold copies as *returns*. If you want to become a writer, Bert," he said familiarly, as if this were not our first meeting, "you've got to learn to adapt yourself to deadlines and schedules. If you can't, I'll find an experienced professional writer for Diego who can."

I appealed to Diego, who was about to return to Mexico and had no time for battle. "You write up the panels that you know so well, and then cut, and cut, and cut," he said. "I'll write an introduction that will give my impressions of California and Detroit and what I painted there, and my feelings about America. You'll have only to write up the panels in the New Workers' School. You've gone over each of them dozens of times with me. All you'll have to do is give each one form and meaning. Let's take his offer and sign it before I leave for Mexico. You'll get half the royalties and a name for yourself as a writer."

It wasn't the advance—only $250 to be divided between the two of us. It wasn't the royalties—that was doubtful music of the future. It was the chance at last to become a free-lance writer. I was caught. There was no time to waste! I signed.

We signed the contract on December 6, 1933, each of us receiving the munificent advance of $125, and the copyright was taken out in Covici-Friede's name on the ground that one of our two authors was a foreigner. We agreed that all the pictures, Diego's introduction, and my texts for the

New Workers' School panels, were to be delivered not later than February 1, 1934. To my surprise, Diego kept his promise, wrote his introduction on the boat, and mailed it at the beginning of February. And no less astonishing, I squeezed the history of some fifteen eras of our country's life as best I could into a thousand words per panel.

I did my part with a mixture of sorrow and joy—the joy (you are now an author!), the sorrow (is that the best you can write and a true account of the history of your country?). The sorrow predominated so that I never liked the book. When the copyright to *Portrait of America* finally expired, Covici having gone to the Viking Press and then to his grave, Friede having gone to Hollywood, and Diego too having died, I renewed the copyright in my own name for the sole purpose of preventing some publisher from reprinting it or making a paperback of it. Since it contains virtually all the paintings Diego did in the United States—the Stock Exchange and School of Fine Arts murals painted in San Francisco; his Detroit frescoes; *Frozen Assets* and the *Drillers* from New York street scenes; the destroyed RCA murals and striking details therefrom; Diego's view of American history in the twenty-one panels in the New Workers' School, most of them since destroyed by the fire in the Unity House kitchen; and even the two small panels from the Trotskyite headquarters—it is now a rarity that can only be secured by getting a bookseller to advertise for it, and paying a consequent premium above the original list price.

I had managed to squeeze in even our black heroes, Denmark Vesey, Nat Turner, Crispus Attucks, Sojourner Truth, Frederick Douglass. This was long before any of our black history courses and black movements had discovered them. But how much can you say in a thousand words about such men and women in a panel on the conflict over slavery, which also contains the honor roll of the transcendentalists and abolitionists, including Thoreau pictured in his prison cell, Emerson, Hawthorne, Greeley, Dana, Lowell, Parker, Godwin, Whittier, Ripley, Alcott, Clarke, Brownson, the Channings, Bryant, Margaret Fuller. . . . And how many of them could Diego actually get into that panel without crowding it intolerably? Moreover, Diego had to find room for at least one of the most enlightened apologists for slavery in the same panel, in this case John C. Calhoun, invincible in senatorial polemics. And I had to find room for Calhoun's two main arguments. In short, the task that Pascal Covici had set me, one thousand words for each panel and three weeks for our whole history, was impossible. The result was the worst writing I have ever set down between the covers of a book.

A WOLFE'S EYE VIEW OF OUR HISTORY

But when Will Bohn, an editor of the *New Leader*, attacked the paintings and my text as a "Wolfe's Eye View of American History," I rallied to the defense of both text and pictures. He implied that it was a gloomy and jaundiced view of our history, full of floggings and lynchings of slaves, hangings, and executions. I submitted an article to the *New Leader* going over the text panel by panel, showing that each panel had things for Americans to be proud of, which, on the whole, predominated over the things to be ashamed of in our history. I pointed out that the shootings in the *American Revolution* panel were true to our history, that the man being shot was Crispus Attucks, a black, who was the first man to die in the Boston Massacre. I underscored the prominence and enlightenment given to the faces of Benjamin Franklin, Thomas Paine, Thomas Jefferson, and Samuel Adams. When it came to panel five, I pointed out that the figures that stood forth were those of Nat Turner, Margaret Fuller, Sojourner Truth, John Brown, and Thoreau in prison. In my text I crowded the names of other transcendentalists, their whimsical crochets and generous dreams. From Emerson I quoted, however briefly, "It is a country of beginnings, of projects, of vast designs and expectations. It has no past: all has an onward and prospective look." And from Thoreau: "All things invite this earth's inhabitants to rear their lives to an unheard of height, and meet the expectation of the land." From the first number of William Lloyd Garrison's *Liberator,* I quoted his opening declaration:

> I will be as harsh as truth, and as uncompromising as justice. . . . I am in earnest—I will not equivocate—and I will not excuse—I will not retreat a single inch—AND I WILL BE HEARD.

And when Will Bohn said he saw too many hangings in the panels, I bade him remember that the first hanging was that of John Brown, and before him stood Abraham Lincoln holding out suggestively to the hanging man the text of the *Emancipation Proclamation.* Then there are two blacks, one burning at the stake and one hanging from a tree in the Ku Klux Klan panel, the Ku Kluxers being offset by a foreground in which are the Radical Republican reconstructionists, Wade, Stevens, and Sumner. And, as I pointed to the only other lynching of a black in panel X dealing with the beginning of modern "trustified" industry in the nineties, I reminded Bohn of the fact that from 1892 to 1904 more than 100 lynchings occurred in our country each year. For me that was the shadow over my America in my boyhood. I never forgot it, and in the early thirties I founded the periodical, *Race,* and with its aid helped to organize a number of interracial conferences in the south which did their small share in the general awakening of the conscience of America in that respect. The founders of the journal included Henry Lee Moon, a black Harlem journalist, George Streator, managing editor of the *Crisis,* Martha Gruening, benefactor of many related causes, Frances A. Henson, Sterling Spero, Loren Miller, Genevieve Schneider and me.

Yet, after I had made my defense of my cramped text and Diego's paintings, I recognized that I was still too much under the influence of the American histories written by the Socialists, James Oneal and A. M. Simons, though in neither "debunker" of American history will one find my attempt at balance which brought into the foreground of each of Diego's New Workers' School frescoes the attractive faces of so many of the great men and movements of our history. Indeed, there is in every one of Diego's panels about the history of a country, which he had had to derive from me and my assistants in such strange fashion, something to stir the pride of any American in the history of our land.

EINSTEIN ON RIVERA

Among the distinguished persons who were excited by Diego's paintings at the New Workers' School was Albert Einstein. As I remember it, he was brought there by Otto Nathan, his guide to many aspects of American life, and later his executor. Otto Nathan does not remember the visit, but was kind enough to send me some correspondence between Einstein, Rivera, and myself when I asked for his recollections. On February 13, 1934, Einstein wrote to Diego concerning the effect on him of the paintings on American history. He wrote the following letter:

> The "New Workers" School has sent me photographs of the paintings with which you have decorated the school. I am glad to take this opportunity to express to you high admiration. I would not be able to name any other contemporary artist whose work has been able to exercise a similar powerful effect on me. I hope that the world will realize more and more what they possess in you. With sincere affection,
>
> Yours,
>
> *(signed)* Albert Einstein

I sent Einstein a copy of *Portrait of America.* In a letter of thanks dated May 27 he wrote:

> This master exercises a strong, demonic effect; he characterizes the spirit of our time more than almost anyone else.*

And Diego sent him a handwritten letter in which he told Professor Einstein how deeply he was moved by a tribute which he scarcely deserved for the little he had been able to do as a painter. He compared his work humbly in the field of painting with "your great strength as a man of science has changed the highest perspectives of human thought, in the enlargement of man's knowledge of space and light."

I did not use Einstein's reaction to advertise the paintings in the New Workers' School. We were getting a constant stream of visitors as it was, although I am sure the flood would have greatly increased had I publicized the Einstein-Rivera correspondence.

* Translations authorized by the Estate of Albert Einstein.

PORTRAIT OF AMERICA BECOMES A BEST SELLER

To my astonishment and delight, and to Covici's satisfaction, *Portrait of America* became a best seller. I knew it was not my writing but Diego's name. All those controversies, all his tall stories, all the publicity, had built up a market for anything from his hand. People were waiting for some pictures by Diego Rivera—any pictures. And great numbers were attracted, too, by the fact that a painter from Mexico could paint a history of the United States, showing such knowledge and insight and sense of balance, and showing that he knew what all our outstanding figures looked like. Reviewers and art critics gave the book more than its due of space and praise. Pascal Covici instantly saw in his mind another book that would be more attractive and pull his firm further out of the red. Diego having gone to Mexico and being notorious for his habit there of rarely opening and never answering the letters he received, was now remote and inaccessible, so Pat Covici had to send for me. "Bert," he said, "congratulations! Your first book is a best seller. Now I have an idea for another book for you to do with Diego. Get him to send you photographs of all his paintings done in his own country, on walls or on canvas. You write a text. It can be short. And we'll have another Rivera-Wolfe book."

I recognized at once that I had the upper hand and began, not to bargain with this shrewd Hungarian who had given me three weeks and a thousand words a panel, but to dictate my own terms. "It's a good idea, Pat, but I'm not going to write another book for you under the same tough and shabby conditions I wrote the first one."

"What do you want?" he asked meekly, expecting me only to up the advance.

"I am a good writer, Pat, always the best in my class, the winner of the Ward Medal in English at City College, and other such honors. But your three weeks' deadline on so compex and unfamilar a subject made a mess of what I wrote for *Portrait of America*. It's the first time I have written anything of which I really felt ashamed. And a thousand words for an entire era of American History!

"Your advance to Diego and me was outrageously low. Diego's name would have been worth a fortune if he had used an agent and gotten publishers to bid against each other."

"I didn't offer a fortune, but I offered speed."

"Well, this time I don't want speed, and Diego doesn't care one way or the other, I want time to do a good book. His portrayal of Mexico is infinitely deeper and more complex than the American History I spoon-fed him. Besides, Pat, I have to go to Mexico to find out what he really painted and where his paintings are, and his drawings. He's a better draughtsman than he is a painter. As for his frescoes, they have to be seen *in situ* to be appreciated, to be interpreted in relation to the architecture and setting in which they are to be found, and in relation to the uses of the building—

"What do you want?" Pat repeated meekly.

"I want a big enough advance to go down to Mexico and spend up to six months looking at and securing reproducible photos of his works and listening to his own tales of what he meant by them. And I want adequate time to write the book. I promise to work as speedily as possible and to deliver the manuscript within a maximum of six months after my return from Mexico.

Covici offered me an advance of $500 for the trip and pointed out that would mean another $500 to Diego, and he urged truthfully that he was "short of funds." Since I was going by a Ward Line Steamship, second class, and would live in Mexico as a guest of my friend, Martin Temple, and since he drew up a contract with no stipulations as to deadline, I accepted his offer. That same day we sent off a contract with his signature and mine for the signature of Diego. Diego was pleased that his views of Mexico as expressed in his murals would be written up by me. He returned the contract immediately with his signature, and, at Covici's plea, promised to wait for his part of the advance until the book had earned its first $500 in actual royalties.

I RETURN TO THE LAND OF PERPETUAL BANISHMENT

I had hanging over my head the order of perpetual banishment from Mexico issued by President Calles, but armored with the lapse of time, with a contract, and with my desire to test the banishment, I made preparations for my voyage. It was late March, 1936, and our friend Martin Temple happened to be in New York on business, so we journeyed together to Mexico. My wife, who had no perpetual banishment hanging over her head, was to join me as soon as her high school, where she taught advanced Spanish language and literature, closed for the summer.

A word about Martin Temple. He was born in Eastern Europe on some Jewish ghetto "street" and came early to America where he got no education except for his disorderly reading and the things he taught himself. He was a Socialist, probably having brought his fragmentary doctrine with him from Europe. He was strong-minded, stubborn and powerful of body. When I first got to know him, he was a packer in a firm where strength as well as packing skill were required. He became aware of my existence because of my antiwar journal, *Facts*, and my position as publicity director of the Rand School, where he attended forum lectures. When President Wilson finally brought us into Europe's war, his conscience bade him refuse to fight, so he went to Mexico which was not conscripting its male inhabitants for war in Europe. True, Mexico declared war on Germany shortly after the United States did, but it limited its warlike acts to such things as confiscating the big German chemical and drug companies in Mexico City, thereby enriching the country and some of its rulers.

But how to get to Mexico when exit was forbidden to men of draft age? Simple for Martin. He went down to the waterfront, showed his powerful body, and enlisted as a stoker for the round trip. He shovelled coal into the furnaces, naked except for a pair of shorts and then, still in good health, jumped ship in Tampico. Speaking imperfect English, Yiddish, and Hebrew, but not a word of Spanish, he started a beggarly life in Mexico.

THE QUIRKS OF MARTIN TEMPLE

Like many a self-educated man he carried in his intellectual baggage a pack of quirks and isms; he was possessed, for example, by vegetarianism at least as deeply as by socialism. Somehow he had gotten the idea from the sudden switch of Woodrow Wilson from peace to war that if people did not make war on other animals by eating meat, or eggs, or hunting animals for their skins, or using certain animal products, man would lose his warlike nature. He had many tabus: no liquor; no soap (an animal product); no salt; no medicine; no doctors except "nature doctors"; fasting for a number of days or weeks as a cure for any ailment or weakness (until near the end of his days, when in Italy he attempted to fast to strengthen himself for a steep mountain climb and was shocked to find that the fasting had made him not stronger but too weak to climb the Alps). He nourished a firm conviction that no ailments or diseases were caused by germs or bacteria, but only by sins of diet—and he had other quirks too strange and too numerous to mention.

Yet, if he heard an idea from someone he respected and it was expounded to him with logic, he was quick to grasp it and would often then drop a tabu that he had lived by for a decade or more. I had two such experiences with him in our ten or twelve day trip on a Ward Line ship. We ate together at a small table, and he worried the life out of his steward by trying to get vegetables cooked to his taste, a baked potato when it was not on the menu, and a proper dessert that met his standards and was the unconscious source of most of his energy. The steward exploded when he sent back all his carefully cooked vegetables because they had salt in them. I thought it was time to take a part in the dispute, and since he always had great respect for me, he listened quietly.

SALT AND WINE

"Look, Martin, you claim to want to eat according to nature. Do you know what part salt licks have played in the course of history? Weak and defenseless beasts risked their lives to get at salt licks, hoping to get a bite or a few licks which they felt they needed, before racing away faster than the beasts of prey that waited at the salt licks to catch them. Surely all these animals lived according to nature. My horse always had a lump of rock salt within reach to lick when he felt the need of it, and it lasted him a long time. Among men, those tribes who had possession of local salt licks or salt mines could barter the salt with emissaries from other tribes who traveled long distances to barter their most precious products or precious metals and jewels for some of the salt which they needed so badly. Whoever told you that in a state of nature men didn't use salt, lacks a knowledge of history and of physiology. The problem, as in so many things, is one of measure: how much is good for you and how much is too much." Whereupon Martin infuriated the steward a second time by saying: "I've changed my mind: I'll take the first plate of vegetables you brought me with the salt in them."

Next I ordered a porterhouse steak and said casually, "A good Pommard, a French red wine, would go well with this if you could share it with me." Martin looked at me quizzically. He was always tolerant of my unholy eating and drinking habits, but share it. . . . !

Having been so successful with the salt, I tried wine. "Martin, wine is not necessary to your body as salt is, but throughout the history of man we know of no people that did not ferment some fruit or grain in order to make wines or other alcoholic beverages. Once more, it is a question of measure. If you limit yourself to dry wines, you get no more than from ten to twelve percent of an entire glass that would be alcohol. The rest would be grape juice. You might be careful with fortified wines like sherry, vermouth, port, or Madeira. To these brandy or some other high percentage alcohol has been added. That's why they're called fortified. And of course I wouldn't recommend to you the hard liquors like Scotch and bourbon. But a moderate amount of wine with a meal will not hurt you."

Martin asked, "What wine did you say you would order with your steak?"

I answered, "Pommard."

He called over the waiter who came expecting trouble. "Waiter," he asked, "what wine would you recommend to go with this man's meal?"

The waiter paused a moment and then said, "A good Pommard would go well."

"Okay," said Martin grandly, "bring us a bottle and two glasses."

"May I recommend a half bottle if they have it?" The waiter brought a half bottle. From then on Martin became a wine drinker, but all his life he religiously abstained from fortified wines and hard liquors. And when I settled down in his home on Edison Street, to my astonishment on the first afternoon there arrived an entire case of Pommard. I drank nothing but first-rate Pommard during my whole stay at Martin's home.

HOW MEXICO RECEIVED THE DEPORTEE

Since President Calles' order of banishment had declared itself "perpetual" and had added that if I ever returned to Mexico I would be given five years imprisonment, followed by a second deportation, I entered the country at the Port of Vera Cruz a bit cautiously. I had a tourist permit allowing me to stay six months, I wore an American cut raincoat and a camera hung over my shoulder with a strap across my breast, and pretended not to understand a word of Spanish as if I had never been in the country before.

The train rose slowly from sea level; climbed through long hours strung end on end into and out of the rich subtropical lands; circled in leisurely fashion around Orizaba's majestic, snow-capped, eighteen-thousand-foot peak; puffed heavily up the arid, now parched, now frozen maguey-dotted meseta slope; crept with hollow-voiced roar on airy bridges hanging over torrential canyon clefts whose walls were jungles of brush; halted for quiet unexpected waits in soundless villages dominated by a church's soaring dome, a maguey grower's baronial castle, or occasionally by a fortress-like textile mill, a once-fortified minehead, or a palatial ranch, all of which even recently still needed fortifications against raids by rebel bands and bandit attacks. When at last our train with two locomotives in front and two in the rear climbed to 12,000 feet above the sea and came to the rim of the valley of Mexico and I saw the great city below me, I thought of how it must have looked to Cortéz and his little band when they got their first glimpse from that same rim of the unexpected great city on the lake, with all its palaces and temples and pyramids and causeways and surrounding suburbs. Their wonderment was set down by Bernal Diaz del Castillo in his *Conquest of Mexico*, whose words had stuck in my mind since first I read them:

> We saw so many cities and villages built on the lake and other great towns on dry land . . . great towers and temples and buildings rising from the water . . . the lake itself crowded with canoes, and in the causeways many bridges at intervals . . . like the enchantments they tell of in the book of Amadís. Before us stood the great city of Mexico, and we—we did not number even 400 soldiers. . . . What other men have there been in the world that have shown such daring?

We began to drop slowly via hairpin turns, through snow tunnels and rock tunnels for over four thousand feet to the floor of the valley of Mexico which, saucerlike, rises up from a bottom of 7,500 feet above the sea. I was not entering it now as Amadís de Gaula, but as one who had been driven from it under escort less than a decade before.

When I got off the train I left Martin, to walk alone in the city I knew so well, to see how it would receive me.

My first impression astonished me. There was a headline running all across the top of the first page of the daily, *Excelsior*, which read:

TODAY THE TRAIN FROM VERA CRUZ
DID NOT FALL INTO THE CANYON!

Ten centavos got me a copy of the paper and I read that, the day before our trip from Vera Cruz, the same daily train had run the same route and had fallen into the steepest canyon on the journey, killing all on board.

I walked down the street, meditating on the amusing idea of such a headline and the ease with which one could disappear from the face of the earth. Suddenly I found myself in the embrace of a labor leader. "Ay, compañero Wolfe, que bueno que está Usted otra vez aquí (How good that you are back here again)!"

Did he not know that I had been deported by President Calles? Of course he did. Had he not been relieved then to see me go? Indeed he had. Then why the *abrazo?* and the warm tone of the greeting?

I was on one of the main streets of the town, not far from the Central Plaza. I continued to walk, and almost every quarter of a block, it seemed, I bumped into another labor leader or *Laborista* politician whom I knew; and was enfolded in a fresh embrace and patted on the back. What had happened that yesterday's pernicious foreigner, vender of narcotics or transporter of Russian gold to Mexico to foment a railroad strike, was suddenly so welcome? I looked again for a newsstand. The afternoon editions were up; the train that didn't fall into the canyon had disappeared, and in place of it, the headline read:

PRESIDENT CALLES DEPORTED FROM MEXICO!!!

Thus while I was on the train that hadn't fallen into a canyon, the President that had deported me was himself flying over my head, deported to the United States by President Cárdenas! He was now the villain (he was even reported, mendaciously I think, to be reading *Mein Kampf* on the plane). He was the villain now, and I, his pernicious foreigner, was being transformed into a hero. A weird coincidence! I couldn't have timed it better.

The next embrace proved it. I bumped into Vincente Lombardo Toledano, who had become head of the Mexican labor movement when Calles' labor lieutenant, Luis N. Morones, was displaced. "Don Beltrán," he cried, giving me a courteous yet intimate greeting along with his embrace, "how good it is to see you here again! Come up to my office," and he handed me an engraved card. "I would like to have you write up our labor movement as it is today for the American press." With every embrace, my memories of Calles' order of "perpetual banishment" grew dimmer. I could stay then my six months, work on *Portrait of Mexico* to my heart's content, and perhaps have some time to make notes for a biography of Diego Rivera. I did not waste any time interviewing fellow-traveller Lombardo Toledano, nor any of the politicians who had embraced me on my brief journey through a main street of Mexico City, but I went at once to Villa Obregón to announce my presence in Mexico to Diego Rivera.

I found Diego with his left eye tearing profusely and covered with a black patch. Always hypochondriacal when he was even slightly ill, he was now terrified that he would go blind and no longer be able to paint. "When one eye goes, the other also goes out of sympathy." He was waited on not only by the usual *criadas* (servants) plus Frida, and also by a tall, large-boned, mannish-looking nurse in full nurse's regalia, hired to sleep in on a twenty-four hour basis to stop the onset of blindness. All she actually did to that end was occasionally wipe his tearing eye and put some soothing drop into it.

"Let's go and eat," said the hypochondriac.

"Martin Temple may be waiting for me with a sumptuous dinner."

"Legumbres y una papa!" (vegetables and a potato) retorted Diego contemptuously.

I called up the vegetarian restaurant which Martin himself had founded out of his own capital, and where the only meat served was the worms in the rolls the chef baked from his own flour.

"We're going to eat in the café Tacuba," I told him.

"I'll join you there around nine o'clock."

Off we went, Diego, Frida, his nurse, and I, in a station wagon driven by Diego's chauffeur, who parked outside the restaurant to wait for us.

The café was crowded—people with drinks and with cups of chocolate and *plomos* (light, delicate, mildly sweet cakes popularly known as "lumps of lead" or "sinkers.") In strode a tall, authoritative-looking man with his wife and his pistol-armed bodyguard. He seated his wife, carefully took a corner seat with two walls to protect his back, then dismissed his bodyguard, putting his own pistol on the table near his right hand, and ordered drinks.

"That's Deputy Altamirano," said Diego, "the next Governor of Vera Cruz." That meant that he was the nominee of the ruling party in Vera Cruz, and, short of a successful rebellion, would surely have the majority of votes counted in his favor. "He has been tipped off by telephone from the Port of Vera Cruz that some gunmen are coming up to get him," added Diego.

"Then why did he dismiss his bodyguard?"

"Es muy hombre." (He's a brave man) "He has his own pistol at his right hand, and his back protected so that they can't shoot him from behind."

Deputy Altamirano took his glass in his right hand and raised it to his lips. At that moment the revolving door in front turned; a man with an automatic pistol in his hand entered, and at a distance of at least twenty feet with cool precision put a bullet into Altamirano's pistol hand, shattering his glass, a second bullet into his temple, a third into his heart, and then, advancing nearer, scattered the other bullets with elegance around the slumping body, only one of eight going into the wall without first penetrating the body. . . . With that he backed out the revolving door and was lost from view.

Diego seized his own pistol and stepped toward the fallen man. Fearing that there were other armed men in the café to protect Altamirano, I struck Diego back out of what might be the line of fire, though he weighed a good hundred pounds more than I did. But there was no cross fire. I looked at my table mates. Martin Temple, who had entered before the shooting, and Frida sat motionless, as if paralyzed. I was startled, however, to see expressions of something like exaltation on the faces of Diego and his nurse, identical expressions as if death were a tremendously exciting experience that fascinated them both as they witnessed it. The nurse leaped forward to take the fallen man's pulse and pronounced him dead, but the excited exaltation did not leave her face. Diego was studying the fallen man painstakingly, with the same expression on his face. Was this another aspect of the Mexican attitude towards death? As for Diego's look, I got the answer the very next day—on the floor of his studio, leaning against a table, was the dead man's body, right hand with the bullet hole which had prevented him from using his pistol, a bullet wound in the temple, one near his nose, one piercing his vest exactly where the heart had been beating, body slumped against the wall, mouth open in the last gasp for breath. Diego had caught every detail and made a finished painting in tempera on masonite. He seemed unwilling to wait for the slower process of true fresco on wet plaster and cement, but had mixed his pigments with some substance like egg white and painted on dry masonite. This bullet-ridden body, slumped lifeless in its own blood, was not merely Deputy Altamirano, the "next Governor of Vera Cruz," was also a symbol of Mexico's turbulence, that I was to witness more than once, where all politicians carry guns, where *madrugar* (to get up first or draw first) is a cardinal maxim, and where deputies use their parliamentary immunity not to assert the independence of the executive, as was its historic function, but to eliminate their opponents. In 1937, when I was writing the text of *Portrait of Mexico*, in Diego's native town of Guanajuato the entire newly-elected Executive of the Miners Union was assassinated *en masse* as they sat for a photograph at their first meeting. Thus was yesterday's election verdict reversed. And the officially stated homicide rate of the country at the end of the first Six-Year Plan under Cárdenas was 118 times that of England, almost 13 times that of Italy, famous for its crimes of passion, and something like five to six times that of the United States. I cannot assure the reader that the proportions are the same today, for the enthusiasm of the Six-Year Plan (one year more than the Soviet Union's Plan) apparently was such that Mexico attempted to give statistics on many things which it had never counted. No one really knows the homicide rate in Mexico for any year because there are whole areas of unorganized territory and jungle where no census taker, no tax collector, and no representative of the National Police can safely show himself. The census figures are filled out by global guesses for the regions where a census cannot be taken. And homicide statistics are even less reliable, since most people know better than to report homicides to the police. Consequently, when I attempted to check these comparative figures for later dates, I found that Mexico did not even report homicide statistics in such places as the *International Crime Statistics* of the police organization, Interpol. I imagine that the homicide rate in Mexico is somewhat lower today, in proportion to the population, but I have found no statistics verifying my speculations.

DEATH AND LAUGHTER

The Mexican folk take death simply and naturally, as they do sex, as they do life as a whole. If anything, death and sex and life are jokes. A Mexican dies silently, phlegmatically, and, to the best of his ability, heroically. In his *corridos* (popular, broadsheet ballads sung in the market place, then sold for a few centavos) his heroes never evade an ambush though they have had a warning. They face death like men, faces toward the enemy and their guns speaking to the last, though the hero be one against an entire detachment.

Perhaps an episode from my personal experience will help to make clear how lightly death is taken. A young man named Enrique Flores Magón, and a friend of his whose name I no longer remember, who belonged to the Young Communist League, were inseparable companions. One of them never visited our home without the other. Indeed, we never saw them apart. But one day Flores Magón came to us without his boon companion. "Where is your inseparable friend?" I asked.

"I killed him," he answered cooly.

"Was it an accident?"

"No, I shot him."

"Why?"

"He dared me."

"What did he say to you?"

"A ver si me matas?" (Let's see if you'll kill me?)

"That's all?"

"Yes, that's all. He kept taunting me so I took my pistol and put it to his temple."

" 'A ver, a ver!' he kept saying to show how brave he was. It was a challenge. He kept it up until at last I had no choice but to pull the trigger."

"What will they do to you?"

"Oh, nothing much. This is a civilized country. Our Constitution forbids capital punishment. The maximum term is five years, but since there was no holdup or any other evil about what I did, I'll probably get two years." He got much less than that, and was back in my house, as cool as ever, within a couple of months.

One popular song to which Mexican soldiers march is called *Valentina*, and it runs something like this. The soldier has been taken prisoner by the opposing side and has been condemned to be shot at sunrise. He declares his love to Valentina, and then boasts:

Oh, Valentín, Valentina,	Oh Valentin, Valentina
Yo también sé morir	I too know how to die,
Pero si me han de matar mañana,	But if they're going to kill me tomorrow
Que me matan de una vez	Why don't they kill me now?

There is something special about death in Mexico as compared with Spain or with any other Latin American country. Spain talks more seriously and frequently and familiarly about death than we do or Mexico does. Her graveyards are filled with skeletons, skulls, and other genuine *memento mori* on tombstones, but it is quiet and somber talk of death. Only in Mexico have I found festive death, death made into a joyous week-long holiday, death and laughter joined together.

We have vestiges of this fiesta in our Halloween, followed by All Saints' Day, and then All Souls' Day. There is some trace left of a festival of death in the pumpkin heads, the masks, the witches' garments, the pranks of *trick or treat,* but it does not occur to children to link these sports up with death or with the *Day of the Dead.* In Mexico, however, the fiesta connected with the *Day of the Dead* lasts for an entire week and is the gayest festival of the year. *Puestos* (bazaar stands) are set up in the local market places and in the plazas, at which you can buy every form of death gift from full length skeletons to candy coffins where a skeleton sleeps uncovered and every morsel can be eaten.

It is hard to explain why the Mexican attitude toward death is so different from that of any other people, though the awesome and magnificent Aztec festival of human sacrifice, the sacrifice of a man who has first spent a year living as a god, is surely a factor. So, too, is the tremendously high death rate that prevailed in Mexico during the twenties, thirties, and forties. I am sure the death rate is lower now with the introduction of modern sanitation, though the extreme poverty of those living at the margin of Mexican society still keeps the death rate high, harshly lessening to some degree the problem of growing overpopulation.

During the first few years that my wife and I spent in Mexico as high school teachers of English, the toll of constant rebellion or revolution, the outbreaks of guerrilla warfare and banditry, the well-nigh universal habit of every *macho* of wearing a pistol and a belt of cartiridges, and the ready use of pistols in settling controversies and in testing a man's daring for fun, all kept the death rate inordinately high for men, and filled the cities with widows working or begging to bring up their children, and with hordes of orphan boys who sold papers or lottery tickets or begged or picked pockets for a living, and spent their nights sleeping in hallways or on sidewalks, kept warm by a few old newspapers or billboards and a half-starved dog.

The tranquil and natural preparation for death among the very aged, and the seemingly inevitable loss in every family of half or more of the very young, have made death a familiar visitor in the average Mexican household. In a world where life is valued lightly, its end is taken lightly, too. Except to exalt a valiant death as one of the noblest acts of living and to find an absurd accidental death to be an uproarious joke, the Mexican people give little thought to life's end. This nominally Catholic people does not live in the shadow of the fear of death, or concern with what comes after.

When villagers tell tales of the dead, they show no preoccupation with Heaven or Hell, but rather think in terms of surviving, the pre-Conquest tradition in which the departed shade undertakes a five-year long journey into an underworld closer to the ancient Grecian Hades than to Heaven or Hell or Purgatory. Often a dog is slain and buried with the deceased to guide him through the perils of the journey. Frequently food and money are included in the coffin. Even those who have gone barefoot all their lives, with unconscious irony may be sandalled in death, for the way is long and hard. The dead require and long for the same things as the living, and may return or linger near the haunts of their life, savoring dimly its pursuits and memories in the bloodless, joyless, sorrowless life of shades.

But when the Day of the Dead rolls round, that is a time for rejoicing among shades and men, for the dead return to the bosom of their families and partake of the pleasures of a family reunion once more. All Saints' Day and the day or two following are "visiting days," in which the dead return to their families and the living return the visit by visiting the dead in their cemetery resting places.

This courteous and loving exchange of visits is a truly festive occasion with no trace of melancholy. In the countryside it is an occasion of repressed and quiet festiveness; in the cities among the predominantly mestizo * inhabitants it has an aspect of carnivalesque hilarity which gives a new meaning to the death's-head grin. And make no mistake about it, it is truly a grin. In fact, the whole city is a-grin with deaths'-heads from the time the *puestos* go up, well before the festive week: skeletons in store windows; skulls dancing in the wind; recently unpopular dead men in caricature; little toy funerals in candy; silver skull stickpins with glinting ruby eyes; skeletons that pop out of boxes when you open them; tiny death's-heads that move their lower jaws rhythmically when touched or jiggled; skeletons with black wire legs and sandals that dance as one moves or the wind blows; death's head brooches for girls and stickpins for boys. Sweethearts give each other skulls mounted on rings. The great popular artist, José Guadalupe Posada, in his day, and artists today, make macabre drawings with epitaphs in verse for people to mail to each other as our boys and girls sometimes send each other comic valentines. Broadsheet ballad vendors abandon their usual stock in trade of outlaws and train wrecks to hawk pink, yellow, green, and purple tissue broadsheets known as *calaveras* (skeletons) dressed in uniforms, armed with brooms as streetsweepers, guz-

* Mixed Spanish and Indian origin.

zling liquor, firing guns, all with appropriate epitaphs to match, doing all the things grotesque and serious that make up the human-comedy of life in Mexico.

On November 1st comes the *Día de los Difuntitos Chiquitos* (Day of the Dear Little Dead), a happy day, for those who died young could not have had time to sin and therefore are surely in Heaven. The table is set for them with all kinds of dainties, fruits, cakes baked in the form of animals, of course skeletons which are known as *pan de los muertos* (bread of the dead), lighted candles, festoons of the yellow *zempasuchitl,* traditional Nahua flower of the dead, and all their favorite fruits and flowers and sweets and toys. The little dead are invited to partake, and then the living celebrants partake with them. What is offered to the deceased are called *ofrendas* and are in many villages given to visitors and to the poor. The whole ceremony has an air of childlike earnestness and subdued joy and color.

PICNICKING IN THE GRAVEYARD

But the most joyous day is the day of the *difuntos mayores,* the adult dead. Then all Mexico goes to the cemetery. There are not nearly enough *tranvías* and buses, so most of them go on foot, in entire families, all laden with their picnic baskets for the dead and for themselves, and with their jugs and bottles and wineskins to accompany the food. Where the distances are great, mule, burro, auto, truck, or cart may also be used for the aged, for the children, and for the pleasurable burdens to be consumed at the graveside or sitting on the grave itself. They carry with them great baskets of food and dainties, as well as jars and bottles and skins of *pulque, tequila,* water, and whatever other drinks may be at hand. They often carry, too, braziers and bundles of charcoal to make hot dishes at the graveside, and fresh flowers of every description.

DON JUAN TENORIO

The dust rises on all the approaches to the cemeteries, and there are vendors at key spots to sell flowers, fruit, drinks, toys, and sacred images, and whatever else may have been forgotten. All the approaches to the cemeteries become one vast country fair and the cemeteries themselves brighten into crowded and joyous picnic grounds. Whole families sit upon the graves or around them, perhaps cry or pray a little for the recent dead, offer those they are visiting food and drink and sweetmeats and toys and flowers according to their age, and partake themselves of the offerings in fraternal communion with the dead, strum upon their guitars, sing folk songs, plaintive and gay, perhaps quarrel a little as the strong drink goes to their heads. When twilight comes, they take their leave of the deceased, dragging sleepy children after them as they stream out in all directions to go to their homes and then, as the night darkens, the whole City of Mexico goes to the theater, all to see the same play though all those who have seen it a few times, although given only once a year, know it by heart. Since there are not enough theaters to encompass an entire metropolis, on every vacant lot a theater for the night is erected of flimsy wood or canvas. Or movie houses are set up playing a film based on the same play and following it as faithfully as it can be followed. All the tents and shanties and theaters are crowded to the doors, with playgoers sitting on the floors, in the aisles, and on the stage.

My wife and I spent the day in the cemetery, familiarly known as Doña Dolores (Our Lady of the Sorrows), envied the funereal-cheerful picnics of the multitude, bought such food as we could get from vendors, dragged our way home along the dusty roads on foot, and, after another snack, we too went to the theater to see the play deemed appropriate to close the week of the fiesta known as the Day of the Dead. The play was José Zorilla's *Don Juan Tenorio.* I had read it but never heard it before, my favorite version of Don Juan being that of the Spanish monk, Tirso de Molina, written in 1630 and entitled *El Burlador de Sevilla o el Convidado de Piedra.* But that night in one of the improvised theaters of Mexico we were destined to see Zorilla's play once, and hear it three times, delivered almost simultaneously with the same lilt and emphasis. Everybody in the theater seemed to know the play by heart, so that we could hear the audience reciting it from memory, all around us we could hear the prompter in his trapdoor box elevated in a curve and open to face the actors, and we could hear the actor, waiting for his lines as if he did not know them by heart, then delivering them as if they were welling up from his own bosom. The triple recitation of every line was a fascinating novelty to us and disturbing to nobody. It seemed to belong as a fitting end to the week-long celebration of death. Why *Don Juan Tenorio?* Because it had swordplay galore and ended in a cemetery where the monument of one of Don Juan's victims found itself a voice, accepted a gruesome invitation to dine with Don Juan, then invited him to return the visit by dining with his victim in the bowels of the earth.

Don Quixote has given Spain its favorite national image and is incarnated in the *Día de la Raza.* But Don Juan expresses an aspect of the Spanish character, too, and he has given Mexico the *Día de los Muertos.* The story of Don Juan originates in the Chronicles of Seville where it is recounted that the Don, after violating the daughter of the Comendador, murders her father in an unequal duel, but cannot be punished because of his noble rank until, as the legend has it, he goes to the church cemetery which his father had willed not to his son, but to his son's victims. There Don Juan mocks the Comendador whose stone monument becomes animated and drags the libertine (*el Burlador de Sevilla*) into Inferno.

The monk, Tirso de Molina, a first-rate dramatist, tried to make of his play a moral legend that warns all libertines that they are doomed to eternal torture in Hell. But somehow the monk-dramatist made of Don Juan a figure more interesting and more expressive of something in the Spanish character than Spanish fears of the fires of Hell. Since then scores and scores of writers in all the literatures of Western Europe, and in pantomime, music, poetry, ballets, puppet shows, and the great opera of Mozart, have continued to celebrate the deeds and misdeeds and fearful punishment of Don Juan Tenorio (this appears to have been his real name), the *Burlador de Sevilla.*

DON JUAN AND DON QUIXOTE

Don Quixote means more to Spain, to be sure, than Don Juan does. Spain has been described by Nietzsche as "the land that attempted too much." Don Quixote has been called the archetype of the Spanish character, as Hamlet has been of the English. He acts instantly on his impulses, for he is possessed by a dream, while Hamlet is the vacillating type possessed by reflection and doubt. Hamlet's indecision is the key to the tragedy in Shakespeare's play, for it is the cause of death of guilty and innocent alike: not only of his stepfather, the assassin, but of the Queen, Ophelia, Polonius, Rosencrantz and Guildenstern, Laertes, and even of Hamlet himself. But Don Quixote's impulsive actions carried out in a waking dream kill no one and do no harm, or only the harm to himself that causes laughter in all beholders and a mere blanket tossing and pummeling for Sancho. But Don Juan never hesitates to bring harm to all who cross his path. His creed is simple and devastating. "*Esta noche he de gozarla,*" (this night I must enjoy her) he says of any maiden he lays eyes on. "If anyone gets in my way my sword will take care of him." When he is warned of eternal punishment after death, his arrogant answer as Tirso writes it is: *Si tan largo me lo fiais* (if my credit is extended for so long a time then I shall spend the rest of my life as I have spent it until now). If Tirso's Juan possesses any virtue, it is *virtus* in the ancient Roman sense of manliness and valor. He is *hombre y macho* and ready to risk his life in each encounter with a maid and her defenders. In this last he knows no mercy and no sense of fair play, as shown by his murder of the aged Comendador. His sword play is but a more ancient form of the gun play I so often witnessed in Mexico. And the Day of the Dead, or the week-long fiesta that has grown out of it, would not be complete if it did not end with the two defiant encounters with the statue over the grave of the Comendador. That Zorilla's play has ousted Tirso's much superior tragedy on the stages of Spain, Mexico, and all of Latin America is due precisely to the change in the ending and the fact that it is the closing moment of All Souls' Day in every Spanish-speaking country.

But as soon as Don Juan's story and image leave Spain for the other lands of Europe, it is reflected as if in a hundred mirrors, proving that Don Juan is in some sense a human archetype and not a mere aspect of Spanish valor or Mexican *machismo.*

Leo Weinstein, a professor of romance languages (French Department) at Stanford, has written what is probably the most remarkable of the books on *Don Juan Tenorio.* In it he lists some 490 versions in countless lands, mostly dramas, but also twenty-eight paintings and motion pictures, and several musical plays or operas including the best known of all, the *Don Giovanni* of Mozart.

Don Juan and the Comendador are in them all, yet they are, as Professor Weinstein aptly calls them, metamorphoses, as if in each land the Don is reflected in a mirror that has a slightly different curved surface to reflect a somewhat different image. Even when *Don Juan Tenorio,* the nineteenth century *zarzuela* written in Spain by José Zorilla, crosses the ocean to Mexico, he is, as we shall see, transformed.

In any case, Spain's Don Juan is not the Don of Hoffmann and Musset and other northern romantics, in love with love, seeking his ideal in vain in woman after woman, and never finding her. Nor is he Byron's satirical Don Juan who is seduced rather than seducing. As Ramiro de Maeztu wrote, "Our Don Juan the rest of the world does not know, and if they got to know him they would deport him as undesirable." Not only is the Don not in love with love; he does not even know what love means. If Tirso's Don Juan should fall in love with one of his victims, he would cease to be the *Burlador,* the libertine, the damned. At every encounter with a girl, peasant or lady, he displays overflowing energy, infinite craft and zeal, immediacy of desire, but no true depth of feeling. His aim is conquest: immediate possession, then indifference or mockery toward the possessed. It is that which makes him a *Burlador,* an untranslatable word, some of whose meanings are violator, ruiner, and above all, mocker. That is the secret of the boastful "bookkeeper's list" of Leporello who in Mozart's *Don Giovanni* assures us that his master, who has taught him how to boast, has enjoyed the satisfaction of his impersonal desire with *mil i tre,* one thousand and three women, in a single land in a single year.

In Tirso, moreover, there is not and cannot be any woman who continues to love Don Juan once he has deceived her. The unique thing about Zorilla's *Don Juan* is that in the end he is not damned, but saved, redeemed by the love of a pure woman after he has betrayed her. And we are sure that he has fallen in love with her innocence, has suddenly come to believe in God, and sees in none other than Doña Inés, the Comendador's daughter, his chance for salvation.

But how can a man be saved in an instant who has deceived so many women and killed so many men? And the one from whom he seeks salvation is a girl who is about to become a nun and whom he raped while she was in a faint after he invaded her room.

Zorilla solves this problem with a different view of theology from Tirso's, with a different idea of love and salvation. Don Juan, moved by the innocence and purity of Doña Inés, kneels before the outraged Comendador and begs for his daughter's hand to right the wrong he has done her. That is, he tells the inflexible Comendador, my only chance of salvation. The Comendador quite naturally asks what concern he could have with Don Juan's salvation, draws his sword, and in the ultimate unequal battle, is slain. Doña Inés dies, too, and both of them and all of Don Juan's victims are buried in the estate which he should have inherited, but which his father's will turns into a cemetery.

When Don Juan returns five years later to visit the cemetery, the shade of Doña Inés appears from her tomb to tell him that she is waiting for him and has decided to share eternity with him, whether in salvation or damnation. Follows the famous scene of the two feasts with the statue of the Comendador, which now take place, appropriately, in Don Juan's private cemetery. When the statue, in the second feast, grasps the Don's left hand in his stony grasp that will not relax, his own daughter, Doña Inés, rises from her tomb to take the right hand which Don Juan has raised to Heaven, crying, "Almighty God, I believe in You, have pity on me, my Lord!" With that appeal, and with that right hand which he has raised to Heaven and Doña Inés has taken in hers, they are both saved. At this point, in the Mexican version my wife and I saw, two doves gliding up on visible wires ascend from the cemetery to the ceiling, which is the promised Heaven. My wife remembers how the audience broke into a storm of joyous applause at this happy ending.

So the nineteenth-century romantics who liked happy endings and found Tirso's play too consistently and unremittingly tragic were satisfied. Thus the Spanish and still more the Mexican view is verified that "God's mercy excels and shines more brightly than His justice" (as Don Quixote put it). A pure love, if only one, and for a mere moment compared with all his outrages, is sufficient in this new version, because as Salvador Madariaga has said, Spanish men—and I might add, still more Mexican men—are "accustomed to have their women do everything for them." So the gayest, the most characteristic, and the most unique and colorful of all Mexico's colorful fiestas ends happily as end it must, and people return to their homes tired and satisfied that death has given them a wonderful week.

37

PORTRAIT OF MEXICO

When I wanted to start work with Diego on *Portrait of Mexico*, he was so worried by the infection in the tear gland of his left eye, so afraid of going blind and no longer being able to paint, that he had arranged to go to a hospital. He had not generally been subject to infections, indeed was always as strong as a master workman on walls needed to be. But during his year in Detroit he had been following a slimming diet prescribed by a Mexican physician that reduced him to a mere shadow of his former self. Here was the diet as I copied it from the doctor's prescription:

QUANTITY OF NOURISHMENT: a) 12 acid foods daily: 4 lemons, 6 oranges, 2 grapefruit; b) 1 liter of vegetable juice; c) two times daily a vegetable salad

MENU: On an empty stomach, fruit salts [a physic]. Breakfast: 2 oranges, 1 lemon. During the day: every two hours an acid fruit. Dinner and supper: a vegetable salad. Vegetable juice should be drunk during the day. Fruits of all kinds, except grapes and bananas. No cooked salads. No sugar or oil in the salads. Every night a bath with epsom salts (½ kilo daily).

To this drastic diet was added liberal doses of thyroid extract. In defense of Mexican medical science I might add that the doctor who wrote that prescription, and whose name charity bids me omit, spent some time studying in Los Angeles, and I must say that the diet smacks more of Los Angeles, California, than it does of Mexico.

In the course of a year of toil, much of it under the hot sun and humidity of a Detroit summer, in a glass-covered museum court where the temperature rose at times to 120° Fahrenheit, Diego's frame shrank until he had lost well over a hundred pounds. His body became flabby, his face lean and sad, his clothes hung about him in elephantine folds. It is a wonder that he got no more than an eye infection. To make matters worse, the wet plaster and cement stayed moist longer in the Detroit summer humidity so that he was able to work longer into the night.

Just before I arrived in Mexico, he had gone to consult an able eye specialist in Mexico City named Rafael Silva. Dr. Silva's first command was: "Diego, reinflate yourself, and never try to disinflate yourself again. Follow your natural appetite. Eat what you want and all that you want." And I, having often watched Diego eat, can testify that his appetite was adequate to the hugeness of his frame and the enormity of his toil on the scaffold. Then, on Diego's insistence, Dr. Silva arranged a room for him in the British Hospital.

Frida was in a bad way, too. When they patched up their divorce in California and remarried, she persuaded Diego at last to help her realize her schoolgirl ambition to "have a child by Diego Rivera." She was pregnant when they arrived in Detroit. At first she rejoiced at her pregnancy and was full of plans and dreams for her coming child. But slender and frail as she was, she did not take kindly to the hot summers of Detroit after a lifetime spent in the cool uplands of the Valley of Mexico, 7,500 feet above the sea. Nor to the American cuisine. She missed the native food of Mexico and limited her meals to birdlike pecks at tidbits supplemented by sucking on hard candies and taking periodic nips from a Three-Star Hennessey bottle she always carried in her purse. She began to complain that "her baby hurt her" but continued to act the gay, reckless girl she had always been. On July 4 a miscarriage and frightful hemorrhaging resulted. Toward morning they rushed her to the Ford Hospital in Detroit to see if they could check the bleeding. As they wheeled her through the basement directly into the operating room, she opened her eyes upon a many-colored ceiling, and in the midst of her agony found the strength to whisper, "Qué precioso!" (How beautiful!).

Frida was heartbroken at the loss of the child, and depressed to the point of melancholia when Diego admonished her that they must never try again. To make matters worse, before she had recovered, her mother became seriously ill, and she took an arduous journey from Detroit only to arrive in time to see her mother die. After many months of feeble health and ill spirits, Frida recovered enough to ask for oils and tin and did a series of oil paintings on tin, such as the simple folk do to paint a church *retablo* when some miracle has occurred to them. She turned out works at long intervals, now on tin, now on canvas, dealing with her fantasies in connection with her miscarriage, paintings strange, witty, sad, and fantastic. They are definitely better than the works she did before the loss of her child. One of them is the celebrated *Self-Portrait* showing her lying in her canopied bed, asleep or perhaps dead, her coverlet and pillow covered with five-pointed leaves with their roots running down into the earth at the bottom of the bed; and on top of the canopy lies a full-length *calavera* or skeleton adorned with fireworks on the lower limbs like a Judas of the Saturday of Glory, but holding in its (her?) hands a bouquet of ivy leaves. Only recently, I received a letter from a collector asking who owned the picture at present and how he could get in touch with the owner to buy it from him. It is a painting that is highly prized by critics and has been much reproduced. When last I heard of it, it was in the collection of A. Conger Goodyear. The reader can see a good reproduction of it in black and white as Plate 157 in *The Fabulous Life of Diego Rivera.*

Once more, as during her first accident and self-taught apprenticeship in painting, Frida was compelled to do her painting in bed. Her doctors, who had never succeeded in arresting the slow decay in her frame, found new reasons for operating on her, and she went along with Diego to the British Hospital where they occupied adjoining rooms. She worked once more on a bed of pain with an easel fastened to her bed. Between the first painting in her life and the last, she had never been free from pain, though always she stood it bravely. She made up for the accidental crippling of her frail body by turning herself into one of the most effective of her works of art. Barbaric pre-Conquest jewels, colorfully embroidered, many-folded skirts, blouses drawn from the Mexican popular costume at its best, strings of brightly colored wool in her hair, her long skirts filled out by many petticoats, skillful and subtle use of paint and mascara and whatever else her artistic sensibility taught her to use to express the flame of joy and creativeness that burned so brightly within her and to conceal the maiming effect of her accident—all added up to an appearance that would have seemed outlandish were it not for the knowing artistry with which she designed and adorned herself.

Diego was embarrassed that neither he nor Frida could work with me on *Portrait of Mexico,* which I had come to do together with him. Hence he was delighted, as I was, when I proposed that while I was waiting for them, I should work on a future biography. "Go to my home," he told me. "You can live there and the servants will feed you and take care of you. My files are open to you. You can read all the letters I wrote and all I received and take any notes you please. You can visit my walls and come and ask me questions. Somewhere in my files you will find photographs of almost everything I have painted. Or you can get copies from Alvarez Bravo, my photographer. I have seen so many foolish attempts at my biography, that I am glad you are going to undertake it. And when you visit me at the hospital, I will answer all your questions."

That was all the permission I needed. I found his letter files in various places, but mostly in a balcony of his studio. Letters had piled up there in startling disorder, more letters than he ever dreamed he had or knew what to do with. Almost the first letter I opened contained a check for him, quite old, that he had never cashed. Later, when my wife arrived and began to help me, she found enough unopened letters containing uncashed checks to make a small fortune.

There were letters from friends; opportunities for exhibitions in museums and art galleries, offers to purchase works of his, or have portraits or other easel work done. There were letters from the Communist party begging for donations at the very time when the party was denouncing him as its arch-enemy. There were individual requests for money, often granted, to help an unknown peasant to buy a mule or a student to have his thesis typed. There were letters from museums, more often unanswered than answered. Letters from artists expressing admiration, acknowledging a debt or gratitude, asking for advice on or criticism of their work sent in the form of a photograph, soliciting a foreword to a catalogue, looking for help in some fight against censorship. There were letters from bores, cranks, people who wanted to know about Mexico's divorce laws, or the cost of living in such and such a village, letters asking him whether he hadn't some "unimportant" sketch or painting which he could spare for a poor admirer with no funds to pay him, letters warning him of plots against his life, threatening letters, letters preaching some new faith or a fragment of some oriental religion—all the wide range of mail that was likely to come to one who was continuously in the headlines.

Everything lay in disorder, important and unimportant, opened and unopened, from crackpots to critics, trash to treasure. Frida had once tried to organize his files and dig him out of the avalanche. She had purchased thick cardboard accordion files, and later, steel cabinets. But I found the cabinets strangely empty for whole letters of the alphabet, although the letter "P" was stuffed and overflowing with opened and unopened epistles. "Why the letter P?" I asked Frida. "Oh, that. We put the important ones there *Para contestar*—to be answered." But the system was abandoned when the letter P revolted and refused to admit another piece of paper.

Especially interesting was Diego's correspondence with young painters. As often as not he had failed to reply, despite a notation in his own hand, "To be answered *cuanto antes*" (as soon as possible). But when he did answer, he was always generous and encouraging to young and struggling painters whose work showed a touch of talent. When Pedro Rendón, doing a mural in the Rodriguez public market, was attacked in the press and his painting threatened with obliteration, Diego wrote:

> I find his painting extremely interesting and am amazed at the unfavorable judgments against it. . . . I am determined to defend his work personally on the field of esthetics and of justice and will appeal to art authorities on an international scale in its favor. . . .

Despite his indisposition to write letters instead of paint, he actually gathered testimonials from local and "international" esthetic authorities on Rendón's behalf, and the frescoes are still in the market.

The range of Diego's sensibility was wide. Painters as diverse as Ben Shahn, Paul O'Higgins, Angel Bracho, María Izquierdo, Caroline Durieux, Kandinsky, Klee, Covarrubias, all received quotable praise from him or an introduction to some catalogue of one of their exhibitions. Even men whose style was far removed from his and whose reputation was already great and their market assured, were pleased at such help. Thus I found this letter from Vasili Kandinsky, dated May 21, 1931:

> Believe me, you have caused me very *great* pleasure with your opinions on my art. You can well imagine that I have periods of great loneliness, but at the same time

I know that it will not always be so. . . . It pleased me greatly to know that you own some of my pictures. . . .

At the other end of the spectrum of artistic fame there was Mardonio Magaña. This humble worker in the arts Diego found when for a brief period he (Diego) was made director of the San Carlos Academy of Art by a vote of the student body, the same academy from which he had been expelled a quarter of a century earlier. Magaña was the janitor of the academy. In his spare time, stirred by all the creation going on around him, he carved sculptures of wood, though his wages barely allowed him to purchase the quality of wood he needed, and his style had no model or precedent among the art students of San Carlos. After Diego looked at his work, sculptures carved on a small scale of perhaps three feet in height yet monumental and life size in their feeling, he raised this simple Indian peasant from janitor to teacher of wood carving. Diego personally purchased some of his sculptures at prices Mardonio would not have dreamed of asking, wrote letters and illustrated articles about him, interested Frances Flynn Payne, and through her the Rockefeller family, in the purchase of some of Magaña's work. Next Diego bought for the old man, already over sixty, a piece of land, an adobe hut, some chickens, some pigs, and a cow, so that Mardonio might be economically independent and fully devote the precious remainder of his life to the exercise of the talents so belatedly revealed. I visited him at his "estate," and it was a joy to see among the garden truck and century plants his beautiful sculptures. Magaña's blossoming from janitor in the art school proved once more that the Mexicans are a people with an instinctive plastic sense, wherever it has not been spoiled by middle-class and American tourist customers' taste.

Many of the letters to Diego recorded lost opportunities. "While you are looking through my papers," said Diego, when I visited him at the hospital, "see if you can find a letter from Jack Hastings about an exhibition I am to have in London. I want to accept, but I have mislaid his letter and don't know his address." I found it in the end only because I looked through every scrap of paper for the purposes of my biography. It was a letter from Lord John Hastings, himself a painter, arranging for an exhibition of Diego's work in the important Tate Gallery in London. But it was lying inside an envelope from our publisher, Covici-Friede. It bore the date March 31, 1935. I answered it for Diego a year and twenty days after he had received it, when the period was long past that the Gallery had offered him. I wrote an intimate explanation to Lord Hastings who knew him well, and a tactful and persuasive apology to the director of the Tate Gallery. I succeeded in getting a new date for the following year, but Diego never did get to exhibit in London. This helps, I imagine, to explain some of the coldness British critics have shown toward Diego's work and the English edition of our *Portrait of Mexico*. To snub the Tate Gallery was something unheard of in the tight little island, as it was in the thirties. I am sure it was not Hastings' fault nor the Tate's; but somewhere in

Diego's files there must be another letter from England labeled in his hand: *Para contestar.*

In one drawer, lying by itself, I found a packet boldly labelled in Frida's hand, *Cartas de las mujeres de Diego.* These I felt I might not look at without special permission. When I asked both Frida and Diego, they said that if I was to be his biographer, of course I had the right to examine them and copy them or take notes on their content. And Diego said, "You may ask me any questions you want about them." My heart rejoiced, for now I felt I really was accepted as Diego's biographer. To write two books with him, illustrated by him, and then to write his biography and find a publisher, which I felt would not be hard, was really a great stride on the road to my ambition, to be a free-lance writer.

In the packet were letters from Frida herself to him; from his two mistresses in Paris, Angelina Beloff, a painter who dreamt of becoming his legal wife and going with him to Mexico or being sent for afterward, and Marievna Vorobieva, another Russian mistress in Paris, actually half-Polish, half-Russian, who bore him an illegitimate child, Marika, whose legitimacy he never acknowledged; and letters from a number of other women, mostly American, who offered to serve as models or gave hints of the extent to which they were attracted to this huge, homely, powerfully creative painter. I asked Diego about his illegitimate daughter, Marika, who became a dancer; he dismissed her laughingly as "a daughter of the armistice," when all Paris went wild in three days of Bacchanalian revel at the news of the war's end, and again referred to her as "the daughter of some Senegalese sharpshooter," implying that his mistress had conceived her during those revels. But I found letters from Marika, which he seemed never to have answered; letters showing that he intermittently sent Marievna money to support and educate their daughter; and letters from such good friends in Paris as Elie Faure, reminding him that his daughter needed help and that it was his duty to support her. When I got a picture of Marika and made comparisons concerning her resemblance to his two legitimate daughters by Guadalupe, I received a warm and grateful letter from Marika. After studying all the, to be sure, fragmentary evidence, I had no doubt that Diego himself was the "Senegalese sharpshooter."

Frida knew there were letters in that packet that had caused her bitter anguish. Several of Diego's casual affairs were carried on while he was wooing her, but the one that was hardest on her occurred seven years after her marriage. It was Diego's affair with Cristina, that caused her to divorce Diego. A lonely and miserable time followed for both of them; Frida grieved endlessly, tried in vain to knit to some other being or interest the raveled thread that had bound her life so completely to Diego's. As the flame of resentment died down, she forgave her younger sister whose protective guardian she was, and told herself that it was Diego that she loved, and that he meant more to her than the things that stood between them. Diego for his part was regretful, tactful, and patient, but he did not give up, for Frida, the standards or ways he had always followed.

Frida's letter to him on that occasion was the most moving one in the whole package. Wiser and more tolerant now as a result of this bitter test of separation, Frida wrote him that she knew on reflection that

> . . . all these letters, liaisons with petticoats, lady teachers of "English," gypsy models, assistants with good intentions, "plenipotentiary emissaries from distant places," only represent *flirtations,* and that at bottom *you and I* love each other dearly, and thus go through adventures without number . . . yet we will always love each other.
>
> All these things have been repeated throughout the seven years that we have lived together, and all the rages I have gone through have served only to make me understand in the end that I love you more than my own skin, and that, though you may not love me in the same way, still you love me somewhat. Isn't that so? . . . I shall always hope that that continues, and with that I am content.

Ella joined me when her summer vacation started at the beginning of June and we spent three happy months together, working on *Portrait of Mexico,* which was getting along splendidly, and gathering the materials for Diego's life story, discounting his tall tales as best we could, and putting together the pictures, some of which I was to reproduce in both books. My wife worked up in the balcony of Diego's large studio now, poring through his correspondence and pronouncements on artists and art and Mexican politics, and all the while keeping her ears open for the tall tales and fantasies and farces that he was telling down below to wide-eyed visitors. She took notes on what she heard that were a priceless aid to me, and when his fantasies seemed too big for me to swallow, she and I and Frida questioned him on the preposterous details. Frida, too, was a great help on both books, for she was on my side and wanted them to be a more or less faithful reflection of his life and work. The two books dovetailed marvellously. The 161 plates that were eventually to illustrate our *Portrait* were a huge portion of his work and of his fantasy and knowledge about the history of his country, thus forming a considerable portion of his life also; the biography, with its 167 plates using some of the same pictures and many different and more personal ones, traced the development of his work as a would-be artist from his childish drawings, through the work of his teachers and inspirers, to his paintings as an imitator of the artists of Spain, to his cubist work in Paris (copies of which I got from his Paris dealer, Leonce Rosenberg), and finally to his late and sudden finding of himself and a style of his own, first in a huge encaustic mural, and then in his frescoes of Mexican life and history, real and imagined.

He had stories to tell of every period that were a delight to listen to, and which were, with careful appraisal on my part of possibility and probability, material for the biography itself. Of course, I had to get to Paris somehow to interview the painters who had known him and to get reproductions of the work he had done in Europe, much of it not available in any other way. Luckily, after I got to the United States, the Communist opposition to which I still belonged wanted to send me to Spain in connection with the Spanish Civil War, a trip which gave me an opportunity to stop en route in Paris and do the Paris research so important to his biography.

Diego's inventions, fantasies, and tall stories were of great help to me in an unexpected way. During the years that I knew him, he had scores of writers and would-be writers who approached him to do his biography. Some wrote so badly that they were utterly unfit for the task. Others were repelled by the fact that he lied as Münchausen would have lied about his life. One by one they dropped off because they could not stand the manifest inventions he was telling them. Or they argued with him about the impossibility of a given tale until both writer and interviewee were in a fury, and the close alliance that is necessary between biographer and subject even in an unauthorized biography such as mine was to be, broke up in mutual antagonism. The tall tales for which Diego was famous were improvised as effortlessly and as naturally as a spider spins his web, their pattern changing with each retelling; they were fables wrapped within fables and counterpointed by their opposite, woven so skillfully out of truth and fantasy that one could not be distinguished from the other, told with such artistry that they compelled the momentary suspension of disbelief. If Diego had never touched brush to wall or gesso, tin or canvas, merely talked and had his talk set down, Baron Münchausen would have had to look to his reputation.

This was hard indeed on would-be biographers, especially on one young woman, who tried to take down every sacred word as autobiography, particularly since he made a number of new inventions especially calculated to offend and shock her young maidenhood. He told her that he had indulged in cannibalism for an experiment of the medical school, eating the thigh of a young woman raw, and that it tasted better than chicken. He followed this by declaring that his favorite cheese was Roquefort, and that the green mold which is part of it was manufactured by incorporating the menstrual material of young maidens. I don't think she outlasted that session.

But this was only a modification of his usual tale-telling, for he seemed always to be probing the cherished beliefs and point of tolerance of his listener. For anthropologists, as we have seen, he invented a pecuniary economy for the Aztecs. When Leon Trotsky was his honored guest, he drove him to distraction by outrageous inventions of facts and doctrines in Mexican politics until the argument ended by Leon Trotsky's packing his bags and leaving his and his wife's goods on the sidewalk while he looked for another habitation.

If I managed to enjoy a friendship with Diego for over three decades and become his biographer it was not because I did not take truth seriously, but because I took Rivera seriously as a creative artist, regarding his wild fantasy and fertile invention as an essential, if sometimes upsetting, aspect of his overflowing creativity and character as artist and man. His life as he recounted it was by no means the least of his works of art, though it had greater formlessness than his more carefully composed images on canvas and wall.

When my wife's vacation period was over, she left for her teaching, and I continued my work alone on both books. I had finished neither of them when my six-month visa expired and I too had to take the Ward Line steamship for New York. But the long period of close intimacy with Diego and Frida, and with Martin Temple, had taught me much about the mysteries of Mexican life.

During the years 1975 and 1976 our newspapers and our Congress made a terrific fuss about the bribing of certain key people in a given country in order to get the country to buy American airplanes or machines and not those of some other country. I know nothing about the countries involved or the deals, but I do know something about bribery by businessmen, foreign and domestic, to get contracts and make deals in Mexico. During my stays in Mexico in the thirties, I witnessed and learned of such bribes large and small and convinced myself that one could get nowhere without knowing the proper officials to bribe and making it seem that his visit to you or yours to him was entirely a matter of courtesy and had nothing to do with business or bribery. A few examples will suffice.

I have more than once witnessed a scene in which a policeman, poorly paid, supplemented his income in the following fashion. Among his tools for the enforcement of the law, he carried in one of his pockets a screwdriver. When a street was comparatively deserted, he would go over to the NO PARKING sign and unscrew it, secreting it in the box in which he stood at his regular traffic station. After a while, a *forastero* (foreigner or stranger to the city) would come along and park his car where the sign had been, then go about his business. When he returned, the No Parking sign was back but his license plate had been unscrewed and had disappeared. He would then go in search of the nearest traffic cop, give him five or ten pesos (ten pesos was then worth five American dollars), and the policeman would courteously and in person go to the car, bringing back its license plate, and himself screw it on. That was graft on a small scale.

On Sunday mornings I was often at the house of a philanthropist who was trying to help the International Rescue Committee to get Mexican residence visas and work permits from the Mexican Government for European refugees. A general used to visit my friend also on Sunday mornings, and they would exchange courtesies, but how much money passed from the hand of the philanthropist to the general I could never guess. But the amount varied with the number of German Jews or people in danger in Stalin's Russia, to be saved. It took some more bribing in the home country, too, and I must say it was easier to help Germans to get out of Hitler's camps than Russians out of Stalin's. One friend of mine who escaped in that fashion from a German camp said to me: "Thank God for corruption."

One last example. In most of the countries of the world where alligators are indigenous, the Government passes a law protecting them against hunting for their skins during the mating season. But Mexico is strikingly more humane than the other alligator countries; it protects them not only during the mating season but forbids hunting them at any time of the year except during the hibernation period, when they bury themselves deep underground and are not to be found by the hunters. One of my friends was in the business of tanning alligator skins, a process which he did so well that every skin he could get found a ready market in the high-priced factories and stores of the United States that made the finest alligator purses and shoes. Each year this man, who was strong, hardy, and brave, and respected by the frequently dangerous natives, would go into the jungle territories and hire hunters to provide him with alligator skins. But the alligators were protected all year except when they were invisible, precisely for the purpose of guaranteeing that each key official in the chain of protection and rule of the region would get a bribe, and a not insubstantial one, so as not to notice that the alligators had been hunted in the seasons when the hunters could find them. Naturally, this man added the necessary bribes to the cost of the skins, and had to bribe any inspector who "chanced" to inspect his factory during the tanning.

I learned much of the personal lives of Frida and Diego, for they both used the same car and the same chauffeur when they went to their assignations. Frida was not falling in love again and again, but her affairs were always brief and never deep, and none of the men she carried on flirtations with meant to her what Diego did. Since the trip to Mexico City from San Angel is long, and a ride in the city to my home short, they always offered me a ride, and, particularly, Frida told me details of her current affairs.

Their chauffeur was a silent Mexican largely of Indian blood. He went where he was told and waited minutes or hours in his car until asked to drive his passenger home again, and never said a word to anyone of where he had been. But one such trip became a celebrated one, for he fell asleep in his car with his feet on the upholstery and projecting through an open window. When he was finally awakened his shoes had been unlaced and taken off his feet by a light-fingered thief, so that he had to drive home barefoot. This was a joke throughout the household including Diego's and Frida's numerous servants. For my part I christened him *mi general,* and when asked *General What?* answered *General Trastorno,* which means General Confusion. The name stuck to him, and he good-naturedly accepted it thereafter.

But neither Frida's affairs nor Diego's belonged in their biography, except where they deeply influenced their art or their life, nor do they belong in the present memoirs either.

Yet when I sent Diego a printer's dummy of his forthcoming biography, he complained of my reticence, saying: "Your book threatens to be really philistine because as regards women, you show only the official ones, and they are not always the more important in the life of a man." He got over his pique when he saw the biography itself. But his letter showed me how really fortunate I was that I had not finished either text before I had to leave Mexico, for I would have had my hands full trying to satisfy him with every sentence. As it was, neither my text for *Portrait of Mexico* nor, what is more important, my *Diego Rivera: His Life and Times* was official, although he helped me enormously with both of them.

Either my mother's God or dumb luck was watching over me when I chose my Ward Line steamship. The first passenger I met and began to chat with proved to be an editor for Alfred A. Knopf, Inc., named Bernard Smith. He asked me what I had been doing in Mexico, and I told him, "Writing a book with Diego Rivera to be called *Portrait of Mexico*" Did I have a publisher? I did. I also had worked on a biography of Diego Rivera.

Bernard Smith showed visible interest, so I told him some of the tall stories and what truth I thought I had extracted from them. We walked for hours pacing the deck and leaning over the rail to the windward, and because we were going through quiet waters on a waveless, windless day, I did not get seasick. By the time we got to the shark-free, blue waters of the Gulf Stream and were watching the flying fish, Bernard Smith said to me: "How would you like to do the Rivera biography for Alfred Knopf?" I expressed my interest, concealing my eagerness. "O.K.," said Smith. "When we get to New York, I'll talk it over with Knopf and draw up a contract for your signature." I was in luck indeed: two books with Rivera's pictures, and then a life of Diego Rivera. I felt it was a sure thing. I had made it as a free-lance writer.

38

THE CIVIL WAR IN SPAIN—I

In 1854 Marx wrote in the *New York Tribune,* "Spain has never succeeded in acquiring the latest French style . . . of beginning and ending a revolution in three days." Spain's Civil Wars of the 19th century bear him out. The century embraced cycles of from three to nine years of civil wars (and one of fourteen years), which kept Spain in almost constant turmoil, but changed nothing. The Spanish revolution which I was going to witness early in 1937 had two prior beginnings. After the Spanish-American War over the freedom of Cuba, Spain suddenly realized that its young men had had the opportunity to observe at close quarters the incompetence and pompous frivolity of the bureaucrats who were Spain's official leaders. The country had been kept in the dark and knew neither the gravity of the Cuban revolt, nor the strength of the powerful country that had come to the support of the Cuban insurgents. They knew still less of the unreadiness of the Spanish Army and Navy and officer class. The Spanish fleet had sailed to its doom armed with ancient cannon that fell short of the ships of the American fleet, and it did not even possess a base, a coaling station, transport ships, or any of the elementary requirements of a modern fleet. When the men came back from disaster, they were yellow ghosts, ravaged by yellow fever and contaminated food. This event produced the first revolution in Spanish thought, the works of those intellectuals who in honor of Spain's catastrophic defeat called themselves the generation of 1898. The disillusion spread through the entire working class and peasantry, and in the other camp produced a determination in the Spanish officer class to unleash a preventive counterrevolution before a revolution might start.

"We must shorten the process of history and make a leap of four centuries to catch up with those who have gotten ahead of us and with whom we have to live," wrote Joaquín Costa of the generation of '98. And Joaquín Maurín, the founder and outstanding leader of the POUM (Partido Obrero de Unificación Marxista), declared, "A revolution is a point of departure. Unhappy is the people who cannot depart, that sees itself obliged to mark time. It will waste itself in stagnation, in idleness. It will vegetate miserably while the rest of the world that surrounds it marches ahead at full speed. Such has been the fate of Spain." No less deeply stirred were the much more powerful Socialist party and its unions, the UGT (Unión General de Trabajadores), centered in Madrid. And equally stirred was the powerful and uniquely Spanish anarchist movement which dominated Catalonia.

In another sense, the revolution that I was going to witness began in the year 1931 when the incompetent Alfonso XIII fell without a struggle, as a federation of the various ex- and antimonarchist forces overwhelmingly won the municipal elections, on which basis they founded a republic. At this, the reactionary generals redoubled their preparations for a preventive *coup d'état* which, after some false starts and ebb and flow of feelings, brought on the military coup of July 19, 1936.

As early as possible in 1937, the American Communist opposition decided to send someone to Spain to get a closeup of the Spanish Civil War, and to carry an important message to Largo Caballero, Premier of the Spanish Republic and Secretary of the General Workers' Union (UGT) which had its center in Madrid. Our group picked me. I spoke Spanish fluently, was immersed in Spanish history and literature, had studied under such great teachers as Pedro Henríquez Ureña, Angel del Río, and Federico de Onís, had published articles in the Spanish language press, and had taught a course on *Don Quixote* in the Romantic Department at Stanford University, when Professor Hilton was the department head. He had chosen me to teach it, put all his graduate students in my class, and had even taken the course himself. This time, when I applied to my government for a passport, they finally gave me one, but stamped it:

NOT VALID FOR SPAIN

Another obstacle to my trip was the "Non-Intervention Committee" which "contained" France and England who, on the whole, didn't intervene, but it was also made up of Germany, Italy, and Russia, all three of whom intervened with all the types of weapons they then possessed (good practice!). But the United States did not ratify the Non-Intervention Treaty. Furthermore, the Non-Intervention Committee seemed to have put the Pyrenees between France and Spain, and it was to France that I went to find out how I could get into Spain without a proper passport and visa.

In lieu of a Spanish visa I carried with me several letters to high officials of the Spanish Republic, one of them potentially very important, as well as a proud heart that would not agree to be stopped by Non-Intervention Committees, the Pyrenees, lack of Spanish visas, or a rubber stamp which proclaimed that my passport was "NOT VALID FOR SPAIN." I also carried a copy of my book, *Portrait of Mexico*, to give to Luis Araquistáin who had himself written, in Spanish, a book on Mexico, and was the Spanish republican ambassador to Paris.

Before I left for Spain I had some business to transact here and in Mexico. From a Mexican daily, *El Demócrata,* I secured a credential as a reporter. Benigno Valenzuela, its owner and editor, agreed that I was to write a series of forty reports from Spain on the Soviet Union, entitled *Rusia en 1937,* at a fee of thirteen pesos per article. If I completed the entire forty articles, I could make a book of them, and *El Demócrata* would pay me an additional two pesos per article. My compensation, not bad for a Mexican correspondent, would be thus fifteen pesos, or seven dollars and fifty cents per article, since the peso was then worth 50¢ American, which meant much more then than it does now, after so many spells of inflation. (At that time one could buy an ounce of gold for $35.00 and the dollar was redeemable in gold on demand.) In addition I got something more precious from *El Demócrata,* a credential identifying me as their correspondent, duly sealed and containing my picture and the signature of Benigno Valenzuela.

I next secured a similar credential with seal and photograph from the European Picture Service. These were the first two documents I was to get to make myself a working reporter and photographer, delegated to Spain to send reports and photographs back to the United States and Mexico. I was soon to receive many more documents, for in a time of civil war every pocket must be stuffed with papers, or you will get nowhere.

Lovestone and I next went to see the well-known Catholic liberal, Frank P. Walsh. He had written the Industrial Commission Report in 1912, and when the Catholic Hierarchy in New York lobbied against the New York State legislature's ratifying the Child Labor Amendment, this famous Catholic layman, with two nuns as daughters, sent telegrams to 100 liberal Catholic laymen in New York State asking them to come out in favor of the Child Labor Amendment, and got 99 favorable responses. Their advertisement in *The New York Times* swung the scales in favor of the amendment in spite of the hierarchy. I knew him slightly, but Lovestone knew him very well, for Walsh had served on the Russian Labor (and Liberal) Commission that visited the Soviet Union in 1927, a commission which Lovestone had contrived to set up.

We asked attorney Walsh what he thought of the refusal of the United States government to sell arms to the Spanish Republic, although it was the duly recognized government of Spain. He answered: "A government which we officially recognize as the legal government of Spain has the right to purchase arms here. The Spanish government was defeated in the courts because it made two mistakes in the choice of a lawyer: their lawyer, Lee Pressman, is a Communist and a Jew, and these two facts played into the hands of those Catholics who support Franco."

I said, "Mr. Walsh, I am about to go to Spain. Will you authorize me to quote you to that effect?"

"Not only that, Mr. Wolfe, but I will give you a letter to the premier, Largo Caballero, in which I inform him that I believe I can still have the decision reversed, and will be glad to serve the Spanish Republic gratis for that purpose." And he called his secretary to take a letter which he immediately gave to me.

That message would give me a splendid entry into the Spanish Republic, but there was still the problem of my passport stamped "Not Valid for Spain." How to get over, or under, or around the Pyrenees? I decided to go to Washington to see the Spanish ambassador, but at that moment *The New York Times* printed the news that he was coming to New York on some business, and gave the name of the hotel at which he would stop. If I remember rightly, it was the Barbizon Plaza. I went to the desk of the hotel mentioned and asked in what room Ambassador Fernando de los Ríos was staying. To my astonishment, they did not ask my name or business with the ambassador, nor call him up to learn if he wanted to see me, but actually gave me his room number. "Just like a Spanish intellectual not to take precautions," I thought, as I went right up to his room.

De los Ríos came to the door in answer to my knock. Seeing a stranger, probably an American who would be unable to speak Spanish, he looked embarrassed, but when I began in Spanish and told him that I knew his work as an authority on 18th-century Spanish literature, his face melted into warmth and he invited me in to sit alongside him on a sort of "loveseat." I chatted with him about Spanish literature for some time until he was completely relaxed, then showed him the letter from Frank P. Walsh and explained Walsh's significance. After that, I asked him to write a letter of introduction to Premier Largo Caballero and another to the Republic's ambassador in Paris, Don Luis Araquistáin, which he promptly did. In Paris, I visited Araquistáin, who gave me a document that was ideal to offset the forbidding words: "Not valid for Spain." It read:

Embajada de Espāna
en
Paris

Embajada de España
Secretaría
13 Mars 1937
No. 722

SALVA CONDUCTO

El Embajador de la República Española en París ruega a las Autoridades de la Repúblic y a las Milicias del Frente Popular dén toda clase de facilidades para la entrada, circulación y salida del territorio español al camarada Beltram Wolfe escritor antifascista norteamericano afecto a nuestra causa en beneficio de la cual va a realizar una importante labor informativa.

Paris, 13 de marzo de 1937
(Signed) Luis Araquistáin

SAFE CONDUCT

[The Ambassador of the Spanish Republic in Paris requests the Authorities of the Republic and the militia of the Popular Front to give all manner of facilities for entry, circulation, and departure from Spanish territory to Comrade Bertram Wolfe, North American antifascist writer favorable to our cause, in benefit of which he will accomplish important informative work.]

These matters being finished, I said to Ambassador de los Rios, "Don Fernando, quiero hablarle, ahora, de un asunto tocando no a mí, sino a Usted. Cuando pregunté al cajero el número de su cuarto, me lo dió sin siquiera preguntarle a usted por teléfono. (When I asked the cashier for the number of your room, he gave it to me without even asking your permission by telephone.) You must remember that your country is in the midst of a civil war. Suppose it was a gunman who asked for your room number. You ought to give instructions that no one should get your room number until he has identified himself and told his reason for wanting to see you, and you have given your approval."

"That's very important," said the ambassador, leaving our little sofa and going to his desk, "I must make a note of it," and he took a little block of notepaper to jot it down. Yet two weeks later, when I went to see him again in the same hotel, they gave me the room number just as freely as before.

Near the end of February, 1937, I set sail for France, armed only with that passport not valid for Spain, a camera and a credential from a photograph agency, a credential from *El Demócrata,* a letter from Frank P. Walsh to Largo Caballero, another from Fernando de los Ríos to Ambassador Luís Araquistáin, a passable knowledge of French, and a fluent command of Spanish. My ship arrived on the first Saturday in March in Le Havre, and the boat train took me to Paris, where, before I even found a *pension,* I bought all the papers I could find in French and Spanish, as well as those two first-rate European journals, *Neue Zürische Zeitung* from Zürich and *Il Corriere della Sera* from Milan, to find out what was happening in Spain. Since the general Spanish scene was familiar to me, almost every sentence brought a rainfall of thoughts and understanding.

I learned that the smallish Catalan Communist Party and the larger Socialist party of Catalonia had united a little while ago, and that the Communists, with their usual consummate skill at infiltration, had already captured the whole outfit, known as the P.S.U.C.* Without losing any time, the newly Communist-controlled Party induced the middle class *Esquerra* (Left Catalan Party) to join it in calling a People's Front demonstration in Barcelona as an act of defiance to the anarchist mass and the POUM. The words, People's Front, or Popular Front, had been ordered by the Seventh Congress of the Communist International. All the slogans proposed for the Popular Front demonstration banners were Communist, too: UNITY, DISCIPLINE, UNIFIED ARMY COMMAND, STRONG GOVERNMENT, SINGLE ORGANIZED ARMY. The POUM, a dissident Communist Party akin to the American Communist opposition, refused to participate in such a demonstration because its slogans were aimed against the POUMist and anarchist militias and patrols fighting at the front and policing the Catalan rear. But the anarchist labor

* Partido Socialista Unificado Catalán.

unions (CNT—Confederación Nacional de Trabajo) and the anarchist ideological organization, which called itself the F.A.I. or Federación Anarquista Ibérica, decided to swamp the demonstration by their sheer numbers.

The anarchist banners read: "Win the War and Make the Revolution; Unified Command—Yes, But Under Working Class Control; Arms Equally for All Units on All Fronts." Clearly, the central government in Madrid, under the advice and compulsion of the Russian agents who were infiltrating Spain, were distribting arms galore to Communist regiments and Communist-controlled fronts or sectors, while next to them fought ill-equipped and ill-clad Anarchist and POUMist regiments. Needless to say, the anarchist banners swamped the PSUC demonstration.

At the end of the first week in March, having held a conference with Brandler,Talheimer, and Borochowicz (three leaders of the German Communist opposition) on Germany, Spain, and Russia; and with Juana Maurín, Paris representative of the POUM, sister of Boris Souvarine; and apparently widowed wife of Joaquín Maurín who had been campaigning in the part of Spain that Franco seized at the outset and who then completely disappeared, I determined to try my luck with the Pyrenees.

First I must say that I was shocked at the ignorance of the Europeans about our Communist opposition in America. And I was even more deeply shocked by the ignorance of Brandler and Talheimer about Stalin and his regime. Brandler was still convinced that Stalin was absolutely right in his internal policy in the Soviet Union, and expected that Stalin would soon recall him and Talheimer to leadership of the German Communist party. Now I understood where Jay Lovestone had gotten his theory to the same effect which lasted from 1929 to 1936. In vain I told the Germans how Stalin had smashed Bukharin, how he had murdered millions of peasants in his forced collectivization. Brandler said that Stalin was right in his fight with Bukharin, who had insisted on a constant reexamination of how the "plan" was going. According to Brandler, Stalin was in the right again in 1932 ("on the basis of the difficulties of 1932") when he killed the peasants and filled up the concentration camps, while even his henchmen, Shatskin and Lominadze, were opposed to him. "True, Stalin was unable to rule like Lenin, but there are few Lenins in history. Better to rule like Stalin than fail to impose his will." First Gitlow, and then I, had fought quietly with Lovestone, but until the actual blood purge of Lenin's old lieutenants, we got nowhere in that debate. In 1936, when Stalin began killing his comrades, I wrote: "Between us and them, a river of blood has flowed that no decent man will cross." And at that point Lovestone agreed with me, and we dropped the name "Communist" from the title of our group, emphasizing our trade union work, and calling ourselves The Independent Labor League of America. But this was 1937, and Brandler and Talheimer were nearer the Russian land than we, yet they still stubbornly held on to their defense of Stalin's regime. "That was the only way he could defeat his opponents," they said, "and their defeat was necessary at any cost."

I argued heatedly and was backed by Leo Borochowicz, while Talheimer showed by his embarrassed silence his own disagreement with his inseparable companion, Brandler.

"What if Stalin dies?" I asked. "Or becomes seriously ill and incapacitated or proves to have been seriously wrong? What if Germany and Japan or some other countries should attack in the midst of the confusion of the internal slaughter? Couldn't practical discussion have avoided even the cattle slaughter of 1932? Can there be a healthy regime in other parties of the Comintern, if there is such a murderous regime in its leading party?"

Then I gave up, happy that Leo was with me and August Talheimer shaken. I changed my questions to Spain. They seemed to know little about Spain and had no underground that could help me over or under the Pyrenees.

I left them and went to the Spanish embassy, my *Portrait of Mexico* under my arm as a substitute for a passport valid for entry. The embassy was crowded to utter confusion by several hundred people wanting to see the ambassador. Clerks and lesser officials formed a sort of human palisade fending them off and trying to find out what each one wanted. There was a great gabble of Spanish filling the entrance halls. I went to the most important-looking officer, acting as if I expected that he would speak to me at once. He addressed me in French and said, "I am sorry, monsieur, the ambassador is busy and cannot receive you at this time. What is your business with him?" He was startled and pleased when I answered him in Spanish. "I do not wish to see the ambassador, sir," I said, "merely to send him my compliments and have you present to him this book. Should he wish to communicate with me at the Hotel Lutecia, I shall be there for the next few days and my phone number is. . . ." He took the number down, thanked me, and went up to the ambassador with *Portrait of Mexico,* which I had dedicated, since I knew he too had written a book, in Spanish, on Mexico: "To Don Luís Araquistaín, a fellow worker in the field, with respectful greetings from the author, Bertram D. Wolfe." I had not been back in my room for half an hour when the phone rang and the ambassador invited me to come to his office for a chat. We had a pleasant leisurely hour of talk about Mexico, Diego Rivera, Calles, Obregón, Morones, Toledano, Trotsky, and Mexican Catholicism. I told him I intended to go to Spain, showed him my defective passport and the letters of de los Ríos and Frank P. Walsh to Largo Caballero. He said, "There are two ways of arranging your difficulties—*agachupinarse o aletear* (make yourself into a Spaniard or fly)."

"Comrade Wolfe," said Araquistáin, concluding the interview, "Would you like to come to dinner at my embassy tonight? It will be a literary dinner. John Dos Passos, Ernest Hemingway, and you would be my guest."

"With great pleasure," and I went back to my hotel to spruce up a bit. Like the other ambassadorial dinners I had been invited to here, the food was superb, the accompanying beverages ample and of the finest. With each course we had a different wine or liqueur. Fine cigars followed, and although I am no smoker, I took a few puffs. And then, to my astonishment, with the coffee, as party favors, there was a ticket for each of us on Air France from Toulouse to Valencia. Over the Pyrenees, indeed!

By discreet inquiry I learned that the Spanish Republic, in order to keep some communication with France, had bought enough stock in Air France to persuade the French to keep some of their oldest and most dubious planes flying to Barcelona and Valencia. True, I had never flown in my life and did not know whether I would be afraid, especially to fly without air pressure over the mighty Pyrenees, and then have Franco taking shots at us with German antiaircraft guns. But *aletear* was much easier than *agachupinarse,* and I was delighted at the unexpected gift; I even thought that the French bureaucrats of the Non-Intervention Committee might be much easier at Toulouse than at Paris. I did not know my French bureaucrat!

I had not met Hemingway before, but we formed a cordial relationship on a first name basis that night. As to John Dos Passos, he was an old friend, whom, as the reader already knows, I had first met in a prison cell on Boston Common, where we were both thrown by the police for demonstrating against the execution of Sacco and Vanzetti that was planned for that very midnight. Since then I had seen Dos in Provincetown where often we both spent the summer. He had come to Spain now on a quixotic personal mission, a search for a single missing man, José Robles, professor of Romance Languages at Johns Hopkins University. Robles had been a resident of the United States for sixteen years and was an American citizen. When the Spanish civil war broke out, he was on vacation with his wife, his son Francisco, age 16, and his daughter Margarita, American-born and 14 years of age. He had never belonged to any party nor participated actively in political life. He had a fine open face, a pleasant personality, discreetness, a Babel of languages, and was generally liked as a disinterested, idealistic scholar and teacher. He offered his services to the Spanish Republic in the field of translation. His knowledge of English, French, Italian, Spanish, and some German and Russian, led the government to make him a liaison officer in the Ministry of War. There he was in contact with newspapermen and military observers, tried to instruct the Russian Ambassador, Rosenberg, and several of his aides, in Spanish, and then became the translator for the Russian General Gorev, and with Gorev's consent continued to meet with and brief American and English newspapermen. Soon the Russian Cheka became convinced that he was being entirely too friendly with foreigners in Madrid. To break his links with the foreigners and satisfy the Cheka, he moved to Valencia, to which the government had already moved, and continued working in what he thought was safety. Then suddenly he disappeared, and even the members of his family in Spain could not get in touch with him. According to one rumor, he had been a witness to the death of the anarchist military hero, Durruti, who was shot in the back at the Madrid Front, presumably by the

Communists who wanted all the glory for the defense of Madrid. According to another report from a sober journalist, a foreign correspondent in Spain, H. Edward Knoblaugh, the following was the occasion of Robles' disappearance:

> One day after I had cocktails with Professor and Mrs. Robles in a Valencian café, Professor Robles was arrested. The sharp ears of counter-espionage agents had heard him recounting a war ministry joke involving the misfortune of a loyalist general who had stumbled into a puddle of water and been forced to change trousers with a much more portly aide.*

Early in the Spring of 1937 this gentle professor disappeared without a trace, and John Dos Passos was in Paris on his way to Spain to try to find out what had happened to him. Needless to say, neither Dos's passport nor Hemingway's was stamped "Not Valid For Spain." They left the next day with the tickets Araquistáin had given them, and within 24 hours were in Valencia while I was fighting my David's battle with the Giant Pyrenees.

GETTING AROUND THE PYRENEES

The very next day I was off to Toulouse. The following morning at sunrise I was to take the plane. Having my doubts as to how I would make out or what would happen to me, I did not write my wife that I was bound for Spain. Instead I had sat in one of the swell hotels in Paris, using their stationery to write a week's letters to her, one dated for each of the next seven days, describing imaginary sights and adventures in Paris. When I had gotten safely across the border, it would be time enough to tell her that I was in Spain, and thus she would avoid all the worries and uncertainties of my coming bout with the Pyrenees. I gave all the letters to Leo Borochowicz and his wife, Elly, and asked them to mail one each day to Brooklyn, in the order that I indicated. True, the letters were strangely empty, for who can write seven imaginary letters full of realistic adventures in Paris, and finish the pack of them in less than an hour? But they would keep her from worrying, as they did.

At the Toulouse Airport I handed a stout and well-fed official my passport and my Air France ticket to Barcelona. He instantly spotted the "Not Valid For Spain" stamp and did not say "Nothing doing," but began an angry tirade against me.

"What do you think, monsieur? Your own government says your pass is not valid for Spain, and you expect me to ignore that? Have you never heard of the Non-Intervention Committee? Why, your government has not even signed our non-intervention agreement! Why not! And if even such a government says 'not valid for Spain' why should we let you cross our frontier?" He threw up his hands in a characteristic French gesture,

* H. Edward Knoblaugh, *Correspondent in Spain,* London, 1937.

then shoved my papers back in my face. I tried to invent new orders from my journal and my photographic agency, but had no cables to show him. He turned away from me in scorn.

I went to the window of the airport, saddened that my ticket was wasted and that *aletear* had failed me. The sun was slowly rising to the horizon and already a splendid glow filled the air. Not a breath of air was moving, not a leaf stirred. What a lovely day to make a first flight! On such a day I was sure now that I would not be afraid of planes, nor altitudes, nor Franco's antiaircraft guns. While I watched them warming up the propeller and motor of the plane, I suddenly heard my bureaucrat yelling again, this time in altercation with an American who could not speak French. I went over to see if I could help him. He had a passport valid for anywhere. He was a medical doctor going as a member of a blood transfusion unit to the front lines in Spain.

The Frenchman was shouting, "Où allez-vous? Mais où allez-vous, à Barcelone ou à Valence?" And the American was holding up two fingers under the bureaucrat's nose and crying senselessly, "Deux, deux, deux."

In a moment I understood. The American was crying in his pitiful fragment of French, "Two, two, two!"

"He doesn't want to know how many valises you have," I explained. "He wants to know whether you are going to Valencia (Valence in French) or Barcelona." Thereupon the American said, "Valencia," and was hustled onto the plane, which took off into the sunlit sky. I had managed to get him on the plane, but not myself, I mused sadly, and went looking for the railroad station to get nearer to the foothills of the Pyrenees. I bought a ticket to Perpignan, a town of some 50,000 inhabitants not too far from the border and big enough to have a Spanish consul from whom I might seek help.

The consul turned out to be a Valencian, and a friend of Joaquín Maurín. My letter from Araquistáin, the name of Maurín, and my easy command of Spanish gave me entrée. "Yes," said the consul, "we have gotten a lot of *their* people over the frontier; I don't see why they shouldn't get one of *ours*." I didn't know whether his word, *they*, had meant Communists or anarchists, but I scarcely gave it a thought. "Check your baggage," he continued, "at your hotel, and tell them you will be gone for a long time. Take only what you can carry in your pockets or on your back, and come here tomorrow night, and I will get you a guide over the Pyrenees."

But first I took the train down to the port nearest to the Pyrenees on the Mediterranean Coast of France, Port Vendres. There I learned that there was a tunnel under these towering mountains through which ran railroad tracks. The French had cut off all use of it by trains since the Non-Intervention Pact. I had time now to meditate whether it was anarchists or Communists whom this Consul's guides had been helping over the Pyrenees. Perhaps it was Communists, and if the guide recognized my name, he might deliver me to the Communist secret service and I would be in trouble before ever I got safely into Spain. I decided to try the tunnel under the Pyrenees, for it was still early in the day.

I followed the railroad until it suddenly lost itself under a great black hole in the mountains with no sign of a light in it. I ventured into it cautiously, step by step, stumbling over the ties in the darkness. Gradually my eyes grew accustomed to seeing dimly in the darkness and I felt my way along the wall of the tunnel. Suddenly, unexpectedly, a shaft of light ahead, and men sitting around a fire in mid tunnel. The *Garde Mobile!* The French, no doubt, had selected the exact spot where the two borders met in the darkness to catch those smuggling their way into Spain to join the International Brigade. I could see the members of the *Garde Mobile* in their uniforms, but to their firelit eyes I was still shrouded in darkness. I backed up cautiously to a turn in the tunnel, and then turned toward the France I had just left, giving up my dream of passing under the Pyrenees. My second failure!

At the appointed hour of the evening, the Perpignan consul, Puig Pujades, took me in his auto and introduced me to my guide. Our conversation, which was brief and cold, was conducted in Spanish.

It was a beautiful moonlit night; finding the way over a pass should not be too hard. My baggage was easy to carry: a few extra handkerchiefs, two extra pairs of socks, two toothbrushes, a tube of paste, all discreetly distributed in various pockets including those of a light topcoat in case it should be cold near the pass. But the face of the guide was sullen, and when I asked him to what point we were headed, or tried to make conversation, he was uncommunicative. Clearly he gave signs that he did not like me, and I began to wonder whether I had led myself into a trap on the coveted frontier of Spain. But the moon was bright. We walked easily over cow paths and narrow roads. We climbed and climbed until at last we seemed to be already in the pass, when suddenly—once more a huge campfire and hugging it, cold in their uniforms, a detachment of the *Garde Mobile.* Again the light dazzled their eyes while the darkness mercifully covered us. The *Garde Mobile* was apparently out in force that night, but we backed down safely the way we had come. When I recgnized features of the town of Port Vendres, we separated. The guide did not even answer my *Adiós!* For my part I felt well rid of him. A third failure, but perhaps a lucky one.

Next morning I bought a local paper. It told the reader that scores of smugglers into Spain had been caught by the *Garde Mobile* the day before, some in the unused tunnel and some in the mountain passes. They would get six months each in prison and then be deported to their native lands. So luck had been with me again. I took a walk through the small towns of Port Vendres and Cerbère, both French Catalonian villages, that is, villages of Languedoc where the language is really Catalan, but the people also speak Spanish as easily as French. Both villages were on the flanks of the Mediterranean, dancing blue in the sunlight, with little harbors, small fishing boats, great cliffs with the white and pink spray of early spring. The tongue, the intonation, the gestures, the appearance, the household speech, the public life, their sympathies in the Spanish Civil War, all marked the Catalán. It was hard to believe that amidst the peace of these fruit-spray covered terraces and hills, just off that mighty mountain range that separated them from the other Catalonia, was an exposed and bombarded bridge, bombing planes, men in death struggle for freedom or for one of two kinds of dictatorship, Franquist or Stalinist.

As I walked, a new plan germinated in my mind. I would try these Catalan-speaking fishermen with my Spanish. If they understood that, I would talk of my mission, show my documents, see if I could get one of them to take me on a fishing boat to Spain. True, the French bureaucrats, persistent, unrelenting, watchful, crafty, and calculating as ever, had taken care of that, too. Every fishing boat had a list of its crew and only they were allowed to go out fishing from Port Vendres. How could I make myself look like a Port Vendres sailor?

I spied a tall, strong, handsome man standing on the edge of a dock, with a silver pin on his jacket, an arm with a closed fist. He had to be at least a sympathizer with revolutionary Catalonia. "Do you speak Spanish?" I asked him. "Sí, señor." "Have you a few minutes to spare to listen to my troubles?" "Certainly." The fact that I was dressed like an American made him sure that I was not going to beg for money. I launched into my story. I told him how I had tried an airplane, the railway tunnel, and a mountain pass, and had still not gotten across the frontier. I showed him my passport, explained its blemish, then Ambassador Araquistáin's letter to Largo Caballero, and was going to continue, but he stopped me with the word, *Basta!*

"I can take care of you," he said simply. "In the first place, get rid of that hat; they'd know you're an American from a kilometer away. Without a word, I tossed my beautiful Borsalino into the water, and pulled out of the pocket of my topcoat my Basque beret which I had taken along on my trip to the mountain pass. He looked at my action with approval. I have not worn an American hat from that day since, for I soon discovered that a beret sits tighter and tighter on your head the harder the wind blows, while a hat has wings and goes flying off into space.

"Come down here to the Plaza tomorrow night at five, dressed as nearly as you can like an ordinary workingman. I'll be standing about where I am now, talking to someone. Don't come near me. Stay a safe distance away, and when I leave the harbor, follow me at the same distance."

"And my baggage?"

"Oh, that's easy. You've noticed, perhaps, that the next town is named Cerbère? Its mayor has the same name as the town. And across the frontier in Catalonia there is a town even smaller named Cervera. Many of its people are members of the same family as our mayor and bear the same name as their little town. On both sides of the frontier they help each other out. The mayor of our town here, besides being mayor, is also a *contrabandista.* Leave your bags at your hotel, and put his name on them. He'll see that they get to Valencia before you do and they will be waiting at the check room in the Valencia railway station with your name on them. You can pick them up whenever you want them."

"What do I pay him for the service?"

"Nothing. After the letters you showed me and the story you have told me, I can see that you are one of ours. On my say so, he'll be glad to help you out."

Our whole dialogue seemed to have something of a dreamlike character, but when I came down to the dock in beret and lumberjacket the next afternoon at five o'clock there he was talking to another man. I could only watch from a reasonable distance and wonder what would be coming next.

Punctually at 5:00 P.M. my new sailor friend shook hands with his companion, then headed for the foothills of the Pyrenees just at the edge of the town. I followed at a proper distance. He took a lonely road with no traffic on it, a road that ran first up, then down, then up again as all foothill roads do. He would disappear over the brow of a hill but when I got to the top I could see him below me starting the ascent of the next hill. Beautiful shrubs and trees lined the road and a glorious sunset was preparing in the west, but I had to keep my distance and my eyes on him, so that I would not lose sight of him. Why did he not walk with me? I decided that some little detachment of the French *Garde Mobile* might pop out of any valley along the way. It seemed something like a half hour that we walked thus far apart from each other, up one hill and down another, until suddenly, when I got to the brow of a hill and looked for him, he had disappeared as if into thin air. "He must have turned down the ravine at the bottom of the hill," I thought, "left and downhill to where the Mediterranean licks the shore." What if I had guessed wrong? I quickened my steps and sure enough, at the bottom of the cowpath running down the ravine, I found a small fishing ship with both sail and outboard motor, and five more men besides my guide. "Juan," he said in a voice of gentle command, "give this fellow your place on the boat and take the evening off. We'll pick you up later at the usual place." Juan obeyed the order without a word and I climbed awkwardly into his seat, noting with satisfaction that the sea was too gentle that night for me to get seasick.

"My name is Per, or in Spanish, Pedro," said my guide. "I am the captain of this fishing boat and have a document from the authorities to fish with a crew of six, myself included. Now you are one of the crew. We can fish all night if we want to, but we must not go out of French waters." And he turned to give orders to his men.

"How easy," I said to myself, "and how lovely, to pass the Pyrenees on the Mediterranean with a red sky and little red wavelets on the sea. The boat chugged quietly, its sail furled; no one seemed to do any fishing. The captain held the tiller and decided the direction of the boat.

We continued to sail for a long time as the sunset deepened and changed colors, until suddenly the ship stopped with a little jolt in a tiny cove. "What a pilot I am!" grinned the Captain. "I'm supposed never to leave French waters, but this cove looks as if it might be Port Bou in Spain. Would you like to get off the ship for a while and touch your foot to Spanish, or rather, Catalonian soil?" I was off in a jiffy. The captain led me deeper into the beach. "You see this footpath?" he asked. "It goes straight up this ravine and over a hill or two. Keep following it until you come to a beautiful, big summer resort. You'll find no one in it but the watchman. Nobody goes to summer resorts during a revolution, and you'll have the place all to yourself. Tell the watchman Pedro brought you and he'll take care of you. It's getting dark. Don't lose sight of the path, and no matter how long it seems, just keep following it."

I offered to pay my passage. Don't you know," he asked me, "that you have been working your way as one of my crew?" Then he grasped my hand warmly, and wished me luck.

The summer resort proved truly sumptuous. I was given a light repast, a room of my own with a private shower and a shiny, highly polished, deep red brick floor. "Have a good sleep" said the watchman. "I'll call you early, for you have a long way to go." He called me before the sun came up, gave me a solid breakfast, then took me to the nearest hill. "You see that path? Follow it, and climb until you come to a railroad, turn left on the tracks and keep going for about thirty kilometers or perhaps one or two more, until you come to the first station. That's Figueras, a big town, you can even get newspapers there with today's news! But first buy yourself a ticket to Valencia."

It was indeed a long climb, and then an enormously long walk along railway ties. When I got to Figueras I had one of the greatest shocks in my life. There on the newsstand lay a paper with the front page headline: "WOLF BERTRAM SE MURIO EN EL FRENTE" (Wolf Bertram Died at the Front).

The sight was at once incredible and upsetting. What if the newsmen in Madrid and Valencia had seen it already? Virtually all of them knew my name and would cable the news of my death to their papers, and an obit would follow. What upset me was the fact that I had not yet let Ella know that I had left Paris and was trying to conquer the Pyrenees. In fact, she was still receiving a "daily letter" from me dated Paris. I wanted to purchase a copy of the paper, but the fact that I had entered Spain irregularly meant that I had no Spanish currency, while Figueras, a town of about 10,000, had no money exchange at the railway station. What a souvenir it would have made, especially if I could have read my obits in the American dailies. But fortunately, Spain is made up of a number of *patrias chicas*, and Figueras was in Catalonia, so that the news of my death never reached the two republican capitals.

As soon as I got to Valencia I changed some currency, sent a long cable to Ella, and purchased for 30 centavos a copy of a pamphlet by Wolf

Bertram entitled *La revolución española de 1936 y la revolución alemana de 1917-18* published by the Editorial Marxista of the POUM in 1937.

In the introduction I learned that Wolf Bertram began his Communist activities in the Austrian Communist party in 1921 and was the editor of its central organ. But when the Communist opposition began in Russia in 1923 and 1924, "Comrade Bertram took the position of Trotsky, for which he was expelled from the Austrian party in 1926." In 1931 a number of disagreements caused him to break with Leon Trotsky. He continued writing in Paris where he adopted the pseudonym Wolf Bertram, and with the outbreak of the Spanish Civil War, went to Spain and joined the POUM, entering into its military section.

But nothing in the pamphlet told me his real name, or how he had come to choose that rather rare and curious combination of names. Later I learned from the POUMists that his real name was Max or Kurt Landau. The POUM military force had been fighting side by side with a Communist detachment on the Catalonian front when Landau was shot in the back by a Communist, because Stalin had sent the word through the Cheka that all "Trotskyists" and all Communist oppositionists should be eliminated. The story in the Figueras paper was a false one, for it had him wounded by the enemy by a shot in the front of his chest, and proclaimed him a hero.

THE BLACKOUT IN VALENCIA

At last a train chugged into the station, old and slow and looking as if the English had sold it to Spain decades ago, and after Britain got through with it. It was headed for Valencia to which the Central government had just moved because they feared that Franco was about to take Madrid. It was crowded, the windows dirty, the seats dusty and occupied, so I stood out on the platform, risking a little piece of coal in my eye as I watched the scenery of Port Bou and other lovely little Pyrenee seaports. I found the people on the train, as I would later find the people in Valencia and Madrid and Catalonia, a brave and gallant folk, full of indignation, and confident of ultimate victory. The train went with incredible slowness, for the tracks and bridges had been repeatedly bombed by Franco's artillery and the roadbed repaired again and again. Some guards rode outside on the fender and watched for rocks that might have rolled down onto the track, leaping off repeatedly to remove them. A trip which before the civil war began would have taken only an hour or two now took all day and far into the night. I had no lunch with me, and still no Spanish currency, but that didn't trouble me. Soon I saw militiamen from the Catalán regiments, or Secret Service, walking through the train and asking everybody for his documents. I had a passport, but no entry visa in it. However, my command of Spanish made things easy as I told them as much as they wanted to hear about my defective passport, my forfeited airplane ticket, my attempt to walk through and over and finally around the Pyrenees. I explained part of my mission, showed them the letter of Ambassador Araquistáin to Largo Caballero and all other authorities. They promptly gave me a "precious" present, a package of "Looky Streakes," a perfect forgery of our Lucky Strikes package, except that there was one grievous error in spelling and anything but tobacco in the cigarettes. After lighting one, I gave them back the rest. Then one of the militiamen brought me a wine-skin made of goat's hide and filled with red wine. I told them I would choke if I tried to drink wine flying through the air and down my throat out of the wine skin. Somebody brought me a not exactly clean glass, and with the Spanish wine as a disinfectant, I swallowed several glasses full, thus assuaging my hunger. Some of the militiamen or secret service or whatever they were went on through the train checking documents. Some of them stayed with me, and the others came back after checking the rest of the train, for they found my case and my account of it enormously entertaining, and a real adventure story which made me fit to be a Spaniard if not a Catalán. "When we get to Valencia," they told me, "we will tell your story to the station militia, and you will have no trouble there. Entry visa or no entry visa, you are in and here to stay as long as you want."

The hours dragged and the train crawled, but we had a gay time together until nine o'clock in the evening, when at last our train gasped its way into the Valencia station. To my astonishment I found the city pitch dark except for a few searchlights scanning the sky to see whether the air raid was over. I was not surprised at the air raid or the blackout, but at the fact that I would have to find my way around a city of half-million to a million inhabitants (the first figure represented the normal population, the second the refugees and the horde of government officials that had come from Madrid looking for habitations). The only light was a little blue bulb high on each light pole which shed no illumination on this city that I had never seen. How was I to find a hotel when every hotel in town, and almost every building, had its iron shutters down?

Everybody but me seemed to know where he was going, and in a few minutes the station was deserted except for a few Catalán militiamen, a number which soon dwindled down to one, who, when he found out my name, disappeared, and came back with my baggage which the Mayor of Cerbére had smuggled in to me. For the first time in my life I really understood why the Romans called baggage *impedimenta*, yet I was glad to get it. I said to the militiaman, "May I leave the baggage with you? I'm going into the city to see if I can find a hotel room. If not, would it be all right for me to sleep on a bench here until daylight?"

Cautiously I entered the darkness of the great city. There should be hotels near the station, but could I find my way back to the railway station and my baggage? I felt my way along the walls and iron shutters and decided to go in a straight line so that I could retrace my steps, at least until I might find some landmark I would recognize against the darkened sky. At last I found it—a bull ring, there was no mistaking that. Its profile was clear in the darkness, and it was round so that I could go in several directions, always making sure to retrace my steps to the ticket entrance. I banged on iron hotel shutter after iron shutter until my hands were sore, but I might as well have been a Franquist invader or a cannonball for all their eagerness to open. At last, a shutter pulled up, a dim light appeared, the sleepy face of a portero or watchman behind it. "What do you want?" he growled first in Spanish and then in Catalán.

"A room and bed for the night."

"Mister, we have somebody sleeping in the barber chair, somebody in the bathtub, and the floor is carpeted with bodies of sleeping men. I couldn't squeeze another body into our hotel," and with that the shutter slammed down and I was alone once more. I felt my way back to the bull ring, and from the bull ring to the station. My bags and my militiaman were still there. "Why don't you come home with me," he said, "and sleep with my son? The bed's a little narrow, but he won't mind, and you can get some rest until daylight and break your fast then." I could have blessed him in every language we had in common, as he seized the heaviest of my bags. We walked off slowly so that I should not lose him in the darkness of this unknown city.

I slept soundly alongside his son, got up early to a good breakfast, then gave the militiaman a few dollars by way of compensation, with which he was enormously pleased. The peseta was sinking rapidly and dollars rising correspondingly. Anyhow, I still had not one cent of Spanish currency. Then I went out onto the streets.

Valencia was a beautiful city, inundated with color and light. It was a weekday, but people were to be seen walking the streets, engaged in eager and animated conversation. One could hear anyone he cared to listen to, for Spaniards do not know how to speak quietly. Nor would one know a war was on, except for the flood of posters everywhere and the union signs of the CNT and the UGT over shops reading "Taken Over and Controlled by the Workers" and the greater eagerness, animation, even elation, visible in every step, every face, every voice. However Madrid may have felt at this moment, Valencia seemed to be enjoying the war.

39

THE CIVIL WAR IN SPAIN—II

My interest in Spain was manifold and grew with each day's experience there. My first task was to deliver the letter from Frank P. Walsh to Largo Caballero in the hope that Spain might be helped by Walsh to use its huge gold reserves to purchase arms in the United States, and thus deliver itself from Stalin's monopoly as the sole source of arms (these arms were not gifts, but were sold to Spain at a high price, and with conditions for their use). Knowing Stalin well, I knew those conditions would in the end be intolerable. My second aim as a student of the International Labor movement was to see, interview, and try to understand the Spanish anarchists who were engaged in the hitherto unheard-of action of taking part in a government as cabinet members of the Republican government of Spain. My third purpose was to see the difference between the anarchist volunteer militias of Catalonia, the first armies to win striking victories and succeed in driving Franco's forces back from almost all sections of the Catalán region; and the largely Socialist and then increasingly Communist forces of Castille, which were being driven steadily back until they held their ground at last at the very gates of the capital, and then only with the aid of the International Brigade recruited from all the countries of Europe and America.

I had spent only a few days at the Catalán front before I perceived how miserably armed these courageous and victorious militias were compared with the magnificently armed batallions of Castille, secretly directed by Russian military experts. Even on the Catalán front, the small detachments of Communist troops were magnificently armed by Russia, while the Catalán militias and those of the POUM had to arm themselves as best they could with daggers, fowling pieces, rifles and pistols confiscated from sporting goods stores, and weapons captured from the enemy, often in hand-to-hand combat. Only the *Guardia de Asalto*, about 6,500 strong in the whole country, and part of the *Guardia Civil* in Barcelona sided with the Republic, but it was the anarcho-syndicalist unions of the C.N.T. that gave the élan to the Catalán fronts. Stalin sold arms both for money and for promised distribution only to the Communists and fellow-travellers and those officers who would be subservient to them. More than once Stalin threatened to stop all sales if the orders of his Russian generals, often dangerously fallacious, were not obeyed.

I intended to return to the Catalán front later, but having gotten my first glimpse of its miscellaneous assortment of pick-me-up and fix-me-up arms, I could not wait to get a close-up view of the situation in Madrid. I must get to Madrid *cuanto antes* (a quaint Spanish idiom which cannot be translated, but means *as soon before as possible*). Easy said, but like all Spanish *hurry-up* idioms, not easy to accomplish.

From Barcelona to Valencia was a mere train trip. The railroad to Madrid, however, had been cut by Franco's troops, and one had to get a good auto and go over one of the two most mountainous countries in Europe to make it. Where could I get an auto, or a seat in one, and a tiny corner in which to stick a diminutive travelling or duffel bag?

A taxi from the coastal cities to the capital of the second highest country in Europe was probly not available and was, in my case, beyond my means. Moreover, Franco had been advancing steadily on the Western front so that his forces were already laying siege to Madrid at the last ravine before the city. They were comfortably lodged at University City, from which they could bombard the capital by day and by night. There Franco had stopped, apparently for regrouping, before taking Madrid. The government of the republic had already fled in fear with all its bureaucrats and their ocean of documents. Only the workingmen and the International Brigade, armed by their own enthusiasm and Russian arms (secretly—most secretly—directed and often commanded by Russian generals and other Russian military experts), as well as a few doughty officials like the premier, Largo Caballero, and members of his cabinet (including the anarchists and other valiant men who stood behind Largo Caballero and refused to flee to Valencia, giving courage to the workingmen to prepare to defend the city street by street, improvised trench by trench, and house by house) still blocked Franco's army. It would be a sight worth seeing if only I could get to Madrid. I decided to present myself to the government of Catalonia, tell them of my mission to see Largo Caballero, and see if they would help me.

Besides some officials of the *Generalitat,* as the newly autonomous government of Catalonia was called in Catalán, I saw an American who looked familiar to me, and with him a woman who could be his wife. She looked pleasant, but he was scowling and arguing in uncertain Spanish with one of the officials.

I told my story and made my request of the first man who looked inquiringly at me. "Franco has cut the railroad," he said to me in Spanish, "but we have a *coche* leaving tomorrow for Madrid. It has two passengers and plenty of room for you and your baggage. It will leave early in the morning, for it is an all day trip."

At this, the American who was arguing with another official left him abruptly and interjected himself into our conversation. "The car," he said, "was assigned to me and my wife for our trip to Madrid. We have a lot of baggage, and there is no room for anyone else."

"Who are you?" I asked.

"Gilbert Seldes," he said importantly, "writing on the civil war in Spain and the International Brigade. It is of the utmost importance that I get to Madrid at once, and I can't wait for you to get packed and ready to go. Besides, the car was assigned to me and there's no room for you in it."

I realized that he was the brother of the far more pleasant and genial George Seldes. Also I could see that Gilbert was going to prove one of the most unpleasant fellow travellers I was ever to meet.

OVER THE MOUNTAINS TO MADRID

But the official we were talking to settled our first possible quarrel by saying in a gentle voice, "The car, comrade, was assigned *by the Generalitat* and belongs to *it*. While you people are on the trip to Madrid, if anyone commands in the car, it will be our chauffeur. Both you and Comrade Wolfe have made good cases for being helped to get to Madrid. This skinny señor will not occupy too much space, nor is he likely to have much baggage. If necessary, we may have to squeeze yet another person in. Trips to Madrid are not easy these days."

Seemingly insensitive to the rebuke, Seldes said, "He can come only on the condition that he comes without baggage and is at my hotel entrance ready to start at 6 A.M. sharp."

I knew that he would be able to have breakfast served in his room, but that 6 A.M. meant no breakfast for me, since the restaurant in my hotel and those around it did not open until seven, but I raised no objection. At six o'clock I was there with a full duffel bag and an empty stomach, and we were off through the blossom-starred lowlands and up into the foothills. There I spied a *fonda* (café), and since my Spanish was more fluent than that of Seldes, I had no difficulty in persuading the chauffeur to stop the car while I grabbed a bite. That was my mistake, for the *fonda* suffered from greater shortages than the coastal capitals, and the only breakfast available was an impossible combination of some sweet sponge cake and some cold snails cooked in garlic sauce, left over from the day before. Garlic always upset my stomach, while the snails, which were rubbery, were something I had never eaten before, and the sponge cake was a miserable companion for snails. Less than an hour had passed when I was compelled to persuade the chauffeur to stop the car again while I gave up my breakfast in the shelter of a tiny bit of woodland. However, around three in the afternoon we came to a farmhouse restaurant known to the chauffeur, where, after the shortages of the coastal towns and the endless rice á la marinera, that consisted of rice with sea shells saved from the day before, and the day before that, and weeks gone by, to give some illusion of protein flavoring to the rice, we dined startlingly like princes royal. "How do they get so much good food here?" I asked the chauffeur.

"They grow and raise their own, send nothing to the cities, and the woman who runs it knows how to cook." At that moment I raised my eyes from my plate to look out the window and spied an orange tree with boughs bent down by their load of ripe, juicy Valencia oranges.

"Could I have an orange?" I asked the waitress, who was also the cook.

"*A esas horas!*" she said in genuine astonishment. In Madrid, I was to find that oranges were served only at night, one to a customer, under the menu title *postres* (desserts), but despite the plural, *postres* was always one and the same single small orange. But after I persuaded the waitress that we strange Americans generally started our day on an orange or its juice or half a grapefruit, she went into the yard, shaking her head in wonder at our barbaric customs, and broke off the tree its biggest bough laden with ripe oranges which lasted for many days.

I got so tired, in time, of the rice with empty seashells that I developed an allergy to rice. "Haven't you anything but rice to eat?" I asked. "No, sir," a Madrid waiter answered apologetically, "nothing except omelettes." I jumped at the chance, and from that day onward lived almost exclusively on eggs, to the endless surprise of the waiter. No good Spaniard could understand my preference. And today I am still the despair of Chinese restaurants by my mere picking at fried or boiled rice.

Thereafter the trip to Madrid was lovely—high tablelands broken by still higher mountain ranges, cut by sheer walls which had been carved by deep, seasonally narrow, and often dry rivers.

Madrid itself communicates with the rest of the country through mountain passes that rise to 4,700 feet and networks of tunnels and an endless variety of high valleys. About half of Spain is dry; the other half moist and fruitful. Madrid, at the very pinnacle, is like a fortress ensconced in battlements. Still higher above it is the Guadarrama mountain range, snow-covered even when I reached it in the spring months. One of the reasons for the deep antagonism between Barcelona and Madrid is that Barcelona is on the Mediterranean. Between the rockbound fortress near the pinnacle and the seaport that is the harbor of the inland sea, real peace could only come through federalism and respect for linguistic, cultural, and political autonomy for the Catalonians.

I soon forgot my disagreeable fellow traveler as I became absorbed in the deep rivers, profound gorges, rocky plains and passes of the tableland, and mountain peaks, of Castille that *Don Quixote* had made immortal. As the dark came on, we arrived at last at the fortress capital.

The knowing chauffeur took us immediately to the bureaucratic center to be put up for the night. I was thoroughly exhausted and ready to accept any hotel with a room and a bed at least until morning. But Seldes became demanding again: "I insist on a good room for myself and my wife at the Florida. It's the center of things. All the other correspondents are there. That's where we'll get our meals. That's where I'll find people eager to be interviewed. That's where I'll pick up the news. That's where we insist on being lodged tonight."

"It will be easier to put you up at some other hotel until tomorrow morning, when someone with authority is here," demurred the clerk.

"Do you know there's a civil war on?" I volunteered gently.

"I insist on the Florida, and a good room tonight," persisted Seldes. He got what he wanted, and I went quietly to another hotel which, although I did not know it, was a mile nearer the front and Franco's headquarters in University City. When I got to my night's abode it was "*rat-tat-tat, pow, rat-tat-tat, pow*" in endless din. "Machine guns and mortars," I said to myself as I lay down fully clothed without bothering to unpack my duffel bag. "I'll never be able to sleep in that racket." I looked around the room with my searchlight and found that the wall facing University City had been shot out with artillery fire, and to conceal the lack of wall and the sky, a huge mattress had been hung lengthwise. "No wonder there's so much noise! But it's better than nothing." I climbed into bed with the music of machine gun and mortar ringing in my ear, and the next thing I knew I was wakened by silence and a shaft of sunlight shining in my eyes. I knew then what I had not known before, that if I were tired enough I could sleep in a trench under fire. I pulled the wall mattress to one side—it was broad daylight in the bright sunshine of Castille.

I walked down one of the boulevards of Madrid from my somewhat battered hotel to La Florida. The besieged city was beautiful even in the midst of civil war. On my way, I stopped to talk with some soldiers on leave. They were wearing pitifully thin garments for such a chilly morning. They told me that they had fought all through the first winter of the civil war in the same thin garments amidst the snows of the Guadarrama mountain range, for no other garments were available.

It was too late for breakfast when I got to La Florida; besides, I had as yet no meal tickets. The hotel proved to have a bureaucratic center, where, when I showed my letter from Ambassador Araquistáin, they began to fill out a whole set of documents: food cards, a document authorizing me to circulate freely through the city by day, another to be out at night after curfew time and in a blackout, another to carry a camera and use it freely, yet another to enter the trenches.

As I turned away from the desk that poured out documents, I bumped into Ernest Hemingway. "Bert," he said, surprisingly, "come up to my room and I'll give you a drink."

"At ten A.M.?"

"Don't be fussy, it's good Scotch, Black Label. You won't find it anywhere else in republican Spain except in my room." I thought with a pang as I had when Gilbert Seldes was so fussy about getting fixed up late at night on his first night in Madrid, "Don't you know there's a revolution on? If only you could see the miserable armament, clothing, and equipment of the Catalán anarchist and POUMist militias who have taken the Barcelona barracks by storm, then spread out over much of northern, eastern and southeastern Spain! Isn't there a shortage of shipping arms and clothes and foodstuffs?" But I didn't venture to rebuke Hemingway. "Do you really drink Scotch at ten A.M.?" I asked.

"I drink Scotch whenever I find a good fellow to drink with. Come on up." I went to his room. What took my eye was his dresser, where a lady of fashion might have had her perfumes, powders, curlers, and other nostrums. It was filled with bottles of Scotch, all Johnnie Walker, most of it Black Label. He poured drinks, yielded to my request to add some cold water, and, considering my lack of breakfast and my mile-long walk in the brisk, sunny air of a spring morning in Madrid, the drink felt good. I was tempted to tell Hemingway that when I had a chance I would buy him a watch which I had seen at a jeweller's in the Statler-Hilton in Washington, that no matter how much you wound it, always showed the time as 5:30—an early drinker's treasure. But again I refrained. We talked of what had brought each of us to Spain at this moment. He was planning to leave at once for the active southern front with John Dos Passos and a cameraman. Together they would make a documentary on the Spanish civil war. I found Ernest full of enthusiasm for the republic (a feeble thing as I already knew); for the Communist party; for the heroism of the Communist leaders who had held back the Revolution to win the membership of the frightened middle classes and bourgeoisie in general, in order to strengthen the Republic, and for everything the Communist party was doing: planning to restrain the anarchists; crush the POUMists; force the militias to form detachments of the regular army, thus obeying the Russian advisers and the new generals, whom the Communists were exalting in their press. I told him that the Communist party was founded in 1921, and that until the Soviet Union proved to be the only country selling them arms—then taking advantage of that fact to build up the Communist party, force on it the new "Popular Front Line," and send a battery of military advisers, secret agents and the like—the Spanish Communist party had never managed to gather more than 3,000 members or win any influence in the trade unions. Hemingway looked incredulous and scornfully indifferent. At least from ten to eleven that March morning, Ernest Hemingway was an ardent all-out apologist for the Soviet Union and an unquestioning fellow-traveller. I wondered how he would get along working with Dos, a gentle and kindly man, not particularly fond of profanity or base expletives as Ernest was, using the English language with care and elegance. Moreover, I knew that Dos had come over to find out about a presumably murdered friend, and that he had already learned that the Communists, under Stalin's order to spread the purges to Spain, had done away with another of his dear friends.

Actually, their collaboration broke down upon a somewhat different issue. In his youth Dos had volunteered for an ambulance unit in France in the European war. In 1917, as a result of his experience with mangled bodies and soldiers plied with drink to make it possible for them to conquer fear and "go over the top," he recorded his revulsion and outrage in

Three Soldiers and in *One Man's Initiation*. In Spain in 1937 he became furious with the cruelties he saw on his own republican side and with the campaign the Communists were preparing in order to start a new civil war inside the republic, thus opening the gates to Franco where the latter had been most effectively repulsed, and he rediscovered, perhaps to his own surprise, the worth of the American democratic heritage. Despite America's cowardly neutrality in the Spanish civil war, marked by its refusal even to sell arms to an officially recognized government, Dos, the man who on the execution of Sacco and Vanzetti "privately seceded from the United States," now more publicly decided that it was "probably the country where the average guy got the better break," and that he was "rejoining his native land."

To Hemingway he proposed that their documentary be truthful and show the sufferings and atrocities on both sides, and defend the anarchists despite their share in the cruelties; because of their courage and ardor. Hemingway began to argue with his collaborator and in a few minutes was uttering foul curses. He wanted to sell the republic, the popular front, and the Communist party as all being without a blemish or defect. Dos Passos tried to resort in his gentle, kindly, always courteous way. The debate got nowhere; the documentary was never made.

The story of their debate and their break, not only on the documentary film, but on the whole nature of war and civil war, reached me promptly. Half the American correspondents in Madrid seemed to want to tell it to me, particularly when they found out that I was a friend and admirer of John Dos Passos. Though their versions differed slightly, all of them seemed to have heard the story from Hemingway—Dos was not given to gossip. Moreover, all of them took Hemingway's side, a number of them tried to assume the brutal manliness of Hemingway, reaching in vain after Ernest's vocabulary concerning Dos, the anarchists, and the "Trotskyites" (by which they meant, as was the Communist fashion, the members of the POUM). But try as they might, they could not attain the "he-man" scatology of Hemingway, who had no equal in this regard among the writers and intellectuals of the period. Nor would any of them have spoken of Dos, as Hemingway had in print, as "that one-eyed bastard."

As I heard these various accounts of their break, to my mind came the fact that the POUM, which the Communists were calling fascist and were preparing to annihilate, had a mere twenty-five or thirty thousand members, of which six or seven thousand were fighting desperately against Franco, with inadequate arms, on the Aragon front. Moreover, Trotsky was attacking these alleged Trotskyites, and they were criticizing Trotsky more effectively than the Communists with their manufactured "spy stories."

And I thought of the greatest of the anarchist leaders, who ten days after the civil war began had the humanity to write of what was happening:

We have confirmed something which hitherto we knew only in history, namely, that the revolution in which uncontrolled and uncontrollable forces operate imperiously, is blind and destructive, grandiose and cruel; that once the first step has been taken and the first dike broken, the people pour like a torrent through the breach, and that it is impossible to dam the flood. . . . How much is wrecked in the heat of the struggle and in the blind fury of the storm! Men are, as we have always known them, neither better nor worse . . . .They reveal their vices and virtues, and while from the hearts of rogues there springs a latent honesty, from the depths of honest men there emerges a brutish appetite—a thirst for extermination, a desire for blood, that seemed inconceivable before.*

I thought, too, of those first few days when the republic, under the aegis of Manuel Azaña, its president, and Martínez Barrio, its premier, refused to arm the workers, lest the power of the state pass into their hands, and attempted to win, and win back, the revolting generals. Azaña told General Mola, who preceded Franco as head of the rebellion, "I am willing to offer you, the military, the portfolios you want on the terms you want." While these fruitless negotiations were going on, mobs of workingmen, and even criminals, were seizing arms and opening the jails both to political and civil law criminals. Impromptu lynching by so-called tribunals, looting by newly-armed criminals, killing of priests (sometimes justified, it must be said, by their turning of churches and monasteries into fortresses of the rebellion), wholesale burning of churches, killing of many decent officials and members of the propertied classes—all was in the order, or disorder, of the day.

In the spring of 1937, about the time of my arrival in Madrid, the "Red Dean" of Canterbury, Hewlett Johnson, was affirming with a straight face as he looked into the eyes of his interviewer, Burnett Bolloten, that "not a single Spanish church has been destroyed or desecrated," while the anarcho-syndicalist organ, *Solidaridad Obrera,* was boasting that "Catholic dens no longer exist; the torches of the people have reduced them to ashes," and an anarchist youth manifesto affirmed that "for the revolution to be a fact, we must demolish the three pillars of reaction: the church, the army, and capitalism. The church has already been brought to account. The temples have been destroyed by fire, and the ecclesiastical crows who were unable to escape have been taken care of by the people." A scholarly and reasonably reliable writer (Antonio Montero, citing names, places, and dates of assassination) lists 6,832 religious personnel as assassinated, while the Spanish bishops claim that the number of churches destroyed or sacked during the first year was 20,000.

Reflecting on these and other matters like them, I felt that in the

* Printed by Federica Montseny in *La Revista Blanca* of July 30, 1936, and reprinted in Burnett Bolloten, *The Spanish Revolution,* whose work while still in manuscript I was privileged to read and to make considerable use of the fruit of his interviews and documentation.

Hemingway–Dos Passos debate I could not but choose to side with Dos Passos.

My first use of all the documents I had been issued was to present myself to the trenches on the edge of the ravine between the partly destroyed by bombardment, but still elegant settlement of West Park, and the Franco forces in University City. West Park had been deserted by its once-fashionable inhabitants as soon as it came under bombardment, but in front of it, and running part way down the western slope of the ravine, the ground had been dug up into regular trenches which were filled with soldiers defending Madrid. My document presented to a local officer got me immediate permission to proceed to the very front line, to take my camera, and to take as many pictures as I cared to. It also got me three soldier guides to show me where the narrow corridors of earth led from trench to trench at concealed and irregular places. Bullets whistled over my head, came closer and closer to my beret, but I was unafraid. As I got nearer the front and the bullets closer to my head, I got the first and only blow administered to me while I was in Spain: it was a not too gentle blow on the back of my neck by one of the soldiers acting as my guide. "Bend your head down, you fool!" he cried in Spanish. "Don't you see that like all Americans you are taller than we are and stick way out of our trenches? Keep your head and shoulders down or you'll lose them in a few minutes. They're poor marksmen, but you present a good target." Humbly I bent my head, and thus I made my way to the front line. There I found a breach in the trench that had been opened by mortar fire, and on either side of it was seated a young soldier with a submachine gun, a huge box of bullets, and another of grenades. They were not shooting at the moment, nor were Franco's soldiers on the other side. One of our defending soldiers kept his gun at the ready in the breach, but low down, while the other was reading a book which he rested on a box of belted bullets. I looked over his shoulder and saw that he was reading a well-printed and well-bound mid-nineteenth century book, a volume of the *Opere Politico-Economiche del Comte Camillo di Cavour.*

"How did that book get out here?" I asked.

"Oh, it comes from a resident of one of those swell West Park homes just behind us. They all fled without taking such things with them, and I can get you almost any book you want from the first row of houses."

"Aren't you fellows afraid of a sudden rush toward the breach?"

"No, not at all. These breaches are opened every so often by a low mortar shell shot. We don't stick our heads into the opening, for they may be watching with a glass. Would you like to look at them?" he asked, and conducted me a few paces to a periscope. Through it I could see clearly, as if near me, Franco's soldiers in their trenches on the East side of the ravine, and moving the periscope a bit, right in front of me and it seemed large as life, was a corpse lying on a slope near the bottom of the ravine. "That corpse," I asked, "ours or theirs?"

"I don't remember now. A number of men are lying on the slopes, some of them ours and some theirs. We can't go down to examine them and bring up ours unless there should be a special truce agreed upon. "But," he added sagely, "There are not many truces during a civil war."

"The ravine seems to slant off from West Park and Madrid and get farther and farther from you fellows and your line of defense. Which way would you advise me to go to see more of the ravine?" I inquired.

"Eastward. To your left. Really more northeast. I'll get you a soldier to guide you. It was good of you to come and visit us and wonderful to meet an American who supports us."

As I left I heard the soldier who was reading say to his comrade, "If you localize them let me know, and I'll drive them *locos.*" Clearly at this moment this was not a battle for Madrid, but a siege of forces that had been stopped at University City.

I found my way out of the trenches near the very edge of the ravine, but beyond the fighting area. Soon the sound of machine guns and occasional mortars dimmed, and I began to enjoy walking on the edge of a peaceful ravine. Then I saw a sight that I shall never forget: at the bottom of the ravine a farmer was plowing. Curious, I walked back closer to the fighting, and even at the edge of the battleground, where stray bullets were whistling over his head, a farmer was plowing for his spring planting and autumn harvest that would help to feed the great city at his side, paying no attention to the exchange of bullets in the battle for Madrid. As I looked at the patient peasants plowing their land in the very ravine over which bullets flew in the fight to determine Spain's future, and to wipe out one party in favor of the other, I told myself: "As long as these peasants plow their land in the midst of mortal combat, Spain will not die."

The sight of those two peasants strengthened my growing conviction that despite the self-deception of the Non-Intervention Committee, the brutality of the Nazi and Fascist support of Franco and the Russian support of the Republic, what I was witnessing was another one of the violent Spanish clashes like the five or six of the nineteenth century, one in which the basic issues were both local and national, so that Franco would never go all out for Hitler, nor try to close the Mediterranean to British and American ships. This view of an old Spanish hand greatly annoyed almost all my American friends, who, forgetting that nationalism existed, were sure that Franco was nothing but a junior partner in an "international fascist conspiracy," and that the Spanish rebellion had started under Nazi and fascist urging. They were sure, too, that if Hitler fell, Franco would automatically fall with him. In vain I told them that if Stalin permitted Franco to win by starting a new civil war inside the Republican camp against the numerically most powerful anarchists and anarcho-syndicalists and the dissident Communist POUM, Franco would establish not totalitarian fascism, but a military dictatorship, and the Spanish people, exhausted by this, the largest of their civil wars, would be glad for a period of peace before another purely Spanish Civil War could possibly break out.

Most Americans and Europeans had come upon Spain's tortured history, full of the self-importance of their own concern with Hitler, Mussolini, and Stalin, and had put the unknown and little understood rhythm of Spain's continuing clashes, periods of exhaustion and rest, then of new violence and conflict, into quite another context, that of un-Spanish European history with its concern for great powers and the balance of power on the European continent. We misunderstood Spain's intermittent struggles: against Napoleon for independence, 1808 to 1814; the struggle for a liberal monarchy from 1820 to 1823—and then from 1824 to 1843; war over the question of republic, 1868 to 1875, merging into the Carlist wars which continued until 1878; in the twentieth century, the unsuccessful military revolt at Jaca, in 1929; the "republican revolution" of 1931; the rebellion of the miners of Asturias, 1934; the military, dictatorial reaction of 1934; and the military coup and the counterstruggle beginning in the storming of the Catalonia barracks, then carried to Madrid in 1936. All this characteristically Spanish turmoil our newspapers and "oracles" tended to ignore, seeing only our own growing torment with what was, we thought, a once-and-for-all fight against "fascism" as encompassing Spain's war of 1936. Hence my declaration that Franco would perhaps not fall just because Hitler did, aroused among my friends and readers only angry repudiation or monstrous incomprehension.

Looking back now at the dispute which began even before I went to Spain, I must make one correction of my view. I did not foresee that Franco would live so long and in due course give the exhausted Spanish people some of that long period of rest they craved. Nor did I foresee the unexpected greater wisdom of Prince Juan Carlos, who has so far, as I write these lines, added liberalization to the period of rest, so that for the present a more than usual peace has settled over Spain, in which the people can hear the quiet wisdom of their poet, León Felipe, or that of their great teacher of the teachers of Spanish literature, Ramón Menéndez Pidal.

THE VERDICT OF EL MAESTRO

Ramón Menéndez Pidal, who died at the ripe age of ninety-nine, was recognized for well over half a century by all Hispanists as the outstanding scholar in the field of the epic, the popular ballad, and medieval literary history, and was the maestro (teacher and inspirer) of all the teachers who in turn have taught those who today lead the departments of Hispanic studies in most of the great universities of Spain, Latin America, the United States, England, and no doubt other European lands. Until 1936 he was the director of the Royal Spanish Academy. My wife and I studied under two of the maestros whom he had formed: Pedro Henríquez Ureña and Federico de Onís.

After a voluntary stay abroad during and after the Spanish Civil War, Pidal returned voluntarily in 1947 and was restored to his post as head of the academy. For the next year his disciples, and the disciples of his disciples, myself included, waited with bated breath to hear what new word he would say after his return to his post in Franco Spain. *The Spaniards in their History* was that new word. It was written to serve as the introduction to a many-volumed history of Spain which has since been published. With erudition, intellectual passion (passion and intellect are ever inseparable in the Spanish mind), with humanism, poetry, and love of his land and people and all that characterizes him, don Ramón in his introduction treated the whole range of Spain's dialogue with its own relatively unchanging spirit. The invariant aspects of the Spanish psyche, he maintained, give Spain its "permanent identity" amid all vicissitudes, but these invariant aspects are "two-faced," having now positive, now negative effects, being now dominant, now recessive.

Thus a basic austerity of spirit may at one time spell detachment from material things and the courage to endure hardship, and at another time apathy and neglect. And so with all the "invariant" traits. However, even for Spain's changing history (though Spain's history is no doubt the most invariant of the histories of the major countries of Europe) this works but poorly. This part of don Ramón's introduction proves continuously enlightening, for the side remarks and the tiny gems of concrete historical analysis imbedded in it, rather than for his thesis as such. It becomes much richer when he enters, for instance, into a detailed analysis of how various monarchs used, or failed to use, the most capable individuals living in their kingdom. As in the works that earned him his supreme reputation, it is when he thus combines precision with poetic and historical insight that his essay takes on the fullness of life. But in all this, where is the new word that his disciples both at home and in exile were waiting for?

It comes at last, stated with the courage that does the maestro much credit, for it is a plea for tolerance of opposition, for a fruitful recognition of the value of difference, and for a comradely collaboration of the "two Spains" in the reshaping of a single Spain which will be whole again, because it finds room both for innovation and tradition, for Europeanization and Hispanidad. In the nature of the theses it is addressed to the party in power rather than to the defeated and exiled, when it speaks, as it does quietly and boldly, of the "demoralizing situation of living without an opposition." Yet in his survey of the long see-saw of Spanish history, we feel that if the other party should win, he would not hesitate to address the same, identical plea to it. Nothing is worse, he writes, than to have to say: "Here lies half of Spain killed by the other half."

LEON FELIPE: POET OF SPAIN'S EXODUS AND TEARS

The other plea for tolerance that I should like to quote here is that of León Felipe, the great Spanish poet who spent almost all his adult life in the Spanish speaking countries outside of Spain, the last thirty years of it in Mexico. Unlike Menéndez Pidal, he witnessed Spain's bitter conflict of 1936 to 1939, close up, for when the civil war broke out, he left Mexico for Spain to read his poetry aloud to the soldiers of the republic on all their fronts and in their places of rest. The close-up view of the civil carnage where Spaniard showed no mercy to fellow Spaniard made him sadder and more intensely bitter than was Ramón Menéndez Pidal. He became truly the poet of Spain's tragedy, and the grief and despair that possessed him filled four successive volumes after his return from Spain in 1939, and colored all the poetry of the last thirty years of his life. He did not know much about world politics nor understand that Stalin, by spreading his purge to Spain and ordering that the Spanish Communists attack the more numerous and more animated anarchists, was thus opening the gates of Republican Spain to Franco's victory. But he wrote a five-hundred line prose poem prophesying the defeat of the republic because of the war of the factions inside it ("syndicalists, Communists, anarchists, Socialists, Trotskyists, republican-leftists") who were tearing the republic apart by their quarrels, who had "used up in a thousand egoistic combinations the letters of the alphabet for their partisan initials and affixed in a thousand different ways on cap and jacket the red and the black, the sickle, the hammer, and the star," each side seizing its private booty without so much as a decree of expropriation, and already planning to flee the shipwrecked land, "stealing the seat of a child in an autobus of evacuation." This prophetic vision is dated Valencia, June 29, 1937 (less than two months after the May Day attacks of picked Communist troops on the telephone exchange in Barcelona), but the republic dragged out its diminishing existence for almost two years more, until March 28, 1939.

The third and greatest of the four book-length poems of the grieving poet, Felipe, on the Civil War (indeed, the greatest of all the poems on the same theme by the Nobel Prize-winning poet, Pablo Neruda) is entitled *El hacha,* (The Axe) subtitled *Spanish Elegy,* dated Mexico, 1939.

It is dedicated without distinction

To the Knights of the Axe
To the Crusaders of Rancor and Dust
To all the Spaniards of the world

thus embacing Franco and his cohorts no less than the warring factions on the republican side. This all-embracing lament for all Spaniards is one of the sources of its greatness. Space forbids my quoting more than a tiny fragment of this long monody of pain. Yet a fragment may serve to give the reader some notion of what these pages of sustained and cumulative pain are like. These lines are from the invocation:

Ah the sorrow
this sorrow of no longer having tears
this sorrow
of having no more tears
to water the dust.
Ah the sorrow of Spain
which is now no more than wrinkle
and dryness . . .
screwed up face
dry grief of earth
under a sky with no rains
gasp of a well sweep
over an empty well . . .
dry dusty weeping
for the dust,
for the dust of all things ended
in Spain
for the dust of all the dead
and all the ruins . . .
for the dust of a race
now lost in History forever!

Dry weeping of dust
and for dust. For dust
of a house without walls
of a tribe without blood
of ducts without tears
of furrows without water . . .
Dry weeping of dust
for dust that will no longer
agglomerate
neither to make a mud-brick
nor to raise a hope.

Oh yellow accursed dust
given us by rancor and pride
of centuries
and centuries
and centuries . . .
For this dust is not of today
nor came to us from abroad
we are all desert and African.

Nobody here has any tears
and for what are we to live
if we have no tears?
For what have we to weep
if our weeping does not bind?
In this land
tears do not bind
neither tears nor blood . . .
Sandy earth without water
wrung flesh without tears . . .
yellow atoms and sterile
of unfruitlessness
vengeful motes
sand quarry of envy . . .
wait dry and forgotten
till the sea overflows . . .

Why have you all said
that in Spain there are
two bands
if there is only dust?

In Spain there are no bands
In this accursed land there are no bands
there is only a yellow axe
which rancor has edged sharp
an axe which falls always
always
always . . .
on any humble union
on two prayers that fuse
on two hands that grasp each other.

The order is to chop
to chop
to chop
to chop until dust is reached
down to the atom.

Here there are no bands
there are no bands
neither reds
nor whites
nor patricians
nor plebians . . .
Here there are only atoms
atoms that bite one another.

From here no one escapes
for tell me, friend ropemaker,
is there any one who can braid a ladder
of sand and dust?

Spain
your envy was mightier
than your honor
and better you have guarded the axe
than the sword . . .

Under its edge
has been made dust
the Ark
the race
and the sacred rock of the dead;
the chorus
the dialogue
and the hymn;
the poem
the sword
and the craft;
the tear
and the drop of blood
and the drop of joy . . .
And all will be made dust
And all will be made dust
all
all
all . . .
Dust of which nobody
nobody
will ever make
either a brick
or an illusion . . .*

* The above is taken from parts of my translation of *The Axe* into English, as published in *TriQuarterly*, No. 16, Fall, 1969.

40

A WRITER, EH?

When the Japanese attacked our fleet and forts at Pearl Harbor, we became involved in a two-front war. We had to fill the waters of the Pacific with fresh ships, the air with fresh planes, the Pacific islands with our men. There was a real shortage of manpower; for ordinary nonmilitary activities we scraped the bottom of the barrel. Hence I, who was trying to make a living as a free-lance writer without doing potboilers, suddenly found myself regarded as proper material for such sacred, albeit miserably paid activities as Grand Juries and Blue Ribbon Juries, the latter used only in possible death penalty cases. One fine day I found in my morning mail a Subpoena to a Grand Jury panel. No help! Moreover, had not our forefathers fought for the rights of indictment and trial by jury so that the common man might become part of the real government?

The Clerk of the Court spun a squirrel cage lottery device and came up with the names of most proper men and women: managers of factories, vice presidents of banks, and the like.

Then the clerk came out with my name, stared at it in speechless astonishment, then said: "A writer, eh?" All eyes in the Grand Jury room turned on me as on a curiosity. At last the clerk recovered his powers of speech and asked: "Where do you work, Mr. Wolfe? What is your business address? For whom do you write?"

"I write at home. I am my own employer. I write books and articles . . . free-lance."

Again bewildered silence, for these were not "real" activities like buying, selling, dealing in money. Finally the judge intervened, asked me a few questions about what it was I wrote, and suddenly I found myself a member of a Grand Jury.

A district attorney appeared and made a plausible case against a presumed lawbreaker. The matter was clear enough to justify an indictment and trial, but a boast by the district attorney aroused my anger. "He was hard to find, and we couldn't even search his home unless he was present to admit us. So I got his local draft board to summon him to clear up some supposed mixup in his conscription, and when he showed up we nabbed him." I had never been in favor of conscription and felt that one of America's best traditions was a volunteer army. But once the draft act had gone through, I thought this was a shameful and outrageous way to use it. When the district attorney withdrew, as was his duty while we deliberated on the case he had presented, I immediately asked the foreman for the floor. "The evidence is sufficient for us to find a true bill," I said, "and I so move. But there is another matter I should like this Grand Jury to take up, namely the trick the district attorney used in getting the draft board to summon the defendant, instead of having the police do their work. It is tough enough, when our country is fighting a two-front war, that we have to have conscription. But appearing before the draft board is a patriotic duty, and it should not be cheapened by using a draft board summons as a police trick. I therefore move that we further adopt a motion to censure the district attorney for using the draft board in this manner to discredit the war activities of our government." The motion was seconded and adopted. Whereupon the district attorney was called in and told by the foreman: "It is the opinion of this jury that you have abused a war arm of our government, a procedure which should not be repeated in any other case." The D.A. flushed, thanked the jury for the True Bill, then began a secret investigation of our proceedings until, somehow, my name was scratched from the Grand Jury list.

My first Blue Ribbon jury case had surprises of another character. Again my name fell out of the squirrel cage and again there was the astonished: "A writer, eh?" Then the judge intervened. "Mr. Wolfe, what do you write?"

"Books. Articles."

"Did you ever write a murder mystery?"

"No, Your Honor."

"You read them, don't you?"

"No, Your Honor, not since I've grown up."

A roar of laughter in the courtroom. Then the State's attorney rose and said, without so much as questioning me, "Accepted by the State, Your Honor." And the attorney for the defense, also liking my answer said, "Accepted by the defense, Your Honor." I cursed my fate, for I had talked myself into becoming juror No. 1 when I wanted nothing better than to get home and finish what I was writing.

THE BANKRUPTCY OF MY PUBLISHER

How I finally talked myself off that jury will not interest the reader, so I shall turn to the next legal problem that being "*a writer, eh!*" taught me about my chosen profession. Everything seemed to be going well, for I had hitched my wagon to a celebrity who attracted controversies and headlines almost as fast as he could paint. Our *Portrait of America* had become a best-seller, and *Portrait of Mexico* was becoming one. The publisher, Alfred Knopf, had accepted the biography of Diego Rivera on which I was at work.

Then I received a note from something called the Outlet Book Company, on Fourth Avenue, where all books go when they die. It read:

> The merchandise to be sold consists of all the assests of Covici-Friede, including the right, title, and interest of Covici-Friede in contracts between itself and the authors, the inventories of bound books and sheets, the inventories of electrotype plates and the right, title, and interest, in, and to, certain works published and unpublished, exclusive however of cash accounts receivable, and furniture and fixtures. . . . The undersigned shall not be obligated for any of the liabilities of Covici-Friede.

That settled it. Obviously, Covici-Friede had been secretly in deep debt to his printer, and now he was being wiped out. And so was I. Of course, the printer was a fool. He was waiting for Covici-Friede to get a book or two that sold well; then he foreclosed on debts and promissory notes. But if he had held on to the deeply indebted Covici, he not only would have gotten paid in full from the mounting sales of the two *Portraits* by Diego and me, but Covici carried with him to the Viking Press, where he became an editor, a book by a promising young author named John Steinbeck, *Of Mice and Men*, and the printer would soon have been getting huge printing orders on books called *Grapes of Wrath, Cannery Row*, and *Tortilla Flat*. But now, all he got was a foreclosed debtor's payment of so much on the dollar, while the Steinbeck books went to Viking Press with a printer of its own, and the Rivera-Wolfe books to the Outlet Book Company.

I puzzled over the note from the Outlet Book Company, and over my contract. There was of course nothing in the contract to compel a publisher to inform a prospective author that he was over his ears in debts, and could do nothing to protect the author if the creditor subsequently foreclosed. As was the custom in such sudden failures, the Outlet Book Company got all of Covici's assets at bargain prices, and the sum paid for them left no room for author's royalties. It was my first lesson in the law of literary property and the rights of unimportant authors. Hence I wrote into my next contract a provision that in the case of the bankruptcy of the publisher, I, the author, should have a first lien on the property of the publisher, a lien prior to and taking precedence over all other forms of indebtedness. Then I notified the Author's Guild, which was working on a new "model contract," that such a provision should be a part of it, and today the Guild attempts to get such a first lien for all its authors.

WHAT I LEARNED FROM ALFRED KNOPF

My new publisher, Alfred Knopf, did not ask to see the manuscript—there wasn't any. All negotiations about terms, possible length, number of illustrations, and the like, were made with Bernard Smith. The contract was signed by Blanche Knopf. But, negotiations about the price of the book were made with Alfred Knopf.

He did not read the book—in fact, he read it only six months or more after it was out. Only then did he write me that he had just read it, that it was a fine book, and that he was proud of having published it. But of course, as a veteran publisher, he was sure he knew all about books, the format, the size of the editions, the price. Yet he had never published art books and so his inexperienced author had ventured to make suggestions.

I proposed that he print a very small edition, 1000 copies, at what was then a high price, $10 or more per copy, to sell to the collectors of art books, and thus pay the cost of the plates. That cost met, I proposed a large edition, 25,000 or more, to be brought out at the price then prevailing for biographies, $2.50 or $3.50. The readers of biographies not accustomed to buying art books, but readily attracted by the adventures of Diego, would snatch it up, and he could continue with further large editions at a smaller and smaller price per copy for him. I asked for a minimum of 160 plates in sheet-fed gravure, which preserves the stroke of the printer's brush infinitely better than the stippled and dotted half-tones so popular with publishers.

In our one meeting to discuss my proposals, he could not conceal his scorn that a novice writer should try to tell a veteran publisher what was what about editions and pricing. He insisted on a huge first edition to sell at $5. In vain I urged that lovers of paintings would gladly pay twice that and that readers of biographies would never pay such a price as $5, twice what they were accustomed to.

I lost my battle, and Knopf his money. He printed his huge edition, but only the art book collectors bought their small quota of approximately one thousand. The rest of the books filled his shelves and floor in several rooms rented at a costly New York City rent, while the metal plates took up space in yet another room. The years rolled by until the War Industries Board, during the later stages of World War II, insisted that he melt down the plates for metal, unless he was going to use them to get out a new edition immediately. Mr. Knopf offered to sell me the plates to get out an edition of my own at my own pricing—but where would I keep them in my little apartment? and how to pay the costs of publishing? I took advantage of the occasion to revoke his copyright lease and wait for another publisher and a better day. Twenty-four years passed and my life of Diego continued to live its feeble and rachitic existence without change. Then suddenly, I received a check for $500 in the mails, informing me that another publisher, who had acquired the rights, had sold them to Crowell-Collier for a paperback edition for an advance of $1000, half of which was my share.

I called up Richard Cecil of Crowell-Collier. "Dick," I said, "that Rivera book is nearly a quarter of a century old. Diego painted many years after I finished it. He has been dead six years and will paint no more. Why don't you give me time to revise the book before you print it? I don't like the style of the author. I write more compactly and effectively now. I don't like his ideas on the relation between art and society; Russia's treatment of its art and its artists has taught me a lot about the artist and the society in which he lives. Besides, why don't we get out a hardcover edition first, which will be reviewed and advertised in the press, and will help the sale of your paperback?"

"Sorry, Bert. We can't wait. Your book is on press already. They will begin running it off on Monday. Besides, where will you find a publisher for a revised edition when you haven't even a manuscript?"

"Dick, give me three days at least."

"Three days!" he laughed. "What will you do in three days?"

"I'll call up three publishers in what I think is the order of their blind faith in me as a writer."

"O.K. You have three days," and he laughed again.

When an author writes seven days a week, he never knows what day it is. I looked at my calendar. It was Friday! I looked at my watch. It said 4 o'clock! And Monday the press would start rolling: where were my three days?

I called up Sol Stein of Stein and Day, and told him my story.

"Why," he said, "what is the matter with the book as it is now? I have a copy, and I learned more about art and Mexico from it than from any other book."

"Sol, if you'll take it, I promise you a gayer and a wiser book."

"*Gayer and wiser*"—I heard him softly tasting the two words as he whispered to himself into the phone. "All right, Bert. You are a pretty self-conscious writer. If you think you can do a gayer and a wiser book on Rivera, I'll take it."

"Fine. But we've got to act fast. I want you to give me an advance of $2,000 and call up Dick Cecil of Crowell-Collier right now. Tell him I am writing a new book called *The Fabulous Life of Diego Rivera,* which will be so much better than the old one that he won't be able to sell his paperback. Tell him you are buying back the rights to the paperback for what he paid for them, $1,000, and that you are sending him another thousand as interest because his capital has been tied up."

"But 100% interest—that would be usury."

"Precisely. Don't argue, Sol. I know he won't take it. But offer it, and right now. He may still be in his office. We have no time to waste."

Sol Stein made his call, and a few minutes later, an astonished Dick Cecil called me up. It was then 5:30. "You've got me licked, Bert. I can't accept the thousand dollars interest, that would be usury. But send me a check for one thousand, and I will return the paperback rights directly to you."

Of course, the first edition, overprinted in number and overpriced by Alfred Knopf, had never died and had been selling slowly and steadily over the years. But I was honest with Dick Cecil and Sol Stein when I said that

I no longer liked it. And I was getting on in years, and when one grows older he begins to think that he wouldn't like to leave behind him a book with which he is not satisfied. It was the last time that I would write on Rivera, and I took advantage of it to write what I had promised, the gayest and the wisest book that such a splendid subject permitted. Thus *The Fabulous Life of Diego Rivera* and its predecessor, between them, have lived in cloth (now sold out) and in paper (selling in lively fashion) for something like forty years, and I am satisfied that I have done the best I could with this gigantic and preposterous figure, his time, his country, and his fellow artists.

A LIBEL SUIT FOR $200,000

But now I must tell another tale of my trouble with the law, this time a lawsuit by Guadalupe Marin, former wife of Diego Rivera, for damage to her reputation to the extent of one hundred thousand dollars in the United States and one hundred thousand dollars in Mexico.

A woman newspaper correspondent, I believe from the Hearst press, had purchased a copy of the first edition in the American Bookstore in Mexico City, then had cultivated the friendship of Guadalupe Marin as a likely newspaper feature story character. After she read the book, she said to Lupe, "What Bertram Wolfe said about you is outrageous. If you were to sue him in an American court, any jury would award you a fortune in a libel suit."

"I couldn't win anything, because señor Wolfe hasn't any money to pay me with."

"That's nothing. His publisher has, and he is equally guilty for publishing the libel."

Lupe had it in for me at the moment, because when I was interviewing her she told me scandalous tales about Diego and about herself, but if they didn't throw any light on his work as an artist, I omitted the scandals. By nature a scandal maker and a scandalmonger, Guadalupe was angry that in my book I had played down her scandals. The chance of making money from my publisher she hadn't dreamed of. Encouraged by the American newspaperwoman, she sold a house of hers, borrowed money from friends, promising them part of her anticipated earnings, shares in her anticipated victory. She set off for New York, for as a foreign citizen she had to bring suit in our federal courts, and New York City was where Alfred Knopf and the money was.

Knopf had a topnotch legal adviser, the firm of Stern and Reubens, who had fought such literary cases as the one over the right of various American publishers to publish Hitler's *Mein Kampf*. They assigned one of their younger members, named Farmer, to handle the case under the direction of one of their two senior members. I received a summons from the Federal District Court for the Southern District of New York, signed by Judge Knox, and one almost as peremptory from Mr. Farmer of Stern and Reubens to come to see him.

I found him an engaging, redheaded young lawyer, not too familiar as yet with the contents of my book. But after preliminary greetings, he was minded to put me in my place. "Mr. Wolfe," he said, "I am your lawyer. You are to pay all legal fees to Stern and Reubens both for yourself and for Alfred Knopf, and any damages the Knopf firm may suffer for libel."

"Why?" I demanded indignantly. "You're his lawyer, not mine, and damages may well be levied on him without being levied on me, or on both of us, only one of whom possesses money to lose to the plaintiff."

"Have you read your contract, Mr. Wolfe? Did you not see that you have engaged to 'hold your publisher *harmless* in any suits he may suffer for your having written libelous matter'?"

Yes, I had read those innocent-sounding words but had no idea that they meant that I was to pay any costs or losses incurred by him for publishing my book if a court should declare any part of it libelous. Still less that I was to pay all his lawyer's fees incurred for defending my book in court. There was no use pleading ignorance of the meaning of those innocent-sounding and benevolent words I had signed, for I knew I would be told: "Ignorance of the law is no excuse for not understanding a contract you have signed with Alfred Knopf." I thought I could prove the truth of everything I had written, and if necessary, could prove that Guadalupe had not a reputation that nothing I had written might damage. I had to think fast. Silent for a moment, I went over to the offensive.

"Mr. Farmer," I said, "I have two or three large questions to raise with you. Number one: Are you prepared to make a nuisance settlement with the plaintiff to avoid the dangers of a large courtroom damage verdict?"

"Yes, certainly, if the settlement cost is not too large."

"In that case, Mr. Farmer, you can be Knopf's lawyer but not mine. A nuisance settlement is an acknowledgment of the guilt of the author. I will not give the plaintiff a penny, but shall try to prove the truth of everything I have said about her. Consequently there is a conflict of interest between me and Knopf. He is willing to acknowledge guilt—*my* guilt as a writer of false libels—if he can get off with a light fine. I am not. Hence neither you nor your firm can act as my lawyers. I shall be my own lawyer and defend my honor as a writer. Knopf will have to pay Stern and Reubens for they will not be defending me."

Farmer looked at me with new respect, but he had his answer ready. "Mr. Wolfe, you contracted to hold Alfred Knopf and Company *harmless*. You could have stipulated restrictions in your contract, but you did not. I am afraid you will have to pay all of Knopf's legal costs, regardless of how well or ill you consider our defense of you. Neither Knopf's nor his lawyer's duty to defend you is stipulated in the contract."

I retreated to my second line of defense. "Mr. Farmer, you cannot begin to defend Alfred Knopf without my help and my detailed testimony. The time I shall have to spend gathering the evidence of the truth of my book both in my memory and here and in Mexico will be very costly to me, a poor free-lance writer whose first publisher has failed and with him all the books I have so far published. If you or Knopf try to charge me with what may prove to be enormous legal expenses, I shall not spend my time and energy helping you or him, for you have said in his behalf that you are not interested in my reputation as a writer, only in Knopf's potential losses. In my head is the only defense you people have. If you want me to devote my time and energy to your case which is not mine, you will get nowhere. Contract or no contract, whether I understood it or not, you have no other defense but the time and energy that I shall spend in your defense."

Farmer looked grave. "Mr. Wolfe," he pleaded, "we will not offer her a big amount as a nuisance settlement."

"It's the principle of the thing, Mr. Farmer. I am a writer and my integrity is at stake, worth more to me than the sum Mr. Knopf may have to pay will be worth to him."

And then my curiosity got the better of me, for I was learning the laws that applied to my field and the meaning of the terms of authors' contracts—"Mr. Farmer, what is the top limit you are willing to grant Guadalupe Marin?"

"Not a cent more than the cost of a round trip from Mexico to New York City, plus normal expenses while living in New York. Perhaps $500 or so."

"That is all you are offering for a woman's honor? Why so little?"

"Mr. Wolfe, you have mentioned hundreds of people in your book, including many artists and politicians. You have told fascinating scandals concerning some of them. If we give Mme. Marin more than the cost of a round trip to New York, who knows how many will sue you and Knopf? Just for the ride if nothing more. No, that is our limit, not a penny more."

"In that case, Guadalupe will sue, and that will drive you closer to me in the defense, and you may help me more. But you will still not be my lawyer. I shall ask nothing for my time and services, but I shall give nothing either 'to hold Alfred Knopf harmless.' "

"O.K., Mr. Wolfe, I shall have to take the matter up with Mr. Knopf and my superiors."

The next day Farmer told me over the phone, "Everything is settled, Mr. Wolfe. You will help us all you can, we will help you all we can. And there will be no monetary obligation between us. And, by the way, Guadalupe Marin has already refused our offer, and the case will go to trial. Only one condition I make to you: No publicity. We don't want the damage aggravated by "malicious libel." Knopf, Stern and Reubens, and you, must all try to keep the trial secret."

"Agreed," said I regretfully, for my hopes of making the book a best seller because of such publicity vanished with that agreement.

The preliminary motions were argued before the brilliant jurist, Judge

John Knox, who resolved all motions of both sides swiftly and reasonably. But when the case came to the trial, Judge Knox had disappeared and a man who had been a loyal Tammany politician and in his later years moved from the post of Commissioner of Docks to a federal judgeship was on the bench. He seemed to know little about libel law, and nothing about the mysteries of life in Mexico. He faced such characters as the beautiful and wild-looking Guadalupe Marin and the author Bertram Wolfe with bewilderment. I think his name was something like Hulbert, and I shall refer to him by that name.

The trial was held under strange circumstances. The Japanese airfleet had just bombed Pearl Harbor and the rumor was spreading through our country that we were utterly defenseless against their attack on America itself, for our Far Eastern fleet and our great fortifications at Pearl Harbor had been destroyed. The Pacific Coast went into an immediate panic, and the governor of California, Earl Warren, prepared an ignoble and illegal deportation of native Americans of Japanese descent, including Issei (Japanese who had been born in Japan), Nisei (native born Americans of Japanese descent), and even some Sansei (Americans of the second generation with Japanese blood in their veins). When Governor Warren had included even some Japanese married to Americans, California felt safe from the "imminent invasion." But the hysteria spread through the country, and our trial in New York City was interrupted by several air raid alarms and air raid drills, with no place to hide that was worth hiding in. Guadalupe's lawyer decided that this atmosphere was favorable to impugning my patriotism and the unreliability and untruthfulness of writings of mine that had nothing to do with Diego Rivera or Guadalupe Marin. Each time this occurred, our lawyer objected to the testimony as inadmissible. Each time Judge Hulburt asked Guadalupe's lawyer what he intended to show by that piece of irrelevant writing from my other books and pamphlets, the lawyer said that it was to prove that I was always unreliable and had no regard for the truth, and each time the judge declared the evidence admissible, while all we could do was pile up objections and exceptions for use in an appeal.

Since Farmer seemed to be unable to block this flood of inadmissible and irrelevant materials from the record, I finally took the floor myself as my own attorney.

Guadalupe's lawyer began reading from *Keep American Out of War*, a book I had written with Norman Thomas. From page 57 he read:

> The "bombshell message," as the historian Beard terms it, came only a week after the House had passed the largest peacetime naval appropriation in our history, giving the Navy everything it had asked for. Why had the Navy suddenly discovered the need for another billion within a week?
>
> This question was put to Admiral Leahy by a member of the House Committee of Naval Affairs, and the honest old sailor blurted out: "I am not accurately

informed in regard to that." . . . The Navy, considering needs for defense, had asked all it wanted and received all it asked. The sudden demand for an increase had not come from the Navy at all, but from the White House, without consultation with the Navy heads.

Farmer made his usual objections, and Guadalupe's lawyer told the judge that "It was manifestly a falsehood that President Roosevelt should not have informed Admiral Leahy, his own naval chief, that a week after Leahy's report to Congress, Franklin Roosevelt should ask for another billion dollars for the navy without informing the chief. Your Honor," said Guadalupe's lawyer, "this shows once more how Mr. Wolfe is reckless in the falsehoods he manufactures in his writings on any and all subjects." Judge Hulburt overruled attorney Farmer's objections, and Farmer made his "exception" for the purpose of eventual appeal. At this point I rose from my seat next to Farmer and said:

Your Honor, if you are planning to admit this as evidence, I shall have to request that you issue a subpoena to Admiral Leahy and President Roosevelt and if possible the member of the House Committee on Naval Affairs who asked Admiral Leahy the question cited in the book by Norman Thomas and myself. I shall also ask for a summons to be issued to Norman Thomas and to the historian, Charles A. Beard. And I shall further ask that you postpone the continuance of this trial until these subpoenas have brought such witnesses, or affidavits from them, to this courtroom.

Judge Hulburt flushed, looked embarrassed, and then said: "The court is adjourned for lunch. All the participants will report back in one hour." At the end of the hour, he had changed his mind and said: "On second thought, I rule the last passage read here by the lawyer for the plaintiff inadmissible and irrelevant to this case." He added some vague words to the effect that no more such evidence should be offered by the plaintiff dealing with books not on trial in the libel suit.

"Your Honor," cried the plaintiff's attorney, "I ask permission to read one more passage from the defendant's writings, one of the highest importance, and will then ask the court whether that single and singular piece of evidence is not properly admissible."

"You may read it," said the Judge. At this the following cross-questioning ensued:

Attorney for the Plaintiff, who had a great pile of my writings on his desk before him: "Mr. Wolfe, did you ever write: The American Revolution was a bourgeois revolution. . . . The Constitution is a capitalist constitution. The Declaration of Independence is bunk?"

I stared at the plaintiff's attorney in bewilderment. Yet he had a piece of printed paper in his hand. What could it be? Surely those were not my words. Finally I answered: "No, Mr. Attorney, those are not my thoughts. Those are not my words. I am sure I never felt that way about the Constitution and the Declaration of Independence. I never made such a declaration either in writing or in speech."

Attorney: "Are you sure you never said . . ." and he read the same words with greater unction than before.

The Defendant (I, myself): "No, Mr. Attorney, those could not be my thoughts or my words."

Attorney: "For a third and last time I ask you: do you swear that you never said, 'The Constitution is a capitalist constitution. The Declaration of Independence is bunk.' Remember, Mr. Wolfe, you are under oath, and when I enter this document into the record, you may have proved to have perjured yourself."

A sudden light went up in my mind. "Mr. Attorney, you are reading from a pamphlet the whole purpose of which is to prove that those words are nonsense. Yes, I quoted those words as 'infantile leftist' and the purpose of the whole pamphlet is to prove that they are wrong. I now remember the pamphlet which you obviously have not read, you only looked for a sentence or two with which you thought you could catch me. The pamphlet in your hand was published in 1926 to celebrate the one hundred and fiftieth anniversary of the Declaration of Independence. If you look at the cover you will see that it is called OUR HERITAGE FROM 1776, and bears as a cover adornment a red flag with a pine tree and a serpent curled around it, and the flag bears the motto *Don't Tread On Me*. It is one of the first flags we used in the American Revolution."

The lawyer collapsed. The judge said, "The document just read to the court is irrelevant to the present libel suit, and I order it stricken from the record." The cross-questioning of the defendant ceased, and the trial proceeded on other rails.

Thus far, Farmer had piled up a number of objections and exceptions on which to base an appeal to a higher court with a more knowledgeable judge, and I had blocked two irrelevant but prejudicial-seeming pieces of testimony from my writings, but actually we were not doing well in the trial. Indeed, we had got nothing on the record for the defense. Every time that Farmer questioned me concerning some passage of my *Life of Rivera* to which the complainant objected and I attempted to answer that the source of the passage in question was something that Diego had told me, Guadalupe's lawyer jumped up and said: "Your Honor, I object to what the defendant is saying as hearsay not binding upon the plaintiff." And Judge Hulburt said: "Objection sustained. Let the defendant's answer be stricken from the record." This procedure continued for two and a half days, and at the end of that time, I had gotten nothing into the record in my defense, since I had naturally, as Diego's biographer, gotten all this information from him. Both Farmer and I were desperate as we went to lunch on the third day. I decided that I must find some way of challenging the rules of evidence that were keeping me from definding myself and leaving my defense a blank.

"Mr. Farmer," I said, "suppose Diego told me these things that

Guadalupe now objects to, in her presence, and she made no objections, even laughed as she listened, does that not permit me to testify to Diego's statements?"

Farmer's face brightened up. "Why didn't you tell me?" he asked.

"Why didn't you ask me?"

"Well, that changes the whole situation. If she was present when these things were said, then she can make a rebuttal, and all the evidence so far blocked can at least be given by you and heard by the Judge. I shall have to start my questioning all over again."

And so we did. Farmer began all the disallowed questions, followed by asking me, "Was anyone present, when Rivera told you this?"

"Yes, Guadalupe Marin herself. And all she did as a rule was laugh."

Guadalupe turned red with anger, became confused, admitted that she was present in several instances. Then her lawyer stopped the proceedings to confer with her and tell her she must deny that she was present. In any case, I was now able to tell my story, and though Guadalupe denied that she had heard Diego say any such thing and denied its truth, the Judge began to get a picture of the kind of woman Guadalupe was. The case now moved splendidly, and I got into the record a complete picture of the plaintiff, always followed by her ineffective denials. Guadalupe denied, moreover, that she had ever posed for Diego. The pictures in my book, though they were not entered as evidence, showed clearly that she had. Later she testified that she had never posed in the nude, but only fully clothed. Diego had painted "only her hands and face," presumably adding the body when she was not around. He had never proposed that she should be his model. Her testimony on this whole matter was so confused that it was finally stricken from the record.

My defense could have rested on the proof of the absolute truth of what the complainant objected to as libelous. But that would have required a visit by me to Mexico, and the securing of Mexican witnesses willing to testify against her. That would have been costly, and while many of them were my friends and would have testified for me, they were not Knopf's friends. Since Knopf was an American, and presumably wealthy "like all Americans," they might easily have decided to testify for her so that she could get substantial damages from Alfred Knopf and Company. So, as the case progressed, I decided on two more lines of defense: 1) that she had not been materially damaged by what I wrote; and 2) that her reputation was such that it could not be damaged by anything I had written. Farmer worked on the material damage question, and I on the nature of her reputation.

The reader might think that by this time, the press would be full of the story. But by accord between Knopf's lawyers, her lawyer, a Mr. Silvester, the judge, and myself, we agreed against a jury trial, against the entry of Diego Rivera's name on the calendar, and other ways of avoiding a sensational story. On the day our trial opened, court reporters read the posted list of trials and found that ours read *Marin vs. Wolfe*, which they passed up for the more interesting-seeming trials with more prominent persons involved. Not a word hit the press until Frida Kahlo, basing herself on my report to her on the trial's outcome, managed to hit the first page of the Mexican dailies with a report of her own.

The material damage matter proved easy. A published statement may be declared by a court libelous *per se,* but then the plaintiff has to prove that the libel in question actually damaged her, and to what monetary extent. If there is no monetary damage, the verdict is usually a "Scotch verdict," awarding the plaintiff six cents in damages to show that she or he was libeled, plus all costs, so that the plaintiff loses nothing material in defending her honor.

Guadalupe, seeing where the trial was moving, or advised by her lawyer, and aware that Judge Hulburt was a practising, and quite likely as so many Irish are, a devout Catholic, appeared in the Court Room tastefully dressed in black as devout Mexican women are when they go to church. She swore that she was a devout practising Catholic communicant, that she did not know what a homosexual was, and that such rough words as *cabron* ("old goat") or *chingar echar el palo* (crude expressions for sexual intercourse) never crossed her lips, and that although she was not legally married to Diego because they did not go through a civil ceremony, without which marriage is not legal in Mexico, being opposed as she was to the Mexican government's antireligious and atheistic laws, she had insisted on being married in a church because she wanted "to be married in the sight of God and according to God's laws."

At this Judge Hulburt adjourned the court for lunch, and when he came back had sitting with him on the bench a Catholic priest in cassock. He leaned over repeatedly to consult this nonlegal adviser, whereupon Farmer made his usual objection and exception for the purposes of a future appeal to a higher court.

First Farmer began questioning me on the language Guadalupe used to me in Diego's presence and to Diego in mine, and then on the general reputation she possessed in Mexico as quarrelsome and frequently foulmouthed. She in turn testified that I lived with Frida's sister, Cristina, when my wife was not in Mexico, and had no residence of my own. The Judge gradually got the idea that Lupe, despite her black garments, was not a refined person and did not have such a reputation as my words could have damaged.

The problem of whether Guadalupe had suffered any serious material or spiritual damage as a result of my book was finally decided by the judge himself, a decision based on two mistakes as to the nature of life in Mexico, which cancelled each other out. In the United States, if the things I had said about Guadalupe had been made to stand up in Court, she might have been fired as a school teacher. Consequently, he considered a number of those statements libelous *per se*. But in Mexico the school officials pay no attention to the private life of their teachers, as long as they are competent and well behaved in the classroom. The judge turned to Guadalupe

Marin and inquired anxiously: "Mrs. Marin, were you a teacher in the Mexican school system when Mr. Wolfe published his book?"

"Yes, Your Honor. I was teaching dressmaking and drawing."

"Did you lose any of your positions as a result of what Mr. Wolfe wrote about you?"

"No, sir, I am still teaching the same classes."

"Then how were you materially damaged by Mr. Wolfe's book?"

A profound silence followed, for Lupe did not know what to say. "That will do, madam," said the judge. It was at this point that the judge made up his mind both as to Lupe's public reputation, and her right to claim damages. He called the court together once more near the middle of February, 1942, and declared that I had proved the truth of many of the statements of which Guadalupe Marin complained, but had not brought into court sufficient proof of certain trivia which he regarded as "libelous *per se*." But he added that the complainant had not proved that she was materially damaged by those statements, nor had she brought in positive proof that they were not true. He therefore entered judgment for Lupe for six cents damages, but without the payment of costs for her trip to the United States or legal costs for the trial. (An ordinary "Scotch verdict" is six cents *with* costs. But Lupe got what can only be called a "double Scotch" verdict.) Her lawyer, Mr. Sulvester, had to pay a fee of five dollars for filing the 6¢ judgment. At this point, Mr. Farmer rose from his chair, walked over to Guadalupe and her lawyer, and counted out in front of them six shiny new pennies. Guadalupe rose from her seat without picking up a penny of her "double Scotch" winnings, walked with dignity out of the courtroom, and as she passed me, leaned over to hiss: "The next time you come to Mexico, I'll have you assassinated!" Frida's article on the trial in the Mexican press was headed in good sensational Mexican style, all across the front page: "NI UN CENTAVO PAGO UN CORTE NORTEAMERICANO POR EL HONOR DE UNA MUJER MEXICANA."

Since then I have been in Mexico three times, but have not yet been assassinated. On the contrary, Lupe eventually issued a statement to the press which *de facto* exonerated me, by saying that Diego Rivera was such a big liar that he had "even deceived his biographer, Bertram Wolfe."

And indeed, there had been at least one respect in which Diego had deceived his biographer. When I first asked him about Lupe's claim that they had been wed in church, if not legally in a civil marriage, Diego's comment was: "I did not go to church with Lupe. She took somebody as a proxy." In a later edition of my biography, thoroughly revised and renamed *The Fabulous Life of Diego Rivera*, I wrote:

> Since it did not occur to me to doubt this, it was thus that I set it down, whereupon Guadalupe Marin was deeply aggrieved. On this and other matters she brought her suit for libel. She did not fare well in the suit, yet I thought I might have been taken in by Diego's proxy story. Further research showed me that Diego

Rivera, in June, 1922, personally entered the Church of San Miguel Arcangel, in the parish of that name in Mexico City and signed the marriage register in his own unmistakable hand. I regret that Lupe's feelings were hurt and here correct the error. . . . And I ask myself: Are there other such errors in this book? Surely there must be, hence in the introduction I have put the notice *caveat lector*. . . . And repeat the same warning in an early page of the first chapter.

41

HOW A BOOK WAS BURNED IN AMERICA

In the Autumn of 1939, when the crops were safely in, Europe went to war again. And as in 1916 and 1917, a good number of our élite were in favor of getting into it, while the mass of the American people were in favor of staying neutral and keeping out of "Europe's bloody wars." This time the president (Franklin Roosevelt) did not lead the peace movement as Woodrow Wilson had done. As in the First World War, I was for keeping out.* When Hitler attacked Stalin, I felt that we should let the two totalitarian powers tear each other to pieces. To be sure, Hitler could penetrate deeply into Russia, since Stalin had killed almost all his officer staff (70% of the entire General Staff from Colonels to Marshals) and did not believe his own or our espionage staffs when he was informed that Hitler was preparing an invasion. But I knew, too, that Stalin had, if nothing else, those great old generals, General Mud, General Distance, and General Winter on his side, and that those generals had defeated Charles XII of Sweden, Napoleon of France, and Darius of Persia. Once the two totalitarian regimes had destroyed each other, I was in favor of America using her magnificent resources to help a ruined Europe to liberate and rebuild herself.

Norman Thomas and I, and a number of like-minded people, formed a surprisingly strong organization called the Keep America Out of War Congress, and, the majority of Americans being in a mood for staying out, Norman and I decided to write a programmatic book together, with the simple title of *Keep America Out of War.* We took the manuscript to Stokes, the publisher who had done so many of Norman's books, and it was instantly accepted by Horace Stokes, the head of the firm. We wrote the book at high speed, for we agreed that I was to write it singlehanded, working into it, in appropriate places, large sections of Norman's speeches and articles printed in the *Socialist Call.* I was still full of the antiwar passion that I had developed during World War I, strengthened by the

* I did not then know about Hitler's "final solution."

fulfillment of the prophecies I had made then as to what total war would do to our country and Europe, and what the preposterous Treaty of Versailles would do to Europe's finances, the world economy, and Germany's mood.

But however fast I wrote, events seemed to move faster, and the mood began to change under Roosevelt's veiled leadership in America.

Horace Stokes was full of enthusiasm for the manuscript; he recognized that it differed in style and power from all the other manuscripts that Norman Thomas had turned in ("all mere speeches but made with a good heart"), and asked me to give him any other manuscript I had in the works or projected.

At this point I should say a word about Horace Stokes to make clear the last battle with the law in which he involved me. Horace Winston Stokes was a frightened boy in his forties who had just inherited the huge publishing firm built up by his father, Frederick Stokes. His father had founded the firm, was its president, judged all submitted manuscripts personally, was elected a director of the National Association of Book Publishers and later its president. He fought with all his might the early book clubs, which he said would discourage young authors and innovation in writing because they would be geared to the taste of the lowest common denominator of book purchasers and to works that everybody was talking about for the moment. He stubbornly refused to submit his own manuscripts to the book clubs except when they specifically asked to see a book he was advertising. When he died at the age of 82, he was the founder and head of one of the oldest houses of New York publishing, and had issued more than 3,000 titles. It was an awesome inheritance, and his son, Horace Winston Stokes, was not equal to the task of carrying on such a firm. In his heart he seemed to know it; he was eager, nervous, and timorous.

Horace Stokes took our book eagerly, without noticing the changing mood in the country. He printed 1500 copies and sent out 300 for review. The notice the book got was nugatory. One reviewer wrote, "If a *book* could keep American out of war, this one would do it." Another said in jest, "Have you seen the new Thomas Wolfe book? With such an author it can't lose." Horace Stokes reported to us glumly after a few weeks, "It is as if I had dropped the whole edition of 1,500 copies noiselessly into the sea, and thrown 300 review copies in after them." When the Japanese attacked at Pearl Harbor, Norman and I told him he could remainder the whole edition.

After the failure of our *Keep America Out of War* book, Stokes unexpectedly sent for me.

"Mr. Wolfe," he said to me, "you are a writer."

"I try to be," I said modestly.

"No, seriously, I mean it. We, my father and I, have been publishing Norman Thomas for years, and everything he writes sounds like one of his speeches. I don't mean to say his speeches aren't good, they're splendid. I approve of his ideals. But whether he writes them himself, or gets a ghostwriter comrade to collaborate with him, his books turn out to be speeches, and read like speeches. I could tell you, Mr. Wolfe, which paragraphs and chapters you wrote of your joint book, and which he sent you from his speeches. And yours are writing. Your style is splendid. Tell me, have you anything in the works that you could submit to us? I should be delighted to publish any book you are planning, or writing now, or have just finished. Have you any manuscripts I can look at or any planned work I can consider for publication?"

"No-o-o," I said hesitantly. "Except maybe just one thing. I wrote a satirical antiwar novel. It was taken by the English publisher, Hale. They sent me a contract all ready to sign, then England declared war on Germany on account of Poland, and Hale begged off—asked me to excuse them because they couldn't publish an antiwar novel in wartime. Now the manuscript is resting in Hale's office and can't be returned to me because of the German submarine blockade."

Horace Stokes pressed a button, and a woman appeared with a notebook in her hand. "Take a cable," said Stokes:

Hale, London, England. Kindly return at once by the first boat at our expense the manuscript of Bertram Wolfe entitled: *WORLD WITHOUT END*. We will take it off your hands and will most likely publish it.

(*signed*) Horace Winston Stokes
New York

It took, I believe, three months, until a ship called the S. S. *Virginia* zigzagged through the submarine blockade and made the Port of New York in safety. On it was the rather slender manuscript of *World Without End*. Horace Stokes took a few days to read it, then announced, "It's not the kind of novel that goes over well generally in America. It is more like an English fantasy. But we are ready to publish it and here's your contract."

"My first contract for a novel," I thought, rejoicing. I signed it, hardly looking at the terms.

World Without End was a novel that dealt with a medical experimenter who discovered, or, through the error of a reporter, led the world to believe that he had discovered, the secret of the indefinite prolongation of life. The world went wild with joy, until they learned that all of their principal institutions were geared to the reasonable expectation of death. The plot was simple, the characters simpler, little more than mere stereotypes needed for the plot. But the adventures of the novel, the story of the story itself and its fate, are strange indeed.

The novel's first setback was the fact that while it was on the press some other writer finished and published a book on the history of the Balkan states and named it *World Without End*. There is no copyright on titles, so that two books on two diverse subjects might come out with the same title on the same day. The only lawsuit that might prevail is one that might prove that one of the two books with the given title had adopted its name to confuse the readers and sell books to readers wishing to have the other one. Otherwise the two books might live peacefully side by side without legal contest. In this case, though I loved the title, *World Without End,* which I had taken from the English Book of Common Prayer, to avoid confusion I changed the name of my novel to the thinner, less resonant *Deathless Days.*

Next a lawyer laid his hand upon my as yet unborn novel in the strangest fashion. He was, as I learned later, a neighbor, a close acquaintance, and the author of a book called *The Law of Literary Property,* which had just been published two years earlier. The author was Philip Wittenberg, and having only recently published the book he was trying to get clients by frightening timid publishers as to the dangers of "publishing a lawsuit." Mine was the most timid of publishers. All this I learned later, but at the moment it became clear to me, by phone calls from terrified Horace Stokes, that some lawyer was trying to frighten him by pointing out passages in my novel that might lead to a lawsuit. Who would be a better prospect than Horace Winston Stokes? His was an awesome inheritance and Horace did not want to run his great publishing house into the ground by publishing books that might end up in a series of lawsuits. Wittenberg explained to him the dangers of the publishing trade and proposed a retainer. Horace countered: "What price will you charge for giving me a sample opinion on a single manuscript first?" The price agreed on, Mr. Stokes handed him my already printed and bound volume, *Deathless Days.*

"But my usefulness, Mr. Stokes, lies in reading manuscripts before they are printed. I eliminate or point out possible grounds for lawsuits; you correct the manuscript accordingly, and we have plain sailing."

"I have no unpublished manuscripts at present. But that makes no difference. Go through this book as if it were a manuscript, and indicate the dangers, and suggestions you might make." After some discussion, Mr. Wittenberg carried off my novel, and began to comb it with a fine-tooth comb to see what he might possibly suggest by way of dangers, real or imaginary. What follows is the plot of my novel.

Dr. William Marisoff, assisted only by a nurse, Mary Mercer, has drained the blood of a very old dog and extracted its cholesterol (the reader should remember that I wrote this in 1939 when cholesterol was not so fashionable). The dog has shown signs of rejuvenation such as a less wrinkled skin and the dropping off of papilloma (warts), and he wagged his tail as he was coming out of the experiment. Dr. Overhouse, the director of the institute, seeing publicity and money in the discreet, still uncertain experiment, forces Dr. Marisoff to report on his modest work to his institute colleagues, and secretly tips off the press. Tony Van Cortlandt, the society editor of the *Morning Graphic,* is compelled to cover the report because he has gotten Teddy Semmel, the science editor, drunk in an all-night binge, and Semmel is in no state to cover the meeting.

Tony is so distracted by the sight of a red-haired girl with green eyes and a saucy tilt to her frankly freckled and unpowdered nose that he can scarcely pay attention to the technical report of Dr. Marisoff on cholesterol and lecithin and other strange substances, particularly after he finds that she is Dr. Marisoff's nurse and that the director, Overhouse, is unable to put her out of the meeting as a "mere staff member" when the gentle Marisoff shows backbone in defending his laboratory assistant, after finding that Dr. Overhouse has violated his promise and invited the press. Finally Dr. Overhouse introduces Marisoff, not as an experimenter on the "dispersion of cholesterol," but on the "prolongation of life." That takes Tony Van Cortlandt's attention from the red-haired, green-eyed beauty to the report of Dr. Marisoff. The more Tony hears of Marisoff's bewildering report, the more exited he gets. First he "borrows" some sheets of paper from the girl at his side, then decides that he can scoop all the other reporters present by phoning in to his paper what he takes to be the biggest news since the birth of the Savior, and he rushes out to phone in the news. By the time Marisoff is finishing his report the *Morning Graphic* is out with an extra edition, bearing the headline which fills the entire front page of the tabloid paper. It reads: DOC K.O.'S DEATH

In vain did Dr. Marisoff try to refute the rumors. Within minutes the world press was ringing with it. And the world went wild with joy. Ticker tape fluttered and fell in streamers all day long. Paper scraps were wafted from towers making snow and butterflies and flickers of merriment in the upper air. All doors spewed forth their human content and panic joy seized the multitude. All schools closed. All labors ceased. Paper streamers appeared with legends like *You for Me for Eternity; Death is Swallowed up in Victory.* All the frenzies that rule the blood woke from their slumbers. Armistice Day and the First of May, the Bacchanal and Halloween and Thanksgiving and the madness of Pan and drunken revelry and church thanksgiving and all the holidays that man had ever celebrated or dimly remembered, were blended into one joyous madness where all celebrated together until the flame of joy and the strength of man and maid became as weak as water, and weariness took joy by the hand and led her unresisting away to rest. The pumps had long ceased to work like all other things and now the rising waters strove in vain to cleanse the streets and obliterate the traces of man's thanksgiving for the conquest of the last enemy, Death, and the gift of eternal life. Then man paused at last to consider how activities should be continued and what tasks resumed and carried on.

First the stock market opened, as it should, for men who trade in stocks are more important than those who produce the things on which stocks in some mysterious fashion are a claim. But there was no controlling the market: it kept booming and booming, requiring closing every few minutes to let the ticker tape catch up with the trading. It reached an all-time high until the ticker tape carried a quite minor bit of news that caused the traders to reconsider their optimism. Shortly before noon the ticker carried a report that the little-known and seldom traded in stock of the Lifetime

Bag Company ("a new bag if it doesn't outlast your lifetime") declared itself in bankruptcy. At first this news was greeted with laughter. But then the thought occurred of pensions for a lifetime that might never end; health insurance and life insurance for the same lifetime; perpetual annuities to an entire aging population. At 1:57 P.M. the board of governors aided by the police succeeded in restoring sufficient order in a panicky market so that the chairman of the board could announce the closing of the Stock Exchange and add: "We will not reopen until the government announces what form of relief it will give us for the astronomical taxation figures implied in annuities to the aged until Judgment Day."

The next industry to awaken to the perils of immortality was the undertakers'. A picket line appeared in front of the laboratory with signs reading:

> We demand the right to live!
> Marisoff is taking our jobs!
> Down with medical meddlers with human life!
> Let the government take over our burial business!
> Socialize the mortician industry!

A great red banner swept by the astonished eyes of Mary Mercer and Tony Van Cortlandt, who were walking near the laboratory, bearing the words in gold:

UNITED ASSOCIATION OF MORTICIANS AND EMBALMERS AND ALLIED TRADES

and beneath it in a wreath of silver surrounded by a golden rectangle was the motto:

THIS EMBLEM IS A GUARANTEE OF A PROPER FUNERAL AND A COMFORTING MEMORY.

Another line swept past in the opposite direction with the slogans and mottos of: tombstone cutters, quarry workers, stone setters, grave diggers, sculptors, caretakers, florists, cypress and evergreen growers, gardeners, wreath makers, silverleaf and goldleaf beaters, carpenters, casket makers, coachmen, carriage makers, wheelwrights, satin weavers, gilt and bronze manufacturers, Cypress Hills and Salem Fields innkeepers, candle and taper pourers, iron chair and tassel casters, shroud and vestment makers, mortuary makers, sodcutters, upholsterers, embalming fluid dealers, watchmen, mourners, *schnorrers*, joss stick vendors, and a serried army of amazonian blondes all in white uniforms like nurses, except for a gold band across their breasts, marching in military precision behind the Lady Funeral Parlor Attendants' Protective and Benevolent League, followed by members of countless related industries, which combined their demand for work or relief at union wages with the demand that only qualified lady attendants should perform certain of the last preparation tasks for female corpses.

A break in the endless procession permitted a grizzly-chinned, ruby-cheeked, bottle-nosed, tatterdemalion sandwich board man to break into the line to march with proud if uncertain step. He was from Fairfields, which firm, despite the suicide that morning of its president, was keeping up the firm's enterprising tradition with a sign in front which read:

Why Walk Around Half Dead
When as Little as
$35
Will Buy a Beautiful Funeral?
No Extras
at
FAIRFIELD'S
where death is brighter

And on the sandwich man's ragged retreating rear were the words:

FREE FLOWERS
AND VESTMENTS FOR
ALL FUNERALS
IN JUNE
Beautiful Booklet
"A Memorable Half Hour"
FREE FOR THE ASKING
FAIRFIELD'S
Where Death Is Brighter

At this point Stokes' lawyer stepped into the action. I received a terrified phone call from Horace Stokes telling me: "We're in deep trouble, Mr. Wolfe. I have been advised that there is an advertising undertaker named Fairchild, and your sandwich man carries in the undertakers' picket line the only advertising sign that is carried in the whole parade. And you have called your undertaker *Fairfield.* I have been advised that Fairchild may feel alluded to and ridiculed to the point of libel. I have also been advised that the head of the Fairchild Mortuary establishment is likely to bring a suit against me, if only to get some valuable publicity out of it."

"Whoever told you that, Mr. Stokes, doesn't know anything about libel law. He would have to prove that he had actually lost customers, and how many he had lost, and that *Fairfield* referred to him. When I chose the name *Fairfield,* I was only thinking of a name suggesting a cemetery. I could just as well have said *Stillfield.* In fact, *Stillfield* is better."

"That's a wonderful thought, Mr. Wolfe. Do you have any objection to my changing it to *Stillfield?*"

"Not at all. But how are you going to change it, now that the book is printed and has gone out to reviewers?"

"Easy, Mr. Wolfe, but a little costly. I shall have to tear out that page from all 1,500 copies, and print another page on which I substitute *Stillfield,* and then handtip in the new page identical in all respects except for the change of name. Then I'll recall the copies from reviewers and send them the revised copy. And, Mr. Wolfe, I want to tell you that the man who gave me that advice is a lawyer and an authority on literary law. He agrees with you that I could win the case, but says it will cost me something like a thousand dollars and a number of days in court to win it."

"O.K. Handtip. I like *Stillfield* better than *Fairfield.*"

A few days later my phone brought me once more the alarmed voice of Horace Stokes. "My lawyer has read further into your book and found more trouble. On page 104 you have your heroine ask whether there is 'anything to a rumor concerning a rich man's will,' and your reporter, Tony Van Cortlandt, answers: 'Well, I got it straight from Winchell, who got it from the cloakroom girl at the Club Carrillon, who is that way'—and he crossed two fingers—'with young Batten of Batten, Barton, Burnham, and Besonovich, who handle the rich man's legal affairs.'

"Now my lawyer informs me that there is a firm with the name: Batten, Barton, Durstine, and Osborn; that Batten is known to be very litigious, and not so long ago brought a libel suit against a young lady when she told a reporter that George Barton, Sr. was the father of her child. My counselor says he can easily win the lawsuits because there's no real case in either of them, but that my cost for appearing several times in court with my lawyer, making motions and filing papers, will easily cost a thousand dollars in each case."

Once more I assured Stokes that his lawyer must be a nut quite ignorant of libel law, but he responded with sudden firmness that his lawyer was a great authority on the subject and had written works of importance on literary law. "Then he is trying to deceive you," I countered. But Stokes was insistent, and we ended the dispute by my agreeing to tear out two more pages from 1,500 copies and handtip in two new pages without the name or the line the lawyer had objected to. This silly censorship is getting to be costly, I thought, but that's Stokes' hard luck, not mine. What else would he find, I wondered, to cavil at?

And then it came! The treasured passage that the mysterious lawyer had been looking for to frighten Stokes into giving him a personal retainer turned up, and on the frontispiece of the book! Many novels contain a routine formal passage on their first page to protect publisher and author against libel. This protective passage generally reads more or less as follows:

> Any similarity between the characters or events in this novel to any person living or dead or any of his actions was not so intended and would be purely accidental.

After running through the book dozens of times and not finding anything to frighten Stokes with, the lawyer had happened to glance at the flyleaf and found that in place of the customary passage I had written:

> I cannot make the usual disclaimer concerning the personages and incidents: they are not wholly fictional. The man here designated as Doctor Marisoff will be

recognized by the informed readers in this field as a genuine thinker and experimenter in the field here ascribed to him. The details of career and character here set forth, however, do not correspond as closely as do the initials to those of the man whose words first gave the author the central idea and impulse to write this book which is, indeed,

GRATEFULLY DEDICATED
to
W.M.M.

The attorney held his breath while he called up Stokes, and Stokes with anxiety called me up.

"Is that a real person?" asked Mr. Stokes.

"Is what a real person?"

"The man to whom the book is dedicated, and a simulacrum of whose name runs all through the book."

"That's a secret until the book is out, Mr. Stokes."

"It can't be, Mr. Wolfe. My lawyer says that if it is a real person you have to get his permission to dedicate the book to him and to say what you have said about him."

"More nonsense from your lawyer, Horace Stokes. If it's a real person, it's his business, not yours or your lawyer's, that I have dedicated a book to him and presented a complimentary picture of him in it."

"Not so, Mr. Wolfe. He can sue me for making fun of his work, for libelling him as a serious scientist, or for invasion of privacy. If he is a real person, you will have to go to him at once and get a letter of permission in writing signed by him, and witnessed by another party, or this time we're in real trouble that no tearing out and tipping in of pages will cure."

"It is a real person, Mr. Stokes, and his work bears no resemblance to the work of Dr. Marisoff, and will never set the world on fire. That's clearly fiction, all of it. He's an old friend, a high school chum of mine, and something he told me in the Fifth Avenue Library suggested to me the funny idea of a world that needs death to exist. Even that was not in the remotest his idea. But since his conversation with me suggested to me the idea of writing this satire on the nature of life and death, as an act of gratitude I dedicated the book to him. That's a secret, and I do not intend to reveal it to him until I give him a copy as a present. He will be surprised by everything in it, including the dedication. And he cannot possibly be hurt or angered or annoyed by this gesture of kindness on my part."

"Mr. Wolfe," said Stokes with unwonted sternness, "you will either get his permission in writing, notarized or signed by a witness, or there will be no book."

HOW THE NOVEL WAS BORN

I had gone to the Fifth Avenue Library one day, as was my frequent custom, to get some materials from the Slavonic Division, then magnificently run by my friend and classmate, Avrahm Yarmolinsky (C.C.N.Y., Class of 1916). By accident I bumped into another classmate that I had not seen since our graduation from Boys' High School, Brooklyn, in 1912. He had won a Pulitzer scholarship at Columbia because someone had tipped him off that to become eligible for a Pulitzer he must excel in Greek as well as Latin, while I, the first member of my family and all my relatives to go above elementary school, had only reluctantly and accidentally studied Latin (a *dead* language, but one that has since helped me to develop my style in English). I did not even know that there were Pulitzer scholarships until they were being awarded and I learned that I was not even eligible because I had not taken Greek. I don't know whether my Pulitzer-Prize-winning classmate, William Malisoff, had gone to a better college than I, though I doubt it.

We exchanged reminiscences and experiences of the days since we had jointly headed our graduating class in Boys' high. "What are you doing now?" I asked, and Malisoff answered solemnly, "Experimenting on the prolongation of life."

"How are you doing that?" I asked skeptically, "And are you having any success?"

"I am underfeeding guinea pigs and rats—feeding them less than they naturally want or require for their natural growth."

"And what results are you having?"

"Not bad. Our experimental animals grow up and mature more slowly. They remain thin and underdeveloped, but they live longer by a perceptible percentile than our control animals who are fed normally and develop faster."

I could not resist the comment: "So you want us to live longer but never live fully at all."

"Exactly," said Bill Malisoff, hearing no irony in my question. "Our control animals eat too much, mature too fast, and don't live nearly as long."

"And don't play as much?" I asked.

"Yes, I guess that's so, they don't have the energy."

"Do they learn the same tricks just as fast? To find the right exit from a maze? To press the right button to get food? or avoid a shock? Are they enjoying life as well? Are they as lively? Are they as healthy?"

"Those things we don't know yet. But they are not important. The fact is that they live longer and that's what we're after—to prolong life, to delay and repel death. We can experiment with such things as mazes and buttons later. Besides, it's up to them to use the longer life we win for them. In any case, we do know that they live longer, that death is delayed, and so we can count our experiment a success. To enjoy a long life is what's important, how you use it less so."

I thought of John Watson who had been at Johns Hopkins, and then gone into business. I thought of his celebrated book on behaviorism and life as conditioned reflexes, published in 1925. I thought how naively I felt that I had finished him off with my "Balance Sheet of Behaviorism" published in the *Virginia Quarterly* in 1930. And here, before me, was another character of the same kind, who thought of deciding things for us, and prolonging our lives merely by underfeeding us and making us live more slowly and more feebly and drag a more meager vitality out longer. *Quid custodet custodes?* Who would watch the watchmen? Who would the watchmen be who would prescribe the quantity and the quality of our diet? How many would there have to be? And how many would it take, and where would they station themselves to prevent us from enjoying an occasional holiday meal, and how abolish the last vestiges of fiestas in our overmechanized, overindustrialized society lest we go on a gastronomic binge? And how would they make up our schedule of calories and gourmet foods? And the temptation of gaiety, or celebration of festivals? Would they have to breed a special troop of overfed and overstrong who might be healthy enough to bury our emaciated frames when we finally died of undernourishment? Would they become a new aristocracy? Or a species of helots and day and night watchmen? Would it become a misdemeanor to enjoy an occasional good meal, rich in food and drink? My head spun with questions and amusement at Malisoff's solemnity. Ideas for a dozen novels were coursing through my mind.

When I found no laughter, and, it seemed to me, no wisdom in Malisoff's retorts, I felt that I had questioned him enough to get his point of view, and I sought to bring our dialogue to a close. This was easy, for he talked only of his experiment, and never thought of asking me what I was engaged in or how I was getting on. I took my leave and hastened to the subway on which I used to do my homework when I was at C.C.N.Y. and could read and think without minding the roar of the trains. I rode to Prospect Park station in Brooklyn, Prospect Park having become my favorite stomping ground at the moment, then paced up and down the peaceful paths and hillocks around the lake, thinking, thinking, thinking about Bill Malisoff and the implications of his experiment on the life of man. I told myself that I had no business thinking of writing a novel, when I had been promised that in six months I would begin receiving an advance from the Viking Press of $100 a month to write a history of the Russian Revolution. Really, I should be making my preliminary studies for it now.

But a wave of self-pity swept over me. I had worked so hard on the three books with or about Diego Rivera. The biography was such a solid and lively work that all the other would-be biographers had stopped pestering him. And *Portrait of Mexico* had been a solid work, too, requiring me to plunge into the archaeology, biology, and geology of the Mexican land, the laws, institutions, history, and temperament of its people, the politics, folkways and attitudes toward life and death, the startling differences between the proclamations and deeds of its rulers, and a hundred things more. I deserved a rest before I tackled that big work on Russia. (Was writing a novel a rest? Would it be fun? Could I finish it in the six months before January first and the first hundred dollar check from the Viking Press? And why worry about Russia now? There were so many books, mountains of them, written about the Russian Revolution and in so many European languages, most of which I could read: all I needed to do was wade through the torrents of books and articles, correlate them, illuminate them with the insights I had gained from my three stays in Russia and my more than five-month long fight with Joseph Stalin. Other scholars could depend only on mendacious documents meant to deceive them, while I could use my insights to go below the surface and interpret the meaning and intention of the falsehoods.)

Could I write a novel? What kind of novel could I complete in six months? Surely I couldn't develop characters and background—scientific and otherwise—and work out a plot that would raise all the questions that had bobbed up in my mind while I was listening to Malisoff. No, the plot had to be simple, yet raise the deepest questions concerning the death and life of man. In America men are afraid to think of death. I must make them think of the prolongation of life and its consequences. But Malisoff's prolongation of life was too melancholy, too smallish, too antilife. I must make men think of the abolition of death altogether, and what it would do to our society.

So I decided to take a six-month rest until January 1 and try my hand at a light-hearted satirical novel. Try to tell a serious novelist that writing a novel is a rest! Or that one could finish a novel in six months. Could I write a half-way decent novel anyway? Presumptuously, I told myself that I might be able to. And as I continued my walk in the deepening darkness in Prospect Park, following remote and unsought paths through a park that had become a deserted forest woodland, a story kept working itself out in my mind, chapter by chapter and scene by scene, almost as if I were watching a movie.

I saw the false news hit the street, saw the country and then the world go wild to learn that science had conquered the "last enemy, death," saw the stock market close in a panic when the little Lifetime Bag Company went bankrupt, watched company after company close in panic when it realized that pensions were thenceforth to be perpetual and taxes mountainous, saw the churches lose their audiences as the notion took possession of multitudes that there would be no more death, nor heaven, nor hell, and I spelled out headlines for myself like:

CREEDS UNITE IN FAITH
IN LIFE AFTER DEATH
Holy War Proclaimed
For Rescue From Body
Of Imprisoned Soul

I watched street-corner sky pilots take up with the Church of the Avenging Angels, which proposed that each faithful servitor take his "slaughter weapon in hand" against those who opposed the coming of God's Kingdom; found names for cults like Death Worshipers, Grave Gladdeners,

Waiters on the Housetop now that the last days had come, Marisophists of the East, Keepers of the Golden Stair, We Shall Now See His Face (the Jewish Messianic Cult that purported to trace Dr. Marisoff's descent directly from David, King of Israel). I thought of the bedlam of the new preachings in Union Square. I thought of the lines of undertakers picketing the Medical Research Insitute and demanding that the government socialize the inhumation, embalming, and mortuary industries, and even saw a few doctors joining them on the picket line. I thought of the panic taking possession of philosophers and thinkers and men of culture as they foresaw the multitude of vulgarians lasting forever, and gradually by their sheer numbers peopling and dominating the earth. Yes, I could see the scenes of the novel growing in my mind, and hastened home to write the first pages. But then I found that it was after midnight and I had forgotten dinner and was tired to the point of exhaustion. I fell asleep with the novel filling my mind, and woke up next morning with whole pages ready to put themselves on paper, as if my unconscious had continued the labors where the conscious had left off. This was not the first time, nor the last, when problems, the solution of which eluded me when I tried to write too late at night, worked themselves out during the night. Things that I had had to leave undone continued to do themselves during the night while I slept—not merely now in the field of fiction, but also in the field of history which has always seemed to me as much of an art, perhaps a tougher one, than novel writing. At any rate, when I woke up next morning I could hardly wait to get at the typewriter and tap out the first pages of a novel entitled *World Without End.*

The novel wrote itself miraculously within less than the six months I had allowed for it. I could have done better had I taken longer, but January first loomed up on the horizon, and with it the expectation of a contract and a monthly advance, and the problems of the Russian Revolution. And so I did what I have never done before, and would never do again until this book. I took the manuscript to a literary agent, Curtis Brown, Ltd., and without waiting for their verdict turned to the problem of Russia. I found a name for my book on the Russian upheaval, *Three Who Made a Revolution: Lenin, Trotsky, Stalin.* I have always found names for my books before I began them, and let the name guide me into the labyrinth of each book's problems. Then I waited for a contract, a hundred dollar check, and a conference with Pascal Covici, now my patron in the Viking Press. I waited and waited but no contract, no message, and no check came from Viking.

Word did come, however, from Curtis Brown. One of their readers, Edith Hazzard, wrote me:

I have read the book and find it interesting and exceedingly well done, but neither Mr. Collins nor I feel that it could be marketed successfully in the United States. Books of this type are not popular at present; even Wells' *The Holy Terror* with all the Simon & Schuster build-up and H. G. Wells' name, sold only 4,300 copies.

The English market is another matter entirely, and we would like to send it to our London office.

I immediately agreed, and they as immediately sold it to an English company, Robert Hale, Ltd. But almost immediately thereafter England declared war on Germany following Hitler's invasion of Poland. My book had an antiwar ending, as follows:

Members of the Federal Bureau of Military Intelligence kidnap Dr. Marisoff from a party. They take him to the chief of intelligence, who informs him that we are about to declare war on a great European power and that the president is putting an entire medical corps at Marisoff's disposition to help him devise a cheap, rapid method of reconditioning all the men between forty and seventy, to make them suitable for conscription. Dr. Marisoff refused to put the science of the prolongation of live at the service of death. When he asks for a bed on which to rest he is maneuvered into the outdoors, and then kidnapped by Tony, who has become aware of the intelligence men who have been surrounding him. He escapes in the private plane of a wealthy patient whom he has succeeded in rejuvenating. And when the President of the United States goes on the air to announce the declaration of war, Marisoff breaks in on a pirate radio station. He announces that he has set up a secret underground laboratory to continue his modest researches on the prolongation of life, after learning from the President of the United States that an attempt will be made "to pervert the very fight we have been making against death to the ends of death itself." More cautious than our newspapers are today, with such secrets as the papers stolen by Daniel Ellsberg, or the more recent publication of the names of members of our Central Intelligence Agency, who have then been ousted or assassinated in foreign countries, Marisoff tells his listeners: "I do not feel that I have the right to say how, since it was revealed to me as a state secret." He concludes his brief broadcast with these words:

So long as man's knowledge and achievements can be used to make him more frightful than the beast, he is not fit to receive the gift of longer life, nor capable of undertaking the collective effort to attain it, nor to make longer life endurable.

This is Doctor William Melius Marisoff broadcasting, in the names of Doctor Jacques Neville and Mary Mercer Marisoff, and in his own name. Further details of our researches will be made available through the writings of Anthony Van Cortlandt. Dr. Marisoff signing off. . . . Good-bye all. . . .

All channels became once more silent. The air was clear at last for the President's historic message.

It was this ending that made it impossible for Hale to publish it in England. And even if Horace Stokes' lawyer had not tangled us up with his "special opinion" on an already printed book, Stokes probably could not have sold a copy either, after the attack on Pearl Harbor.

Under the persistant pressure of Horace Stokes, now thoroughly alarmed by his lawyer, I went to the home of William Malisoff with a copy of *Deathless Days* lent me by Stokes, and asked him, as the publisher's lawyer had insisted, that he give me in writing, witnessed by a third party or by a notary, a signed statement that he would sue neither Stokes nor me. Malisoff asked to keep the book overnight, and read it through. Next morning he told me, "Bert, my wife and I liked the book very much. I was flattered by the implied picture of me in your book's hero. I am glad to promise you, and to guarantee, that I will not sue either you or your publisher because of anything in your novel. But I cannot give you such a signed statement in writing."

"Why not?"

"Well, you see, I am also a scientific research worker for the Consumers' Union, which is dominated by the Communist party. If they found out that you had written such a friendly book about me, and that I had been close enough in friendship with you, they would hold it against me, and I might lose my job. It is my principal source of income. But I give you my solemn word as a friend and old schoolmate, that I will never sue you or your publisher. And I authorize you to tell this to your publisher orally."

In vain did I argue the question with him: he would not sue, and he would not sign, nor give me a statement in writing.

I called up Stokes and gave him the news. There was an ominous silence at the other end of the phone. I repeated again and again Malisoff's promise that he wouldn't sue. But Stokes said with a voice expressing both alarm and firmness, "Mr. Wolfe, you'll have to get his promise in writing, or there will be no book."

I BECOME MY OWN LAWYER

The next event was a phone call from attorney Philip Wittenberg, the author of the book entitled *The Law of Literary Property*. Would I come to see him at his home? He was an old acquaintance, not exactly a friend, but well known to me. He lived in the Heights section of Brooklyn, not far from me. "Bert," he said after an exchange of greetings, "I have recently been advising your publisher, Horace Stokes, on your novel, *Deathless Days*. I didn't want to do it; I wanted to give him a trial opinion on a still unprinted manuscript. But he offered to pay me for a sample opinion so as to decide whether my opinions were worth his giving me an annual retainer. I answered that my usefulness consisted in editing out of as yet unpublished mauscripts possible formulations that might impel someone to sue him. But he said: 'I have no manuscript just now, treat this book as if it were a manuscript and give me a sample opinion.' I went through it looking for formulations that might lead an exceptionally litigious man ignorant of the law to try to sue him. I wanted to frighten him a little, so I picked on trivia, told him that they would not be grounds for a successful lawsuit, but such a person might sue and Stokes' time in court and court costs might stand him in a thousand dollars or so before I succeeded in getting the case thrown out of court. When I told him these things, I did not dream that I was dealing with a timorous nut. When you failed to get the man to whom you had humorously dedicated the book to give a statement in writing that he would not sue, unknown to me, Stokes took his handyman and his office staff and had them carry every copy of your book down into the cellar, then watched while the handyman burned every last one of them. When there was not one single copy left, he called me up, informed me of his action, told me I had proved my usefulness to save him from publishing lawsuits, gave me an annual retainer, and ordered me, as my first job, to sue you for the sum of $2,800 for the costs of printing and then burning all the copies of your book. I am ashamed to bring such a suit against you, Bert, and sorry to have gotten a poor author into such a mess, but it is my job and I shall have to do it."

"Come on, Phil," I retorted. "You know that I have a countersuit for nonfulfillment of contract."

"Have you, though?" taunted Wittenberg. "Did you ever know a writer who knew enough about the law to draw up a contract spelling out specific performance and permitting a suit for such specific performance of the contract, which is the only contract suit which will hold in court? Did you spell out specifically the meaning of the term, *to publish?* I'm willing to bet that all your contract says is that the publisher 'agrees to publish.' He could print two copies on toilet or tissue paper, display them for sale at $500 apiece in the windows of a bookstore, and the law would hold that he has published."

"Have it your way," I said to Wittenberg, and turning on my heel, left his home.

Since I could not afford a lawyer, I decided to use the same lawyer Horace Stokes had just hired on a permanent retainer. I went straightway to the Montague Public Library and took out *The Law of Literary Property,* by Philip Wittenberg. I read it through from cover to cover, and was ready for battle. Had he not taunted me on the legal helplessness of authors, I would not have known what the nub of the case should be. But the taunt had done its work.

I sat down, and without bothering with all the verborrhea of legal documents, I wrote my "brief." Wherever there was a difficult point, I quoted directly from Wittenberg, putting his words in quotation marks. But instead of saying whom I was quoting, I would write: "This matter has so far never been adjudicated by the courts, but those knowledgeable in the law would presumably recognize that the following is a sound statement of the probable law in this matter"—and then would follow with the quote from Wittenberg.

But the gem of my brief was matter supplied by the application of my sharpened wits to the taunt that Wittenberg had made:

It is notorious—I wrote—that authors do not know enough about the law to draw up a contract specific enough to be enforceable in the courts by a *Suit for Specific Performance.* For instance, they rarely know enough to impel them to define the word, *publish,* but leave it in limbo for the publisher to decide how many to publish, in what form, on what kind of paper, with what kind of cover, at what price, or in an edition, or how many copies. But in the present case, there has already been a meeting of the minds of author and publisher on all these matters. Author and publishers have agreed in writing and in oral description and action that *publish* means at the very least a *first edition of 1,500 copies, with a cloth cover, a jacket drawing by an artist reputable in the publishing trade, and at a price of at least* $2.50. I therefore give the publisher two weeks to notify me that he agrees to the retention by me of the advance already paid me (which is small compensation for all the work I have done on the novel, *Deathless Days,* otherwise known as *World Without End*), agrees further to the return to me of all rights in my manuscript, and the dropping of any suit against me which he may have had in contemplation. Otherwise, I shall, at the end of two weeks, open suit against Horace Stokes & Co. for compliance with all the terms to which we have agreed orally and in writing and action as defining the publication of the work, *Deathless Days.*

Philip Wittenberg took one look at my brief, and then hastened to advise his new employer, "Mr. Stokes, I have read Bertram Wolfe's 'Brief,' a copy of which I suppose he has sent to you, and I advise you to give in to him at once on the demands he is making. He has us on the hip."

I sent a copy of my newly-recovered property to Luís Alberto Sanchez in Chile, who had published in Spanish a translation of my *Biography of Diego Rivera,* but by the time his translator had stumbled through and translated my book with the aid of a Spanish-English dictionary, Chile had declared war on Germany, and the diffusion of the book had become "untimely" there.

I contemplated sale in my own country, but after Pearl Harbor, it became "untimely" here also. So, aside from one copy which I have in Chilean Spanish, I have only the single copy that Stokes gave me to show Malisoff, and there is a second copy I coaxed from the production man before the book was officially out, to give as a present to Sheba Strunsky Goodman on her birthday. That copy resides happily in the Goodman home in Washington, and the other copy remains in my possession. Hence the book exists in one of the most highly limited editions in history. I guard my copy jealously, and so do Mac and Sheba Goodman theirs. If any publisher should be interested in getting out a second edition, I shall be glad to let him have it, perhaps with an introduction which I would entitle "The Story of a Story."

At any rate, this is the first instance in which, not being able to hire a lawyer, I represented myself, and despite the adversary nature of law suits, used my opponent's lawyer as my own, too. And this is the second time that I won a case when I was too poor to hire a lawyer. A publisher who would burn an entire edition of a printed book without consulting the author or his lawyer obviously was not made for publishing, and Horace Stokes soon disappeared from the field.

As for me, I toted up the sum of my fortunes to the date of the burning of my novel. My two books written with the pictures of Diego Rivera as illustrations, *Portrait of America* and *Portrait of Mexico*, had been swallowed up in the bankruptcy of Covici-Friede, and had disappeared from the market. My life of Diego Rivera published by Alfred Knopf was a good-looking book, but it had been printed in too large a first edition with too small a price to pay Knopf for his plates and to get out a cheaper edition thereafter for readers of biographies. For all practical purposes as a means of income, free-lance writing for the first quarter of a century was a flop. And my solitary novel, *Deathless Days*, had been totally consumed in the furnaces of Horace Stokes. In short, I was virtually bookless and penniless, and my half-decade of writing had left me where I started—with nothing. At this moment of the nadir of my fortunes, I disinterestedly opened my morning mail and found that I had become a "WHO." I looked at the letter uncomprehendingly, and the fancy struck me that the sound of W-H-O must have come from an owl sitting on the solitary tree growing in my back yard. Then I shook my head, rubbed my eyes, and took a second look at the letter in my hand. It was from Marquis and Company, who informed me that my name had been accepted for *Who's Who in America!* Penniless and bookless, but a "WHO."

A FAREWELL TO BERTRAM D. WOLFE

BY SIDNEY HOOK

I want to say a few words of farewell to my old friend and comrade-in-arms, Bert Wolfe. I got to know him sixty-one years ago, when I was a fledgling high school student and he a fledgling teacher—not yet twenty—at the same institution. Our paths have crossed and recrossed many times since then.

There will be other occasions for proper memorial meetings to Bert, celebrating and evaluating the significance of his life's work, his contributions to scholarship, and the vitality of his writing and speech in which no one has ever found a dull or unclear sentence. This morning I shall speak of Bert as a human being, as a person of many careers and talents—the man of political affairs, the scholar, the man of letters—and also as a man who could survive the shipwreck of his early hopes, and with indomitable courage forge a new outlook continuous with the democratic tradition whose ideals have always inspired him.

It is true that Bert's lifelong passion was politics. But it was politics with a difference, because it was aware of the dimensions of human experience that transcend the narrow politics of factional and partisan bias. His varied friendships were testimony to that. They span more than five decades of his life and extend to many areas of the world. So long as you had a sense of the human condition, of its grandeur and tragedies, it made little difference to Bert what you believed about first things or last; and so long as you believed in human freedom, to Bert all differences about a regulated or unregulated economy and similar questions were negotiable, a matter not of either-or, but of more or less.

Bert was always a humanist, even in his salad days as a revolutionist, in the sense that he saw problems and events in an historical perspective. He always related the specific to the universal, the local to the general, the exceptional to the rule to which it was an exception. One of his early heresies was denounced by the political pope of the Kremlin as "exceptionalism."

This respect for the individual and unique was particularly impressive in that aspect of Bert's intellectual activity of which he himself was quite modest, and concerning which not many of those who admired his political and historical works were aware. I refer to his literary criticism, notably his studies of Cervantes and other eminent figures in Hispanic literature, down to his magnificent translation of, and commentary upon, Leon Felipe, whom he interpreted as "the poet of Spain's exodus and tears." His treatment of literary themes was always fresh and insightful and illustrated the capacity for empathetic identification that made him a remarkable teacher, whether he was inside a classroom or on a platform.

Those who knew Bert for any length of time soon realized that he was a natural born teacher whose gifts were enhanced by the discipline of art. He had a flair for the dramatic, and an effortless ease in exposition, which flowed from conscientious preparation that marked his deep respect for his students and auditors. Bert was a master of improvisation when he had to be, but never as a result of his own choice. The range and depth of his erudition were always surprising, and were the source of apposite illustration that both amused and instructed. In personal relations his wit was always kindly, although when it was necessary, he could use it as a devastating polemical weapon against the enemies of freedom.

It is the qualities of Bert's life during the last decades, the period during which most of those present here got to know him, that are of the greatest moment to us. Bert came to the Hoover Institution as a Senior Research Fellow in the twilight years of his life, almost at the Biblically allotted span of human existence, at an age in which most human beings rest from their labor—all efforts spent. But Bert's verve and energy continued to be remarkable, drawn from an inexhaustible source. He knew no holidays or regular hours, whether at home or in his office.

What strikes one who is familiar with Bert's long career are the varieties of courage he manifested. There was first his moral courage in rethinking his ideas. "To consider challenges to one's first principles," Oliver Wendell Holmes once abserved, "is the mark of a civilized man." To face such challenges is not easy. Our natural tendency is to immunize our basic beliefs from the refutations of experience. Bert was not one of those who moved into the future backwards—a pallbearer of the dead past wrapped in stale dogmas that explained away embarrassing evidence. He did not hesitate to modify once firmly held views when the evidence required it.

There was also his intellectual courage in applying his critical mind to new problems. He realized that the world was more complex than anything we can ever say about it. He refused in his maturest outlook to categorize in absolutes or to substitute labels and wholesale solutions for the multiple problems that beset us. He tried to understand the world piecemeal, to make it better and freer, aware that even with all our intelligence and effort, as necessary as they are, it requires luck for our modest successes.

Beyond all other forms of courage in Bert's life was his spiritual courage—his triumph over the limitations of his body, that was more skeleton than flesh. He was a frail and ailing man, always in pain and sometimes in torment, and kept alive by the ministrations of his devoted wife, Ella, who has shared the long journey with him together from childhood days in a union that only a poet can do justice to. When one said Bert, one said Ella, too. She was always the sustaining presence in the trials and crises of his life, a genuine partner in all his works, without whose labors they might not have come to fruition.

Physicians often proclaimed Bert a medical miracle. At least three times his spirit pulled his body back from the verge of death. It was as if its fierce determination to continue with its tasks refused to let go of the precarious vessel through which it reached others. It is truly symbolic that only fire could quench the mortal flame of his spirit. But the flame of his spirit burns on not only in the works he has left behind but, it is to be hoped, in the memories of the readers and listeners of his many publics.

What was the flame of Bert's spirit that remained constant during the stations of his political pilgrimage—a pilgrimage initially inspired by the outbreak of the First World War, which he regarded as a needless slaughter from its very first day to his last reflections upon it just a short time ago? The flame of his spirit was his love of individual freedom, not individualism as a doctrine, but freedom as a personal and yet shared responsibility. It enabled him to overcome all the allegiances that falsely promised to achieve freedom by means incompatible with the justifying end. It enabled him to recognize when his early dreams had become transformed into nightmares, to brave the obloquy of fanatics devoid of a sense of reality as well as the scorn of cynics, for whom all visions were mere illusions. And it helped him to re-establish its continuity with the legacy of the American Revolution, which in a memorable essay during our Bicentennial year, he maintained had not received its proper recognition as the only great revolution in history that did not devour its children.

Bert Wolfe was not a conventionally religious man. But he had an abiding faith in the inextinguishability of the desire for freedom, regardless of the heavy layers of cement with which the tyrants of the world seek to smooth over it. His faith was a form of natural piety periodically renewed when he heard the dissenting voices—fearless however few—from the major and minor Gulag Archipelagos of the world. Yet Bert was not a wishful thinker or foolish optimist. He knew that there could be no guarantee of victory in our struggle to remain free—that habit, love of comfort, and the desire to survive at any and all costs increase the odds against freedom. But he was also convinced of one thing—that whatever the vicissitudes of the future, so long as *we* do not haul down our own colors, so long as we do not strike the flag of freedom, the enemy cannot prevail. The future still remains open—and what it will be depends to some degree upon what we—who pick up the torch of Bertram Wolfe's flame—do or leave undone in the unending struggle to which he devoted his life.

INDEX